012   £2:00

SOCIAL WORK IN BRITAIN: 1950–1975

To K. E. of H. and S. K.
with gratitude

The author and publishers wish to thank the Trustees of the Carnegie United Kingdom Trust for a generous contribution to the publication costs of this volume.

Social Work in Britain: 1950–1975

A Follow-up Study

VOLUME 1

EILEEN YOUNGHUSBAND

London
GEORGE ALLEN & UNWIN
Boston   Sydney

First published in 1978

British Library Cataloguing in Publication Data

Younghusband, Dame Eileen Louise
  Social Work in Britain: 1950–1975.
  Vol. 1
  1. Social service – Great Britain – History
  I. Title
  361′.941   HV243   77–30674

ISBN 0-04-360043-3 *Hardback*

Printed in Great Britain
in 10 on 11 point Times
by Unwin Brothers Limited
The Gresham Press, Old Woking, Surrey

Acknowledgements

The Carnegie United Kingdom Trust sponsored and published my two post-war inquiries: *The Education and Training of Social Workers* (1947) and *Social Work in Britain* (1951). The Trust's generous sponsorship has also made possible this present study of some developments between 1950 and 1975. Thanks are also due to the Gulbenkian Foundation for kindly administering the grant.

I am indebted to Elizabeth Irvine for a substantial contribution and to Sylvia Watson and Fred Jarvis for sections on professional associations. Many organisations and individuals have generously contributed information, read draft chapters and given advice or permission to quote. They include Age Concern, the Association of British Adoption and Fostering Agencies, the Association of Directors of Social Services, the Association of Teachers in Social Work Education, Geraldine Aves, Mary Barker, Barnardo's, Rose Mary Braithwaite, the British Association of Settlements, the British Association of Social Workers, Sibyl Clement Brown, Megan Browne, Zofia Butrym, the Carnegie United Kingdom Trust, Derek Carter, the Central Council for Education and Training in Social Work, Olive Chandler, the Church Army, the Church of England Board for Social Responsibility, the Community Development Project Information and Intelligence Unit, the Community Relations Commission, Joan Cooper, Joan Court, Anne Cronin, the Department of Health and Social Security (Social Work Service), the Family Service Units, the Family Welfare Association, the Group for the Advancement of Psychotherapy in Social Work, Phoebe Hall, Florence Hollis, Robert Holman, the Home Office, Dorothy Howell-Thomas, Elisabeth Hunter, the Inner London Probation and After-Care Service, the Institute of Marital Studies, the Institute of Social Welfare, David Jones, Robin Huws Jones, the Joint University Council for Social and Public Administration, Ann Kelly, Bessie Kent, Margaret Lester, Katharine Lloyd, the Local Government Training Board, P. J. MacRae, Joan Matthews, Eric Miller, Richard Mills, the National Association for the Care and Resettlement of Offenders, the National Association of Probation Officers, the National Council of Social Service, the National Marriage Guidance Council, the National Institute for Social Work (including the librarians), the National Society for Mentally Handicapped Children, the National Society for the Prevention of Cruelty to Children, the National Youth Bureau, George Newton, Priscilla Norman, Jean Nursten, Pamela Page, the Personal Social Services Council, Dorothy Pettes, the Polytechnic of North London, the Pre-School Playgroups Association, Colin Pritchard, the Prison Service Staff College, Hilda Rawlings, Helen Rees, Gordon Rose, Margaret Roxburgh, Eric Sainsbury, the Salvation Army, the Scottish Office (Social Work Services Group), Ian Sinclair, Adrian Sinfield, Muriel Smith, Jean Snelling, the Social Science Research Council, the Social Work

Advisory Service, the Southern and Western Regional Association for the Blind, Harry Specht, Marjorie Steel, Sara Stevens, Janie Thomas, T. Treunheuz, the Welsh Office, Reg Wright. I am also grateful to the many who helped, knowingly or unknowingly, by discussions about the past, present and future of social work and by keeping me well briefed on some activities without any specific request: they include the National Children's Bureau, the Tavistock Institute of Human Relations and the Calouste Gulbenkian Foundation. I am also indebted to the Home Office and to the Controller of Her Majesty's Stationery Office for permission to use Home Office material and to quote from Stationery Office publications, especially the Seebohm and Younghusband Reports.

Eileen Younghusband
November, 1976

Contents

PART TWO: DEVELOPMENTS IN SOCIAL WORK STRUCTURE

List of Tables

PART ONE   SOCIAL WORK IN SOME MAJOR SOCIAL SERVICES

Chapter 1

Changes in Social Work
Between 1950 and 1975

INTRODUCTION

This is a lop-sided history because inevitably it pays more attention to some
events than others and because it is impossible to discuss the employment
of social workers without reference to the services in which they worked:
though this is not a history of the social services as such. Aspects of service
provision, lacks and achievements are described because these were the
milieu within which social workers functioned, though they themselves were
only an element, even if an increasingly significant one, in a broad social
welfare spectrum. In some situations social workers were primarily the
service, in others they were only relevant to a marginal number of clients,
in yet others they came slowly onto the centre of the stage or else made
little headway.

The focus is on changes over the twenty-five years between 1950 and
1975, as by degrees new attitudes about the nature of social need resulted
both in more services and a change from officials administering the regulations to social workers giving a professional service. This study aimed to
discover what social workers actually did at different periods, as well as
what was discovered about their appropriate use. Thus much space is given
to medical and psychiatric social work, and to the child care and probation
services, which were primarily manned by social workers. Periodic research
or inquiries at the time gave glimpses of common assumptions and practice
and of agency policies and professional social work aims. There are specific
references to Scotland and occasionally to Wales if substantial differences
existed: but the study did not cover Northern Ireland.

This is a story full of tensions, of unrecorded achievement in the lives of
individual people, of blind spots and irrelevant intervention, or of the little
that was sometimes enough. It is also the story of a profession's struggles to
understand many different kinds of people better in their family and social
circumstances, their reactions to long-continued stress or depriving circumstances or sudden crises, and how it might be possible to substitute a benign
for a vicious circle. This included a fitfully recognised need to combine
practical help with understanding of human behaviour. Clients included
people able to function if given sufficient support and others who at some
point in their lives lacked adequate natural support systems or were too

gravely damaged socially and emotionally to function without skilled help. The list grew longer throughout the period as more needs were identified or social change resulted in fresh problems. By the 1970s it included children whose homes had failed them, homeless people adrift, people displaced by urban renewal or living in blighted urban areas, isolated old people, battering parents and their children, severe marital conflict, one-parent families, multiproblem families, joyless children, some persistent offenders, the violent or the apathetic, addicts, alienated, inadequate or mentally disordered people, and others whose problems were both discrete and related. The record here shows that social work had made progress in uncovering the degree and variety of personality damage from which different people suffered. Some recorded experiments to reverse the process showed positive results with certain individuals, sometimes a holding operation (which might be too costly for general application), or a failure by any available combination of individual and group methods or environmental 'manipulation' to effect relevant change. Over the twenty-five years, social work in such situations had reached the stage of more accurate identification or arrested deterioration and a wider range of 'treatment' methods but only limited prescriptions for prevention or 'cure'.

Interest in prevention grew, particularly prevention of damaging childhood experiences or of dereliction in old age. Some pointers were maintaining the child in his home, temporary removal with support to the parents, or permanent removal and resettlement. These pointers were hard to apply partly because accurate and continuous assessment, or criteria for judging how much support was enough or ineffective with particular people, or what was the indication for a quick clean break were lacking. New forms of prevention included play groups, a more flexible youth service, group activities and the whole range of community development to enrich people's experiences, social relationships and control of their affairs. These developments, hailed as creative innovations, in the late 1960s and early 1970s were strikingly similar to settlement activities in earlier periods though with more systematic attempts to study group dynamics and interaction.

There were many reasons why the number of social workers increased in child care and probation and advanced professionally in psychiatric and medical social work, but made little headway in the care of the physically and mentally handicapped (including the blind and deaf) and old people. Probation and child care may have received more public resources because they attracted more political interest, whether through the nuisance value of delinquency or the emotional appeal of unprotected children. Conversely, the old and the handicapped were thought of primarily in medical and social-security terms or as the concern of many active voluntary organisations. Moreover, they were the responsibility of a government department and local authorities primarily concerned with health and it only began to be realised in the mid-1960s that health and social care were complementary. Their sheer numbers also became dauntingly apparent later and for too many social workers they had neither the interest nor the challenge of family conflict and child deprivation or delinquency.

When poverty was rediscovered after the first welfare state enthusiasm died down, it became obvious that chronic poverty, bad housing, limited employment opportunities and blighted urban areas called for large-scale action far beyond the bounds of social work. In any event, it slowly became clear that social work could only be effectively practised from within agencies with a range of resources including group work, day centres, aids to daily living, financial help and appropriate residential care. Social work was earlier a handmaid of medicine but later this became a partnership in the prevention of social handicap, especially with psychiatrists and paediatricians, in relation to emotionally and socially damaged children and adults. Interdisciplinary co-operation increased as it became obvious that no one profession could go it alone. The relations of social work to education were still little explored by 1975. New bridges were school counselling, an altered concept of education welfare, and community work, while throughout the period the youth service had a foot in both camps.

Social work only spread in the local authorities after 1948; it largely created the child care service, won its slow way in health and welfare and then became the key profession in the social work and social services departments. But, except in a few sheltered situations in voluntary organisations or public services, social workers struggled with over-large workloads, never free of 'the danger of being lost in mediocrity and administrative mazes' (Butler, 1976).

The advances recorded in this study were due to more generous social attitudes, more accurate identification of need and a wider range of services, more interdisciplinary action, more knowledge in the behavioural sciences, a wider range of social work intervention and more and better-qualified and supported social workers. None the less, at many points the knowledge and skill and quality of service that could ideally be provided far outstripped actual resources. But social work is a profession only at its beginning and this study is mainly a chronicle of early stages in which clearer perception, more finely differentiated knowledge and skill revealed greater complexities.

THE CHANGING SOCIAL SCENE

By the early 1950s the weight of a deterrent and incompetent poor law had been lifted; some of its shadows remained but it was thought that new legislation providing better education, health, housing and social security, coupled with full employment, would abolish most social problems.

The standard of living rose markedly between 1950 and 1975 and most people 'had never had it so good'. But some remained persistently caught in the trap of poverty, in particular low-paid, unskilled manual workers, single-parent families, old people and the handicapped. National insurance, supplementary benefits and family and other allowances raised minimum standards, but many did not apply for means-tested benefits and life on the margin continued. All through the period there were stop–go policies in government spending.

There was full employment until the 1973 world recession and galloping inflation. Mobility in employment, coupled with geographical mobility, separated many families physically and broke up old, close community networks. Family members might keep in touch by telephone or a periodic visit, but not be easily available for daily practical services or help in illness.

The mother's confinement was a persisting cause of children having to be received into short-term care as more confinements took place in hospital.

Early marriage, divorce and remarriage and sometimes responsibility for two sets of children, coupled with smaller family size and increasing employment of married women also meant that fewer were free to cope in an emergency. A more equal age distribution of the sexes resulted in a higher marriage rate, and at an earlier age, so that the family was 'at risk' for longer, while many services lost their reliable spinsters and families their maiden aunts or daughters. Even so, the family and local community remained the main personal social service. For example, the vast majority of old and handicapped people were looked after by friends and relations, even though until 1971 the personal social services were too fragmented to plan comprehensive support for families and communities. There were great changes in the age structure of the population because of earlier high birth and survival rates and advances in medicine which kept more old and handicapped people alive. For instance, the number of old people increased from 6,850 million in 1951 to 9,055 million in 1971. Poliomylitis and tuberculosis were conquered but many other handicapped people lived longer.

All these changes had significant consequences for the social services. In a sense, this twenty-five years was an exercise in learning to support the family better, to make its tasks tolerable to the giver and receiver rather than taking responsibility from it. This had to be attempted at a time when, paradoxically, higher housing standards and the policies of some housing authorities, coupled with women's employment, made it difficult for the family to look after additional family members or to take in foster children or lodgers.

WHAT SOCIAL WORK MIGHT BE LIKE IN THE 1950s

Changing practice in medical and psychiatric social work, child care and probation are discussed in later chapters. The most substantial source of information about actual rank-and-file practice in different services was Rodgers and Dixon's study, *Portrait of Social Work* (1960). In this northern county borough in the mid-1950s there were 72 social workers, among whom 5 had had a professional training and 42 no training of any kind. In any event, training was not considered important compared with being good with people, sometimes 'taking a firm line, standing no nonsense' and 'not allowing people to get away with it', being experienced and knowing the regulations. Some classed themselves as social workers without any idea what this meant. Casework was common sense 'requiring no special skill or methods so that any worker feels himself equal to it' (p. 158). It tended to be equated with home visiting and such visits, however brief, constituted a claim to know all about the family's circumstances. Supervision and consultation were almost unknown and co-operation rare and sporadic. Some people were natural social workers, kind and patient, tolerant, persistent and undefeated. They did not always act wisely but their efforts to help were untiring. Others expected too much too quickly and had no conception of why they failed to make people exercise their responsibilities or that other methods might be more effective. Some became intolerant and wrote off 'non-cooperative' families or were personally hurt at 'ingratitude'.

Matrimonial work was light-heartedly undertaken by anyone, with unrecorded consequences. People were 'supervised' by those in authority who knew what was for their moral good and made no attempt to draw them into decisions about the direction of their lives. 'There is one type of chief officer who thinks of social work as a means of getting people to do things – of making them observe rules and regulations. For him it is the business of social workers to see that people do as they are told and to make them realise they will be punished if they don't' (p. 163).

An Association of Psychiatric Social Workers' (APSW) publication (1956*b*) said of untrained and unsupervised workers:

'Some of these workers have very good natural gifts of sympathy and sensitivity. Their lack of training makes it difficult for them to detect the basic difficulties underlying the presenting problems. In these circumstances they may be inclined to offer premature advice and reassurance, to impose apparently reasonable plans upon their clients rather than to explore their feelings and needs in a way that will help them to find their own solutions.' (*The Essentials of Social Casework*, p. 6)

Probably agency policy largely determined good or poor practice. It might either contribute to staff development through regular discussion of difficult cases, or leave individuals to fulfil administrative requirements in their own way without a framework of professional support or supervision. Moral judgements stifled curiosity and a heavy paternalism hung over non-professional social work. There was much independent uncoordinated visiting, lack of clarity about function, contradictory advice or information, inadequate communication and no common code of ethics.

Over a large part of the field, case records were rudimentary. In the mid-1950s the Younghusband working party (1959) found these 'poor or non existent' in the health and welfare services owing partly to pressure of work and lack of clerical help, but also because untrained and unguided workers had no idea of their value. They might consist of a card index of name, address, age, source of referral and nature of request. Confidentiality might be little regarded, for instance in a county office the records were kept on the counter at the reception desk with names and addresses clearly visible. In 'welfare visiting' there was little concept of initial assessment to clarify the nature of the need and objectives, to be followed by periodic assessment of change. Conversely, under the Home Office Probation Rules there was an approved assessment form: each interview and the case history were written up as well as periodic summaries of the probationer's progress.

These two examples illustrate the uneven state of service recording even in the mid-1950s, and therefore the lack of data for assessing the nature and geographical distribution of need, the people who received several services, the quality of the service provided and its outcome. There were many efforts to standardise records but real progress only began after social services reorganisation. The later Martin Report (n.d., but actually published 1974), after reviewing various systems of local recording for Scottish national statistics, recommended that a unit return should be made on every open case which had required some service in the previous year, a 'case' being either an individual or a group of clients. Returns should include basic information about those concerned in the case, the reason why the department was involved, what action was taken and the service provided. This system was introduced in Scotland in 1976 and thus it would be possible to discover over a period of time what individuals, families and communities received which services.

This was part of the process, throughout the twenty-five years, from impulsive and unexamined activities to systematic assessment, recording and review, including criteria for closing inactive cases. Professional social work deserves credit for making assessment (social diagnosis) a fundamental of practice and devoting much effort to refining this in the light of new knowledge. Later this was made more precise by the concept of a contract with the client about limited goals for joint action. In the far-off days of Charity Organisation Society principles this had been called 'making a plan with the applicant'. These gains were counterbalanced by rapid staff turnover and lack of continuity of relationship with clients.

FROM WELFARE TO SOCIAL WORK

The extent of poverty, the range and depth of social need and environmental blight and the amount of knowledge, skill, resources and drive that would be required to combat them came to light by degrees later and was but at its beginnings by the mid-1970s.

What was sometimes called 'the social dimension' or mental health was only gradually identified. It is significant that there is no word for this 'social dimension' or 'social care' in the English language. This added to the confusion and rivalry before, during and after the Seebohm inquiry into the personal social services, which were in some respects no more 'personal' than health or education. By and large social care was regarded as something private or as an attitude, a concern for welfare, rather than as a practice based upon knowledge and skill. Indeed such a practice was for long ignored or held to be impossible, or undesirable prying, or to destroy fellow-feeling and personal concern. Hence some local authorities' reluctance to employ trained social workers, hence also Wootton's strictures (1959).

The first stage in the 1950s included some constructive experiments in personal social services and personal care by voluntary organisations, or voluntary effort often on a religious basis. The change finally came with the recognition that the social/personal element in human functioning was amenable to systematic inquiry, professional intervention and the provision of a range of services for assessment, treatment and prevention – if the compassion, the drive and the skill were there. This change partly resulted from the experience gained by medical and psychiatric social workers and family caseworkers in their work with specific groups, whether in child and family relationships, or with mentally disturbed or ill people. The probation service and the 1948 Children Act were early breakthroughs and the only ones to advance independently of medicine, though with its help. In so doing the ideological foundations were laid for the later personal social services.

The earlier concept of 'welfare' became popular none the less. In a confused way it meant to treat people with courtesy and to have concern for them as individuals with different needs and personalities, and thus it became the matrix from which social work could grow. The transformation of 'welfare' into a professional service, which was bound to happen, resulted partly from the experience of fieldworkers in some statutory services; from some enlightened voluntary organisations which concentrated on specific social problems, like the Family Service Units (FSU), the Edinburgh Guild of Service and the Institute of Martial Studies (IMS); and from the application of new knowledge in psychiatry, paediatrics, sociology and criminology.

What essentially happened, and went on gathering momentum through the period, was that curiosity burst free from the static or moralistic assumptions of an earlier period. Full employment and better living standards made it possible to concentrate more on people facing chronic or intermittent social or personal crises or deprivations. Some misfits were no longer told to pull themselves together or written off as moral failures. The boundaries between the deserving and the undeserving became blurred and social workers began to ask why they and not the client had failed. But throughout the period both social workers and public opinion continued to show more interest in some groups than others.

Those twenty-five years record when and how society became able to 'see' and take legislative action about some social problems that had been there all the time. Deprived children became visible in 1948 and the chronically sick and disabled dimly in 1970. But the old, one-parent families, the homeless, prisoners and their families, the chronic poor and young people adrift only passed fitfully across the stage. Services existed for them and knowledge about them but the necessary quality, universality and drive was lacking except in some voluntary organisations. For example, the Curtis Report (1946) and the Maria Colwell inquiry (DHSS, 1974d) had explosive consequences, but revelations about back wards of subnormality hospitals, the living death suffered by some young chronic sick or isolated old people caused hardly a ripple, while the plight of the very poor and the homeless was known but not faced.

The great changes that finally resulted in social work and social services departments and significant extensions to the probation and after-care service, began in the 1960s and accelerated until the outburst of initiative from many sources between 1965 and 1968 heralded a new era. At last paternalism was waning and there was a Trojan horse in the penal system. Much detail in the following chapters records new attitudes that finally burst into action in the mid-1960s. Often this action revealed that the tools were lacking, that, for instance, there was little knowledge of how to prevent or cure social handicap, which might require as much skill in its own sphere as medical treatment.

Residential services were primarily for education or medical treatment or reform or punishment until, in the early 1950s, homes for children and for old people began to take on a more positive nurturing role. Neglect of staff and staff shortages delayed developments at the very time in the 1950s and 1960s when there was a swing away from custodial residential care, and finally the recognition that this was a particularly skilled form of social work. By 1975 there had been no systematic study of all forms of residential care for children and young people and the effect of different patterns of organisational structure, care and staff training. This range included community homes, boarding schools, residential special schools for handicapped or maladjusted children, children's wards of subnormality hospitals, sick children in hospital, long-term hospital care for the young chronic sick, borstals, and hostels of various kinds for adolescents.

SOCIAL WORK LOOKS AT ITSELF AND ITS METHODS

Social work had looked at itself before the 1950s but did so more consistently in the outburst of energy characteristic of the post-war years. Naturally it first tried to learn more about individual and family behaviour. It was dazzled by the key to many inexplicable responses offered by the concepts of unconscious motivation, maternal deprivation and the mechanisms of defence. Only casework existed as a technique, but at national conferences of family casework agencies and professional associations there was regular discussion of social issues, for example bad housing or the iniquities of hire-purchase firms. In other words, social work techniques were more limited than social work concerns.

There were numerous definitions of social work throughout the period. The following (Swithun Bowers, 1949) was widely accepted in the 1950s: 'Social casework is an art in which knowledge of the science of human relations and skills in relationships are used to mobilize capacities in the individual and resources in the community appropriate to better adjustment between the client and all or any part of his total environment' (p. 417). This definition recognised the importance of the social environment and of adjustment as a two-way process, though not specifically of family and social relationships. It was expanded but not fundamentally changed by a British Association of Social Workers (BASW) 1975 definition:

'Social work . . . extends its interest beyond the immediate issue to understanding the clients' background, social situations, motivation, attitudes, values, personality and behaviour and attempts to encourage development and change by a wide variety of methods which amongst many others may well include the development of strong relationships with clients, insight-giving techniques, behaviour modification and practical help.' (*Social Work Today/BASW News*, 1975c, p. 317)

The period when professional social workers were small bands of freedom fighters on alien ground was succeeded, too quickly for comfort, by demands that they should occupy whole territories. They had always been in short supply and apt to cluster together, whether geographically or in particular services. In these years there was an unremitting struggle to increase numbers in some traditional social work services and to extend these over the whole country. The results were disappointing not, as in the late 1940s, for lack of candidates but because of training bottlenecks which hindered a sufficient supply of recruits from flowing through to meet an unsatiated demand.

THE EFFECT OF THE SOCIAL ENVIRONMENT

In the 1960s, a series of action research studies, some summarised later, coupled with more knowledge about the consequences of social change, showed the extent to which social circumstances generated 'private sorrows'. Some people overcame these and others survived. In helping those who floundered social workers began to face the stigma of coercing helpless people into conformity. In any event, it became obvious that if many individual deviants were reacting normally to abnormal circumstances, or some so-called inadequates coping heroically, the sensible answer was to change their circumstances. Hence a stronger emphasis was placed on social action and social reform in social work thought. A [1974] BASW working party report on social action said that 'the problem [*sic*] clients have are as likely to be related to the situation they are in as to any inadequacy in themselves' (2.1.6). But the situation they were in might result in anxiety, stress and depression which prevented the children from receiving good mothering. So an external situation might lead to defective personality development – and so on through the cycle of deprivation. None the less copers and non-copers might live alongside each other in the same street.

Many studies showed the high proportion of sufferers from almost every form of social malaise in social classes IV and V. But Davies (1969) and Goldberg (1967) found families of young offenders and schizophrenic patients in reasonable material circumstances, and Goldberg and Neill's (1972) action study showed that all social classes responded to social work in an acceptable setting. The IMS had similar experience (personal communication). The Community Development Project (CDP) teams also found little personal pathology in socially deprived areas. But there was much evidence of depression, apathy, loneliness, chronic anxiety, boredom, strained relations and outbursts of violence related to oppressive poverty and debilitating living conditions. Those in other social classes had better material standards and freedom of choice but might be under-represented in the personal social services because they used other services or were less likely to be identified, not because they were free from personal, relationship or social problems. Many people in all classes bore such burdens with dull resignation, unaware that any relief was possible. Others had little or no access to essential services or would only respond in a socially acceptable setting; hence experiments in placing social workers in child welfare, family planning or other clinics, in general practice teams, in schools, in youth employment bureaux, or as unattached workers in streets, pubs or market places. This also made early identification or crisis intervention possible. There was discussion about vulnerable points in the life-cycle where support was important, for example early childhood, entering employment, marriage and the arrival of the first baby, retirement and bereavement. But there were only isolated experiments in making social work services easily accessible at those transitional points.

Community work and social action by many social workers was motivated by anger at the suffering of the overburdened and powerless poor. Hadley, Webb and Farrell (1975) made a strong plea that mental suffering, irrespective of poverty, should be a concern of social services departments: 'Loneliness is one example, it is a virtually universal condition; most people experience it as a problem at some time and consequently a wide cross section of the population might be persuaded to use a service which offered advice and support during these periods of isolation and loneliness' (p. 195).

Aims shifted from encouragement of self-help activities in the 1960s to politically motivated social action by local people to increase their share of outside resources and more power in decision making. Not all community workers agreed with the BASW working party on social action [1974] that 'material deprivation and social powerlessness on the one hand, and emotional deprivation and personal inadequacy on the other, are both valid grounds for social work help' (1.5.1).

Several succeeding chapters stress the slow development of conceptualised group work compared with casework, followed by the boisterous arrival of community work in the late 1960s. The joint effect of this and of widened responsibilities in social services and social work departments (and indeed in the penal system) was that social work lost grip of its identity. It sought unsuccessfully for a core and let go the happy certainties of an earlier group of creative caseworkers in the 1950s, but by the mid-1970s it had not found a clear professional identity between the poles of social action and psychotherapy. Many social workers were troubled that the pendulum had swung too far and that while there was a proper indignation about material deprivation a concern with the relations between people's inner and outer worlds was not being kept in proportion. These conflicts and uncertainties could be healthy stages in the growth of a profession if some balance was achieved between them.

In spite of attempts throughout the period, there was neither clarity nor agreement about those situations which should only be handled by qualified social workers, sometimes in consultation or as members of interdisciplinary teams. Failure to use trained social workers effectively wasted very scarce resources, hindered improvements in professional practice and gave people inappropriate service. Moreover, the identification of the social services departments with material help delayed the development of a citizen service.

After the first period when trained social workers were not always acceptable and the second stage which was characterised by demands for a 'fully qualified' service, came a further period when more experience of providing universal public services showed that such manpower aims were unrealistic and inappropriate. At first the use of ancillary workers and volunteers was resisted in situations where they were a threat to social workers' not-yet-recognised professional skill. Later it became obvious that ancillary workers and volunteers could strengthen professional practice and give effective and different personal help. The key was assessment of individual needs and the best way to meet them. A still unresolved question was whether every client needed skilled intake assessment or whether this could be made for some people by other staff trained to identify danger signals that required professional assessment.

Community work, using group work and combined with casework, began to make a considerable potential contribution to the early identification of people at risk, for instance families at breaking point or isolated old people; in mobilising local volunteer effort in co-operation with the public service; and in identifying and meeting local needs or local people's priorities, indeed to foster natural processes of give and take.

Feelings of worthlessness, isolation, depression, inability to make lasting or satisfying relationships, or overwhelming stress resulting from sudden crises or long strain were universal. Social work had no more claim than psychiatry to cure or prevent universal human ills. But in so far as these were caused by poverty and social neglect it became an accepted professional duty to press for social action. By degrees social work objectives as such became more limited, based upon a more differential assessment and more precise aims of seeing people through until they could cope, or giving long-term support with periodic intervention, or devising means of forestalling or alleviating breakdown. Social work grew increasingly self-conscious but remained clear that spontaneous concern for clients and accurate empathy combined with skill and knowledge comprised its art.

Sociology, social psychology and social work experience throughout the period showed that the individual's interaction in a variety of group situations was crucial for a sense of belonging and identity. As a result, much social work aimed to strengthen natural groups or create new groups and work within them. Indeed, the social network and group membership became central concepts in social work and contributed to a theory of preventive action. A wider range of social work treatment possibilities were thus evolved during the mid-1960s, including the flexible use of social work methods with individuals, groups and communities and integrated methods teaching. These methods included family therapy, short-term casework and the development of social work skill in strengthening natural support systems and social networks, learning how to use and support volunteers, making it more possible for the family to cope, helping to change negative social attitudes that increased isolation, forecasting the consequences of social change like rehousing schemes, making the case for more day nurseries, or acting as welfare rights advocates. These new (but not exclusively) social work functions entailed research, social data collection and case analyses for social planning and action. They required new dimensions in training and much expansion of almost non-existent post-qualifying training.

Most new knowledge that found its way into social work practice continued to come from psychiatrists, paediatricians and sociologists or other academics. From within social work itself fresh practice knowledge came from the few social workers in research teams, those who worked in agencies where advanced and recorded practice was possible, and small groups and individuals who analysed and published their findings. In the later period, improvements in practice were held back by a career structure which discouraged the good practitioner from remaining in practice – a regression from the 1950s – which weakened interest in knowing 'why' and 'how to do' and ran the risk of turning social workers once again into officials rather than professionals.

From the 1950s, some experienced professional social workers made a careful assessment of family dynamics and the distribution of roles and relationships as a prelude to considering where to intervene, at what point environmental change or direct casework help (or later family therapy) might bring about a better realignment in the family constellation and release pressures. These studies and a few creative experiments based on making close relationships with social casualties showed the depth of their personality damage, though sometimes growth was possible in a therapeutic environment or with long-term personal support. It was essential for social work practice to reach this level of conscious understanding if help were to become more than first-aid or symptom oriented, and if the service was not sometimes to be an expensive waste of time that left much human misery unalleviated. But although by 1975 pockets of advanced practice existed, the public services were too overwhelmed to make proper use of and extend work of this standard in disturbed relationships. Unfortunately knowledge gained from hopeful experiments pioneered by individuals or financed by trusts or public funds were often not followed up or related to each other. Two exceptions from the 1970s were the series of Home Office experiments in probation based on earlier research studies, and the National Society for Prevention of Cruelty to Children (NSPCC) action research on non-accidental injury to children (1976a).

The family emerged more clearly as the matrix of close personal bonds, of nurture, socialisation and life-long responsibilities. Conflicts between parents and children and between married partners spilled over into the practice of social work everywhere. Mothers and children took more and more of the limelight but fathers, who seemed to be almost non-existent in the 1950s, continued to be largely ignored. They were occasionally consulted if they were fathers of illegitimate children, or more often about becoming foster or adoptive fathers and they were admitted to one-parent family status. But mothers definitely had the edge on them in social work literature and practice. Apart from the persistence of the IMS, astonishingly little research or consistently recorded social work practice was invested in marriage and family relationships. The importance of the mother in child nurture or deprivation was well recognised, but the crucial contribution of fathers to normal or pathological personality development only began to be clarified in a few unconnected studies referred to in later chapters.

JARGON

By comparison with 1975, jargon was almost non-existent in the 1950s, apart from the unlovely terms 'casework' and 'supervision'. An Association of Social Workers Conference report (1953) recorded objections

'to the term 'client', which has a specialized meaning, both to the lawyer and to the prostitute; no convenient substitute was found, and the word is therefore used in inverted commas throughout this pamphlet. It was hoped that social workers would neither create technical jargon, nor adopt the use of officialese, but would always try to express themselves clearly in simple English.' (*Notes on the Ethics of Social Work*, pp. 2–3)

This was a forlorn hope: the clients lost their inverted commas and even generated client groups or target populations, that is people suffering from some disability that could cause them to need social work help. Those who advocated re-naming social workers 'social practitioners', or 'social servants', or Mary Richmond's 'sociotrists', on the grounds that 'work' could be assumed, got nowhere. 'Areas' spread far beyond their geographical boundaries; 'fields' took on human capacities to think and feel; and the 'interface', 'images', 'models', 'low profiles', 'high risks' and 'intervention or innovative strategies' multiplied. Like other professionals, social workers evolved their shorthand for internal communication and external mystification. Over the years many social workers mixed sociological and psychiatric jargon with their own, larded these with American clichés, and lost interest in trying 'to express themselves clearly in simple English'. BASW was an honourable exception.

SOME CHANGES IN THE SOCIAL SERVICES

With some shining exceptions, the 1950s and 1960s were characterised by limited public services, by waiting lists and by inaccessible and unpublicised services. Different local authorities provided what the interests and imagination, activity or inertia of councillors and senior staff dictated. Voluntary organisations showed much drive on behalf of some people like the blind, whereas the mentally handicapped were neglected. Anything might be better than it had been previously, and the aim of providing truly universal, personal social services was still only a hope to some people by the 1970s and an impossibility to others. Yet preventive services began with home helps and meals on wheels for old people, then spread in a limited way to children. Early identification of crises or action to prevent breakdown was sporadic, but changed attitudes in the 1970s resulted in publicity for services, local offices, surveys to identify people qualifying for help and action to provide it. After the Seebohm and Scottish reorganisation and changes in local government boundaries, it was obvious that neither the small-scale services of the 1950s and 1960s nor social work training had produced an infrastructure able to bear the weight of massive reorganisation, changed attitudes, large-scale provision and new duties, What had been done for education by the 1944 Act and for the NHS by the 1946 Act could not so easily be done for the personal social services at the time of the 1968 and 1970 legislation. Both education and health had well-established professions with accepted status and traditions, advanced studies and research. But there was only limited professional education for social work at a basic level when the local authority children's, health and welfare services started, and the race against time continued in the 1970s. Moreover, needs and how to meet them were peculiarly elusive in the personal social services, because

'Needs do not exist in fixed quanta, present in the community and awaiting measurement. Any attempt to estimate needs has to come to terms with the fundamental part played by contemporary judgments as to the range and nature of social and personal problems to which some response on the part of the public services is deemed appropriate. Such judgments vary quite startlingly over time, and may also differ markedly as between the relevant professions and the wider public.' (Martin Report, p. 26)

'SOCIAL DEVICES'

In the 1950s resources were confined to some casework, foster care for children, a few 'aids to daily living', home helps, meals on wheels, a few reception centres or other means of assessment, welfare visiting, a few hostels, some clubs, sheltered workshops and day training centres for the handicapped, and homes for children or old people. Although more varied residential institutions were started later, reliance on them grew less and their warehouse function changed as more alternatives were devised to keep people in the community, preferably in their own homes. These piecemeal developments for different groups of people included day hospitals, various day care centres, night care, short-stay homes, weekly boarding, more home helps and meals on wheels, play centres, 'sitters in', night sitters, and other attempts to substitute part-residential and part-family care to avoid institutionalisation and to help the family to carry the burden of looking after old or handicapped people, or single or overburdened parents to keep their children. Short-stay homes and recuperative centres were part of the same provision. In the early 1970s intermediate treatments, community service orders and day training centres were started as alternatives to community homes, borstal or prison.

Reception centres for assessment were intended to be part of the children's service from the start. Child guidance clinics were also used for diagnosis and so were remand homes and classifying schools for children before the courts. Probation officers' social inquiry reports were a form of assessment, as were discharge discussions between psychiatrists and mental welfare officers or PSWs at mental hospitals. Case conferences, co-ordinating committees, case committees and youth employment bureaux conferences for school leavers served the purpose with differing competence. These efforts sprang from a new understanding that it was crucial to assess a person, his family and his situation as fully and accurately as possible before deciding what was wrong and taking action. It was some time before it was thought relevant to include the chief actor and his family in the diagnostic discussion. Capacity to make good initial assessments became an increasingly important element in social work training. Multidisciplinary assessment was available in a few assessment centres for some people in the 1960s but only spread slowly, largely because of extreme staff shortages. For instance, in Scotland there were efforts to set up multidisciplinary regional assessment teams to assess the health, educational and social needs of children. As was stressed in *Living with Handicap* (Younghusband *et al.*, 1970), it was essential that the team should not only work out an initial treatment plan, but also review this at stated intervals in the light of the current situation. Obviously such all-round assessment and review was much needed for the physically and mentally disabled, old people and offenders in their family situations, as well as for children. In many instances good assessment was nullified because the necessary range of treatment facilities, including skilled social work, did not exist. But none the less multidisciplinary assessment had emerged as an essential 'social device'.

Each 'device' spread to more people, for instance day training centres originally for mentally handicapped people became dynamic experiments for persistent offenders; day centres started for the elderly were extended to drug addicts, alcoholics and homeless vagrants; foster homes for children became supervised lodgings for old or mentally disordered or handicapped people. At each beginning there were naïve ideas about the task but experience demonstrated that much knowledge, skill and consultation were necessary to achieve positive results.

Aids to daily living made it possible for handicapped people and their families to be more independent. Toy libraries, play groups and play buses helped to meet the need of small children for imaginative and creative play and a few local authorities lent toys to child minders.

By degrees several devices were combined, for instance a family advice centre might provide advice, counselling, play groups, discussion groups, welfare rights and landlord and tenant information, a meeting place and sometimes a neighbourhood community development project. There were also suggestions that local authority area offices and advice centres might be linked with clinics and health centres, with housing advisory centres and facilities for voluntary organisations.

The Central Council for Education and Training in Social Work (CCETSW) working party on day services (1975*a*) found that

'Day services currently cater for the needs of people of all ages from infancy to old age. They include people with conditions which give rise to intrinsic handicaps (e.g. blindness, deafness, cerebral palsy, mental retardation) which may be lifelong or acquired, and extrinsic handicaps (homelessness, social deprivation, drug addiction, apparent unemployability). They may require day services because of some personal problem which inhibits their normal functioning (e.g. depression) or because circumstances over which they have no control have changed (e.g. the death of a supportive relative).' (para. 5.42)

As in residential care, the focus was shifting from 'somewhere to be' to individual assessment, the setting of a series of limited objectives focused on achievement and awareness of self and others in order to make possible satisfying living experiences and better social functioning. Ideally day services were closely linked with domiciliary and other services.

By the mid-1970s there had been no comprehensive study of all these different and often isolated social devices, their significance and what they were or might be 'good for', singly or in combination, for different people in different circumstances as elements in social services provision, and of course including members of other professions.

In addition to strengthening local neighbourhood resources, another type of social device resulted from the lowering of 'them' and 'us' professional barriers, fresh understanding about communication hazards, and the sheer shortage of professional 'helpers' which led to new uses of volunteers.

Discussion groups for multiproblem family mothers, or would-be adopters or foster parents, or prisoners' wives were variations on the same theme. The potentialities of this 'device' were only beginning to be explored in relation to specific groups by the mid-1970s.

SOCIAL WORK MANPOWER

The social work employment scene in 1975 was very different from 1950. The increase in numbers (only partial figures are available for the 1950s) must, of course, be related to population changes and the growth of services. Promotion prospects were far removed from the one or two steps up the ladder in the early 1950s. Table 17 (see chapter 21, p. 304) shows that some social workers' salaries increased tenfold in monetary terms between 1950 and 1975. The number of trained social workers in local authority service had increased from a handful in 1950 to 9,558 in 1973 (Birch Report, 1976, table 3). But only 40 per cent of fieldworkers and 60 per cent of senior staff in social services departments were trained. In central government departments in 1950 there was a chief social welfare officer in the Ministry of Health and chief inspectors in the Home Office Children's Department and Probation Division. By 1975 only the chief probation inspector remained as such. Scotland had a chief social work adviser in the Social Work Services Group, and the DHSS director of social work services was about to become the chief social work officer. This appointment as chief professional adviser to ministers and the Department on social work and social services, which was only open to qualified social workers, was made in 1975 at deputy secretary level with a salary of £14,000 a year and a staff of 130. Most social workers were called officers until the 1970s when they all became social workers except in the probation service.

Both the first and second Carnegie reports (Younghusband, 1947 and 1951) stressed the need for job analyses. There were few subsequent attempts at these, partly because there were no accepted yardsticks for good practice. Periodic protests about the use of trained social workers for clerical tasks and attempts to assess workloads were a form of job analysis, but there was no recorded experimentation with varied deployment of professional or other social workers in direct or indirect service, using or not using ancillary or 'indigenous' workers, working independently or as members of interdisciplinary teams. The issue became urgent with the range of demands on social services departments and the shortage of professional social workers. The Birch Report (1976) pointed out afresh that job analyses were needed to distinguish between tasks suitable for qualified social workers, people with other trainings, and the untrained. It also thought that the tasks required of qualified and other social workers were so diverse that study was essential to discover how qualified social workers were actually used. It classified the range of staffing thus:

(a) Professional social work is one amongst a range of services required and should be more explicitly defined and appropriately used; and in some instances the term social worker should be limited to those who are qualified;

(b) Needs not requiring social work can and may be better met by staff with different types of training;

(c) Community based services demand close involvement with the local community and its own resources; and

(d) Different sectors of service need closer integration for example, between field and domiciliary services, and between residential and day care provision. (para. 6.2)

It was hoped that these questions would be clarified by a research project on social work practice being conducted under the auspices of Oxford and Aberdeen Universities.

CONTINUING TASKS

Throughout the period, the social, health and prison services were plagued by dreary, barrack-like, nineteenth-century buildings, sometimes in remote country districts, which embodied custodial attitudes and made it well-nigh impossible to implement modern ideas about small groups of staff and residents in close contact with the outside world and, in varying degrees, democratically run. Unsuitable buildings exercised a stranglehold in the years after the war when fresh building was either prohibited or later increasingly costly, and in spite of great efforts, some of them were still in use in 1975.

If this study seems overloaded by developments in the late 1960s this is because, as has been said, something momentous happened between 1965 and 1968 which released energies still active by 1975, in spite of massive economy cuts. The social work profession had leapt from the margins to the centre and was faced with a challenge to do the job to which it had always laid claim. This looked far more demanding than in 1950, because experience gained in the past twenty-five years made social work more aware of what it faced in attempting to provide services that ranged from remedial treatment and support to preventive action in collaboration with the other helping professions and from within large bureaucratic structures.

Chapter 2

The Child Care Service,
1948-1971

DISCOVERIES IN THE 1950s

The 1948 Children Act made it mandatory for counties and county boroughs to set up a children's committee responsible for child care and to appoint a children's officer. Individual care was to be provided for every child who had no home or who could not remain at home, either temporarily or permanently. This created an even more pioneer situation than the later Seebohm reorganisation, but similar upheavals accompanied the transfer of staffs and buildings to the new children's departments. The history of the child care service from then until it was merged with the social services departments in 1971 consisted in trying to discover how to reverse the odds against children whose homes had failed them; to lessen or prevent the trauma of separation, whether for short or long periods, or grossly inadequate parenting; to provide substitute, family-type care whether in institutions or foster homes; to forestall emotional stunting in institutions and to give the children a better start in life than they would otherwise have had.

The following account shows not only the ups and downs, the task that grew more rewarding and more daunting with fresh knowledge, the constricted resources, the individual achievements, the extremes within discernible trends, the uneven progress revealed by research studies, but also the steady commitment that created the children's service and made it responsive to individual needs. To our loss, individual children's histories were neither systematically recorded nor analysed. Much that was learnt in those years was embodied in good practice by some departments, though not in others, for example Packman's (1975) account of developments in Oxfordshire Children's Department or Parker's (1966) and other studies discussed in Chapter 4.

When the children's service began it was still assumed that children must be rescued from inadequate families, the slate wiped clean and the child given a fresh start. By degrees it was realised that parents lived on inside the child, that his identity was bound up with his origins and hence that everything possible should be done to strengthen home ties. In the pre-1948 public services for children it was thought that to provide food, clothing, shelter, education and moral training was sufficient. New understanding of the emotional needs of children began to seep through in the late 1940s with explosive consequences over the years for the child care service. Perhaps the essential change was from stereotyped assumptions about a child care régime to observing, questioning and experimenting to try to find the right answer for very different individual children and their families.

The new children's departments started with much public goodwill because of the strong feelings aroused by war-time evacuation, the Dennis O'Neill case and other revelations of child neglect and the Curtis Report's findings, though there was considerable resentment from the health and education departments and some trepidation at the influx of women children's officers with chief officer status into local government. The new service was also influenced by the experience gained from the small group of trained social workers stationed in evacuation regions by the Ministry of Health, and by the Home Office Children's Division inspectorate. A considerable number of children were in the care of voluntary organisations, some of which were national and had a wide range of resources, some local, some with a single purpose, for instance responsible for one children's home or placing babies for adoption. Much of what follows about changing practice applies to voluntary organisations as well as local authorities.

The stocktaking by the new departments from 1948 revealed scanty or non-existent records, an unknown number of children in various forms of care, separated siblings, unrecorded and lost relations. This was coupled with inadequate or non-existent facilities, notably children's homes that were often large, overcrowded, understaffed, barrack-like institutions, sometimes part of the old workhouse and characterised by 'dirt and dreariness, drabness and over regimentation' (Curtis Report, 1946). Children might be grouped according to age and moved when they were 2, 3, 5, or 11 or recalled from their foster homes at 8 or 14 to residential schools or training. Siblings of different ages might be separated in such homes: children also suffered the double trauma of being moved to strange situations at the same time as starting or leaving school. Some overworked staff gave unstinting care to children, though they might be rigid disciplinarians. Apart from Dr Barnardo's and the National Children's Home, training of residential staff was unknown.

The new emphasis at that period on family group homes and reception centres was a reaction from receiving children into care at a point of crisis and, without assessment of their individuality and needs (except for a health check), sending them to large and often isolated children's homes. Comparatively few reception centres were set up because of building restrictions and because views differed as to their merits when compared with the double upheaval they represented for the child. (Residential care is discussed in the following chapter.)

Fortunately Bowlby's *Maternal Care and Mental Health* (1951) fanned the winds of change. The response to this study was enthusiastic, especially in the child care and probation services, and in varying degrees in the other helping professions and in the teaching of social work students. It reinforced the swing away from children's homes but was sometimes misinterpreted to mean that any natural mother, no matter how unmotherly, was superior to any alternative, whereas the crux of the matter was a secure nurturing role rather than a biological relationship as such. As Dr Hilda Lewis (1954) commented in the only child care action research study of this period, 'Unfortunately dogmatic statements about ill-effects of maternal deprivation often leave out of account the emotional hazards and harms children may suffer from bad mothers and indifferent mother substitutes, or the variety of sources (including the father) from whom children may draw the love and support necessary for their happiness' (p. 75). Though many subsequent studies refined the original hypothesis of maternal deprivation, they none the less demonstrated the damage suffered by those infants and small children denied a stable relationship with an 'attachment figure' over a sufficient period of time.

The struggles by this small and unproven service for resources in the local authority structure were affected by the status and understanding of councillors on the children's committees: indeed, 'the members had to be committed and knowledgeable and to deal with a mass of case detail which was, in fact, a way of enabling members to consider children in care as individuals, with personal needs and problems' (Packman, 1975, p. 32). Another crucial element was the tact, diplomacy and wisdom of the children's officer, often a woman new to local government who had joined a group of male chief officers at a time when the medical officer of health and the director of education each thought that the children's service should have been given to them. Good provision was made for children's officers in many local authorities but Rodgers and Dixon (1960) have described what sometimes happened:

'The first children's officer appointed in the town was a woman, a trained almoner with a classics degree and a social studies diploma . . . To begin with she was offered a desk in the typists' room in the health department but, protesting about this, she was permitted to join the health visitors. For five months she worked quite alone but then a full time clerk was appointed and two months later a junior clerk. Demands for a child care visitor met strong opposition, the establishment committee being unwilling to authorise the new position. Eventually, however, after ten months, a woman visitor was appointed and nine months later, in January 1950, a man joined the department to deal with the older boys and for general clerical work. In 1954 a second woman visitor was appointed and since this time, although the staff have changed, the establishment of the department has remained unaltered.' (pp. 69–70)

This northern town had a population of nearly 100,000. By 1969 the total population was unchanged, though it included more children but, in addition to a children's officer, there were by then a deputy, 2 senior and 7 child care officers, 2 student social workers and 3 trainees. The residential child care staff had doubled (Rodgers and Stevenson, 1973).

Children's departments in the 1950s were learning how to provide a personal social service within the local authority structure, a setting where trained social workers began to be employed for the first time in substantial numbers. In the early days neither staff nor committee members knew what would be demanded of a service dedicated to the well-being of children and acting wholly or partly *in loco parentis*. Necessary services to meet the needs of deprived children had to be discovered step by step and had often to be fought for throughout the 1950s. There was confusion about objectives and the importance of working co-operatively with parents, while at the same time meeting legal requirements and sanctions especially in relation to fit person orders (later, care orders). These regulations themselves were a safeguard to professional practice and by degrees they were based on experience of loopholes. In the 1950s, the previous assumption that a personal social service could only be provided by voluntary organisations began to be disproved.

One of the biggest advances in thought in this period was the concept of continuity of care and an attempt to fuse preventive and remedial services through far more selective and differentiated provision which took account of the developmental needs of individual children and the maintenance of personal relationships. This tremendous change from the pre-1948 services governed by inflexible rules resulted largely from the influence of social work. In many departments much effort and imaginative provision was invested in trying to discover what was best for individual children and in providing appropriate nurture before the stage of 'too little and too late' resulted in irreversible damage. New knowledge about the underlying causes of behaviour was increasingly applied in the best practice. Often children were severely damaged before they were received into care, yet the child care service had no power to intervene earlier so that, if possible, support to the family could keep them at home. Naturally, standards varied greatly. The point is not that high standards were universal, but that they became possible for the first time. Knowledge was not recorded or tested by research, but it was accumulated and spread through frequent consultations and conferences, through the Home Office inspectorate, informal and in-service training and the activities of the professional associations. In the most advanced children's departments, women – and sometimes men – with considerable drive, imagination and intuition, knowledge and training, together with an ability to carry their committee and staff with them, pioneered children's services in which some children in care or supported in their own homes got a better start in life than they would have had otherwise, and later sank into the background as 'ordinary, good-enough' husbands and wives, fathers and mothers.·

Foster Care

The Curtis Committee's extreme emphasis on adoption and foster-home placement was partly a revulsion from what the members had seen in many over-organised and regimented children's homes. Under the 1948 Children Act all children in care were to be fostered unless this was 'not practicable or desirable for the time being' (section 13) and there was detailed control over some aspects of fostering under the Boarding Out Regulations. The search for foster homes was more successful in some areas than others, partly owing to local traditions or the lack of them about fostering, to the housing situation, to women's employment in the locality, to the low level of boarding-out allowances, and to shortage of child care staff.

In 1949 35 per cent of children in care were boarded out: by 1960 this had risen to 48 per cent of a larger number. In Scotland, the proportion remained fairly steady at about 60 per cent throughout the period but fell to 52 per cent in 1970. It is impossible to judge these percentages in terms of the quality of child care in this period without more detailed analysis than was undertaken of the factors making for success or failure under different conditions. Some later research studies are discussed in the following chapters.

As time went on, there was more careful choice of foster homes, greater effort to find the best one for a particular child or to keep siblings together, as well as experiments in boarding out handicapped children, coloured children, short-stay children and babies and toddlers. About two-thirds of the children in care were under school age and this, coupled with the pressure to close children's homes in old poor-law buildings, together with a shortage of foster homes, at first led to more residential nurseries being opened in England and Wales. But by 1963 60 out of 142 local authorities had no residential nurseries. Short-stay fostering also became steadily more significant.

Preventive Work

The Curtis Committee thought the question of whether deprivation could be prevented 'of the utmost importance and we hope that serious consideration will be given to it' (para. 7). Some authorities were driven by sheer frustration to find ways to undertake preventive work. At first this was officially regarded as beyond the scope of the 1948 Children Act, but it was clearly absurd to take no steps to prevent family breakdown and only to act when there was an application to receive the child into care. The first family caseworker was appointed by Oxfordshire Children's Department in 1952 and another by Oxford City next year. It is significant that in 1954 8 per cent of all children in care came from homeless families (this fell to 5·2 per cent in 1970), yet the children's department could officially do nothing to prevent homelessness or forestall other forms of family breakdown. In some authorities where co-ordinating committees worked effectively there might be agreement between the children's, health and welfare departments – sometimes also the housing authority – and voluntary organisations about concerted plans to help individual families, but this depended on relations between different officials.

The *Eighth Report on the Work of the Children's Department* (Home Office, 1961) indicated that by the late 1950s preventive work was demanded by the logic of circumstances.

'There are many ways in which children's departments seek to avoid the separation of a child from his family: often the help of relatives or neighbours is sought or the parents are advised about the various welfare services, such as National Assistance, home helps and day nurseries, which may enable them to keep their children with them. Long and intensive case-work may be necessary to enable a family to keep together and maintain a reasonable mode of living. Time spent on a family in difficulty, primarily in the interests of the children, and with a view to avoiding their separation from their parents, may both help to reduce the demand which the parents make on the services of the community and in the long run ensure that the children do not repeat their parents' mistakes.' (para. 9)

This was an advance on Home Office Circular 160 of 1948 which said 'To keep the family together must be the first aim, and the separation of a child from its parents can only be justified when there is no possibility of securing adequate care for the child in his own home.' But children's departments were not empowered to pursue this 'first aim'. There were different opinions as to whether the 1948 Act should have been more broadly drawn or whether the limited goal of attempting to meet the needs of deprived children was the necessary first step to avoid diffuse aims. The Children and Young Persons (Amendment) Act, 1952 required local authorities to investigate allegations of neglect, which gave them some slight power to do preventive work. But in spite of individual successes, neither this nor co-ordinating committees gave local authorities sufficient power to meet family need or make difficult decisions when services were fragmented, staffs overloaded and views divided.

Under the 1948 Act the child care service had a duty to work with the family or guardian (if any) of children actually in care so that they might go back home as soon as possible. Throughout the 1950s it became increasingly clear that this often meant much work with relations (though there was no power to give material help), as well as with foster parents and residential staff. This included arranging periods at home while the child was still in care. It began to be recognised that parents often felt their parental failure acutely and needed help with their guilt and anxiety if they were not to disappear altogether. Their confidence might be further undermined by housemothers and foster parents, but they might also be accepted and family bonds strengthened.

Complex judgements in child care entailed assessing change over a period of time, the present in the light of the past, and forecasting the future: and to decide for some children the point at which they would be more greatly damaged by the maintenance or severance of a tenuous bond. There were few objective criteria on which to decide, thus children might be left in an uneasy no man's land or calculated risks be taken. Differing views in the child care service increased the conflicts of the work and the amount of skill and judgement demanded of child care officers. This added to the strain of responsibility, greater perhaps than in any other branch of social work, and led to long working hours.

The Social Survey Study on *Children in Care and the Recruitment of Foster Parents* (Gray and Parr, 1957) found that on any given day 40 per cent of the children had been in care for over five years.

Trained Child Care Officers' Workloads and the Deployment of Staff
During the early 1950s some local authorities had to be induced to employ trained staff, and newly qualified child care officers might lose heart after a series of unsuccessful interviews. Some authorities preferred experienced local men and women who 'know our ways', attitudes varied in different

parts of the country, and also the capacity to recruit and pay trained staff. In addition, there was an unduly slow increase in new appointments owing to economic stringencies in the early 1950s. Later in the decade the economic situation improved and the growing complexity of child care resulted in vigorous demands for more trained staff. It then became obvious that trained staff and student fieldwork placements attracted more trained staff. Thus by the end of the decade a few authorities had 100 per cent trained child care officers (including a county with a staff of one), many had a mixture, while a depressing number had recruited no trained child care officers.

The Curtis Committee's proposed staff/children ratio of 1:10 in children's homes and a caseload of 100–150 for boarding out officers (renamed child care officers in 1954) showed little understanding of what a reasonably enlightened children's service would actually need. By the late 1950s caseloads ranged from just over thirty to about ninety, though what constituted a caseload had not yet been defined. Many children's officers had both deputies and assistant children's officers for administration and residential care; while some children's departments had appointed specialised adoption officers and family caseworkers for preventive work (officialdom was increasingly turning a blind eye to this). The staff/children ratio in children's homes had also improved considerably. Many larger or more scattered authorities had set up area offices with easier access for parents and foster parents and a better chance for child care officers to know and be known in the neighbourhood. In these offices or in small children's departments teams working together under a senior were able to discuss and support each other, which improved performance and added to shared experience. There was also a varying amount of psychiatric consultation available in some areas, whether from child guidance clinics or otherwise.

Conflicting Views and Values

In such highly charged situations as parent/child relationships there continued to be profoundly different views and values. Some stressed the fundamental importance of the natural family and the strength of the blood tie. This was partly a reaction against the previous 'idea that a child could be "rescued" by a neat surgical operation which removes him from his inadequate and unsatisfactory family situation for good and all' (Packman, 1968, p. 203). None the less some families were unable for various reasons to care properly for their children. Some children's officers had become more conscious of the deprivation and permanent emotional damage which children could suffer in their own homes from rejecting, unloving, immature, incompetent or grossly overburdened parents. They contended that views about 'not letting parents get away with it' were sometimes upheld at the expense of the children. There was thus within the children's service a conflict about what constituted the welfare of the child and the circumstances in which a child should be received into care. This might be compounded by inadequate social diagnoses that failed to reveal the diverse reasons why parents parted with their children. There were also few intermediate alternatives between 'preventive' casework and receiving a child into care. In particular, children's departments did not control the home helps or day care services nor the allocation of housing or temporary accommodation. It was indeed often local authority policy not to offer temporary accommodation until a family was literally on the streets.

It is strange that in a field where so much was at stake there should have been only the small-scale studies summarised in the next chapters and no publicly sponsored, large-scale research into various aspects of family welfare and child care. Thus in some departments crucial decisions could depend on individual, unverified experience and opposing values not put to the test of objective inquiry, while in other departments there was careful work and discussion amongst colleagues. Throughout the period there was a striking difference between the standards achieved by different local authorities.

THE 1960S AND EARLY 1970S

The Ingleby Committee
Pressure from social workers, the Magistrates' Association, the Council for Children's Welfare, the Fisher Group, and various others who knew that many children were unprotected and families unsupported against impossible odds, led to the setting up of the Ingleby Committee on Children and Young Persons in 1956. Its terms of reference included the whole operation of the juvenile courts; 'the prevention of cruelty to, and exposure to moral and physical danger of juveniles' and 'whether local authorities . . . should . . . be given new powers and duties to prevent or forestall the suffering of children through neglect in their own homes'. In its Report (1960) it pointed out that to prevent neglect was essentially a negative approach as against the positive one of trying to ensure that every child got the best possible chance. 'It is thus the duty of the community to provide through its social and welfare services the advice and support which such parents and children need' (para. 8).

It recommended the setting up of family advice centres as a central and non-departmental point of reference where advice, information and skilled diagnosis would be available. It was several years before such experiments were made and then in widely differing forms. The Committee also recommended that local authorities should have a general duty to prevent or forestall child neglect and should be empowered to do preventive casework and provide material help. The Committee stressed that there should also be adequate arrangements to make the services known and easily available, 'a door on which to knock'. This was in sharp contrast with the views of some that widely known and easily available help would loosen family bonds and make it easy for parents and other relations to get rid of their responsibilities (see also chapter 15).

The Children and Young Persons Act, 1963
Section I of the Children and Young Persons Act, 1963, based upon the Ingleby Report, required local authorities through the children's department to ensure that advice, guidance and assistance (exceptionally help in cash or kind) were available to promote the welfare of children by diminishing the need to receive them into or keep them in care or to bring them before a juvenile court. This section was energetically implemented by some

authorities and little if at all by others. None the less prevention, rehabilitation and reception into care began to be accepted as related aspects of a
single service. The Act also extended the grounds on which a local authority
might assume parental rights over a child in care under section 2 of the
1948 Act. Throughout their existence most children's departments were
heavily involved with the care of delinquent and 'pre-delinquent' children
and with efforts to maintain their links with their parents. This responsibility
was reinforced by the 1963 Act and contributed to the thinking behind the
1969 Act.

Much planning and discussion naturally preceded the Act. Some children's
officers forecast correctly that it would double the demand for child care
staff and could result in more not less children being received into care
temporarily to relieve family stress. In some authorities there was considerable and sometimes imaginative effort to keep children at home in spite of
a parent's illness, desertion or death. For example, the 'flying angels' scheme
in Cornwall provided foster mothers, housed in dormobiles and paid as
houseparents, to care for children in their own homes who would otherwise
have to be received into short-term care. From 1955, the London County
Council sometimes provided a full-time home help for 'problem' families.
In Kent a family help service provided a temporary 'mother substitute'. In
several other authorities there was close co-operation between the children's
department and the home help service.

The power to give material help resulted, for example, in provision of
household goods, payment of hire purchase, gas and electricity debts, or of
fares for a relative to come to look after the family during the mother's
illness. It also led to closer links with voluntary organisations, to early
warning arrangements, to rent guarantees and advice on household budgeting to prevent eviction, and to co-operation with housing authorities – or
clashes over the ethics of letting some tenants 'get away' with non-payment
of rent. Some children's departments ran family rehabilitation centres
themselves or provided 'welfare' housing for homeless families and those
at risk of becoming homeless. These families were given help in household
management and child care to prevent family breakdown.

The new duty to 'advise, guide and assist' was not limited to individual
casework. The family advice centres which were set up by many authorities
ranged from an advice service in the children's department to some creative
experiments in neighbourhood family advice centres with play groups,
crèches, classes and discussion groups for mothers, and sometimes community development activities, notably advice about housing policies,
leisure activities for young people, adventure playgrounds and provision of
play space. Holiday schemes for mothers and children were another way
of lessening stress (Leissner *et al* , 1971). In short, much that the settlements
had pioneered was rediscovered and a wider range of day care services began
to be evolved intermediate between 'straight' casework on the one hand and
reception into residential care on the other. The aim was to get into 'at
risk' situations as early as possible and to have available a range of easily
accessible and acceptable support services. The volume of work to prevent
family breakdown grew by leaps and bounds. In 1970 46,000 children were
admitted to care and 220,000 supervised in their own homes. Some families

only needed help over a crisis but for many others long-term, intermittent or continuing support was essential to keep the family intact. Matrimonial or financial problems and difficulties between parents and children pre-dominated and there was much chronic poverty beyond the power of children's departments to remedy.

Child care officers were active in these and other forms of advice centres, as well as giving more sophisticated casework help focused on the family as the unit rather than the individual child. Thus the range of their activities and their caseloads both increased. A typical result was that

'Our officers are carrying impossible caseloads . . . they are working longer hours at tremendous pressure and some of them, particularly the younger ones, are almost at breaking point . . . It seems very sad that these trained officers of good strength and quality should be at risk of becoming dis-heartened so early in their career, and this is what often happens when they find that the pressure affects the quality of their work for the clients they wish to serve.' (Hertfordshire Children's Department, *Annual Report, 1965–66*, p. 8)

Numbers and Needs

In 1960 there were 1,100 child care and senior child care officers of whom 28 per cent held the CTC letter of recognition and another 30 per cent a social science qualification. The ratio of CCOs to the population varied from 1 : 28,000 to 1 : 3,500. By 1964 local authorities had appointed nearly 400 extra field staff, probably as a result of the 1963 Act. By 1970 out of the total of 3,368 child care officers, 1,579 were professionally qualified in one way or another, while another 554 had a social science qualification. In 1965 the Home Office awarded a Declaration of Recognition of Experience to child care officers and senior administrative staff with nine years of appropriate experience by the age of 40 to fourteen years by the age of 45. This was in line with the scheme established by the CTSW for the health and welfare services. In 1968 a similar scheme was introduced on the same terms for staff in the residential care of children.

There were 61,729 children in care in 1960 and 70,187 in 1969: this con-tinued to be a national average of slightly over 5 per 1,000 of the total population under 18 (7·2 by 1974), though with variations from 12 per cent to 1 per cent within this average. By 1974 there were 91,300 children in care, of whom 29,400 were in foster care and 15,600 living at home (DHSS, 1975*a*, *Annual Report 1974*). Multiple problems usually led to children having to leave home. The biggest single reason for children coming into short-term care was family illness, particularly of the mother; this included the mother's confinement in hospital rather than at home. Other reasons were: unemploy-ment, illegitimacy, poorly housed, low-income families, mental illness, death, desertion, divorce, separation, abandonment, and being newcomers to an area without close friends or relations. Naturally the population of children in care was closely related to the adequacy or otherwise of com-plementary or related services, for instance provision for homeless families, for unmarried mothers, of home helps, recuperative holidays, sufficient social security payments, all-round support services like those given by family service units, day nurseries and play groups and help by neighbours and relations. These were usually insufficient to meet the extent of child care need.

The foregoing summary owes much to Packman's important study *Child Care: Needs and Numbers* (1968). She and Power estimated for the Seebohm Committee (1968, appendix Q, p. 348) that in 1966 one child in twenty-two was receiving special help for physical, mental or social handicap, but that at least one child in ten would need special educational or mental or social help before it reached the age of 18. Research was urgently needed to establish the number of individual children requiring help of all kinds and the number of such children actually receiving this from various sources.

Assessment, Decision making and Planning

Some of the difficulties of deciding whether and when to receive a child into care, coupled with the lack of resources for preventive work, have already been discussed. There might also be insufficient information for proper assessment and for a decision based on sound evidence to be made at a special case conference. The number of reception centres with facilities for interdisciplinary diagnosis of children's personality and developmental needs increased throughout this period, but their success depended on whether appropriate subsequent treatment was available. Various studies in the period suggested that children's departments were often forced to receive children into care when this could have been prevented by more adequate resources, and that at the crucial point of reception there were often too few options, including foster parents, and too little pooling of services with other agencies in order to make the best plan for the individual child. A full psychosocial appraisal and sensitive work with the child and his family in this crisis period could be decisive in determining whether he ever went home again. The age of the child, and thus his memory time span, was also crucial in relation to the effect on him of separation; this added to the importance of quick placement for children who needed new parents. Pugh (1968) commented: 'Many of the lost, isolated children in children's homes with no one in the community who writes to or visits them are in the situation because the living network of relationships which surrounded them at the time they first came into care was not captured on paper and placed in the files for later use' (pp. 34–5).

Rowe and Lambert (1973) also found stereotyped reviews, poor record keeping and considerable differences in the adequacy of the assessment and decision-making procedures in the thirty-three statutory and voluntary agencies they studied. The study itself was undertaken soon after reorganisation, so some comments refer to generic teams but others and the records themselves to children's department work. Records tended to be superficial and lacking in assessment of situations, personalities or problems. There were individual instances of excellent recording. 'Nevertheless the situation seemed serious, both in terms of current social work practice and because of the importance of preserving the personal histories of children being brought up in care' (p. 93). Sometimes there were 'high standards of service with warmth and concern for clients, interesting new projects and united, forward-looking teams of workers' but 'unfortunately a much more typical comment was "on the whole . . . very little real casework is done, simply crisis work . . . or a united team almost too tired to care" ' (p. 78).

In the three departments studied by George (1970) of the twenty-eight CCOs (half of whom were trained)

'. . . trained child care staff performed their duties in much the same ways as their untrained colleagues. It seemed as if parts of the theory of social work in general and of foster care in particular have been absorbed in the conventional wisdom of the child care profession and, as such, they have influenced the work of trained and untrained child care officers. There was no evidence, however, that much of the detailed knowledge in foster care theory, which is not part of the conventional wisdom of the profession, was being applied by the trained staff. The marital adjustment of foster parent applicants for example was generally regarded as an important criterion for accepting or rejecting the applicants, but there was no evidence that child care officers had a detailed knowledge of what constituted marital adjustment or how it could be assessed.' (p. 226)

None the less it is hard to see how standards of good practice developed unless these were based on substantial experience in well-staffed departments with provision for professional consultation about decision making and study of individual children's needs. For example, Ballance (1975) gave a good account of the work of an experienced CCO in a progressive children's department (pp. 76–96).

The two largest groups of the 2,812 children under 11 in long-term care studied by Rowe and Lambert (1973) were illegitimate babies and small children and sibling groups from disorganised families, usually where at least one parent had only a limited capacity for parenthood. Sibling groups were the most difficult to place in foster homes, the children were often likely to be in and out of care and it was hard to find foster homes able to take two or more children. Most had already been in care for most of their lives, 61 per cent were expected to remain until they were 18, and half had been under 2 when they were last admitted to care. Not surprisingly, the children most often in and out of care also had the most unsettled lives at home; these were the cat-and-mouse children who had no legal protection or on whose behalf some local authorities were slow to assume parental rights under section 2 of the 1948 Children Act. The CCOs concerned thought that 626 (22 per cent) of these children needed a substitute home, but over one-third had already been in care for four years or more. On a national scale this amounted to about 7,000 children. 'Since nearly two thirds of those needing family care were over five years old and most of them had been admitted as babies or very young children, the delay in getting them settled in substitute families had itself created a serious obstacle to successful placement' (p. 75).

About one in three of all the children had behaviour problems but a much higher proportion of those who had had four or more moves. It seemed obvious that some of these behaviour difficulties had been intensified while the children were in care, though the records were too inadequate to show the extent to which problems existed previously. In spite of the difficulties of finding substitute family care, especially when many of the children were siblings, boys or coloured, the percentage needing this varied from 3 per cent in one authority to 45 per cent in another. There did not seem to be any obvious reasons for what were probably complex inter-related factors.

The quality of the work in children's departments thus varied widely for reasons which included individual CCOs' performance, workloads, filing and record keeping, departmental organisation, consultancy services (including psychiatric consultation), group support and supervision and the range of available resources (including finance).

The Children and Young Persons Act, 1969

The two White Papers and other moves which finally resulted in the Children and Young Persons Act, 1969 are discussed in chapter 15. This Act (which applied to England and Wales) was based on the current, though not universally accepted, philosophy that juvenile courts should be a last resort service rather than the mixture of welfare agency, casualty clearing station and court of law that some had become. Avoidance of court proceedings was a major objective. This was to be achieved by informal co-operation between services and within the family – indeed this was a basic aim at every stage. The Bill was acutely controversial: basically different attitudes about the care or control of young delinquents and whether the depraved were also deprived flared into life as it went through Parliament, and were not allayed by subsequent events.

The juvenile police liaison scheme pioneered in Liverpool was made general, and there was to be close consultation between the police and the social services department before a child was brought before a juvenile court, in the hope that voluntary co-operation by the child, his parents and the school would make his appearance unnecessary. In the following years this co-operation varied greatly in different areas.

Court proceedings were only to be taken after the child's background had been considered and if he was not receiving the care, protection and guidance he needed and was neglected or ill-treated, or in moral danger, or not getting efficient, full-time education, or had committed what would be an offence in an adult, *and* if he was in need of care or control which he was unlikely to receive unless the court made an order. Children's departments were on the way out when this section came into operation. The age at which offence proceedings might be instituted was to be raised by stages (it became 12 in 1973). By degrees supervision orders were to be made to the children's (later the social services) departments for children up to 14 and at the discretion of the court to the local authority or the probation service for those between 14 and 17. Social services departments became responsible in 1974 for supervising children up to 13 – an additional caseload of about 2,000. All forms of residential care, including remand homes and approved schools, were merged in a single comprehensive category of community homes. By another major change approved school orders were abolished in favour of care orders. These could be used more flexibly because the local authority would now decide whether at any given time it would be best for a child to be at home, in a foster home, a community home or elsewhere.

As a result of the Act, local authority social workers began to serve in juvenile courts. The new system started just when social workers were pre-occupied with reorganisation, ex-CCOs were trying to learn new jobs and other social workers to pick up child care expertise. The result was anxiety, annoyance and tensions between the magistrates and social workers who succeeded experienced probation officers but were unfamiliar with court proceedings, the rules of evidence and the preparation of court reports. In some areas regular meetings between the magistrates and clerks, the social services departments and the juvenile liaison police gradually improved relations, particularly when social workers were given in-service training in juvenile court work and some were regularly allocated for court duties.

The success of the Act largely depended upon an increase of resources and a constant or decreasing number of children in trouble, whereas unfortunately there was a reverse equation. Police cautioning increased considerably in some areas so that fewer children were brought to the juvenile courts. The number of extremely disturbed children and adolescents were thought to have increased and many subject to care orders were said to be 'running wild in the streets' because resources, including secure accommodation in community homes and places in residential special schools, were wholly inadequate and staff often unobtainable. There was much controversy as to whether the philosophy of the Act was unrealistic and only appropriate to emotionally disturbed children with family problems and not to children whose delinquency was environmentally caused, or whether the Act was sound but had never had a chance. It was calculated by the Home Office that 1,000 additional CCOs would be needed to implement the Act, which was of course intended to be operated in conjunction with section I of the 1963 Children and Young Persons Act.

A House of Commons Expenditure Committee reviewed the working of the Act and recommended (1975) that courts should have power to make 'secure care orders', that attendance centres should be continued and expanded, that the transfer of responsibilities from the probation service to social services departments should be halted, that secure accommodation should be provided in every area, that there should be more imaginative plans for intermediate treatment, and that 'urgent attention' should be given to this and other forms of day care.

Community homes, intermediate treatment and regional planning committees are discussed later in chapter 3.

The Home Office Children's Department Inspectorate
Throughout the period the Home Office Children's Department inspectorate played a crucial part in discovering the needs of children in care, in supporting children's department staffs, helping to raise standards, especially where these were unacceptably low, and themselves profiting from the experience of the best services. To an increasing extent they provided a consultant, reinforcing service across the whole field of child care and many took part in in-service training and ongoing negotiations between the training inspectors and universities and colleges of further education. This changing role of central government in providing advice, guidance and

professional services, based on experience, made it all the more necessary for the inspectorate to have a wide – and sometimes specialist – up-to-date knowledge of both the theoretical underpinning and practical application of an increasing range of child care services. By 1969 there were about 100 inspectors (including the training inspectors) in the Home Office Children's Department working from seven regional offices.

CHILDREN'S DEPARTMENTS 1948–71: AN UNFINISHED AGENDA

When the children's departments came to an end in 1971, great strides had been made since 1948 in clarifying the needs of children actually or potentially deprived of nurturing relationships, and of children with behaviour problems which resulted in efforts to provide similarly for the deprived and the delinquent. Translated into operational terms this included discovering what should be the nature of preventive services, good residential care, fostering and adoption, though much remained to be discovered, applied and tested. Inevitably in the total deployment of resources a wide range of early preventive services was needed, coupled with systematic efforts to study and support foster and adoptive homes, to match these with individual children, to implement the best of what was known about residential care, and to work with natural parents. There was an evident need for well-informed decision making at the right point in time based on all the relevant evidence, reinforced by resources to implement the decision. The Home Office *Report on Dorset County Council Child Care Service* (1966a) contains a valuable account of the administration, staffing and services of a children's department in that period.

The nature and importance of interdisciplinary team work and interdepartmental co-operation also became clear through successes, failures and calamities throughout the period. Later this was brought into the limelight by the death of Maria Colwell, killed by her stepfather in 1973 while she was under social services department supervision, and in various ways the responsibility of the education and health services and the NSPCC. The Report of the Committee of Inquiry (DHSS, 1974d) was an illuminating case study of family and neighbourhood interaction; organisational structures; faulty administrative procedures and professional judgement; failures of communication with Maria herself and between services; failure to observe significant symptoms, to co-operate systematically and to take action, partly because of too great an emphasis on family rehabilitation and the blood tie. The report concluded:

'There was no question at any time . . . of anyone deliberately shirking a task; there was no shortage of devotion to duty. What has clearly emerged . . . . is a failure of system compounded of several factors of which the greatest and most obvious must be that of the lack of, or ineffectiveness of, communication and liaison. A system should so far as possible be able to absorb individual errors and yet function adequately . . . Many of the mistakes made by individuals were either the result of, or were contributed to, by inefficient systems operating in several different fields, notably training, administration, planning, liaison and supervision.' (paras 240 and 241)

Voluntary societies are discussed in chapter 18. They continued throughout the period to play an essential part in a comprehensive child care service. They moved from trying to provide a non-selective general service, or running one in narrow isolation, to pioneering new and imaginative ways of enriching family life socially, or providing substitute care for severely physically, mentally or emotionally handicapped children. They, like the public authorities, discovered that application of good practice depended upon a sufficient number of well-qualified and well-supported staff.

In 1948 the child care service started with an amended agenda: it ended with an extended and unfinished agenda in which accepted good practice had still to be made universal, tested and improved. The task in 1948 was to work a sea change in the care given to children deprived of a normal home life, and to discover what good substitute care for individual children might mean. But this became an excursion into prevention, and into new methods that resulted in breaking down the barriers between services for delinquent and other youngsters, between the child's family and residential and foster homes, between residential and day care, between previously accepted ideas about suitable treatment for any given group of children, between the child, his family and the local community. In these wide horizons devoted continuity of care for the individual child might become blurred and a sense of direction confused. It was utopian to think that a 'best' solution existed for every damaged child, but more could be done by clarity about that 'best', determination to work towards it, and an organisational structure that made this possible. Services for children had to face the upheavals of the 1971 and 1974 reorganisations when child care often stood still or regressed because specialist skills were diluted and scarce resources allocated to other parts of the social services which had struggled less actively for these in the 1950s and 1960s. Yet at least a framework of legislation existed 'which allows a social services department to develop a many sided comprehensive child care service, incorporating prevention, protective, treatment, care and rehabilitative functions for all children in trouble' (Drake, 1975, p. 88).

This embodied 'the simple straightforward motive of attempting to meet their need for love and happiness' (Winnicott, 1964, p. 11). 'You can't give children love by Act of Parliament', said Margery Fry when the 1948 Children Act was passed. But love and children can be brought together, and love be refined by knowledge and supported materially and by clinical judgement. So it also proved true that 'love is not enough' and that you cannot give some children love without Act of Parliament.

Chapter 3

The Child Care Service Continued: Residential Child Care; Community Homes and Children's Regional Planning Committees; Youth Treatment Centres; Intermediate Treatment

RESIDENTIAL CHILD CARE IN THE 1950s

The claims that houseparents (mostly women in children's homes), or house-masters or mistresses (mostly men in boys' approved schools and borstals) should primarily provide substitute parental care in the former, and 'build character' in the latter were based respectively on ordinary family or public school assumptions. This was a great advance on the Curtis Committee's findings of

'a widespread and deplorable shortage of the right kind of staff, personally qualified and trained to provide the child with a substitute for a home back-ground. The result in many Homes was a lack of personal interest in and affection for the children which we found shocking. The child in these Homes was not recognised as an individual with his rights and possessions, his own life to live and his own contribution to offer. He was merely one of a large crowd, eating, playing and sleeping with the rest . . . Still more important, he was without the feeling that there was anyone to whom he could turn who was vitally interested in his welfare or who cared for him as a person.' (para. 418)

Poor salaries and poor accommodation made residential child care unattractive. Understaffing and limited education also resulted in too much time being devoted to domestic chores rather than to child nurture and stimulation.

In 1955, Sibyl Clement Brown, then director of child care studies at the Home Office, completed an unpublished study of a sample of trained house-parents in different sizes of home and staff composition. Her findings (quoted by permission) showed that the chronic shortage of staff was partly due to the unpopularity of residential work, to the isolation often experienced by staff (who yet lived at close quarters with each other), and to the fact that while the house was the staff's home as well as the children's it was not made home-like. Assistants, in particular, complained that they were neither included in discussions between home and field staff about the work nor helped with their own problems as houseparents.

Senior staff moved less frequently than juniors, which might mean that some people went on changing jobs until they found the group where they fitted in. In any event, many left altogether after two to five years. The effect on the children of staff shortages and turnover was probably most serious in small family group homes with only two or three houseparents. There was much emphasis at the time on recruiting married couples because these would provide a more natural home for the children. Observation of people at work showed that quite contrasting personalities could be success-ful in work with children, though tolerance and warmth of feeling for both adults and children were essential, coupled with readiness to learn, good health and physical energy.

In the 1950s, the ill-effects of rapid staff turnover became more obvious, and also the problem of the staff who stayed for years, long after they had lost sufficient physical vigour and emotional resilience, because the children's home was their home too and they could not afford the cost of independent accommodation. Inadequate accommodation in children's homes – and lack of separate housing for married staff – continued to affect recruitment and staff contentment throughout the period. In 1962, the Government Social Survey undertook for the Home Office a study of housemothers and assist-ant housemothers (published 1964). As in the Clement Brown study, assist-ants complained that they were infrequently consulted or told about plans for individual children. They also continued to complain about long and irregular hours – a vicious circle of supply and demand – poor living accommodation and problems of staff relations.

All voluntary homes had to be registered with the Secretary of State and were, like local authority homes, subject to inspection and regulations. As the standard rose in the children's departments, the number of children in the care of voluntary organisations fell. It was 33,000 at the time of the Curtis Report and 11,500 by 1971.

RESIDENTIAL CHILD CARE IN THE 1960s

By the 1960s there was much discussion and better clarification of the essential nature of the task or tasks, in residential child care, largely stimu-lated by the Central Training Council in Child Care (CTC) training pro-gramme, the Residential Child Care Association (RCCA), the Association of Workers with Maladjusted Children and by much closer team work with the Association of Children's Officers (ACO) and the Association of Child Care Officers (ACCO).

All-age homes made the task more complex, and the gap between 'knowing' and 'knowing how to do' widened. The family group home idea of the early 1950s had been based upon a theoretical assumption about creating a 'normal' family. This had strengths and weaknesses which could now be compared with a variety of other patterns. The strengths were considerable where a wise and mature single woman or married couple ran the home (or the husband went out to work), who got on well with junior staff and in the local community and gave a home with continuity to a mixed group of children. There were not enough such people to go round. In residential child care situations there were also considerable problems of too much or too little concern for a married couple's own children, though obviously the children in the home needed to live with adults of both sexes. There were also complex and insufficiently studied relations between adults and children in which some dynamics of family life were re-enacted. Staff relations also depended to some extent on whether people with different personalities played complementary or conflicting roles and whether the children experienced consistent or inconsistent methods.

Restrictions on building had been eased by the late 1950s, so that a greater variety of provision was possible for children with different needs and staff with varied preferences. Homes for twelve to twenty-five children, divided into smaller units, found some favour, since this meant less sense of rejection for the children when an individual staff member left, while group life was possible to a greater extent than in a very small or very large home. This was all part of the changing emphasis from trying to create a substitute family to remedial treatment. 'For the staff, the practical details of living are a fundamental part of a total process of living and growing which each child and staff member experiences within the group. The staff are concerned with the total process and with the need to understand it more fully in order to enhance its value and effectiveness' (Winnicott, 1968). This changed outlook shifted the emphasis from cooking and household tasks in the family group home where the staff were often too busy or too unaware of the child's world to communicate with him. Provision of domestic, catering, administrative and maintenance help began to be taken for granted, though it was assumed that everyone would take part in domestic activities and practical tasks as part of community life.

The old idea of treating all the children alike and 'not having favourites' had been succeeded by an understanding that an individual staff member could help an individual child by having the time to listen and the ability to hear, thus developing a personal relationship in which the child was given care and understanding. This individual caring function was consistent with the whole group of staff and children providing a holding and nurturing experience in which individual children could find themselves and come to terms with their life experience. This might include shared responsibility between staff and older children through discussion of basic problems of living, self-expression and agreed action about day-to-day activities. The aim became to intensify interaction and communication between staff and children.

The pendulum had swung from the old idea of the 'complete break with the past' to perception of the dangers of blurred identity and therefore the child's need to know about his past, to experience his own individuality in the present and to take part in plans for his future. All children in care experienced the shock of separation, often also of rejection, and of earlier, sometimes irreversible, deprivation and consequent damage. Many had families to which they would return sooner or later and who were to be encouraged to visit and have the child home from time to time if possible. At all costs the child must be prevented from becoming institutionalised or incapable of forming sustained relationships. This meant a double and demanding task for residential staff in a highly charged and often competitive situation.

In 1969, a study group of ACO, ACCO and RCCA produced a much-quoted report on the *Residential Task in Child Care* (RCCA, 1969) in which it clarified the demanding professional task in residential child care. It said:

'Not only the children, but also their parents, relatives and friends require sympathetic help and support from residential staff. Matrimonial disharmony, frustration caused by homelessness or poverty, mental illness, anti-social attitudes, alcoholism, aggression, depression, shock and distress in parents produce their impact on children and staff alike. If the child and the community are to be protected from too much damage, the staff need to be able to absorb and deflect negative or harmful attitudes and to make good use of positive relationships which they will help to develop.' (p. 8)

More flexible use of residential care also meant that some children might only be resident at weekends or during the week or come daily to give some hard-pressed family a break. For some other children, their only hope of continuity, of growing roots, of having a springboard for the future, lay in the staff of the children's home. This made it all the more important that both staff and children should be part of a local community and have pets, plenty of activities, their own possessions and outside friends.

It was thought that the emphasis on foster home placement and on keeping children in their own homes as long as possible, resulted in a higher proportion of difficult and damaged or physically or mentally handicapped children or children from one-parent families being admitted to children's homes. They were of all ages from babies to late adolescents, they might have suffered from neglect or indifference, from parental breakdown, from rootlessness or from poverty: the older children might be drifters or delinquents, hostile to adults, addicted to drugs or alcohol or be pregnant. Thus the overall residential child care task was to learn how to give nurture and remedial care to this range of children and young people. This obviously included being able to build up relationships and to communicate, to talk with, not to, them. A much higher staff/children ratio began to be accepted, particularly in residential nurseries (where these continued) and in special provision for disturbed adolescents. For instance, the study group report, *Residential Task in Child Care* proposed ratios of between 1:2·2 in children's homes generally and 1:1 in those providing intensive remedial care. These were calculated on the amount of time each child needed care every twenty-four hours. As a result of this and the Williams Committee findings (1967), the National Joint Negotiating Committee (NJC) reduced the working week but owing to staff shortages some might work much paid overtime. Average staff ratios in 1972 were 1:1·5 in residential nurseries, 1:2·5 in reception centres and 1:3 in other children's homes (DHSS, 1972*a*, Circular 35/72).

Several action research projects, notably *Growth to Freedom* (Miller, 1964) and *A Place Like Home* (Wills, 1970), demonstrated the profound damage suffered by delinquent and maladjusted adolescents and the degree of understanding, tolerance and ability to absorb hostility demanded of the staff. This, like many other child care situations, showed the need for psychiatric and social work consultation. By degrees a number of local authorities appointed consultants to their children's homes to give individual and group consultation to staff and to take part in in-service training. Homes' consultants were also appointed to take responsibility for some of the household management side of administering children's homes. Indeed, by the late 1960s it had already become necessary

'. . . to clarify the functions of caring staff compared with others and to look again at the confusion of ideas which exists as a result of the 'substitute parenting' theory of the past. If residential establishments are to be seen in the future as therapeutic communities the whole concept of training and the roles to be played by staff directly involved in the caring process will need to be reassessed.' (*Residential Task in Child Care*, pp. 17–18)

Cooper (1967) discussed the use of residential situations to enable children to experience caring group relationships, friendship groups and interest groups, and thus to grow through group relationships. This included the use of the group for the management of tensions, to help withdrawn or aggressive children to get on with others, to feel free to express anger and allow the group to absorb it. Talking about deeply felt needs and deprivations was difficult for children who had not experienced this at home, thus staff had to be sensitive to non-verbal communication and start with informal discussion of shared daily experiences as a means of demonstrating to children a capacity to listen and to understand the feelings behind behaviour.

In the late 1960s a working group of children's officers, an approved school headmaster and members of the Home Office Children's Department Development Group worked on a community homes project and produced a report (1970) embodying concepts, principles, practice and attitudes which they thought were generally relevant to residential child care. Their views once again emphasised the highly professional nature of the task. This essentially consisted of creating a warm and accepting planned environment which would in itself be therapeutic, as well as creating an appropriate milieu for a variety of treatment in which easy communication and shared participation between adults and children would become possible as a result of satisfying personal relationships. Free communication would lessen the risk of some children perpetuating their previous sub-culture of resistance, distrust, aggression and hostility towards adults. Specific remedial skills might be needed with some very deprived children with poor social and emotional adjustment. The community home experience should include work by residential staff and fieldworkers with the child's family as a whole (where it existed and was not wholly rejecting). Frequent group discussions were necessary to enable the staff to function as a team, to absorb inevitable tensions and to cope with staff changes. These were enormous yet realistic demands which pointed to the need for more support, training and consultation and higher salaries and status than residential staff received.

These Angel Gabriel-like aspirations were achieved in some situations, but on the whole acute staff shortages persisted, with the consequent appointment of some unsuitable people, coupled with long hours and weariness that sometimes increased staff tensions and reacted on the children. The employment of part-time, non-resident staff increased in spite of some difficulties. Such staff had their own outside lives and interests; their daily living and their work were not inseparable with no boundaries between their personal and professional selves. Sometimes part-time workers also brought the children and other staff into contact with the local community. In addition, it became more usual for full-time staff to live out, i.e. the children were resident but not necessarily all the staff.

The Williams Committee's national inquiry (1967) showed that nine out of ten local authority homes contained fewer than 20 children. Most voluntary homes had 11 to 20 children, though over a third had 21 to 50. The ratio of full-time staff to children was 1:4. Over four-fifths of all care staff were full-time and four-fifths were resident. Eighty per cent of the care staff were women and nearly two-thirds of the total staff were single women. A substantial majority of heads of homes were satisfied with their accommodation, except for the problem of privacy. Seventy per cent of all full-time care staff had no qualification other than experience. This did not take account of in-service training courses. Fifteen per cent in local authority homes and 23 per cent in voluntary homes held the CTC residential child care certificate. In local authority children's homes with ten children or less, only 18 per cent of the assistant staff left annually compared with 33 per cent and over in every other size of children's home run by local authorities. The reasons for leaving included long hours of work and evening and weekend duties when other people were free. Previous surveys showed a working day of thirteen and a half hours in children's homes, i.e. a seventy-five-hour week. Eighty-five per cent of heads of homes said their hours of duty were sixty to seventy hours a week and that they were on call day and night. This was the actual situation in which local authorities and voluntary organisations had to struggle to apply increased understanding of the needs of children in residential care: in some situations the pressures were so great as to be almost out of control by 1975.

Berry (1975) on the basis of much experience made a strong plea for regular group and individual staff consultation with a well-qualified and experienced consultant who, instead of direct contact with the children, would give support to the staff in dealing with their problems. A higher proportion of residential workers in the very good than in the inadequate units in her study had substantial opportunities for individual or group discussions with senior staff or outside consultants, and thus support for staff clearly affected the quality of child care. There were frequent or fairly frequent visits by social workers to twelve out of the forty-four homes studied. Many staff felt neglected by fieldworkers or that they were used as a dumping ground, cut off, left to their own devices. Seventy per cent of the children were more or less isolated from the local community, often on account of the situation of the building. Parents were usually encouraged to visit but such visits were infrequent, often because children were going home regularly for weekends and holidays, but about 25 per cent had no parental contacts.

Residential care included hostels for young people in care (see volume 2, chapter 14, section on 'Hostels for Young People in Care').

COMMUNITY HOMES AND CHILDREN'S REGIONAL PLANNING COMMITTEES

Under the Children and Young Persons Act, 1969 approved schools, detention centres, remand homes and assessment centres were brought together with children's homes in general under the title of community homes. It was thought that wider planning was necessary than even the future enlarged local authority areas could provide, thus twelve children's regional planning committees were set up for England and Wales with responsibility for surveying total needs in the region for various categories of children and young people, from residential nurseries to treatment homes for severely disturbed adolescents. Plans were to be drawn up, based upon what local authorities and those voluntary organisations which decided to accept assisted or controlled status were able to provide at the time or later. These plans were to be submitted to the Secretary of State and amended from time to time. By degrees these committees appointed professional advisers or development officers to stimulate surveys and fresh provision. These surveys revealed some severe shortages, especially of provision for disturbed adolescents and of secure accommodation for those who it was thought could not be given care or control otherwise, though this view was contested. The problem was intensified by the lack of varied intermediate treatment facilities, also a regional planning committee responsibility (see below).

Children's regional planning committees' national average figures forecast an overall need for 2·72 places per 1,000 of the population under 18. The implementation of these plans was bedevilled by inflation, staff shortages and building problems. There was also confusion about the role of the committees, i.e. whether they must simply accept local authorities' plans or could initiate agreed criteria for the assessment of need and monitoring of services. The committees had power to rank priorities for regional projects, and by 1975 some were extending their planning activities to other parts of the child care service, for instance fostering.

YOUTH TREATMENT CENTRES

For a number of years there had been controversy as to whether residential care and treatment for severely disturbed and sometimes violent children and adolescents was primarily the responsibility of the child care or national health services. Approved schools were sometimes disrupted by such children, while mental hospitals did not provide facilities for unruly adolescents, indeed only rarely for younger teenagers in adolescent units.

Finally the controversy as to whether they were primarily psychiatric or social care cases was resolved by section 64 of the 1969 Children and Young Persons Act, under which the Home Office (later the DHSS) could itself set up and run youth treatment centres which would combine hospital, children's home and approved school facilities under secure conditions. It was intended that three such centres should ultimately be set up, catering for both sexes and an age range from 12 to 19. The aim was to provide long-term care in varying degrees of security, so that badly damaged boys and girls with very disruptive behaviour (the proportion of such girls in most categories of disorder was higher than that of boys) might achieve some adjustment, and more be learnt about the causes and treatment of severe disturbance. It was hoped to create a therapeutic milieu, using group activities and environmental therapy, as well as group and individual psychotherapy together with social work with the families. There was to be. progression from a maximum security zone, through semi-security to completely open conditions. Various forms of research were to be built in. The staff was to consist of a psychiatrist as director and members of other relevant professions. It was thought essential that the staff should become a cohesive team which would give support and strength to very damaged young people and develop a capacity for interdisciplinary treatment that would integrate care, control, management and therapy. This plan was produced by two working parties on the assumption that such boys and girls were untreatable in any existing régime, and that many would become severely delinquent or a life-long charge on community resources. The case for these costly youth treatment centres was thus argued on both economic and humane grounds.

In the event, only one treatment centre, St Charles, Brentwood, was opened, though by 1975 others were planned at Birmingham and Wakefield. The adolescents at St Charles had the characteristics of explosive violence, grossly impaired capacity for relationships or for guilt about their behaviour, as described in *Youth Treatment Centres* (DHSS, 1971d). It closed for a time as a result of various stresses and problems including a partly unsuitable building, the difficulties of welding a multidisciplinary staff into a team with a common philosophy and working methods; and the highly disruptive activities of the first youngsters. It reopened in 1973. The director described the aims and processes in detail (Edwards, 1976) when the centre was almost full and the staff had evolved 'a working treatment philosophy' and 'excellent work was being carried out' (p. 5). Good assessment was essential to eliminate all but the small group whose disturbance and delinquency could only be managed and treated by total security. This secure régime must provide both a therapeutic environment and a range of treatment techniques.

INTERMEDIATE TREATMENT

The Children and Young Persons Act, 1969 enabled juvenile courts to include in a supervision order a requirement that the boy and girl should take part in some local activity for a total of a month in a year, or else be resident somewhere for up to three months in a year. This became known as intermediate treatment, i.e. 'intermediate' between casework at home and residential care. Children's regional planning committees were responsible for encouraging provision of facilities in their regions by social services departments and voluntary organisations, and notifying these to the Secretary of State so that they might become available to the juvenile courts. Intermediate treatment with a court order was controversial because it was argued that to join a youth club or engage in any other regular activity ought to be wholly voluntary rather than a decision with a sanction behind it, and that a range of opportunities should be available irrespective of a court appearance. Conversely, it was said that many young people would never go near an organised group unless they were actively encouraged to take the initial plunge, and that it was up to the social worker to decide the right group or other activity for a particular young person and those who ran it to help him or her to find satisfaction in the group or in some individual venture. Not surprisingly, something as new and demanding had a slow and confused start: in some local authority areas no scheme had been notified by the mid-1970s, or else only existing traditional forms of youth service which young people could join in any event if they wished. But by 1975 intermediate treatment had gone through some of its earlier confusion and many social services departments had appointed intermediate treatment officers with special responsibility for discovering the resources of the neighbourhood and stimulating action to meet the needs of very different young people, from those who were bored into delinquency in a dreary and frustrating neighbourhood to disturbed and habitually delinquent adolescents, and whether or not they had been before a juvenile court. They would be 'those who need a more group-oriented or practical activity approach to their problems than can be provided by casework supervision alone' (DHSS, 1973b, p. 16). There were many efforts to engage the interest of children at risk, as well as those for whom court orders had been made. It was hoped that children who had been before the courts might be successfully introduced to activities provided for other young people and would continue these after the compulsory period was ended (DHSS, 1972b).

An intermediate treatment condition enabled the social services committee to meet the cost. But in any event, a range of preventive facilities could be used for children at risk under section I of the Children and Young Persons Act, 1963. A number of such experiments, including activity groups, camps, holiday schemes and centres for adolescents with plenty of adult attention and enjoyable things to do were described in *Intermediate Treatment Project* (DHSS, 1973b). The DHSS was criticised for concentrating on traditional youth organisations, and regional planning committees for the unimaginative projects in their regional schemes. In short, that most activities made available were more suitable for non-offenders than for those for whom intermediate treatment was designed. As in other services, the need was recognised for various 'intermediate' resources, for example there were considerable lacks in provision for 8- to 14-year-old children, for some adolescents, and of holiday activities. None the less good schemes existed, for instance Hertfordshire intermediate treatment staff had initiated and provided an outward bound centre in Wales, a narrow boat, and a youth training workshop. In 1971, the National Children's Bureau started a five-year, intermediate treatment action research project jointly with seven social services departments. Each was in a family advice centre with a wide range of services for children and young people, integrated with the social and community work functions of the centre.

The essential aim of intermediate treatment was to provide closer and more varied support based upon skilled assessment of the individual child's needs, with better chances for good relationships and creative activities and to counter boredom. It was hoped by these means to change attitudes, behaviour and motivation, to repair earlier damage and give the youngster a better life chance. It was also hoped to bring about environmental change and lessen the gap between a casework service and residential care. The *Eleventh Report from the House of Commons Expenditure Committee* (1975) said:

'teaching a child in its own community is almost always more humane than removing it from its home and . . . if delinquency is environmentally determined, removing a child for a time from his damaging environment only to return him to it will not in many cases 'cure' his delinquency. This argument would certainly go far to explain the high recidivism rates of most forms of custodial care.' (para. 114)

The range of intermediate treatment might include special interest groups, adventure activities, remedial teaching, outlets for physical energies, community service and group counselling, combined with individual and family casework. It was also essential that there should be communication between everyone concerned in remedial schemes, though in practice this might not happen. Children's regional planning committees intended to monitor various forms of intermediate treatment to assess their effectiveness, what seemed to work best with whom and why. But by 1975 there was no common plan for this and the inherent difficulties of such monitoring were not resolved.

Different ideas about the nature of intermediate treatment were held by 1975, though five years' experience showed that it must be more varied and flexible than was originally contemplated. To some extent it was yet another attempt on a broader scale to capture the allegiance of the 'unclubable' for whom many small projects had been run over the years. Some young people found satisfaction in ordinary youth clubs provided they were carefully introduced, received special attention in the early stages and were accepted by the other members. Others responded well to adventure holidays, though there were quite unreal expectations of what objectives could be achieved in one week, and the results were not always consolidated by well-planned continuing support. There were other young people with some individual need or ability which must be discovered and nurtured. There were yet others whom only imaginative and very skilled special forms of intermediate treatment could hope to capture and hold. The essence was thus the ability to understand individual boys or girls in their family, peer group and social situation, and sometimes, as part of their treatment, to be able to introduce (not 'refer') them to the right form of group activity where they would feel wanted, enjoy activities, make relationships with others and become more free, friendly and self-confident.

When youth clubs lacked the manpower, or for other reasons were not able or willing to accept disturbed or anti-social boys and girls, they sometimes lent their premises to social workers with these groups, thus solving a problem of accommodation. In other instances, a social worker might go regularly to a club in order to support and help a small group of boys under supervision.

The experiments with group counselling for children and adolescents, already well under way, fitted into the concept of intermediate treatment, indeed such groups were sometimes thought essential to bring about real change in aggressive or withdrawn behaviour. Aplin and Bamber (1973), in discussing the Group Work Counselling Service in Bristol, pointed out the urgent need for combined educational and casework experience in order to understand the individual and family needs of children with social and emotional difficulties. Some children could become absorbed into ordinary, good leisure activities, but others needed a planned programme geared to their needs, for example group experiences and individual counselling, coupled with family casework.

Thorpe and Horn (1973) explored different forms of intermediate treatment and the variety of possible means of expression compared with casework interviews based on fluency in the use of words, an unfamiliar medium to many working-class adolescents. For instance, regular short periods away from home for well-selected small groups enabled the social workers to know the children in an ordinary give-and-take situation, to experience acting-out behaviour and the assumption of different roles in the group, as well as giving its members a chance for enjoyment and achievement. This form of treatment within the community was a more systematic, more consciously used form of the summer camps and group discussions pioneered earlier by the probation service and the Settlements. Intermediate treatment – and other provision for young people – relied increasingly upon a combination of activities and discussion.

Residential intermediate treatment could vary from weekends away as part of the total programme to up to three months intensive residential experience, sometimes a long distance from home. The first type, of which the long-established Northorpe Hall near Leeds was a good example, consisted of regular residential weekends and summer holidays, combined with casework and group activities in the home environment to reinforce good and stimulating experiences as part of day-to-day life. The second type, which might sometimes be a substitute for longer residential care (for instance Tyn-y-Pwll), was intended to provide a consciously planned and skilfully handled 'total' experience. Other examples were Hafod Meurig outward bound courses and others of the same type and the NABC and NAYC adventure and other planned holidays. There was more attempt by the mid-1970s to assess what was or could be accomplished and consolidated by these residential experiences.

Chapter 4

Child Care, Continued: Fostering; Child Protection; Child Minders and other forms of Day Care; Adoption; the Children Act, 1975

The following chapters discuss some other aspects of child care in greater detail.

Changing trends in fostering in the 1960s resulted from new light on its complexities. Theory was based upon experience and studies of the dynamics of family life, but was not sufficiently tested by field research. Only two large-scale studies were undertaken, the Social Survey statistical study *Children in Care and the Recruitment of Foster Parents* (Gray and Parr, 1957) and *Children Who Wait* (Rowe and Lambert, 1973). Unfortunately the Home Office research unit undertook little child care research compared with the series on probation. The foster care studies by individual researchers – Trasler (1960), Parker (1966), George (1970), Napier (1972), Adamson (1973) and Thorpe (1974) – were carried out in only one to three children's departments at different points in time and consisted of small samples. They provided the only systematic knowledge available because of the failure to undertake research into what constituted successful fostering. They related only to long-term fostering, whereas there were many more short-term placements from which children returned home, and an indefinite number in between. These considerable limitations which resulted in emphasis on some negative aspects must be borne in mind. Yet in the period experienced practitioners could quote examples of good foster homes which had met the needs of children, even where the parents had kept in touch, and the children been successfully returned to them.

Traditional long-term fostering was based on the assumption that nurture in a family met the developmental needs of children best unless their behaviour difficulties or physical and mental handicaps were too great. Even so, there had been successful attempts to foster such children, with extra support for specially selected foster parents. About half the long-term placements studied by Trasler, Parker and George broke down within five years but, only twenty-nine out of seventy-nine of those studied by Napier. Breakdown usually happened within the first six to eighteen months, thus this was the period when the most skilled support was needed after placement. Napier found it impossible to assess from case records the amount of preparation leading up to the placement. He thought it likely that all the factors he, Parker and George measured were 'irrelevant compared with the professional skill and interest of a child care officer, not only during the pre-placement period but during the period immediately after the placement' (Napier, 1972, p. 188). This important factor was not studied.

George, Adamson, and Rowe and Lambert all emphasised the ambiguous role of foster parents in our society. They commonly regarded themselves as substitute parents, while their neighbours might think they were 'in it for the money', and the children's agency that they were understudies for the natural parents. A number of obligations were specified in the agreement which they were required to sign but no rights, and the child might be taken from them at any time by the placing agency (whether statutory or voluntary). Unless the child was in care under a court order or a parental rights' resolution he might also be reclaimed without notice by the natural parents from a children's home or a foster home. The Houghton Stockdale Committee's recommendations (1972) about removal, custody and adoption (embodied in the Children Act, 1975 – see below) were controversial. It was feared that they might make parents hesitate to let their children go into care or social workers to use foster care where parental ties should be maintained.

In circumstances where the pain of rejection and separation might be inevitable, an emerging guide line was the primacy of the child's welfare and that he belonged where his psychological roots lay, not necessarily with his biological parents as such. This assumption was based upon child care experience, upon the work of Bowlby (1969 and 1973) on attachment, separation and loss, on the findings of Winnicott and others, and on slowly changing social attitudes about contingent rather than absolute parental rights. Yet like any other clear-cut solution in this field it was highly controversial, as Holman (1975) cogently argued.

Several research studies brought to light the haphazard nature of much of the search for and study of foster homes. There were instances in which applications were not followed up for months, if at all (George, 1970; Adamson, 1973) or else some applicants withdrew who with more discussion, help and support might have become successful foster parents. George, Rowe and Lambert found a lack of systematic, continuous planning for foster home recruitment and no whole-hearted attempts to find sufficient substitute families. This often depended on the initiative of individual CCOs, who might only begin to look for a home when a particular child was already in care. Most CCOs were overburdened and the search for or follow up of potential foster homes was apt to rank low on their list of priorities. Advertisements usually produced many unsuitable applicants and a number of withdrawals. The majority of suitable foster parents wanted a baby or small child for semi-adoption, whereas many older children needed substitute homes, often for an uncertain period. It was necessary both to have foster parents ready to take children and to find special homes for particular children.

There were sometimes very good preliminary foster home studies before acceptance, but this often rested upon one or two interviews and frequently the husband and the rest of the family were not seen. George (1970) found that most of the twenty-eight CCOs' records he studied were a vague series of stereotypes with almost no evidence to back up impressions. The reports 'never presented the applicants as real persons where their past experiences enlightened the understanding of their present lives and where the past and the present provided important clues for the understanding of the applicants' future in relation to the foster child' (p. 141).

There was little discussion of motives, though in all child care literature the whole family's attitudes and motives were thought to be crucial. Matching the child to the foster home was regarded as an essential ingredient in successful long-term placements. Yet here, too, George (1970) and Parker (1966) found no discussion recorded on the files, and concluded that there would only have been limited matching for the psychological needs of the child and the foster parents.

There had always been concern about many social workers' difficulties in communication with children, and George found that the case files contained almost no record of any discussion between the CCOs and the child about fostering and his reactions, yet the CCO was the child's continuity at that crisis point when he faced another separation demanding adaptation to unknown people. It may be that all these CCOs knew more, sensed more, discussed more, and did more than they recorded but frequent staff changes made good recording all the more necessary. Conversely, Goodacre (1966) found in a county children's department 'records on foster children in which emotional factors and assessments of relationships . . . were a paramount feature' (p. 88). Trasler (1960) also found that 'the case papers contained a great deal of valuable material concerning the child, his own family and his foster parents . . . These were detailed, skilfully and accurately written and often illustrated by a keen insight into the relationships and problems of a foster family' (p. 10). Dinnage and Kellmer Pringle (1967) also identified as key factors in successful foster home placement that the CCO had time for interviews, reflection and consultation and the ability to select and match well.

Emphasis on maintaining the child's links with his natural family, and if possible strengthening it for his return, made the child care task immensely more difficult. Several surveys stressed the importance of more support for the natural parents. This was essential to reassure them about their continuing importance in the child's life. Mapstone (1971), in a sensitive article, described the feelings of natural parents and the off-putting and frequently misinterpreted behaviour to which this might give rise. The child was caught between conflicting loyalties, the foster parents had strong feelings, and the CCO must struggle to understand all the cross currents but not identify with one group against another. One reason for breakdown seemed to be the child's reaction to losing his own family and it was always important to help him to talk about this and the foster home. Contacts with the natural parents, together with uncertainty about the length of the placement, the impact of conscious and sub-conscious feelings, and the consequent insecurity, all made a trustful and loving relationship more diffi-cult. These factors were probably an element in various survey findings that some social workers and a few agencies disparaged parents' capacities and kept them out of the picture. Rowe and Lambert (1973) found that only 5 per cent of all the children in their study saw both parents frequently, and that 1,150 children out of 2,812 never saw either parent. The longer they remained in care, the more likely they were not to see their parents. George (1970) and Napier (1972) also found no parental contact in about half the long-stay placements. The three departments George studied made very limited attempts to help natural parents. Sometimes parental visits were stopped or made difficult. But in another department Adamson (1973) found that efforts were always made to keep in touch with members of the natural family. CCOs often tried to help foster parents to accept natural parents' visits, but many regarded this as the hardest part of fostering. More children returned to their own families from residential homes than from foster care, though the latter might have included more children without families.

Thorpe (1974) interviewed 121 children who had been in foster homes for over a year and the parents of 60 children, and also discussed with foster parents and social workers their attitudes towards parental visiting. She found that only 32 children had any clear idea of their family background and why they were in care and 26 had almost no understanding of their situation. More children who understood their family situation, and who were in contact with their parents, showed evidence of well-being than the others. There was a statistically significant relation between their adjustment and their knowledge about the department's function; conversely confusion and anxiety resulted from limited knowledge. There was no evidence that contact with natural parents was harmful and most children enjoyed it. The foster parents were overwhelmingly against the idea of re-establishing lost contact. Few natural parents felt encouraged to maintain contact; they thought social workers had lost interest in them, they were often unsure of their rights and lacked the confidence to make the first move. Many children wanted to see their own parents even when they were settled in the foster home. Thorpe also found social workers were ignorant of the natural parents' and children's desire for contact – they only talked alone to 30 per cent of the children – and sometimes feared that contact might lead to a tug of love situation. Many parents lived in poor accommodation, had low earnings or were unemployed, and nearly half were lone parents. 'Often their sense of failure was reinforced by their contact with social workers and the children's department' (p. 694), and nearly two-thirds did not know their child's whereabouts. There were practically no plans for family rehabilitation, though half wanted this and 70 per cent of parents were caring for their other children. In many instances, this seemed to indicate a preventable drift into long-term care and to the filial deprivation of parents separated from their children.

The 1955 Boarding Out Regulations required foster homes to be visited by the children's department within the first month and then on a scale rising to three months. At its best this continuing casework relationship between the CCO and the child, the foster family and the natural parents (if available) allowed difficulties to be aired, and a better understanding and more security to develop. It also gave CCOs more evidence on which to make difficult decisions about leaving or removing the child in a doubtful foster home. All placements had to be reviewed every six months. This might be a formality or an opportunity to make new plans for a child; for instance Holman (1973) recorded that in the departments he surveyed special six-monthly reports were studied by both the children's officer and the committee.

Group methods (combined with individual interviews) slowly began to be used for the assessment, support or education of foster parents or adopters. There were fears about using an unknown method which might get out of hand, thus there was an urgent need for training in the use of groups. Bull and Bailey (1971) described a foster parents group and the learning which took place between the members. By the late 1960s a number of children's departments were running discussion groups for foster parents, and this was later extended by the social services departments.

Both experience and research studies showed that foster parents fell into three groups. Firstly, there were the quasi-professionals who took a succession of babies and toddlers for short periods or the long-term care of emotionally disturbed or handicapped children. Secondly, there were those foster parents who would work closely with the agency and the natural parents to reunite the family, whether the children were with them for short or long periods: Trasler (1960) found that foster parents who acted as uncles and aunts or grandparents were often more successful in this. Finally, there was the traditional long-term placement where the child was grafted into a substitute family. Childless and older couples often made successful foster parents. George and Napier found (unlike Parker and Trasler) that if foster parents had children close in age to the foster child this did not affect success or failure.

Parker and Napier both found the child's age at placement important for success or failure. But this did not apply to children under a year old, possibly because foster parents could accept them more easily. Legitimacy or illegitimacy were irrelevant under the age of 4 but significant later, probably because older illegitimate children had had a more deprived background (Napier).

Dinnage and Kellmer Pringle (1967) suggested in relation to foster parents' motivation that 'Possibly, it is not only the intensity or the kind of adult need which should be considered, but its combination with other personality characteristics – insight, perseverance, or simple good sense – that has the over-riding influence in determining outcome' (p. 15). The following is typical of good fostering experience: '. . . the vast majority of foster parents quite unselfconsciously and with great patience and care, provide the setting of a home for the children to grow into responsible and creative adults, and very often are able to understand the difficulties, which is perhaps the hardest task of all' (Hertfordshire Children's Department, *Annual Report, 1965–66*, p. 17).

There was much discussion throughout the period about the low allowances paid for fostering and the wide variations in these between local authorities. Its cheapness had been a merit in the eyes of the 1952 Select

Committee on Estimates, but the old argument that payment for a service, as distinct from an allowance to meet (or fail to meet) expenses, would substitute mercenary motives for love was slowly giving way to the view that some types of foster parents should be paid a quasi-professional fee. A few children's departments paid a lump sum in addition to the basic allowance to specially qualified foster mothers who could take several children, or provided rent for a bigger house, travel expenses, extra furniture, repairs, and so forth. In a research project to place adolescents with severe problems in foster homes (Hazel and Cox, 1976), the foster parents could be paid up to £50 per week for a demanding task, including work with the adolescent's family. The foster families were organised in groups which met frequently and selected, trained and supported participating couples. Only one placement out of twenty-one was terminated in the first year. Factors crucial for success were the professional skill of the project staff and a strong sense of collective responsibility in the group. Several other local authorities began to experiment with this type of fostering.

There were also experiments in partial fostering, by which a child living in a residential institution might go for holidays and weekends to foster parents. This was a more realistic variation of the earlier ambiguous 'uncle' and 'aunt' scheme.

In 1974 the DHSS set up a working party to produce a *Guide to Fostering Practice* (1976*b*). By this time social services departments were beginning to appoint specialist social workers for foster parent recruitment and assessment. Specialist liaison officers were also appointed to maintain links with foster homes and in general to strengthen the services: some were senior officers with wide responsibilities for fostering and adoption. As with other specialist appointments, there were considerable problems in integrating their duties with the general work of the department.

Several local groups of foster parents came together in 1974 to inaugurate the National Foster Care Association which quickly spread. Its main objectives were to improve the quality of service given to children in care and to work for an effective share in policy making by foster parents.

The most important elements in successful fostering which emerged from practice and research appeared to be: careful selection, preparation and continuing support for foster parents (especially in the early stages); the age of the child at placement; his previous experiences of nurture or deprivation; the degree of preparation for and support he received before, during and after the foster home placement; and how his relations to his natural parents were handled. Research studies also showed that the policies of different children's departments had a crucial effect on standards.

CHILD PROTECTION

The protection of privately fostered children had always been inadequate. The 1948 Children Act made notification mandatory for children under school-leaving age placed privately for reward for more than one month by someone who was not a relative or guardian: further modifications were made by the 1958 Children Act. The Children and Young Persons Act, 1969 extended the definition to include children whose care and maintenance was undertaken without reward, in some circumstances extended the minimum period of fostering to more than six days, and did not require notification of movements of individual children in regular foster homes; but it gave local authorities new powers to make requirements and prohibitions. It was the duty of all but regular private foster parents to give fourteen days' notice before they took a child, except in emergency situations. The local authority could then inspect the premises, impose certain conditions, and prohibit the keeping of foster children if either the premises or the foster parents were unsuitable. The local authority had a general duty to satisfy itself about the well-being of these foster children; to visit them from time to time, and to give advice about their care and maintenance. Children could only be removed by bringing them before a juvenile court and producing evidence of neglect or extreme unsuitability. These provisions were largely ineffective in many areas because many private foster parents did not know of or evaded their obligation to notify and detection was far from adequate, while overburdened CCOs were apt to put child protection visits at the bottom of the list, not least because there was little effective action they could take. None the less by the mid-1970s a few social services departments were providing an effective child protection service.

There was little published information about private fostering until Holman's pioneer study (1973) of a matched sample of 100 private and 100 local authority foster homes. In comparison with the total population of children in local authority foster homes, those privately fostered tended to be placed at an earlier age and to experience shorter placements. Many parents of privately fostered children were overseas students, though, as in the past, some were British deserted wives or husbands, or unmarried mothers. CCOs assessed over half the private foster homes as unsuitable or doubtful, but a quarter would have been accepted by the local authority. These foster parents were usually inadequately and erratically paid and the foster children were in poorer and more overcrowded physical conditions, indeed more generally at risk. Both groups of foster mothers gave as their main reason for fostering love and concern for children: '. . . the overriding impression is of a well-meaning sincere attempt to help children and of a high valuation of affection, security and family life' (p. 71).

None the less, and despite the fact that the children were more frequently visited by their own parents, over one-third showed symptoms of emotional deprivation against one-quarter of the local authority children. There was no attempt to match the child and the foster home or to introduce him gradually to it. By and large the foster fathers showed little interest in the children compared with their local authority counterparts.

Only 8 out of the 100 placements had been notified (as the law required) to the local authority before the child arrived. CCOs felt that they had no clearly defined duties or roles compared with the supervision, support and education requirements in local authority placements. Over half the children had been seen by CCOs less than twice or not at all in the preceding twelve months, and 95 per cent had not been seen alone against 23 per cent of the local authority children. It was very rare to give practical help or advice about behaviour difficulties, although the research interviews showed that a number of foster mothers and natural parents badly needed help. Indeed, only 43 per cent of local authority foster mothers had received supportive and educational help. In short, 'the most unsuitable private foster mothers, the least participant foster fathers, the children displaying the most adverse conditions, the single natural parents with no support of a partner, were not given compensatory help through extra visits' (p. 237).

No child in the study sample was removed nor unsuitable foster parents prohibited from receiving children, probably because this required court action and evidence for this was hard to obtain. Not surprisingly, Holman concluded that 'In Britain it is easier to get a child than an extension on one's garage' (p. 262).

The Commonwealth Students Children's Society strove to promote better standards of private care for the children of overseas students (Stapleton, 1976).

CHILD MINDERS

Women's employment steadily increased and at the 1971 census 588,000 women with children under 5 were working. Of these, 92 per cent were wives in married couples, 7 per cent widowed, divorced, separated or deserted, and 1 per cent single mothers. In consequence, large numbers of small children were placed daily, sometimes for long hours with child minders. Child minding was regulated by the National Health Service Act, 1946 (section 22) and the Nursery and Child Minders Regulation Act, 1948 (amended by section 60 of the Health Service and Public Health Act, 1968). Child minders had an obligation to register with the local authority and were visited before registration, though they might or might not be visited subsequently. For various reasons many child minders did not register. In the homes of unregistered child minders there was no control over standards of health, safety or personal care. Some minders provided excellent care but others might take too many children in overcrowded conditions, impose strict discipline, and fail to meet emotional needs or provide toys or other stimulus. But there were many good child minders who provided proper care and a continuing relationship in a family setting. Some were eager for training, motivated by love of children, and anxious to change the poor image of child minders.

The Finer Committee (1974) stressed that

'the conditions in which some of the children are kept, even if they are representative of only a small minority of cases, show how bad 'caretaker' conditions for children can be; and some standards in this area are lower than society should tolerate. Moreover, even where standards are satisfactory, private arrangements of this kind lack the security of public provision and can well produce harrowing problems for the lone parent who has to rely on them . . . An unmarried mother told us that after obtaining addresses from shop-window advertisements she took her child from door to door, asking whether there were any vacancies; the minder would look the mother and child up and down before answering and if the answer was 'Yes', the fee would then have to be discussed. Nor are the problems solved once the child has been placed. If, for example, she has illness in her own family the minder may, without notice, discontinue the service; on the other hand, if the mother is late collecting her child or through illness misses a day, she may find that the minder refuses to accept the child any longer.' (para. 8.113)

The Committee thought that all forms of full-time day care were unsuitable for children under 3. In any event, their mothers should be involved in services for them and the child should be looked after by someone whom he already knew before his mother left him. Even between the ages of 3 and 5, children should only be separated from their mothers for part of the day. Day foster care, pioneered by some local authorities, should become general. Local authorities should recruit, employ and supervise child minders who should be given in-service training and play equipment to increase their understanding of the children in their care. This was already being pioneered by a few local authorities. Some of the children should go to play groups or nursery classes. Day fostering should also be available for school children before and after school hours and in the holidays. If private child minders were to continue they should be given the same help as that for local authority day foster care.

A 1973 DHSS selected sample survey (1975c) showed that registration was often a formal procedure, with few subsequent visits. Where an area team social worker was given responsibility, child minders were encouraged to register, a high and consistent standard maintained, and embryonic day foster care developed. Child minders might also be used instead of short-term care or in conjunction with a day nursery. By 1975, several local authorities had social workers responsible for child minding who recruited and trained child minders, placed individual children, arranged payments, gave individual support, and ran groups for child minders where they supported each other and learnt about child development. Some local authorities also loaned toys and safety equipment. There was thus a dawning recognition of the need for shared responsibility between parents, child minders and the local authority. This might lead to a public service of child minders, recruited, registered, supported, supervised and paid a salary by local authorities and integrated with other services for the children and their families (Community Relations Commission, 1975, *Who Minds?*).

OTHER FORMS OF DAY CARE

The number of local authority day nurseries decreased steadily after the Second World War on the assumption that mothers should stay at home when the children were small. However, there were circumstances in many one-parent families, or others, where the mother (or father) had to work or for some other reason could not care adequately for the child, and also mothers increasingly went out to work from choice. The result was a greater demand for private fostering, nursery classes and child minders providing part- or whole-day care.

By 1969 there were 21,000 places for children in day nurseries against 72,000 in 1944. The 1973–83 DHSS ten year plan suggested an increase to about 34,000 places. By 1975 there were nearly 26,600 places in private and voluntary day nurseries. All forms of all-day care were highly controversial from the point of view of the well-being of the child. The Finer Committee thought that day care facilities concentrated on the need of the mother for someone to take care of the child during her working hours rather than on the child's needs.

Day nurseries did not provide young children with regular mother substitutes because of staff shortages and frequent staff changes, so that children might be isolated from their parents for most of their waking hours. The Report thought that nursery classes and play groups were child centred and welcomed the proposed considerable expansion of nursery schools for children from 3 to 5. It said:

'Playgroups have helped mothers as well as children. They have enabled many mothers to escape from the loneliness and inertia they may experience at home into the activity and companionship they may enjoy at work. In planning together and working for their children's needs mothers are able to gain in skill, self-esteem and confidence in themselves as parents. This aspect is of particular significance to lone parents who can so easily become detached from the community. In the comradeship of united effort for their children, groups of isolated and lonely parents can grow into a 'caring community' which may go far in providing a substitute for the wider family group and circle of friends which many of them lack, both for the parent and the child. In this kind of atmosphere, arrangements can be made for baby-sitting and for positive help in times of trouble, for example, if a mother suddenly goes into hospital. In many areas, also, mother and toddler groups for children under 3 are emerging and these are particularly valuable in helping parents to a fuller understanding of child development and play needs, and in strengthening relationships between parents and children, at the time when the children's need for mental stimulation is at its greatest.' (para. 8.116)

Measures to make it possible for children to be cared for in their own homes should in the Committee's view include relief mothering to keep a family together, home helps to get the children off to school and to cover the gap between their's and their parent's return, and day fostering.

Pre-school play groups are discussed later in connection with one-parent families and voluntary organisations (see chapter 18 below, and volume 2, chapter 17).

The 1973 DHSS survey (1975c) showed (pp. 14–18) that most social services departments had appointed play-group advisers and supervisors of child minders. These and day nurseries were under the direct management of the residential/day care section, and thus in some isolation from field services. In a few authorities this responsibility was delegated to social workers or specialists in the area teams. It was then an area team resource closely related to applications for care, and social workers began to understand the value and use of these services. It was clearly essential to make senior appointments of persons with ability and understanding to advise the management team on necessary services for young children related to needs uncovered by the area teams.

Developments by 1975 included the increasing use of day nurseries to help socially handicapped children and their families, experiments with family day care centres to meet family needs rather than only providing substitute care for the children, and nursery centres which combined day care with nursery education.

ADOPTION IN THE 1950s, 1960s AND EARLY 1970s

The number of adoptions increased in the late 1950s. This partly resulted from foster placements which developed into adoption and the placement of children with a view to adoption. Local authorities' power to arrange adoptions without necessarily receiving the child into care was clarified by the 1958 Adoption Act which also extended the grounds for dispensing with parental consent.

Contrary to earlier views, experience showed that the crucial factor in successful adoption was not a long probationary period but skilled and thorough work before an adoptive couple was accepted and a child placed with them. Their motives, attitudes and health were more crucial than an expressed willingness to give a home to an unwanted child. The focus began to shift from finding the perfect baby for childless couples to finding a good home for a child. There were also some early attempts to place older or handicapped children for adoption. These changes resulted largely from the experience of the best local authorities and voluntary adoption agencies: some others continued to employ untrained staff or use committee members, the local vicar's wife or other voluntary workers, and sometimes to conduct their inquiries by correspondence. More careful and sophisticated placement policies began to displace the view that only the robustly healthy and alert baby was suitable for adoption. This had been coupled with a mystique about matching and some ill-founded fears about hereditary taint. The result here, as elsewhere, was a demand for far more skilled and experienced child care workers, whether in local authorities or voluntary agencies. A number of registered adoption societies were moral welfare associations which worked with and on behalf of the mother as well as the child. Many mothers and small agencies alike, faced extreme financial and other difficulties in placing the child with a temporary foster mother pending adoption. Throughout this period and later the then Standing Conferences of Societies Registered for Adoption (later the Association of British Adoption and Fostering Agencies) was the national forum and standard-setting body.

The Hurst Committee (1954) was clear that 'The primary object at which all should aim in the arrangement of adoptions is the welfare of the child, and adoption should therefore be approached as a means of finding the right home for a child rather than of satisfying would-be adopters' (para. 19). This was a substantial change of attitude, but it only referred to the making of an uncontested adoption order and not to dispensing with the natural parents' consent, though the Adoption Act, 1958 embodied the Committee's recommendations about extended grounds for doing so. The Committee feared that to give paramount importance to the welfare of the child could result in any parent who temporarily gave up the care of a child being permanently deprived of him. 'Apart from the possible value of the blood tie . . . the importance of preserving parental responsibility is such that the parents' claim should not be reduced for the sake of giving greater claims to prospective adopters' (para. 119). But what about the well-being of children caught between these rival claims of adults? This debate swung back and forth over the years in regard to 'tug of love' cases in which parents refused consent to adoption or children were removed from foster parents.

For a short while in the early 1960s, there were sometimes more available children than would-be adoptive parents. In a situation where services were local, unevenly distributed and often unduly restrictive, this could lead to an unsuitable placement, for example with a woman who had no experience of children but was mourning the death of her dog (Adamson, 1973). The number of adoption orders reached its peak in 1968 and thereafter began to decline as the number of available children steadily decreased though the proportion of adoptions by natural parents increased. The decrease in adoptions by non-relatives was thought to be due to 'the pill', legalised abortion, more liberal social attitudes to unmarried parenthood and some provision of flatlets for unmarried mothers; though the financial, housing and social disabilities suffered by one-parent families remained considerable. Conversely, adoption became more socially acceptable so that not only infertile couples but those with their own children tried to adopt.

Triseliotis (1970) studied the actual practice of statutory and voluntary adoption agencies in Scotland in 1965 against the yardstick of current social work theory. Only two of the twelve agencies had three or more interviews with adoptive parents and there was little attempt to assess personality and attitudes. Decisions were usually made on standard and stereotyped factual information related to income, occupation and physical living conditions, coupled with the views and value judgements of individual workers, usually based upon their experience and hunches rather than a general body of knowledge. The scant information in many case records was as much due to routine procedures as staff shortages. In a majority of cases the natural mother was only interviewed once, and only one agency attempted to see the putative father. There was little information about the natural parents or the child's background, though most agencies believed strongly in the power of heredity. The majority of records made no reference to the child as such. Most voluntary societies were extremely short of funds. Many had not changed their objectives since they were founded and did not carry out continuous reviews of their work in the light of fresh knowledge. Thus they failed to formulate their practice into a body of working principles and much of their work remained adoptive-parent oriented rather than child centred. The shining exceptions were a children's department and a voluntary agency which consistently used, and indeed helped to pioneer, the best current practice in relation to the child, its natural parents and would-be adopters.

Goodacre (1966) found that half the voluntary adoption agencies she studied in an English county only interviewed applicants once and might use a local contact (often a doctor's or vicar's wife) for the home visit. Some societies required applicants to have a committee interview in which brief, factual questions were asked. On the other hand, in the local authority children's department at least three visits were paid to the applicants in their own home by qualified CCOs. These were supervised by a senior and all final decisions were made in consultation with the children's officer. Packman (1975) described the practice in Oxfordshire where a panel of senior social workers, the adoption officer and the investigating CCO considered each case. Group interviews for would-be adopters had also started.

In 1966, voluntary societies placed twice as many children as local authorities. By the early 1970s there were 63 voluntary adoption societies in England and Wales (8 in Scotland), while 96 out of 172 counties and county boroughs in England and Wales acted as adoption agencies (Houghton Stockdale Report, 1972, paras 32–3). A 1966 sample survey quoted by the Houghton Stockdale Committee (para. 82) showed only 4 per cent arranged by third parties but some of these were extremely unsatisfactory and the Committee recommended that they should be made illegal (para. 92). The big national child care societies and a few others provided a comprehensive service (though with various limitations on grounds of religion). They, and ACCO, the Standing Conference of Societies Registered for Adoption, the National Children's Bureau and individual researchers were all trying to clarify the needs over time of the child, the natural parents and the adoptive parents, and thus what constituted a good adoption service. Even in comprehensive child care agencies adoption tended to be an isolated service. The increasing tendency to appoint specialist adoption officers could reinforce this, even though it had obvious strengths in adding to and spreading knowledge derived from experience.

Adoption placements were often too long delayed through trying to ensure the baby's physical fitness and normal intelligence. The result was to deprive adoptive parents of some initial satisfactions of parenthood, while research findings were demonstrating that the development of intelligence was closely related to the stimulus the young child received. Experience favoured early placement for the development of close relationships and to save the child from separation and discontinuities of mothering, yet more older children were also successfully placed. As a result the focus shifted from the child to be placed to the adoptive parents because

'all investigators have found that the personal qualities of the adopting parents are of paramount importance. Included here are attitudes not only to the child itself, but also feelings about adoption in general, about illegitimacy and about the reasons for not having a child of their own, be these infertility, impotence or any other circumstance. The age, income and social class of adopters are far less important'. (Kellmer Pringle, 1967, p. 23)

As in foster home placements, this emphasised the importance of a thorough and skilled assessment of would-be adopters. For a long time the most responsible adoption agencies had also been considering their obligations to applicants, who had often been under much stress about childlessness and might then have to face a rejection which seemed to affirm their inadequacy. There were a few examples of discussion groups for would-be adopters which gave both the couples and the agency some idea of whether or not adoption was appropriate. In the past, adoptive parents might be rationed to one child on the grounds that it was not fair to give them more because of the shortage of babies, but this created one-child families and good practice swung to placing successive children in an adoptive home, not necessarily with childless couples.

The shortage of babies available for adoption, contrasted with the number of handicapped, coloured and older children in care needing permanent homes, led in the late 1960s to far more flexible attitudes about adoptable or non-adoptable children. Obviously there were great advantages in this, financially and for the welfare of the child, but a large investment of the time, imagination and skill of the most competent CCOs was required to explore a new aspect of child care. A well-planned action research project on the adoption of non-white children was undertaken between 1965 and 1969 (Raynor, 1970). A follow up at the end of the project showed that, as tested on a comprehensive rating scale, of the fifty-one, non-white children adopted into white or non-white families, most of the children were doing well, indeed only three situations gave any cause for concern and even these had positive aspects. The children were to be followed up periodically. The project soon discovered different standards and procedures between agencies, with some desperately seeking adopters while others had no available children. In due course, initiative by the project resulted in the Adoption Resource Exchange in which the member agencies agreed to work to common high standards in the placement of non-white children. Numbers grew rapidly from the original six in 1968, and its resources were extended in 1972 to other 'hard to place' children. By 1975 there were eighty members. In 1973, the south-east Scotland resource centre was started on similar lines and mainly dealt with older or handicapped children.

The strain on the natural mother of deciding whether or not to part with her baby – and indeed the conflicts or fierce partisanship suffered by CCOs and moral welfare workers – showed the need to free the mother as much as possible from financial anxieties, isolation and forebodings, and to help her to make up her mind as soon and as clearly as possible about the baby's future. Her right to refuse consent even on the day of the court hearing was intended to protect natural parents' rights but in practice it could add to indecision and guilt, while the adoptive parents often did not dare to let themselves become too fond of the child during the probationary period for fear the mother would change her mind. This led ACCO (*Adoption – the Way Ahead*, 1969a) and others in the adoption field to argue that the mother's right to withdraw consent should cease once the child was in an adoptive home.

As in foster home placements, but in differing ways, it was crucial to place the child in an adoptive home that could meet his changing needs throughout his childhood, taking account of the feelings and attitudes of the adoptive parents themselves and other family members. In the probationary period when responsibilities were fragmented between the adoption society, the welfare authority and the guardian or curator *ad litem*, the adopters were usually too apprehensive to discuss difficulties. It had been thought that the initial adjustment would be made in this period and that once the order was made adopters should be free from interference. This assumed that the order magically made them just like natural parents, but experience showed that adoptive parenthood was different. Apart from comments by relations, friends, neighbours and other children, and fears about 'bad blood', there was the problem of telling the child he was adopted. This caused such anxiety to adopters that sometimes they faced it too late or not at all. McWhinnie in her retrospective follow up of seventy-eight adopted adults (1967) described their memories of intense curiosity as children about their parentage. In an account of a series of group discussions (1964–67) with adoptive parents, she concluded (1968) that the best age for telling was between 3 and 4½ when most children ask many questions about where babies come from and adopted children can easily accept having been born to a different mother. She (like others) found adoptive parents were eager to come to discussion groups which aimed at the expression and modification of attitudes, thus helping the couples to function better as adoptive parents. These discussions helped adopters to overcome many uncertainties and problems and to find support. There was much fear about possible difficulties in adolescence and a desire to meet again then when adopted children especially want to know about their origins as part of their identity. The project on the adoption of non-white children found that couples gained considerable support and reassurance from discussions in preliminary and post-adoption group meetings. An increasing number of children's departments began to run such discussion groups for adoptive parents.

The only large-scale longitudinal studies of random samples of children born illegitimate and of adopted children were undertaken by Crellin *et al.* (1971) and by Seglow *et al.* (1972). These recorded the situation at birth and nine years after of 145 children in the 1958 cohort (all babies born in a particular week) who had been adopted. Most of the children were illegitimate and a much higher proportion of such children in the total cohort were born to very young mothers who had less ante-natal care and whose babies were of low birth weight. This group therefore had a comparatively poor start and posed the question of whether a good home environment could reverse the process. When the children who remained with their mothers were followed up at the age of 7 their physical development was normal but their abilities and attainments were lower than the rest of the cohort. They had experienced more substitute or supplementary care owing to their mothers' employment and difficult and unsettled family circumstances. Five times as many had suffered separation from home and twice as many were maladjusted.

About a third of all the illegitimately born children were adopted, usually in infancy. The adoptive parents were interviewed personally when the children were 8 to 9. The children's environmental circumstances were better than that of the cohort children in general.

'The great majority of adoptive families were thought to be meeting the needs of their adopted children satisfactorily at the age of about nine years. This is all the more remarkable in view of the children's early vulnerability; community attitudes to adoption; the misconceptions regarding the influence of poor heredity; and the fact that there is certainly room for improvements in adoption practice.' (Seglow *et al.*, 1972, p. 152)

About 21 per cent of the children had been privately placed. Their progress did not differ significantly from those placed by adoption agencies. The authors comment on the poor light this shed on agency standards against 'relatively haphazard' placements. Only 6 per cent had not yet been told they were adopted. Only a very small number were unsatisfactorily placed but 'every child in this group was very unhappy and probably should never have been adopted by those particular parents' (p. 125). It was intended to do a further follow up when the children were adolescent.

In the late 1960s the Advisory Councils on Child Care for England and Wales and for Scotland set up a joint committee to prepare *A Guide to Adoption Practice* (1970*b*) to help to increase knowledge and raise standards. It recognised that good standards would not be achieved overnight but 'In the past, lack of clear guidance and proven facts has resulted in sweeping generalisations and decisions arrived at on the basis of subjective hunches. Rigid rules have arisen as protection from the anxieties of uncertainty. There is now a growing body of knowledge gleaned from accumulating experience and from research findings' (para. I.14). It outlined good practice in relation to natural parents, prospective adopters, the child himself, the administration of an adoption service and the legal processes. It emphasised the key role of casework in adoption services and also referred to some weaknesses in the law.

The Houghton Stockdale Committee (1972) drew attention to the lack of adoption services in some parts of the country and the many voluntary agencies which were primarily concerned with unmarried mothers or with would-be adoptive parents, whereas adoption should be part of a wider family social work service and children should not be unnecessarily relinquished for adoption.

THE CHILDREN ACT, 1975

The limitations of the Hurst Committee's proposals in 1954 and the more radical recommendations of the Houghton Stockdale Report (1972) became the requirement in the Children Act, 1975 that in reaching an adoption decision a court or adoption agency should consider all the circumstances, first consideration being given to the need to safeguard and promote the welfare of the child throughout his childhood. This 'first consideration' could clarify decisions to dispense with parental consent where a child was in and out of care, the parent or parents were too unstable ever to make a home or a plan for him, might have no contact with him, but would not consent to adoption.

Some sections were not to come into operation until resources were available. Local authorities would be required to provide a comprehensive adoption service, counselling about adoption problems and temporary accommodation for pregnant women, mothers or children. Approval of voluntary adoption agencies was to be transferred from local authorities to the Secretary of State and made dependent upon an effective contribution to the adoption service and the number and qualifications of the staff. This would supercede almost automatic registration by local authorities. The parent or guardian might not remove a child without twenty-eight days' notice (unless the local authority consented) if he had been in the care of the authority or a voluntary organisation for six months or more. These were long-needed safeguards against sudden removals. A local authority might also pass a parental rights resolution in relation to any child who had been continuously in its care or that of a voluntary organisation for three years or more.

If there seemed to be a conflict of interests between the child and his parent or guardian in any court proceedings, the court might appoint a guardian *ad litem* to act on behalf of the child. This was the independent children's advocate so necessary, for example, in some applications to revoke a care order when, as in the Maria Colwell case, the local authority could not be both party to the proceedings and able to play an independent role.

A court would be able to make an order freeing a child for adoption in general if each parent or guardian agreed or if the court dispensed with their consent. An additional ground for dispensing with consent to adoption was that the parent or guardian had persistently or seriously ill-treated the child and rehabilitation was considered unlikely. If the applicant to adopt was someone with whom the child had lived for five years or more no person might remove him before the case was heard.

A new category of custodianship orders could be used as an alternative to double relationships created through adoption by relations. These orders might also be made to other people with whom the child was living. They required the parent or legal guardian's consent and were revocable. The court itself might decide to make a custodianship order instead of an adoption order.

There was much controversy about the time-limit clauses of the Bill and some doubts about the new category of custodianship. Some also contended that this was an Act to take children away from their parents rather than making it more possible to keep them by fuller use of the 1963 and 1969 Acts and by implementation of the Finer Report's proposals. This ignored the importance of the sensible use of a flexible range of resources.

Chapter 5

Training for Child Care: Child Care Officers; Residential Child Care

Early Stages in the 1950s

The child care service started with so much goodwill that from 1947 six universities had been willing to set up *ad hoc* specialised courses in child care for candidates with social science qualifications, despite their doubts about vocational training in the universities. Students had no doubts and some of the best and most active wanted to train for the new child care service. At the beginning of the 1950s the child care courses at two universities were discontinued for fear supply would exceed demand, while another decided to end its child care course: thus only those at LSE and Birmingham and Liverpool Universities remained. In 1950, there were seventy-seven boarding out officers in training but later annual output fell to the mid-forties. By the end of the decade there were three applied social studies courses at LSE and Southampton and Birmingham Universities, but with only a small number of places for child care students. Thus training contracted, the early impetus was lost, and the imbalance between supply and demand worsened throughout the 1950s when more local authorities began to demand trained staff as these first-qualified social workers demonstrated what was meant by a service to meet the needs of individual children. In 1959, the Association of Children's Officers (ACO) pressed the case for expanded training as a result of figures collected from children's departments. The Association rejected arguments for financial economy and that it would be wrong to draw too heavily upon the diminishing number of educated women coming into professional work in general. The Association also contended that skilled child care officers reduced the need for residential care.

Theory and practice were concurrent on the applied social studies courses, while in the child care courses theory and some term-time experience preceded the three months full-time fieldwork at the end. The term-time experience varied from a one day a week attachment to a children's department or child guidance clinic to the significant study of coping and non-coping large families undertaken in Birmingham by the tutor to the course and her students (Shapiro, 1965). The teaching about casework in child care had to be built up from scratch, drawing largely on war-time evacuation and child guidance experience, and by degrees with material from the new children's departments. There was some outstanding theoretical teaching of various subjects on these courses. At first most children's departments thought it was the tutors' responsibility to relate theory and practice, thus there were long, hard struggles to persuade local authorities to accept students for fieldwork and to change 'a period of attachment' into supervision by selected CCOs given time and training for the purpose. By the mid-1950s about twenty-four children's departments were taking students in the long vacations. The 1956 Home Office memorandum of guidance on *Training in Child Care* (unpublished) said that the students' progress in learning

' . . . calls for sustained attention by one person . . . This involves regular weekly discussion between student and supervisor . . . In the long run this important work of training will be found to justify the special allocation of staff time, and in the larger children's departments the appointment of additional staff. Experience with a number of students enables such a supervisor to develop wisdom in training and a standard in the assessment of students.'

There was some controversy when LSE merged its child care course with the applied social studies course, because this decreased the number of places for child care students and some in the child care world preferred the sharply focused, specialised child care courses which they thought provided a more reliable foundation for practice.

By the late 1950s children's officers had had enough experience of foster home placements to know how much skill this needed. They therefore began to take a more active interest in training. The Central Training Council in Child Care asked ACO to collect information about the total numbers of CCOs and wastage rates and the results gave a depressing picture which reinforced the case for more training.

Expansion in the 1960s
Up to 1960, students were selected jointly by the CTC and university representatives, in addition to subsequent selection by individual universities. There was also a general meeting between CTC and university representatives at the end of the summer to decide whether each student should receive the CTC certificate in child care on the basis of university recommendations. When this practice was discontinued in 1962 the CTC letter of recognition was substituted.

Pressure by ACO and ACCO and the sheer weight of evidence demonstrated that a great expansion of training was essential, and the CTC set up a working party of its members to make an energetic exploration of every possibility. It was agreed that the first aims should be to increase the number of university places and to concentrate on new recruits. It was hoped that by 1963 about three times as many students would qualify each year, and then untrained staff could be seconded to train. In 1964 ACO and ACCO submitted to the CTC an urgent joint memorandum about the lack of trained staff and the 'breakdown of standards' in the child care service. Subsequently, at the request of the Home Secretary, local authorities were asked to assess their staffing needs. The CTC was aiming to train 300 students annually by 1968 which seemed to be the maximum for whom places could be provided on one- or two-year courses. The local authority associations thought this was insufficient but there were financial impediments to a faster rate.

As a result of the new drive for expansion there were discussions between the CTC and every university with an appropriate department that might be willing to start or enlarge a course if additional funds were available. In 1960 the University of Liverpool initiated an eighteen-month course for graduates in non-social science subjects who otherwise had to take a social science course followed by one in child care. Later, several other universities started similar courses. These integrated courses were subsequently lengthened to two years for reasons discussed in another chapter. (See volume 2, chapter 1, section on 'Professional Courses in the 1960s'.) The first post-graduate, two-year master's degree 'generic' course started at York University in 1966.

Until 1960 the training of child care officers was concentrated in the universities, but it was obvious that these could not increase numbers indefinitely in addition to meeting equally pressing demands from other branches of social work. In that year the LCC decided to take action to meet its own needs by setting up a two-year course at the North Western Polytechnic on the lines of the Younghusband working party proposals (1959). Before the course started the CTC agreed to recognise it and to put forward candidates. There were 133 applications for the eighteen places on the first course. Thus the principle of integrated (i.e. combined social studies and social work) two-year courses with concurrent theory and practice was accepted and others were started both in university extramural departments and in colleges of further education. Ten years later when the CTC came to an end there were twenty-three such courses (including three in Scotland).

A clearing-house system was set up in 1964 which made possible for the first time an unduplicated count of applicants for training. Of the 410 students who started courses in that year 146 were seconded. By the end of the decade authority was given for the output of CCOs to be increased to 1,100 a year by 1973. This staggering advance over previous figures resulted largely from pressure to train more staff to implement the Children and Young Persons Acts of 1963 and 1969. It followed earlier struggles to prevent reduction of CTC output target figures. The result was that 575 students qualified in 1970 against 50 in 1960. The minimum age of admission was 23 (formerly 25) but the age range of students on the two-year courses remained fairly constant at 30 to 45.

It soon became clear that to expand training on the scale of the late 1960s demanded a total strategy with different parts related to each other. This included trying to spread courses from the south and midlands into the then desert areas of the north-east, Wales and Scotland. It was also obvious that the strategy must include cultivating fieldwork resources, which were limited by lack of supervisors, accommodation for students and inadequate standards in some local social agencies. Whether these placements could have been increased more quickly over the field as a whole is a moot question. From 1961 the Home Office was able to pay a *per capita* supervision fee of £125 a year for each student, which obviously stimulated local authorities to provide more supervision. Three years later a CTC survey of all qualified CCOs who might supervise students showed that many were not being used and that most supervisors only had one student. This survey, like the similar one in the probation service, stimulated the setting up of student units. The first such unit financed by a local authority was started in Essex Children's Department in 1957 for students on the LSE applied social studies course.

The Local Government Training Board (LGTB) became responsible from 1967 for the salaries of staff seconded for training and also for payment for supervision, but there was dismay when, being short of funds, its grant was fixed at £1 a day. In 1969 it agreed to finance two student units jointly in children's and health and welfare departments. Next year Home Office funds were made available for a number of units in voluntary organisations able to offer casework, group work and community work. The first five were in three family service units, Liverpool Personal Service Society and the Blackfriars Settlement. (See also volume 2, chapter 4.)

In this expansion of fieldwork it also became obvious that there was a greater dearth of child care officers competent to supervise students than could be overcome through supervisors' groups run by child care course tutors. Thus in 1966, as part of the total effort to increase training facilities, the entire CTC in-service training programme for the year was concentrated on supervision.

The total training strategy also included much consultation and support to new or enlarged courses and participating children's departments by the CTC training inspectorate, and indeed by experienced social work teachers in the locality. As time went on, almost every type of course had been started that would attract candidates. Naturally this led to a swaying battle between quantity and quality and differing views as to whether the one letter of recognition guaranteed an acceptable minimum standard of achievement. In any event, this was not clarified or related to the changing demands of the task in any precise way. The problem of achieving, maintaining, indeed improving standards needed constant initiative and ingenuity to combat scarce resources and overwork.

There was steady pressure on the CTC from local authority and professional associations to run part-time qualifying courses for serving officers. Finally, it agreed to start these experimentally, provided that in two- to three-year courses the same ground was covered as in a one-year, full-time course. This would entail day release, several short residential periods and a supervised field placement not in the employing authority. The first course was planned for Sheffield but had to be cancelled for lack of candidates; another at Keele ran for several years and then became full-time at the request of employing authorities. Others in Middlesborough and London were more successful in recruitment. One year, full-time courses to enable long-serving, unqualified CCOs to qualify (and incidentally have a better chance of promotion) were provided in several extramural departments and two colleges of further education or education (the latter in Scotland). Admission was restricted to health visitors, qualified teachers and serving CCOs over 27 with at least three years' experience in the field who could show evidence of continuing study. There were constant demands to lower the minimum age, but difficulties arose when it was discovered that a few local authorities were recruiting untrained people, employing them till they reached the minimum entry requirements and then seconding them to train in one year instead of two.

Courses which were part-time in the first year and full-time in the second were run in London, Ipswich, and Preston for several years for experienced serving CCOs. They were the forerunners of the phase III courses described later (see volume 2, chapter 7, section on 'The Central Council for Education and Training in Social Work'). At the other end of the scale, three-year, full-time courses for young entrants of 18 or over were started in 1969 at Moray House College of Education, Edinburgh, and Thurrock Technical College in Essex.

The Home Office White Paper *The Child, the Family and the Young Offender* (1965) forecast a demand for an additional 1,000 child care officers. An emergency course was inevitable to train such numbers in addition to all other possible expansion. There was a good deal of opposition to this in the social work world. But an imaginatively planned emergency course was started in 1968 to recruit older candidates already settled in their localities and to avoid undermining recruitment to existing courses or drawing on their fieldwork placements (the second objective was not altogether met). It was to run for five years (later extended to eight). Candidates of 35 or over might be serving, unqualified child care officers but the primary aim was to attract new recruits, who were appointed by local authorities or voluntary organisations (preferably in 'desert' areas) for secondment to take the course. All candidates were interviewed and finally selected jointly by the employing authority, the CTC and the North Western Polytechnic. Each agency requesting a place for a candidate on the course had to agree in specific terms to provide supervised fieldwork in the second year for new entrants. The first year (on a Home Office grant) consisted primarily of lectures, seminars and tutorials on sociology, human growth and development, social policy and administration, and social work method, reinforced by role play and a practical project on one day a week (more practice was added later). The second year (on salary) consisted of supervised fieldwork in the employing agency and regular group discussions with tutors to the course. The letter of recognition was awarded on successful completion of both years. During the initial planning year the tutors had regular sessions at the National Institute for Social Work Training to study educational objectives and methods and curriculum planning. The course was staffed by 22 tutors (2 part-time) to 200 students. This made it possible for two tutors to have continuing contact with the same group of twenty students in the second year and also to work regularly with the local supervisors and keep them abreast of what was being taught on the course. Two sandwich courses at a six-month interval were also planned for children's officers, supervisors and tutors taking part in the emergency courses. Over the years this close relation between the course and the local authority or voluntary organisation also made a substantial contribution to in-service training. In time, the educational content of the second year was also increased. From 1972, when the course had become generic, students returned to the Polytechnic for a day a fortnight; they continued to undertake individual projects and also submitted two case records as part of their final assessment.

The number of initial inquiries for the first course in 1968 (resulting in 1,900 applications) made some self-selection procedure necessary. This was achieved by a stringently worded statement about the work of a CCO and by inviting potential candidates to lecture/discussions where they could ask questions about the course and the job. One hundred and eight candidates were accepted out of 230 interviewed, and 92 finally started the course, including 60 men and 70 new recruits. This same number was repeated in 1969 and 1970. There were 76 in 1972 and 1973 but 52 in 1974.

Subsequently two other emergency courses on the same lines were started at Leeds Polytechnic and Llandaff College of Education, primarily for candidates in the north-east and Wales. The three courses had places for 175 students a year. When the last course ended in 1977 approximately 1,000 students would have qualified. Much was learnt on these courses about the professional education of intelligent mature students with varied educational backgrounds.

The number of CCOs sponsored by the Home Office to take advanced courses remained at between four and eight annually throughout the period. In 1967 ACCO proposed an advanced course to include casework supervision and administration. This proposal made no headway, but in 1971 a CTC committee discussed the need to provide advanced training for senior people engaged in management, consultancy, teaching and research. So far very little progress had been made and some attempts to provide advanced courses had collapsed for lack of candidates, largely because senior staff could not afford to train on student grants and local authorities were reluctant to second key staff.

In the early years of the decade comparatively few graduates trained but in 1968 around 500 were unable to get places on child care courses alone. Existing university applied social studies courses for graduates were expanding and new ones were started in several polytechnics for holders of social science qualifications, while three additional universities started courses for graduates. All this was not enough and in 1971 a new type of emergency course for graduates was proposed. There were to be four courses, each taking fifty students. Each course would have five tutors and five supervisors jointly appointed with neighbouring local authorities. These would be responsible for supervising groups of students as well as for some tutorial work. Theory and practice would run concurrently with fieldwork placements in casework, community work and residential care. This proposal was overtaken by new plans when the Central Council for Education and Training in Social Work (CCETSW) got under way.

There was naturally continuing pressure to provide qualifying training for experienced but unqualified staff. In 1970 a joint working party of the CTC and the Council for Training in Social Work (CTSW) produced a three-phase training scheme for those over 35 with at least five years' experience. This was implemented by the CCETSW (see volume 2, chapter 7).

This was the total training pattern for qualifying courses for child care officers when the CTC came to an end in 1971, with an unfinished agenda to be carried on by the CCETSW. Over the years since 1947 it had discovered how to work in an active partnership with the universities and colleges, the local authorities, the staffs of the courses, field teachers and members of related professions, the professional associations and voluntary organisations. Its growth was both cause and consequence of more knowledge and skill in child care since 1947. After the contraction of the 1950s it worked with energy and determination in the 1960s to expand numbers and to pioneer new ways of training.

The 1947 basic content of courses consisted of the psychological and physical development of children, principles of child care and the law relating to children: some courses also included the dynamics of family life and work with those in need of help. By 1970 the minimum content had become:

(a) human growth and behaviour: including social influences on behaviour; child health/paediatrics; physical and mental handicap; and elementary psychopathology;
(b) the environment of social work: including social policy and administration; the sociology of organisations; social control and disorganisation; methods and results of social inquiry; law and administrative procedures in relation to child care practice;
(c) principles and methods of social work (including ethics); the specific application of social work theory and practice to child care (CTC memorandum, unpublished, 1971).

In the absence of follow-up studies and evaluation, it is not possible to answer two key questions, i.e. the relevance of training to the changing task; and what (if any) differences there were in the performance of students with different backgrounds from the range of courses of different lengths and on different patterns. This is regrettable because these courses grew more rapidly than any others at a crucial period in the evolution of social work education. Educational method was improved, probably most of all in fieldwork; lecturers on established courses understood better what students needed; theory and practice were more closely related; supervisors were selected and trained; local authorities accepted a teaching obligation and student units were established (see volume 2, chapter 4).

The tremendous training effort of the 1960s resulted in 46·9 per cent of child care officers in England and Wales being professionally qualified by the end of the decade, with a range from 27·9 per cent in Welsh county boroughs to 66·2 per cent in English counties in the south-west (DHSS, 1971b). Many more had taken in-service training or staff development courses. More men trained as time went on but there was a heavy marriage mortality rate amongst women. By and large, the child care service had not lost the zest with which it started in 1948 but it had learnt far more about the demands of the work and some of the elements in good training.

No training was available in Scotland for boarding out officers other than one-week, in-service training courses until 1960. A number of Scottish students trained in England and a child care stream was added to the

Edinburgh University course in 1960 and later to the Glasgow, Aberdeen and Dundee University applied social studies courses. The courses in colleges of education were referred to earlier. In 1968 when the Social Work (Scotland) Act was passed, there were 60 professionally qualified CCOs in children's departments out of a total of 305.

Courses for Child Care Officers, 1971

The number of students in child care officer training was about 1,500 on over eighty courses when the CTC came to an end. The main divisions of students and of courses is shown in table 1.

Table 1 *Main divisions of students and courses*

	Students	*Courses*
Courses in applied social studies		
1-year course		
17-month course	329	39
2-year course		
Courses for mature students		
1-year course	71	5
2-year course	674	20
Emergency courses	175	3
3-year course for students aged 18	32	1
Part-time course	44	1
	1,325	69

The balance was made up by students on courses in Scotland, on 4-year degree courses and a small number taking advanced courses.

Source: CTC memorandum, 1971 (unpublished).

Table 2 *Number of child care officer students trained during the life-time of the Central Training Council in Child Care, 1947–71 (England and Wales: Scotland in brackets)*

Year	Students successfully completing training	Year	Students successfully completing training	
1948	61	1960	50	
1949	82	1961	68	(4)
1950	77	1962	124	(6)
1951	72	1963	171	(4)
1952	56	1964	166	(8)
1953	44	1965	235	(9)
1954	46	1966	242	(12)
1955	47	1967	326	(20)
1956	59	1968	400	(32)
1957	60	1969	485	(50)
1958	47	1970	575	(68)
1959	47	1971	715	(90)

In addition, a large number of child care staff had taken short courses.

TRAINING FOR RESIDENTIAL CHILD CARE

The 1950s

The urgent plea of the Curtis Committee (1946) for training of residential child care staff resulted the following year in the fourteen-month courses, started even before the CTC came into existence in 1947. It was obvious that trained staff in children's homes were as important as field staff in learning how to meet the needs of children in care. Thus persistent efforts were made throughout the period to increase output in spite of continuing problems of recruitment. These were largely caused by the low status, heavy responsibilities, long working hours and unsatisfactory living conditions of residential staff (see also chapter 3). The whole history of this training must be understood in terms of the conflict between the pressure to produce more trained residential staff and the problem of how to make any real headway. In these circumstances in-service training was crucial. The CTC provided a substantial programme of short courses all over the country (see also volume 2, chapter 5) and their part in raising standards was an essential complement to the full-time courses.

During the 1950s the CTC sponsored fourteen-month courses, including those run by Dr Barnardo's, the National Children's Home and 'the nuns' course'. These gave a predominantly domestic and practical training, coupled with study of the normal growth, development and health of children, but with little stress on the particular needs and background of children suffering from the trauma of deprivation and separation. The emphasis on 'home making' – however necessary at the time – reinforced the assumption that separate and different courses were needed for houseparents and boarding out officers. None the less even in the CTC's first year the question of joint courses was raised on the Council.

A 1947 CTC memorandum on training said a housemother should be

'. . . a person who is competent to take charge of a 'family group' of 12 to 15 children of mixed ages and sexes, either in a small scattered Home or in a larger Home where such a group would form a 'family' within the total group. The basic idea is that staff of this type should be so trained that in addition to having domestic and other skills they should be able to meet the needs of the child as an individual in a satisfying personal relationship.'

It said of the study of child development:

'This subject should be placed first in the curriculum. In addition to the study of the nature, development and needs of the normal child, this subject should particularly include the study of the child in relation to normal family life, the special circumstances affecting the child cared for outside his own family whether for short or for long periods and the role of the adult acting as parent substitute. Under this heading should come also the function of play in the child's development, the contribution made to his development by school as well as home and some recognition of his spiritual needs. Students should be trained in the observation of children and in the keeping of simple records.'

In discussing practical work it said:

'It is clear that there are not sufficient Homes of high standard to provide what would be ideally desirable for the training of students. Even during their preliminary two months' testing period students will inevitably be placed in Homes which will have shortcomings as well as satisfactory features . . . it is the personality and attitude of the staff that has more significance than any other one factor . . . As well as having a good atmosphere, staff with understanding of children's needs, and spare accommodation (a very rare feature), it should, also, ideally have a good age range of both sexes, sound contacts in the community, and above all a Head capable of dealing with students . . . It is, however, the development of their capacity to make a substitute home that it is particularly hoped housemothers in training will learn.'

Home Office inspectors were expected to find suitable children's homes and 'see the student there and give her such further instruction and guidance as may be required'. Would that supervision had proved so simple! In practice, the tutors negotiated placements and visited their students.

In 1948 Leila Rendel, founder of the Caldecott Community, said in a far-sighted memorandum to the CTC:

'I hope we shall not lose sight of the fact that we must enlist in the service well-educated girls who are prepared to go through a fairly long and extensive training that will fit them: (a) as qualified assistants in any type of children's homes; and (b) later if they wish as heads of homes, or larger children's communities which for many years will exist; and alternatively (c) as out-door workers in the field of boarding-out care, or other more definitely administrative work.'

Twenty years later the first joint course was started (see below). She commented that the housemothers she met on one of the three-week refresher courses

' . . . were kindly, hardworking people, almost over anxious to learn . . . Most of them . . . had a shrewd innate wisdom that was refreshing. Their limitations were mostly due to their 'shut in' overworked existence, and the majority had stood the test remarkably well. Small homes and hostels of ten to twenty children have considerable dangers, for, unless life for the staff is adequately provided for, it must and does tend to warp the adults and so react on the children.'

Later in the period new, small independent units and family group homes increased the responsibilities of individual houseparents. Efforts to keep siblings together, as well as changes in policy, were resulting in more all-age children's homes, so that in the same home there might well be both a baby and an adolescent who was going out to work. Efforts to keep families in touch resulted in more short-stay children, while increased boarding out led to more emotionally disturbed children in children's homes, or children so upset by leaving their own home that they could not tolerate a foster home. As a result, the course curriculum began to include more study of very young children and adolescents and, to a limited extent, of maladjusted children.

The 1953 CTC *Notes on the Training of House-Parents of Children's Homes* said:

'House parents need to be able to combine the good 'mothering' of children with the successful running of a home . . . House-mothers are generally responsible for the planning of meals, for cooking and for organising and taking part in the arrangement and cleaning of the home. Housefathers generally take more responsibility for house-hold maintenance, and for the upkeep of the garden. Both take a share in all the day-to-day interests of the children.' (p. 1)

The main subjects in the curriculum were: child study, all aspects of the care and upbringing of children, including religious guidance, recreation and child health; home making; social services; and general and special interests, recreation and hobbies. Teaching was based upon the study of children who did not present unusual difficulties. About half the time was given to practical work but its content, the kind of experience students should have to develop skill and how to relate this to the study periods were not discussed in the *Notes*.

The 1956 Home Office memorandum of guidance on Training in Child Care (unpublished), said that students had three to four periods of practical work within a total of six to seven months and that tutors arranged this to give each student 'a variety of experience in different kinds of homes', though it was 'not possible for each student to see every kind of home'. This 'see all sides of the work' approach was general in this period. The importance of designating supervisors was more generally accepted and cautiously approached in the memorandum:

'As so many houseparents are sharing in the practical training of students, authorities may wish to consider whether they can help their staff further in this important work. Where many staff are employed it may be desirable to appoint a person with the special duty of helping them to develop their skill; in this way, the responsibility could be linked with provision for guiding young houseparents, and for keeping more senior houseparents in touch with modern trends.'

The memorandum suggested that a talk at the beginning and 'further talks at a half way stage and at the conclusion of the students' stay were sometimes useful'. Supervision was not necessarily provided in the residential situation itself. It often consisted of two or three talks with the children's officer or the tutor to the course. Home Office inspectors and tutors discussed the students' needs with senior staff on their visits. Newly appointed staff commonly complained that they had little chance to talk over their work and their problems.

The progress of the residential child care courses was reviewed twice yearly at meetings between all the tutors and Home Office inspectors. In 1956 annual conferences were started for tutors and heads of children's homes used for practical work, but these were for general discussion and it was a long time before individual staff members were designated as supervisors. They began to be given some training for the task from 1966, mainly on CTC short courses. This meant that students had varied, though sometimes superficial, experience in their practical work but little planned help in coming to terms with its impact on them. Sometimes, where there were close links with the course, practice was well planned and stimulating, but conversely a student might be told on arrival that someone was ill or on holiday and that she was in complete charge of a group of children or she might be used mainly for domestic duties or as relief staff, or else be left to find her own way. The Curtis Committee (1946) had suggested that theory and practice should be concurrent, but the lack of accommodation in children's homes made this impracticable from the beginning. Another impediment to improving the quality of supervision in children's homes was that no payment was made.

In the early 1950s approved schools were being closed owing to the fall in juvenile delinquency, believed to be due to a new, stable post-war situation. This was rudely shattered by a steady rise from 1955 onwards and new approved schools were hastily opened. There was an extreme staff shortage and the whole situation was made more urgent by the disturbances at the Carlton Approved School in 1958. This resulted in a public inquiry and much pressure to increase training, and several courses were started specially for approved school staff, including work with difficult adolescents.

By October 1950, 355 students (including 56 men) from eleven courses in England and Wales had gained the CTC certificate in residential care and there were 204 students in training. The Curtis Committee had estimated the necessary output at 300–400 annually. But the local authority courses were hardly ever full, in spite of widespread publicity, and early in the 1950s two were discontinued for lack of candidates.

In 1957 the length of the training was reduced from fourteen to twelve months because most candidates already had experience of children's homes. The Residential Child Care Association (RCCA), amongst others, was steadily trying to raise standards and ACO was now fully aware that houseparents needed much more than domestic skills. In 1958 it sent out a questionnaire which revealed that there were 3,043 residential child care staff of whom only 9 per cent had the CTC certificate, though many more had taken short courses. There were 274 vacancies.

The 1960s and early 1970s
By 1960, 2,036 students (including 264 men) had qualified. By 1970 numbers on qualifying courses had doubled to over 400 students and the target output to 420 a year. In 1968 the Home Office started to require returns showing the total number of residential child care staff in employment and the proportion of trained to untrained staff. By 1970 the total was about 15,500, of whom 14 per cent were trained.

In Scotland in the early 1950s there were only short refresher courses for staffs of children's homes and one-week courses for boarding out officers.

But from 1960, students on the one-year residential child care courses at Jordanhill and Moray House Colleges of Education worked for the CTC certificate.

The Underwood Committee on Maladjusted Children (1955) recommended that 'house-staff' should take the CTC residential child care courses and from 1962, at the request of the Ministry of Education, the courses became the recognised training for the child care staffs of special boarding schools for maladjusted and physically handicapped or educationally subnormal children. Changes were made in the curriculum and some students had practical work placements in residential special schools.

Two advanced courses were started at Bristol University (1960) and Newcastle University (1963) for students who were already qualified and experienced in residential child care. These courses enabled those who took them to stand back and look at residential child care in greater depth and in relation to current research and thought about children, and also to prepare a thesis on some aspect of their own work. Later a third course was started at Glasgow University. By 1970 a total of 199 students had received the CTC advanced certificate in residential care (see also volume 2, chapter 3, section on 'Post-Qualifying Courses').

Tutors to residential child care courses were subject to constant strain and overwork: the recognised staff/student ratio was 1:15, though sometimes there were up to twenty-five students on a course. These tutors were single-handed – apart from part-time specialist teachers – until second tutors began to be appointed as a means of expanding training. There was an overwhelming shortage of people qualified to train residential child care workers. As part of the intensified drive in the mid-1960s to increase the number of students very substantially, a few tutors in residential child care took the course in educational studies at the National Institute for Social Work Training. This and the advanced courses in residential child care were the only obvious sources of further training to enable people with experience in children's homes to become better equipped to teach.

In the 1960s more local authorities appointed homes advisers to residential staff on the lines recommended in the Government Social Survey Report undertaken in 1962 and published 1964, and by the Williams Committee (1967). These advisers could obviously have an important influence in raising the level of work in children's homes and like local authority training officers they had to discover and fulfil new functions. In 1970 at the request of the CTC, the National Institute for Social Work Training started a three-month pilot course for a group of homes advisers to help them to explore and define their role and to work out methods of staff support. It was hoped that eventually there would be a one-year course for qualified people taking on what could be a key role in residential care of all kinds.

For several years ACO had advocated some form of preliminary child care training for school leavers, and local authorities were running a variety of junior courses in child care. The CTC was against any kind of training that would commit school leavers to go into residential child care, but in 1966 it approved a pattern of education based on two-year further education courses for 16 to 18 year olds. These continued the students' own education and introduced them to the principles of child development and residential child care. The course led to the preliminary certificate in the residential care of children. By 1970 54 courses had been approved and 778 students awarded the certificate. By 1974 there were 83 courses and 735 certificates were issued in that year alone.

There was unremitting pressure for residential child care staff to receive the Home Office Declaration of Recognition of Experience which had been made available to long-serving child care officers. This was finally agreed in 1965 and 1,600 declarations were awarded by the end of the eligibility period. This was a necessary recognition of long service but it left untouched the training of the very large number of unqualified residential child care staff who needed something more substantial than short courses which were not necessarily closely related to their day-to-day experience.

Probably the most thorough and imaginative in-service training course in any branch of social work was devised to meet this need and a national programme was launched in 1967. The course was designed for residential child care staff in children's homes of all kinds, approved schools and boarding special schools for handicapped (including maladjusted) children. Each employing body providing a study course was to appoint a member of its staff approved by the CTC as a study supervisor. A number of short courses were arranged for these study supervisors to help them in the planning of the in-service training courses and in their role as teachers. They were responsible to the appropriate chief officer for working out a programme, taking account of local resources and individual needs, and relating the teaching closely to practice.

A guide syllabus issued by the CTC outlined in detail the areas of study to be covered in each approved in-service study course. The syllabus and the related teaching notes were intended to help study supervisors and those who taught in the courses to think about and plan the subject matter to be presented. Each was to use the material in his own way, adding to it from personal knowledge and experience, and adapting it to the needs and level of understanding of the particular group of residential child care staff in order that the material might be relevant to their own current experience. This was to be done in the live learning/teaching situation with the fullest possible participation of the students themselves. The guide syllabus specified the minimum number of hours to be devoted to each group of lecture/ seminars, practical subjects and private study: each participating body was free to plan the time span of a particular course, for example to organise weekly study days or to alternate periods of full-time study with weekly or fortnightly seminars. The pattern of subjects in the guide syllabus was planned as a basic minimum applicable to staffs in all types of residential child care. Study group supervisors were responsible for choosing seminar leaders with an intimate knowledge of residential child care, coupled with an understanding of the content of the study course being undertaken by members of the group.

The total study course covered a minimum of 220 hours, of which at least 60 hours was for private study (with books and other reading material made available). The three sequences of the course were (a) understanding children and young people, (b) the practice of residential child care – this course was spread over at least twenty-five weeks to ensure its relation to practical experience, (c) the social framework. Each course lasted for a year and most were run at colleges of further education. Students who completed a course received the national certificate of attendance at an approved in-service study course.

The scheme was welcomed by employers and by residential child care staffs, and the BBC broadcast a series of talks on child care to launch it. The scheme expanded the provision of substantial in-service training and the participants were stimulated by the chance to discuss their day-to-day experiences in a group in relation to the teaching, and thus to extend their understanding of children and reduce their own sense of isolation. Like most good in-service training, it acted as a stimulus rather than an alternative to further training and many participants later applied for full-time training. By 1970 there were 84 approved courses run by local authorities and voluntary organisations and 2,698 certificates of attendance had been issued. The existing scheme was phased out in 1975 and succeeded by a more broadly based pattern.

The success of the scheme led to the institution in 1970 of a part-time, one-year qualifying course composed of one day a week and five residential weeks for candidates who held the preliminary certificate or the certificate of attendance, coupled with at least one year's experience in residential child care, and with the personal qualities and abilities required to study at a professional level. The theoretical studies were the same as in the full-time course and there was provision for supervision of the student's own work. Successful students received a residential child care certificate (part-time). By the end of 1970 there were three courses in colleges of further education with forty-five students. Ten additional courses were planned for 1971.

During the 1960s views about the role of residential child care staff began to change from a mixture of domestic home making plus substitute parenting, which perhaps inevitably characterised the earlier period, to a more complex professional role which demanded that each child's individual needs should be sensed and met in a group situation. In this situation the child should experience warm and direct feelings towards him, yet his own parents should be built up and reinforced if this was realistically in his interests. Informal group discussions and children and staff involvement also used the strengths of group interaction. These higher demands coupled with a chronic shortage of candidates made selection all the more difficult, particularly when warmth, enjoyment of children, ability to accept both hostility and attachment with maturity and self-awareness, sensitivity and a sense of proportion all seemed essential. This was a far cry from the days before 1947 when senior staff were often selected because they were strict disciplinarians and able to keep order.

It was clear that some staff had to be employed in children's homes who could not achieve the necessary level of professional performance. This seemed to point to different levels of training with the opportunity for individuals to progress from the 'basic' to the 'professional' course. Even before the Williams Committee Report (1967) there had been discussion about two-year courses. The alternatives were to extend the one-year courses to two years or introduce residential child care into some of the two-year courses for child care officers.

The University of Leicester decided in 1968 to offer a residential work option in its applied social studies course but this did not attract candidates. In 1969 a general, two-year course in residential care on the lines of the Williams Committee's recommendations was started at Enfield College of Technology. Students intending to go into residential child care received the CTC certificate. The following year Manchester University extramural department's two-year child care course became integrated so that students could qualify as social workers through study and experience of both field and residential work. They received the CTC letter of recognition and were eligible to join BASW. It was hoped that this kind of training would raise the status of residential work. But by 1973 only six students, all from one course, had taken this option.

The Home Office *Community Homes Project Report* (Home Office, 1970) considered training from the angle of what ·the staff would need in order to practise the 'fundamental principles of therapeutic care'. It said:

'. . . the residential community worker should be responsible for creating and maintaining an environment which provides some of the positive experiences of good home life and a supportive framework for individual treatment, and which is also in itself therapeutic. In such an environment every aspect of a child's day is used to help to heal the effects of past damage and to promote emotional and social growth. The purpose of training is to enable him to fulfil these responsibilities.' (p. 36)

Residential community workers (the term used in the Report) must understand themselves, their own needs and motivations, and be able to meet the children's needs rather than using them or their relationships with colleagues to meet their own emotional needs. They should be trained to observe, record and interpret behaviour in order to assess a child's needs and take part in a treatment plan that involved the child and his parents. The main theoretical study should include:

(a) The individual child – emotional, physical and social development within the family context and including underlying causes of personality disturbance.
(b) Structures and patterns of society – cultural variations in behavioural norms and ethical concepts; the formation and development of communities and groups, including the dynamics of family life and its place within the community; the effects of change on society and family life; cultural and sub-cultural groups.
(c) Communities and residential institutions – patterns of social intervention and group processes, leadership in groups and the mechanisms which operate in group situations amongst both staff and children; anxiety, stress and resistance to change.
(d) The residential community worker as a social worker – the professional attitudes and values and the scope and limitations of social work; residential care and treatment as a social work method; the nature and use of all supporting services.

The Report thought that essential practical skills included making individual relationships and using these therapeutically, but it did not sufficiently explore how this should or could be related to the ability to understand and use the dynamics of group and intergroup situations in community homes. It stressed the value of taking part in some community activity, including direct observation of the life of the street and the family unit, and of group processes in student training and that 'the training of a residential community worker should be similar in extent and status to that of other professional workers in related fields' (p. 39).

This Report, contrasted with the 1947 CTC memorandum, illustrates the growth of knowledge and understanding of the task in residential child care. But a daunting gap remained between aims and the possibility of fulfilling them.

By the time the CTC came to an end in 1971 it was suggested that the aim for the total residential child care staff might be for 30 per cent to be professionally qualified, 40 to 50 per cent to be qualified on part-time courses, and for the rest to take the in-service study course or to be young staff with the preliminary certificate. There should also be extended opportunities for advanced study leading to a higher degree; as well as a good range of in-service training and staff development.

The CTC decided in 1971 that residential work was part of social work and that training should be of equal length, standard and qualification as that of CCOs. This was a great step forward in thought compared with 1950, but the problem of implementation had still to be solved. The CCETSW continued the existing residential child care courses and in 1974 558 students qualified, together with 37 on the three advanced courses.

Table 3   *Annual output of trained residential child care staff, 1960–72*
Certificate in the residential care of children

Year	Annual Output England and Wales	Scotland	
1961	175	20	(7)
1962	213	18	(24)
1963	244	22	(10)
1964	275	18	(22)
1965	269	27	(24)
1966	303	35	(24)
1967	296	29	(24)
1968	287	45	(24)
1969	289	45	(27)
1970	321	54	(32)
1971	326	50	(32)
1972	334	53	(30)

Figures in brackets refer to the senior courses in residential child care (including the course at Glasgow University).
Source: *Setting the Course for Social Work Education 1971–1973* (CCETSW, 1973).

In 1970 the total residential child care staff in local authorities was 7,524. Of these 834 were qualified. There were 1,969 staff in voluntary organisation homes, of whom 422 held the CTC certificate or senior certificate (DHSS, 1971*b*, pp. 28 and 39). By 1970 2,397 certificates of attendance had been issued under the in-service training study scheme, (*Setting the Course for Social Work Education*, 1973*c*, CCETSW, p. 30). Many staff had also taken various short courses.

Chapter 6

The Probation and After-Care Service, 1950-1975

PROBATION IN THE 1950s

By the early 1950s the probation service was entering a post-war era of more generous provision resulting from a great wave of social reform. In a post-war climate of opinion the Criminal Justice Act, 1948 at last implemented the recommendations of the 1936 Departmental Committee on Social Services in the Courts of Summary Jurisdiction and instituted the administrative structure within which the probation service continued to operate in the 1970s. The Act embodied the profound change in attitudes towards offenders which throughout the period from 1950 to 1975 resulted in new non-punitive and non-custodial experiments and to a growing volume of research in criminology. These changes, forecast in the 1936 Committee's Report, resulted from the interest in penal reform of a succession of Home Secretaries and their officials, the informed advocacy of individual members of both Houses of Parliament, of the Howard League, the Institute for the Study and Treatment of Delinquency, the National Association of Probation Officers (NAPO), the Conference of Principal Probation Officers, the Probation Advisory and Training Board (the PATB, later the Advisory Council on Probation and After-Care, ACPAC), the Advisory Council on the Treatment of Offenders (ACTO), and many other groups and individuals. The 1948 Act abolished a number of harsh prison practices, introduced attendance centre orders for offenders under 21, which were the ideologically confused forerunners of intermediate treatment, and also made it possible to insert a mental treatment requirement in probation orders. The consequent 1949 Probation Rules left far greater professional discretion to probation officers, while more principal and senior probation officers began to be appointed. Many probation officers realised that their work with children before the juvenile courts was in fact family casework with the parents as well as the child, and that (as child guidance clinics knew) the child's anti-social behaviour was frequently a symptom of troubled family relationships. The service was also coming to grips with the practice of matrimonial conciliation as laid down in the 1948 Home Office Memorandum.

NAPO had embarked upon its independent existence, with leadership which made it increasingly influential throughout a decade when, as later, it continued to struggle with ethical dilemmas in attitudes to offenders and the role of social work in an authoritarian setting. The Probation Division of the Home Office took every opportunity to increase in-service training; while the first step away from an isolated specialist training and towards a common professional qualification was taken when both the Home Office and NAPO supported the first applied social studies course at LSE in 1954. The able men and women who had trained in the immediate post-war years were also coming to the fore as leading members of the probation service. Thus the early 1950s were looked back upon by some as the golden age of probation. It was a period of rapid development in staffing, changing from a predominantly part-time to a whole-time service and sometimes achieving a standard of office accommodation and clerical assistance not gained by the other social services until later. Crime rates, including juvenile delinquency, after their post-war spurt declined steadily until the mid-1950s, thus for a short time probation officers were less heavily overburdened with court inquiries and new cases. The number of direct entrants decreased dramatically to three in 1955. Thereafter the brief respite was over.

NAPO said in its annual report for 1958, that it was

'concerned about the growing pressure of work on probation officers, the widening range of duties accruing to them, the effect of the increase of crime, the acute shortage of officers, the failure to keep the Service manned to meet its current needs and the apparent lack of any attempt to assess, and plan for, its future requirements in the light of developments in case-work over recent years. These difficulties have been allied to serious discontent about the inadequate pay of probation officers and constant frustration in the effort to remedy this situation.' (p. 2)

Criminologists and researchers in general had failed to forecast the sudden increase in crime from the mid-1950s onwards.

The courts were making more use of social inquiry reports though no question of probation arose, and even before the Streatfeild Report (1961) had clarified 'the fundamental difference between assessing culpability and pursuing the other objectives of sentencing: namely that where the court is seeking to reform, to deter or to protect, it is seeking to control future events rather than to pass judgment on past events' (para. 269). Obviously to do this entailed a difficult personal and social assessment of the offender, coupled with sound judgement about his probable future behaviour under given circumstances. Later the Morison Committee (1962) pointed out that probation officers 'are not now equipped by their experience, and research cannot yet equip them, to assume a general function of expressing opinions . . . about the likely effect of treatment' (para. 41).

Matrimonial conciliation work also increased in amount and difficulty. The Matrimonial Proceedings (Children) Act, 1958 made court welfare officers available at every court in England and Wales where divorce cases were heard, and the court had to be satisfied about arrangements for the children. This court welfare duty was placed on the probation service. In addition, voluntary cases, for example advice about troublesome children, voluntary supervision, and so on increased by about half. This – which could be paralleled in other services – showed how, in the absence of a comprehensive personal social service, the people without a pigeon hole over-flowed everywhere. In Scotland the range of functions undertaken by the probation service was much narrower, though court welfare officers were appointed there too.

In addition to these extended duties, the growing body of knowledge in the psychology of deviance, in sociology and criminology resulted in a steadily increased demand that this should be used, thus adding to the personal demands on probation officers who in addition 'have to stand up to the hostility of delinquents, to be constantly let down by them, and . . . [undertake] long term unrewarding work with immature, dependent and inadequate people' (Braithwaite, 1959, p. 30).

Of course, neither training nor the knowledge itself were sufficient to bear the weight of the demands, nor were there any effective criteria for determining success in probation, or for that matter in any other branch of social work. The measurement of success by the completion of the probation order without a breach or a further offence within two years was easy to establish – if the offender was caught. But he might not be, or he might have had a temporary breakdown, or changed the symptom of his maladjustment, or family conflict or community attitudes to delinquency and difficulties of getting employment might weight the scales too heavily against him. From the late 1950s onwards the probation service was giving active support and encouragement to the pilot research and evaluation studies undertaken by universities and the Home Office Research Unit.

Because of the more generous provisions of the welfare state and full employment, there was less pressure on probation officers to concentrate on probationers' material needs. This heightened the demand for better understanding in terms of social and personal problems and for more selective responses to individual probationers, who might suffer from emotional difficulties, personal inadequacies, unsatisfactory peer group and family relationships, a constricting environment, and entrenched anti-social attitudes. The problem of how to 'motivate the unmotivated', how to change negative social attitudes towards offenders, and whether reconciliation was possible between casework principles and use of authority all exercised probation officers in this period.

Perhaps British social workers had been less troubled than the Americans about the use of authority – and indeed more apt to exercise it with too little concern for the mixture of hostility and dependence which it often generated. In the 1950s probation officers were discovering an accord between casework and authority, They pointed out that child care officers and other caseworkers also used it; that without an element of compulsion they would never see some probationers at all and thus would be unable to make a relationship with them; that everyone had mixed feelings about authority but these had to be faced and its positive aspects clarified. Indeed, many probationers were unaware of their need for help (displacement as a defence being common amongst offenders), their own part in putting themselves at odds with society, or that people in authority could be helpful rather than a cause of fear, suspicion and resentment. Many probationers needed the firm, consistent and benevolent control which they had never experienced. Later, the preliminary study in the Home Office Research

Unit probation project (Folkard *et al.*, 1966) found that 'success rates tended to be associated with the use of low control, but many of these cases may have been good risks who did not need much control in any case' (p. 41). It also concluded that 'for some types of offender the control and regulation of behaviour may be the most appropriate and effective type of treatment, and an adequate theory must take account of the alternative treatment approaches that might be used' (p. 43).

At a time when probation officers and other social workers were struggling to analyse the different meanings of authority, the dangers of its use without adequate self-awareness, and the ways in which it might be used constructively, students were also beginning to question whether this, and other casework techniques, were used in many subtle ways to bring about conformity to current – and not necessarily just – social values. In any event, probation officers were members of an ill-assorted team of magistrates, clerks, the police, lawyers, local authority officials, and prison officers and borstal and approved school staffs. These people with diverse roles, trainings and attitudes also epitomised society's ambivalent attitudes of punishment, deterrence and reform towards offenders.

Current thought about casework in probation was thus expressed in *The Probation Service*, a textbook produced by NAPO in 1958:

'If behaviour is influenced, often unconsciously, by feeling rather than by rational thought, it is by a change of feeling rather than by rational argument or exhortation that any permanent change in attitudes and behaviour must be sought. If the way people feel about themselves and others is largely determined by their early relationships it may be through new relationships that scars can be healed and a change of feeling achieved. Thus the relationship between caseworker and client, which has always been accepted as a basic factor in giving this kind of individual help, is now seen as of overriding importance. It is recognised as a vital means of healing to be used consciously for the good of the client, whose feelings, hostile as well as friendly can be accepted as an essential part of the process of growth or recovery. In addition an increased awareness of human motivation has thrown light on the reactions of the caseworker as well as of the client. This has given the former a clearer appreciation of his own feelings and of the pressures to which he himself is subject in his relations with his clients. Such feelings, if unrecognised and uncontrolled, may distort and misdirect the relationship, but if accepted cannot merely be controlled but can often be• used to enrich the caseworker's understanding and ability to help.' (King, 1958, pp. 48–9)

This is an account of the one-to-one relationship so vehemently challenged subsequently.

The inherent tensions of acting as a servant of the court and as a caseworker on behalf of the offender were doubtless faced in specific situations but resolved pragmatically, unfortunately without recording and analysis as a basis for principles of practice. Probation remained the only form of social work in which intake decisions and allocation were made by lay people – the courts – which decided whether probation was likely to be effective.

THE MORISON COMMITTEE

For several years NAPO and others had been pressing for a committee of inquiry into every aspect of the probation service. This was reinforced by periodic questions in Parliament and letters to *The Times*. Finally in 1959 the Home Secretary announced the setting up of a departmental committee (the Morison Committee) 'to inquire into and make recommendations on all aspects of the Probation Service in England and Wales and in Scotland'.

Its Report (1962) was a comprehensive document. One criminologist said that it included every aspect of the service except what probation officers actually did, but detailed studies of actual practice were a later development in any branch of social work. The Committee concluded that probation was essentially a social service of the courts and should continue to be administered by local probation committees under the general control of the Home Office in England and Wales, and with each individual probation officer's appointment subject to confirmation after the first year as a result of a probation inspector's report (in the 1960s probation and after-care committees were given this responsibility). Modern developments in casework and the appointment of principal and senior probation officers had made detailed supervision of individual cases by case committees no longer appropriate. It was, however, important for magistrates to be kept in close touch with probation officers' work and problems and the consequences of probation, and for the service to see its activities through the eyes of lay people with varied experience. This was a statement for a particular service of the perennial problem of how to educate those ultimately responsible for the quality of a service.

The Committee rejected specialisation, though it thought that a group of officers' particular aptitudes, interests and experience should be taken into account in allocating work. It considered but rejected the idea that because of recruitment difficulties there should be an assistant probation officer grade at a lower standard of selection and training. Indeed, the Committee thought that 'the need was to raise rather than lower the standards of selection and training' (para. 278). Undoubtedly this was correct in itself but the Committee failed to analyse the range of tasks in probation and consider whether some of these could be performed by ancillary workers. At the time they reported, the proposal to use in-service trained welfare assistants in the health and welfare services produced negative reactions in other services, which stressed the universal difficulty of their clientele, failing to distinguish between overall responsibility and delegation of certain tasks. Ancillary workers were finally introduced in 1968.

The Report pointed to the

'. . . major changes in the ways in which probation officers establish and use the personal relationships on which their success depends. This development has not been unique to the probation service. It has taken place, as understanding of human behaviour has deepened, wherever social workers operate through personal relationships: and it has imported into the practice of social work a new and highly professional approach described by the term 'social casework'. It is significant that the 1936 Committee could describe the supervisory functions of the probation officer without using this term. To-day, the probation officer must be seen, essentially, as a professional caseworker, employing, in a specialised field, skill which he holds in common with other social workers; skill which, if it opens up to him hopes of constructive work which were not enjoyed by his predecessor of twenty years ago, also makes more complex and subtle demands upon him, reflecting, as it does, growing awareness of the difficulty of his task.' (para. 54)

The Report described the creation of this relationship in the following terms: 'Casework, as we understand it, is the creation and utilisation, for the benefit of an individual who needs help with personal problems, of a relationship between himself and a trained social worker' (para. 56). This assumed that all change was to stem from the influence of the probation officer on the offender and ignored the potency of the environment. Moreover, all the views quoted assume that probation officers subscribed to the idea that they should, or did, use a relationship with probationers to bring about greater self-awareness and thus changes in attitude and behaviour. Subsequent research studies showed that this frequently did not happen.

PROBATION IN THE 1960S AND EARLY 1970S

After-care, prison welfare, parole and other major developments are discussed separately in the following chapter. Apart from the question of salaries and its indirect effect on establishments, relations between the service and the Home Office improved in the post-Morison period. This was achieved by frequent meetings between officials and representatives of NAPO and principal probation officers, and through working parties, seminars and conferences all of which led to more co-operation and mutual understanding and created a forum for the development of new ideas and much experiment. At the same time, the PATB took a much more active part in planning the future establishment and other organisational and material needs of the service, and in setting targets which proved to be a considerable stimulus to achievement.

The new developments were also part of the trend towards trying to change offenders' behaviour in their social environment rather than taking them out of it without any very constructive results. This made it crucial to discover how to motivate different types of offender towards non-delinquent solutions in their own setting. Hunt (1974) commented that 'services traditionally concerned with the treatment of offenders have been occupied with problems of the deteriorating urban environment, with marginal employability . . . with the pathogenic family and with the criminogenic sub-culture' (p. 108). It was obvious that in many instances casework alone was insufficient and that, although there were many non-delinquents in delinquent neighbourhoods, new methods and resources were needed to overcome the combination of personality factors and destructive social settings. This also needed a sociological perspective which would 'take account of the view that behaviour can be influenced by changes in the social setting in which the individual lives, and by changes in the role which he performs in the groups of which he is a member' (Folkard *et al.*, 1966, p. 42). It became clear in time that this entailed concentrated community action and community work beyond the scope of the probation service on its own. Many probation officers became conscious of the importance of community involvement and later took part in the community development activities discussed in volume 2 (see chapter 18). In the service, as elsewhere, new emphasis was put on delinquent groups and on isolated offenders incapable of ordinary social relationships.

Systematic group work in probation was a tentative voyage of discovery by a few probation officers rather than the conceptualisation of theory or practice. It was not introduced from outside as casework had been a decade before and did not arouse the same anxieties and hostility as 'deep casework', but it failed to spread. By the late 1960s the former had become 'traditional' or 'classic' casework and was shot at for its rigidities, its inappropriateness and inadequacies for many offenders. In this period probation practice met the same challenges as social work in other settings, but criminology and research studies were further advanced and more comprehensive psychological and sociological field research was available to the probation and after-care service than to other social workers. In particular, the substantial series of Home Office Research Unit studies on probation aimed to construct typologies of offenders and the outcome of different treatment methods.

If the 1950s were the golden age of the probation service, then the 1960s and early 1970s were the years in which it was required to spread further afield. Indeed, from being one element in the treatment of offenders, the probation service entered into almost every aspect, often as the crucial element in new efforts at rehabilitation rather than punishment, and as part of the whole swing away from residential custody towards treatment in the open. In that period it became responsible for the voluntary after-care of offenders, for prison welfare, for parole, for the administration of community service orders and day training centres, for extended duties regarding children's welfare in divorce cases, and for close co-operation in greatly increased hostel provision for adult offenders and ex-offenders. It lost much of its juvenile court work but in England and Wales it entered a new era in which it was no longer predominantly a court service, though it kept its close links with the magistrates. These widened responsibilities were welcomed as such by NAPO, but there was protest and anxiety because they followed each other thick and fast at a time when the service was severely undermanned, when there was a good deal of bitterness over salaries and when responsibilities were not matched by more comprehensive, conceptual underpinning and training. This series of reforms resulted from years of effort by penal reformers, but probation officers were afraid of being pushed into becoming part of an essentially punitive penal system rather than having a chance to use the dynamic that might change it.

DILEMMAS IN THE PROBATION SERVICE

The service was indeed rent during the 1960s by a crisis of identity, in which probation officers were forced to think out their role and where they belonged in the whole field of social work. NAPO played an ambivalent part in the discussions in the Standing Conference of Organisations of Social Workers. Probation officers agreed that they were social workers – but were they akin to all those others, or was it so important to maintain their link with crime and the judicial system that they should only join a federation or else go it alone?

The service was further disturbed by the Kilbrandon Report (1964) and the setting up of the Seebohm Committee. The majority view, as expressed in evidence to that Committee, was that a probation service independent of local government control was essential, even though it might become a centralised service closely related to other parts of the penal system. The minority wished to integrate the probation service with local authority personal social services in order to make it clear that probation officers were social workers, and offenders were people in need of social work help rather than a class apart to be labelled black sheep and segregated. If probation officers were in the local authority service they should be specialists in dealing with delinquents of all ages (Editorial, *Probation,* November 1966, pp. 109–10). After the publication of the Seebohm Report the controversy continued in and outside the service as to whether or not it should be merged with the social services departments, as was done in Scotland in 1968.

The Seebohm Report (1968) pointed out the dangers of 'unplanned overlapping' and urged that 'the Government should undertake an immediate examination' of its recommendations as they affected the probation and after-care service. The mills of God grind slowly but by 1972 the Home Secretary announced that it would remain a separate service. Probation areas were to become coterminous with local authority areas after local government reorganisation in 1974.

The 1969 Children and Young Persons Act also caused a good deal of concern about the probable end of the longstanding relationship with juvenile courts and of work with young people. This would remove the more hopeful cases from probation officers and leave them with increasing numbers of recidivists and hard-core offenders.

Davies (1972) suggested that the probation service had two objectives, the organisational objective was to achieve an efficient and smooth-running system, the second or functional objective was to maintain and improve the effectiveness of the service. It continued to set itself and achieve high organisational standards, for example in record keeping, working relationships with the courts, absorbing wider responsibilities, providing adequate staff supervision but maintaining the autonomy of mainstream officers, and combining reorganisation of areas with the establishment of local sub-offices. Assessment of whether or not the functional objective was being achieved depended on the standard by which it was measured. Ordinary probation officers, it was suggested, regarded themselves as being concerned with the supervision or oversight rather than 'treatment' of offenders in the community. 'Indeed the exercise of oversight over disturbed, inadequate, wilful and deviant men and women in the complex and hostile social network which constitute their living environment, and to be able to claim that this objective is being achieved day by day is still something of which the probation service can be proud' (Davies, 1972, p. 318). And some probation officers had achieved far more than this with individuals. But was 'oversight' without favourable change in the probationer or his environment enough? Various developments suggested that 'treatment' might after all be the aim and that probation's effectiveness should be tested by its effect on the client. Innovations related to this included selective treatment methods, reduced caseloads and specialisation for some officers.

By the mid-1970s probation officers were recovering from a fit of the doldrums and feeling more secure *vis-à-vis* social services departments, but they saw themselves in the future as being primarily either social workers or criminologists.

Whether or not probation and after-care in England and Wales should indefinitely remain isolated from the rest of the personal social services also remained an open question. Views differed as to whether this was an anachronism or whether the service gained strength, thrust and clear purpose from concentrating on a range of adults whose distinguishing feature was a criminal conviction. No comparative studies were undertaken of the separate services in England and Wales and the Scottish unified service. What may or may not be desirable in principle is not necessarily expedient at a given time, and the overburdened social services departments of the early 1970s would not have been in good shape to absorb probation and after-care with all its extended functions. The service itself changed after 1974 when areas were enlarged to coincide with local government reorganisation and the small, intimate local services of the past with their close relation to particular courts ceased to exist.

The research studies and action research projects described in the following chapter added some knowledge about different types of offender and their environment. There were also the beginnings of systematically recorded treatment based upon research findings and designed to change clients' attitudes. 'This might point to more structured use of different methods . . . directed largely to learning and problem solving; acquiring social skills and survival skills; gaining insight into one's own behaviour and feelings, and into other people's' (Wright, 1974, pp. 103–4).

The Criminal Justice Act, 1972 imposed a wider range of new responsibilities on the probation and after-care service for suspended sentence supervision orders (there were 2,000 of these by 1973), community service orders, day training centres and hostels. Indeed Davies (1973) suggested that the way was open for 'a locally based correctional system which would increasingly usurp the function of prison as a reformative enterprise' (p. 196). If so, the probation and after-care service would find itself managing, though on a smaller scale, a range of resources similar to those of a social services department. At the same time, prisons would increasingly follow *mutatis mutandis* the pattern of other residential institutions in catering only for highly disturbed, dangerous or habitual offenders who either for their own sake or the protection of society required residential custody or treatment. The end of this story is not in sight. It could mean increasing convergence or increasing divergence between services specifically for offenders and the general social services.

Probation officers, like other social workers in a time of change and conflict, continued to have divided views as to whether the offender or society was sick; whether they were or should be agents of social control; whether the most significant insights came from psychoanalytic theory or sociology; and whether or not more research and better training and practice could clarify or even solve some of the intractable problems of delinquency.

THE SCOTTISH PROBATION SERVICE

At the time of the Morison Report the probation service in Scotland was more constricted than in England and Wales. It was regarded as a minor local authority activity rather than a court service; probation officers had a limited range of duties and there were no whole-time officers north of Aberdeen. The Morison Committee sadly recorded: '. . . the impression that some Scottish Probation Committees favour maturity and local know-ledge at the expense of academic training in selecting new entrants to the service, and look upon the university trained social worker as a person who is less likely to take a firm line with his charges than is a "practical, common sense" type of officer without an academic background' (para. 339). It recommended enlarged probation areas and that members of the judiciary should play a more important part on probation committees.

Salary scales in Scotland were lower than those in England and Wales until later on, following the Morison Committee's recommendations, they became uniform. In 1962 there were 181 probation officers in Scotland. The Morison Committee thought the service should expand to 220. By 1968 the Scottish probation service was meeting increased demands from the courts and had taken on statutory after-care of young offenders and responsibilities for parole. There were 336 whole-time probation officers of whom about one-third had completed the Jordanhill one-year probation course and many others had qualified for the declaration of recognition of experience on the same conditions as social workers in the child care and health and welfare services. Others who became probation officers before 1960 took courses covering 300 hours of tuition at Edinburgh University for the declaration of training and experience.

In 1969 all the powers and duties of the probation service were transferred to the new social work departments. Under section 27 of the Social Work (Scotland) Act, 1968 local authorities were required to prepare probation schemes for the approval of the Secretary of State and to allocate functions to officers named in a court duties list.

MANPOWER STRENGTH OF THE PROBATION SERVICE IN ENGLAND AND WALES AT VARIOUS DATES

In the 1950s casework developments and changes in the services were altering the role of senior officers from primarily administrative duties to supervision as a teaching/consultative function. Many older officers had little to teach but their own experience, and younger officers eager for principles of practice often regarded supervision by them as an unhelpful waste of time. It also created tensions when officers who had taken a modern casework course or had had good in-service training were promoted over the heads of older colleagues. The Morison Committee's proposals were aimed at increasing the number of senior and principal probation officers. They also recommended that some tutor officers responsible for several students should be appointed in the senior probation officer salary grade (para. 318).

In 1959 there were 62 principal, and 159 senior probation officers in a total service of rather over 1,800. This gave less than an 8:1 chance of promotion. By 1961 there were 241 principal, deputy principal and senior probation officers; and by 1971 there were 706 with a 4:1 chance of promotion. The Home Office aimed at one assistant principal probation officer to thirty-five probation officers and one senior to five main grade officers. The structure of the service consisted of principal (later chief) probation officers, assistant principal and senior probation officers.

The wastage of probation officers was steady at less than 5 per cent a year until 1954. It then rose to slightly over 6 per cent a year for the remainder of the decade, and to 7·6 per cent in 1971. The wastage of probation officers with university qualifications hovered between 8 and 10 per cent. A good deal of the movement was into the child care service and later into social services departments. Well-qualified, 'mainstream' probation officers were often appointed to middle-management posts in these services, but no social worker from another service was appointed as a senior probation officer, though the Probation Rules as amended in 1968 made this possible. None the less a survey for the Butterworth Inquiry (1972) showed that 'the probation service is characterised by a high level of vocation and commitment. Most officers saw themselves in a job which was fulfilling and provided the basis of a lifetime career; they were unambivalent in their concern for the offender and in their sense of responsibility for developing a variety of methods and treatment' (p. 55).

At the end of 1969 average caseloads were 52 for men and 42 for women. These did not take account of social inquiry reports or various other responsibilities. The number of social inquiry reports actually doubled in the 1960s, whereas the number of mainstream officers only increased by 79 per cent. These national caseload averages concealed considerable differences, for instance table 13 of the Morison Committee Report (1962) showed that in 1960 119 probation officers were carrying caseloads between 80 plus and 100 plus, and even in 1971 the Butterworth Inquiry disclosed some caseloads of 80 or more. It recommended that the main grade should be recognised as a career grade with adequate remuneration so that officers should not be compelled to abandon casework to improve their salaries, but should have a proper chance to develop specialist skills.

National standards in the service, stimulus and support in pioneering new responsibilities were a responsibility of the Home Office probation inspectorate. By the end of the 1960s there were twenty-nine Home Office probation inspectors, of whom ten worked the whole time on training. Responsibility for detailed confirmation inspections of newly appointed qualified staff ceased and was passed to principal probation officers, and the purpose of Home Office inspection shifted from details of the work of individual probation officers to the management of the service and the promotion of good practice.

Table 4 *Strength of the Probation Service (England and Wales)*
(full-time officers)

Date	Men	Women	Total	Trained on appointment	Direct entrants
1945			about 750	23 men and 96 women trained between 1945 and 1949	
1949	—	—	905	75	26
1950	656	350	1,006	84	29
1951	685	371	1,056	66	23
1952	731	382	1,113	68	27
1953	765	395	1,160	56	29
1954	789	411	1,200	70	6
1955	801	412	1,213	57	3
1956	829	418	1,247	63	20
1957	861	430	1,291	50	46
1958	938	453	1,391	77	58
1959	1,013	489	1,502	107	53
1960	1,135	498	1,633	91	114
1961	1,234	528	1,762	104	92
1962	1,333	565	1,898	92	105
1963	1,434	600	2,034	129	67
1964	1,566	601	2,167	171	81
1965	1,678	632	2,310	260	57
1966	1,874	683	2,557	250	57
1967	2,006	739	2,745	212	139
1968	2,168	792	2,960	290	82
1969	2,298	874	3,172	342	59
1970	2,411	941	3,352	333	114
1971	2,547	1,061	3,608	265	139
1972	2,735	1,204	3,939	407	122
1973	2,983	1,344	4,327	467	123
1974	3,079	1,464	4,543	455	53
1975	3,117	1,558	4,675	538	55

The number of prison welfare officers rose from 92 in 1966 to 294 in 1972.

Sources: Home Office, *Reports on the Work of the Probation and After-Care Department, 1962–5, 1966–8, and 1969–71* (HMSO). Also Morison Report (1962), *Report of the Departmental Committee on the Probation Service* (HMSO) Cmnd 1650 and Home Office communications.

Chapter 7

Some Major Developments in the Probation and After-Care Service in the 1960s and Early 1970s

THE DIVORCE AND MAGISTRATES COURTS WELFARE SERVICES

The divorce court welfare service provided by probation officers had expanded considerably since the 1950s. The number of inquiries undertaken at the request of judges in divorce proceedings grew from 880 in 1960 to 8,026 in 1971 (Home Office, *Reports on the Work of the Probation and After-Care Department,* 1962–5 and 1969–71). Under the Family Law Reform Act, 1969 the Chancery Division had power to commit children to the care of the local authority or to place them under the supervision of a probation officer. The court welfare officers already had a duty under the Matrimonial Proceedings (Magistrates Courts) Act, 1960 to supervise the children of parties to matrimonial proceedings if ordered by the court. There was a similar duty in the High Court under the Matrimonial Proceedings (Children) Act, 1958 where there was a custody order for the child. In 1961, 576 such children were being supervised and 9,350 by 1971 (ibid).

AFTER-CARE

The Maxwell Report (1953) on voluntary after-care concluded that it was ineffective for local discharged prisoners' aid societies to try to give help (often very limited) to all discharged prisoners. It recommended that scarce resources should be concentrated on those prisoners most able to benefit, and that for this purpose the appointment of welfare officers financed from public funds should be extended to all prisons by the National Association of Discharged Prisoners' Aid Societies (DPAS). Experimental appointments were made at four local prisons in 1955 and extended to all prisons by 1961. But, owing to the limited resources of DPAS, after-care continued to consist largely of short-term material help; moreover, these welfare officers were in anomalous positions, neither part of the prison staff nor an outside social service. From the beginning of the decade, prison discharges reached a new peak and it became clear that voluntary prisoners' aid societies, which relied primarily on volunteers and limited and untrained staff, could not cope.

The Advisory Council on the Treatment of Offenders (ACTO) report on *The Organisation of After-Care* (1963) regarded as 'patently illogical' a system under which staffs engaged in voluntary after-care were employed by voluntary societies (though largely paid from public funds) while compulsory after-care under the Central After-Care Association was undertaken by probation officers. It accordingly recommended that statutory and voluntary after-care should be united and undertaken by professional social workers in a reorganised and expanded probation service. It regarded prison welfare as an essential part of good after-care but did not think this should continue to be provided by a voluntary organisation. This view was accepted, with the result that the Probation Division of the Home Office became the Probation and After-Care Department in 1965 and by degrees the probation service took over responsibility for voluntary after-care from the discharged prisoners' aid societies and for statutory after-care from the Central After-Care Association, and consequently for prison welfare.

Shortly after the publication of the report, provisions of the Criminal Justice Act, 1961 whereby offenders released from detention centres became subject to twelve months' compulsory supervision by a probation officer were introduced in 1964. By 1967 all borstal licensees were subject to two years' compulsory supervision. The work of the isolated approved school welfare service was also transferred to the probation service and children's departments. In the attempt to build bridges between these institutions and after-care it became increasingly the practice for probation officers to visit prisons, borstals and detention centres to get to know those for whom they would be responsible, to discuss their difficulties with them and with prison welfare officers, social workers and other staff. This also gave probation officers themselves a better idea of life in penal institutions and its effects. A consequence of these contacts was a considerable increase in the number of ex-offenders who went to see a probation officer on discharge, even though the majority went for one interview only and primarily for very necessary material help. In borstals there were often discussion groups to talk over plans and possibilities with offenders. Probation officers designedly exercised little control or supervision of licensees. This permissive supervision after the intensive training programme in borstal did not help licensees with severe problems of family life, work and leisure: nor probably could it within its own resources (Davies, 1974, p. 6). In any event, there was no evidence that intensive after-care produced better results. The borstal failure rate rose steadily in the period under review, possibly because to an increasing extent only the hard core of young offenders were committed to borstal. Success was claimed for an experiment in using borstal boys on community service volunteers projects. By 1968 all after-care constituted over 15 per cent of probation officers' caseloads. All these changes involved a major task of reorganisation and expansion, particularly in London.

In the early days of after-care in the probation service the Home Office Research Unit study (1965–6) *Explorations in After-Care* (Silberman *et al.*,

1971) examined provision in units set up in Liverpool, London and Manchester to provide a specialised after-care and casework service. Most clients were casual callers at the units within a month after discharge from prison. They came because of pressing needs for money, work and accommodation and most of them were unmarried or separated, homeless recidivists under 40. They were not representative of the total population of discharged prisoners. About three-quarters were in contact with a unit for three months or less and few for more than six months. This bore a striking similarity to the length of stay in after-care hostels discussed in volume 2 (see chapter 14, section on 'Hostels for Those before the Courts'). Many lived in common lodging houses or reception centres. Probation officers had little pre-release contact with prisoners and nothing was known about many of those who turned up at the units, while the general lack of therapeutic and remedial resources meant that even after a correct diagnosis little could be offered; moreover most clients wanted material aid rather than help with personal problems. The report summed up the situation thus:

'One of after-care's most outstanding requirements is for a conceptual and theoretical framework which is adequate to the tasks which confront it. The complexity of the emotional and social problems presented by large numbers of discharged prisoners requires considerable skills and experience on the part of those who deal with them, and if the best use is to be made of the available material resources they must be employed with insight and understanding. It is undeniable that a discrepancy between concern and goodwill on the one hand and lack of fundamental knowledge as how best to help discharged prisoners on the other hand constitutes one of the most conspicuous features of this field of social work.' (p. 46)

Some clients were both unemployable and homeless on account of their emotional difficulties, which also made them unreliable, unpredictable and often prone to alcoholism, drug dependence and gambling.

'It seemed that with many men the achievement of any positive long-term results was impossible without treatment on all three levels, either simultaneously or consecutively, according to their needs . . . the psychopathology of clients, although it is of essential importance, was hardly dealt with at all in a systematic manner, with the result that the clients themselves defined their difficulties in terms which were anything but related to their personality problems.' (pp. 34 and 38)

Imprisonment had frequently aggravated these problems. The situation was summed up in terms which also applied to other 'casualties of the welfare state'.

'The need to refer the client elsewhere meant that he was often treated as an assembly of different needs rather than as a unique individual with a history and problems of his own. This splitting-up process, which reflected the administrative division of the various welfare and medical facilities, may have reinforced the client's own opinion that his problems were only short term rather than long term. Moreover, it often resulted in diffusion rather than co-ordination of effort, and for this reason its effectiveness may have been low in relation to its cost. The client was referred from one authority to another, and repeatedly had to explain himself anew to different persons, all of whom had to reassess him in respect of their particular functions. Although many clients had great difficulty in coping with these situations, there were some that exploited them in order to play off one authority against another. In any event, instead of meeting a concerted approach to his problems, the client was forced to fit into a confusing network of agencies and found himself parcelled out among the various statutory and voluntary bodies.' (p. 42)

These were the clients who, along with their non-delinquent fellows, also turned up in temporary accommodation and the psychiatric and local authority services. Prisons and common lodging houses were the last refuge for them, as long-stay hospitals were for the physically and mentally handicapped. Various estimates showed 25 to 35 per cent of ex-prisoners as having nowhere to go on discharge. To be a prisoner one day and a responsible citizen the next inflicted too great a strain on men and women with limited capacity to cope with stress. For those with social support and material means after-care seemed to be a private affair; for those without these the problem was compounded because 'in addition to the cold plunge, there is added the fact that they have never learned to swim and society provides them with virtually no aids to survival' (Davies, 1974, p. 137).

VOLUNTEERS IN THE PROBATION AND AFTER-CARE SERVICE

By the mid-1950s volunteers had been largely excluded from the probation service. But new after-care responsibilities and the first and second Reading Reports, *The Place of Voluntary Service in After-Care* (1963 and 1967), changed the picture. By degrees volunteers began to be recruited in different parts of the country and many probation officers' doubts and suspicions were lessened by experience of the volunteers' quality. They were divided into volunteers in general and 'accredited associates' formally appointed by probation and after-care committees to provide support for considerable periods. The most substantial experiment was in London, where in 1966 a voluntary organisation, Teamwork Associates, was established to recruit, select and train voluntary associates for the Inner London Probation and After-Care Service. Everything had to be learnt from scratch. Barr (1971) described the process. Surprisingly there was no difficulty in obtaining suitable volunteers. Final selection was made after training rather than by interview and discussion groups before acceptance for training. By degrees some local teams were constituted under the guidance of consultant probation officers; in any event all associates were responsible to a probation officer, some had considerable independent responsibility, and others shared cases with a probation officer supervisor.

Outside London volunteers were usually recruited direct by probation officers and by the early 1970s there were over 2,000 volunteers in the probation and after-care service and it was thought that this number would soon double.

The use of volunteers ultimately spread far beyond after-care, so that they were working with prisoners long before discharge, with prisoners' wives and families (who were also the concern of the Prisoners' Wives' Service), with probationers, with men released on parole and with matrimonial cases. All these included difficult 'hard-core' cases. The commonest reason for referral was the need for support to overcome loneliness or to give the client some sense of belonging. Associates had to be prepared for rejection, over-dependence, aggression and dramatic crises in their efforts to act as companions, to support and befriend badly damaged people. 'Most associates . . . are concerned to befriend someone whose life has, until now, been a misery to himself and to others, and to try to bring some happiness into his world by enabling him to form . . . a stable relationship with someone whose motives, so far as he is concerned, are disinterested' (Holden, 1964, p. 125).

The second Reading Report (1967) thought it vital to give the very highest priority to ensuring that 'the bonds which make a family are sustained and strengthened' because if this was ignored 'the efforts of social workers . . . will be largely sterile' (paras 63, 64). Continued social work could both support the wife and help to ease some of the problems of re-adaptation when the man returned home – and make it more likely that a home existed.

Some argued that prisoners' families were clients in their own right and that prompt contact should be made with them whether or not the prisoner consented. The National Association for the Care and Rehabilitation of Offenders (NACRO) found that some probation services were using volunteers (Vercoe, no date of publication) both for long-term contacts and specific purposes, conversely a minority of probation officers were actively hostile to the use of 'well-meaning but inept volunteers'. Twenty-one prisoners' wives' groups were located, some run by volunteers; only about 7 per cent of probation officers used them. Some others had fundamental objections to them or thought they were 'just hen parties'. They were primarily seen as morale building and as helping wives with practical difficulties, also to discuss visiting and the wives' fears about their husbands' release. Volunteers also looked after the children while wives visited their husbands or they ran play groups near the prison.

PRISON WELFARE

After much discussion it was decided in 1966 to staff the prison welfare service by secondment from the probation service. The alternative would have been to appoint a small, civil-service class of social workers in the prison service, but it was not thought this would recruit staff of the necessary standard compared with the probation and after-care service where there was wide scope in the work and better career prospects (Home Office, *Report on the Work of the Probation and After-Care Department*, 1962–5, para. 101).

In 1967 local probation and after-care committees took over from the Prison Department serving social workers in remand centres and borstal allocation centres as well as in detention centres, and became responsible for filling these posts by the secondment of probation officers, usually women. At the time of the takeover seventeen of the forty-six social worker posts were vacant.

Secondment as a prison welfare officer was usually for two or three years. The seconded officers (who might be women in men's prisons) were members of the prison team with responsibility for helping offenders in the prison situation, in their relationship with individuals and organisations outside the prison, and with plans for after-care, as well as for working with prisoners' families, many of whom were severely affected by the imprisonment of husbands or wives, fathers or mothers. Unfortunately, for various reasons family work had a low priority, although it might play a direct part in modifying the offender's behaviour, and families might be in great need of help and support.

A major problem was the relations between the prison welfare officer, the governor and other prison staff, and the outside probation service. Prison governors had general responsibility for the service given in the prison by the seconded officer, who however had the right of access to his local senior or principal probation officer on any professional matter. The latter was responsible for the professional content of his work but was often isolated from day-to-day decisions and developments. Clearly there were inherent tensions in this division of responsibilities, in introducing probation officers into prisons and in clarifying their role and function as prison welfare officers. For many individual officers there were also problems in being answerable to two masters.

The Home Office defined the function as including unhurried initial interviews with every prisoner; on-going casework where desirable (sometimes including visits to prisoners' families in the locality); membership of reception, review, home leave and hostel selection boards; training of prison staff; and supervision of probation and other students (Home Office, *Report on the Work of the Probation and After-Care Department*, 1966–8). The 1963 ACTO report on *The Organisation of After-Care* had proposed that after this 'unhurried initial interview' the social worker should then 'take steps to solve any social problems left behind and to preserve family ties'. Could it ever have looked as simple as that?

The number of prison welfare posts rose from 101 in 1965 to 294 in 1972. The target ratio in the early 1970s was 1 prison welfare officer to 100 prisoners and the average ratio in 1972 was 153, with a range from 53 to 350. The unhurried initial interview was seldom possible and much of the work was simply a response to requests for a series of practical services and information, when

'. . . to assume that a prisoner should not be involved even in contributing to the solution of his own problems, to send him away until someone else produces answers only adds to the depersonalisation already inherent in an institutional experience, and particularly in a custodial situation, a situation further aggravated by the implication that someone else knows how to solve the problem better than the prisoner himself.' (Appleyard, 1971, p. 109)

These routine tasks could well be carried out by ancillary workers or else by attaching selected prison officers to work with prison welfare officers. There was discussion as to whether such prison officers were capable of learning to carry out welfare duties, including counselling, though staff shortages made it difficult to use them in these ways. One possibility was a welfare team based on prison officers with their valuable daily contact with prisoners and with the prison welfare officer in a consultative role. This was controversial.

Action about prisoners' immediate problems seldom led to constructive long-term relationships and the pressure of these routine tasks prevented the development of professional skills within the prison. On the other hand, immediate problems which arose from being separated from their environment were a main cause of anxiety to many prisoners. The authoritarian nature of prisons aroused hostilities which led many to deny their anxiety and need for help. Orthen (1975, p. 90) thought that to reduce rather than to work through anxiety was a questionable social work aim.

The introduction of probation officers into prison raised the whole question of whether or not the prison system and social work were fundamentally incompatible with each other, whether indeed a system designed to protect society necessarily damaged the individual. Sanders (1963) said '. . . we see daily the tragic results following the incarceration of individuals in subcultures totally unreal in terms of everyday living. It is little wonder that breakdowns occur so quickly on release however skilful the after-care worker is in his efforts towards the resettlement of the offender' (p. 84).

Other contributions to *Probation* during the 1960s stressed the impossibility of giving more than first-aid in local prisons because of the rapid turnover of prisoners (though there was no reference to crisis intervention theory). It was also argued that it was unreal to talk about casework in prison where people were depersonalised, deprived of freedom of choice, decision making and responsibility, made dependent (with inevitable regression), subjected to extreme discipline, cut off from relations, friends and their familiar milieu, unable to do themselves or anyone else a good turn. In this total situation individuality and responsibility were denied. This denial was alien from social work which stressed the uniqueness and worth of the individual, helping him to become more aware of social reality and able to take more responsibility. In this setting a prison welfare officer could only hope to undo some of the harm by limited help to individuals. This was likely to result in superficial contacts and to the prison staff neutralising and isolating the alien body. Thus it was an illusion to talk of being a member of a non-existent treatment team or substantially influencing the prison régime. No doubt the situation varied to some extent in different prisons according to their ethos and whether or not they were open or closed prisons, obsolete and overcrowded or in modern buildings.

These views of some prison welfare officers were thought by others to devalue governors, assistant governors and prison officers, many of whom wanted to develop treatment rather than solely custodial roles. The prison welfare officer's focus on the one-to-one relationship and the prisoner and the outside world, left out of account needs which sprang from the structure of the organisation and the total environment. This raised the whole question of the functions of assistant governors, whether indeed in time the prison should become treatment-oriented with no real dichotomy between different roles and objectives. These discussions and controversies amongst prison welfare officers seemed to be essentially related to the question of how to bring about system change in prisons, institutions in which the staff was faced with inherent contradictions and confusions of purpose. When the probation service took over prison welfare, the Home Secretary of the day spoke of the 'antiquated and obsolete prison system', and Alexander Paterson had already said years before on the basis of his experience as a prison commissioner that 'You cannot train men for freedom in conditions of captivity'. These views were shared by a large body of enlightened opinion both within and outside the prison service. (For a discussion of the neglected role of prison officers see Thomas, 1965 and 1972). The aim, some said, should thus be a shared treatment situation in which no one was excluded. The setting was an integral part of social work, and prison welfare officers who came from a different setting had to discover how to use the legal and administrative framework to provide opportunities for treatment, to use instead of denying the prison setting. The conflict of interest between the welfare of the offender and the protection of the public also existed in probation, but it was far more acute in prison welfare and parole. Some recidivists were not accessible to help while at liberty, whereas when they were in custody it might be possible to help them to face and come to terms with themselves. Many inmates saw their problems as primarily material or being let down by others, i.e. they had a distorted sense of reality which resulted in a limited ability to tolerate frustration, to find socially acceptable satisfactions and to feel concern for others. Under what circumstances they could be helped to come to terms with the deprivations and personality defects which underlie such attitudes was still a moot question. (For a full contemporary discussion of the issues see NAPO, *Social Work in Prison*, 1968a). The practical problem was to create the milieu and discover the methods which could make possible a treatment function in prison. Thomas (1972) commented, 'The prison officer saw the post of welfare officer as one for which he was admirably suited' but the effect of introducing specialists 'was to narrow the role of the officer, to heighten its coercive overtones and to contribute to its definition as starkly custodial' (p. 199).

Pratt (1975) analysed role strain for PWOs when Home Office circulars were 'idealistic and superficial' and did not define the PWO's place in the prison hierarchy. To do so would have obvious advantages but in the current state of experimentation and ignorance about the best methods of social work practice in prison it would only hasten conformity. He argued that 'the present situation is . . . a vitally important preliminary stage, during which a role for social workers in prison will be slowly established by practice' (p. 382). In any event, PWOs were constantly tempted to resolve their role conflict by sliding into conformity or siding with prisoners instead of coping with the conflict. This included recognition that 'the client' was partly the prison system itself as well as individuals and groups of prisoners and staff. There were analogies here with social work in hospitals.

The need for better and more frequent communication between the prison and probation services led in 1972 to the appointment of a second deputy principal probation inspector at the Home Office with special responsibility for developing social work in penal institutions and for after-care. There were also to be more regular contacts locally and regionally and a probation adviser post was created at Wakefield Staff College.

A Home Office report (1975*b*) on *Social Work in the Custodial Part of the Penal System* affirmed generally accepted aims for the treatment of offenders as better self-understanding, preparation for return to the community, and learning to accept and deal responsibly with the consequences of behaviour. This necessitated creating a 'humane, dignified, constructive and participatory environment which looked outward to the community'. But individual treatment was 'no longer thought to be realistic'. BASW criticised this over-simple, either/or approach which apparently discounted the tentative findings of *Social Work in Prison* (described below). It pointed out that prison welfare officers' official caseloads were 1:100 whereas 1:40 would be a more realistic figure; and that they had restricted access to prisoners. The Home Office supported the Prison Officers' Association's proposal for an expanded role for prison officers, who felt resentful and undervalued. It envisaged the development of wing teams which would review individual situations and cases, co-ordinate effort and meet the danger of the intermittent and unco-ordinated attention of an array of individual specialists. BASW acknowledged that prison officers were skilled in managing very difficult prisoners and understood the prison culture, nevertheless their background and training did not equip them for social work practice. It supported NAPO in opposing the suggestion that prison welfare officers should become consultants and thus run the risk of not being directly involved in the institution.

There were continuing difficulties about prison welfare officers' joint responsibility to their chief probation officer and the prison governor, without a sufficiently clear definition of duties and accountability.

PAROLE

A Government White Paper on *The Adult Offender* (ACTO, 1965) proposed that some prisoners who were not a risk to the public should be released on licence before the end of their sentence. The idea of a parole system was generally accepted. NAPO was in favour but protested strongly against the hasty introduction of the scheme with little consultation or preparation at a time when recruitment was falling, the service was 200 below strength, was stretched to the utmost in any event, and had not yet absorbed after-care and prison welfare, and when it was essential that a venture as hazardous as the early licensing of prisoners should be undertaken with sufficient resources and support. The additional duties that the system would require included service on local review committees and individual interviewing of prisoners; preparing home surroundings reports in the prisoner's own locality, which often meant visits to his family and inquiries about likely jobs; and finally supervision (on similar conditions as in a probation order) of those who were licensed. In spite of protests, the Government of the day decided that the probation and after-care service had the capacity to take on parole at once. In the event, the number of prisoners released on licence made little difference to individual probation officers' caseloads.

The Criminal Justice Act, 1967 provided for an independent Parole Board to advise the Home Secretary about the conditional release of prisoners on licence to serve the remainder of their sentence under supervised and supportive conditions in the community. Parole was for selected prisoners who had served one-third of their sentence or twelve months. A separate Board was constituted for Scotland. Local review committees were also set up, every eligible prisoner was interviewed individually to help him to prepare his case for submission to the review committee, which made a recommendation to the Home Secretary in the light of all the evidence available. These reports were then considered by the Parole Unit in the Home Office and the most likely ones sent on to the Parole Board. In 1968 there was a backlog of 4,700 prisoners to be considered in an entirely new system where it was essential not to take risks that would lead to a public outcry. Of the total, 1,032 were assessed by local review committees and 480 were referred to the Board who recommended that 385 (plus another 21 subsequently referred) should be released.

The *Report of the Parole Board for 1971* reviewed experience since 1968. Of over 8,000 prisoners who had completed their period of parole by the end of 1971, only 6 per cent had been recalled to prison for further offences or for otherwise breaking a condition of their licence. In spite of a steady increase in the number of prisoners recommended for parole, the failure rate remained constant at 5·6 per cent. A data bank was established in 1969 in the Home Office Research Unit so that research could be based on the social and criminal characteristics of all prisoners eligible for parole from the start of the scheme. The risk of reconviction could also be statistically estimated by a prediction formula based on variables known to be related to reconviction rates and this resulted in several hundred prisoners being paroled who were not recommended by review committees.

NON-CUSTODIAL PENALTIES

The ACTO report on *Non-Custodial and Semi-Custodial Penalties* (1970) reinforced efforts to find constructive alternatives to imprisonment, which was often a costly failure, for the rehabilitation of homeless, unemployed, alcoholic, drug dependant, isolated or inadequate offenders. The report recommended a system of day training centres, hostels and community service orders. Under the latter, offenders would be required to perform a specific number of hours of service to the community in their spare time through a scheme administered by the probation and after-care service. This was intended as an alternative to short custodial sentences which would enable the offender to go on living and working in the ordinary community. It was launched by the Criminal Justice Act, 1972, under which community service orders might be imposed for from 40 to 240 hours within twelve months on offenders who consented and were judged suitable after social inquiry reports. An order would result in some deprivation of leisure 'for a constructive and outward-looking purpose which will enable the offender to give something back to the community against which he has offended'

(Home Office, *The Criminal Justice Act 1972, A Guide for The Courts*, 1972, p. 2). Maybe society had offended too. In any event, the scheme was regarded by some critics as hastily introduced legislation without sufficient experimentation, as moralistic retribution, as a punitive imposition on working-class offenders – or alternatively as a sentimental attempt to make silk purses from sows' ears. The 1972 Criminal Justice Act also included day training centres (discussed below) and a considerable increase in the number and range of hostels to be run by the probation service.

The range of community service possibilities was explored by a working party of the probation and after-care service in discussion with voluntary organisations and some public authorities. The agreed tasks included manual activities such as land reclamation and clearance, community projects, constructing adventure playgrounds; making children's toys, or redecorating houses for older or handicapped people or the homeless; and also tasks which included personal relationships such as work with the physically or mentally handicapped, or old people, or children, or in youth clubs. The intention was that the work should be useful in itself and that offenders should work with ordinary volunteers.

Before the scheme was made general in 1975 it was tried out experimentally in six urban and rural areas. The Home Office Research Unit carried out an initial assessment (Pease, 1975) of experience in these six areas to discover what had been learnt and what changes were indicated. Evaluation to show whether community service had produced measurable changes in offenders' behaviour would obviously only be possible when sufficient time had elapsed. It was essential to search actively in the locality for a wide range of tasks, assess what kind of offenders were likely to respond as a guide to social inquiry reports to the court, to match the offender to the task and the setting, and to ensure adequate supervision and good relationships. In every area there was a senior probation officer (community service officer) in charge of the scheme (in London an assistant chief probation officer) and main grade officers entirely employed on community service. In some areas full-time ancillaries were employed as supervisors, in others supervisors were paid sessionally.

During the review period, 307 offenders completed orders satisfactorily, while 114 were unsatisfactory: of the latter significantly more had already experienced custodial sentences. The majority of offenders felt that the experience of community service had been worthwhile and more positive than imprisonment. All community service officers mentioned the benefits gained by both the offender and the community. For many offenders it had been a positive rather than negative experience, doing something useful rather than hanging around. The cases quoted suggested that important factors were good social interaction, the feeling of being valued, of having something to give (especially to children and handicapped and old people), of gains in self-confidence and the discovery of unrecognised potentials. The Report said of one man, what may well apply to a number: 'It is thought that a counselling service such as would have been afforded him on probation would not have benefited him a great deal, and deprivation of liberty could have damaged him even further' (p. 46). In a number of instances offenders continued to work voluntarily in the organisation after the order ended. The Report in its summing up concluded that 'at best, community service is an exciting departure from traditional penal treatment' (p. 70). Further experimentation would show whether for some offenders (including middle-class offenders) this could be an effective form of 'intermediate' treatment.

THE YOUNGER REPORT ON YOUNG ADULT OFFENDERS

The Younger Report on *Young Adult Offenders* (1974), impressed by the failure of custodial penalties to produce any better results than treatment in the community, recommended the abolition of custodial sentences as such for young offenders between 17 and 21, and 'a deliberate switch of resources into a new system of control in the community' (para. 21). Committal to a detention centre, borstal or prison should cease and be succeeded by a custody and control order, which would include an initial period of custody if the court thought this was inevitable. The period in open or closed penal institutions should aim 'to motivate the offender to change his attitudes and to give him opportunities for exercising choice' (para. 57) in spite of 'the intrinsic difficulty of providing training or treatment which will fit the offender . . . to face the problems of managing his own life on release' (para. 17). Custody might be necessary to prevent the offender from committing more crimes and to give both local resentment and the offender himself a chance to cool off. It was thus to become a short adjunct to learning to live in the community rather than the reverse. Its length would be decided (with a few exceptions) by a licensing advisory committee in the light of the offender's response. The committee would include the governor of the establishment, a probation officer and two other local people. The real weight would fall on the subsequent control part of the order in the ordinary community. This might include a wide range of requirements about living arrangements, employment, and so forth, including liability to recall into custody. Custodial and other resources should be grouped to the greatest possible extent on a neighbourhood basis.

The alternative, a supervision and control order, would develop and expand non-custodial treatment but with strict conditions laid down by the court and used at the discretion of the probation officer, who should also be able to apply for a warrant for temporary detention up to seventy-two hours if a serious breach had occurred or was likely, or an offence had been committed. A major increase in resources would be essential, including more probation officers who would intervene more vigorously in young offenders' lives. More hostels, flatlets and approved lodgings would also be necessary for homeless offenders, those unable to cope without residential support, or to get on at home, or keep out of trouble in the neighbourhood. More day training centres and other resources would also be essential.

These proposals were a leap in the dark. Supervision would increase the control function of the probation service, though obviously lessen its severity within the penal system as a whole. At a time when many young probation officers saw themselves as the allies of the offender against the court, the service was faced once again with having to think out whether control of behaviour was consistent with dedication to the client's well-being. Many more probation officers and hostel wardens would be needed to take on non-custodial supervision orders and reduce workloads. The Younger Report emphasised that these changes required adequate facilities and 'must not get off to a limping start'.

There were mixed reactions from NAPO, the Conference of Chief Probation Officers and BASW. All welcomed a shift to community treatment; all were against seventy-two hours' detention in a penal institution; all had doubts about the control element. The Conference of Chief Probation Officers pointed out that typical young adult offenders did not respond to 'arbitrary severity' and that social control should be a positive relationship which produced a change in the offender's social functioning. NAPO thought that the Report had 'serious defects' unless its proposals were 'considerably modified'.

HOME OFFICE RESEARCH UNIT STUDIES OF PROBATION AND THE SOCIAL ENVIRONMENT AND SOCIAL WORK IN PRISON

Research Unit studies in the 1960s on the social environment of young offenders and social work in prison are analysed in detail here because they cast light on actual situations and broke fresh ground for social work theory and practice.

THE SOCIAL ENVIRONMENT INCLUDING THE 'IMPACT' EXPERIMENT

Two studies by Davies (1969 and 1975) analysed the social environment as it affected the lives of 515 probationers aged 17 to 21 placed on probation in 1964. In the sample, 37·3 per cent of probationers were reconvicted within twelve months, but there was no association between reconviction and the length of the order. Sixty-two per cent were inadequate people on a general measure of inadequacy. The 20·8 per cent who were emotionally disturbed had the worst failure rate, conversely the 34·5 per cent who were neither inadequate nor disturbed had the best chance of keeping out of trouble.

Under 5 per cent were homeless and only 8·3 per cent were living in hostels or lodgings: both had reconviction rates of about one in two. Seventy-three per cent were living with parents or parent substitutes. Relations between the parents were satisfactory but without strong family cohesion. Fifty-one per cent of the probationers whose parents were fundamentally compatible had good probation relationships, compared with 30 per cent whose parents quarrelled, and just over 16 per cent where the parents were separated or divorced. Good father/son and good probation relationships were closely associated, and vice versa. Almost half the fathers had 'the worst possible' relationship with their sons.

'In general, mother/son relationships were rather more positive than those between father and son; but there was overwhelming evidence that it was the latter association which was the crucial one insofar as it was most closely linked with the lad's failure or success on probation. Easily the most important family factors in the successful avoidance of further trouble are that the father should be firm but kindly, and that there should be mutual warmth and affection between him and his son.'

'Parental over-indulgence was common, and was linked with reconviction. Over the whole sample of single men, only 9·4 per cent had firm but kindly discipline exercised by both parents.' (Davies, 1969, p. 118)

Those who came from ill-kept homes, indicative of poor family functioning, tended to have weak or disturbed personalities and high failure rates. Overcrowding was rare and in general material standards were high. Most probationers and their families were well in the mainstream of Britain's economic affluence in the 1960s and they tended to be home-centred at weekends. None the less 41 per cent were unemployed when they were put on probation and almost 70 per cent had employment problems during the course of probation, some being virtually unemployable. Few of them had anti-authority feelings about their employers. A large majority were free from severe stress as measured on a stress score, but stress was closely related to reconviction or other failure on probation.

Group membership only caused problems to about 10 per cent but one-third mixed mainly with delinquents. Neither previous convictions nor the type of offence affected the probationers' relationship with the probation officer. It was, however, markedly linked with his 'life at home, at work and within his peer group' (p. 107). 'Those probationers with the most trying home situations tended to have the greatest personality problems, to be unemployed and to mix mainly with delinquents' (p. 118). Since these complex factors were statistically associated with the likelihood of reconviction the report thought it essential for probation officers to take them into account in considering treatment aims.

The findings posed considerable problems for casework because

'Social work has traditionally emphasised the concept of client self-determination: through a casework relationship, the probationer is helped and encouraged to solve his own problems and to counter the negative aspects in his environment. If, however, the casework relationship varies proportionately with the quality of the probationer's environment and with the limitations in the probationer's personality, then a tricky problem is posed for social work theory and practice: the main instrument for diagnosis and treatment in casework – the interpersonal relationship between worker and client – is rendered relatively ineffective when the need for it is most pressing. Those probationers with the greatest problems are least likely to achieve the best relationship with their supervising officers; and conversely the clients with whom officers have a good relationship are the ones with the fewest personality problems and the most effective support in their environment.' (p. 109)

If this was too narrow a statement of the range of casework techniques, the study yet raised the whole issue of the extent to which accepted probation methods – or indeed any other known methods – were appropriate where there were severe environment problems and/or serious personality difficulties. This and other studies also began to identify the neglected but crucial role of fathers in nurturing and socialisation processes.

The indications were that some probationers whose problems lay primarily in their own personalities needed more intensive and varied treatment, coupled with changes in their social environment. But for others detached and unorthodox group work and casework in their own environment on the lines of *The Wincroft Youth Project* (Smith *et al.*, 1972), coupled with other resources, whether in the probation and after-care service or elsewhere, might be necessary to bring about any effective change in very complex situations.

'The approach of preventing and treating the social disorder of delinquency within the community . . . is part of a gathering confluence of thought and policy in many personal social services, that proposes that the patient or the client, whether an individual or belonging to a group or network, should be helped to function adequately within his normal circumstances . . . Assistance needs to be directed not only towards the client but also towards the groups or communities of which he is a member.' (Smith *et al.*, 1972, pp. 264–5)

In *Social Work in the Environment* (1975), Davies studied the probation case records of the same group of young men from the angle of the probation officers' activities in relation to home, employment and friends. Most clients presented a multitude of problems but the officers' freedom to help was limited by time, other pressures, lack of resources, or knowing that effort spent on some environmental factor would produce no result. None the less 'There is of course no doubt that probation officers help individual clients and their families at times of crisis and in response to specific needs, and there can be little doubt that their efforts are often appreciated by those who benefit, and that they succeed in relieving immediate pressures' (p. 93). The records were divided into probationers with fewest environmental difficulties (failure rate ·14) and those in the worst environmental circumstances (failure rate ·56). There was infrequent home visiting and an almost total absence of intensive home-treatment plans seemed to result mainly from pressure of work. 'In some . . . cases there was evidence of "classic" casework, but, so far as the remainder of the sample was concerned, home visits were undertaken only occasionally, and in general the role of the officer in the home appeared to be relatively superficial, and not particularly treatment-based' (p. 21).

In a fair-sized minority of cases the father's attitudes towards the probationer improved considerably. There was also a positive relationship between the amount of probation officer involvement and freedom from reconviction for those with low or high support at home. The probationers whose officers did most in the home had better results but possibly probation officers became involved in the home situation of those who for various reasons were most likely to succeed. There was minimal contact between probationers' girl-friends and the probation officer. There was also no evidence of the probation officers' systematic contact with the wife, whether or not there were difficulties in the marriage, though in many cases there were a number of matrimonial problems.

There was a good deal of discussion with probationers about work and some intervention about employment with a number of young men prone to unemployment. The reconviction rate was high amongst those with low job stability, though active intervention by the probation officer appeared to make little difference. None the less 19 per cent showed very much better job stability at the end of the probation order. A small minority suffered from material hardship or lack of accommodation. Probation officers tried to help if this was essential. But

'. . . attempts at relieving material stress occurred spasmodically and only briefly, [and] . . . cases which required more intensive and persistent work could not possibly be helped . . . The question still remains, however, whether it is the probation officer's task to help in the alleviation of material stress and, if so, how it can be achieved more effectively and whether the facilities, resources and knowledge available to the service need to be supplemented or reorganised if officers are to give adequate help to the client in need.' (p. 70)

The single factor most indicative of potential recidivism seemed to be the probationers' tendency to mix mainly with delinquents, but in the records there was an almost total lack of contact with the probationers' contemporary friends and in only one instance were there group discussions with other probationers.

'It is the recognition of the complexity of breaking into the probationer's peer-group associations that has led some people in social work to advocate a greater use of group-work techniques in supervision. Such an approach might enable the probation officer to get closer to the real life situation of his client . . . A great deal more work needs to be done before we can understand how social workers can effectively intervene in an alien environment.' (pp. 75–6)

The report concluded that

'There is little evidence from this research that environmental treatment within the current probation context secures any significant reduction in the level of environmental stress in the lives of probationers . . . No positive association was found between the focus of the probation officer's casework interviews and the resolution of his client's environmental difficulties or the level of his reconviction rate.' (p. 97)

Environmental intervention was far from being a simple matter when clients were living in situations where 'the stresses cluster and react on each other'. Any effective intervention in more difficult environmental situations required a greater investment of community resources than probation officers had at their command. When the degree of environmental stress was limited

'. . . it is possible that the personality of most clients . . . is still more resilient than the resources of any helping agency, and hence that the policy of non-intervention is not only as feasible but as valid as any other approach in the present state of knowledge. There are, however, many individuals whose personalities cannot cope with environmental stress, but society at present is able to do no more than pick them up each time they fall and give them another chance of 'proving' themselves. Always among probationers there are some who succeed who have failed before, and the system may yet be better than any alternative. But there would still seem to be a need to explore all possible avenues of development with a view to achieving greater success for an activist approach among bad-risk cases.' (p. 100)

The tentative findings of this and other research studies were tested in a new experiment, IMPACT (intensive matched probation and after-care treatment), launched in 1971 as a Home Office Research Unit action research experiment (Folkard *et al.*, 1974). Its purpose was to discover whether some types of high-risk offenders with previous convictions would respond to intensive situational treatment based upon a mixture of support, control, and environmental modification. High-risk offenders with two or more previous convictions placed on probation were randomly allocated for experimental or ordinary treatment in order to study the differential outcome. An initial assessment form included social background and demographic, stressful or delinquent variables in the probationer's situation, while the Eysenck extraversion-introversion and neurotism-stability personality inventory, coupled with the self-administered Mooney Problem Check List attempted to clarify personality variables. The project was a joint effort between the researchers and the probation and after-care services in five experimental areas, three urban and two mixed urban and rural.

In ordinary practice, office interviews were the predominant form of treatment. In IMPACT the aim was considerable, direct, practical interaction in family, work and leisure situations, also using ancillaries, volunteers and other agencies and resources. The probation officers selected for the experiment had small caseloads of about twenty and no other duties. In Sheffield and London separate units of five probation officers were set up; in Liverpool the unit consisted of two prison welfare officers working in the prison. In Staffordshire and Dorset there were individual 'experimental' probation officers in local offices.

The aim was to help probationers with their problems and to control unacceptable behaviour. Support and control were measured for the experimental cases on situational assessment and quarterly summary forms. The main emphasis in evaluation was primarily on reconviction, but included rated changes in family relations, work and leisure (Folkard *et al.*, *IMPACT*, 1974). The response of probationers varied from marked dependency to apathy or annoyance at too much attention. Planning and use of group activities were much stressed in London and Sheffield, for instance groups for adolescents, for 'loners', for wives, for those with drink problems, and play groups for children. Volunteers and ancillaries helped with these and it was hoped that peer-group learning and better capacity for communication would result from them.

The Mooney Problem Check List and various other methods placed real onus on probationers to decide how the order should be used. There was more home visiting than usual as part of the situational treatment; this revealed problems and strengths earlier and often made it possible to work with the family in various ways rather than relying mainly on verbal discussion with individuals in office interviews. In at least one unit, there was sophisticated use of joint matrimonial discussions, and of conjoint family therapy in which the family's energies could be mobilised to tackle root causes of its problems (Thornborough, 1974). 'Experimental' probation officers met probationers on their own ground in pubs or cafés or in their own homes on a more equal footing and often for practical activities. Ancillaries and volunteers were also used in these ways. The London unit had its own premises where probationers could relax and talk, read, play darts or other games, or look at television, or make a hot drink. These valuable aids to better communication had, of course, long been used by family service units, some family advice centres, settlements and community centres.

All 'experimental' probation officers had frequent supervision from the team senior, while in the London and Sheffield group discussions everyone assessed each case and individuals found themselves forced to think and plan more systematically, to question what they were doing, what were the consequences, and whether some alternative would give better results. In these units a strong team spirit developed, which had a significant effect. In some situations a man and a woman probation officer shared the supervision of each probationer.

By 1974 the 'experimental' officers felt that probationers who were sufficiently motivated or in need had benefited from the extra amount of time these probation officers could give them. Getting out and doing things with probationers and involvement in the family situation enabled probation officers to show caring behaviour on a more equal footing in various situations, which also changed probationers' attitudes. Probation officers had the advantages of manageable caseloads, time to plan treatment and carry it through in relation to the needs of each probationer, i.e. to do better focused and evaluated casework.

In spite of the high proportion of situational contacts in the experimental cases at the end of the project 'the results showed no significant reconviction rates between the experimental and control cases, therefore producing no evidence to support a general application of more intensive treatment' (Folkard *et al.*, 1976, p. 22). 'Subsequent conviction as a measure of outcome has many deficiencies' (p. 17). The experimentals showed earlier improvement than the controls in family, finance and homes (p. 16) but there was 'no solid evidence . . . that experimental treatment produced more beneficial results than control treatment' (p. 17). Older, more extroverted, less neurotic control-group probationers with relatively more previous convictions tended to do better; control probationers with low and medium scores on the Mooney Problem Check List did significantly better. Assessments of the probationer's criminal tendencies made by probation officers at the beginning of the order were also statistically significant. On these last two findings, offenders with moderate or high criminal tendencies and average or few personal problems did significantly worse in terms of reconviction rates under intensive treatment, though offenders with low criminal tendencies and many personal problems appeared to do better under such treatment (Folkard *et al.*, 1976).

DAY TRAINING CENTRES

Day training centres were the first opportunity the probation service had had to develop alternatives to imprisonment. Four experimental centres were started in Sheffield, Liverpool, Pontypridd and London. Offenders were placed on probation with a condition to attend a centre for sixty days on five days a week. At the Inner London centre ('Day Training Centres, First Report', Inner London Probation and After-Care Service, 1975) there was a staff of seven probation officers, art therapists, remedial teachers and others, including psychiatric consultation for a group of twenty-five participants. The aim was to encourage the participants to examine and take responsibility for their behaviour. This was attempted through close personal relationships between the staff and small groups of eight participants, and a demanding but stimulating programme aimed at helping them to become aware of the connection between their feelings and their behaviour. The basic working units were small groups led by probation officers in which members worked out expectations for their time at the centre and assessed their achievements. There was much use of art and music therapy to heighten communication, awareness of self and others, and imaginative reflection. Role play and intergroup activities in which long-buried feelings were explored were also important. Practical activities included art and pottery, and there was remedial teaching and various community activities, while the whole group took part in decisions about the running of the centre. Most participants were offenders between 21 and 45 with long delinquent histories but some commitment to change in spite of rigidly stereotyped views of themselves and others.

In the first year, 81 men were assessed for training centre orders of whom 56 were single and 25 married, though only 11 had fairly stable marriages, and 38 per cent had been separated from their parents before they were 15. Fifty-seven orders were made in the first year and sixty-six in the second, but the centre was still under used. It was too early by 1975 to measure success by reconviction rates. But 'Many have been damaged to such a degree that their capacity to function on their own has been gravely and perhaps fundamentally impaired . . . Many experienced themselves and their potential for growth for the first time. Much of this cannot be achieved without stress and anxiety and parts of the programme can be extremely painful' (p. 21). But 'dormant skills have emerged, or re-emerged, sensitive and warmer feelings have been aired without fear, learning has become easier and failure not so debilitating' (p. 20). This was unlike prison where it was easy to avoid looking at oneself or one's relationships, to deny responsibility and remain isolated. The Home Office Research Unit undertook research into changes of attitude at the four experimental centres. If the staff could maintain their early enthusiasm and continue to learn better how to fulfil their aims, there seemed hope that this civilised experiment might prove an effective alternative to imprisonment.

SOCIAL WORK IN PRISON

In 1968 the Home Office started an eighteen-month experiment at two Midland prisons, which it was hoped would begin to identify the place and potential function of social workers in prisons, the necessary numbers, the supporting services they needed, and how they should be deployed. The prison welfare officer staff in these prisons was increased to 1 to every 100 prisoners. Some results were published five years later in a Home Office Research Unit report on *Social Work in Prison* (Shaw, 1974) (see also Sinclair, *et al.*, 1974). The research was undertaken at a low-risk open prison and a high-risk maximum security prison. It was intended to discover: (1) whether prisoners were prepared to accept a series of regular interviews with the caseworker and, if so, what they thought of the experience; (2) whether prisoners who received regular casework were less likely to be reconvicted than those who did not; (3) if so, what kinds of prisoners were most likely to benefit; and (4) how they did so. It was hypothesised that those who formed a significant relationship with their caseworker would benefit most; that 'prisonised' men, sub-cultural offenders and psychopaths would not respond; but that the neurotic and the verbal and intelligent would do so because casework relies heavily on techniques for the treatment of the neurotic and is a 'talking treatment'.

Two groups, an experimental and a control group, were randomly selected from all men due for release from the two prisons in 1969 – seventy-five men in each group. The welfare officers saw the men in the experimental group for an average of fifteen sessions over six months and for considerably longer than in the average of six sessions for the controls (i.e. those seen in the normal routine). When they were interviewed later by the research workers the experimentals were significantly more likely to speak favourably of their caseworker and to say they had discussed personal as well as practical problems. A follow up of all the men two years after their release showed that significantly fewer of the experimentals had been reconvicted, i.e. 57 per cent against 76 per cent. None of the hypotheses about types of prisoner were confirmed, neither did the 'successful' experimentals have a better relationship with their caseworker than those who were reconvicted. One statistically significant factor, however, came to light: amongst the ninety-nine who had taken the Eysenck personality inventory test, the experimental 'successes' were more introverted than the control 'successes', while the experimental 'failures' were more extroverted than the control 'failures'. All the introverts in the control group were reconvicted but in the experimental group the majority were not. Checking with the control prior risk of reconviction score showed that introversion amongst the experimentals was significantly associated with success, even taking prior risk into account. There was little difference in the proportion of extroverts reconvicted in the experimental and control groups, which suggested that they were unaffected one way or the other. The 'successful' introverts in the experimental group had significantly better relationship scores than those who were reconvicted, but in this group this was negatively correlated with prior risk scores. This suggested that introverts with good prior risk scores were less likely to be reconvicted and more likely to have a good relationship with their caseworker. Conversely, the extroverts with good relationship scores were rather more likely to be reconvicted than the rest. The experimentals did not report having received any more material help or help with jobs and accommodation than the controls. But 'As a result of their greater contact with welfare officers, the attitudes and behaviour of the experimental group differed significantly from those of the control group' (p. 93). It was not possible to know whether this was due to casework as such, or more frequent contacts and more attention. The caseworker might have been the only person to offer a warm, personal relationship in prison and this might be more significant to introverts than it would be in the outside world, partly because they found it difficult to join the prison culture and might be less satisfied with themselves than extroverts and therefore more highly motivated to change. A casework relationship might also be more relevant to problems of introverts, who had difficulty in making contacts and might benefit from encouragement to express themselves.

It was also apparent that the location of the welfare officer either in a wing or in a separate administrative block facilitated or impeded communication. If inmates saw the PWO frequently and could easily go to him for practical help, they were more likely to be willing to talk about their personal problems than if they had to go to a distant office.

This was an important study because it seemed, unlike most, to identify circumstances in which a relationship with people of certain personality types made a significant difference. The report concluded with some reflections on the implications of prisons as a whole:

'Many other staff are involved in social work, the chaplain, assistant governors, principal and senior officers, and some basic grade staff: their involvement should not be sacrificed to the expansion of welfare departments. The tentative findings of the present study, which are supported by those of other investigators, indicate the potential of uniformed staff and instructors for developing their role – a fact which has long been recognised by the Prison Officers' Association. The welfare officer has no monopoly of good relationships with the inmates. The practical benefits to be gained from greater involvement of other staff in social work are clear, not least that it would relieve welfare officers of work which does not require their special expertise. This in turn would allow them more time to select cases in need of intensive treatment, and to support other staff in dealing wih requests and applications. It would lead to increased communication between staff and the welfare department, a development essential to proper planning of on-going treatment and also for helping staff to handle day to day situations in the prison. Greater involvement of staff in social work has implications for the men too. If, as seems clear, it is the attitudes and organisation of the staff which largely determine the relationships between inmates and staff, then greater understanding and communication between staff is essential.' (p. 103)

This had dynamic implications for prisons as social systems. It ignored the constant tensions between security and 'welfare' which confused prison staffs, but was in line with new concepts about the role of all staff in personal, therapeutic roles in institutions.

The differences in reconviction rates for extroverts and introverts were further explored by McWilliams (1975) in a follow up of 230 offenders placed on probation or not under supervision during 1966–8. He found that of those who scored high on extroversion and neuroticism, 71 per cent on probation and 70 per cent not supervised were not reconvicted within three years; while of those with low extroversion and high neuroticism scores only 19 per cent were reconvicted against 79 per cent in the low neuroticism, high extroversion category. This added to other evidence that some degree of anxiety was essential to successful treatment and that it was correspondingly difficult to achieve success with extroverted, aggressive clients.

By 1975, then, there had been only a decade of exploratory research action studies and attempts to test out some findings in practice. Probation could not reverse the extensive damage suffered by some people while imprisonment might increase it. For others, hopeful action seemed to lie in intensive efforts to increase their own self-awareness and more satisfying relations with others. But these were early explorations in which, as with recorded experiments with other groups, there might be secondary change for the better but not the desired alteration in particular behaviour.

Chapter 8

Probation Training

It is impossible to read contemporary material of the 1950s without sensing the excitement about the new methods and the new learning, the new knowledge that would shed light on much incomprehensible behaviour and the new casework skill that would give probation officers more insight, more sense of direction and achievement in their work. In future, so it was generally said, they would be working 'at an intensive level', would need 'scientific consultation' and 'every opportunity to increase their knowledge and skill'. The problem which exercised the Home Office Probation Division and at least an influential part of NAPO was how to get from 'here' to 'there'. Supervision as a teaching/learning process in relation to day-to-day practice seemed to be crucial but a difficult exercise in logistics when the field was so wide and resources so limited.

The Home Office Probation Division made active use of the American social work teachers who came here in the 1950s and of every university or other refresher course, as well as running its own in-service training. Both it and NAPO arranged local discussion groups, seminars and case conferences for probation officers, often led by psychiatrists or by others from outside the service. Some of these groups met weekly for about a year and generated a powerful dynamic for change. Since 1948 there had been discussion about the possibility of some form of casework supervision in the service, especially for newly appointed probation officers. The main difficulties in the way of this were the shortage of people with training and experience in supervision, the pressure of staff shortages and high caseloads, and doubts and dissensions about 'deep casework'. But the Home Office and NAPO actively campaigned for supervision of probation officers as an educational rather than a checking process. The NAPO 1956 Annual Conference adopted a statement on 'the place of supervision in probation casework' in which it was recognised that experienced officers must be given training in supervision, preferably by being supervised themselves. The statement said: 'The real solution in the task of improving standards of service offered to clients may lie . . . in the use of casework supervision within the service itself' (*Probation*, September 1957, p. 98). There were fears that supervision would result in probation officers losing responsibility for their cases and being told what to do, and fears too of being found inadequate. Yet the skill of good probation officers was being wasted because they were not sufficiently articulate to communicate it. The statement concluded by suggesting that as a means of using scarce resources, trained supervisors should be seconded as full-time casework tutors to supervise other probation officers on their supervision and to take case discussions with local groups.

In order to give principal probation officers some idea of new advances in casework, the Home Office ran the first short course on supervision at Birmingham University in 1954 and subsequently all principal probation officers took similar courses at other universities. These were followed by regional courses for senior probation officers. The Home Office also ran special training courses for supervisors (known as tutor officers in the probation and after-care service). There were a number of refresher courses for serving officers, but in spite of fairly generous provision it was well-nigh impossible for management to release sufficient staff for such courses and at the same time meet the heavy demands of pre-service training. This could only have been achieved if the service were fully staffed. The long-standing demand that every officer should be able to take a refresher course at three- to five-year intervals was only met in the 1970s. The NAPO textbook (King, 1958) said:

'In recent years, various courses have been arranged for probation officers which are especially helpful to those undertaking training. In some areas these have taken the form of group meetings with a psychiatrist, whilst in other areas extra-mural courses have been arranged at universities with visiting Fulbright scholars as tutors. In addition, short courses for training officers have been arranged at Rainer House [the Home Office training centre in London] and a small number of officers have been able to take full-time advanced courses lasting one year. It is important that courses of these kinds should become more generally available in the future, since they can contribute greatly to improving the quality of supervision offered by training officers to students and it is at this point that the best hope lies of improving the standards of the Service and ensuring its future development.' (p. 137)

By the early 1960s experienced probation officers were becoming more willing to accept supervision, while newly qualified officers who had had good supervision tried to get appointments where this would continue. Extended training during the first year after appointment, through reduced caseloads and regular supervision, began in the probation service earlier than elsewhere. It was hampered by staff shortages and lack of probation officers competent to supervise, but the then revolutionary principle was accepted.

As part of its concern about qualifying training, NAPO sent statements to the PATB in 1954 and 1958. It thought that all candidates except a few exceptional older people should take a social science qualification as a basis for professional training, that there should be more, and more systematic, in-service training and an end to direct entry of untrained recruits to the probation service. After initial hesitation it, like the Home Office, supported the principle of 'generic' training in the first applied social studies course and later pressed for the extension of these courses. It recognised that the success of practical training depended on the students' potentialities, the skill of tutor officers and the facilities at their command. Great care was therefore necessary in their selection and training.

Far more was beginning to be expected than in the past when

'. . . the student on 'practical work' had a rather passive role and was frequently an observer of another person's activity. He watched, listened and accompanied an established worker whilst the latter went about his normal duties. The implication was that the student would see and hear what was done and that this would later be supplemented by discussion with the worker, so that eventually the student in his turn would be able to function in much the same manner as the established worker. Such a method of training had obvious limitations.' (ibid, pp. 133–4)

The demand that tutor officers should become fieldwork teachers pre-supposed a new and time-consuming role, yet they often carried a heavy caseload as well as trying to meet students' needs, which created an almost unbearable two-way stretch. In the view of NAPO:

'It must now be recognised that potential tutor officers require specialised training. This might take the form of a year's course in advanced case-work, but impressive results have already followed attendance at extra-mural courses in casework and supervision undertaken in connection with certain Universities under the guidance of Fulbright scholars and others skilled in casework, and at the Home Office courses for tutor officers, though these have been regrettably short. Every officer charged with the responsibility of teaching casework should have had a thorough training for this duty through a specialised full-time or part-time course or by con-tinuous training on an in-service basis.' (*Probation*, June 1958, p. 143)

The Association hoped that no one would be used as a tutor officer unless he had taken a special course and that the short courses provided by the Probation Division would only be regarded as sufficient if they were followed by regular tutorials or supervisory sessions for several months. These views supported and reinforced the policy being actively pursued by the Home Office and the PATB.

The pattern of student training, which remained unchanged for some years, was based on a rigorous Home Office selection procedure of inter-views and leaderless discussion groups worked out several years earlier by the National Institute of Industrial Psychology. Successful candidates under 30 were required to find places on university social science courses: this was followed by about nine months of specialised Home Office training based on Rainer House, London, or from 1954 an applied social studies course. Those over 30 took the Rainer House one-year course only. The general pattern of this course for both groups of students was a one- to three-month orientation period in a probation office and sometimes experience in a family casework agency, followed by the three-month theoretical course at Rainer House and then a further four to five months of practical work. The following description of the Rainer House course is based upon the NAPO 1958 statement on training (*Probation*, June 1958) and an unidenti-fied contemporary account.

In the initial orientation period the student was to be introduced to probation, to learn about the function of probation officers, court procedure and office routine, and to pay visits of observation to other related social services. He was not intended to be responsible for any cases. This period gave the student his first impression of probation and he needed plenty of time for discussion. He should be learning how to observe and to gather factual information systematically; he should have responsibility for some direct service and not be allowed to become frustrated through inactivity. In practice, there was no uniformity amongst tutor officers about the use of this period. Some allowed students to have a normal caseload and get on with it, others did not allow them near a probationer. Thus students might arrive at Rainer House with very different experiences in the orientation period, which added to the difficulties of relating theory to practice.

By the late 1950s the syllabus of the three-month theoretical course consisted of lectures, seminars and tutorials on the law, criminology, human growth and development, biological and physiological aspects of sex, casework, matrimonial conciliation, institutional treatment and after-care, together with social administration for non-social science students. The lectures were given by doctors, psychiatrists, university lecturers and psychiatric social workers. NAPO thought that probation officers should take more part in the teaching. In its view the lecturers were often first rate, but they came in from outside, there was no co-ordination between them and they had little idea what others were teaching. The result was a lack of cohesion. This complaint ignored periodic discussion meetings between lecturers and probation inspectors. The latter had all been probation officers and their tutorial classes were intended to relate theory to practice. The syllabus was heavily overloaded, which could cause considerable strain to older students. The integration of theory and practice would only have been possible if lecturers had been more *au fait* with the fieldwork and the tutor officers had known what was being taught. Although many members of NAPO had trained on this course, it said in its 1958 statement that it was only aware of the subjects not the content, and that tutor officers gained most of their knowledge from students. There was pressure from NAPO and elsewhere to appoint a full-time tutor at Rainer House to hold the course together and to co-ordinate studies. This was not done until 1966.

In the final four- to five-month fieldwork period students were expected to learn the practice of casework in the probation service through taking responsibility for selected cases, applying their theoretical knowledge, and developing skill in various aspects of the work including interprofessional co-operation. The students went to different parts of the country, thus the link between the theoretical course and the tutor officers depended mainly on contacts with the training inspectors. The NAPO memorandum proposed that these final placements should be lengthened to seven months.

By the end of the decade all second-placement tutor officers had taken a Home Office one-week course in supervision. These were followed by similar courses for first-placement tutor officers. Even though these were too short, they still spread the concept of supervision. The NAPO 1958 statement pointed out the advantages of 'group training' (i.e. student units, introduced in the first applied social studies course) for both students and tutor officers; and that 'in the applied social studies and mental health courses each stage in training is planned in relation to what precedes and follows it so that a progression of learning results' (p. 144). It proposed an experiment on these lines for Home Office probation students, apparently realising that the Rainer House course hovered between in-service and professional training.

THE TRAINING PROPOSALS OF THE MORISON COMMITTEE

Some evidence to the Morison Committee on the probation service (1962) suggested that there was too much Home Office control of probation training, in that a government department selected students, provided and ran training courses and inspected new probation officers before their appointments were confirmed. This, it was said, made students anxious, and they also resented being taught and subsequently inspected by representatives of a central authority whose maintenance grants were inadequate. The Committee dismissed these objections which it thought did not 'outweigh the advantages of using the knowledge and ability of inspectors in an educational role' (para. 297). It also rejected the idea of an independent training council under which training would cease to be the responsibility of a government department. While the Committee was sitting, the Bill to set up a Council for Training in Social Work for the health and welfare services was before Parliament. The Morison Report recommended that 'there should be the fullest possible co-ordination of probation training and refresher courses with the Council's schemes' (para. 296). This did not happen.

It also drew attention to

'. . . the growing responsibilities of the probation service on the one hand, and on the other to the rapid advances in the sciences of human behaviour. This means that the pressure to turn knowledge into operational terms will steadily increase in the probation service as elsewhere. As a result, increased knowledge and professional competence will be demanded of probation officers in the years ahead. Training is the primary means by which this knowledge finds its way into probation practice, and a serious situation would arise if the training which probation officers received were at any time insufficient in length or quality to bear the weight of new demands and new knowledge.' (para. 292)

The Committee re-affirmed that whenever possible probation students should take a university training. But

'The evidence showed that some students under thirty, although having a valuable contribution to make as probation officers, were not best suited by their educational backgrounds to university courses nor likely in future to be admitted to these . . . Such students and others might more profitably take one of the new two year courses.' (para. 307)

It said:

'. . . assignment to training according to an age limit appears to us, even with the occasional exceptions now admitted, to be artificial; and, having regard to the range and complexity of the probation officer's work, a one-year training seems to us far from ideal. We accordingly recommend that, from the earlier possible date, every probation officer should receive not less than two years' training before appointment. In the immediate future there should be greater flexibility in the choice of training. One year Home Office courses should continue for the present though in . . . reorganised form . . . but candidates over thirty should be considered for university (three years) training if they are willing and are accepted by a university. Admission of such candidates, under thirty, to two year courses should also be arranged.' (para. 308)

It commented on the overwhelming weight of evidence it had received about the unsatisfactory consequences of separating theory and practice on the Home Office course; and also that the whole pattern of a course that was concentrated in London with fieldwork in different parts of the country was a disincentive to potential candidates with families, who might well be recruited if a number of training courses existed in various localities. The Committee therefore thought it would be desirable to participate in the new two-year courses being started in extramural departments and colleges of further education. It said:

'We have no doubt that there will remain a need for a centre in London where specialised training . . . and also refresher training of serving officers, . . . can be carried out. But we recommend that the Home Office should seek the co-operation of colleges of further education and of extra-mural departments of Universities in developing courses of probation training at provincial centres.' (para. 310)

PROBATION TRAINING IN THE 1960s

The Probation Division was against these proposals because it feared that older recruits whom the service needed, some of whom were earning fairly high salaries and had family commitments, would not take a two-year training. This objection had substance when inadequate grants were a severe deterrent to older candidates. It might have been met by re-introducing training on salary sooner (this was done in 1970 but did not in the then climate produce a flood of applicants). In the Probation Division's view there was a valid case for preserving the one-year training for older students, followed at intervals by short in-service courses to enable them to integrate their experience with learning at a more advanced level than they could cope with as students. This assumption, like many other views about the length and content of training, was untested by research although a control group was soon available. The alternative of two-year training for most students but one year for those with certain qualifications was adopted elsewhere but not in probation. In the early 1960s it was not evident that, as happened later, large numbers of older men and women would come forward to take the two-year child care and certificate in social work courses. These recruits included new entrants and staff seconded to train (including trainees). It was argued, against continuing criticism, that the Home Office courses fulfilled their function in the two decades after the war in that they brought a greater proportion of trained staff into the probation service than into other social services. But later, so it was argued, the increasing complexity of social work problems and the better standard of two-year professional courses made the transition necessary.

Under an interesting scheme which operated for a few years in the early 1960s, candidates over 25 with university entrance qualifications were appointed to the London Probation Service and then given a two-year, full-time course which combined probation training with the London University external diploma in social studies. In 1963 a specialised one-year probation course was started by Leeds University extramural department, followed by Leicester University in 1964 and next year by Bristol and Southampton Universities. These courses fulfilled a Morison Committee recommendation that training should be provided in universities and colleges of further education as an alternative to the Home Office one-year course. They brought probation students into general educational institutions, made concurrent fieldwork possible, and had full-time tutors. But they were started as one-year specialised courses. In 1968 and 1969 respectively they were combined with the child care courses at Leicester and Bristol Universities and lengthened to two years, but confined to students between the ages of 23 and 30. The Leeds and Southampton University one-year courses for older students continued separately until the early 1970s.

In contrast with the 1950s, by the mid-1960s there were about fifty-five probation students a year on the one-year or seventeen-month university applied social studies courses. Of the 283 students who completed training in 1965, 18·5 per cent took one of these courses and 67 per cent the Home Office course.

A recruitment and training sub-committee of the PATB (which became the Advisory Council on Probation and After-Care – ACPAC – in 1965) set about a vigorous recruitment and publicity campaign to try to meet the acute shortage of probation officers and progressively decrease the number of direct entrants. The Home Office decided that the age below which candidates were required to take a social science qualification before the probation course should be lowered from 30 to 27 and later to 23. The decreasing number of social science certificate and diploma courses was a major element in plans for two-year courses for students under 30. Over that age it was assumed that they could be satisfactorily trained in one year, even without related past experience or qualifications. By 1968 there were thirty courses recognised for probation students, against three in 1960.

A survey of all available final placements showed that expanded training would only be possible if some probation officers supervised several students. Thus student units were set up in 1964 with the creation of special senior probation officer (training) appointments for the supervision of groups of six to eight students. The number of units rose from twelve in 1966 to sixteen in 1968 (with four more under consideration). This made possible group teaching and resulted in closer links with educational institutions as well as increasing the number of student placements.

By the early 1960s a total of thirty probation officers had taken the Tavistock Institute advanced course in casework, indeed the service was at the time more active than any other in giving leave on salary to those accepted for the course, encouraged by the Home Office who had earlier paid the cost from training funds. But set against the total number of probation officers this figure shows the continuing inadequate provision for advanced training in this service, as elsewhere. The numbers actually fell after 1965 when local probation and after-care committees were empowered to second probation officers for various forms of post-basic training but showed little enthusiasm for doing so.

IN-SERVICE TRAINING

The extended duties of the 1960s resulted in a considerable need for in-service training related to parole, after-care, prison welfare, and the use of volunteers; and to give a greater understanding of group and community behaviour. As in other services, experienced officers needed opportunities for continuing education both on specific topics and aimed at all-round professional development.

The following main forms of in-service training were provided between 1960 and 1968:

(a) One-week refresher courses at universities and colleges of further education. Between 1966 and 1968 there were ten such courses taken by 168 probation officers.
(b) Nine residential courses for student supervisors were taken by 217 officers.
(c) All senior probation officers took a one-week residential course during the first year of appointment.
(d) The Family Discussion Bureau course on matrimonial work was taken by eighty-nine officers between 1966 and 1968.
(e) When the probation service was to take over prison welfare, the Prison Service Staff College at Wakefield arranged three-week courses to give small groups of experienced probation officers an understanding of prison conditions and the problems of institutionalisation and resocialisation, especially for homeless prisoners without relatives or friends. By 1968 these courses had been taken by 116 officers.
    (*Reports on the Work of the Probation and After-Care Department*, 1962–5 and 1966–8.)
(f) A few principal and senior probation officers were regularly sponsored to take the three-week senior course in criminology at Cambridge University Institute of Criminology.

In the late 1960s the training committee of ACPAC reviewed provision of in-service training, especially for newly appointed officers and for experienced officers to keep up with new developments and extended duties.

It thought that this should primarily be the responsibility of local probation and after-care committees. It naturally found considerable variations in different parts of England and Wales and that close co-ordination would be necessary to provide training on a regional basis. It was thus decided to appoint four regional training officers from central funds to co-ordinate and develop training provision for serving officers in each region. Regional committees were established and the first appointments made in 1969. Later, numbers were increased. Their functions were to plan for the training needs of newly qualified officers and for regional in-service training courses for main-grade officers according to their particular needs. The aim for newly qualified officers was that in their first year they should have reduced caseloads, together with support, guidance and consultation to consolidate their training. There should be local group induction meetings, supplemented by regional residential courses, planned jointly by regional training officers, tutors to professional courses and senior probation officers. This would give past students a chance to look back at their training in the light of subsequent experience and tutors to hear their views. Similar opportunities were needed throughout the probation officers' first two years of service.

IN-SERVICE TRAINING FOR DIRECT ENTRANTS

The first general type of training for direct entrants started in 1959, mainly in the north, with a residential one-month course, followed by regular group meetings, a long residential weekend and a second residential month a year after the first. There were roughly two courses a year, each for thirty to thirty-five students. They were run with the help of four university extramural departments and a college of further education: Sheffield University helped with a course on a slightly different pattern. It was also necessary from time to time to run day release courses lasting about twelve months. These imposed a much greater strain on students. Direct entrants with a university qualification took the three-month theoretical part of the Rainer House course. An imaginative scheme was devised in 1960 for four consecutive groups of direct entrants appointed to meet the extreme shortage of staff in the London Probation Service. This gave them the equivalent of the Home Office one-year training spread out over their first two years of service.

The Morison Committee recommended that 'every effort should be made to release direct entrants for a full length training as this became possible' (para. 328). This was not implemented, indeed a direct entrant wishing to take a qualifying training had to resign from the service in order to do so. Ten years later the Butterworth Inquiry (1972) once more recommended that direct entrants should be seconded for professional training.

When the Central Council for Education and Training in Social Work came into existence in 1971 and took over probation training, the Home Office felt it no longer had the resources to continue to run courses for direct entrants. Over 1,000 had taken in-service training through Home Office courses since 1959. In 1973 direct entrants became the responsibility of the regional training officers but the following year, when these in turn were unable to continue this training, the Home Office passed on the responsibility to chief probation officers.

NEW IDEAS ABOUT PROBATION TRAINING IN RELATION TO SOCIAL SERVICES REORGANISATION

The Conference of Principal Probation Officers publication, *The Place of the Probation and After-Care Service in Judicial Administration* (1968) concluded that 'a broadly based pre-service professional qualification should occur [*sic*] in established educational centres alongside students committed to other social work disciplines' (p. 7). This should be followed by continuous in-service training.

'The provision of non-institutional treatment involves a range of methods which require of the probation officer the ability to use individual casework, to understand and make therapeutic use of groups, especially when providing support in institutional situations; to work with and within the community . . . Since most forms of social breakdown can be traced to similar general origins, the treatment of offenders, diagnosis, and matrimonial conciliation, require extensive knowledge in the field of sociology and individual and social psychology.' (p. 17)

In the same year NAPO published a *Statement on Training* (1968*b*). It pointed out that the Home Office one-year course, which still trained most probation officers, was different from other forms of social work training because it was not in a general educational institution, it consisted of separate periods of theory and practice, and the theoretical part was staffed by Home Office inspectors and outside lecturers. Close links between the course and fieldwork supervisors were impossible. On other courses, continuous and parallel theory and practice helped learning and probation officers knew how much they gained from the support of course tutors and other supervisors. Yet the Home Office course was training larger numbers than ever before, whereas courses in different parts of the country should be expanded so that the London course lost its key position, as indeed was Home Office policy. NAPO thought that training should be extended to two years, with a one-year course for 'a small and specially selected group' of people with substantial relevant experience. The statement (agreed before the Seebohm Report appeared) concluded that 'the existence of three major training councils is wasteful of resources and prevents any overall planning of social work training as a whole . . . The Association therefore favours the establishment of a new Social Work Training Council, independent of any government department and financed from public funds' (p. 6). In saying this, it foreshadowed the CCETSW which from 1971 unified all social work training. Probation training was assimilated by degrees, it became non-specialised though with special options, and probation students worked for the general certificate of qualification in social work (CQSW).

EXPANDED TRAINING FROM THE 1970S

By 1970 it was clear that the existing target output of 350 students a year for England and Wales would not meet projected new appointments and the envisaged rate of expansion in the probation and after-care service to carry out new duties, so the planned annual output was raised to 550. This resulted in an expansion of existing courses and plans for three 'emergency' one-year courses at Birmingham, Manchester and Newcastle upon Tyne Polytechnics (followed by a fourth course at Enfield College of Technology a year later) for candidates over 27 with some relevant experience. It was hoped that each course might take thirty to thirty-eight students, though there was a good deal of local concern about adequate fieldwork arrangements in areas which were already heavily overburdened. There was also disquiet about new one-year courses being started in polytechnics which already had two-year courses, and the lack of plans for continued learning and super-vision under the aegis of the course tutors in the first year of employment. The courses started in 1971. When the CCETSW assumed responsibility for all qualifying courses, planned supervision in the first year of employment and a periodic return for further study were introduced as part of the assess-ment for the award of the CQSW until these and other courses could be lengthened to two years. It was also planned that the London Training Centre (the Home Office course) should end when possible. By 1974 eighty-one courses recognised by the CCETSW were training probation students: they had places for 737 in 1973 against just over 600 in 1971. As pre-viously, students who had not taken a probation option were eligible to apply for probation appointments. But in 1975 probation committees were required to appoint probation students before recruiting from other sources.

When the training committee of ACPAC was about to come to an end it prepared a memorandum on those 'specialised features of probation train-ing' which should be taken into account if future courses were to produce social workers competent to enter the probation and after-care service. It was assumed that there would be various essential options for those intend-ing to enter 'one or other branches of the social work profession'. Fieldwork in a probation and after-care department, coupled with a 'short period' in a penal institution, were essential to provide direct experience and to give reality to academic discussion. These should be reinforced by comparative teaching about 'the various branches of social work', and here knowledge of the penal field was vital. While all students would presumably study family law, intending probation officers must also study their role in the administration of justice and criminal law and procedure. They also needed 'more than a superficial knowledge of the natural history of anti-social behaviour and of the theories which seek to explain its various forms', coupled with elements of forensic psychiatry. The CCETSW report on *Legal Studies in Social Work Education* (1974a) commented that much law essential for probation officers was also necessary for other social workers. But it was especially important for intending probation officers to study a wide range of legislation on sentencing and the treatment of offenders, on domestic proceedings, the principles of the criminal law, court procedure and various types of punishment.

A Probation Consultative Group to the CCETSW was set up to advise on the content of social work qualifying courses which made provision for Home Office sponsored probation students.

CONCLUSION

Basic training and an increasing range of in-service trainings were pioneered by the Home Office between 1936 and 1971. The foregoing account of developments needs to be appraised in conjunction with the steadily increasing range of responsibilities placed upon the probation and after-care service on the one hand, and on the other the limitations imposed by finance, training facilities, recruitment, staffing establishments and some local probation committees' lack of interest in training. This led to a mounting backlog of vacancies in the service, and consequent overwork. The situation was also bedevilled by the unexpected and persistent increase in crime from the mid-1950s. This service, like others, was chronically short staffed and there was constant pressure to train students as quickly as possible, but not to lower selection standards. By 1970 74·2 per cent of serving officers in England and Wales had had at least a one-year training as against 65·9 per cent in 1960. This was a much higher proportion than in other services. There were opposing views as to whether one-year courses purchased quantity at the expense of quality. Unfortunately recruitment efforts failed to attract enough university students to fill available places on applied social studies courses, though in time the situation improved on courses for 'non-relevant' graduates. Sociology students were said to be hostile to the control functions of the probation service.

In the circumstances, neither training nor conditions in the service matched new demands on probation officers for skilled psychosocial 'diagnosis' and 'treatment', not only of individual offenders but of families, groups, the social environment and the delinquent sub-culture, together with a wider and more differentially deployed range of treatment methods. Although the variety of in-service training courses and provision for staff development steadily expanded, this was not matched here, or elsewhere, by more demanding advanced courses, apart from a few places at the Institute of Criminology, the Tavistock Institute of Human Relations and two or three universities. None the less much learning undoubtedly took place through staff meetings and in discussions with the Home Office (including the Research Unit) and through NAPO, the Conference of Principal Probation Officers (from 1971 the Conference of Chief Probation Officers) and contacts with local universities.

It seemed clear that for the service to become increasingly effective and attractive as a career, probation officers should be able to gain a wide and well-informed view of related social problems and to specialise in particular aspects. There was consultant and specialist backing from the forensic sciences but too little from within the service itself, coupled with opportunities for advanced study and practice.

TRAINING TARGETS

A total of 562 probation students completed university applied social studies courses from 1965 to 1971. In spite of great efforts the total number of available training places of all kinds was not filled. Table 5 shows output and target figures.

Table 5   *Training output and targets, 1969–74*

	1969	*1970*	*1971*	*1972*	*1973*	*1974*
Output	325	265	341	427	482	468
Targets	350	350	350	550	550	600
				(630 places available)	(732 places available)	(737 places available)

PROBATION TRAINING IN SCOTLAND

In the 1950s untrained probation officers were appointed and sent to take a three-week course in Glasgow. This was obviously quite inadequate and in 1960, as a result of pressure from various quarters, the training became a one-year course. After a short independent existence, it was transferred to an educational institution, Jordanhill College of Education, and theory and practice ran concurrently. Local probation committees had to appoint from the national Probation Register and then lose the candidate for a year for training before he was actually at work. There was thus a strong incentive to pass all students at the end of the course; while an unexpected vacancy could only be filled by attracting a probation officer from another area. Under this system recruitment of candidates with a social science qualification was almost unknown. The mixed good and bad result was that 'all entrants to the Scottish probation service had a minimum of full-time professional training . . . but at the expense of opportunities for more prolonged training' (Morison Report, para. 328). Two hundred and seventy-three students completed this training between 1961 and 1970.

The Morison Committee recommended that pre- and post-entry training should run alongside each other, until a two-year, pre-entry training could supersede the existing pattern. This only finally happened in the 1970s after probation officers had become part of the social work departments. The Scottish Home Department arranged sufficient one-week refresher courses for every probation officer to take one every three years.

Chapter 9

Medical Social Work in Hospital, General Practice and the Community: Training for Medical Social Work

MEDICAL SOCIAL WORK IN THE 1950s

A leading article in *The Times* (13 May 1951) suggested that, with the coming into being of the National Health Service, the hospital almoner was finally free to discard her preoccupation with preventing financial abuse of the voluntary system and to devote herself to the medical social work for which her training had fitted her: 'This was to study the patient's background and his reactions to illness with a view to assisting in the many personal and practical problems which are associated with illness.' This entailed close co-operation with doctors and, in the acute shortage of almoners, the article suggested that priority should be given to those departments where the medical staff really wanted medical social work for their patients and were willing to co-operate. Actually, almoners had been responsible since 1920 for assessing patients' capacity to pay, rather than 'preventing financial abuse', but this meant that they were often looked upon as collectors of fees rather than social workers.

The Cope Committees on Medical Auxiliaries, reporting in 1951, reiterated that 'the work of the almoner should be regarded as one of the essential elements of a complete hospital service, and indeed of a complete health service' (para. 115). The Report analysed the extreme imbalance between supply and demand, and concluded that recruitment was being affected by poor salary and promotion prospects and lack of regular grants for students. It did not even consider the radical proposal that almoners should only be available to those hospital departments prepared to make proper use of them. But it pointed to the wasteful use of almoners' time: '. . . for instance she might be required to register patients on their first attendance at hospital, to give out and file medical notes, to organise appointments for clinics, to arrange for motors and ambulances, all of which could well be done by a clerk' (para. 126).

In a spirited minority report several of the so-called 'medical auxiliaries' surveyed by the Cope Committees pointed out that some recommendations were

'. . . based on the assumption that doctors can, by virtue of their medical training and experience, satisfactorily plan and control the curricula of training and methods of work of the professions under review. From our experience this is not in accordance with the facts. We agree that members of our professions must work closely with the other specialists in the team treating the patient, of which team the doctor is the undisputed leader. This, however, presupposes a very different basis of association from that which the report assumes. Almoners, being primarily social workers, bring into the health services knowledge and experience learned in the social science departments of universities and in fields of social service other than health.' (para. 583)

The Institute of Almoners refused to accept the plums offered by the Report – recognition of training and registration – as medical auxiliaries. In 1953 the Ministry of Health indicated that almoners would not again be so classified or registered. This was a stage in the long battle by medical social workers to establish themselves as part of an independent profession rather than auxiliaries to another profession. Kelly (1961) said of this period:

'Many of the older generation must remember the constant and speedy interviews accompanied by rapid notes of relevant social factors which somehow served both administrative and social purposes. Often hospitals required us to see every in-patient, sometimes every out-patient too, . . . while at the same time remembering her main function as a social worker and assessing whether the patient was in need of social help. It is a . . . tribute to the older generation, that they did do extremely valuable social work despite administrative pressures . . . what they did, . . . they did through the strength of their own personalities. Their warmth and genuine desire to help overcame enormous obstacles and many of them had an almost uncanny knack of spotting where help was needed and seeing that it was given. We did not talk about the use of a professional relationship in those days, but such relationships were made and used helpfully though . . . usually superficially.' (p. 349)

During the 1950s the Institute of Almoners continued to struggle with the Ministry of Health over erratic and inadequate grants for student training and to negotiate with universities to start medical social work or applied social studies courses. It was hamstrung in urging new hospitals to start departments by the shortage of almoners, but it tried to clarify with hospital management committees the appropriate functions and status of almoner (or social service) departments.

In order to discover what changes had taken place since the National Health Service, the Institute set up a committee in 1951 to inquire into almoners' duties in hospital social service departments and to make recommendations. It conducted a national survey by questionnaire, with 311 completed returns out of 413. The survey report (Institute of Almoners, 1953) showed that almoners were still responsible for many small administrative duties in a number of departments. The Institute recommended that they should not undertake the supply of appliances or arrangements for transport. It was intrinsically desirable that they should interview all in-patients and take social histories for the medical staff but shortages made this impossible. Only 8½ per cent of the almoners surveyed saw all new out-patients, but particular clinics, for example for maternity cases, were more generally covered. In nearly half the departments all in-patients were seen; in the rest they were referred by the medical staff or seen after discussion with the ward sister. The report concluded that there should be careful selection of work rather than routine interviews: to see all in-patients was extremely time-consuming in relation to the amount of social work discovered and could leave no time for casework with those who needed it. Doctors should be responsible for deciding what almoner service was needed and almoners should only do referred work, except in special circumstances.

'The almoner is essentially the medical social worker whose job it is to study the patient's social background and his reactions to illness, with a view to assisting in the solution of the many personal and practical problems which are associated with illness. The fullest use of her skill is made when she is giving help to patients where the doctor believes their anxieties or personal difficulties are closely associated with the illness for which the patient is being treated. Problems which require listening, helping the patient to sort out worrying situations, to face the future and possible readjustments to his life or the limitations of his disability can only be dealt with by the medical social worker.' (ibid, p. 66)

The 'only' is probably intended as a statement of primary function rather than a denial of the help given to patients by some doctors and nurses; though the assumption that the medical staff would identify anxieties and personal difficulties was not borne out by later studies.

The almoner, said the report, will also be required to arrange for a wide variety of practical forms of help for patients. Ideally almoners should conduct the initial interview but owing to staff shortages some could only be dealt with on a superficial level by less well-qualified workers, i.e. clerical workers of good calibre working in the department. There should be a clear assessment of those tasks which required the almoner's personal attention and those which could be carried out by clerical staff. There was no suggestion that clerks needed in-service training for what was obviously not a purely clerical task. Later, the Manchester Regional Hospital Board and the University started an in-service training scheme for hospital welfare workers (see chapter 22, section on 'Social Work Assistants').

This survey was an attempt to get departmental priorities right and allow time for casework. It had a considerable influence in helping almoners all over the country to sort out their departments and get rid of unnecessary duties. Its recommendations were backed by the Ministry of Health. There was much heartburning at the time about the need for referral, selection of patients and how initial decisions about referral were made.

In 1952 the Ministry actually discontinued its subsidy to the Institute of Almoners (it was reinstituted in the following year), with the result that students' fees had to be increased and a number were lost to training. In that year 87 almoners qualified, the smallest number for years, yet there were 250 advertised posts (of which 54 were new). It seems even more shocking in retrospect than it did at the time that a professional association should have been expected to provide from its present and future members' subscriptions or fees much of the cost of training for a public service, which in any event paid notoriously low salaries. These salary scales were confined to almoners on the Institute's register, which was no doubt an incentive to train.

The Institute in its *Annual Report 1956–57* recorded 'the most important change in the last ten years' as a demand for medical social workers from doctors prepared to co-operate with a social casework service, contrasted with those who wanted the beds cleared quickly.

The whole question of the most effective setting for medical social work was also being discussed more generally as a result of the quick turnover of hospital beds, the obvious need for 'pre-care' and after-care and support for patients' families. But by the mid-1950s there were only seventy almoners employed in local authority health and welfare departments, nearly half of them for the considerable personal and social problems arising from TB. There were only two in local authorities in Scotland and one in Wales. There had been an almoner at the General Practice Teaching Unit in Edinburgh since 1949. There was also an almoner at the Darbishire House Health Centre in Manchester, appointed to help with the social problems which arise in general practice. These remained isolated pioneer projects until a few more followed in the 1960s. Social work in general practice is discussed below.

THE 1960s

The Institute's *Annual Report 1963–64*, when it changed its title to the Institute of Medical Social Workers (IMSW), commented that

'. . . the retention of this out-of-date title creates an artificial barrier between almoners (medical social workers) and the wider field of social work to which they belong by virtue of their training as well as by the nature, aims and methods of their work. The general emphasis now, borne out by training trends and by the recommendations of the Younghusband Report, is that all social workers are first and foremost members of the profession of social work with a corporate body of knowledge and experience. Only secondarily are they subdivided according to their specialised fields of work such as psychiatric social work, child care, probation or medical social work.' (p. 5)

During the 1960s the Institute was active in promoting a unified social work professional association, through regional and national joint activities with other social work associations and university social work staffs (see also volume 2, chapter 12).

For several years its annual reports drew attention to the heavy marriage wastage of women social workers since men were not attracted to medical social work on account of the low salaries. Indeed, throughout the period the annual reports complain of struggles to increase inadequate salaries and to try to get them onto the same basis as local authority scales. There was much dissatisfaction with the new salaries awarded in 1966, which gave inadequate immediate pay increases for people with long service. The following year a new scale considerably improved career prospects and from 1970 new entrants received a salary comparable to those paid to local authority social workers with similar qualifications, though nothing was done to improve the position of experienced workers.

Three significant studies, *The First Two Years* (Moon, 1965), *Medical Social Work in Action* (Butrym, 1968), and 'The Social Needs of the Physically Sick' (Carter, 1976) cast light cn the use of medical social work in hospitals, its limitations and the directions of necessary change.

In order to clarify the nature of the task in medical social work, the IMSW undertook an inquiry into what actually happened to newly qualified workers in the first two years. The survey covered seventy-six MSWs who had qualified in 1961–2. The majority had suffered shock from the impact of the hospital setting itself. In their view the training had not prepared them for the realities of everyday life for a social worker in hospital, and supervisors and tutors had protected them from the impact of the hospital setting. Casework classes and teaching about human growth and development had been interesting, but settings classes were either forgotten or remembered as being very dull, except for one course on social administration in which hospitals were compared with other organisations, illustrated by case discussions on administration, which had helped them to see the effect on social work of the framework in which it was practised.

Most felt that their training had contained 'too much teaching about human problems and ways of helping through case-work, whereas the place of social work in hospitals, and collaboration with medical and nursing staff remained, as one put it, "like a vast uncharted sea on which we must embark without equipment – not knowing where we are going – or how to get there" ' (*The First Two Years*, p. 52).

They all thought that to work satisfactorily it was essential to come to terms with the hospital setting. This meant recognising the limitations of and the scope for social work in institutions which do not make a consistent demand for it and where constantly rushed and often inaccessible staff might well be ignorant about or not interested in social work. There were different attitudes in different units, for instance MSWs in ten out of seventeen orthopaedic units felt they were part of the team and in two out of four dermatology units. On several other units the majority of referrals came from consultants who asked MSWs to investigate social situations or arrange social services, and recognised that they had skills in helping patients with various problems related to medical care, for example they were often expected to help patients whose state of mind was affecting their treatment. It was more satisfactory if the consultant himself first talked to the patient about attitudes and feelings affecting treatment and how the MSW could help with these. If a consultant made a request for services to be arranged, these requests carried with them the same authority as one for a drug or appliance, i.e. they personally prescribed certain social services, and were irritated if the prescription were questioned or slowly carried out.

Unless there had already been social planning about discharge, MSWs were often regarded by consultants as slow and unhelpful when they were asked to make urgent discharge plans for patients whose emotional state and domestic background had deteriorated or changed since admission, even though their medical condition had improved satisfactorily.

There was often close co-operation between consultants and sisters with the result that between them they had a variety of ways of helping patients with their feelings. MSWs' attempts at this were usually not recognised and occasionally strongly disapproved of. In some situations there was close co-operation with and referrals from ward sisters. This could be a lively and challenging professional relationship but there was a danger of sisters being possessive about patients. They sometimes challenged the aims and methods of social work and there were often rivalry situations.

Many of the MSWs interviewed found that they had lost sight of their casework training and not increased their skills, though those who had supervision in their first jobs were better able to integrate training with their work. They often found themselves in buffer positions in which they were ignorant of the social services, though they had a responsibility in the department to act as a co-ordinator. Training had not prepared them for this so it was liable to seem a chore rather than a major part of their function. This made them feel anxious and appear inefficient so that they frequently felt they were not doing enough and that as a result of anxiety to fit in they would lose sight of their proper role. Most said that they were spending a good deal of time on work which a clerk could do. Some thought their discussions with tutors and supervisors during training had reduced their confidence, making them feel 'enveloped in clouds of feeling' but not helping them to recognise their role more clearly or to be more practical. Some experienced a constant burden of doubt and worry as to whether they were doing all they could to ensure that the medical and nursing staff made better use of social work. They did not want to become too passive or ingratiating or too inclined to accept the *status quo*.

This study demonstrated typical reactions of most newly qualified workers to the strains, frustrations and uncertainties which face them; especially if they have been prepared for a task which differs from the way it is perceived by more powerful professions in the setting. It reaffirmed by implication that in much medical practice concern with the effect on people of the crisis situations of illness is not central to treatment. At the same time, those consultants and sisters who were aware of the effect of the patients' feelings might regard the MSW as an intruder rather than a colleague. These were familiar dilemmas of interdisciplinary co-operation. They were also related to the network of communications in the highly complex organisation and hierarchial structure of hospitals.

The study also showed the imbalance of one-year courses which emphasised 'exploration of feelings' and 'use of a relationship', but included too little knowledge of the social services and good after-care planning as essential elements of practice, and did not stress an intelligent understanding of and ability to work in administrative situations. Indeed it appeared that MSWs were being equipped to work with individual patients, to some extent in isolation from the setting, but not to understand different roles and role conflicts, the hospital as a social system, and within this their own contribution to it in terms of human relations.

This study naturally led to lively discussions within and outside medical social work circles. Conclusions drawn from it were that most newly qualified workers required much support in their first two years of practice to consolidate skill and to appreciate the wider application of their particular expertise, to learn to communicate with colleagues in related professions, and to operate effectively at an organisational as well as an individual level in a particular setting. Newton (1966) commented: 'It is clear that the newly trained medical social workers find difficulty because they seem to have a rather narrow and somewhat perfectionist view of themselves as long term caseworkers and do not have the broader perspective of social work as a general enabling profession with a high degree of casework skill as one of its professional tools' (p. 14). This was but one example of the growing pains of social work in this period.

As a result of these discussions, IMSW students went to social administration classes at the LSE; while the help for newly qualified MSWs which had existed for years in some hospitals was more widely extended. If medical social workers needed to re-think their role and function, it was also obvious that changes were required in the perceptions of medical and nursing staff. It was often said that these tended to defend themselves from the impact of human suffering by concentrating on the physical aspects of treatment and were more impressed by the remarkable advances in the sciences allied to medicine, than by the unproven assumptions of the behavioural sciences. None the less many members of the medical profession were conscious that in actual treatment and in the whole milieu of the hospital, account must be taken of the social, emotional and economic accompaniments of illness. A future role for MSWs might be not only to help individual patients and their families, but also the medical and nursing staff and the hospital administration so far as these other aspects of illness were concerned.

Butrym (1968) undertook a small study of the content of medical social work practice in a London teaching hospital. The results showed that many referrals were for straightforward services and she herself calculated from an analysis of records that about half the patients referred did not require the knowledge and skill of a trained medical social worker, though in some instances considerable knowledge of community resources and competence in their use was necessary. Over two-thirds of cases lasted under a month, and over 70 per cent entailed from one to seven interviews. This compared with an average of under six interviews revealed in the later York University study of eight hospitals (see below). An attempt to evaluate the work, both quantitively and qualitively, was fraught with difficulty because of the lack of agreed criteria for judgement, which inevitably resulted in subjective assessment, while, 'the system of recording failed in many instances to provide even the basic data from which deductions concerning the nature of social work activity . . . could be made' (p. 49). This was compounded by the failure to distinguish between routine cases and work which demanded full use of professional skill. The lack of agreed criteria for analysing the content of social work also affected attempts to arrive at reasonable workload figures. This was further obscured by the different policies of individual MSWs about carrying forward or closing inactive cases.

This study reinforced other evidence about patients' difficulties in communicating with medical and nursing staff, resulting from the inadequate training of doctors and nurses about emotional and social factors in illness. This raised the question of what care functions, especially related to reduction of stress and anxiety, should be assumed by staff directly responsible for patients and in what circumstances social work help was more appropriate. The study also suggested that many patients were not being referred for social work help who needed it, while MSWs were overburdened with routine cases suitable for welfare assistants. This particular hospital was atypical in that it did not employ these, which resulted in MSWs being overloaded with routine work and having little time to help patients with their problems and anxieties. The eleven doctors and eleven ward sisters interviewed valued medical social work, thought patients' social needs were important, and were doubtful about their own ability to identify and refer the right patients. 'Only the medical social workers themselves could remedy the position by making themselves accessible to these patients' (p. 98). This was the familiar dilemma of who is equipped to spot a need for social work.

The Seebohm Committee (1968) said:

'A more fundamental source of difference between medicine as a whole and social work lies in particular contrasting developments in the two professions . . . social workers are of course concerned with practical measures. They also set store by skills that could help patients better to understand their situation and the adjustments that may be needed, and in the professional training of social workers much importance is attached to the acquiring of personal insight and understanding. Medicine is ever refining its objectivity and technology, which increasingly are the basis of its authority and of the responsibility that it takes on behalf of the patient and society. In relation to their joint concerns, these two approaches are as different as they are obviously complementary: they are needed often by the same patient and at the same time. Yet, while medical education has emphasised the primacy of clinical and laboratory science, in the past this has rarely been balanced by study of the emotional aspects of illness and of the relationships between sick people and those around them. Nor have the social components in precipitating illness, and in prognosis, had anything like adequate attention. The result often has been that doctors are ill-trained themselves to deal with the psychological and social factors in the management of illness and the prevention of chronic disability and dependency: nor do they know how to get help from social agencies and to collaborate with social workers – who have *their* contribution to make and a professional responsibility to do so. That doctors do not recognise this responsibility is at the root of many difficulties . . . Another factor in poor collaboration is the common assumption that the doctor must be leader in any team of which he is a member . . . On the other hand . . . many social workers need to learn far more about the doctor's job and what is happening in medicine today. Furthermore, what appears to doctors to be a lack of interest of many workers in the social services, and even among the academics, in evaluating the results of their work is a recurrent irritant.' (para. 694)

The impending reorganisation of both the NHS and the personal social services raised afresh the issue of the maldistribution of MSWs, whether geographically or between hospitals, for example teaching hospitals or hospitals for the chronic sick, or even between different medical specialities. There were still great inadequacies in continuity of service for patients and their families before they went into hospital, while they were there, and particularly after discharge.

Largely on the initiative of the IMSW, the DHSS agreed in 1968 to finance a four-year research study at York University into the social needs of the physically sick and the role of MSWs (Carter, 1976). Replies to a questionnaire on the deployment of MSWs showed that in September 1969, 954 of the respondents were in hospital and 123 in local authority health and welfare departments, the majority in the south. Nearly 80 per cent of local authorities employed no MSWs. In addition to the MSWs, the other hospital social workers were: 49 with the CSW (only 4 per cent of all CSW holders), 231 with a social science qualification, and 375 unqualified. The ratio of hospital beds to MSWs varied from 225 in the N. W. Metropolitan Region (76 in a London graduate teaching hospital) to 1,156 in the Welsh Region. Thus even in the most favourable circumstances the Institute of Almoners' 1949 working party target of 1 almoner to 75 beds in general and teaching hospitals, and 1 to 300 beds in hospitals for the chronic sick was very far short of achievement twenty years later (see also chapter 20, section on 'Almoners'). There were 43,000 beds in hospitals with no MSW. Conversely, 'In one county in which 218 social workers are employed 75 (34 per cent) work in hospitals . . . It is questionable whether such a situation represents a rational distribution of resources in response to needs' (Carter, 1971*b*, p. 6).

Until 1970 CSW holders were not intended to take senior posts. Replies to the study questionnaire showed that they were commonly regarded as professionally qualified. Of 271 respondents who were unqualified social workers, (47 per cent of the total non-teaching hospital social work staff) only 148 were responsible to an MSW, while 83 were in charge of the social work department. No one questioned their contribution as such, but to have no systematic in-service training and to be in unsupported charge of a department was another story.

Analysis of referrals to total admissions in the eight hospitals showed that only just over 11 per cent of patients had direct contacts with social workers and then usually for less than six interviews. The number of patients referred varied from 5 per cent to 16 per cent of total admissions. During the study 455 patients in four hospitals were interviewed in hospital and subsequently at home to assess their needs and whether these were met. Nearly half reported serious problems, but of these only 18 per cent saw an MSW. The commonest causes of worry were about the illness, money, arrangements at home on discharge, employment and dependent children. Only 30 per cent of all worries were discussed with the hospital staff and 34 per cent of patients with serious worries were thought by nurses to have none.

There was close agreement between doctors' and nurses' assessments. Patients reported much support from friends and relatives but the least-visited patients had most worries. The typical patient with worries, i.e. most at risk, was likely to have been in hospital for over a month, to have had previous difficulties, to have been admitted to a medical ward and to have comparatively few community supports. Neither patients nor doctors and nurses expected that personal worries would be discussed. A general score composed of several factors showed that 10 per cent of patients had many worries and had made a poor adjustment.

Interviews in the same study with doctors and nurses about the MSW's most appropriate functions showed that these were primarily thought of in material terms, especially related to discharge, and only about a quarter suggested assessment of a situation or relief of stress. They were strikingly unaware of casework functions related to patients' anxieties and adjustment as seen by MSWs. 'They aren't doing practical things, sorting out forms and things like that. They act more as amateur psychiatrists' (Carter, 1976).

In teaching hospitals, where many more social workers were employed, there was no significant difference in the number of problems detected and referred. None the less excellent team work sometimes existed, and this and the Butrym study showed a good deal of mutual respect between social workers and other staff. Neither study sufficiently analysed these satisfactory situations and the reasons for them.

Of the discharged patients interviewed, all but a small minority thought they had been discharged at about the right time. Forty-six per cent reported severe or medium worries. Of these only a minority had seen an MSW at any point and few had any form of social work support after discharge.

Common findings in the three MSW studies were that:

(a) medical social work cannot be effectively exercised where professional co-operation is not institutionalised and referrals are a hit or miss affair;
(b) provision of practical services is an important function of a social work service which could largely be undertaken by welfare assistants under supervision; and
(c) if caring and treatment functions were combined in the medical staff it should be more possible to detect problems requiring skilled psycho-social help by social workers, who should become consultants in the social sphere.

Social work was moving towards better understanding of the impact of large institutions on people and the part that social workers might play in humanising the hospital as an organisation, for instance by studying the quality of the patients' day, especially in long-term hospitalisation (Hall-burton and Wright, 1974, pp. 107–8).

For many years MSWs had struggled to achieve competence and recognition that would enable them to make their independent professional judgements as colleagues not subordinates of doctors. This was particularly difficult to achieve in the hospital setting where everyone else in greater or lesser degree took orders from the medical profession: and when in any event something as intangible as casework was difficult either to describe or demonstrate in contrast to mobilising material help or services. The independent judgement of some MSWs was accepted by some consultants on account of their obvious ability; while the Moon and Butrym studies showed that a significant minority of doctors appreciated the distinct professional contribution of MSWs. But this was not general. Problems of effective referral remained unsolved, while medical social work was a peripheral service in hospitals and MSWs (who did not normally visit outside the hospital) could do little to lessen the isolation of the hospital from community resources. There were also unsolved questions as to whether hospital MSWs should only be concerned with personal and social problems directly related to the illness – and where the line could be drawn, for instance in connection with disturbed family relationships or unsatisfactory living conditions. Many thought the logical solution was to locate hospital social work in the new social services departments.

THE LAST STAGE BEFORE REORGANISATION

The IMSW welcomed the suggestion in the second Green Paper on the NHS (DHSS, 1970*b*) that the social work staff of hospitals might transfer to the local authorities and be made available to hospitals and the community health services. This would make it possible to provide a single social work service for ill people, with continuity of care and an improvement in the links between hospital and community services. Questions about the proposal were included in the York University survey, since there was resistance amongst some MSWs to transferring to local authority service. The replies showed that 84 per cent of the 917 respondents were satisfied with their present posts. This contrasts strongly with the findings of *The First Two Years*, which perhaps demonstrated the difficulties of initial adjustment to a complex professional role rather than the feelings of MSWs as a whole. Fifty-five per cent of the respondents were favourable to the idea of local authority employment and 29 per cent unfavourable. If they were transferred, 61 per cent would want to spend all or most of their time in hospital. Their views were also dependent upon the professional standing of the projected social services departments. 'Having battled to establish professional identity, perhaps with only moderate success, in a highly professional clinical setting, MSWs have no desire to fight a similar battle in a "lay" setting' (Carter, 1971*a*, p. 266).

Responses by community-based MSWs stressed the advantages of being able to see a case through, to work with the whole family and with a wider range of colleagues. Transfer to the local authorities would not necessarily solve the perpetual problem of patient discharge against the advice of MSWs, although the new social services departments would be responsible for providing some of the conspicuously lacking continuity of care. This would include social work with the patient and his family at the time of diagnosis, before he went into hospital, while he was there and after he came home, aimed to give help in the personal and family crises that result from illness or surgery and often lead to severe psychological stress. It would also facilitate co-operation with general practitioners.

It was argued that long-term, full-time secondment of MSWs would allow them to become accepted as part of the hospital; while, instead of merely acting as go betweens, their base in the social services department would give them greater independence and enable them to be more effective because they were members of the department which provided community resources. The transfer might also clarify for both hospitals and social services departments the range of supporting services or intermediate care needed to facilitate quick discharge from hospital. Whether MSWs seconded to hospitals would be in a better or worse position to contribute to 'humanising' hospitals as such and helping patients with their personal and family anxieties and fears remained an open question. The IMSW in its final annual report (1968–9) said:

'The fundamental issue facing medical social workers at the present time is whether they are to remain in the employment of hospitals or whether they are to enter the new social service departments which everyone wishes to see created. All medical social workers are anxious that hospital social work should be extended not curtailed. We need good departments able to cater properly for the needs of patients and able to contribute to teaching in all hospitals and not only in the limited number fortunate to have such a service at the present time. The real disagreement within the profession is whether this aim would be better achieved if the Local Authorities had a responsibility to provide the social service in the hospitals or whether maintaining the present position would be likely to get a better recognition for hospital priorities. There is undoubtedly a very sincere difference of opinion within the profession on this issue but at the end of the year under review it seemed likely that the majority of the profession would accept that the right solution was for medical social workers to be part of the Local Authority Department and seconded in sufficient numbers to ensure a reasonable service to the hospitals. The Department of Health's views on this issue were eagerly awaited.' (p. 6)

Later, a number of MSWs swung away from this policy, preferring that area health authorities should have their own social workers. But in spite of sharp differences of opinion, in 1972 the BASW Council affirmed its support for the transfer.

In 1971 the decision to transfer social work in hospitals to the social services departments was announced and the transfer took place in 1974 (1975 in Scotland). There were a few experiments by mutual agreement earlier (notably in Southampton and Coventry) so that some useful experience was gained. Many MSWs remained in hospitals on long-term secondment, but as members of social services area teams.

Thus came to an end a stage of medical social work history from 1948. In those years MSWs struggled valiantly with limited resources and inadequate support, but unfailing commitment to the patients' social well-being, to develop good practice in partnership with doctors and nurses.

SOCIAL WORK IN GENERAL PRACTICE

Individual general practitioners often worked closely with mental welfare officers in relation to psychiatric patients. But many found the fragmented personal social services a confusing jungle. In any event, to refer particular patients for services which the doctor had identified as necessary was different from a partnership in social aspects of the medical diagnosis and treatment. It was well known that many patients went to their general practitioners suffering from social or psychological problems and a few pioneer studies explored the advantages and pitfalls of attaching social workers to general practice teams, notably Paterson (1949), Dongray (1958), Collins (1965), and Forman and Fairbairn (1968).

The advantages were reinforced by the Seebohm Report (1968):

'Survey after survey has shown that many family doctors do not seek help from social workers nor use social services that are available: they often do not know about them, or do not understand or value them. Yet the family doctor is concerned with much of the serious psychiatric disorder, functional illness, and family failure in the community, and a large part of his effort is devoted to the long term care of the chronic sick and handicapped and their families. Moreover, much of the work of the social service department will "present" only in the setting of family practice (for example with maladjusted children), and many social problems (e.g. marital difficulties) may best be treatable there. Realistic attempts at prevention in the social field, whether in detecting early trouble or intervening at times of crisis like bereavement, will often have to be based on family practice and organised as a joint effort of doctors and social workers. General practice today is in touch with a higher proportion of those who are in difficulties than any other of the social services and it needs the full support of them all.' (para. 692)

There were more attachments late in the 1960s resulting from DHSS grants for a few experimental projects and part-time attachments of social workers from local authority health departments. The study of *Social Work in Scotland* (1969) (Department of Social Administration, University of Edinburgh) suggested that 'about 10% of all hospital and general practitioner patients seemed to need support or action by social work services and that a large proportion of such patients went to their family doctors with a variety of complaints' (p. 66).

The attachment requested by the Caversham (London) general practice team and financed by a foundation grant became a five-year action research project undertaken by the National Institute for Social Work. Its findings (Goldberg and Neill, 1972) showed that a general practice is an acceptable place to which people go and therefore a good early identification and pick-up point for psychosocial problems. The social worker's clientele was evenly distributed across all social classes, although the professional classes more often wanted to discuss family problems. Possibly the image of social work as a service for social failures and the deprived, deterred middle-class people from seeking help if this was only available in social agencies.

There were various situations in which patients could more effectively receive social work help in the practice than being referred elsewhere. Significantly, the number of self-referrals increased rapidly until by the final period these were the largest single source of referral. Problems included crises caused by illness, especially terminal illness, bereavement, anxiety about retirement, early marital difficulties and adolescent problems, and by chronically physically or mentally ill patients and others with persistent personality problems who were often carried in this, as in other practices. The project revealed a number of gaps in services, even in one of the most progressive local authorities in the country, particularly for the chronically sick and mentally disordered. When the research project came to an end a local authority social worker was attached part-time to the practice.

Subsequently, an increasing number of social services departments began to establish systems of social work support for general practices in health centres. But the coverage was still very thin by the mid-1970s. A discussion paper (Ratoff *et al.*, 1974) prepared for the British Association of Social Workers (BASW) and the Royal College of General Practitioners Standing Joint Liaison Committee explored the differences and conflicts in assumptions, views about roles, working situations, authority, accountability and confidentiality which often resulted in a poor relationship between GPs and social workers. Each had a limited understanding of the other's basis of knowledge, working methods and concern with different aspects of human functioning. This led to mutual frustration through attempts to communicate without a common frame of reference. Social workers were ill-equipped to understand medical diagnoses and GPs might concentrate on physical malfunction to the neglect of psychological and social aspects. But this was changing so far as new generations of doctors were concerned. Another source of conflict arose because doctors were expected to arrive quickly at diagnoses and treatment, whereas social workers wanted first to understand a person and his situation. An increase in interdisciplinary seminars and teaching and discussion groups was desirable. The discussion paper also foresaw an expansion of the few social work student placements in general practice teams, and the development of teaching general practices with field placements where social work, medical, nursing and health visitor students would meet and learn together.

HEALTH SOCIAL WORKERS AND HEALTH SERVICE REORGANISATION

The report of the DHSS working party on *Social Work Support for the Health Service* (1974*f*) explored means by which local authority social services departments and area health authorities could forge an effective partnership. It was significant of a changed world that the report referred to social workers rather than MSWs, PSWs, MWOs and SWOs. Although it is discussed in this chapter, it applied equally to hospital PSWs. It affirmed that 'the health service will continue to need the support of social workers with specialised skills in working alongside health service staff in health settings. There must be no question of these skills being dissipated or devalued in the future' (para. 14).

It clearly recognised the difficulties of effective working between two professions and two massive and complex systems, but thought these difficulties could be reduced by sound organisation and by an understanding of the tensions to which each was subject, though 'in the end effective partnership in the care of patients rests on personal understanding and co-operation by individual doctors, nurses and social workers . . . We therefore regard good communication between health and social services as the single most important feature for bringing the two services into partnership' (paras 15 and 89). This was very different from casual and infrequent contact between doctors and a changing number of different social workers. 'The future development of social work support for the health service should build on this pattern of teamwork and seek to extend it to areas where it does not exist' (para. 19).

A BASW statement quoted in the report said of social work in hospital

'Many [patients] need help to tackle the social and emotional problems which complicate ill-health and its treatment, which can affect the sick person at any stage of his illness. They may contribute to the causation of disease or arise from it. Anxiety concerning personal problems may impel a patient to postpone or refuse treatment or may retard progress towards recovering. The illness or admission to hospital of one member impinges on the whole of his family. Social work support may be needed equally for the patient and for his family.' (para. 25)

'Medical social work is a professional service based on the understanding of the psycho-social implications of illness and handicap. All patients who face the problems of physical helplessness, deformity and mutilation, incurable progressive illness and death, experience anxiety, fear, loss and grief. Awareness of the emotional responses to characteristic problems of illness, of handicap and of medical care, and ability to remain in close relationship no matter how distressing the situation, are the particular attributes of medical social workers. They have a responsibility to know and understand the medical situation and the implications of this for the patient and his family, the problems it presents for them and the potential stresses it brings. Medical social work can be preventive in help given with foresight of the probable social consequences for the patient and his family, including mobilising practical resources and services on his behalf.' (para. 113)

The working party described the contribution of social work to the hospital clinical team from the angles of diagnosis, treatment, discharge and after-care.

The importance of general practice as a key pick-up point for social work and identification of severe social problems was at last fully recognised in this report. The working party, while aware of the shortage of qualified social workers and the many pressures on directors of social services made 'a strong plea that experimentation in the field of social work and primarily health care should receive urgent consideration by the professions and by the health and local authorities' (para. 44).

The working party's analysis of teamwork bears quoting because it represents enlightened thinking in the 1970s about interdisciplinary teams:

'We suggest that teamwork in a clinical situation means that all members of the team accept that each has a professional contribution to make in his own right; and that it is both the right and, equally, the responsibility of each member of the team to make that contribution if the patient needs it. Such a responsibility derives not from the prescription of the head of the team, but from the right of the patient to have the benefit of all the team's skills as he needs them. We believe that if these principles of teamwork are accepted then doctors, nurses and social workers will find it much easier to work together as partners than has sometimes been the case. In particular, the social worker will not feel that his access to the patient is contingent upon the direction of any other professional in the team (e.g. the doctor or the ward sister), but derives from his responsibility to the patient to make available the skills that he needs . . . it is inherent in the idea of partnership between professions that none can prescribe to others in matters which lie within those others' professional competence. However senior a doctor and however junior a social worker (and the balance will not always be this way round) the relationship requires an acceptance that ultimately each professional is the best judge of what it is right for him to do and the way in which he does it.' (paras 33 and 34)

This was a far cry from the Cope Committees' assumption of medical supremacy over auxiliaries.

The working party seems to have found the professional issues less daunting than the organisational problems of ensuring the vital continuity of care when local authority area teams were geographically based, while hospitals took patients from wide and loosely defined catchment areas.

Each local authority social services department appointed a senior social worker near the top of the ladder, responsible for arranging social work for the area health authority. And each area health authority appointed a specialist in community medicine and a nurse responsible for arranging health service support for the local authority. These were responsible for planning health services for the elderly, the physically handicapped and the mentally ill or handicapped, and had various important liaison functions with the social services department. The local deployment of social workers was intended to make experience and knowledge available to the health authority, and to ensure that inexperienced social workers should learn under skilled professional supervision about the needs of patients and their families.

Social workers could continue to specialise in hospital work by full-time secondment if they so wished. But social work in the health service was integrated with the rest of the local authority social services. It had been the practice in hospitals for senior and principal social workers to carry caseloads, it was hoped this would continue. Social workers in hospitals (as in schools or prisons) would have to learn to maintain administrative accountability inside the institution and professional accountability outside it, the key problem of agency services in a secondary setting. In general, the skill and knowledge needed in the health service were general to social work but with special emphasis on 'the impact and consequences of illness and handicap for the patient and his family . . . study of the hospital as an institution and its relations with other services and . . . the roles and responsibilities of other professional workers' (para. 138).

This seems to expand in greater detail Sir Charles Loch's comment to the Hospital Almoners Association in 1906 that 'When the proposal to appoint Almoners was first made it was advocated on . . . grounds . . . that the patients would be altogether better dealt with – the home and the patient and the means of helping thoroughly – all being taken into account' (Snelling, 1970).

Not surprisingly, after the transition, in which different local authorities developed different systems, there was a range of reactions by health social workers from satisfaction to difficulties in understanding local authority practices, coupled with a feeling that the quality of service was suffering. There was also concern about inter-agency rivalries. None the less the chance existed for social work in health care to assume a far more comprehensive role than ever before.

TRAINING FOR MEDICAL SOCIAL WORK

Much of the history of training for medical social work was part of the change in university professional courses (see volume 2, chapter 1). In the 1950s the Institute of Almoners was the largest professional social work training body in the country and it struggled manfully for the improvement of social work education and its transfer to the universities. The debate amongst almoners about training gathered strength in the 1950s, with a good deal of conflict between old ways and new ideas, especially as to whether students were being 'taught to probe and pry', indeed to 'psychoanalyse patients' when, as was generally said at the time about 'American casework' method, 'We British do not wear our hearts on our sleeves'.

The 1949 Institute of Almoners working party report had said: 'It has been suggested that the intensive casework study carried out in the training schools might lead students to lose interest in the many small services which patients require' (p. 97). Students themselves were sometimes tactlessly eager to do something they called 'pure casework', so new ways caused tensions on both sides. By degrees, over a period of time and not without dust and heat, the Institute and leading almoners' departments pioneered the change from apprenticeship training to professional courses of related theory and practice.

As a result of the 1949 working party's recommendations, the Institute of Almoners played a leading part in the efforts to get post-social science, professional, one-year casework courses started in the universities. Its negotiations with Edinburgh University led in 1954 to a medical social work stream parallel with the already well-established mental health course. It was active in the preliminary discussions which finally resulted in the Carnegie course at LSE and later in those which led to the applied social studies courses at Southampton and Birmingham Universities. The slow growth of these university courses, however, meant that the Institute had to continue to train the majority of medical social workers itself, although its policy since the 1949 report had been to transfer professional training to the universities on courses of which it approved. It also continued to approve – or disapprove – particular university social science courses as a basis for professional training. This caused some university resentment, but as the most popular career choice of social science students the Institute had a powerful voice. As Snelling (1970) commented, 'The constant anxiety over many years of keeping its own course going on a shoestring, for as long as was needed, meant that the Institute had no resources to promote the expansion of training' (pages not numbered).

The American MSWs invited by and attached to the Institute or to hospitals in the 1950s took seminars and discussion groups all over the country. As in other fields, these were eagerly attended and they gave supervisors and other experienced almoners a grasp of casework as a coherent practice based upon a better understanding of human behaviour, especially of responses to the stress of illness. A small but steady stream of almoners went to work in American hospitals and brought back new social work methods and a hearty respect for the national health service with its freedom from pressures to finance patients' treatment. The interest amongst training almoners and others in knowing what students were being taught also influenced their own practice. This process had started in the mid-1940s when Australian MSWs came over here, having taken a training originally pioneered by almoners from this country and combining it with American experience. They and the American visiting MSWs had the knowledge and time to make a considerable contribution to professional teaching in the 1950s, and in a manner which was acceptable to many leading practitioners.

In 1959 a supervisors' standing committee was set up. It encouraged local self-help groups on student supervision and organised national study days. This was reinforced in 1960 by a nine-day summer school for supervisors run by the Institute's teaching staff. This successful venture was continued annually, and conferences, special study meetings, refresher courses and study overseas became established and regular events.

In 1965 the Institute's student training course was redesigned and based on greater London in order to relate classroom teaching and practice more closely than when students had also gone to a number of centres outside London for fieldwork. The theoretical studies at the Institute continued to be social casework, the field of medical social work, the dynamics of human behaviour and medical information. By 1967 there were places for MSW students in seventeen university social work courses (including Scotland), though there was a severe shortage in the south-east.

In 1967 the IMSW, the Association of Psychiatric Social Workers (APSW) and the Council for Training in Social Work (CTSW) took up urgently with the DHSS, the Joint University Council for Social and Public Administration (JUC) and the University Grants Committee (UGC), the shortage of places for MSW and PSW students on university courses. This resulted from the lack of grants for staff salaries and other expenses compared with Home Office grants for child care and probation students. These representations led to the UGC making additional grants available to certain universities,

Table 6 *Numbers of medical social workers trained, 1950–71*

Almoners

	1950	1951	1952	1953	1954	1955	1956	1957	1958	1959
IA	93	106	87	77	131	64	81	71	54	57
Universities	–	–	–	–	13	20	19	24	26	32
	93	106	87	77	144	84	100	95	80	89

MSWs

	1957–8	1958–9	1959–60	1960–1	1961–2	1962–3
IA/IMSW	71	54	57	53	53	48
Universities	16	22	24	18	35	46
Recognised overseas qualifications	8	4	8	7	5	8
	95	80	89	78	93	102

	1965–6	1966–7	1967–8	1968–9	1969–70	1970–1
IMSW	39	35	37	–	–	–
Universities	50	40	25	85	63	33
	89	75	62	85	63	33

Sources: Institute of Almoners/IMSW *Annual Reports*, and *Setting the Course for Social Work Education 1971–1973* (CCETSW, 1973).

while others agreed to step up student numbers without a grant. The result was an increase of over 100 in the number of places available for MSW and PSW students. The Institute's training course finally ceased in 1970 when LSE agreed to increase the number of MSW students on its applied social studies course to twenty-five and to continue some of the Institute's fieldwork placements. By the early 1970s there were over forty student units in hospitals in the country as a whole. Thus it took twenty-one years to implement the Institute of Almoners' decision in 1949 to transfer its training to the universities. During that time it made a considerable direct and indirect contribution to better professional education. But, as is clear from this chapter, students were often being prepared for work with individual patients of a kind not always effective in the hospital setting.

Chapter 10

Social Work in the Mental Health Services[*]

SOME MOVES IN THE 1950s

The mental health services covered people suffering from any form of
mental disorder or handicap. Obviously medicine was the primary profession, but social work increasingly played a complementary role when from
the 1950s the profound influence which the family and social environment
had on the well-being and level of social functioning of mentally disordered
people became clearer. Psychiatric social workers contributed to this, particularly through their energy and initiative in pioneering earlier community
care schemes as regional representatives of the then Provisional National
Council for Mental Health (from 1946 the National Association for
Mental Health, NAMH). The earlier Mental After-Care Association and
other voluntary organisations were already running a few hostels, and some
mental hospitals had started halfway houses. 'These resulted in new thinking
about ways of providing services in the community for the mentally ill, and
a search for new instruments or facilities with positive rehabilitative
functions' (Titmuss, 1970a).

After-care functions under the Lunacy and Mental Treatment Acts were
usually assigned to duly authorised officers (DAOs) whose traditional concern was to remove psychiatric emergencies, i.e. patients whom they considered unfit to remain at large, to hospital, frequently by compulsion. Some
of these men had a poor-law background, some had nursing training, but
many had no training beyond the short induction courses offered by the
NAMH, having learned their know-how from their untrained predecessors.
They operated on the assumption that people were either sane, to be left
alone, or insane and 'subject to be dealt with': but this assumption was quite
inadequate for the new functions of preventive work and after-care, which
called for a social frame of reference, a fuller recognition of the complexity
of human motivation and behaviour, and particularly of family and social
interaction. They had to make difficult decisions, sometimes in dramatic
situations, and, if there was no case for statutory action, they had to leave
the disturbed person and his family without social work help. Discharged
patients might also deteriorate and have to return to hospital if no adequate
community care service existed. Some of the few senior PSWs found that

[*]See also Chapter 11.

one of their most important activities was to re-open 'abortive' files, point out the need for further intervention, and teach techniques of relieving tension and helping families to contain or help their sick member.

The Royal Commission on the Law relating to Mental Illness and Mental Deficiency (1957) concluded that 'social work for patients who are not receiving hospital treatment, including those who have left hospital is essentially the responsibility of the local authorities' (para. 603). It also thought that social work with the families of in-patients was desirable. This expansion of local authority community care services would greatly increase the demand for social workers and of trained staff for homes and hostels. Its recommendation about local authority responsibility for community care was embodied in the Mental Health Act, 1959. This legislation required local authorities to provide a full range of residential and other services to reinforce the swing to community care (see also volume 2, chapter 14).

The growth of a community care service for the mentally disordered and handicapped was slow and uneven. There were outstanding experiments in psychiatric social services in Birmingham and Middlesex local authorities which received direct referrals from many sources including the National Assistance Board. There were a few well-integrated local authority and hospital schemes with joint use of medical and social work staff, regular case conferences between psychiatrists, PSWs and mental welfare officers, and a comprehensive after-care service. In these situations mental welfare officers in effect received a good in-service training. In some other localities there was no co-operation, and mental hospitals claimed to do their own after-care. This was undertaken by mental nurses whose main responsibility may have been to see that the ex-patient was taking his drugs and attending an out-patient clinic regularly. They usually did not know the local social environment or social services and might or might not be concerned about the other members of the patient's family. This form of after-care also ran counter to new understanding that mentally ill or handicapped people needed help with personal problems, with family and social relationships, and with work. None the less there was a vicious circle in that hospitals would not refer patients for local authority after-care unless good provision was obviously available. This was easier said than done in view of the manifold difficulties of hostel provision, the heavy expense to the local authorities against centrally financed regional hospital board services, and the strain on families of 'containing' mentally disordered or handicapped people in their homes without adequate community care services. Community care was also needed for mentally ill people who refused to enter hospital voluntarily and could not be compulsorily admitted. In such circumstances there was often no help available at all for the person and his family.

No action was taken about training for mental health social workers following the Mackintosh Report (1951). The Younghusband Report (1959) said of this inertia:

' . . . we cannot but deplore the time lost in the years since the Mackintosh Committee stressed the urgency of the situation. Even a series of modest experimental courses in the last few years would have helped newly recruited duly authorised officers and mental welfare officers to undertake the difficult and important work which awaited them, and would also have produced a useful body of experience on which to base recommendations for training. We have much sympathy with the disappointment and frustration felt by these officers who have waited so long and done so much to try to bring about opportunities to train in their chosen field of work.' (para. 226)

For years various organisations had been pressing for training and the NAMH had done what it could by running induction courses.

MENTAL HEALTH SOCIAL WORKERS AND COMMUNITY CARE IN THE 1960s

In 1961 returns to the Ministry of Health showed that 1,128 mental health social workers were employed by the 146 local authorities in England and Wales or about 0·024 per 1,000 population (Ministry of Health, 1963, Cmnd 1973 para. 84). The revised estimates submitted by local authorities to the Ministry of Health in 1966 (Cmnd 3022) envisaged a need for 2,625 by 1975 (or 0·05 per 1,000 population) against an actual 1,606 in 1965, of whom 139 were PSWs and 135 held the then new certificate in social work (CSW). Some local authorities planned ratios of over 0·13 by 1975 but others only 0·02 (paras 53–4). The Ministry of Health gave no guidelines for these estimates, which were probably based on what local authorities thought they could afford rather than on objective assessment of need. By 1970, i.e. before the Seebohm reorganisation, there were 1,808 mental health social workers, of whom 197 were PSWs and 365 held the CSW (Jones, 1972, p. 364). They were usually responsible to a principal mental health social worker.

It was agreed that many more mentally disordered or handicapped people could live at home without damaging strain for themselves and their families, given a range of supportive services, including social work, clubs, day hospitals, and short periods of residential care. Children were especially vulnerable when either parent, but particularly the mother, was mentally disordered. Goldberg (1960, 1966a, 1967) in a series of social work studies of young schizophrenic patients and their families concluded that 'some understanding of the whole family constellation is essential before any plan for treatment can be formulated' (1967, p. 25). She went on to outline a framework for family assessment and the related treatment questions, but said 'The answers to these questions can only be found by trying different methods in relation to defined circumstances and building up objective evidence of the differences in outcome. Systematic understanding of family functioning and of how to bring about changes are so rudimentary as yet that any kind of dogmatism is out of place' (1967, p. 27). This thorough assessment and differential, carefully recorded treatment with its acknowledgment of ignorance contrasted strongly with usual practice and suggested much wasted and ineffective activity of little help to clients. Various studies showed that intense emotional relationships with the patient's family contributed to his illness, militated against recovery and perpetuated relapse.

The mental hospital 'open-door' policy, partly made possible by new drugs which controlled symptoms, led to a comparatively rapid discharge rate of schizophrenic and other patients into the community and often resulted in a revolving door. This policy also made many types of local authority and voluntary accommodation necessary, including attempts to board out mentally ill people in private families. Voluntary organisations and local authorities were also experimenting with group homes where residents lived without resident staff. Sometimes these were bed-sitters near a staffed home.

Brown *et al.* (1966) studied over the course of five years schizophrenic patients discharged from three mental hospitals. Most of these were discharged to their families, but those living apart from their families were found to be significantly less subject to early relapse, while those returning to their families of origin were at greatest risk. Although many parents bore severely disturbed behaviour with great fortitude, the level of anxiety and the quality and intensity of relationships within the family often contributed to a recrudescence of the illness. Patients returning to their wives relapsed less rapidly and less often, although there was a high rate of marital breakdown. Few wives of schizophrenic patients had a chance to discuss their marriage with an experienced counsellor or be given advice about how long an extremely distressing situation might last. About one-third of the married women patients were thought by their husbands to have affected the children. Social workers at two of the hospitals helped just over 25 per cent of the patients but only 2 per cent at the third hospital (which had one untrained social worker). Shortage of social workers was not the only factor limiting services; there was also a tendency to neglect or avoid patients who were hostile or failed to take advice. Closer contacts with community care services did not result in lower morbidity or greater family cohesion, apparently because of insufficient attention to the social milieu. This failed to prevent social handicaps which were not necessarily part of the illness itself, i.e. personal attitudes and habits of hopelessness and truculence, resulting in negative reactions by others. This study clarified the important principle that rehabilitation should consist of minimising primary disabilities and preventing secondary handicaps. These efforts needed to be continuously applied but after discharge there was little systematic attempt to measure handicap and plan the environment. After-care consisted of supervision rather than treatment or rehabilitation. Many families with a mentally ill member, whether or not diagnosed, 'settle back into apathetic acceptance of a situation of tension and potential crisis simply because they cannot conceive of a solution to it and no active help is offered' (Brown *et al.*, 1966, p. 214).

This study and recorded hostel experience (see volume 2, chapter 14) began to clarify the aims and necessary skills in after-care for psychiatric patients, but good standards were only reached in a few instances.

The Seebohm Report (1968) said of the mid-1960s:

'The widespread belief that we have "community care" of the mentally disordered is, for many parts of the country, still a sad illusion.' (para. 339)

'The families of mentally disordered people tend to suffer from interrelated social disabilities which are often caused or aggravated by the mental disorder, which may precipitate breakdown or incapacitate the family for caring for the chronically sick member. The social worker should be concerned with the whole family, learning how to make a family diagnosis, and be able to take wide responsibility and mobilise a wide range of services.' (para. 353)

The Committee also found that

'The distribution of professionally trained mental health social work staff is uneven. There are also wide variations in the loads of work carried by mental health social workers in different areas . . . In some areas, care of the mentally ill is separate from care of the subnormal; in others it is combined. In a few authorities social workers are employed jointly by the local health authority and the hospital authority to provide an integrated service to the hospital, the child guidance clinics and the mentally ill and subnormal in the community. In most areas, mental health social work is a specialised function.' (para. 275)

This function included home visiting and social support for mentally disordered people and their families, mobilising other services, involvement in admission of mentally ill people to hospital, and working closely with GPs and hospital psychiatrists.

By 1967 there were for England and Wales as a whole 71 day care centres for mentally ill people temporarily or permanently unable to work and 247 social clubs. A number of local authorities made no provision. Local mental health associations and the NAMH ran or promoted clubs for ex-patients and hostels, after-care and homes for mentally confused old people. In total these made a considerable contribution to the development of mental health services. Nearly 185,000 mentally ill or retarded people were receiving local authority mental health services, in close co-operation with mental hospitals and GPs. Workloads must have been high but, as usual, they varied considerably from place to place and no information was available about the quality of service. Some local authorities employed consultant psychiatrists jointly with hospital boards. These worked closely with mental health social workers (Seebohm Report, 1968, Appendix F). But in relation to total need the Report found 'nothing short of a manpower crisis in the mental health service'.

THE EARLY 1970S

It was clear by now that the aims of both day care and hostels should be to provide sheltered conditions, social and educational activities, relief of family strain, help to clients to adjust to work and develop self-confidence, particularly in relationships with others. This meant assessing each person's level of functioning, a continuous process in which he himself must be motivated to reach better levels. This was a highly skilled task.

The 1971 census of mental hospitals showed that a new group of long-stay patients was coming into existence, about two-thirds needed a sheltered environment in the community but often there was nowhere for them to go.

There had been several experiments in the 1960s in boarding out patients from psychiatric hospitals. For example, a boarding-out scheme was started at Severalls Hospital in 1963 (King's Fund, 1970, pp. 22–3). Some of those successfully boarded out had been in-patients for up to forty years. Patients and hostesses were matched for social background, interests and religion; a holiday was arranged at the home and if this was successful the patient was discharged. There was social work after-care to support the patient and the hostess, and the patient could return to hospital if necessary. A similar scheme was described by Smith (1975) under which 100 long-stay patients were successfully boarded out in twelve months. After-care and supporting services were essential, including day hospitals, industrial and occupational therapy, outside luncheon clubs, women's institutes and church groups and visits by social workers and psychiatric nurses. In Dorset in 1974, a senior social worker was appointed to resettle long-stay psychiatric patients. The hospital prepared them for community living and provided after-care. Some might go for a short period to a hostel, they were then resettled in flats or bed-sitters on their own or with others, or with specially selected landladies who received close social work support. There were other examples in different parts of the country. Day centres came to be accepted as an essential part of a co-ordinated resettlement programme for former psychiatric patients. To meet the local shortage in Dorset a psychiatrist devised a travelling clinical team in 1974 which provided a day centre service in different places on different days. The team included a hospital social worker and collaborated closely with local social workers. It used all the community facilities, including voluntary helpers to bridge the gap between hospital and community care and reduce the hospital re-admission rate. There were a few other travelling day treatment centres by 1975. (Information supplied by the Director of Social Services, Dorset County Council.)

There were also various schemes to prevent the need for admission to a psychiatric hospital. For example, in Northampton (1970) joint teams were started for each area, composed of the mental hospital clinical team (including a social worker) and a social work team headed by an area mental health social worker. Members of the social work team visited patients in their own homes, attended hospital out-patient clinics with the psychiatrists and ran clubs for the patients and their families. Careful assessment and preparation reduced the need for hospital admissions through the social worker's close contact with families.

More services were started from the late 1960s and expanded in the 1970s for drug addicts, alcoholics, disturbed adolescents and the newly bereaved, whether at psychiatric hospitals or elsewhere. They were run by statutory services or voluntary organisations like Alcoholics Anonymous, or as individual ventures. They included day centres, self-help groups, crisis intervention and shopfront projects, with emphasis on counselling and group therapy. Some youth consultation and other centres were non-medical with a walk-in appointment system. Social workers in these teams might have had previous experience as probation officers, PSWs, MSWs or unattached youth workers. They developed a high level of expertise and contributed much to knowledge in largely unexplored fields. There were experiments in the use of volunteers for the actual work with clients. Small groups of these met regularly with experienced social workers to discuss the nature of bereavement or whatever might be the purpose of the service, and the ongoing work with individual clients.

There was much opposition to the Seebohm reorganisation, which separated mental health social workers, hostels and day care and other services from the other local authority mental health services (after 1974 the area health authorities). In some new social services departments social workers kept their old specialisations for a time and when generic caseloads were introduced they often acted as consultants to those with no experience of mental disorder, or provided an emergency service. Many local authorities ran in-service training courses which included the nature of mental illness and subnormality, the key role of psychiatrists, the services provided and the nature of social work with patients and their families. There were severe setbacks in many authorities where social workers unaccustomed to work with the mentally disturbed were unfamiliar with the regulations and procedures, afraid of the patients, not supported or given in-service training, and had little chance of gaining experience (Danbury, 1976).

The DHSS White Paper (1975*b*) *Better Services for the Mentally Ill* summed up the situation thus:

'By and large the non-hospital community resources are still minimal, though where facilities have been developed they have in general proved successful. The failure, for which central government as much as local government is responsible, to develop anything approaching adequate social services is perhaps the greatest disappointment of the last 15 years. As a result the balance of existing facilities – health and social services – bears increasingly less relation to acknowledged needs. Hospital staff have, rightly in one sense, come to see their role as an active therapeutic one and the hospital as a place for providing medical treatment and nursing care. So they have become increasingly unwilling to act as social care custodians for those who would not need to remain in hospital were supporting facilities available in the community. But we have to face the fact that adequate supporting facilities in the community are not generally available.' (p. 14)

There were widely differing views about contributory causation of mental disorder, thus summarised in the White Paper:

'Drug treatments continue to be widely used, and have played a major part in facilitating the decline in length of in-patient stay for many patients, and the rapid growth of day and out-patient treatment. It has to be recognised, however, that research has still not shown the precise mechanism by which these drugs have their effect. Some argue that drugs are used too much – particularly in the treatment of neurotic illness; that they treat symptoms only and ignore underlying social, psychological and environmental causes of mental illness, for which psychological methods are more appropriate. In particular, some stress the importance of family and personal relationships as a factor in causing mental illness and argue that often it is society or the family which is disturbed rather than the individual patient. Others are equally convinced of the importance of biochemical factors in causation and argue that from this viewpoint drug treatment is the logical remedy. The issues are widely discussed and debated; but what seems beyond doubt is that mental illness is a highly complex phenomenon, taking many forms and caused by a variety of different factors.' (p. 13)

By 1975, contrasted with the early 1950s, social workers were no longer regarded as unimportant or not mentioned at all. Indeed the foregoing White Paper said that 'the unifying element . . . is the professional skill of the social worker, whether deployed in fieldwork, in primary care, in residential or day care, or in hospital' (p. 23).

This chapter shows the enormous task of filling in gaps in the services, setting right the 'misplacement' of buildings and staff, and helping to change public attitudes towards mentally disturbed people. It was an open question whether in the future sufficient social workers and holders of the new certificate in social service would be willing to take on the tasks, especially for the mentally handicapped, that society had assigned to them. None the less, though services were still grossly deficient in quantity there had been some substantial gains in quality as a result of more knowledge and well-planned pioneer projects. The multicausal factors in mental disorder still remained obscure from the biochemical to the familial and societal. The systematic identification and reinforcement of family and social networks – which could be destructive or non-existent as well as supportive – was barely at a beginning, and social workers might not come into the picture until the disorder had reached crisis proportions.

THE MENTALLY HANDICAPPED

The preceding section also applied largely to mentally handicapped people. For example, their families were in much the same plight, except that there was no hope of improvement, the situation could continue for years, and enormous strains were often faced by all members of the family if there were no adequate supporting services. While people with a mild degree of such handicap could achieve relative independence in favourable family and social circumstances, the more severely subnormal, if not cared for in hospital, were a great burden to their families. Parents urgently needed help at the time they suspected mental retardation in their child or it was diagnosed, yet for many there were no services until the child became 5 and was diagnosed as unfit for an ordinary school and might be sent to a training centre (later a special school). A careful medical and social assessment was needed to determine whether the child was severely subnormal or, as sometimes happened, autistic or suffering from extreme emotional disturbance. The practical questions were the child's own personality and the extent to which family and social influences could contribute to or retard the development of intelligence, self-confidence and social competence. Some emotional and practical problems of rearing a child with any handicap were similar, so was the range of social and other support services they needed. These are discussed in chapter 13 on 'Social Work and the Physically Handicapped'. Physical mobility, but limited intelligence and possibly emotional immaturity created special problems in adolescence.

Todd (1967) stressed that for all but the most severely subnormal person social functioning depended upon 'his own personality and the extent to which he can accept his handicap; the attitudes of . . . his family or intimate friends and their ability to provide the emotional environment that he needs; and the attitude of society' (p. 9). There was a statutory obligation to visit mentally handicapped people under statutory guardianship or supervision, so at its best mental welfare officers might support families over long periods of time.

Tizard and Grad (1961) in their study of 250 families with severely sub-normal children found that the majority were cared for at home, though with inadequate support. Twenty nine per cent of the 100 families with children in hospital thought they could have coped if sufficient support services had been available.

Tizard and Grad (1961), Tizard (1964) and Morris (1969) exposed the sub-human conditions in some hospital wards, the inappropriate care for many patients, and the numbers who could be more effectively cared for in small residential homes, lodgings or their own homes, given full supporting services. King *et al.* (1971) studied routine patterns of daily life for mentally retarded and physically handicapped children who would spend much of their childhood in hospital wards or children's cottage homes or hostels. The wards lacked warmth and homeliness, toys within the children's reach, or personal possessions (sometimes including clothes). The cottage children had far more freedom and personal attention and their care was related to their individual needs. In several of the children's homes and hospital wards there was no difference in the severity of handicaps, but the children in the homes were noticeably more advanced in feeding skills and speech. There was no evidence that the child-oriented units were better staffed or that the staff had had more training: the institutional practices in hospitals were not due to staff shortages. Over 80 per cent of the housemothers had been in the same cottage for a year or more but there was a heavy turnover of junior staff. Heads who were child-care trained were more likely to talk to the children, interact with them, less likely to reject them than those who were nurses: ' . . . these findings suggest that the type of training received by staff exercised a powerful influence not only on the way in which they carry out their duties, but also on the patterns of care maintained in their units' (King *et al.*, 1971, p. 188).

Jones (1975) studied hospital and community services in a region in relation to each other. There were only three whole-time (one qualified) and four part-time social workers for all the mental subnormality hospitals in the region, too preoccupied with work related to admissions and discharge to undertake other work with patients, their families and the community. There was a total of at least twenty-one qualified social workers in the region, most of whom were in acute general hospitals. She endorsed other findings that care of mentally handicapped people did not primarily involve medical knowledge and skill and concluded that 'the professionals we have are not the professionals we need'.

By the early 1970s there were about 60,000 mentally handicapped people (including 7,500 children) in long-stay hospitals, with a further 1,500 physically handicapped children. There were 43,000 places in local authority training centres for children and adults but only 5,000 (1,300 children) were in local authority residential care. Many authorities still made no provision, though a wide range of facilities were needed – homes, hostels, sheltered housing and boarding out. It had repeatedly been emphasised that the problems of many mentally retarded people were social and emotional, not medical, and that they should be treated as people not patients, but a change in the balance of 'misplacement' required determination and different buildings when

'The punitive or neglectful attitudes of the past have left a legacy of old buildings, poor facilities, understaffing, overcrowding, inadequate provision of all sorts, and a lack of elementary amenities in the niggardly provision which has been made so that it will be difficult to change or make good. Yet similar difficulties were rapidly overcome in large part by Local Authority Children's Departments twenty years ago, and comparable changes could rapidly occur in the mental health services also.' (King *et al.*, 1971, pp. 23–4)

Bayley (1973) brought out the grim reality of some situations in his 1970 study of fifty-three families in Sheffield with severely subnormal adults aged 16 to 71 living at home. Half were incontinent, almost wholly unable to speak, needing help with washing, feeding and dressing and unable to be left alone. The mother's life was dominated by the sheer grind of coping with the daily routine 'but there were many instances of regular whole-hearted and effective help from husbands, relatives, friends and neighbours' (pp. 351–2). None the less nearly half received 'none or "precarious" help. The families often needed a great deal of support over a very long period measured in decades rather than months' (p. 352). Half the families found mental welfare officers little or no help because they could not meet the families' most pressing need, relief from the daily grind, the essential chores of caring day in and day out for the mentally handicapped person. The urgently needed day care was not available, which made the social work help that could be – and was very infrequently – offered irrelevant and 'the burden that the mental welfare officers were expected to bear totally unrealistic . . . casework help only makes sense when a family's basic needs are met' (pp. 359 and 361). The grossly inadequate help available led in some instances to intolerable family strain or admission to hospital that could have been avoided if official services had reinforced care by the family and neighbours.

The DHSS White Paper *Better Services for the Mentally Handicapped* (1971a) found that progress had been made in pioneering the quality of services but in quantity they were 'grossly deficient'. The number of places in adult training centres was 'quite insufficient' and many people were at home without training or occupation. Three-quarters of the staff were untrained and practically no training had existed until the Training Council for Teachers of the Mentally Handicapped was set up in 1964. About 170 people qualified yearly for its diploma. (Its functions were taken over by the CCETSW ten years later.) The White Paper gave an honest appraisal of a deplorable situation. It pointed out that 'apart from junior training centres (now special schools) for children, to which most local authorities gave first priority, only a small start had been made towards providing in sufficient quantity . . . practical help and advice, for families with mentally handicapped children living at home' (p. 13). Its proposals would have halved the number of adults in hospital and increased the number in residential homes and lodgings from 4,850 to 36,800, besides far more day training centre and other local provision. Obviously this was a programme for a generation, when for lack of other resources people were 'still pressing upon overcrowded hospital waiting lists' and the patients themselves, their families and the nursing staff bore the brunt of the deficiencies. Yet all experience showed that many families supported by friends and neighbours wanted to care for disabled members if the task were made bearable. BASW calculated (1974) that 2,400 social workers would be needed to implement the White Paper's policies.

By 1975 much was known about the plight of the mentally handicapped and their families but as before there was little social work interest in working with them.

Chapter 11

Psychiatric Social Work: Training for Psychiatric Social Work

(by Elizabeth Irvine)

During this decade the demand for PSWs spread far outside the bounds of mental hospitals and child guidance clinics. Perhaps this masked or perhaps added to 'the dual nature of the work . . . a source of considerable conflict in the minds of those who practise it, tempting them to retreat in one or other direction from that point of convergence of psychiatric and social where, in our view, their true strength will always lie' (Ashdown and Clement Brown, 1953, p. 249). Indeed, there was continuing discussion as to whether PSWs were primarily social workers or therapists. Many of them, particularly those in child guidance clinics, regarded their work as what Florence Hollis later termed 'a psycho-social therapy'. Psychoanalytic theory had come to occupy an important place in their training, and the dominant 'diagnostic' (or mainline Freudian) school of social work in the USA continued to have great influence.

At the same time certain indigenous developments could be distinguished. In particular, the English (Kleinian) school of psychoanalysis had influenced the training of a number of PSWs through the teaching of certain analysts and through fieldwork placements at the Tavistock Clinic. Whereas teachers of the 'diagnostic' method focused attention on the ego and in many cases enjoined on students the need to avoid the development of a transference from client to worker, those influenced by Kleinian theory considered that this was impossible, since elements of transference entered into all relationships, and particularly those with professional helpers. The client who brought his problems to a professional helper was bound to bring into the relationship hopes, fears and defensive strategies first learnt in relation to loved or hated parental figures. At least some of these attitudes would be relevant to the problem brought for help, and frank and friendly discussion of them could help many clients to gain insight into their habitual misperceptions of others and the self-defeating behaviour arising from such distorted perceptions.

These were clearly the preoccupations of people who regarded themselves as therapists. It has been argued that they were over-represented in the budding literature (The *British Journal of Psychiatric Social Work* was launched in 1947). Bree (1970) pointed out that only 16 per cent of PSWs had appeared in print by 1960, more than half of them only once, and expressed the view that this articulate minority were seriously unrepresentative of the silent majority, whose work was more spontaneous and intuitive. She described her view of professionally mature practice as 'unselfconscious attention to the other's [i.e. the client's] experience', and said: 'I believe this stage . . . was reached by many of the early trained PSWs who stayed long enough in one type of post to see their work in relation to the whole setting: clinic or hospital, the patient's own environment, the neighbourhood, general attitudes and relevant legal procedure; but they cannot describe it and are usually apologetic in talking about it' (p. 176).

Those PSWs with a psychoanalytic orientation certainly had the advantage of a ready-made conceptual framework and language which were perhaps unduly impressive and had the unfortunate effect of inducing an apologetic attitude in many people whose work, however successful, did not lend itself to formulation in such terms. None the less a number of PSWs, mainly those working with the mentally ill or with delinquents, published descriptions of a diversity of methods, adapted with great flexibility to the needs of each client and directed often by intuition more than by theory. A number of workers reported that with this kind of client it was not enough to be a good listener, encouraging the client to freer communication; and it might be particularly inappropriate to encourage the expression of fantasy, which might only increase the client's confusion and distress. This kind of client needed the very opposite, help in perceiving and holding on to reality. Instead of a passivity modelled on that of the analyst, the worker needed to be more active in the relationship, presenting herself more as a real person, revealing some of her thoughts and tastes to the client, and leaving no room for doubt about her concern and sympathy for him (Ratcliffe and Jones, 1956). Nor was talking and listening enough in many cases; it might be useful to take an agoraphobic patient for a walk to the shops, to accompany or drive patients to doctor or dentist, or to visit a child in hospital or boarding school. It appeared that not only were these shared experiences valuable in themselves and a most convincing proof of concern; they also favoured communication, in that many clients talked more easily and freely on such occasions. Here we see many of the traditional methods of social work, with their therapeutic value directed and enriched by deepened insight into the meaning of each situation for the client, whether or not the worker formulated this insight in terms borrowed from psychoanalysis. Non-verbal communication received more attention and the concept of the 'corrective relationship' began to emerge.

Mental hospitals were rapidly emerging from a period when their function had been largely custodial into a phase of enthusiastic absorption in shock therapies, brain surgery and chemotherapy. The new treatments resulted in the early discharge of a growing number of patients after relatively short spells of in-patient treatment, not necessarily because they were well, but because their symptoms had diminished sufficiently to be contained in the community (see chapter 10 on Social Work in the Mental Health Services). Many of the patients returning to the community were in need of considerable after-care, in the form of social care and support. Questions then arose as to the most appropriate role for the PSW; whether this was to ensure liaison between hospitals or clinics and the local health service, to act as consultant on psychiatric aspects of social care, or to join the local mental health services.

In the hospitals themselves the demand for social histories remained strong, on account of their vital contribution to the natural history, chronic or acute, of a progressive disease. Lip service was paid to Adolf Meyer's more global picture of the individual grappling successfully or unsuccessfully with problems and crises in his social roles and relationships, but only a minority of psychiatrists seemed to take this seriously in practice. These were the best friends of the PSWs, and valued their support in demonstrating the dynamic significance of past experience and of the tensions and conflicts in the family and social situation. Moreover, PSWs were also working hard to demonstrate that with such a frame of reference it was often possible to modify the current reality to some extent, to enable families to cope with patients and patients with families, by understanding and relieving the anxieties and resentments, the ancient grudges, which so often contributed to the patient's disturbance and jeopardised his reintegration into family and community.

This kind of work presented new technical problems. Social workers trained mainly for the individual interview were tempted at first to avoid family interviews as far as possible, but then had to deal, in conflicted family situations, with the anxieties and rivalries aroused in every member by an outsider's private contact with every other. In particular, workers had to be alert to the desperate or subtle attempts of both patients and relatives to enlist them as allies, and to find ways of resisting these while demonstrating a genuine sympathetic concern for the suffering and the welfare of each party.

However, work with families was slow to develop and in 1954 an APSW survey of the functions of PSWs in fifteen mental hospitals found that their subjects were spending from 36 to 88 per cent of their interviewing time with in-patients, from 10 to 69 per cent with out-patients, and only up to 18 per cent visiting outside the hospital. This suggested that as PSWs became better accepted in the hospital they were being increasingly assimilated into a patient-centred culture and drawn away from their traditional concern with families. This recognition of a direct therapeutic role for PSWs with patients arose partly, perhaps, because they saw only selected patients, and thus had more time to spend with them than a doctor with a large caseload; but in some cases psychiatrist and PSW co-operated closely as a therapeutic team, each having regular and separate interviews with the patient, with different and clearly defined functions. Sometimes also they saw themselves as playing paternal and maternal roles respectively. Unfortunately nothing was written about these interesting forms of collaborative therapy.

Assimilation in the therapeutic team focused on the patient perhaps went furthest of all in those hospitals which adopted the structure and culture of the therapeutic community. These offered stimulating and exciting new experiences and possibilities and called for considerable adaptation of traditional professional roles, including that of the PSW, who became increasingly absorbed in contributing to the various meetings which were the staple therapeutic activity of these communities, adapting their traditional casework skills to the demands of a community where private communication was devalued. At this time the intense absorption of the therapeutic community in its own processes was often reflected in a corresponding lack of interest in families, both as regards their needs and problems and their potential contribution to the rehabilitation of the patients, and the PSW received little encouragement or support in her concern for them. Family therapy (see below) developed mainly in child guidance clinics.

A number of other hospitals also set up therapeutic groups of various kinds in which PSWs were often invited to act as co-therapists with psychiatrists. This called for a knowledge of group dynamics which was not included in PSW training. Some managed to get training, or at least experience, of therapeutic groups elsewhere, others learnt on the job, sometimes with help from their psychiatric partner (though sometimes he, too, had no specific training for work with groups). We have seen that the Mental Health Act, 1959 imposed the major responsibility for the social care of the mentally ill on local health authorities.

While duly authorised officers (DAOs) were grappling with the difficult transition, and before any adequate training was provided for them, a small number of PSWs began to join the local authority mental health services as reorganised under the Mental Treatment Act, 1930. Their numbers rose from eight in 1951 to twenty-six in 1959, plus some shared appointments (Younghusband Report, 1959, para. 804). Pre-care and after-care afforded an opportunity to return to the focus on the patient in his family which had been eroded in many mental hospitals. These professionally trained workers appeared as rivals claiming superior status, although they were often younger and less experienced than the DAOs, and were sometimes paid on the lower NHS salary scale. The DAOs, who had much to learn, were reluctant to learn it from relatively inexperienced rivals, most of whom were women, and who often refused to undertake the statutory duties of the DAO.

In 1958 the APSW set up a working party on the functions of PSWs in the adult field. The evidence from the mental hospital sector showed that the developments described above were far from general. Demand for the traditional, full social history was declining in favour of 'assessment of particular areas of a patient's social functioning. With the reduction of the average length of stay of patients in hospitals, short term casework is increasing in importance, while tasks requiring less skill are beginning to be undertaken by hospital welfare officers' (report unpublished). Relations with psychiatrists were frequently a problem; they 'vary in the extent to which they will allow PSWs to handle a case in their own way. Some try to direct what action should be taken, and expect their ideas to be carried through.' Some objected to PSWs working with cases which they had not referred, and some apparently would not even discuss their recommendations (or instructions) with the PSW or consider any alternative suggestions as to the appropriate social work treatment. Yet on the other hand (and presumably elsewhere) PSWs were involved in the training of medical students.

The section on the mental health departments of local authorities insisted at some length that a great number of variables made it impossible to generalise about the service. 'Referrals come mainly from mental hospitals and GPs and attempts to constrain the PSW's freedom seem in each case to come from the administration. For casework, with its flexible and permissive approach . . . to be fully accepted in a mental welfare department may imply something of a revolution in outlook.' 'There has been controversy as to whether PSWs employed by the local health authority should also act as DAOs, and in fact a few are doing so . . . The large majority of these emergency situations are dealt with by the DAO', and it is suggested that 'in some cases for which admission to hospital is not arranged it would be appropriate for the latter to refer the patient to the PSW, who might work with the patient and his relatives either towards admission or out-patient treatment, or towards the resolution of the tensions or anxieties which had brought about the crisis of referral'. One of the recommendations reads as follows: 'For the purpose of carrying out some of his duties, the PSW in community care, although working in the public health department, should have freedom to operate as a non medical social worker' (i.e. not as part of a medical or psychiatric team). Selection of cases was particularly important in pre-treatment and preventive work, and also in after-care, which should be undertaken only for positive reasons, since routine supervision was a waste of time, and might even do more harm than good. Selection for after-care should involve close co-operation between the PSWs in the hospital and community and the patient's psychiatrist.

PSYCHIATRIC SOCIAL WORK IN THE 1960S AND EARLY 1970S

Mental Health Services in the Community
Many PSWs attached to mental hospitals had been much opposed to the transfer of after-care from the hospital to the local authority, but once this had become a *fait accompli* growing numbers of them began to move away from hospital to local authority. By 1966 the PSWs in these services numbered 182, about 25 per cent of the total APSW membership. The proportion of men in the profession was also rising, and reached 12 per cent by 1962 (Timms, 1964). These tended to be attracted particularly to the local authority services, partly because the local authority salary scale compared very favourably with that of the NHS and partly because of the greater professional autonomy in local health departments. Men also tended to gravitate rather quickly to senior posts, of which Timms found that they occupied 30 per cent in 1962.

Some mental welfare officers (MWOs) who had trained as PSWs, returned to senior positions in which they were well placed to perform a bridging function between the two groups. By the mid-decade the rivalry between PSWs and MWOs had largely subsided, and in a growing number of authorities the PSW was accepted as leader of a social work team providing, for those MWOs who had not yet been seconded to courses, a good deal of informal in-service training. At least one authority employed an experienced

PSW part-time to organise induction and refresher courses for all its MWOs. On the other hand, no sooner was the tension between PSW and MWO well on the way to solution than another problem arose between PSWs in the familiar settings and those in the community services, who mostly worked without the benefit (or constraint) of a psychiatric team, and some of whom had adopted and published original and unorthodox methods.

In the community setting, clients were accepted who were far from willing and often totally lacking in insight. The service was essentially one which reached out to the reluctant, sometimes by assiduous home visiting, sometimes by meeting the patient outside the office, in restaurants, parks or a public house. The PSW in the community also reached out by exposing more of his personality in a relationship which established greater social closeness without losing its professional focus. (Some hospital-based PSWs also adopted similar methods but they remained more characteristic of work in the community.) Despite the pressing demand for a great increase in the number of PSWs, particularly in the community services, and the acute shortage of student placements, it was not until 1968 that the APSW brought itself to accept placement in a local authority mental health service in lieu of one in a mental hospital, mainly on the grounds that students in such a placement would not have the benefit of a psychiatric team (although the amount of teamwork in many hospitals was rather notional).

The policy of community care for the mentally ill was supported both by financial and by genuinely humanitarian considerations; but the focus was on the patient, and there was at first little concern for the families to which many patients returned. Little attention was paid to the risk of conflict between policies of community care and preventive mental health, in terms of the strain imposed on relatives and particularly on children. Early accounts of a local mental health service expressed a sense of departing from tradition in working with patients rather than with relatives (although as we have seen, many PSWs in the hospital service were doing likewise). Where work with relatives was described, it was nearly always undertaken in the interests of the patient, although Goldberg (1957) and Jones and Hammond (1960) touched on the problem of conflicting interests between a severely unstable patient and those of spouse and children.

Irvine (1961 and 1964), writing from a base in child guidance, demonstrated with clinical material some of the pathological processes which can be initiated by the diagnosis and recognition of mental illness in a parent, even apart from the impact of the illness itself. She argued that the patient's relatives, even if not already disturbed, should be seen as vulnerable people at risk from such disturbance, with a claim to consideration in any programme of preventive psychiatry, and she particularly stressed the threat to the healthy development of children. By 1964, Sainsbury reported on a research project on community service and the home care of psychiatric patients, one of the findings being that children were adversely affected in over a third of the families studied. In 1966 Thompson, writing from an integrated child guidance and mental health service, described a programme with a focus on family interaction as studied by a multidisciplinary team. She also made the point that while a hospital or clinic may be legitimately patient focused, a community service should be 'concerned with prevention and the welfare of the whole community, with those who are referred for help and with those who are not' (p. 21). Such an outlook led to co-operation with all the other agencies in the community, 'and seems to take us outside the area in which we were specifically trained and require modifications of our techniques' (p. 21). Even in individual casework, the traditional model 'has to be freshly adapted to each case. There is no standard procedure, no understood psychiatric social work role, no one team; and for each case a fresh framework, a fresh treatment process, an appropriate team of workers has to be found, requiring chameleon like versatility in the PSW concerned' (pp. 21–2).

However, as Hunter (1964) said:

'It is interesting to note the sort of stereotypes which we PSWs have of each other, for example the assumption that only PSWs employed by local authorities provide 'community care' or again that PSWs in child guidance clinics commonly use 'advanced casework techniques'. Traditionally the role of a PSW in a mental hospital was to be concerned mainly with the relatives . . . though this has never really been so. During the last four to five years there has been a considerable increase in the number of patients referred to PSWs directly, and I was interested to find that my current caseload of 52 contained 43 direct referrals of patients themselves, most of whom were out-patients, or had been discharged from hospital or contacted through a domiciliary consultation.' (p. 183)

While he expressed particular concern about the children of mentally ill parents, the cases he presented illustrated intensive casework with isolated adult patients who at the time were refusing to attend out-patient clinics, but accepted casework treatment in the home.

In 1964 both Hunter and Hammond showed PSWs in mental hospitals working with great autonomy with the full confidence of the psychiatrists, who supported them as consultants on request. Hammond reported a case where she was asked to investigate a referral and advise as to whether a psychiatric examination was required or whether it would be more appropriate for her to handle the case in the community. She commented:

'We are now learning to look at the needs of the family as a whole, whether they be social, psychological or economic needs . . . We are beginning to use our skills that we have acquired in our 'psychiatric era' in new ways, which take into account the social factors with which we were at one time preoccupied . . . In the field of mental hospital practice, three main areas of development emerge . . . the growing consideration of the needs of families as units . . . a greater awareness of the needs of children in families where there are mentally ill parents; and . . . a realisation of the need to use psychiatric knowledge derived from the adult and child guidance field in either setting.' (p. 128)

Her case material shows a flexible technique of dealing at different times with individuals, dyads or triads according to the wishes of the families.

In view of the drift of PSWs out of mental hospitals, Hunter (1969) carried out a postal survey of the 70 PSWs then listed as employed in these hospitals. Of the 47 respondents, all but 8 had trained in specialist PSW courses. The majority thought that they functioned as medical auxiliaries in part of their work, but not all of it; all except 8 of the older PSWs considered their work to include psychotherapy. Only 26 felt that their role and function were understood by more than a minority of their psychiatric colleagues, although most of them had regular opportunities to discuss cases with psychiatrists at least once a week, and 29 more often.

They all continued to see the patient and/or his relatives after his discharge, and half reported that over 50 per cent of their work was with patients only. Concern for the children of patients was not very strong, only 27 respondents said that they always tried to ascertain the effect of the patient's illness on the children in the family; 19 did this sometimes; and 1 never. They were also asked whether their psychiatric colleagues took into account any damage to the children which they reported. The proportions were similar: 24 said account was usually taken, 17 sometimes, and 2 'seldom'. Thus it seems that the mental hospital teams were becoming less exclusively patient-centred, while the community mental health services still had some way to go, especially in regard to children.

Group work was developing: 27 PSWs were participating in this activity, while 17 acted as group leaders. Twenty-three assisted formally in the training of mental nurses, and many others informally. Four took part formally in the training of junior medical staff, and 28 informally. Seventeen provided formal consultation to other social workers, and nearly all informally. Thirty supervised social work students, having taken between them 105 students in the previous year.

Sixteen of the respondents were already planning to leave the mental hospital service, and only 24 firmly intended to remain. Financial factors were clearly important: 34 of the subjects were dissatisfied on this score. Dissatisfaction was particularly strong among the 16 aged under 40, 9 intended to leave the service and 4 more were undecided. In addition to salaries, some were dissatisfied with working conditions and 5 resented lack of understanding of their role and function.

The Politics of Child Guidance

Despite the high respect in which child guidance was held by PSWs there was much external criticism of the service. It was alleged that most clinics did not work with the family as a whole, and that they provided a luxury service of long-term psychotherapy which suited many middle-class families but was not acceptable to most of the working class, who were apt to be alarmed at the offer of long-term therapy, taking it as an indication of very serious disturbance in the child, which they were unable to accept. In particular child guidance clinics were said to have nothing to offer to the large number of children in severely disorganised families which confront the social services with their greatest problems. The external critics seemed to have read very little since the publication of the only British book on the subject (Burbery, *et al.*, 1945). It was certainly unfortunate that no other books had appeared, but a study of the appropriate journals would have revealed considerable developments in both family therapy and consultation (see below).

There were at this time three types of child guidance clinic: some in hospitals, some entirely under local authorities, and some jointly administered by these authorities and the regional hospital boards (RHBs). To a foreigner this might have looked like a typical piece of British confusion and lack of logical system, and some British bodies soon began to try and tidy it up; but there was real substance in the view that 'the varied administrative settings reflect – and help to condition – the variety of approach to problems of maladjustment' (Ryan, 1967, p. 23).

In 1962 the British Medical Association proposed that all local authority clinics should be transferred to the hospital service for integration in a hospital-based child psychiatric service. This was strongly opposed by the doctors in the local authority health service and by the NAMH (1965) on the grounds that the local authority setting provided better opportunities for preventive work, for diffusing the valuable ideology of child guidance throughout local authority services, and contributing to the study and treatment of disorders of children predominantly expressed in the social and educational field. It was also argued that the existing variety of settings encouraged flexibility and ready response to the needs of the local community (although other critics complained that this left much to be desired).

In 1967 a Child Guidance Special Interest Group (CGSIG) was set up by PSWs engaged in that service, with the purpose of confronting the various comments and proposals from outside the service, which were often remarkably ill informed, with accurate information about the service and clarification of the structure and functioning of the multidisciplinary team. Until that time the main champion of the traditional pattern of child guidance was the NAMH, which was a direct descendant of the Child Guidance Council. But for all the notice which was taken of it by the various critics and redesigners, the NAMH might have been Cassandra. The creation of the Group was timely, for there was much to be done. The Seebohm Report (1968) suggested that child guidance clinics should invest most of their resources in diagnostic and consultative services, and Rehin (1969 and 1972) proposed that the child guidance team should be broken up and its members distributed among other services.

Early in 1968 the CGSIG undertook a comprehensive survey by questionnaire of the structure and functioning of child guidance clinics, to which we are indebted for many of the facts in this chapter (*The Child Guidance Service,* CGSIG/BASW 1975). One hundred and twenty-one replies were received, representing all types of clinics in England and Wales provided by local authorities or in hospitals. It also emerged that from 42 per cent to 54 per cent of a PSW's caseload consisted of cases in which the child was not receiving any direct treatment, and casework with the parents represented the only therapy provided.

A working party was set up in 1970 to consider and recommend plans for the future of the child guidance service. This was composed of representatives of the Royal College of Psychiatrists (Child Psychiatry Section), the British Psychological Society BASW (represented by the CGSIG) and the Association of Child Psychotherapists. This body circulated to all the relevant government departments a joint statement urging that the child guidance team should not be broken up, as suggested by Rehin, and should continue to provide treatment as well as diagnosis and consultation for members of other professions; also that whatever authority was to employ the PSWs should ensure their full-time attachment to their clinics. It became a major function of the working party to reply to the departments concerned, correcting their misunderstandings and emphasising the nature and importance of teamwork, and the need for consultation to have a basis in current therapeutic experience.

Eventually in March 1974 a further Joint Circular (DES 3/74) was issued which conceded that 'there are many more needs to be met than was at one time thought' (p. 3). It stated that 'psychiatric social workers have been an integral part of the Child Guidance Services since their inception . . . They have contributed to the development of services for children and their families, and the experience and expertise gained in the work have made a considerable contribution to social work training' (p. 4). There was a serious shortage of all the professions concerned, but ways must be found 'to extend help to more children with behaviour, emotional or learning difficulties and their families' (p. 5), apparently by economy in the use of scarce staff time and by greater flexibility. As well as providing assessment, diagnosis, consultation and treatment, the service must also provide 'help and general guidance about problems of child development and behaviour to parents and to other people in regular contact with children, including health visitors, general practitioners, teachers, social workers and residential child care staff' (p. 5).

Consultation
At an APSW study course in 1960, a number of the members were found to be somewhat disconcerted by the recent impact of what were then unfamiliar expectations that they should contribute to the mental health training of health visitors, or support and guide voluntary workers in making friends with patients. The speakers, however, gave encouraging accounts of consultation with social workers in health services and with the staff of a boarding school for maladjusted children, and of helping mental nurses who wished to carry out the after-care of certain patients. Two further study courses in 1966 and 1967 focused respectively on 'Trends in Social Work Services and Implications for Psychiatric Social Work' and 'Meeting the Needs of the Disturbed Child'.

It emerged from the papers presented on these occasions and from other publications, that consultation had two aspects: propagating the ideology of child guidance and mental health on the one hand, and on the other dispelling stereotypes and unlinking the client's or the pupil's problems from the personal associations which might be blinding the consultee to the needs of his client. It seemed that different consultants emphasised one or other of these aspects, but that they were probably both present in varying proportions.

Parsloe (1967) stated that many other caseworkers now shared the knowledge base of which PSWs had once had a monopoly, so that their contribution as consultants now needed to be more specifically focused on the effect of psychiatric illness on children and families, and the therapeutic expertise which they had gained by working closely with other members of the therapeutic team. However, there were still at that time and continued to be a great many untrained social workers, while the brevity of training courses, in view of the proliferation of the concepts and theories which they attempted to communicate, left many trained workers with an indigestible mass of information somewhat loosely related to the practical tasks with which they were confronted. Moreover, even the best-trained social workers continued to feel a need for consultation, not so much to gain further information as to clarify the psychodynamics operating between their clients and their intimate social networks, and between their clients and themselves. Help of this kind might be provided by a psychiatrist for one or more PSWs (Ratcliffe and Jones, 1956) or by an experienced PSW or other caseworker for colleagues in the field.

Certainly the demand was increasing. Skynner (1967), a leading exponent of consultation with a base in child guidance, reported a growing demand for this service, which in his experience was demanding a heavy investment of consultant time. He emphasised the educational aspect of consultation which enabled other professionals to share the knowledge and experience accumulated in the child guidance service and thus to carry, having new insights into the problems of and needs of their own clients or pupils, a growing share of the treatment load. He also pointed out that consultation required a heavy investment of the consultant's time, and that results were only gradual and not very visible in the early stages (very much like the results of psychotherapy).

The Seebohm Committee seems to have been oversold on this line of thought, and suggested that much more time should be devoted to consultation, at the cost of reducing the treatment function to a minimum. The CGSIC and its various allies had to explain repeatedly that effective consultation depended on the continuing therapeutic experience of the consultant. A question on this was included in its 1969 survey. Replies from 101 clinics (including departments of child psychiatry) revealed 'a prodigious amount of activity, in spite of staff shortages and high caseloads'. It appeared that different agencies approached different members of the clinic team for consultation. The greatest consumers were schools and children's departments: maternity and child welfare clinics received rather less consultation, but the PSW was the major consultant for these agencies, operating in half these situations single-handed. She also played a major role as consultant to education welfare officers, although the total number of these consultancies was relatively small.

The reference above to 'high caseloads' may surprise, in view of the widespread belief that PSWs enjoyed the privilege of small caseloads, being protected by the waiting list from the harsh winds of unmet need. In fact it was found that over 60 per cent of head, senior and single-handed PSWs had caseloads over forty. It was also found that in 35·9 per cent of the cases carried by this group of PSWs, casework with the parents was the only service provided, while this figure rose to 47·1 per cent for PSWs below this level.

Other Developments

Group work was proliferating in certain clinics. For instance, a child guidance clinic in the home counties reported (personal communication) that in 1975 it was running groups for mothers of children receiving speech therapy, and of children attending a day centre for the severely disturbed, parents of school phobic children, parents with marital problems, and others who had difficulties with only one of several children.

The *Journal of Psychiatric Social Work* contained occasional glimmers of new theory and its application in social work, for example on the uses of role theory, learning theory or socio-behavioural theory. There was also a growing concern among PSWs in child guidance about the tendency to neglect the many children with severe problems whose families were unable, for social or personal reasons, to use the child guidance service in its traditional form. Walker (1970) drew attention to the importance of intake methods in rendering the service acceptable or otherwise: the value of allowing direct access to parents, without third-party referral, and of treating the unheralded appearance of a distressed parent as a crisis in the sense defined by Gerald Caplan, as an opportunity for immediate and skilled intervention. This concept of crisis as the optimal moment for intervention was exerting an increasing influence in child guidance thought and strategy, and in many branches of social work. Walker also showed that a child guidance service which responded rapidly to parental appeals for help was in a good position to recognise mental illness which had not yet come to official attention, and to help such parents to seek the appropriate service for their own illnesses.

There had been a tendency to reserve child guidance for children whose parents were capable of considerable co-operation with the clinic, attending regularly and thus requiring little home visiting, but uneasiness was growing about the children thus excluded. Howell and Parsloe (1966) described a case in which the PSW took the child patient to and from her appointments by car, and invested a great deal of time in working with the parents at home. Ford (1966) expressed much concern about such families, but saw no alternative but long-term supportive casework in the home (which would have reduced still further the number of cases dealt with). This seemed to others a dubious solution, since it would call for a high investment of scarce PSW time in the kind of work which had been pioneered by the Family Service Units (FSU) and could be most appropriately provided by increasing their number, or by special teams set up in the child care services.

During this decade there had also been a growing focus on family interaction, and some interesting articles about a form of closer teamwork with families, in which the boundaries between the various therapist/patient or PSW/parent dyads were made easily permeable (Elles, 1961 and 1962). However, the process described was still very time-consuming, and it caused some surprise when Roberts (1968) reported on a method which produced quite rapid improvement in a number of families of the FSU type. This was conjoint family therapy in the form which Skynner (1971*a*, *b*, *c*) had developed on the basis of group analytic theory. It seemed that this made sense to the kind of family which was usually hard to reach and time-consuming if reached. Families incapable of frequent, long-term, regular interviews could often be induced to keep a small number of more widely spaced appointments, attending as a whole family, which proved to be less threatening for them than individual interviews. On such occasions, the family dynamics could be observed in action and it was possible to increase the family's understanding of some of the forces at play. This in turn could bring about at least small shifts in the family equilibrium which facilitated better functioning and helped the family to make better use of their regular social workers in the community. Here at last were methods by which the child guidance clinic could treat the kind of family which made great demands on the social services and with which the family most needed help.

The use of conjoint family interviews was by no means restricted to work with this type of family, but was found to be helpful in work with the whole range of cases, including the middle-class families which made use of child guidance but not of other services. Some clinics used such interviews mainly in the diagnostic phase, in which the parents and professionals worked towards an agreed definition of the problem and the formulation of a therapeutic contract. They were also used at strategic intervals in cases where two or more members were in individual treatment, when the need arose to facilitate fuller communication between them. A particularly effective use was made of them when help was sought for pre-school children; in these cases an exploration of the parental anxieties and the involvement of the child in the family dynamics often resulted in a rapid improvement of the child's symptoms, thus making prolonged treatment unnecessary. Most of the publications on this subject came from London; but the CGSIG survey found that in 1969 forty-six of the clinics responding offered this type of treatment, twenty-six of which were outside London (see also volume 2 chapter 8).

Numbers and Distribution of PSWs in 1969
As the total number of PSWs increased, a number of provincial centres began to attract sizeable groups. The APSW published a final list of its members in 1969, on the eve of entry into BASW. The total number of its associates now amounted to some 1,350, including guest members and a small number of qualified PSWs who no longer subscribed to the Association. One hundred and sixty-nine were working overseas. Some of these were British PSWs working abroad, while others were foreigners who had either come to Britain for PSW training or, having trained in their own countries, had worked for a time in the UK and retained their membership on going home. A considerable number had retired, or had temporarily withdrawn from professional work for family reasons.

PSWs were now more evenly spread over the country as a whole, for instance Lancashire had 87, Warwickshire (including Birmingham) 41, and Yorkshire 66. Analysis of the distribution by fields of employment in England and Wales showed 334 PSWs in child and adolescent psychiatry units (mainly child guidance clinics). Those working in psychiatric hospitals or psychiatric departments of general hospitals now numbered 189, a good many of whom worked part-time in the child guidance service of the hospital or in the local authority mental health service, thus providing a useful link between hospital and local authority. A further 12 worked in clinics providing out-patient treatment only for adults. Two hundred and nine were employed by local authorities; 80 of these were concentrated in London, but only eight counties now had no PSW in their mental health services. One hundred and thirteen PSWs held senior positions, while a number worked part-time in two services, particularly in hospitals and local authority services.

In Scotland, 23 PSWs worked in child and adolescent psychiatry, 30 in hospitals, and 7 in community care; and PSWs played an active part in planning the reorganisation of social work services.

PSWs were also making a major contribution to social work training. Fifty-nine were teaching in universities, mainly on applied social studies courses, but also on the few remaining specialised PSW courses and some on specialised child care courses. Forty-eight were teaching in colleges of further education on child care and CSW courses.

A considerable number were engaged in other fields of social work. Many of these had been seconded by their services to take a mental health course as a form of further training, while others had originally trained as PSWs and worked for a while in the mental health field, but had been recruited by other services as a way of raising casework standards. Thus 28 were employed in children's departments, of whom 22 held senior positions, and 10 in probation services, of whom 8 were in senior positions. Eight were attached to schools for maladjusted children, one as deputy head mistress, the rest as social workers. Seven worked in the FSU and others in a wide spectrum of voluntary agencies. Six PSWs worked in the DHSS social work service, 1 as a deputy chief social worker and 3 as regional social work officers.

Research

A popular reproach against PSWs was that they were too absorbed in helping individuals and families to spare time for research. It is true that in 1969 only thirteen were listed as employed in full-time research, but a survey of the professional journals revealed that a number carried on part-time research in relation to their clinical work. Some PSWs engaged in full-time research allowed their membership of the APSW to lapse, while a number also did full-time research for a year or two and then either returned to professional practice or moved into teaching. However, at various times these PSWs made major contributions on such subjects as the family relationships of young men with duodenal ulcers and of young male schizophrenics, the school as a factor in juvenile delinquency, the emotional problems of young deaf children and those suffering from severe burns and their respective families, factors affecting the rehabilitation of schizophrenic patients, and hereditary and experiential factors in mental illness. A PSW was also employed on the evaluation of the Belmont Neurosis Unit in the 1950s, her contribution being a follow up of discharged patients; several PSWs were involved at various times in the research team directed by Bowlby which explored with increasing refinement the results of the separation of young children from their home and parents. Outstanding among these was James Robertson, who introduced film as a method of recording, and who combined research with a persistent campaign of professional and public education which resulted in the widespread relaxation of the restrictions traditionally placed on the visiting of children in hospital by their parents.

In concluding this section it seems appropriate to quote once more from Bree (1970):

'Some PSWs have, through teaching and working for general social work development, helped to bring into being a profession of social work of a quality which was once the PSW's special achievement. We shall always have cause to be proud of this and of those among us who have worked consciously and conscientiously for a general professional organisation which could include all trained social workers. At the same time those PSWs who staffed the classical or pioneer clinical settings, without which there could have been no demonstration of the quality of the work, were establishing themselves as members of the therapeutic team and demonstrating (to colleagues and patients, if not to policy-makers) the value of the specially trained and expert workers in the field of serious mental disorder. These may now justifiably see themselves as specialists within the social work profession; not now because of specialist training only but as the result of committed, continuous, concentrated experience in a particularly difficult field.' (p. 176)

These were the hopes of many PSWs on the threshold of a new era in 1970, but some of them were disappointed. The specialist qualification, and consequently the specialist training, perished in the great post-Seebohm reorganisation, although psychiatric settings continue to make an invaluable contribution to the generic training of social workers. But this contribution is itself contingent on the continued attachment of social workers to hospital or clinic, which was still in 1975 a matter of some conflict and anxiety.

TRAINING FOR PSYCHIATRIC SOCIAL WORK

In 1950, the mental health course at LSE had only recently become independent of the Commonwealth Fund of America, which financed it from 1929 till 1947. It was now one of three courses training PSWs (see volume 2, chapter 1).

Recognition by the APSW of eligibility for membership was accepted as the sole hallmark of a PSW, so that each new course had to negotiate for recognition of the qualification it awarded. As courses began to multiply, special machinery for evaluation was required, and in 1954 the Association set up a Standing Advisory Committee on Training for Psychiatric Social Workers (SAC) to advise it on the adequacy of proposed new courses and to review existing ones periodically. The application of Liverpool University for recognition of a PSW stream in its diploma in socal administration well illustrates the problems of expansion. In an area where PSWs were very scarce, it was agreed that the only hope of early improvement was to start a local course which might appeal to students with strong local ties. But the shortage of PSWs implied an even greater shortage of suitable supervisors. In this context the SAC formulated its first draft criteria for acceptable fieldwork placements – and none of the local mental hospitals measured up to them. Recognition was withheld (to the fury of local politicians) although students were already taking the course. The deadlock was eventually resolved by arranging a block placement (instead of the usual concurrent one) to enable students to have their practical training for adult work at the North Wales Mental Hospital which was already accepting students from Manchester on the same basis.

Other universities also found it difficult to provide, within an accessible distance, both adult and child guidance placements of suitable quality as stipulated by the APSW. This was a major factor limiting the expansion of training, another being the difficulty of obtaining grants for students, which severely limited the numbers on the newer courses particularly. These small numbers fluctuated from year to year under the constraint first of one factor then of the other.

The LSE course was by now in a stronger position; its reputation was established, and it had the advantage of two major units for fieldwork training, the Child Guidance Training Centre and the social work department of the Maudsley Hospital. It had many more applications than the newer courses and of the thirty students enrolled in 1954, twenty-one had grants from the Ministry of Health.

As demand for PSWs further outstripped supply the APSW was subjected to mounting pressures to relax its admission standards. The Association's first attempt to ease the situation was made in 1950, in the form of a 'trainee scheme' by which would-be PSWs worked for a year or two in a psychiatric setting, under the supervision of a PSW approved for this purpose, before applying for PSW training. To become a trainee on the salaries offered showed great motivation for professional competence, since in view of the chronic shortage of PSWs it would have been easy for those concerned to be appointed to PSW vacancies without a PSW training. A number of people called themselves PSWs, since the title was not protected: the APSW therefore decided to entitle its members 'Associate of the Association of Psychiatric Social Workers' (AAPSW) to distinguish them from the unqualified. The trainee scheme provided a useful supplement to the PSWs in the field, although when a trainee took one of the recognised courses he simply replaced another applicant who might otherwise have been selected, but with the advantage of previous specialised experience and supervision. The shortage of appropriate placements was a limiting factor here too, especially as most trainees wanted to work in London, where they were in competition with students for places, rather than areas at a distance from a course. However, the number of trainees gradually increased as new supervisors were found, some of them in local mental health services which were not yet recognised as student placements. By 1957 60 trainees had been placed, of whom 38 subsequently qualified as PSWs, and 4 were still in training. A modest result for a great deal of organising, on account of the problem of combining rapid expansion with maintenance of high standards.

The mental health courses awarded a specialist qualification and most PSWs took up work in the mental health field, but courses were also taken by a few qualified social workers seconded from their own services to gain further knowledge in the psychiatric field. By 1959, as the shortfall of PSWs steadily increased, the APSW was induced to approve a temporary modification of its criteria in favour of MWOs and untrained social workers in hospitals for the mentally ill and subnormal. The same year saw a plan for accepting graduation from one of the new courses in applied social studies as a partial qualification for PSW status. Students on these courses were often younger than PSW students and might have had one psychiatric placement but not two. Social workers who had qualified with one such placement were now allowed to qualify as PSWs by undertaking a further four-month placement in the complementary psychiatric setting, to be organised by the university where they had trained. In 1964 this scheme was modified, enabling them to qualify by working for a year alongside a qualified PSW in the complementary setting; it also included social workers who had taken the advanced course in social casework at the Tavistock Clinic.

Those who attributed the shortage of PSWs to the restrictive practices of the APSW might with advantage have considered the chaos surrounding the financing of students. In 1960–1, of a total of 57 students, 16 had grants from government departments and 18 from local education authorities; 12 were seconded by their employers on salary, and 3 on partial salary. Secondment by employers was gradually increasing and accounted for twenty-five students in 1964.

A number of applied social studies courses eventually managed to qualify students as PSWs by providing within the course the traditional pair of psychiatric placements, but this was precarious. A course might have supervisors for two or three PSW students one year, and none the next. It was becoming increasingly hard to find good placements in adult work, because of the drift of potential supervisors into local authority mental health services, which the APSW was slow to recognise as acceptable alternatives to mental hospital placements. By 1963 under 50 per cent of PSWs were employed in clinical settings and almost 40 per cent by local authorities; but it was not until 1968, as part of a much wider relaxation of placement requirements, that the APSW brought itself to accept a local authority placement as appropriate preparation for work with mentally ill adults; placements in child care and probation were also accepted, provided that at least one placement for each student provided experience with a psychiatric team.

In addition to the LSE course, only three other specialised courses for psychiatric social work existed: in Edinburgh University Department of Social Studies and in Manchester and Leeds University Departments of Psychiatry. The further expansion of PSW training – other than Liverpool – took place on applied social studies courses. At each university, training was shaped not only by the orientation of the tutors, but also by a number of pulls and pressures which varied from place to place according to the academic setting and the local resources and balance of power. The psychoanalytic approach, with its emphasis on the psychogenesis and dynamic meaning of symptoms, was confronted on the one hand by an organic model of mental illness where social and emotional problems were regarded only as precipitants or as stresses to be mitigated as far as possible; on the other hand it was increasingly confronted with sociological explanations of behaviour and in some universities with other psychological models, such as learning theory. In departments of psychiatry the organic approach tended to predominate, and in departments of social administration or social studies the sociological and other models derived from the social sciences. But the available fieldwork placements exerted a balancing influence, since students had to have some comprehension of the theoretical bases of the practice of the agencies in which they were placed. However strongly the local psychiatric services might stress the organic approach (and there were, of course, a number in which the psychodynamic approach was represented) child guidance clinics always demanded an appreciation of emotional factors and the dynamics of family relationships.

Training for psychiatric social work appropriately reflected the demands of future practice in a field where a number of models and theoretical systems were in operation. The eclectic nature of the courses gave students a basis of knowledge from which to choose their own model, while enabling them to adapt if circumstances obliged them to work in an agency with an uncongenial approach.

The expansion of training exerted a constant drain on the pool of acceptable supervisors into teaching posts. As Professor Kathleen Jones said in her chairman's address to the APSW in 1967, the demand for PSWs as teachers was a tribute to the high standard of their training, but the field was correspondingly depleted. 'In the past three years alone, the number holding such posts has almost doubled. An additional fifty PSWs have been taken out of the field, and they tend necessarily to be the more senior members of the Association, with wider than average experience and better than average academic qualifications' (p. 62). The volume of the drain may seem surprising, but it included not only teachers of PSWs but also lecturers on applied social studies, child care and CSW courses. Despite these problems by 1970 twenty courses were recognised as competent to train PSWs.

From time to time efforts were made to provide advanced training or to extend it to two years, but these remained pipe dreams. The best that could be done was to organise refresher courses and study weekends, which attained a very high standard (see also volume 2, chapter 5).

In 1965 a pilot course in group work was organised by the Association jointly with the Association for Group Psychotherapy (AGP), on a day-release basis. This course became an annual event, though the AGP gradually took it over entirely and made it interdisciplinary.

The Content of Training

The content of courses varied from time to time and place to place around a stable core of basic subjects: general psychology, psychiatry (with some, but not much, attention to subnormality), the psychology of personality, the mental health services and psychiatric social work (or casework in psychiatric settings). At LSE there was a marked increase in the 1950s in the time devoted to normal child development and child psychiatry. Sociology made an early appearance at LSE, sometimes focused on a single problem such as crime, sometimes as a general 'sociological approach to social problems', but mostly focused on 'the role of the social worker in relation to social problems'. The psychology of family relations was introduced in the late 1950s, largely taught by members of the Family Discussion Bureau (later the Institute of Marital Studies), who sometimes narrowed the subject to marital relations alone. They none the less contributed a distinctive orientation to transactions across the ego boundaries of family members, and their influence spread to a number of other courses, thus preparing the way for the later developments in family therapy. Casework was always a central subject, but group work and community work were late arrivals in the absence of any concerted scheme for sending groups of social workers to learn these methods in the USA, as had been done for casework. Group work was introduced at LSE for a short time in 1957, but vanished from the curriculum from 1960 to 1969 when it was reintroduced, together with a parallel introduction to community work.

Table 7   *Number of psychiatric social workers trained, 1960–9*

1960	1961	1962	1963	1964
41	55	65	69	73
1965	1966	1967	1968	1969
86	88	101	114	129

Source: APSW *Annual Report*, 1960 (not included in earlier reports) and *Setting the Course for Social Work Education 1971–1973* (CCETSW, 1973).

Chapter 12

Social Work and the Elderly

INTRODUCTION

Social work with elderly people only developed slowly. It was largely unrecorded and with little study of their special social work needs. This chapter is thus largely a summary of related services and the better understanding of old people's needs as these developed in the twenty-five year period covered.

THE 1950s

Old people came into the limelight in the 1940s, perhaps because war-time conditions made their vulnerability more obvious. The National Corporation for the Care of Old People was set up after the war to administer Nuffield, air-raid distress and other funds to promote new ideas and experiments and to help establish a better standard of service for old people. The National Old People's Welfare Council (founded in 1940) effectively campaigned for many different aspects of old people's welfare. It brought a variety of individuals, public authorities, voluntary agencies and professions together, held annual conferences, ran refresher courses, inquired into particular aspects of old people's welfare and acted as a pressure group. It also promoted and serviced the many local old people's welfare committees which came into existence all over the country to bring together statutory and voluntary agencies working for the welfare of old people so that they might create a pattern within the multiplicity of services. Some committees faced problems of working on a shoestring, sometimes with intense resistance to co-operation.

Local initiative, especially to help the housebound or confused or frail, included spontaneous voluntary care for elderly neighbours, provision by the churches, community associations, women's institutes, local schools and factories, and many others. These activities and the considerable, though still inadequate, rise in social security benefits helped many old people to remain in their own homes or with relatives. A margin of financial independence, when it existed, maintained general independence and decreased family resentment. During the whole period only 2 per cent to 5 per cent of all old people were in residential care, indeed the vast majority were looked after when they needed it by their own families or neighbours.

The 1948 National Assistance Act abolished the poor law and transferred to local authority welfare services the provision, direct or through voluntary organisations, of residential accommodation for old people in need of care and attention. Much of this was in public assistance buildings and for a long time much unsuitable accommodation had to continue in use. Energetic efforts, largely by voluntary organisations, to open more homes for old people after the war when building restrictions were still in force often resulted in isolated and physically unsuitable country houses having to be adapted and the myth accepted that old people preferred to share bedrooms with several others.

There was no power to provide social care for old people in their own homes, other than as an incidental part of domiciliary health services including home helps. But some go-ahead local authorities regarded social care as a means to prevent or postpone an old person's need for residential care and attention – at the same time that children's departments were stretching the 1948 Children Act in a similar good cause. Otherwise, home helps, district nurses, health visitors, general practitioners and friendly visiting by a local old people's welfare committee, the churches, or other voluntary organisations or neighbours were thought to fill the bill. Geriatric and other health services for old people and numbers of homes and later sheltered housing, clubs and day centres all increased by degrees. Some of the most active National Assistance Board (later SBC) area offices did much to further individual old people's welfare. Settlements and family casework agencies also knew the amount of personal support and practical help some old people needed to sort out their affairs and to keep their courage and independence of spirit alive as they grew more frail. But there was no tradition of such a personal social service in local authorities. Townsend (1957) studied London County Council (LCC) officers' reports in the welfare departments on admission to welfare homes. These gave a brief summary of physical and social conditions based on a visit to the old person's home, for the officers usually concentrated on the home environment and were not required to discover anything about relatives or alternatives to admission to a welfare home. This contrasts with a mid-1970 view that

'When old people apply for admission to a residential home, it is essential that the matter shall not be treated lightly or superficially. It will be necessary to ensure that the client knows what is involved in this step – the loss of independence, the reduction in personal identity, the limitation on privacy and the restrictions of community life. Unsatisfactory living conditions are not a valid reason for admission to residential care, still less should an old person be over-persuaded by friends, relatives or even her doctor that 'you'll be far better off in a home'. Such an application may be a completely accurate statement of need, or it may be a cry for help because of other worries or needs; what is important is that the client is not encouraged to abandon her home too easily and that, first of all, every other possible solution is explored . . . The patient has not become suddenly very frail, more often there has been a breakdown in help given by family or neighbourhood which has left her unable to cope once the support is withdrawn.' (Speed, 1974, p. 130)

Townsend (1957) found that old people with daughters and other nearby women relatives made the least claim on the health and welfare services and isolated people a disproportionately heavy one. Most lonely old people were widowed and single people, usually men, living alone. There were multiple causes for loneliness, but 'desolation' was related to bereavement and separation from close relatives. These were also the largest proportion of old people admitted to hospitals or homes, or needing home helps. Conversely, grandparents with families close by played an important part, especially in looking after children. 'The greatest usefulness of many old people is in a heart kept young' (Fry, 1966, p. 9). Old people were the largest vulnerable group in the population and for many of them the health services were of primary importance because of their physical or mental disabilities. But many others were independent and, in any event, old people were no more all alike than middle-aged people or children.

In the mid-1950s 83 per cent of local authorities co-operated with voluntary organisations in providing services, for example old people's welfare committees, the British Red Cross Society, and various religious bodies (Younghusband Report, 1959). Many Darby and Joan clubs were started in the 1950s and some old people's clubs expanded into day centres with a mid-day meal, other services, warmth and companionship.

THE 1960s

In spite of great advances in the preceding ten years, the Seebohm Committee (1968) found these services in many areas 'underdeveloped, limited and patchy' (para. 293). A large number of homes were provided by voluntary organisations as well as local authorities. Standards varied considerably from modern, well-planned and well-run buildings to others that were old, badly designed, with too few trained staff and 'primitive accommodation' for them. Some homes in old converted buildings 'still had unattractive dormitory accommodation' (NCCOP, 1973, p. 15). Townsend (1965) pointed out that warmth, comfort and attention did not compensate for being mixed with strangers from other localities and backgrounds, expected to share most events of daily life, loss of occupation and separation from family and friends. By 1965 there were over 7,000 old people's clubs run by voluntary organisations and 115 local authority social centres (with 308 forecast for 1971) (Ministry of Health, 1966, para. 70).

Townsend and Wedderburn (1965) found in their large-scale survey that the vast majority of old people were cared for by relatives, including more than four times as many severely incapacitated old people living at home as were in institutions. Many more needed support services in the home.

By 1962 there were nearly 84,000 places in old people's homes, a number of these unfortunately still being in old public assistance institutions. By 1975 there were over 99,000 residents in local authority homes and 33,319 places in 1,019 voluntary homes.

Sheltered housing (or grouped homes), i.e. flatlets or bungalows with a warden, began in the 1940s and spread rapidly so that by the 1970s they were an important element in care for elderly people. Townsend and Wedderburn (1965) estimated that there were 30,000 to 40,000 old people in such housing in 1963. Figures were not available for the early 1970s, though by 1974 about 3,000 wardens were employed by local authorities and a number more by voluntary organisations. These schemes combined suitable housing within the local community with oversight intended to vary with each old person's needs, to ensure provision of services, and to prevent unnecessary admissions to homes for the elderly. Sometimes failure to clarify wardens' tasks and to support them created uncertainty about their responsibilities and too much control or too little stimulating activity. The main duties included general support to tenants, communal activities, dealing with emergencies, administration, and maintenance of buildings and equipment. The training committee of the National Old People's Welfare Council ran the first training course in 1962, a four-day residential event for wardens. Subsequently local authorities, voluntary organisations and the CCETSW ran short courses taken by a small proportion of wardens. An Age Concern working party made proposals for training through spaced short courses which would include the natural processes of ageing and human needs and relationships; services and facilities; home safety and other practical matters. This resulted in a programme of short residential courses.

Meals on wheels were started by local voluntary effort and greatly extended by the Women's Voluntary Service (WVS later the WRVS). Local authorities were not empowered to provide this service until the National Assistance (Amendment) Act, 1962. The WRVS ran it for one to five days a week on an agency basis for many local authorities. Sometimes meals were provided at or delivered from a day centre or luncheon club or were part of a wider home support service. These meals supplied nutrition, a contact for isolated old people and, at least theoretically, a means of spotting deterioration or emergencies. Books on wheels, the 'telly' and transport to clubs or day centres kept other doors onto the world open. Day centres – as opposed to clubs open for shorter periods – were obviously valuable. Their numbers increased and a few well-equipped centres provided meals, chiropody, hairdressing, recreation, outings, occupational therapy, baths, and a library and advice facilities.

The National Corporation for the Care of Old People, realising that local authority estimates of future needs for community care had been inadequate, offered to sponsor an inquiry to determine need. This was carried out by the Government Social Survey, with the support of the Ministry of Health and the Scottish Home and Health Department. It was undertaken by Amelia Harris (1968) in thirteen local authorities.

Difficulties in making a general analysis of needs included practical difficulties in meeting them, as well as different local authority policies about circumstances in which help should be given, for instance whether a home help for an old lady should also clean the working daughter's room, so lessening the strain of caring for her mother. Using as criteria for home help services that an old person was housebound, or had difficulty with shopping and cooking and there was no one else who could regularly give this help, the survey findings showed that the service needed to be increased from 40 per cent to 400 per cent in different localities to deal with new cases, but excluding additional time needed by existing recipients.

There was a shortage of suitable housing for old people in all the thirteen areas and some had no sheltered housing. Hardly any of the areas made any attempts to help old people with all the practical arrangements for moving and settling in. There were varied reasons for admission to residential homes, but the majority of applicants were single women or widows over 75 who could not look after themselves at home or thought they were too great a burden on relations. The survey estimated that at least one in five old people need not have been in residential homes if suitable housing had been available. It was the exception not the rule for old people to have a chance to visit the residential home before they went into it, though they would probably spend the rest of their lives there. Yet a high proportion of residents liked the homes. As one said: 'It would take a stick of dynamite to shift me.' Others disliked the food or the lack of privacy or other uncongenial residents. Twelve per cent were unhappy, especially about having to share rooms but some of these might have been discontented anywhere. Only 3 out of the 500 residents interviewed complained about the staff, while many spontaneously spoke of their kindness and attention. This is a common finding amongst people in residential situations. It may illustrate 'the snare of gratitude' but also the kindness and devotion referred to by the Williams (1967) and other committees.

Some people on waiting lists had made other satisfactory arrangements or been dead for up to a year. The survey estimate of need for residential care (i.e. not better housing) showed that in seven areas out of thirteen, no extra places were needed but in three others the number should be more than doubled. Unless far more adequate housing was also available, welfare departments would be forced to continue providing for those who were really the housing department's responsibility. Many homes took short-stay residents to enable the family to have a holiday. The proportion of people over 65 getting meals on wheels ranged from 1·9 per cent to nil. Two meals a week was the commonest number. In every area, social welfare officers had caseloads 'far in excess of what they could reasonably be expected to deal with' (Harris, 1968, p. 58). This was the only (and oblique) reference in the report to social workers. In this it did not differ from other studies in the 1950s and 1960s. For example, Townsend and Wedderburn (1965) did not refer to welfare officers in their 1962 survey of the use of health and welfare services.

THE 1970S

The well-being and continued contribution of retired people had become a major concern, since retirement might last for up to thirty years and numbers were steadily increasing. In 1971 94 per cent were in private households, 200,000 were in old people's homes, and 220,000 in hospital, the remainder were in hotels or boarding houses. This gives some idea of the size of the problem of providing a sufficient range of services. Better domiciliary and other services and a longer expectation of life were resulting in more frail old people in homes for the elderly, and many old people still remained in hospital because no suitable alternative was available for them elsewhere. Too little was known about the circumstances or needs of old people living in hotels and boarding houses. It was likely that regulation was required since some were in effect unregistered old people's homes. It was also likely that many old people living alone or in hotels, hospitals or nursing homes needed someone to give personal support, practical help, and act as protector and advocate. There was also concern about the large number of mentally impaired old people suffering from neuroses, depression and dementia. There was an unknown number of homeless old people drifting between hostels and reception centres or sleeping rough.

Age Concern (formerly the National Old People's Welfare Council) became independent from the National Council of Social Services (NCSS), co-ordinated the activities of some 1,100 local groups, provided a comprehensive information service, had a team of advisory officers, ran a training department and campaigned effectively on behalf of old people through the mass media, in government circles and elsewhere. In co-operation with other national organisations, and through widespread discussion groups, it produced a series of reports on different aspects of old age and undertook three research projects in preparation for a manifesto on the place of the retired and elderly in modern society published in 1975.

Domiciliary welfare services for the elderly were only made mandatory in 1971 when section 45 of the Health Services and Public Health Act, 1968 was implemented.

The DHSS Social Work Service Survey of *Development of Services for the Elderly* (1973a) found 'wide variations in the response of society, and of local communities, to the needs of elderly people, and it is generally accepted that the quality, extent and availability of services of all kinds is uneven and subject to considerable constraints' (p. 2).

Most social services departments had arrangements for co-ordinating services for the elderly. These ranged from improvements in previously static services to comprehensive planning. In some authorities there was a lack of clarity about roles and functions; in others senior officers were appointed to co-ordinate services for the elderly. A variety of means were used to identify elderly people in the area, including various small research projects. This raised the further problem of how to keep information up to date, devise reliable recording, review methods and meet identified needs. The main priority groups were people over 75, those living alone or housebound, the very frail or mentally infirm, the isolated, those newly discharged from hospital or in need of residential care, the elderly sick and disabled, and the recently bereaved. There was also little attention to the needs of some elderly middle-class and professional people living on fixed incomes at or below the poverty line who would not think of asking for help: ' . . . these are in need but so are the better off whose incomes can keep them in food and shelter but cannot buy them sheltered housing or adequate home help or home nursing . . . who are as subject as any to bereavements and loneliness, to arthritis or heart trouble or mental deterioration' (NCCOP *Annual Report 1974*, p. 29).

It was generally intended to develop social work support for elderly people and their families, but often this was still an aspiration because of work pressures. Several authorities had projects to board out elderly people in families: a device which had been pioneered years earlier by an energetic local council of social service. There was universal agreement that it was necessary to identify people in need of help. Some social services departments had increased their staffs, but the quality of service and matching this to need was more problematic. The two greatest impediments were financial and staffing difficulties, while services were not well planned in inter-relation with each other, for example day services and sheltered housing co-ordinated to forestall admission to an old people's home or a geriatric ward. Moreover, many old people did not know what was available locally or were reluctant to apply for help.

The home help service was an effective means of making it possible for old people to go on living in their own homes, of counteracting loneliness and identifying deterioration. 'Good neighbours' organised as volunteers were sometimes paid a small sum to be responsible for keeping an eye on several old people in the street or performing regular services for an individual. Help in the home to support relatives or for old people living alone included household tasks and shopping, friendly visiting, letter writing, reading, collecting pensions or changing library books, transport, meals on wheels and night sitting. Meals on wheels services were increasingly run by local authorities and the coverage was extended from two to five or exceptionally, seven days a week. They might or might not be an integral part of a wider home support service. The DHSS survey revealed increased concern for the quality of life in old people's homes and improvement of previous low levels of staffing so that staff could spend more time with residents and change institutional patterns of care. There were also the beginnings of more group activities. Many residential homes offered day care for small numbers of frail old people.

A local survey of old people in Highfields, Coventry, in 1971–2 showed that over half suffered from some ailment which frequently caused problems of mobility. Many took an optimistic view of their health, which resulted in their going out more and being visited more than those with a pessimistic view. Most of those who needed help with personal care received this from relatives, friends or neighbours; only 11 per cent were helped by statutory agencies. A number received no help from anywhere and about 12 per cent were unvisited by either friends or relations. Nearly half were on supplementary benefit and many more appeared to be eligible but had not applied. Rather over half had had no holiday for several years but a number disliked the idea of group holidays. About one-third complained of loneliness, many of these were single or widowed people. Those who were visited infrequently, less often said they were lonely than those visited frequently. Action was taken on these findings in 900 cases, which led to much help which might not otherwise have been given.

Age Concern conducted a survey (1974) of a national sample of 2,700 old people living in private households. Only one in ten were living in households of which they or their spouse were not the head. Five per cent were permanently housebound, 8 per cent had a home help, 18 per cent were in touch with a 'welfare worker'. One-third went regularly to clubs, though only a minority belonged to old people's clubs. Ninety-six per cent were satisfied with the services they received. Twenty-five per cent felt some loneliness, particularly women over 75; in over half the onset followed bereavement. Two-thirds were helping others in some way, by baby sitting, shopping, visiting, gardening, and so forth; the same proportion were always happy to go on holidays but few had one regularly. Eighty-seven per cent were satisfied with their accommodation. About 40 per cent were happy to be retired and the vast majority 'did not get fed up with it'; interestingly there was little difference in this between men and women or across age groups. This survey showed fewer old people living with relations than was often supposed: the majority were managing satisfactorily, but many were in need of further support.

The DHSS *Consultative Document on Priorities for Health and Personal Social Services in England* (1976a) proposed, in spite of severe financial stringency, a doubling in the coming period of day centre places, home helps, meals on wheels, and an increase of 2,000 places a year in residential homes.

The range of old people's needs went far beyond social work as such, but none the less it is surprising to find how little was written in these decades about social work with old people, apart from Goldberg's important study (1970) discussed in volume 2 (see chapter 11, section on 'Two Action Research Studies of Social Work Effectiveness'). Professional social workers, like others, found it hard to accept the limited goals, inevitable deterioration, and need for continuing service in work with old people. Speed (1974) pointed out that

'Too little has been said in the past about the value of casework or a casework approach with older people. They face many problems including the crises of retirement and bereavement, both associated with a great deal of pathological depression not always diagnosed or treated. They live in a rapidly changing world in which they are asked in addition to make drastic adjustments at a time of life when this is most difficult. There may be no better example of the need for social work skill than the vulnerability of the older person forced by circumstances to consider accepting full residential care.' (pp. 129–30)

These were some of the crisis points in ageing. The following aspects had also become clear since 1950. In spite of much poverty and widespread failure to take up means-tested benefits, old people were better off than before the war, though many found it hard to manage, particularly in the winter, and had little freedom of choice. Their families and neighbours were by far their greatest support, even though post-war housing policies and greater mobility in employment had sometimes weakened close links. Their natural support systems were sometimes inadequate, often required reinforcement, and old people might need practical help in getting services or making and carrying out decisions; many were frail or confused and needed someone reliable and knowledgeable to protect them from neglect and apathy. It was especially important to mobilise inter-related services on their behalf, whether home helps, meals on wheels, transport, clubs, day centres or holidays; to care for their physical needs; and to keep them in touch with other people. Indeed, it had become obvious that activity and continuing give-and-take relations with other people were usually vital to mental health in old age. Inadequacies in any given service (including transport) could limit freedom of choice and block other services – especially hospital beds.

Like all social work, services to old people required thorough initial assessment, decisions about possible objectives for individuals, help to create the right social milieu especially in institutions, and a mixture of practical services and emotional and personal support that gave old people a sense of being valued and cared for, an incentive to go on trying to make life better. Direct social work intervention tended to be brief and crisis-oriented, whereas well-chosen, trained and supported volunteers could often create continuing and unhurried relationships with old people.

The disabilities of the elderly eroded independence and freedom to choose at different ages for different old people – though never for some. The severest hazards were failing health, pain and fatigue which restricted mobility and independence. The maintenance of psychosomatic good health, provision of good housing, and every other means of combating disability were therefore essential to lessen the hardships of old age, together with maintenance of social contacts, morale and a feeling of being wanted. 'One of the main difficulties of planning for the care of the ageing person is . . . to respect their personalities while grouping their infirmities' (Fry, 1966, p. 6). Loneliness, though not peculiar to old people, was increased by constrictions, separation and bereavement. Hadley *et al.* (1975) concluded that the chief causes of loneliness were loss of a single close relationship, the slow erosion of a close family network, or having always been a 'loner', but the whole concept was complex and little explored (see also chapter 19).

What had been learnt about old people's well-being in the preceding decades showed that social work had an essential role to play, not only at the onset of old age but in those changing inter-relations between personality and the social environment which either weakened or strengthened morale.

Chapter 13

Social Work and the Physically Handicapped

INTRODUCTION

Social work with physically handicapped people developed slowly between 1950 and 1975. Therefore this chapter covers social work employment rather than discoveries in the practice of social work with people suffering from diverse handicaps of different degrees of severity. In any event, greater contributions to improved services for handicapped people were made by the education, health and employment services – and by advances in technology.

THE 1950s

Voluntary effort on behalf of handicapped people increased steadily in the post-war years (see chapter 18). Local authority health and welfare services also expanded, but their social work was largely unexplored country until in 1955 a working party was set up to inquire into 'the proper field of work, and the recruitment and training of social workers at all levels . . . in the local authority health and welfare services . . . and in particular whether there is a place for a general purpose social worker with an in-service training as a basic grade' (Younghusband Report, 1959, para. 1). The Report said that it was 'the first review of social work in a complex series of services which evolved independently and have reached different stages of development. We found ourselves . . . considering the functions of social workers in nine or ten, rather than in two distinct services' (para. 16). This was due to piecemeal historical development of legislation; to the lack of interest by the general public and politicians and thus the low priority given to the 'welfare' aspect of these services; to divisions according to mental or physical handicap, i.e. classification along medical not social lines; or because social reformers had been active about some needs while others remained comparatively neglected and invisible. There was also a tendency to isolate different groups for special, often separate, provision according to age, handicap or social failure. The simplicity or complexity of individual, family and social problems did not necessarily coincide with the classifications of medicine or the social services. There were limited services for the mentally ill, the mentally handicapped, the blind, the deaf, 'the general classes of the handicapped', the old, the homeless, and in some local authorities, help for unmarried mothers and their children or for problem families. Provision – and efforts to improve it – included home help services, care and after-care and residential accommodation for certain people in need of care and attention or who were homeless. Only those who knew these services in the 1950s can realise the degree of separation between them, the 'different and special' attitudes and the resistance of many social workers (mostly untrained) with each group to the idea that any amalgamation of services might be possible or desirable. Some medical officers of health in combined departments and chief welfare officers in others were pioneering better services, and there was some movement in other health and welfare departments to try to remedy the deficiencies of what were frequently limited and static services.

This was the period when the claim of health visitors, and of others on their behalf, to be both in practice and principle the 'general purpose social worker' was at its height. This claim was understandable because in services staffed by the untrained they had a professional training with common standards (even though for different work); and because medical officers of health naturally preferred health visitors who spoke or at least understood a common language. Home teachers of the blind had the existing training (see below) and a good deal of experience. Deaf missioners employed in what was usually an agency service were almost the only people able to communicate with the deaf. A number of other fieldworkers had come over from public assistance in 1948. More than 40 per cent of these were over 50 years old by 1956. In a world where no qualifications had been provided for them, they looked back with nostalgia to the certificate of the Poor Law Examinations Board, though this was mainly based on a minute knowledge of relevant legislation. Many felt neglected, with little hope for future prospects or for the attraction of the service to a new generation.

Officers already in these services said that they would not advise their children to follow them because of lack of esteem, poor promotion prospects, comparatively low salaries, heavy responsibilities and long working hours. In this vicious circle it was difficult to attract scarce, trained social workers yet the situation could only be altered if they were available and well used. Lack of training and an ill-defined professional function naturally affected recruitment and it rarely occurred to newly qualified social workers to go into a health or welfare department. There were also no fieldwork placements in these departments, which meant that students did not have experience in them compared with hospitals, child guidance clinics, probation, child care and family casework. Moreover, in these local authority departments professional social workers were often in an administrative hierarchy where they might not be free to plan their own work, make decisions, sign their own letters, or have direct contact with other services because communication was only permitted via chief officers, i.e. up and down an administrative ladder. 'To venture forth into a health department of a local authority, perhaps as the only almoner amongst a group of administrators, health visitors and social welfare officers, catching an occasional fleeting glimpse of the deputy medical officer of health, without a room for interviewing, private telephone or filing cabinet, is not a very tempting prospect' (Goldberg, 1961, p. 102). The situation as it was in the 1950s for the blind, the deaf and the general classes of the handicapped is briefly described below.

The functions of home teachers of the blind were to ease the initial shock of blindness, which might lead to severe depression, to restore confidence and teach blind people how to cope with many different aspects of daily living, in short to 'teach the blind to be blind'. This often entailed difficult personal and social adjustments as well as practical help. Home teachers also tried to help the family to readjust and learn not to overprotect the blind member. Practical help might be needed in addition to personal and social adjustment. In 1957 there were 814 home teachers (including 70 in Scotland). Most were single women who held the home teaching certificate of the College of Teachers of the Blind. Unfortunately, candidates for the examination were not required to take one of the available training courses as a condition of sitting the examination. There were thirty-five senior posts (fifteen held by men). Twenty-two per cent of registered blind people were also mentally or physically handicapped and over 60 per cent were aged over 65. The social clubs which home teachers spent a good deal of time in organising were valuable, but more understanding of how to counter withdrawal and apathy was needed. The working party thought that group-work skills were also essential to enable social clubs to fulfil their potential. Local authorities were increasing their own services, but also made considerable use of voluntary organisations. The haphazard growth of services had resulted in many anomalies.

Local authorities required the consent of the Ministry of Health to use home teachers for work with other handicapped people. Many were questioning the wisdom of providing a separate service for the blind when all handicapped people had much in common. This view was not shared by organisations for the blind in the 1950s. They argued that only specialised, full-time workers could help blind people and their families to adjust to and accept the handicap. They also argued that welfare officers with home teacher qualifications would not be satisfactory because blind people would resent being visited by someone also concerned with other handicaps, especially mental illness or deficiency. The strength of the feeling and the identification of many home teachers and voluntary organisations with the blind partly sprang from fear that the considerable gains in blind welfare since 1920 would be submerged in other backward services and that the quality of technical services would deteriorate.

Services for deaf people had been pioneered by the churches and voluntary organisations. They were difficult to provide and problems of communication resulted in a high proportion of agency agreements with voluntary associations for deaf welfare services. By 1956 a handful of authorities had started a few services by enabling a welfare officer to learn to communicate with deaf people. There were only 8 of these against the working party's estimate that 150 to 200 were needed. Voluntary organisations employed about 160 of whom most were men. There was a considerable danger, particularly in agency agreements, of the worker becoming as isolated as deaf people themselves. Problems of communication often resulted in tensions between the deaf and their relatives, friends, neighbours and workmates. For social work in this field, fluency in communication and understanding of the psychology of deaf people were essential, whether in work with individuals or in the clubs which existed for the deaf. There were fewer ordained missioners to the deaf than in the past and fewer people able to interpret the deaf to the world at large and the world to the deaf. Work with deaf people had been pioneered by the churches, but they and their families were now almost the most neglected group in the social welfare field, indeed the deaf and their acute isolation were a blind spot of society.

The working party said: 'In the present limited state of knowledge there is . . . a most urgent need for further research and imaginative experiment in discovering and meeting the individual needs of deaf people and in exploring means by which they can be brought more closely in touch with the community' (para. 692).

Under the National Assistance Act, 1948 local authorities could be required to submit schemes for the welfare of other handicapped people. This included ascertainment, help with personal problems, social and recreational facilities, practical assistance in the home, facilities for transport and holidays, help in finding employment, and sheltered employment in workshops or at home. The trouble was the limited use of these powers, particularly for the 'substantially and permanently handicapped' who were not blind or deaf. For example, so far as ascertainment was concerned, in 1957 two comparable local authorities had 22 and 232 handicapped people on their registers; a county with its own service had 335 registered handicapped people, while a voluntary organisation covering the same county had 994 such people. Although ascertainment and need for services were not synonymous, at least ascertainment was the first step to discovering need. The Piercy Committee (1956) estimated that there were about 140,000 substantially and permanently handicapped people in England and Wales needing welfare services against 65,000 on local authority registers at the end of 1957. The Committee's aim was a welfare service able to give sufficient aid to handicapped people to enable them to share in the life of the community. But by the late 1950s only the fringes had been touched.

At first there was emphasis on providing services, on social and craft centres, sheltered employment, gadgets and aids to daily living, holidays and structural adaptations to the home. The aim was occupation and interest and greater mobility as well as making life easier for the family. Valuable though these services were if well planned, some welfare officers saw that it was also necessary to recognise and ease family tensions and try to modify family attitudes. The enormous frustrations and isolation of handicap were too often dealt with by bright reassurance or incitement to 'grin and bear it'. Most of the work was undertaken by welfare officers with other duties. They made preliminary visits to assess needs, including the type of services required. They then arranged for these services and kept in touch, though rarely in relation to a thorough assessment of the person in his family and social circumstances. But as one experienced investigator commented: 'Although one could observe their genuine enthusiasm in gathering new knowledge and developing a new service, there was the danger of failing to see the handicapped person and his family and of concentrating instead on the handicap itself' (Younghusband Report, 1959, para. 549).

So far as handicapped children were concerned, social workers in the health and welfare services (other than those in child guidance clinics) did not usually come into the picture until the handicapped boy or girl (including educationally subnormal and maladjusted pupils) left school. Health visitors and school welfare officers were responsible up to that point.

All health and welfare services had a significant social work element but were obviously at different stages of development, for example by the late 1950s services for the physically handicapped were seen to be far more complex than in the myopic or regimented past. This was another aspect of increased clarity about the wide-ranging purposes of the services, including the importance of early intervention and helping people to live more independently. The relations between people and their social milieu were also better understood, so that there was recognition that they should be kept as part of their families and the community for as long as possible, though what this might entail was yet unexplored. Good work was possible at a certain level, for example when district welfare officers were well known in the area and to local general practitioners so that much work came their way which was not necessarily covered by statutory services. Yet specialisation could consist of separately administered services, sometimes in the same department, with staff engaged solely in that service, and often with little contact between them. In the mid-1950s about 60 per cent of mental welfare officers had no other duties. Most local authority almoners were specialised in TB or VD work. Services for the blind and deaf were almost wholly specialised.

The heart of the problem in these diverse services was how far the distinctions corresponded to human needs or were primarily administrative categories. In attempting to answer these questions, the working party concluded astringently that 'the existing sectionalisation of these services no longer makes sense administratively, in economy, or from the point of view of social work' (para. 553). It added that the key lay in staff training. There would be little point in grouping functions without staff qualified to meet related needs more adequately through understanding what was common and what special in a variety of human situations.

The field investigations for the working party brought to light the wide range of services and many problems from the simple to the complex in social workers' caseloads. The Report concluded that sound work was being done at a level within the worker's ability and the constrictions of heavy workloads – some at a very good standard – but much of it required a higher level of skill, competence and impartiality than could be expected from untrained workers. Analysis of necessary skill was essential to clarify function. Many people were able to cope, given a home help or support in a crisis; others could contain a difficult situation over a long period with the support of a skilled social worker and periodic alleviation; but some individuals and families might need well-directed support for considerable stretches of time. It was not possible to generalise by the nature of the crisis or disability because a significant factor was the strengths of the person or family and the social supports around them. It was thus necessary, as the Ingleby Report (1960) also emphasised, to assess the situation correctly and the degree of skill needed to help effectively, including a range of available resources.

In the light of this analysis, the working party came to the controversial conclusion that the total content of social workers' caseloads throughout the health and welfare services could be divided into three categories: (a) people who needed information or advice, material help, or periodic visits to keep in touch and assess whether changed circumstances made different help necessary; (b) people who should receive systematic help from a non-university trained social worker; (c) people with problems of special difficulty who needed the service of a professionally qualified and experienced social worker. In the light of subsequent experience these categories as such appeared to hold true, though not the distinction between university and other training. The 1975 analogy would be with holders of the CQSW and the newly started certificate in social service. The working party concluded that staff with a general training in social work could be responsible for a broader grouping of social work functions. Psychiatric social workers, almoners and family caseworkers should have a caseload of difficult cases (a 'case' was defined as a situation not a person), act as consultants to other staff, supervise newly qualified social workers, and take part in in-service training. In time it was hoped that some staff would also be qualified in group work and community organisation.

The categories did not refer to given symptoms, for example unmarried parenthood or handicap, but to the presence (or comparative absence) of personal, family or social crises, or inability to cope with the situation. Thus any given person or family might be at different points in time in any one of the three suggested categories. This implied an expectation, not clarified in the Report, that many people might be in intermittent or regular contact with the service over long periods of time, as was accepted in general medical practice. No data existed in the late 1950s on which to estimate percentages in each category, though obviously there would be a higher proportion of psychiatric cases in the special difficulty category. It was likely that the brunt of the work would fall on what the working party called 'trained' as distinct from 'professionally trained' social workers. Although the Report did not say so, this distinction was made in order not to shock the susceptibilities of the professional associations which had struggled to establish that social workers needed a university training, and whose co-operation was vital – and as it proved, forthcoming – for the implementation of the new training proposals.

This working party's findings finally brought social work with handicapped people into the mainstream of social work. All its recommendations were interdependent and intended to be implemented as a whole under five headings: the increased demands likely to be made on the services in the future; the improvement of working conditions; the better deployment of resources and co-ordination of effort; the provision of training; and the need for research. The Report was criticised for putting the main emphasis on the treatment aspects of social work practice with almost no reference to management (still called administration). This was a valid criticism, though few social workers were engaged in management in that period.

THE 1960s

In 1960 it became mandatory for local authorities to provide welfare services for the 'general classes of the handicapped', but the results were very uneven. Some local authorities only registered handicapped people who applied, others only those for whom services were available. Sally Sainsbury (1970) regarded welfare officers as 'in some sense the pivot of the local authority welfare services' because they assessed people for registration and thereafter must visit them at least annually to provide services (if available) or arrange admission to residential care. She found considerable disagreement amongst welfare officers themselves about their role. Those who were trained social workers were conscious of disabled people's unmet psychosocial problems. But some older welfare officers reacted sharply against intruding into people's lives and thought their task was to lay on other services. Caseloads varied widely but averaged about 350 in London at the time of Sainsbury's survey (1965).

Social workers with the blind (home teachers renamed) faced a difficult transition period. They were not professionally qualified social workers, yet they had more teaching skills than those qualified on the new certificate in social work (CSW) courses. About fifty students a year took the certificate of the College of Teachers of the Blind but this was to be discontinued and it was feared that in time less adequate technical services would be available for blind people. Training for mobility officers seemed likely to be extended to cover social rehabilitation and means of communication, but this would not cover all the education and technical service needs of blind people.

Goldberg (1966*b*) saw as the nub of the problem that

'the introduction of personal and client centred casework services into the administrative setting of the local authority, which used to be mainly concerned with the provision of more impersonal services for legally defined categories of persons, posed difficulties. The nature of the social needs with which the social workers deal demands decision making and a wide range of discretion at field level, whereas formerly decisions were made mainly at the top.' (p. 74)

These decisions were commonly made on paper by untrained administrators. She gave detailed case examples of good (and sometimes less good) work by welfare officers. This study, which was part of the attempt to introduce modern social work in the welfare services, analysed for the benefit of chief welfare officers and others in the service the ways in which handicaps and disability affect people and their families, how other reactions were affected by social supports or pressures, and how social workers could help them to express their feelings and meet their personal and practical needs. Many chief welfare officers and the Institute of Social Welfare co-operated actively in efforts to modernise these services.

Attitudes began to change in the 1960s with the first training for social workers in the health and welfare services, short courses and conferences for senior and chief welfare officers and medical officers of health, and a variety of in-service training.

The Seebohm Report (1968, paras 316–35), referring to the mid-1960s, commented that services for the physically handicapped were in urgent need of development. Expansion of services and experiment depended on individual initiative rather than any national advances. Although the most liberal authorities had made progress, yet they suffered from lack of trained staff and other resources and were too often dealing mainly with crisis situations. The Committee found that whilst there had been great advances in medical services and special education, professional social care for handicapped children and their families had not developed to the same extent, for example for school leavers. Also 'the current provision for the social care of chronic sick people is seriously inadequate and we consider that the social service department must develop a more imaginative and more effective pattern of community support for these people and their families' (para. 374). The Report recommended that the social services departments should take over responsibility for social work and occupational therapy for physically handicapped people and their families, the provision of residential and day centres for them, and home helps, meals on wheels, holidays and a sitters-in service (para. 325).

By the time of the Seebohm reorganisation some senior officers were experienced and professionally qualified. Social workers in these services felt less devalued as they began to be accepted as part of the mainstream of social work, and their function by degrees ceased to be assessed in either medical or vague 'welfare' terms related to the provision of specific services. In some authorities the welfare services were in the health department, in others they were under a separate committee and chief officer. There was a more realistic approach to specialisation and attempts to discover what was common to various handicaps and what special, for instance communication with the deaf and teaching mobility to the blind were clearly special skills, but deaf and blind people shared some personal and social disabilities with other handicapped people.

THE 1970s

Both the Seebohm Report (para. 328) and the National Children's Bureau study *Living with Handicap* (Younghusband, *et al.*, 1970) stressed the importance of early identification, comprehensive and continuous assess-ment, and interdisciplinary and agency co-operation with the family and the handicapped person to diagnose, to assess need, give appropriate co-ordinated service, and revise plans from time to time. Yet good assessment teams could merely cause frustration if the services they recommended were not available. Social workers had a recognised key role, both as members of assessment teams and in helping handicapped people and their families to achieve a better adjustment, to lessen isolation, to provide emotional support, aids to daily living and practical advice about the management of handicap. The same proposals were made in the White Paper *Better Services for the Mentally Handicapped* (DHSS, 1971a).

Both reports recommended that the proposed social service departments should have continuing responsibility for co-ordinating agreed treatment and for the social care of the handicapped person and his family. The Seebohm Report said: ' . . . there must be one service with a long term responsibility, generally extending in time beyond the limits of the responsibilities of other services (with the important exception of the family doctor) for the social care of the handicapped individual and his family. The social service department must carry this continuing responsibility' (para. 328). This responsibility would be heightened at crisis points like the birth of a handicapped baby, chronic illness or accidental disablement of an adult, the transition from home to school, the disillusionment of seeking employment, facing the inevitability of deterioration and sometimes residential care, or any other major change in family circumstances.

Some argued (*Living with Handicap*, 1970; *No Childhood*, Council for Children's Welfare, 1975) that children abandoned in long-stay hospitals – who were not protected by the Children Acts – should be received into care by the local authority or, if they were infrequently visited, have a friend or guardian statutorily appointed with some independent responsibility for their well-being. The same general argument applied to adults.

The Harris survey (1971) of disabled people, carried out by the Office of Population Censuses and Surveys for the DHSS, revealed more than 3 million people over the age of 16 (and not in hospital or other residential care) with some degree of physical, mental or sensory impairment. For various reasons this was probably an underestimate. More than one-third needed some form of social support and over 356,000 were severely handicapped people needing considerable support. Only 12 per cent of the total were registered with local authorities.

There was a very considerable potential advance when under the Chronically Sick and Disabled Persons Act, 1970 local authorities were required to discover the numbers and needs of substantially and permanently physically handicapped or mentally impaired people in their area, and to publicise information about available services. In 1973 the DHSS Social Work Service undertook an inquiry into the development of services under this Act in a random sample of thirty-five local authorities (Browning and Hope-Murray, 1974). Every authority had taken some action to identify disabled people, using the Harris survey as a general guide. Methods ranged from sophisticated research sample surveys or house-to-house visiting by volunteers to authorities which thought it more sensible to improve existing services than to raise false hopes by uncovering more unmet need. Diversity of sampling methods and widely different classifications of handicap made it impossible to compare findings, but every survey revealed many hitherto unrecorded disabled people. Most were elderly women and the commonest disabilities were rheumatic diseases, visual and hearing handicaps and nervous disorders. Most surveys only included people over 16 not in residential care. It remained to translate the findings about numbers into analyses of need and what combination of services, type and level of skill, and means of periodic reassessment was required. It was impossible to deduce from the statistics how many social workers were needed and the surveys gave little attention to the social and emotional aspects of disablement (CCETSW, 1974*b*). By

1974 there were 679,200 people on local authority registers against 404,800 in 1970.

Problems of identifying numbers and need were illustrated by an intensive survey of a small area in Kensington and Chelsea (Kensington and Chelsea Social Services Department, 1974). Wide publicity and inquiries of voluntary organisations, GPs, local publicity and other inquiries identified an additional 12 handicapped people, but a further 43 were found through visits to every household, i.e. a total of 55 as against the 52 already known to the service. Twelve of the 55 needed some service against additional service needed for 20 of those already known. This last figure showed that those supplying any one service do not necessarily know about or report a need for other services. About one-third of the known handicapped people in the survey had a social worker, but some were only visited about every six months.

Initial action by local authorities after reorganisation was concentrated on increasing the number of field social workers, of all kinds of day care, of residential care units for young handicapped people, and of other services including home helps, aids and adaptations, holidays and meals, though the sheer number of elderly handicapped people sometimes obscured the often more pressing claims of the young chronic sick. It was hoped that the transfer of health social workers to social services departments might strengthen limited expertise in this field, for example as consultants, and to help improve a situation in which practical services were largely supplied by social work assistants, but emotional needs and complex family situations were constantly ignored (Browning and Hope-Murray, 1974).

After the Seebohm reorganisation, services were more critically appraised than before by stronger committees with professional officers and the beginnings of corporate planning. Looking at the personal social services as a whole clarified the size of the problem, the need for a comprehensive approach, and the range of necessary action and resources. Many thought that services deteriorated after reorganisation, a specialised service was not the answer but the specialised knowledge and expertise which was often lacking. For example, deaf people continued to be poorly served and there was a serious shortage of social workers able to communicate with them. Many local authorities provided their own services and about fifty professionally qualified social workers were working with deaf people by 1975.

Aids to daily living and information about them were improved and home adaptations more widely provided for handicapped people of all ages. Special housing lagged far behind need, but there were more experiments and more recognition that handicapped people's needs changed as their condition grew worse. Social clubs and day centres (there were 832 social clubs and 191 day centres in 1972) took more people out of their isolation and enabled them to do things together, though many preferred to join ordinary adult education activities or clubs according to their individual tastes if this were made possible. There were large numbers of handicapped people in social services departments' caseloads but many social workers were reluctant to work with them and often had no experience. They needed knowledge specific to handicap, chronic disability and rehabilitation, the characteristics of various handicaps, their natural history and fluctuations, what therapeutic and remedial measures were available and what it meant to live with handicap. More specialised skills were necessary in direct work with deaf and blind people. Some social services departments were appointing principal social workers responsible for co-ordinating and developing services for physically and mentally handicapped people. This included liaison with health-care planning teams and voluntary organisations, as well as appraising and making recommendations about the range of care for handicapped people and helping other staff to provide this.

Rose (1970) described the great advances in higher education for blind children, the opening up of ordinary employment rather than sheltered workshops, and the increase of technical aids to mobility, work competence and recreation. The College of Teachers of the Blind certificate was discontinued in 1973 after it had existed for fifty years and some 600 students had qualified. A new six-month course for technical work with blind people took its place, run by the regional associations for the blind. This course was mainly taken by welfare assistants seconded by local authorities. Some CQSW courses had optional lectures on the deaf and the blind, while a few qualified social workers took the specialised, post-qualifying courses in work with deaf or blind people. The CCETSW working party on people with handicaps (1974) identified the function of trained social workers to include personal help to handicapped people and their families; assessment of the general situation and specific needs; to provide care, support, advice and guidance; to plan and co-ordinate services. Their activities should be undertaken alone or with members of other relevant professions (p. 18). Social workers should take additional post-qualifying training for work with people who needed specific expert help including technical skill, for example with the pre-lingually profoundly deaf (p. 31).

Obviously the health, education, housing and social security services, as well as the social services department, often needed to give substantial combined help. General strategy consisted in identifying points of crisis or continuing pressure, and making available at the right point in the right way whatever services in combination with each other would be most likely to make the burden tolerable, or personal growth and satisfaction more possible.

IMPLICATIONS OF THE SOCIAL AND EMOTIONAL CONSEQUENCES OF HANDICAP FOR SOCIAL WORK

The social isolation and emotional frustrations of severe handicap began to be more honestly faced in the social services during the 1960s and 1970s. Obviously different handicaps imposed different limitations, but severely handicapped people faced the psychological and social consequences of being different, isolated, not able to live an ordinary life, sometimes a burden, not regarded as quite a complete human being, sometimes debarred from the world of work, subject to the hazards of mobility, of circumscribed horizons, of frustrations and pain which ordinary people do not face. This meant that they had specific and general social needs, urgent at crisis points, or intermittent, or continuing over long periods. More babies born with severe multiple handicaps survived these, and other handicapped children might suffer early separation from their mothers for short- or long-term hospital care and might also lack normal stimulation and socialisation. Such children sometimes developed more immature personalities than those who had lived ordinary lives before they were handicapped by accident or disease processes. There were, indeed, considerable differences between being born handicapped and becoming disabled later. The latter had to cope with shock, depression and readjustment to a more constricted life. Obviously physically handicapped people had widely different personalities, from the dependent and self-absorbed to those who achieved control of their lives against great odds. The multidisciplinary study *Living with Handicap* (Younghusband *et al.*, 1970) concluded that

' . . . the physical, emotional, educational and social aspects of the child with special needs must be kept in constant balance with each other . . . The wide range of handicapping conditions . . . some slight, some severe, some temporary, some permanent, means that it is more appropriate to plan in the light of a child's all round needs and functional capacities in everyday life rather than a too exclusive emphasis on the nature of the defect.' (p. 9)

The tremendous family strains also became more obvious to social workers as more were trained to understand family interaction and strengths, as well as ambivalence, hostility, guilt, frustration and stress. The initial crisis for the parents was the birth of a handicapped baby or the diagnosis of handicap in a child who did not pass the normal developmental stages. At this crisis point parents needed to talk again and again about their shock, sorrow and bewilderment, sometimes their guilt and anger, and apprehensions about the future. Handicapped small children were usually protected from the social impact of their difference but school life, whether at an ordinary or special school, sharpened this when they were not mobile like other children, could not play active games, led a more sheltered life, were more apt to be left at home with mother. Their limitations could also change the whole character of family outings and holidays. 'The most terrible thing is to know it will never get any better . . . Truly a handicapped child is a handicapped family' (Letters from mothers of handicapped children quoted in *Living with Handicap*). The parents had to face the fact that, unlike normal children, the handicapped child would create more not less demands as he grew older. They might cope admirably and the child thrive, or they might unite to protect him in a devoted possessiveness which stifled his development, or disastrously reject him, or else the partners might be divided, with resulting strains on the marriage.

A handicapped child might be happy and find fulfilment at school, but there was another crisis period for many handicapped school leavers when they found their fantasies about work choices shattered by the competition to find and hold a job and the sheer practical problems of getting to and from work. The generous spending on special education was not matched in early childhood or at the difficult stage of transition from school to work. Tuckey *et al.* (1973) in a National Children's Bureau study of 253 physically handicapped school leavers in 1968 concluded: 'It seems essential that all special schools have attached to them social workers, possibly seconded

from the Social Services Department of the local authority which is responsible for the welfare of all those who are handicapped, among whom the
young special school leaver has an important place' (p. 40).

These young people's friends were mixing freely with others of the opposite
sex but it had been assumed that marriage was out of the question for
those with crippling handicaps.

'There is a surprising failure to recognise the acute problems of isolation
from their peers that confront many of the more seriously handicapped
adolescents, who face, often without the chance to satisfy them, the normal
urges of young people for companionship, relations with the opposite sex,
sport, enjoyment of leisure pursuits, travel, spending money, achievement,
and the prospect of their own future home and family.' (*Living with
Handicap*, p. 21)

The whole situation was, of course, worse still for the housebound, young
chronic sick and those in hospital wards or residential homes where they
might spend the rest of their lives (see also volume 2, chapter 13).

Handicaps caused by accident or disease later in life could also have
devastating consequences for the family's standard of living, the husband's
ability to hold a job or the wife's to run the home. In extreme cases this
resulted in an almost impossible burden on the other partner, or in family
breakdown. The presence of a severely handicapped family member inevitably had repercussions on the children, particularly when parents had
neither the time nor energy to respond properly to their needs. There were
also parental fears about what might happen to the handicapped member
when they were dead. 'I can't get over the sight of those men lying there
doing nothing . . . It breaks my heart to think my son might be put there'
(Sally Sainsbury, 1970).

The vast majority of handicapped people of all ages were living at home.
But the over-riding assumption that family life was better than any alternative, unless proved otherwise, was fortunately combined with the realisation that temporary absence can make the heart grow fonder and intolerable strains made more bearable. Thus more play groups for ordinary
children began to take a few who were handicapped; sitters in, home helps,
day centres, short-stay hostels or foster home, and special holidays sometimes
made it possible for the family to have a break or go off on its own, or
surmount illness or crises.

The CCETSW working party (1974) found that the reactions of handicapped people themselves showed their resentment at the lack of status
accorded to them, the failure to develop individual people's latent capacities
and skill, the lack of practical assistance, of comprehensive assessment in
which they themselves and their families were involved. 'They were highly
critical of the information given to them by professionals . . . about services,
prospects, rights, etc. They stressed the urgent need to train workers to
locate, evaluate, record and up-date comprehensive and accurate information. They looked to social workers to provide relevant details as soon as
required and to secure and make aids, services and practical advice available
without undue delay' (p. 16). They also expected social workers to be

knowledgeable about the nature, process and characteristics of specific handicapping conditions and their psychological consequences, and to be able to give practical assistance, not just verbal advice.

Pressure grew in the 1970s for a committee of inquiry analogous to the Curtis Committee (1946) into the needs of physically and mentally handicapped people deprived of a normal home life in long-stay care. In 1975 the DHSS set up a Health Advisory Service team to inquire into the needs of handicapped children in long-stay hospitals.

By 1975 the social work and related needs of physically handicapped people, including those who were blind or deaf, were more clearly identified. But provision and increased social work expertise did not match knowledge about what was needed.

Chapter 14

Training for the Local Authority Health and Welfare Services in the 1950s, Proposals for a New Pattern and the Council for Training in Social Work

THE SITUATION IN THE 1950s

In the 1950s no training was available for the vast majority of social workers in the health and welfare services unable to go to university. The exceptions were the Josephine Butler House moral welfare courses, the examinations of the College of Teachers of the Blind for the home teaching certificate, the diploma or certificate of the Deaf Welfare Examination Board, some refresher courses run by the NAMH, and those for matrons of old people's homes run by the National Old People's Welfare Council. These were all limited, separate and specialised, but they represented the struggle of voluntary organisations to fill a vacuum by providing some kind of training for particular groups.

By the mid-1950s it was generally agreed that planned and systematic training was necessary for social workers in these services, indeed that current social services' demands could not be met without training. Nevertheless, influential people still denied the need for this even in mental health work; or thought that the health visitor was the ideal, general-purpose social worker. There were also different views about length, the form of training and those who should be trained. Some wanted a professional standard, others failed to grasp the size of the problem or to go further than proposals for a few months of narrowly based, in-service training.

The urgent case for training was argued by welfare and mental welfare workers, who had had no chance to train since the vacuum left when the Poor Law Examinations Board ceased to exist in 1948. They thought that a national qualification would help recruitment and recognition that the social work function demanded both training and a high sense of responsibility, and that hard work, devotion to duty, and kindness to the mentally or physically handicapped and the old were insufficient without good training. As often happens, it was the officers with the best potentialities and experience who wanted adequate training.

In 1953 the Ministry of Health Advisory Council for the Welfare of Handicapped Persons set up a committee to consider the training and qualifications of social workers with the physically handicapped. Its memorandum (unpublished) assumed that staff dealing with the welfare of the handicapped should be as efficient as other types of officers in the social field, and made detailed proposals for a one-year unified course for work with all kinds of physically handicapped people. The Minister decided that a comprehensive review of social work throughout the health and welfare services would be preferable, and in 1955 set up the Working Party on Social Workers in the Local Authority Health and Welfare Services (the Younghusband working party), whose terms of reference were quoted in the last chapter.

THE YOUNGHUSBAND WORKING PARTY'S TRAINING PROPOSALS

The working party's Report said of the 1950s

'There . . . lies behind us a long history of failure to take the vigorous action necessary to provide trained social workers for the health and welfare services. Neither local authorities nor voluntary organisations ought to be expected to provide training facilities of the necessary magnitude, whilst it is also evident that the university social science departments cannot meet the need. The position has become increasingly acute during the ten years since 1948 for a number of reasons . . . These include the rapid expansion of local authority services for the general classes of handicapped persons, and the Piercy Committee's conclusions as to the need for further development; the Report of the Royal Commission on the Law relating to Mental Illness and Mental Deficiency and a comparable review in Scotland; expansion in social work with families including 'problem' and homeless families; the increasing proportion of elderly people in the population: and the wider public who now use these services . . . A high proportion of officers in welfare departments . . . are reaching retiring age [and] new recruits to the services, by and large, have no recognised qualifications. Thus . . . welfare departments will become the only local authority departments staffed with officers without a recognised qualification. The same is also to a large degree true of [social workers in] health departments.' (para. 857)

Four training possibilities suggested in evidence faced this working party in trying to decide on recommendations that would bring training for social work in the health and welfare services into the main stream. These were: (a) a series of specialised trainings, which would have been contrary to current trends; (b) a social science qualification for every social worker, this was unrealistic and inappropriate from both the training and staffing points of view; (c) short courses lasting a few months, followed by brief in-service training, which would be inadequate to meet the demands on the services; (d) the Joint University Council (JUC) proposal of a new type of course outside the university to give a comprehensive training for 'welfare workers'.

In weighing up these different suggestions, the dilemma was either to pitch standards too high to be attainable, or too low to be relevant, or to propose a training which would be too complex for some situations and too simple for others. Finally the solution seemed to be to apply to training the working party's division of users of the service into three categories, i.e. complex cases; those who needed a competent social work service; and others who could be served by welfare assistants under the supervision of qualified social workers. This would result in two avenues to social work training: university professional courses on existing lines and a new general training related to but outside the university; with, in addition, systematic in-service training for welfare assistants, some of whom would go on later to full training. Refresher courses were also needed for all workers.

The Report recommended a new training which should consist of two-year, full-time courses of theory and practice, with supervised fieldwork for about half the total time. The Report suggested that some might think this too short, remembering that existing teacher training was to be lengthened to three years, that health visitor training took four years, and occupational therapy three years. The theory should include:

(a) human behaviour – how people function in their physical, psychological and social aspects, with sufficient 'usable' knowledge about health and disease;
(b) social and economic circumstances, social structure and common social attitudes, especially towards handicap;
(c) the social services (including voluntary organisations), and the various forms of social care and treatment, and the principles and practice of administration;
(d) the principles and practice of social work (this would be primarily case-work, but later group work and community organisation should be added);
(e) other optional skills, including moon, braille, handicrafts, and com-munication with the deaf.

There should be emphasis on the needs of old, handicapped and mentally disordered people within a framework of a broad understanding of indi-vidual development, social functioning, and the structure and operation of the social services. Specialised training was only desirable if it followed on from general training, or was of a higher standard: but the general training should give a chance for more detailed study according to a particular student's bent, for example students interested in mental health should have fieldwork placements in the mental health service and study this subject more thoroughly.

In services where there were almost no trained social workers the problem was how to get things moving quickly. It was proposed that about fifteen selected welfare officers and mental welfare officers a year, with good education qualifications, should be seconded to take a one-year, specially planned and staffed course leading to the full qualification. 'It . . . should on no account run for more than five years' (para. 915). Of course it did, but that is part of a later story. Other officers should be eligible for leave of absence to take a two-year course. Of the estimated total of 3,150 officers in the health and welfare services in 1956 with a whole or partial social work function, about 1,125 should train. Officers over 50 and with fifteen or more years' experience in a social work appointment should be recognised as qualified by experience. They should still be eligible for refresher courses.

New recruits should either take the certificate before appointment or else first be employed as welfare assistants and then seconded for training. Within seven years about 570 students should start training annually to allow for wastage and expansion. On the basis of thirty to forty students in each course, this would mean that a total of about thirty two-year courses should be provided by degrees as this became possible.

The JUC suggested in evidence to the working party that a 'central welfare training council' should be set up to sponsor and promote training for 'welfare workers from many different fields', i.e. for other public services as well as health and welfare. The working party could not comment on the merits of a comprehensive proposal outside its terms of reference. However, it consulted 21 organisations about the suggestion for the health and welfare services and found 16 in favour, 4 non-commital and only 1 against. The majority saw the value of a training council to establish common national standards when it was clear that no existing organisation had the resources to provide or sponsor training on the necessary scale. The working party recommended that a 'National Council' should be set up quickly as an independent representative body financed from public funds and with its own staff and premises. It should be responsible for promoting and recognising a sufficient number of courses for the certificate in social work (CSW). It would have to decide how to achieve national standards and work out criteria for the qualifying award. It should both promote in-service training and itself provide short courses; conduct publicity campaigns and in other ways stimulate recruitment; make available teaching material of various kinds; and invite suitable colleges of further education or 'other educational establishments' to run the general certificate in social work courses. This would include discussions with local authorities, mental hospitals and other agencies about good facilities for supervised practical work. Opportunities for both theoretical and practical training should be available (or capable of being provided) in any particular locality before a course was agreed. Further negotiations would include discussions with the colleges and the local authorities about student numbers, staff (including secretarial staff), the curriculum and the necessary accommodation, library and other teaching resources.

The Council would inevitably be a large body if it covered all the relevant teaching, training, employing and other interests. The Report hoped rather vaguely that the universities would be prepared to consult with the Council 'about the training and employment of students taking the appropriate university courses'. It also hoped that no unnecessary barriers would separate one type of student from the other. Beyond this it could not go, though as Collis

(1961) commented: 'When the Younghusband Working Party proposed the setting up of a National Training Council many saw this as an opportunity for the government to appoint a body which would cover all social work and not just one for health and welfare services. If ever there was a time for a national policy for the recruitment and training of social workers it is now' (p. 8). But this was not to be for another ten years.

THE COUNCIL FOR TRAINING IN SOCIAL WORK 1962–71 AND
DEVELOPMENTS IN TRAINING FOR THE HEALTH AND WELFARE
SERVICES IN THE 1960s

There was a risk that the Younghusband working party's proposal for a two-year course might be rejected by social work professional associations. For this reason the working party made an unfortunate distinction between professional and general social work courses. But, in the event, the APSW welcomed the report on the day of publication; other professional social work associations and the Institute of Social Welfare also quickly supported it. The LCC almost immediately decided to start a similar course for child care students, which later received CTC support. It was obvious that even a considerable expansion of university places could not meet the demand and there had to be an alternative entry to social work education, though with the extreme shortage of trained social workers some argued that it was more important to train larger numbers on one-year or in-service training courses for specialised jobs. This would have left those services in limbo, but acceptance of the proposal for a two-year course of related theory and practice set the pattern for social work education outside the universities, and later the barrier between the two types of training ceased to exist.

In the early 1960s the new venture was full of imponderables – the educational standard that could be achieved, how the courses would fit into colleges of further education, who would teach, what candidates would apply, how supervision could be planned, and above all what level of performance the students would reach at the end.

In the summer of 1960 the Government announced its acceptance of the Report's recommendations and its intention to introduce legislation to set up a Council for Training in Social Work. This became the Health Visiting and Social Work (Training) Act, 1962 which also set up a Council for the Training of Health Visitors. The two were linked like Siamese twins by a requirement in the Act that each should have the same chairman. The Council for Training in Social Work was independent of, though financed by, the Ministry of Health; and it might be extended by order in Council to fields of social work other than health and welfare. There were also committees of the Council for Scotland and Northern Ireland. As a matter of government policy, there was no power to give grant aid from central funds either for courses or for student training. But the Council, local health and welfare authorities, and indeed the Ministry itself, were given power to undertake or promote relevant research.

In the meantime, there was no clear authority to start these courses until the 1962 Act, though the situation was urgent. But in 1960, on the initiative of the Ministry of Health, energetically supported by the Ministry of

Education, action was taken to inaugurate a few pilot, two-year courses. Similar initiative was taken by the Scottish Education Department. The authority of the Ministry of Education was needed to start a course in any college of further education and it gave valuable initial help in finding colleges willing to pioneer a course. In addition, a small group of leading people in the social work field was invited to advise on the planning of the courses. Certain colleges in England were then visited by the Welfare Division of the Ministry of Health for detailed discussion about what would be involved, and to reinforce willingness to start such an untried type of course if the college could fulfil various conditions. It was also essential for the local education authority to be willing to meet the cost, for a college to want the course and to have some idea of what was involved, for the surrounding health and welfare departments to welcome it, and for supervised fieldwork to be potentially available in social work settings. This last stipulation was a considerable stumbling block, since there were practically no qualified social workers in health and welfare departments and therefore medical and psychiatric social workers in hospitals had to be asked to help, together with the probation service and voluntary agencies.

In the event, four courses were started in 1961 in London, Liverpool, Birmingham, and (to some extent independently) Glasgow, with professional social workers appointed as tutors in charge. In one instance, the Joseph Rowntree Memorial Trust subsidised the salaries of both a college tutor and a supervisor in a family casework agency to enable a course to start.

Teaching in the social sciences, social administration, and the principles and practice of social work all ran concurrently with fieldwork, thus students were constantly helped to apply what they were learning. There were considerable difficulties in finding competent lecturers, particularly in human growth and development, at the low fees which colleges were empowered to pay (one psychiatrist tore up his cheque and returned it to the education department). In spite of much goodwill, there were also difficulties in colleges of further education owing to shortage of accommodation, of library space, of telephones and of clerical help. Moreover, considerable adjustment was necessary in college ways of working in order to accept that a staff member was necessarily out of the college for a good part of the working day because fieldwork was as important as classwork, and thus that 'contact hours' had to be differently calculated. Tutors, of whom there were initially one and later two or more to each course, carried a very heavy load because they were responsible for the general planning and administration of the course, for student selection, for finding and periodically visiting fieldwork placements, for supervisors' meetings, for close contacts with and support for other lecturers, for teaching their own course, for tutorials, for reports on students and for some in-service training.

There was no difficulty about student recruitment for the first courses, even though the students had to take it on trust that by the time they qualified there would be a Council authorised to give them a national award. Seventy-four students successfully completed these first courses, including the one-year course at the National Institute for Social Work Training (NISWT) described below. Most of the students, both men and women, were in their mid-twenties and had more experience of working in big organisations than many university students. Their reliability was favourably commented upon in their fieldwork placements.

The Council for Training in Social Work (CTSW) held its first meeting in late 1962, initially without its own staff or premises. It decided to adopt the generic approach to training recommended by the working party Report and not to produce specialists. It was primarily concerned with social workers for the health and welfare services of local authorities and voluntary organisations, but it aimed 'to train social workers whose knowledge and skills enable them to work in a variety of ways with individuals and groups within the community' (CTSW, *Annual Report 1967*, p. 4). Its early tasks were to establish working relations with existing and prospective courses, to institute procedures for the approval and review of courses and for the award of the certificate in social work (CSW). For the first few years it appointed two assessors to each of the courses in order to achieve a national standard for the award. The test consisted of three set examinations, a long essay, a detailed report from the tutor to the course on the student's performance over the whole period, coupled with the fieldwork reports. In these courses, as elsewhere, the submission of supervisors' reports to external assessors slowly helped to raise the standard, to substitute actual evidence of performance for generalised statements, and to establish expected norms of achievement. Over the years the failure rate was fairly constant at $2\frac{1}{2}$ to 5 per cent and, coupled with withdrawals, a wastage rate of 7 to 8 per cent.

On most courses, students had a prolonged observation period that included a project, followed by three substantial fieldwork placements, as against two for the one-year university students. This and other factors, including the excitement of a pioneer venture, established from the start a level of performance a good deal higher than had been foreseen. By 1967 about one-third of placements were in local authority health and welfare departments (CTSW, *Annual Report 1967*) as against almost none in 1961–2.

The official staff/student ratio was 1:15. By 1968 the actual ratio ranged from 1:6 to 1:15 and there were between one and seven tutors to each course. As a national average, there were over the years about four times as many applicants as places on courses. The student body consisted of about 40 per cent trainees, 30 per cent seconded officers, and 30 per cent new recruits. All the extra costs for CSW courses were borne by the local education authority pooling arrangements, but by the Home Office for child care courses in colleges of further education, as in universities. This created problems.

Naturally there were difficulties in assimilating these trained social workers into health and welfare departments. This was helped to some extent by consultations with senior officers as to how they should be used. Some wanted to work in hospitals as a result of their fieldwork experience, but for a time they were graded as 'unqualified social workers' on the Whitley scale. This insulted their dignity as much as their pockets. Later they were recognised as trained social workers, and there were some places on CSW courses for students who meant to go into the hospital service.

The Council's target was twenty-five, two-year courses in different parts of the United Kingdom, and progressively to expand the number of places on these courses to an annual intake of 25 students (with a few taking 40 to

70 students annually). By 1965 there were nineteen, two-year courses with an annual output of 149 students, a remarkable development in four years. The output had risen to 479 by 1971, including students on courses at Moray House, Jordanhill and Robert Gordon's Institute in Scotland, and a course in Northern Ireland.

In addition to the National Institute one-year course, three others were started in 1965 for officers over 35 with at least five years' experience in the health and welfare service. There was controversy about these courses: some held that older officers without background studies could not assimilate the necessary range and depth of knowledge and skill in less than two years; others disagreed and argued that in any event it would be unjust to deprive them of the chance to train, provided there was stringent selection. The courses included study of administration and staff supervision. Their success owed much to the courage and initiative of these older students when

'It is usually much harder to transform a role which one has exercised unquestioned for years than to learn a new one . . . Learning to be a social worker involves relinquishing some of the short cuts . . . and the defensive manoeuvres of premature advice and facile reassurances by which anyone without special training is apt to protect himself against the suffering of those with whom he has to deal . . . above all it may be hard for someone . . . to accept . . . that he remains an untrained person and must go to school to qualify himself for his work.' (Irvine, unpublished paper on 'Community Care')

Like all seconded students, they also faced difficulties when they returned to their familiar departments feeling different people but were not always encouraged to use their new abilities. There were five such courses by 1970; they were initially to run for five years but were extended for a further two years and succeeded by the phase III courses described in volume 2 (see chapter 7, section on 'The Central Council for Education and Training in Social Work').

There was pressure to introduce part-time qualifying training by evening courses and correspondence. This was stoutly resisted by the CTSW which insisted that theory and practice must be closely related to each other.

Older workers in the health and welfare services who fulfilled certain conditions about length of relevant service, were eligible for a declaration of recognition of experience. This once-for-all operation was completed in 1966 and some 1,500 applicants qualified.

Some additional knowledge and skill, for example in communication or help with mobility was needed in social work with deaf or blind people. A panel of the CTSW worked assiduously from 1963 on this issue, trying to clarify true points of difference as opposed to entrenched specialisations. It was obvious that specific knowledge was needed, especially in the neglected field of communication with the deaf, and to clarify what was common and what different in the effects on personality and social functioning of blindness, deafness, and other severely handicapping conditions. The outcome was that three-month courses for work with blind or deaf people were started for qualified social workers. Unfortunately, there were limited incentives to take these courses and the intake remained extremely small in relation to demand.

The College of Teachers of the Blind certificate was discontinued in 1973 after it had existed for fifty years and some 600 students had qualified. A new six months course for technical work with blind people took its place, run by the regional associations for the blind. This course was mainly taken by welfare assistants seconded by local authorities. Some CQSW courses had optional lectures on the deaf and the blind while a few qualified social workers took the specialised post qualifying courses in work with deaf or blind people. The CCETSW working party on people with handicaps (1974*b*) identified the function of trained social workers to include personal help to handicapped people and their families; to assess the general situation and specific needs; to provide care, support, advice and guidance; to plan and co-ordinate services. Their activities should be undertaken alone or with members of other relevant professions (p. 18). Social workers should take additional post qualifying training for work with people who needed specific expert help including technical skill, for example with the pre-lingually profoundly deaf (p. 31).

By the time the CTSW was merged with the CCETSW in 1971 a total of 2,495 certificates in social work had been awarded, many to untrained workers seconded to take a course. Developments in residential social work sponsored by the CTSW are discussed in volume 2 (see chapter 13). Although the CTSW had no responsibility for university courses, it had yet pioneered successfully in two new fields: social work education (including residential social work) in colleges of further education, and in health and welfare services. It thus had a major share in bringing social work in these services into the main stream.

Chapter 15

A Family Service:
Foreshadowings of Seebohm:
the Seebohm Report

STEPS TOWARDS A FAMILY SERVICE IN THE 1950s AND 1960s

The public services of the 1950s and later were mainly designed to meet
specific needs in particular circumstances at given moments in time, rather
than being concerned with people in their family and social circumstances,
with any necessary continuity of support and with preventing breakdown
rather than trying to pick up some of the pieces: they were indeed symptom-
rather than person-oriented. The classic example was families evicted
for non-payment of rent when the children might have to be received into
care, or the father fend for himself while the mother and children were
expensively housed in Part III accommodation. The costs in human and
financial terms and the difficulties of reuniting families, which were often
already fragile, began to be used in arguing the case for flexible preventive
services.

There is interesting material about general attitudes in the 1950s in the
report of two field studies undertaken in Oxfordshire and Northumberland
(financed by the Carnegie United Kingdom Trust) to discover whether there
was a need for a voluntary family casework service in rural areas (Smith
and Bate, 1953). The assumption that a case needed proving, implied that
no unmet family welfare problems existed in rural areas, or that a family
casework service would not be acceptable, or that the existing statutory
services plus good neighbourliness met every need. Results showed bad
rather than good neighbourliness in villages towards problem families or
'awkward old so and so's'. They also showed that members of different
professions, who said there was little evidence of overlapping or unmet
need, were reluctant to admit gaps in services or their own inadequacies,
or were unable to recognise unmet need or that deep-rooted problems cannot
be treated as a secondary responsibility of someone whose hands are already
overfull. When actual case material was examined there was ample evidence
of help given too late, spasmodically or not at all. There were many
instances in which the problem was one of poor family adjustment rather
than an episode of sickness or delinquency in one individual.

There was failure to take early preventive action, while specialist workers with particular functions might each perform their allocated roles quite competently without achieving any lasting result. There was also a 'tendency to pass people from one social worker to another as if they were sacks of potatoes, not human beings who need above all things stable and intimate relationships' (p. 28).

Difficulties preventing co-operation included different levels of skill and training, differing attitudes, departmental and personal jealousies and a feeling that to pass on a difficult case implied incompetence. It was abundantly clear from the two studies that there were many family and personal needs not being met by existing social services. There was indeed, said the report, an obvious need for a social general practitioner or family casework service. In Oxfordshire its findings produced the evidence on which a family caseworker was appointed in the children's department in 1952 and by 1955 'it was estimated that his efforts had kept fifty children from thirteen families out of care' (Packman, 1975, p. 56). By then Oxford Children's Department also had a family caseworker. Hertfordshire had stationed one in the clerk's department, and Chesterfield had the only family casework service run by a local authority.

The findings of this small investigation were confirmed by many subsequent studies down to the Seebohm Report. The investigators failed to recognise that a family caseworker – or many family caseworkers – would be ineffective on their own. But they realised, as perhaps the Ingleby Committee did not, that quite as important as 'a door on which to knock' is a door on which you would not mind the neighbours seeing you knock.

Jeffreys (1965) concluded that some ineffective results were due to the piecemeal growth of social welfare services with consequent ill-deployment which resulted in 'some workers with no formal education after the age of 16 and little in-service training . . . accepting responsibility for the support of individuals and families with a formidable array of complicated psychological and social problems', while 'university trained social workers were sometimes working intensively with small numbers of people whose behaviour was far less disturbed' (p. 308).

The Canford Families (1962) was an in-depth action study undertaken in a poor urban area from 1956–9. The purpose was to help the family as a 'living entity' by means of a social service for parents and children. In the fragmented state of the social services it proved necessary to set up an independent voluntary agency for this purpose with a team of professional caseworkers and group workers. The focus was on understanding the dynamics of the family group and how social work intervention could help to strengthen members in the performance of their social roles. Fathers were included to an extent not usual at the time. Therapeutic social group work with the children was also a significant innovation. Long-term intensive casework was assumed to be essential, though it was recognised that short-term work might often be necessary in a permanent family service agency to which people could return at need. Family stress resulting in child deprivation, matrimonial disharmony and symptoms of mental disorder clearly demonstrated the need for a family service (and for more general reform of a debilitating physical and social environment). Unfortunately, there was no research design for the project and no plan for it to be taken over by any more permanent service so although the demonstration resulted in valuable new practice techniques it did not lead to action.

CO-ORDINATING COMMITTEES

The joint Home Office, Ministries of Education and Health, and Scottish Home Department Circular of 1950 (Home Office Circular 157/50) requested local authorities to designate an officer to be responsible for mobilising the interest and concern of the relevant statutory and voluntary services in the problem of children neglected in their own homes. By 1956, when local authorities were asked to supply information about their arrangements all but twenty-two had set up some kind of co-ordination machinery. Forty-nine per cent of the designated officers were children's officers, 30 per cent medical officers of health, and 18 per cent county or town clerks. Some committees were concerned only with 'problem' families and not other families under stress. Other committees also considered cases of old or physically handicapped people (Younghusband Report, 1959, para. 1,068).

Experience showed that co-ordinating committees as such should not deal with individual cases, which could only be effectively considered by the workers directly concerned. In practice even this was far from easy when workers had different backgrounds, training or no training, and strong but varied ideas about desirable conduct. 'It is likely to lead to more constructive action in studying these situations to try to assess the strengths in the family, and how to work with them rather than to single out weaknesses in order to condemn them' (Younghusband Report, 1959, para. 70).

By and large, not enough use was made of co-ordinating machinery, too few cases came within its scope and others were sometimes referred too late (for example, after eviction had actually taken place). Sometimes it was even a matter of pride to keep essential information from another department rather than to exchange this as a routine. Co-operation was more likely to be effective when workers in different departments knew and trusted each other than when fieldworkers had to pass reports or questions up and down an administrative hierarchy. One of the values of co-ordinating committees was that they gave chief officers an idea of the range and complexity of some social problems and the unreality of any claim to go it alone. Nevertheless, the Seebohm Report (1968) said in regard to co-ordination in general that 'the impression is of very limited success despite the expenditure of much time and energy' (para. 70).

THE INGLEBY COMMITTEE

There was pressure on the Government in the 1950s to set up a committee of inquiry into children neglected in their own homes and the need for a comprehensive family service. (See also chapters 2–5 on the child care service.) In particular, the Magistrates' Association, the Council for Children's Welfare and the *ad hoc* Fisher Group were pressing for this, and the two latter bodies worked together to advocate 'a statutory service of help to the family'. Finally in 1956 the Committee on Children and Young Persons (the Ingleby Committee) was set up to review the juvenile courts and related services and 'whether local authorities . . . should . . . be given new powers and duties to prevent or forestall the suffering of children through neglect in their own homes'. Five years later its Report summed up the situation thus:

'Nearly all the services which have some bearing on the family have come about piecemeal and on an *ad hoc* basis; they have arisen to cope with specific problems as those problems have made impact on the public consciousness and conscience. As long as those services are organised in something like their present form, their effective co-ordination is clearly essential. The present arrangements for co-ordination, valuable as they are, have proved to be only partially successful. Not unnaturally, there still exists a certain amount of inter-departmental rivalry in this field; it was apparent from some of the evidence we received, and its existence is common knowledge. There is a tendency too for those who first make contact with a family at risk not to call in further help, or to defer doing so with consequent delay in bringing the co-ordinating machinery into operation. In some cases this may be due to failure on the part of the field worker to recognise the need for further help, or to the belief that the worker who first makes contact with a case should continue to deal with it as long as possible . . . Much of the difficulty which at present exists, apart from that attributable to the shortage of skilled casework staff, is due to inter-service rivalries and above all to failure to analyse the different processes involved.' (para. 37)

These processes the Report distinguished as the detection of people at risk; the investigation and diagnosis of the problem; and treatment, i.e. the provision of facilities and services to meet the families' needs and to reduce the stresses and damage they faced. The first involved a widespread 'spotter' function; the second, skilled and objective diagnosis by a unit in the local authority, an independent family advice centre; the third stage, treatment, should be the concern of existing services. The weaknesses of this dichotomy were obvious. Indeed, the Ingleby Committee itself went on to say:

'It may be that the long-term solution will be in a reorganisation of the various services concerned with the family and their combination into a unified family service, although there would be obvious and formidable difficulties either in bringing all their diverse and often specialised functions into one organisation, or in taking away from the existing services those of their functions relating to family troubles in order to secure unified administration of those functions. Any such reorganisation at local authority level might well involve a corresponding reorganisation of the functions of the different government departments concerned. These are matters well outside our terms of reference, but we urge the importance of their further study by the Government and by the local interests concerned.' (para. 47)

It was said at the time that the strength of departmental rivalries prevented the Ingleby Committee from grasping this nettle. It was sharply criticised for this by the Council for Children's Welfare, the Fisher Group and others who had been campaigning for a family service. Like all such inquiries of the period, it was a departmental committee and no more able than any of the others openly to tread on Tom Tiddler's ground.

Another suggestion current at the time, and revived later in some evidence to the Seebohm Committee, was that there should be departments of social work to provide a common casework service for other departments. In any event, social work with families was likely to grow, though only a few local authority children's and health and welfare departments were attempting to meet the need, partly because of shortage of qualified staff. By the end of the 1950s inadequacies of structure, resources and trained staff were all obvious, together with the need to recognise the common elements in social work in scattered services; the piecemeal, fragmented and often ineffective provision of services; and the more precise analysis of the situation entailed in detection, assessment and treatment. Attempts in the 1960s to provide community care also emphasised the importance of the family and the need for comprehensive support services.

JUVENILE DELINQUENTS AND FINAL STEPS TOWARDS THE SEEBOHM COMMITTEE

Throughout the 1960s young delinquents continued to be all unwittingly the most effective pressure group for changes in ways of dealing with them and for a family service. They had to their credit the Children and Young Persons Act, 1963 which resulted from the Ingleby Report; and next year a Labour Party Study Group, chaired by Lord Longford, produced *Crime: A Challenge to Us All.* This recommended the setting up of a family service, and that children under school-leaving age whose needs were not met by the family service should come before family courts which should also have jurisdiction in other family matters. There should be youth courts for young offenders from 16 to 21. Soon afterwards several members of the study group found themselves in power in the successive Labour Governments of 1964–70. One result was the perhaps too hastily produced White Paper *The Child, the Family and the Young Offender* (Home Office, 1965). This proposed that juvenile courts should be abolished in favour of family councils for those under 16, appointed by the local authority through the children's committees and composed of social workers in the child care service and informed laymen. There would also be family courts to hear cases disputed by the child or his parents; and young offenders' courts for those aged 16 to 21. The children's departments would become responsible for supervision of children under 16, and approved schools as such would be merged with other residential provision. It was calculated that this change would require about 1,000 additional social workers. The White Paper tactlessly suggested that some might transfer from the probation and after-care service. Rather naturally this, and the proposal that probation officers should no longer be responsible for children and their families, added to the storm caused by the suggested abolition of the juvenile courts. There was practically no support for family councils appointed by the interested party – the local authority children's committee – and composed of child care officers and others.

The probation service protested that it already knew, as adult offenders or as matrimonial cases, many of the families that local authority social workers would visit if they became responsible for wayward children. Three years later the Seebohm Report tipped the scales the other way by suggesting that the after-care functions of the probation service would overlap with that Committee's proposed social service departments. 'Who is the overlapper?' was indeed a recurrent theme in the 1950s and 1960s: an odd situation when as Sir Keith Joseph said at the ACO annual conference in 1967 our personal social services were 'islands of welfare in a sea of confusion'.

A less tumultuously negative reception was given to the White Paper's proposed 'small independent committee to review the organisation and responsibilities of the local authority personal social services and consider what changes are desirable to ensure an effective family service' (para. 7). This became the Seebohm Committee.

This ill-fated White Paper was superceded in 1968, before the Seebohm Report was published, by the more trenchant *Children in Trouble* (Home Office, 1968*a*). The abolition of the juvenile courts was obviously too much of a hot potato in England and Wales so the White Paper tackled the problem by analysing the purpose of courts. It concluded, as the earlier White Paper had done, that children should be 'spared the stigma of criminality' and that usually the matters alleged were not in dispute. From the latter premise it drew the conclusion that a substantial amount of juvenile misbehaviour could be dealt with by a partnership between the police and the children's departments through juvenile liaison schemes. Children should only be brought before a juvenile court because it was alleged that certain specified circumstances existed and the child needed care or control which he would not otherwise receive. These proposals were more acceptable, partly perhaps because of the amount of emotion that had spent itself on the earlier White Paper, though the juvenile court magistrates naturally objected to proposals to curtail their powers, and probation officers to losing by degrees their sixty years of close association with the juvenile courts.

In the meantime, discussions about a family service grew livelier in many different groups and a number of influential pamphlets and discussion documents were produced and widely read. They included two Fabian tracts and *A Family Service and a Family Court* (Council for Children's Welfare, 1965). The various pamphlets put forward plans for a unified and extended service for families with children and children without families. But Professor Titmuss in an important speech at the 1965 Congress of the Royal Society of Health contended that the reorganisation should not be based 'on biological or sociological criteria – like the family – or as an element in the pattern of needs – like health or rehabilitation' but on 'the need for services irrespective of age, family background and relationships . . . it follows that we require a department of social services . . . which would effectively bring together within one administrative structure all social workers in the employ of a single authority'. This was the solution later proposed by the Seebohm Committee and more comprehensively embodied in the Social Work (Scotland) Act, 1968.

The Standing Conference of Organisations of Social Workers *Discussion Paper No. 1* (undated) said

'The case for a unified social work service receives further support from the nature of social work itself. Social workers of all kinds have increasingly come to realise that they are dealing not with specific problems or handicaps but with people, and not with people in isolation but with people in a social situation, particularly a family situation. All social work has tended to become family social work. Many influences have contributed to this trend – the development of social work thinking and practice, dynamic psychology and more recently findings from sociology, social psychology and anthropology.' (p. 4)

As a result of these and other indications of tides flowing in different directions, coupled with much behind-the-scenes pressure, the Committee on the Local Authority and Allied Personal Social Services was set up in 1965 'to review the organisation and responsibilities of the local authority personal social services in England and Wales and to consider what changes are desirable to secure an effective family service' (Seebohm Report, 1968, para. 1).

The Royal Commissions on the Reorganisation of Local Government in England and Wales and in Scotland were still at work and the Government's proposals for the reorganisation of the National Health Service had not been framed.

THE SEEBOHM REPORT

Naturally there was much discussion, clarification of ideas, preparation of evidence and strongly conflicting views now that at last a committee had been set up which could look at the personal social services as a whole and was bound to recommend reorganisation in one form or another. Even its broad terms of reference excluded, lamentably so some thought, the probation and after-care service, medical social work in hospitals, and central government departments.

The Seebohm Committee's appointment and the Report itself constituted a watershed. By the late 1960s enough experience had been gained and attitudes had changed sufficiently since 1948 to make possible new organisational structures able to carry the weight of a personal social service as comprehensive as the education, health, housing and social security services. The Report was thus consistent with the spirit of the times in its diagnosis, and its prescription not only for remedy but for advance into a future free from the stigma of poverty and not bound by Hobson's choice, a future in which any citizen would use the service.

The Committee cast its net wide. It said in its Report (1968): 'We decided very early in our discussions that it would be impossible to restrict our work solely to the needs of two or even three generation families. We could only make sense of our task by considering also childless couples and individuals without any close relatives: in other words, everybody' (para. 32).

The Committee found many inadequacies in existing statutory services. There was insufficient provision of residential accommodation, of day care, of home helps, of foster homes, and of meals on wheels; and a limited range of services whether for people who needed social work help or continuity of support. Sometimes there was good assessment but the recommended treatment was simply not available. Some groups, like alcoholics or socially inadequate people, were hardly provided for at all. Consequently there were many weaknesses in the quality of provision, partly caused by lack of trained staff, coupled with high caseloads and lack of knowledge about what would achieve the desired results. These weaknesses were further compounded by legal and administrative structures which divided people, who often faced inter-related problems, into categories for which separate services or none were responsible. Some services did not provide simple information about the service, though better publicity without adequate resources would result in demands that could only be met by leaping from crisis to crisis. Existing office accommodation was poor, often with no local offices and frequently entailing a long journey that was almost impossible for mothers with young children or for old or handicapped people. The reception facilities were often bad.

The reasons for these shortcomings were: first, lack of resources, including trained manpower, residential accommodation, office space and other goods and services; secondly, inadequate knowledge about many social problems and the forms of provision that effectively meet or prevent them; and thirdly, insufficient provision for the systematic collection and sharing of basic data. The social care services had been comparatively neglected at a time when there had been great advances in the health and education services, for example the Committee found that only 0·72 per cent of the GNP was spent on both the children's and welfare services in 1965–6.

An adequate personal social service was also dependent upon better housing, adequate social security benefits and a good health service. Preventive work required a broader view of social and individual problems than was then common, including better forecasting of changing social need; for example, the growth of immigrant communities, the rapid increase in child minding and the changing age structure.

Various alternative forms of reorganisation faced the Committee:

(a) The existing structure but with more effective means of co-ordination, for example a committee, representative of the personal social service committees, to be responsible for policy, planning and priorities.

(b) A family service for children, whether or not in their own families (including education welfare and the child guidance and youth services, accommodation for homeless families, day nurseries, family casework and care for unmarried mothers and their children); and a welfare service for old and handicapped adults. Alternatively these welfare services might be combined with health departments since social and health needs in these groups were closely related.

(c) A social casework department which would act on an agency basis for other departments.

(d) Absorption of the personal social services in enlarged education and health departments.

(e) A social service department to meet the social needs of individuals, families and communities so comprehensive as to provide an effective family service (paras 117–38).

The Committee chose the last of these alternatives, some said without full consideration of the others, thinking it essential that the service should unify social care responsibilities; attract additional resources; lessen the risk of people falling between two stools; and ensure the development of a comprehensive approach to family problems.

It recommended that the new social service departments should incorporate:

(a) the child care service;
(b) the welfare services;
(c) education welfare and child guidance services;
(d) the home help service, mental health social work services, adult training centres, other social work services and day nurseries, provided by local health departments, and supervision of child minders;
(e) some social welfare undertaken by some housing departments.

The new departments should also provide play groups for children under 5, ensure proper social care for unmarried mothers and their children and an effective diagnostic guidance service for children under 5 and for adolescents, in co-operation with the health and education services.

Reorganisation would enable the services to:

'(a) meet needs on the basis of the overall requirements of the individual or family rather than on the basis of a limited set of symptoms;
(b) provide a clear and comprehensive pattern of responsibility and accountability over the whole field;
(c) attract more resources;
(d) use those resources more effectively;
(e) generate adequate recruitment and training of the staffs in skills which are, or may become, necessary;
(f) meet needs which are at present being neglected;
(g) adapt to changing conditions;
(h) provide a better organisation for collecting and disseminating information relevant to the development of the social services;
(i) be more accessible and comprehensive to those who need to use them.' (para. 111)

The result would be:

' . . . a new local authority department, providing a community based and family oriented service, which will be available to all. This new department will, we believe, reach far beyond the discovery and rescue of social casualties; it will enable the greatest possible number of individuals to act reciprocally, giving and receiving service for the well-being of the whole community.' (para. 2)

The Report was emphatically in favour of statutory social service committees with undivided responsibility and a chief officer who would give his whole mind and time to the work of the department. He and other chief officers should work as equal members of a team under the leadership of the Clerk in the manner suggested by the Committee on the Management of Local Government (Maud Committee, 1967). This was the principle of corporate management widely adopted later.

The chief social service officer should be 'an effective administrator, the leader of a group of people with widely differing backgrounds, able to take a broad and informed view of the needs the service ought to be meeting and capable of looking outwards, well beyond the limits of his own department and authority, and well into the future' (para. 618). So far as qualifications for these new appointments were concerned, though no single profession combined the ideal range of skills, most of the chief officers should be professionally qualified in social work (including residential care) and have had training in management and administration at appropriate points in their careers or alternatively be administrators knowledgeable about social work.

The Report made the controversial proposal that – as since 1948 in the appointment of children's officers – local authorities should be required to consult the Minister about the composition of the short list for these chief officer appointments and take account of his observations before making an appointment. This was later implemented and in several instances local authorities were required to revise their short lists, and some re-advertised.

New concepts of administration were essential:

'If the services are to meet effectively the complex range of individual, family and community problems, then effort devoted to investigating the needs of an area, and to the overall planning and co-ordination of services and resources, both statutory and voluntary, is clearly of the utmost importance. The staff of the social service department will need to see themselves not as a self-contained unit but as part of a network of services within the community. Thus effective co-ordination with other services and individuals and the mobilisation of community resources, especially volunteers, to meet need are as important aspects of the administration of the social service department – and demand as much skill – as its internal management.' (para. 478)

Comprehensive, area-based teams were also essential to give an effective family service. Each area office should be controlled by a senior, professionally trained social worker with a grasp of administration and wide powers of decision. These area teams should have available specialised resources, advice and support from the head office as well as clear statements on practice and general policy. Seebohm and other staffing assessments are discussed in chapter 20.

The Committee obviously had difficulty in deciding whether social service departments should have power to give financial help in a wider range of need than was already possible under the Children and Young Persons Act, 1963. After weighing up the issue of principle they finally decided that there was a case 'for an additional limited residuary power enabling the social service department to give financial help in emergencies to households where only adults are involved' (para. 604). This proposal was not implemented in subsequent legislation, so there remained a general power in Scotland but not in England and Wales.

It was argued in evidence that progress had come through specialisation, for example by enabling children's departments to concentrate on caring for children at risk or deprived of a normal home life, and thus there would be a reduction in standards of service following reorganisation. But the Committee thought that 'a family, or individual in need of social care should, as far as is possible, be served by a single social worker' (para. 516). This was the sentence that caused much trouble later about 'generic case-loads'. Perhaps the Committee over-reacted against 'the rigid classification implied in the present symptom-oriented approach'. But the Report went on to say, 'There would sometimes be good reasons for involving other social workers with a family or even with an individual – for example in some problems involving adolescence or in some marital problems' (para. 519). A field-level social worker should be enabled to pursue 'concentrations of interest' in particular aspects of the work.

'Specialisations will be necessary above this level, not least to help in the advancement of knowledge. Officers with specialised knowledge and experience, and in many instances further training will be required as consultants, . . . as the service develops specialisations will cluster differently and new types of specialists emerge to meet new problems and needs and fresh conceptions of how these might be tackled.' (para. 524)

The Report stressed the importance of other staff, for example occupational therapists, nursery nurses, supervisors of adult training centres, residential social work and domestic staff, home helps and home help supervisors and the administrative and clerical staff. Professional workers should be used as economically as possible. Their work should be examined rigorously to discover what parts of the total task could be undertaken by welfare assistants.

Although it was outside the Committee's terms of reference, much evidence supported its view that one central government department should be responsible for the personal social services. Controversy raged later as to whether this should be the Department of Health and Social Security (created in 1965), or the Home Office. The former was responsible for social work in the health and welfare services as well as hospital social workers, while the latter had effectively pioneered the child care service and was also responsible for probation and after-care, juvenile delinquency services and the adult penal system. In the event, the Siamese twins were separated by transferring the Children's Department from the Home Office to the newly created Local Authority Social Services Department (LASS) of the DHSS. This included the amalgamation of the Children's Department inspectorate with the DHSS social welfare staff, renamed the Social Work Service, and no longer acting as inspectors. The Seebohm Report saw this role as being 'not so much regulatory as promotional, educational and consultative' (para. 649). It also thought it desirable, as others had done earlier, that there should be free movement between the central government inspectorate and local authority services.

The Committee recommended that there should be a single new advisory council for the personal social services under an independent chairman to act as the central forum for discussion of policy in the personal social services, advising the appropriate Minister and promoting development, training and research over the whole field. It should have a real measure of freedom, an adequate staff and financial resources. In the event, training became the responsibility of a separate Central Council for Education and Training in Social Work, discussed in another chapter. In 1973 – three years late – the Personal Social Services Council for England and Wales came into existence as an independent publicly financed body to advise on policy issues, to provide information and guidance and to promote the development of services. From the start it regarded itself as 'a watch dog and a constructively critical and independent voice for the personal social services' (Personal Social Services Council *Report 1975*, p. 10).

The proposals of the Royal Commission on Local Government in England and Wales (1968) for much enlarged local authorities were accepted in principle by the Government. This created a dilemma as to whether the Seebohm plan for the reorganisation of the personal social services should be implemented before or after general local government reorganisation. On the one hand, there was the problem of facing two major upheavals in a short period of time, on the other the impetus for Seebohm reorganisation might be lost if it were not carried through quickly; and the small, separate personal social services might be swamped in massive local government changes. Moreover, a good deal would be learnt in the interval before local government reorganisation if the new departments had had time to find their identity and establish their relationship with other departments and outside bodies. 'A great deal of work will be needed to reorganise the existing constituent parts into a coherent whole and the full potential of the new service will only emerge over a period of years and with an increase of trained staff and other resources' (Seebohm Report, 1968, para. 670). This indeed proved true.

The Seebohm Committee's ideal that 'all forms of relevant help should be available to any child and family who need them, without the rigid and sometimes permanent classification that the present system involves' (para. 188) was still far from being attained by the mid-1970s when economic recession hit the public services. It remained, however, as an ideal with the 'rigid classification' abolished and the means of implementation potentially if not actually available.

In spite of many criticisms, perhaps the Report's most important achievement was to give reality to the concept of a personal social service, to show convincingly the potential range of social care, and to clarify what this would mean in terms of organisation, variety of provision and staff training.

Thomas (1973), using extensive knowledge from unpublished sources and personal memories, analysed the moves leading up to the Seebohm Committee, how it actually set about its task, together with conflicting pressures while it was sitting, after the Report was published and during the passage of the Bill through Parliament. Hall (1976) surveyed the same ground in far more detail in a research project with access to unpublished material and interviews with members of the Seebohm Committee and others.

Chapter 16

The Seebohm Report's Reception, the Local Authority Social Services Act, 1970 and the First Years of the Social Services Departments

There was criticism of the Committee's predominantly social as opposed to health membership. The Report was taken to task for paying lip service to an 'effective family service' but devoting little attention to the family as such compared with old people, children and the physically and mentally handicapped. It was also criticised for passing cursorily over the youth service. Critics complained that it assigned key roles to social workers without clarifying the nature of social work; recommended sweeping changes without sufficient discussion of alternative patterns of reorganisa-tion; did not suggest that these should be tested before universal implemen-tation; and took too little account of health interests. Like other committees of inquiry, it was also taken to task for not undertaking research, including inquiry into consumers' views, but it faced the recurrent dilemma that to do this would further delay a report already said to be overdue. This was the usual reason given for not doing what ought to be done independently of the urgencies of government committees of inquiry. When the Report appeared it was naturally hailed with enthusiasm by social workers and their supporters. Indeed, 'Seebohm' became as much a rallying cry in some quarters as 'Beveridge' had been over twenty-five years earlier. Predictably, many doctors were far from enthusiastic about proposals to tear apart what to them were essential elements in the health service. Some politicians were also against the proposals.

A few local authorities jumped the gun by bringing their health, welfare and children's services together under the medical officer of health. Social work associations fiercely contested a form of integration which would have resulted in medical rather than social direction of these services. Pressure for and against 'Seebohm' legislation mounted and a Seebohm Implementation Action Group came into being on the initiative of ACCO and the Child Poverty Action Group and supported by professional social work and other organisations. Pressure group activities by the opposed health and social work interests went on throughout 1969. Meanwhile, the second Green Paper on the reorganisation of the NHS appeared and the Report of the Royal Commission on Local Government was published. The Government of the day decided to implement the Seebohm Report's proposals, and after threshing out difficulties about what to include in a comprehensive personal social service, political decisions were finally made on the criterion of where the primary skill lay. Though the Seebohm proposals aroused strong feelings, these were not on party political lines and in the event a short Bill went through 'on the nod'. This was the Local Authority Social Services Act, 1970 which unified the personal social services in one department and established social services committees. The location of child guidance clinics, social welfare in housing and education welfare did not require legislation and was left to local authority decision.

An interdepartmental social work group of Home Office and DHSS officials was established to advise local authorities. It played a crucial part in the appointment of chief officers by emphasising that directors should be qualified social workers with substantial management and administrative experience in the social services. Some proposed appointments of administrators without social work experience and of senior medical officers were contested – in the last resort by ministerial objection – though others went through.

Reorganisation entailed much structural change, the fusing of unequal resources and the appointment of social services committees. Promotion prospects and salaries shot up overnight. But there was much anxiety, stress or jubilation in human terms. Sometimes the children's officer and the chief welfare officer were competing in their own authority for appointment as director of social services or else trying their luck elsewhere as directors or deputies, sometimes by choice and sometimes *faute de mieux*. This was a harsh game of musical chairs for some who were left out altogether, or turned down by their own authority and forced to face for months the uncertainties of other interviews. Conversely, some people applied for and were appointed to a succession of more lucrative posts before they actually started work. In this situation, the clamour for higher salaries and status seemed to obscure concern about 'a better deal for the client'. Of the 174 directors appointed when the social services departments started in 1971, 58 were children's officers; 79 welfare officers; 10 from central government departments; and the rest were probation officers (2), social work teachers (3), medical practitioners (5), from Scottish social work departments (8), local authority deputy or assistant clerks (4), mental welfare officers (2), and voluntary organisation staffs (3): 21 were women (Smith, 1972). The large number of welfare officers appointed was thought to be due to their substantial local authority and administrative experience and local councillors' ambivalence about children's officers who were often professional women. In addition, there were many appointments of assistant directors, principal social workers, area team leaders and senior social workers. Some of these were specialised posts, for example with responsibility for field services, or residential care, or community work, or research and intelligence, or in-service and other training.

The perhaps too quickly amalgamated new departments faced the problem of trying to hold previous work together while coming to grips with new tasks, with such problems as whether to try to amalgamate staffs before setting up separate and perhaps scattered area teams; and of how to bring together separate residential institutions. This homogenising of services naturally affected the percentage of qualified staff. For instance, in one local authority the children's department which had a 97 per cent qualified child care field staff found itself absorbed after reorganisation in a new department with health and welfare social workers of whom 3 per cent were qualified. Thus some services were depleted and others gained. Naturally there were fantasies about 'those other people', much hostility, unwillingness to build up a more general caseload, and many difficulties of welding together staffs with different outlooks, loyalties and working methods. For many people this was a crisis situation, there was often acute anxiety and depression and sometimes disillusionment with the 'Seebohm ideal'. There were inevitable strains and stresses and considerable uncertainty about roles and functions in the process of coming to terms with and finding one's feet in reorganised services where new structures and ways of working had to be created from initial confusion.

Working parties and other devices helped to identify client needs across the board. Slowly people from different departments became less hostile and generated sufficient trust to work together. At first, in some departments specialised caseloads continued but by degrees they became more generic with some specialist workers used for consultation. Much unmet need was uncovered by the new social services departments which now had greater resources, for instance day nurseries for children living in their own homes. In addition, the Chronically Sick and Disabled Persons Act, 1970 gave local authorities responsibilities for discovering handicapped people in their areas and providing a range of services for them, while under section 45 of the Health Services and Public Health Act, 1968 local authorities were required from 1971 to provide welfare services for old people. This was part of strong central government pressure to hasten community care, including the proposals in the White Paper on *Better Services for the Mentally Handicapped* (DHSS, 1971a). The Children and Young Persons Act, 1969 had given local authorities wider responsibilities for children either actually or potentially in trouble, for community homes and intermediate treatment, for progressively taking over from the probation service responsibility for court inquiries and supervision orders and for implementing care orders. In practice, local authorities found themselves acutely short of the necessary range of treatment facilities, especially for disturbed adolescents (see chapter 3).

These new legislative responsibilities were desirable in themselves, but at a time when all the complexities and strains, the exploration of new territory and the shortages resulting from massive reorganisation were in full flood they seemed like last straws. Indeed, some people thought these added commitments delayed the cohesion and effectiveness of the new departments, increased disillusionment, and made even survival itself an achievement. There was an increase in social services expenditure from 0·5 of total public expenditure in 1953 to 0·8 in 1968 and 1·6 in 1974 (Personal Social Services Council, 1976b, p. 6). The personal social services were manpower-intensive and in 1973 67 per cent of total expenditure in England was on staff (73 per cent in the probation and after-care service). From 1975 inflation and recession resulted in retrenchment, drastic cuts in spending and a period of nil growth. None the less the social services departments' big budgets gave them more political power in local authorities.

THE EMERGING PATTERN OF SOCIAL SERVICES DEPARTMENTS

In 1972 three months after reorganisation a study was carried out in four area offices of Southampton Social Services Department by Neill *et al.* (1973) and repeated in 1975 (Neill *et al.*, 1976). In 1972 57 per cent of social workers were professionally qualified against 49 per cent in 1975. All senior staff held a professional or relevant qualification in both periods. The proportion of unqualified fieldworkers had doubled from one-fifth in 1972 to two-fifths by 1975. In 1972 and 1975 there were about twice as many women as men in the field staff, but in senior grades men outnumbered women by two to one in 1972 and by four to one in 1975. By 1975 57 per cent of staff no longer worked in the same offices, but anticipated mobility had slowed down and only a third planned to change their job within two years against half in 1972.

In 1972 social workers were still carrying specialised caseloads and ex-CCOs had much smaller caseloads than ex-social welfare officers. The majority of social workers thought specialisation would continue indefinitely and preferred this. In 1975 most had mixed views. In 1972 the vast majority of child care cases were in specialist caseloads, but only half by 1975. The majority of physically disabled and elderly clients were still in specialised caseloads in 1975.

In 1972 no attempt was made to separate dormant cases from those needing much work. Most fieldworkers with 40 to 200 cases felt under much pressure. The feeling of pressure arose from 'unsorted caseloads, unclear goals for social work intervention, and lack of criteria for assessment, allocation and for closure of cases' (p. 460). In 1972 there was apprehension about taking on unfamiliar work, possessiveness about specialisms and little trust in the ability or interest of others. Integration had also revealed many gaps in services. It seemed likely that a future specialism would be intake, assessment and short-term intervention.

In both 1972 and 1975 most social workers, given the choice, preferred work with children or in interpersonal relationships, and only a quarter wanted to work with old or physically or mentally handicapped people, yet the majority of the Department's caseload consisted of the least preferred groups and only a quarter of child care cases.

The average number in caseloads was 92 in 1972 (with a range from 20 to 375) and 57 in 1975. In 1972 no qualified caseworker had more than 76 cases against many more carried by unqualified social workers. By 1975 the position was reversed: qualified social workers had an average of 52 cases against an average of 43 carried by unqualified workers. Fieldworkers still felt under pressure, largely because of lack of clerical services, problems of deciding priorities, and standards and anxieties about communication with management.

Neill questioned whether 'the work preferences of social workers reflect similar attitudes among social work teachers [and whether] social work with the elderly, the disabled and mentally disordered [was] taught with as much imagination and conviction as is social work with children and families' (1976, p. 14).

A review of referrals to an area team was undertaken by the National Institute for Social Work (NISW) in the same Department in 1973 (Neill, 'Study of Referrals', 1976, mimeographed). At first any social worker had to do intake duty but later intake teams were formed, composed of social workers anxious to become skilled in intake, assessment and short-term work. Self-referrals were the largest group; two-fifths of all referrals were dealt with at intake without being allocated to social workers' caseloads but one-third were allocated. There was no independent assessment of these decisions and their outcome. One-third of all referrals were widowed, separated or divorced people. There were multiple problems in many cases: housing in 39 per cent; financial difficulties in 19 per cent; problems of family relationships, child care, emotional disturbance, isolation, mental disorder or juvenile delinquency in 89 per cent; physical disability, illness or frailty in 62 per cent and need for services, aids or adaptations in 48 per cent. These problems often required extensive knowledge of departmental and other services and the law, but there was no easily accessible information system. In two-fifths of the closed referral cases some action had been taken to provide the necessary service; another quarter were closed because neither resources nor time were available. Great efforts were made to provide regular supervision, which helped to lessen feelings of stress and crisis. The area teams were now in local rather than central offices and had become familiar with the local community and its changing needs which helped them to build relationships with other agencies and professionals.

Much of what follows is based on the DHSS Social Work Service Study (1974e) of the organisational structure and response to clients' needs in a representative sample of thirty-four social services departments. Many were still suffering instability and pressure from the 1970 reorganisation and facing anxieties about 1974 local government changes. In the larger authorities the increase of management levels, particularly of specialists, created confusing patterns of communication alike at the centre and in area teams, especially since clients frequently needed more than one service. Assistant directors played a co-ordinating role most effectively when they were in close touch with area teams and also members of the director's management team. Where roles and responsibilities were clearly defined throughout the department, this helped area teams to cope with continued anxieties. But this and close support for inexperienced workers was frequently lacking. The role of senior social workers included management and professional supervision responsibilities, but many of them were newly appointed and in urgent need of training for these different roles. Trainee social workers were usually supervised and unqualified social workers were given supposedly straight-forward cases. Qualified social workers carried a heavy load of complex cases, which reduced the time they could give to supervision, though there was urgent need for professional supervision and consultation. Rowbottom *et al.* (1974) thought that supervision should clarify the task in specific cases but there were problems of keeping a balance between professional and departmental controls across a whole range of social work situations and clarifying specialist functions.

Varied administrative systems persisted, sometimes with new and old ones running parallel, because of resistance to change or a policy of achieving integration at a manageable pace. Many newly recruited social workers were inexperienced practitioners and ignorant of the department's administrative procedures. In such circumstances persuasiveness and aggression were alike at a premium.

An easy flow of communication demanded formalised procedures for the smooth supply of resources to area offices. Not surprisingly this was often lacking. Personal contact and motivation were essential and could be facilitated by regular area team meetings, though these were often so dominated by allocation of new work that there was no time to discuss a case in depth or general community needs. Some assistant directors and principal social workers could not visit often enough to become familiar with the pressures, workloads, problems and changes in the area, but where they did so area teams were able to examine heavy workloads more objectively, to express anxieties about low professional standards and to feel that their views were known and understood. Residential and day care staff did not take part in meetings between the director, assistant directors and area teams.

It was essential for communication to flow between the director, specialists and area teams, from one area to another, and between the department and other statutory and voluntary agencies. Whatever the formal system, personality was a key factor – those who were or were not communicators – and area team leaders who pursued autocratic or *laissez-faire* policies.

The enormous increase in demand made it vital in estimating resources to analyse geographical, demographic, social and historical referral patterns. Functional or geographical departmental organisation were the two main alternatives adopted. The advantage of assistant directors and staff responsible for specific services was that they could concentrate on these. But several divisions of a department could be involved in one case. Standardised procedures were thus required for co-ordination. Many authorities adopted the alternative of geographical organisation with divisional directors responsible for a range of services. In any event, supporting activities were essential, for example staffing and training, research and evaluation and such specialist services as assessment centres. Functional organisation became increasingly unwieldy after the 1974 local government reorganisation.

Corporate management became general, with chief officers meeting with the chief executive to discuss general planning, priorities and allocation of resources. Obviously education, housing and personal social services were all closely related and required corporate consultation and planning. This also led to 'more emphasis on explicit definition of objectives; on the formulation of policies and programmes designed to attain the objectives; and on devising measures to indicate the consequences, successful or otherwise, of policies in practice' (Martin Report, p. 11).

AREA TEAMS

By 1974 the pattern of area teams was well established with an area team leader and deputy and several senior social workers responsible for groups composed of trained and untrained social workers, social work assistants and trainees. When the centre did not provide effective support and oversight and clear lines of communication and accountability, area teams sometimes became largely autonomous and the centre ill informed about social needs in an area, with resultant variations in policy. There were also problems about the degree of responsibility to be exercised by fieldworkers. Where fragmentation had been prevented, the area team's close identification with its neighbourhood could produce a lively service. Some area teams had started interdisciplinary groups to consider specific issues, for instance young people's problems or social needs in a neighbourhood. Some departments were experimenting with small, highly local units, and indeed with social workers in a mobile office who stayed for several days in a street and got to know local people. Area teams usually covered populations of 30,000 to 70,000 and had staffs of twenty-five to thirty social workers.

Area team problems were most acute in inner-city areas with poor amenities, a shifting population and little social cohesion or family support. This resulted in constant overwork, high staff turnover, and too few qualified and experienced social workers. For example, in 1975 one such area team, undermanned and without a single qualified staff member, reached the end of its tether and went on strike; and another picketed the town hall.

The shortage of trained social workers perpetuated the situation in which some area teams were well staffed but others were below establishment. There were also many complaints about the effects of rapid promotion and quick staff turnover which nullified continuity of care, development of skill, and support for less experienced social workers. This made the most effective deployment of manpower all the more urgent, including the appropriate use of social work assistants, volunteers and home helps.

INTAKE SYSTEMS

It was still common for clients to be interviewed initially by a clerical receptionist and then seen by the duty officer, who was faced by overwhelming numbers and a daunting range of problems. Hall (1974) studied earlier situations, in which receptionists without training and often with no privacy for interviews might request information in public about clients' personal problems and even decide whether a client should be seen, when and by whom.

There was much experiment and debate about intake. Should this be undertaken by changing duty officers or a permanent team? If the latter, should it consist of skilled social workers, or others with adequate professional support? Was the pressure so great in busy offices that social workers should only have short spells on intake, with a senior social worker undertaking more detailed assessment, followed by discussion at an allocation meeting? Many of the people interviewed at area offices primarily wanted information or simple advice or a service, i.e. they did not need social work help, though they might properly be a social services responsibility, so could the first contact be made by non-professionally qualified staff if they were given clear outlines to detect danger points, knew when to consult professional social workers, and were supervised by them? Some intake teams also undertook short-term casework and allocation for longer-term work. The subject required much further study because it was crucial for good professional practice, the management of and a quick response to demand for services. The essential elements were initial screening of applicants, professional support, accurate and easily available information about and ready access to resources, and disciplined recording. Studies of consumer reactions (Mayer and Timms, 1970; Sainsbury, 1975b) brought to light clients' fears about asking for social services, their flustered difficulties in communication, and the hurt to their self-respect if they were not received with courtesy and patience.

REFERRALS AND QUALITY OF SERVICE

High referral rates and the variety of referrals, coupled with staff turnover and few qualified and experienced social workers, forced many teams to concentrate on short-term crisis intervention or palliatives and made long-term or intensive support impossible, for example of mentally ill people or families with complex problems. Some professional social workers were also forced by pressure of work to function below their capacity and the newly qualified might spend their time on superficial or first-aid work, with resulting frustration and loss of skill. There was much concern about the effect of this on competent assessment, continuing care, review and professional decisions on closure, even though more clients received some service. Social workers expected supervision or consultation and where this was systematically provided, together with analysis of workloads and appropriate allocation, it helped to develop a professional culture, the best use of manpower resources, and less feeling of stress and crises.

After acceptance of a case there was no set pattern of follow up and supervision, apart from consultation in a crisis. When an immediate need had to be met it was not common practice to assess the situation and decide whether other help was needed or the case could be closed. Lack of thorough and continuous assessment based upon a weighing up of the total situation led to failure to identify the trouble in personal and environmental terms and to respond appropriately to changing situations. Some departments had plans to review all current cases and to prevent closure merely because work had ceased, rather than as a recorded professional decision. This was essential for reliable statistics, accountability, relations with clients and other agencies and also for the management and analysis of workloads. A good records system was also essential for daily referrals, assessment, allocation, use of resources and the written memory which recorded the review of cases, the history of clients and the services they received. There was support for the view that in order to build up knowledge, initial and periodic assessment should clearly distinguish between the actual needs of the case and what could be provided.

SPECIALISATION

'Generic' practice went further than the Seebohm Report envisaged. Its view that so far as possible a family or individual should be served by a single social worker 'was a plea that one social worker should take primary responsibility for each case, not that every social worker should be able to deal with every eventuality' (P. Hall, 1976). How, it was argued, could a fieldworker carrying a general caseload get enough experience of old people, marital discord, selection of foster homes, adoption placements, mentally disordered or physically handicapped people, children at risk of non-accidental injury, welfare rights, complicated legal requirements, alcoholism, communication with children or disturbed adolescents, or indeed adequate skills in work with individuals, families, groups and communities? It was also argued that far too many complex situations demanded a level of social work expertise and practice well beyond that of unqualified or newly qualified social workers.

The general idea that Seebohm reorganisation had resulted in the abandonment of specialisation was a misreading of the Report. In fact there were a variety of experiments with the use of new or existing skills. These included special appointments for community work and intermediate treatment, and of home help organisers. But the merging of previously separate systems had created a situation in which, for example, a mentally disordered client's children might equally need care; or a physically handicapped man and his family might need marital counselling and help with child nurture. Thus logically no social work specialisation was valid except on the basis of skill in working with universal human realities. 'Unless we quickly encourage and develop more "oases of quality" in social work practice, we shall soon run out of people who know what good social work practice is – they will have died or retired or fled up the hierarchy for the money or to escape present basic grade frustrations!' (Butler, 1976, pp. 2–3). There were serious gaps in general and specialist competence, notably with the handicapped, the mentally ill, children and their families, difficult adolescents and the elderly. It was important to keep in balance a broadly based family service operating through area teams, i.e. the team not necessarily the individual worker was generic, and attention was paid by central management to problems of particular types of client.

Rowbottom *et al.* (1974), in their discussions with social work staffs about professional freedom, found universal agreement that they exercised delegated discretion rather than professional autonomy but that the nature of social work involved judgement or choice within certain policy, managerial or legal constraints.

THE 1974 REORGANISATION

When the new departments were beginning to see light at the end of the tunnel they were faced in England and Wales with a reorganisation of local government which reduced the number of relevant local authorities to 47 non-metropolitan counties, 36 metropolitan districts in the 6 metropolitan counties, and the existing 33 London boroughs. The London boroughs and some other authorities were unaffected by boundary changes but by and large there were major upheavals, fresh appointments of chief officers and other staff, some early retirements, and fresh uncertainties about emerging policies and practices. In the event, 98 men chief officers and 10 women were appointed in England (these figures include the unaffected London boroughs). In the eight new Welsh authorities 7 men and 1 woman were appointed, of whom in 1974 4 were professionally qualified social workers (see also chapter 17 on Scotland). In England in 1975 (the first year for which information was available) 52 directors were qualified social workers. The pattern of assistant director responsibilities and of research and intelligence units remained largely unchanged, but with more appointments at senior levels of specialists in the care of the handicapped and elderly. Under the National Health Service reorganisation in 1974 joint consultative committees and health care planning teams were set up between area health authorities and social services departments. Some of the 1971 uncertainties, confusion and heartsearching were gone through again, though by this time the essential structure had been created and gaps between needs and resources were drearily familiar. By 1975 cuts in public spending and a period of nil growth were resulting in constricted services and some unfilled staff vacancies. Many clients of the social services were among the most vulnerable people in the community and needed special protection in a period of economic recession, all the more so because the personal social services were services at the end of the line and there was nowhere else to go if they failed to provide. In all this welter of need there were pockets of good practice, of new experiments and imaginative service, while some thought that a pause for careful assessment of existing facilities and efforts to discover what could be done without fresh resources might be used constructively. In any event, the departments were only beginning to discover how to fulfil their function or, indeed, what the function and its boundaries might be.

The DHSS *Consultative Document on Priorities for Health and Personal Social Services in England* (1976a) was the first attempt 'to establish rational and systematic priorities throughout the health and personal social services' (p. 1). It proposed a series of targets for modest growth and stressed 'the crucial importance of joint planning by health and local authorities' (p. 1).

It was hard to weigh up the common complaints that services for children, the mentally disordered and the blind especially suffered from reorganisation. This was likely in areas that had provided good services in a particular field, and then found these pulled down when they were diluted with inexperienced and unqualified workers. Earlier chapters in this study suggest that the golden age in the past was a myth, that there was more rationing by the purse than in the 1970s, that the needs of the old and the handicapped were only met to a limited extent, and that sustained work of real quality, although it mercifully existed, was not general. It is not possible to estimate whether the greatly increased resources at first made available to the social services departments matched or fell behind rising expectations, massive new demands, and high administrative costs. There was general confusion about SSD aims, boundaries, priorities and the ability to give a professional service. But the Seebohm reorganisation was but five years old by 1975 after a painful birth and a stressful infancy followed by deprivation. At least, as Aneurin Bevan said of the NHS at its five-year landmark, it had 'made suffering articulate'.

Chapter 17

Developments in Scotland leading up to and following the Social Work (Scotland) Act, 1968

THE MCBOYLE AND KILBRANDON REPORTS

In the 1960s Scotland came to grips with problems of a family service and tribunals for wayward youth. It stole a march on England and Wales and achieved more revolutionary change with less turmoil. The reasons for this are complex. The Morison Committee (1962) thought that 'a principal cause of the failure of the probation service to develop in Scotland as it should have done is that it has been regarded not as a court service but as a relatively minor local authority service' (para. 246). Moreover, few justices of the peace acquired judicial experience and there were only four juvenile courts in Scotland served by lay magistrates. Thus the proposal to take young people out of jurisdiction of the courts did not arouse strong possessive feelings amongst magistrates, the conviction that no one else understood or could do the job so well. In addition there was only one central government department, the Scottish Office.

Scottish members of NAPO fought against being merged in a comprehensive social work service but the vast majority of social workers, including a considerable minority of Scottish probation officers, wanted probation to be included.

The McBoyle Committee of the Scottish Advisory Council on Child Care in its *Report of the Committee on the Prevention of Neglect of Children* (1963) recommended that a comprehensive family welfare service should be set up to avoid overlapping and gaps and to make the best use of scarce, trained social workers. The Kilbrandon Report (1964) dealt with juvenile courts and the categories of children brought before them. Like other inquiries, it found little difference in delinquent children and those in need of care, protection or control. It concluded that 'the shortcomings inherent in the juvenile court system can . . . be traced essentially to the fact that they are required to combine the characteristics of a court of law with those of a specialised agency for the treatment of children in need' (para. 102).

It accordingly recommended the setting up of juvenile panels composed of lay people which would be independent of the local authorities and not a court of law. A new official, the reporter, should decide on all the evidence whether a child need be referred to a children's hearing as being in need of compulsory measures of care. Where the grounds for referral were disputed the case would be submitted to the sheriff in chambers and if the grounds were substantiated the child would then be dealt with by the children's hearing. The panels should have wide discretion based upon the child's needs and should be able to vary (or terminate) an order from time to time in the light of the child's progress. Existing social services for children, including the child care service, should be reorganised into a new comprehensive social education department within the general education service. 'The child's supervision . . . would in fact involve the application of family case-work and would . . . most commonly be entrusted to the qualified social workers who would form a substantial element of the social education department (para. 237). The child guidance service, school welfare, residential schools and children's homes would all be under one authority. The Report referred to proposals for a 'comprehensive "family service" catering for the needs of adults of all ages, as well as those of children in the family' (para. 246). But it would have been beyond its terms of reference to come to grips with this wider issue.

There was criticism in Scotland that two separate committees of inquiry were commissioned to explore essentially related issues of child neglect and child care or control. The Kilbrandon Report was much discussed on both sides of the border because of its calmly radical approach. Many welcomed the juvenile panel proposals, though some thought that inarticulate people would be intimidated into agreeing to measures which could entail continuing authoritarian control over their lives. There was profound controversy about the social education department proposal which would have made social care a comparatively minor responsibility of a department whose primary concern was education. It was also regarded as incompatible with mounting pressure for a comprehensive family service.

NEXT STEPS

In 1965 the Secretary of State for Scotland announced that the government intended to implement the Kilbrandon juvenile panel proposals. He also instituted a working group composed of the local authority associations and civil servants, together with three independent advisers (two of whom were social workers) to draw up plans for the reorganisation of the local authority social work services. The subsequent White Paper, *Social Work and the Community* (1966) proposed the setting up of comprehensive social work departments 'based on the insights and skills of the profession of social work' (para. 10). There would be considerable flexibility of deployment in these departments but the use of specialist skill would continue to an extent which the later Seebohm Report (1968) did not envisage. The new departments should plan their services so that the distinctive needs of each community could be met, and advice from social work departments be provided to other local authority services about the social impact of their policies. This emphasis on general planning of services relevant to each area and the allied concept of promoting the welfare of communities and individuals coincided with an increasing interest in the place of community work and community development in social work services. The probation service would become part of the social work department on the grounds that 'the main duty of the probation officer – personal social work with the offender and his family in the community – is basically similar to that of other social workers' (para. 28). The argument for bringing probation into the social work departments was indeed the same as for other services. School welfare would also come in, but in assessment centres and child guidance clinics educational psychologists would be on the staff of the education department and social workers on the staff of the new department.

THE SOCIAL WORK (SCOTLAND) ACT, 1968 AND ITS IMPLEMENTATION

These proposals were embodied in the Social Work (Scotland) Act, 1968. This was more all-inclusive than the later 'Seebohm' Act of 1970, not least because of the famous comprehensive section 12 (i) 'it shall be the duty of every local authority to promote social welfare'. This gave local authorities a free hand to do so in their localities in whatever way they judged most effective. It ranged from power to make cash payments to individuals to a duty not only to help social casualties but to go far beyond this to the active development of social well-being. This entailed a positive role in co-operation with voluntary organisations to encourage individuals, families and groups to help in solving problems. Community development and comprehensive social planning by local authorities and related services were thus essential. Probation and after-care were transferred to the social work departments, which also became responsible for providing a social work service to the new children's hearings.

The fifty-two new departments were headed by directors of social work. Each local authority submitted a list of applicants to the Secretary of State for Scotland who indicated those considered suitable by qualification and experience, from which the local authority made its appointment. A professional advisory service was set up to help and advise local authorities, which had no long tradition of professional social work. This was created in 1967 as the Social Work Services Group (SWSG) by bringing together relevant parts of the Scottish Home and Health and Education Departments as an independent entity directly responsible to ministers for implementing the Act.

The Scottish Advisory Council on Social Work succeeded the Advisory Council on Child Care and the Scottish Probation Advisory and Training Council. It was composed of individuals appointed by the Secretary of State because they had a contribution to make, not because they represented a particular interest.

When the initial decision was made, and before the Act was brought into operation by stages, conferences were held to study the task ahead. This included not only problems of reorganisation but also the nature of satisfactory community life, the best means of achieving this and what would be the necessary resources and most efficient organisation. The social work services committees started to meet in 1968 and the directors began work early the following year before the new departments finally came into existence in November 1969.

As a third element in the total planning, a working party was set up on the initiative of Edinburgh University Department of Social Administration and financed by the Joseph Rowntree Memorial Trust to examine the possible effects of the Act on the development of social services in Scotland. Its report (*Social Work in Scotland*, 1969) explored in practical detail the organisation of a social work department (including area teams) and the importance of thorough assessment and review of cases and of the unified social work service interacting closely with environmental planning, education, housing, health, justice, police, employment and social security services. It also considered the role and functions of voluntary organisations, children's hearings, training, staffing and research.

These are the dry bones but they give no idea of the sense of release and pioneering which the two reports, the White Paper and the Act generated in Scotland. For years the personal social services in Scotland had been static, sparse and old-fashioned, but now they were given the potential to become amongst the most advanced in the world. The very fact that few resources of trained manpower existed and that the children's panels had to be started from scratch added all the more drive to the stocktaking and planning.

A period of intense and unremitting activity followed. There were few models of local authority social work comparable with the best children's departments in England and Wales and fewer qualified social workers went into local authority service. The Scottish social services in general were not attractive to students with university qualifications owing to poor status, salaries and conditions of service. In 1968 out of a total of 959 local authority staff (including probation), 292 held professional qualifications, including 164 who had taken the one-year probation course. Thus two big leaps had to be made simultaneously – the creation of the service and its infrastructure and equipping the social work staff at every level. The problems faced by Seebohm reorganisation in England and Wales two years later were in some ways greater in Scotland. These were: extreme staff shortages in relation to an overwhelming increase in demand, promotion which took experienced people away from direct service to clients, and anxieties amongst specialised social workers about wider client responsibilities. Nevertheless, thanks to the professional, administrative and financial resources available to the SWSG, the active help of universities and other educational institutions, the professional associations and the local authorities themselves, and in consequence of consultations and widespread in-service training the later Martin Report (n.d., but actually published 1974) found a steady increase in the range and quality of services, 'a continuous concern to respond to the needs of clients as effectively as personal skills and departmental resources permit; there is also a notable absence of complacency, and a constant anxiety to improve services both quantitively and qualitatively' (p. 9). By 1974 1,122 staff of social work departments held professional qualifications against 1,063 not so qualified, and excluding residential and day centre staffs (SWSG, *Scottish Social Work Statistics*, 1974, p. 52).

The policy of decentralisation into area teams was difficult to implement owing to shortages of staffs and premises. But wider powers made it possible for rural authorities to stop appointing part-time staff, who might also be registrars of births, deaths and marriages or inspectors of weights and measures. The social work departments were required to make a court service available and, whilst many previous probation officers undertook the duty of court officer, most authorities deliberately extended the function of the supervision of offenders to all fieldwork staff. The departments became responsible for prison welfare in 1973. About 50 to 60 social workers were necessary to achieve a 1:100 ratio, but there were only 13 prison welfare officers in post at the time of the transfer. The number had risen to 23 full-time and 3 part-time by 1974.

There was a steady increase in community work appointments but differing views about its nature. By 1975 there were about fifty such appointments in the Strathclyde region. Possibly greater emphasis on this in Scotland resulted from section 12 activities. This section included providing advice to health, housing, education, planning and other authorities about the social implications of their services and of environmental change. The giving of help in cash or kind to anyone in need, if this would prevent greater expense, showed that this was often an indispensible preliminary to effective social work help to people in poverty.

There was no ten-year plan in Scotland, but in 1972 social work departments were asked to submit plans up to 1975 and more generally to 1978 in consultation with other departments, hospitals and voluntary organisations. These were to be based on the *Proposals for Development of Social Work Services* (1972) issued by the SWSG. Local authorities were asked to assess how far they were meeting their main responsibilities and what were the chief gaps and inadequacies. Details of priorities for development under all headings were then to follow, including action to stimulate and support community self-help.

For the first time research on a substantial scale began to clarify the needs of those using the services, their organisation, effectiveness and staffing. This was financed from public funds and undertaken by the SWSG, and the universities (including an inquiry in the Grampians region conducted by a Brunel University team into area team organisation and client views of service provision).

Increased training resources primarily depended on more fieldwork student units. At first these were held up by extreme shortages of qualified supervisors, but the chapter on fieldwork describes the rapid subsequent developments (see volume 2, chapter 4). Table 8 shows staffing achievements between 1970 and 1974.

In 1975 the social work departments faced another upheaval when local government reorganisation reduced their number from 52, to 9 regions and 3 island authorities. In the preceding year 29 of the 52 directors of social work held a professional social work qualification. After reorganisation 9 of the 12 directors were so qualified.

Other aspects of social work and training in Scotland are discussed in various relevant chapters.

Table 8   *Staff in Scottish social work departments, 1970–4*
(whole-time equivalents)

	HQ and fieldwork	Day centres*	Residential*
1970	1,365	1,440	4,368
1971	1,532	1,512	5,131
1972	1,804	1,609	5,328
1973	2,110	1,866	6,024
1974	2,530	1,950	6,958

*including administrative, clerical and domestic staffs.

The figures for 1973 include 30 community social workers, 10 training officers, and 27·9 fieldwork teachers (whole-time equivalents). The figures for 1974 include 50 community workers, 11 training officers and 38·6 fieldwork teachers (whole-time equivalents).
Source: Social Work Services Group, *Scottish Social Work Statistics*, 1970, 1971, 1972, 1973, 1974 (Edinburgh, HMSO).

CHILDREN'S HEARINGS

Under the Act, the children's panels on the lines of the Kilbrandon Committee's recommendations were served by reporters who organised the panel's work, decided whether or not a child should be brought before it as being in need of compulsory measures of care, arranged hearings and communicated the decisions reached to the relevant parties. Regular review of cases dealt with by the children's panels was mandatory. The panel members were recruited and selected by an imaginative plan of advertising, interviews and training (see also chapter 19). Advisory committees were appointed to advise the Secretary of State as to the most suitable members to be appointed. Over 3,000 candidates applied in 1970 and 850 were trained. Later this training was organised regionally at universities. More panel members were recruited from time to time until by 1975 there were 1,450. About half the children notified to reporters came before children's hearings, of these, supervision orders were made in 1974 for 46 per cent and 10 per cent were sent to residential institutions. Each hearing lasted about forty minutes and good communication was said to be established with most parents and children. Unsuccessful efforts were made to build in research from the beginning into the two different systems north and south of the border and to develop criteria for measuring their effectiveness.

Chapter 18

Voluntary Organisations Related to Social Work

INTRODUCTION

All the services surveyed in this study resulted originally from voluntary effort, and voluntary organisations continued to play an essential part in them. A number are referred to in other chapters. It is impossible to do more than glance at major changes with illustrations from a few, long-established or metamorphosed voluntary organisations. These examples do not evaluate the size, importance or influence of any given organisation in relation to other perhaps equally significant examples.

By 1975 a great and increasing amount of voluntary effort existed both locally and nationally to provide general co-ordination or specific services for particular groups of people. This concentration was a strength when an organisation knew in depth about some need, but it could result in demands for one group being pressed without thought for wider social policy implications or the claims of people with other less well-publicised needs.

Voluntary organisations had various functions from the social work point of view, though many ranged far beyond social work alone. They provided specialist services which were part of the resources available to social workers, whether direct provision like pre-school play groups or old people's homes; or an information and advice service, like citizens' advice bureaux (CABx) or the Disabled Living Foundation; or pioneer ventures that opened up new perspectives, like the National Association for the Care and Resettlement of Offenders (NACRO) new careers project; or pressure groups, like the Child Poverty Action Group; or sources of fresh knowledge and interdisciplinary co-operation like the National Children's Bureau or Age Concern; or a focus for general voluntary and statutory co-operation like the National Council of Social Service (NCSS), the Scottish and Welsh Councils of Social Service, local councils of social or voluntary service (CSS and CVS), and the Volunteer Centre.

TENSIONS IN THE 1950S AND LATER DEVELOPMENTS

In the early 1950s voluntary organisations and local authorities were struggling free of war-time constrictions, though not always of paternalism, into a new era of enormous social change, new attitudes and general welfare state provision. Many voluntary organisations continued to operate on the old pre-war assumptions; some were afraid that their funds would dry up if the welfare state abolished material need and their functions would be taken over by public authorities. Others were determined to go on attempting to provide a general service, for children for example, being convinced that public authorities would only make cold, impersonal provision, as indeed they often had under the poor law. Conversely, some local authorities wanted nothing to do with voluntary organisations which in their view dispensed charity with strings attached, whereas the local authority would provide a citizen service. In these circumstances local grant aid to voluntary organisations varied from nil to situations in which some local authorities gave 100 per cent grants to voluntary organisations to provide an agency service, particularly for blind or deaf people. In these agreements, the local authority handed over actual responsibility for the service to the agency's specialist workers, who were isolated from the local authority staff and usually not trained social workers. Moreover, the authority itself was not discovering how to operate the service and thus was not always competent to judge the quality of what was provided or able to learn more about clients' needs.

In time, local authority committees grew less suspicious or less wholly trusting and each side discovered how to work better with the other. In some circumstances a national voluntary organisation might be able to provide a specialist service for clients of whom there were too few to make this possible in a given area. The quality of voluntary organisations' services probably varied more widely than that of local authorities'. Many small, local voluntary organisations, in particular, were run by volunteers and the idea persisted that the voluntary principle would be destroyed by the employment of paid, professional staff. Voluntary organisations might also suffer from inertia, vested interests, lack of resources and a fatal tendency to equate aspiration with achievement, though organisations with assured funds could be immovably self-satisfied. None the less many voluntary organisations, whether new or revitalised, showed the flexibility and freedom to experiment, the drive to meet need in new ways traditionally claimed for them. Some voluntary organisations offered a high standard of service which could give the chance of client choice, particularly to those who thought a voluntary agency more personal than a public service, or preferred one with a religious affiliation or connected with a particular professional group, so that birds of a feather could sometimes find solace together. Some of the best pioneer experiments were undertaken by voluntary organisations, usually with grants from trusts or public funds, often with university help, and at a standard well in advance of general provision. Indeed, voluntary effort became increasingly a main source of fresh discoveries about human behaviour in social contexts of particular concern to social workers.

SOME EXAMPLES OF VOLUNTARY ACTION IN VARIOUS FIELDS

Dr Barnardo's and Other Child Care Organisations
By degrees, as local authority child care services improved, the national

societies for children became less competitive with public authorities.

Barnardo's was the largest social work voluntary organisation in the country. Its tradition of Christian care for destitute children had included foster home placement, adoption (from 1949), and help to some mothers of illegitimate children; but the emphasis was on long-term care for children apart from their families in residential homes all over the country. It was a long, hard struggle for Barnardo's to abandon the image of the ever-open door for any child in need, to concentrate on specialist services, and to try to keep children in their families.

After several changes it was finally set on a new course by a policy report (1969) which clarified guidelines aimed 'to provide and develop in consultation with statutory authorities and other agencies selected services for children in need and their families on a regional basis' (p. 3), because 'voluntary services should select and contribute both geographically and functionally where needs are greatest and resources least adequate' (p. 4). 'A voluntary society . . . must be in close touch with the contemporary situation . . . and be sensitive to the ebb and flow of change within it' (p. 20), therefore Barnardo's should 'narrow the field of [its] activities and increasingly specialise' (p. 4). Under the new policy, comprehensive divisional teams were located in selected areas with considerable freedom to respond to local needs. In consequence, the number of day centres for children steadily increased and some of these became a base for family casework, parent involvement, play schemes, play buses, holidays and clubs for adolescents (Bywaters, 1973).

Barnardo's adoption work was increasingly concentrated on hard-to-place children, and a phone-in service was started in Leeds to answer any query related to adoption. Foster homes included professional foster parents. The number of 'ordinary' children's homes was steadily reduced to 25 by 1975, compared with 38 special schools and homes (including 6 former approved schools), 9 hostels for adolescents, and some provision for homeless families and unsupported mothers. By 1975 the staff included 150 social workers, of whom 80 per cent were qualified, and 1,300 residential staff, with 20 per cent qualified (personal communication). The working party had lamented 'the regrettable absence of evaluation of child care practice and of original research into child care problems' (p. 6). Subsequently, several research projects were financed and efforts made to solve problems of evaluation. The entire emphasis was to be on steadily increasing the quality of service.

The National Children's Home, the Church of England Children's Society, the Crusade of Rescue, and others went through similar struggles to recognise that the era when children had no other safety net was mercifully past, so that now they could pioneer new services and also concentrate on families rather than all too often losing track of the parents. By the mid-1970s they had moved beyond a concentration on the deprived or neglected child; first to his family, then to the environment. This led to pioneer projects which included imaginative experiments in family counselling, play programmes, group work and community development projects in deprived areas. Residential homes largely served children with special needs.

The same processes of change were undergone with greater or less struggle by a number of other voluntary organisations. This was only possible in an age of improved public services, more knowledge, changed attitudes – and greater humility.

The National Society for the Prevention of Cruelty to Children

Throughout the period the aim of the NSPCC continued to be to protect children who were neglected, ill-treated, physically assaulted or in other ways likely to be injured in their physical and emotional development. The methods by which it pursued these aims changed substantially between the 1950s and 1970s.

The first women visitors were appointed in 1948. By 1962 there were nearly 300 men inspectors but only 37 women visitors. In 1961 the recruitment policy of the Society was changed as a result of the setting up of a new training department. Previously, inspectors had largely been recruited from the police and the services. From this date, inspectors began to wear their uniform less frequently, until its abolition in 1969. The attitudes of both children's departments and the juvenile courts varied, probably in line with their experience of individual inspectors. Some found them helpful in preventing family breakdown, in giving support to inadequate families, and working with the hostility of parents, even acting on occasions as independent advocates to public authorities. Sometimes, indeed, 'the cruelty man' was an important source of help in the neighbourhood. Sinfield (1961) said:

'In some towns at least people will approach the NSPCC officer – "the cruelty man" – for advice on many different issues completely unrelated to his job – to solve matrimonial disputes, to explain the details of a hire purchase agreement or to persuade a firm to set payments at a lower level, to intervene with a local social worker or to settle arguments with the income tax authorities.' (p. 33)

Conversely, there was sometimes friction when inspectors were rigid, old-fashioned and authoritarian, too prone to remove a child to a place of safety in unnecessarily dramatic circumstances.

The controversy as to whether or not it was desirable for a voluntary society to have power to institute court proceedings in care or protection cases was at its height while the Ingleby Committee (1960) was sitting, and later when fresh legislation was pending. In the event, the power remained, though the controversy was an effective stimulus to preserve the values in the public image of the NSPCC but to modernise its practice. An important dynamic was the new training department which moved the Society's work from an inspectorial service to a service focused on an understanding of family dynamics and the use of casework skills; not only working with the parents but with the children as well. This often required the difficult process of combining, in a therapeutic way, care and control as a social work function. From the inauguration of the new training department no officers were allowed to practise in the field until they had successfully passed the Society's social work course, which aimed to give a general social work base, but focused on child and family protective social work, with a particular emphasis upon the understanding of the psychopathology of parents who put their children at risk, and the most appropriate casework skills to help the families concerned.

From 1964, initially two, later increased to twelve, casework supervisors were appointed to supervise newly appointed staff. From 1962 a staff development programme was initiated, which included secondment to child care and CSW courses, and later 'phase III' and other CQSW courses. A variety of in-service training programmes were also run locally and nationally. Women visitors' training was originally separate from that of inspectors, but from 1965 they were trained on the same course and by 1969 the total staff became more balanced between the sexes. Newly appointed, professionally qualified social workers were given a four-month orientation and further training courses before they began to practise in the Society. All field staff took four-day refresher courses every year. There were also courses for first-line managers, originally evolved from industrial training experience, and largely consisting of simulation exercises. By the mid-1970s the Society's Training School was running a fourteen-month, full-time course for its student inspectors, awarding an internal certificate in child protection and family social work. This course was focused upon an understanding of the causation of situations that put children at risk and included the teaching of family and marital interaction, casework, and human growth and development. Teaching was also given on the integration of law and casework and a positive use of authority, as well as group-work techniques, the use of community resources and play-group skills. It also undertook a substantial programme of staff development and ran a variety of short courses and conferences for social workers and members of other professions on various aspects of child care and general social work (see also volume 2, chapter 4).

By 1975 there were 246 fieldwork staff, of whom 82 were professionally qualified, 95 had taken the NSPCC fourteen-month course, and 25 held the Home Office letter of recognition by experience. There were 13 supervisors in student units and 7 in child treatment units.

The Society continued to be closely involved in the detection, reporting and supervision of children at risk, but in far more constructive and sophisticated forms (see volume 2, chapter 16, section on 'NSPCC Initiative'). Its preventive activities included play groups, holidays and community work. It made its work widely known through multidisciplinary action research, conferences and publications.

The Family Welfare Association

The family casework agencies had always been local, though on good terms with each other. Their standards varied, some were simply relief-giving agencies, but others, like the Liverpool Personal Service Society, consistently pioneered new ways of meeting need. Rooff (1972) recorded the changing history of the London Family Welfare Association (FWA). By the 1950s it was immersed in the struggle to discover an identity that belonged to the present and future rather than the past, that would enable it to experiment with new and more relevant services, and that would have a fund-raising appeal. It was torn by domestic conflicts between 'new' and 'old' caseworkers, in which the old clung to Charity Organisation Society principles while the new were dissatisfied with irksome methods carried over from the past and casework that was primarily relief-giving. There were conflicts with committee members who wanted cases to be reported in detail and to make decisions about treatment. The FWA Council and the central office were also torn and unable to provide a forum for effective discussion and decision. A review committee with external consultants resulted in a report (1960, unpublished) with proposals which breathed some new life into this stronghold of social work. In spite of confusions, student supervision reached a high level and a number of leading social work practitioners passed through and made their contribution to the FWA. Several pioneer projects were undertaken which were both cause and consequence of the FWA changeover from primarily a grant-giving agency to a new concern with emotional problems in family relationships. This required caseworkers with a substantial understanding of psychodynamics. In consequence, more psychiatric and casework consultation was provided, some of it from North America. Shortage of funds made it necessary to contract the number of district offices in the 1960s. Finally, out of many struggles and much reorganisation a new FWA emerged in the mid-1970s. It was a pioneer in marital and family therapy, though including single people, adolescents and one-parent families. Clients were expected to work on their own problems, in a belief that they had potentials for change which casework could help to liberate. In 1975 a separately administered, fee-paying, private counselling service was started. The aim of the revitalised FWA was to provide a high standard of professional service and to add to knowledge through student training, seminars and publications.

Voluntary Organisations for Old People
Other, newer voluntary organisations found the journey into the mid-twentieth century less of a painful landslide. For instance, the National Old People's Welfare Council (at first, part of the National Council of Social Service), and local old people's welfare committees had an obvious co-ordinating, pioneering, pressure-group and good-neighbour role to play on behalf of old people. The effort to provide more old people's homes was very different from the anxieties suffered by organisations forced to find new roles for their children's homes. Local old people's welfare committees were also examples of a local co-ordination, pressure-group, innovating role, strangely enough one never assumed by the child care organisations. Age Concern (the National Old People's Welfare Council under a modern title) continued as the acknowledged spokesman for old people to public authorities, and indeed to the public itself. (See also chapter 12.)

Voluntary Organisations for Handicapped People
National and local voluntary effort made an enormous contribution to services for handicapped people through hundreds of organisations, large and small, from the long-established Central Council for the Disabled to small local societies. The organisations for the blind included the work of

the regional associations for the blind, clubs, holidays, guide dogs, the Royal National Institute for the Blind, the National Library for the Blind, St Dunstan's and residential special schools.

The Spastic Society provided a comprehensive family service through a national assessment centre with panels consisting of a doctor, a psychologist and a social worker; a regional social work service; holidays; clubs; careers and employment advisory services; a housing association; residential schools; further education centres; industrial work and training centres; adult residential centres; hostels; holiday hotels; a medical information unit; research; publications; training and short courses; and various other activities.

During this period many more self-help groups came into existence to improve their own or their children's circumstances and to press for better services: they included the Muscular Dystrophy Group and the National Society for Autistic Children, as well as many others. Some general national voluntary organisations, like Barnardo's, developed more services for handicapped young people, and the National Association of Youth Clubs (NAYC) started its successful PHAB (physically handicapped and able-bodied) clubs and holiday centres. Some handicapped children were included in Pre-School Playgroups Association (PPA) play groups, while adventure playgrounds for handicapped children and the Handicapped Adventure Playground Association were started. Cheshire Foundation Homes for severely disabled people spread all over the country, and the residents in one of these pioneered a degree of self-government and independence not then achieved elsewhere.

In addition, the Disablement Income Group pressed for pensions for disabled people; the Disabled Living Foundation provided advice, information and demonstration services. Research was undertaken by the National Foundation for Research into Crippling Diseases and other organisations for the handicapped.

The National Association for Mental Health (NAMH) came into being in 1946. It inherited the war-time experience and enthusiasm of a group of psychiatrists, PSWs and others for community mental health. Strong lay support also helped to set its course. Its influence was crucial in broadening concepts of mental health and improved conditions in mental hospitals at a time when attitudes were becoming more liberal. This influence was exercised through its annual conferences, special groups, training activities, co-operation with many other statutory and voluntary organisations, and publications, of which *Do Cows Have Neuroses?* (Bingham, 1961) was one of the most widely read. It was concerned with the treatment and care of mentally disordered people and their families. It pressed for better community care, more child guidance clinics and other provision for maladjusted children and for the mentally handicapped; and the extension of health concepts beyond the bounds of mental illness. It ran two pioneer approved schools for maladjusted girls of high intelligence, a home for mentally frail old people, and two hostels for mentally handicapped school leavers. In 1970 it changed its title to MIND and concentrated increasingly on inquiries, campaigns, general publicity, information and pressure-group activities. A number of local mental health associations – over 130 by 1975

– brought interested organisations and individuals together for study and action and sometimes themselves ran homes, hostels, day centres and social clubs.

The National Society for Mentally Handicapped Children, which campaigned for better services for such children, had a number of residential homes and over 400 local societies by 1975. Many members were parents of handicapped children. Some societies provided homes, hostels and day centres in co-operation with social services departments, and ran play groups, holiday schemes, parents' discussion groups and toy libraries, and published guides to local services and surveys of parents' needs. The National Society produced journals, other publications and films, ran conferences and provided a scheme for the recruitment and training of voluntary welfare visitors who gave support and information about the complexities of public services and grants to parents of mentally handicapped children. It also pioneered a trustee scheme for the personal interest and care of mentally handicapped people after their parents' death.

The National Association for the Care and Resettlement of Offenders
The Government decided in 1966 that prison welfare and after-care should be transferred from the voluntary discharged prisoners' aid societies to the probation service. In consequence, the National Discharged Prisoners' Aid Society was disbanded but a new organisation, the National Association for the Care and Resettlement of Offenders (NACRO) was established with grant aid from the Home Office. Its aim was to be vigorously involved in crime prevention, to strengthen and advise local voluntary associations, and to provide information, training and consultant services. The resettlement of offenders also logically included the prevention of further offences. This meant acting as a national forum with an active concern about alternatives to prison and wider preventive schemes for those liable to break the law, to improve the environment in which they live, and especially to prevent deprived and deviant youngsters from drifting into crime. From time to time, NACRO ran field projects to improve non-custodial services and prevent crime. These experiments included accommodation for single homeless people, day care and medical services, workshop employment, day care for drug addicts, and a national advice service for offenders who wanted to improve their education. It also gave assistance and advice on the use of volunteers, landlady schemes, housing associations, employment, education for offenders, and liaison with central and local government. From almost its beginning, it was actively concerned with the training of staffs of hostels for offenders and many took its training courses (see also volume 2, chapter 14, section on 'Hostels for Those before the Courts'). The new careers movement aimed to give selected ex-offenders training and a career in the human services, largely by employment as ancillaries or 'linkers' with in-service training but also with a longer training period for a few. The aim was to make the maximum use of their first-hand experience (see also chapter 19). NACRO was an outstanding example of the new voluntary organisations started in the 1960s which could look questioningly at the present and future, unfettered by past assumptions. Its Scottish counterpart (SACRO) was equally active, for example in finding accom-

modation for homeless ex-offenders and the training of volunteers in after-care.

Radical Alternatives to Prison (RAP) was a pressure group composed of prisoners, ex-prisoners and sympathisers which aimed to promote alternatives that might in time supersede imprisonment with all its ill effects.

The Pre-School Playgroups Association

The comparative neglect of the under fives and their mothers began to trouble many people in the early 1960s. One consequence was that groups of mothers came together locally to run play groups for their children. This resulted in the Pre-School Playgroups Association (PPA) set up to increase public understanding of the needs of the under fives and parents' own part in meeting them; to encourage rich and stimulating play provision for all children under five, and to promote the formation of play groups and the involvement of parents in them. In time it also included fathers and child minders, and provided for more handicapped children and children of working mothers. By 1975 there were 9,400 member play groups in England and Wales attended by 360,000 children. Of these, three-quarters had active parent involvement on a rota system and/or on elected committees. Ninety per cent of play groups paid sessional fees to supervisors and assistants. Only one in every four play groups was grant-aided by local authorities. The PPA play groups were sometimes accused of catering for 'middle-class mums' – as though their small children had no need of play groups. But in 1975 12 per cent of play groups were in poor areas and 40 per cent in mixed areas, against 10 per cent in better-off areas (PPA, *Facts and Figures*, 1975).

The PPA movement spread like wildfire, especially when in the late 1960s the DHSS gave a grant which trebled its annual income. This enabled it to increase its headquarters staff and to appoint area and regional organisers (this work was already being done by volunteers), some part-time play group advisers, play-group and child-minder organisers, tutors, training and development officers, and others. It is not easy to expand at this rate and maintain efficiency and a sense of direction. But this was a movement served by dedicated and competent people with a realistic sense of direction. By 1975 there were 376 branches and 34 county associations. Its publications, including the monthly *Contact*, were full of practical information about play groups. Training of both helpers and supervisors was obviously crucial and the PPA actively promoted good training, including foundation courses and courses for tutors. In 1974 there were 833 courses largely run by local education authorities. Information was not available about the students' backgrounds nor how effectively the courses met their needs.

The Scottish PPA also spread rapidly, thanks to vigorous and imaginative leadership and grant aid from public funds.

Settlements

At their most effective, settlements were a power in the neighbourhood because they were local multipurpose agencies not subject to remote control. Their residents worked with local people of all ages in an equal partnership, belonged in the neighbourhood and made friends in it. But the role of settlements was implicitly challenged by the spread of the welfare state which seemed for a time to make voluntary effort irrelevant. Many settlements disappeared from the 1950s, but others weathered the storm because they had strong local roots and key residents were widely respected locally.

Individual settlements might have had close links with the church or a university. A 1950 survey by the British Association of Residential Settlements (BARS, 1951) showed that the main activities still consisted of clubs for children, young people and adults of all ages. The settlements' value lay in their knowledge of the neighbourhood and its social problems. Thirty-six out of 112 settlements in the survey gave social science students experience of the normal life of the neighbourhood, though the nature of this experience was not clearly stated and no training existed for settlement work.

The settlements went through a fallow period in the 1950s, often continuing the same activities but without developing new expertise or fresh projects. Then came a period during the 1960s when family advice centres, community development projects and other experiments were discovering independently what settlements had pioneered – but with a fresh zest and often with more skill, because many of the best social workers were by then in the public services and people from other professions were also attracted by new experiments in community work. Some settlements also began to pioneer new ventures, notably Blackfriars, Liverpool University and Bristol Settlements. Settlement wardens had often been middle-aged women of considerable local standing and independence. But by the 1960s most settlements were non-residential and their directors and other staff were usually young, committed and articulate. Settlements also became part of the effort to train students in community work and several had publicly financed student units.

A Gulbenkian Foundation grant acted as the catalyst for a group of south-east London settlements to come together under effective leadership to rethink their purpose. In 1971 a national development team was appointed and settlements met regularly to overhaul the constitution and structure of BARS, which changed its title to the British Association of Settlements and Social Action Centres (BAS), and in 1973 defined its purpose as being 'to encourage and enable people to move towards the vision of a caring, sharing society; to bring about the maximum involvement of the group, neighbourhood or community in solving the problems that concern them, in participating in the decisions that affect them and in running their own affairs' (BAS, 1973, mimeographed).

Significant new experiments were initiated by individual settlements, especially in arts, crafts and drama for people living in deprived neighbourhoods. Local, self-help schemes were encouraged and also play groups, welfare rights services and alternative educational projects. Amongst the latter, Cambridge House pioneered an adult literacy teaching technique later widely adopted as part of an adult literacy campaign launched in 1974.

Religious Organisations
Church organisations continued to run homes for children and old people, to act as adoption agencies, and to provide the moral welfare (later family

welfare) services discussed in volume 2 (see chapter 17).

Many struggled to keep their specifically religious ethos in the residential or other forms of care they provided, yet often without demanding a religious affiliation. Others provided for those who preferred this, for instance in old people's homes for members of given denominations. Some priests, clergy, ministers, nuns, and women parish workers trained as social workers. Impetus to discussion and action in a changed social climate came from the Social Responsibility Board of the British Council of Churches, the Anglican and other denominational boards, the Roman Catholic Social Welfare Commission and local councils of churches. Some local social responsibility committees or boards and ecumenical groups started good neighbour schemes to help people in many kinds of need, sometimes in co-operation with local authority services. Individual clergy threw in their lot with, campaigned about and started pioneer ventures for, the homeless, the desperate, drifters and the down and out. Many practising Christians thought that they could work more effectively in lay voluntary organisations or public authorities. Individual Christians and the churches, like other religions, retained their concern for people's spiritual well-being, but attitudes very different from those of the past broke down the barriers between secular and specifically religious services.

It is also important to remember the work of the Jewish community and of the Jewish Welfare Board, and much activity by other religious groups, especially for ethnic minority groups.

The Salvation Army and Church Army continued to provide, among many other activities, shelter and concern for many people at the end of the line, but they were not in the mainstream of new experiments.

For the Salvation Army, like others, these decades were a period of much adaptation, with closer co-operation with the public services and changed methods. Grants from public funds took a burden off the staff and made it possible to provide a better service. But recruitment declined to about 100 new recruits a year. The general growth of professional social work resulted in more emphasis on training, and on improved practice. The Salvation Army continued to provide a large number of beds in hostels for homeless single people, sheltered workshops, and long-stay accommodation for ex-psychiatric patients. Old buildings were rebuilt or modified and new hostels for smaller numbers replaced old premises. Services for alcoholics increased from the early 1960s including rehabilitation and detoxification and assessment centres, together with after-care and help for the families. There were also projects for young drug addicts and for battered wives. The Mayflower Home for neglectful mothers and their children was an alternative to prison much used by the courts in the earlier period. By 1975 the goodwill services (previously slum work) operated from 26 centres in densely populated areas and more generally from 200 social service centres. These offered neighbourhood services, play groups, mothers' clubs, day nurseries, children's clubs, services for old people and the handicapped, workshops, day centres, holidays for children and families, and emergency accommodation. No doubt the Army could rightly claim that 'its well known image enables lonely and needy people to relate to it with a degree of trust and security' (personal communication).

Much of the pre-war Church Army work went over to other specialised organisations. Three counselling centres were opened later; the number of old people's homes increased, including two short-stay centres, and it was one of the first to start sheltered housing for elderly people. It continued to run a number of welfare hostels.

Both the Salvation and the Church Armies continued their own training colleges. In the 1960s Salvation Army training lasted for nine months, two officers were seconded to take a two-year social science course at Bristol University and four the London University extension diploma (part-time). It welcomed the Younghusband Report (1959) and worked on plans to start its own nationally recognised course, but this was against CTSW policy and thus it decided to second staff to two-year courses and to develop a training for cadets appropriate to the Army's needs. An officer was seconded to take a Birmingham University course and in 1966 became responsible for developing social work training during the second year of what was by then a two-year residential training at the International Training College. The syllabus included human growth and development and mental disorders; the social services; principles and procedure for officers; pastoral counselling; and practical work consisting of four months at the end of the first year, weekends during the second year and varying periods related to practical work and projects. With staff shortages in the 1970s, cadets were sent to CTC in-service courses instead of the above courses and about ten each year took the certificate of attendance; a smaller number took the part-time CTC certificate in residential child care. By 1975 the possibilities of the Certificate in Social Service (CSS) course were being explored. One officer was completing a CQSW course and others had taken CCETSW short courses in residential social work, but staff shortages made a secondment policy difficult. The Salvation Army's social officers needed: 'Self awareness, the right attitudes and approach, a body of working (and workable) knowledge, and social work skills' (personal communication).

The Church Army Training College three-year syllabus (revised in 1975) included a substantial amount of religious knowledge; study of man in society, including aims and methods of the social sciences, human personality and development, and the social services; professional studies related to Church Army work; and field training covering about forty weeks in all, some in social work centres. Some officers took the Josephine Butler House course during its life-time. Later, the policy was to help officers to take a CQSW or one-year, residential child care course. In 1975 2 officers were taking CQSW courses, 1 a one-year residential child care course, 6 in-service training courses for residential workers, and 1 a pilot CSS course.

There was a remarkable similarity in the two training programmes and an impression of ambivalence about social work training. This was ascribed to lack of manpower and financial resources. Possibly there were also doubts about the value of professional social work in each Army's practice because their main *raison d'être* was evangelism. They remained outside mainstream developments in professional social work: but at their best they knew much about compassion, care and continuity.

The National Council of Social Service, Councils of Social Service and Citizens' Advice Bureaux

The NCSS and its Scottish counterpart had long been established as national forums for co-operation between voluntary agencies and with public authorities. The Council described this function in its 1974–5 *Annual Report* as being

' . . . to encourage and support voluntary social action by individuals and groups . . . by bringing together the voluntary organisations at national level, both collectively and in interest groups, for discussion and expression of views to Government and other bodies and for joint action; by assisting comparable bodies to carry out similar functions at village, neighbourhood, district and county level with a view to assessing and helping to meet community needs and, where necessary, encouraging community action; by providing means of co-operation and communication between voluntary and statutory services concerned with social action in the fields both of policy and practice; by providing consultancy and information services for national and local voluntary organisations and by promoting and, if necessary, undertaking research and experiments in social action, by establishing and providing the secretariat for certain representative voluntary organisations for as long as such help is necessary . . . by taking initiatives itself in the field of social action when it feels it is the relevant body to do so.' (p. 3)

This summed up a very wide range of activities and a diverse structure to support them. The NCSS was also a pioneer in community development and related in-service training (see also volume 2, chapter 18). It had a considerable influence in certain directions where its middle-of-the-road rather than radical image might be a strength, though it was sometimes criticised for being too conformist.

Councils of social service (sometimes renamed community councils or councils of voluntary service) steadily increased in the period. Some were small local agencies running one or two services though

'To be effective at all, the CVS had to work on a large scale, maintaining links with a wide variety of voluntary and statutory bodies, collecting and monitoring data on new developments or research on specific issues and providing the administrative back-up to make this possible. This implied not just full time staff, but staff who were sufficiently versed in their subject to be able to discuss issues with senior administrators in other agencies, especially statutory bodies. Whether we like it or not, the professional is here to stay in our present social service set-up.' (Lansley, 1976, p. 51)

These functions of co-ordination, servicing and promotion, helping voluntary organisations to formulate common policies and pursue common aims, and at the same time promoting new activities and giving support to informal, self-help community groups were not always compatible. Ideally a CSS worked in close partnership with the local authority, exchanging information but also critically appraising the effectiveness of services and bringing pressure to bear for more resources.

Local government reorganisation was a major challenge to the CSS, which to remain effective had to expand to cover the new local authority boundaries – with all the tensions that this rebirth involved. It meant improved communication and increased staff to give a more efficient professional service through extended activities, for example working groups on specific problems like homelessness or the needs of handicapped people. These enlarged CSS were usually only possible with grants from public funds and trusts.

Volunteer bureaux and consumers aid centres were examples of new services pioneered by the CSS, which were also pioneers in the development of community work from the mid-1960s. The London Council of Social Service was outstanding in its promotional and consultancy work, while many other CSS started neighbourhood schemes and became more aware of their own activities as a form of community work. Other direct services might include Citizens' Advice Bureaux, youth activities, adventure playgrounds, legal advice centres, efforts to meet the special needs of elderly and disabled people, minibuses and holiday schemes. The rural community councils had the same general aims in relation to rural communities, including conservation, environmental problems, and encouraging the formulation of local views about neighbourhood or wider development plans.

Citizens' Advice Bureaux (CABx) became part of the social scene during the war. By 1973 they numbered 566, largely staffed by volunteers for whom the NCSS CAB service provided training. In 1973 there were about 250 paid organisers, and 185 other paid staff in the bureaux (including 4 full-time solicitors). The number of advisory officers was being increased so that each might be responsible for about thirty bureaux. The NCSS provided a regular information service, the citizens' advice notes (CANS), which enabled CABx to give up-to-date and accurate information, though they were sometimes criticised for not acting as clients' advocates like the more militant Child Poverty Action Group (CPAG) advice centres and 'rights stalls' in busy streets. But they fulfilled other important functions and their national returns were indicative of people's current concerns.

SOME CHANGES IN THE 1960S AND EARLY 1970S

In the 1960s and 1970s many voluntary organisations became more conscious than in the past of their duty to face the difficult task of educating the public about the needs of particular people and modern methods of help, rather than relying on emotional fund-raising appeals. This function of education was not discharged by local or central authorities, while the findings of independent inquiries reached few people. Education was made technically easier by the growth of the mass media and through films produced by many voluntary organisations. It was characteristic of pressure groups like the CPAG, with its powerful advocacy, its detailed knowledge of the confused tangle of welfare rights, its ability to give accurate advice, and to influence action about the plight of families on or below the poverty line. Shelter made visible the appalling family life of homeless or grossly ill-housed people, while others like the National Council for One-Parent Families or the Howard League battled on with fewer resources to back up a good cause.

Practically all voluntary organisations of standing in the social services field were grant-aided from public funds by the 1970s. By this means, good innovations like the PPA, NACRO and the Volunteer Centre achieved a range of services and size of operation which would have been impossible without such help. They became, indeed, sources of information, centres of excellence, and means of responsible pressure. Some small organisations doing a useful job were forced out of existence by inflation and many more would have ceased to exist without public funds. A number of new experiments were started jointly by voluntary organisations and local authorities which would have had neither the resources nor competence to start on their own. Intermediate treatment projects, or projects of combined community development groups, and casework in deprived areas were examples. The post-1948 public services demonstrated that voluntary organisations had no monopoly of freedom to experiment but they were more flexible, could be more informal, unorthodox, free to try something out, take risks, make mistakes, change course and rectify mistakes or withdraw. Some experiments contributed to national action, for instance unattached youth workers or the NSPCC battered child research project. This experimentation which often flowed from a voluntary organisation's single-minded concentration on particular people or problems, for example the Family Service Units (FSU) (see volume 2, chapter 15), enabled it to be selective in ways not appropriate for public authorities, and by being highly specialised to gain more expertise about particular life circumstances and disabilities.

There was little self-evaluation study or sophisticated forward planning before the 1960s by voluntary organisations. Later this helped to clarify aims and the use of resources more precisely in the light of changes in consumer needs, sometimes to resolve conflicts between old and new points of view, to change publicity and money-raising activities and attitudes towards professional services, and sometimes led to a wholly new orientation. In 1973 an independent committee was set up with trust funds under the chairmanship of Lord Wolfenden to examine the role and functions of voluntary organisations in the last quarter of the twentieth century. Its questionnaire to voluntary organisations requested both factual information and self-evaluation of effectiveness. It had not completed its inquiry by 1975.

Some social services departments appointed organisers to discover all the voluntary organisations in the area and attempt to co-ordinate their activities with each other and with local authority services. An astonishing number of such organisations were revealed, sometimes small with limited purposes and duplicating each other, sometimes providing a valuable complementary service. There were examples of local authorities seconding professional social workers or offering consultative services to voluntary organisations, as well as giving small to very large sums in grant aid.

For a period in the 1950s and 1960s voluntary organisations found much difficulty in recruiting and retaining trained social workers because financial rewards, promotion prospects, and work satisfaction were greater in the public services. By the early 1970s this began to change when some social workers, disillusioned by conditions in social services departments, were attracted by the greater freedom and chances to innovate offered in voluntary organisations. For a long while voluntary organisations had paid the nationally negotiated salaries and change of employment and promotion was possible within them. Yet, like public authorities, they were faced by an absolute shortage of qualified social workers.

In the early 1950s voluntary organisations were claiming to provide a better service than local authorities, though problems of accountability were not solved then or later. In the intervening years each became sadder and wiser, recognising that the problem of the respective roles of public and voluntary service had no neat solutions in conditions of continual social and economic change where time-lags of history also persisted. Sometimes voluntary organisations were giving services that were a local authority responsibility. For though by the mid-1970s severe cuts in public spending were reducing the quality and range of public services, a local authority might also pay a voluntary agency, for example the FWA and the FSU, to give a higher standard of social work service to a few clients than it itself could provide. Some other voluntary organisations, though also greatly affected by inflation, could maintain the quality of their more specialised services with limited coverage. Thus in some respects the wheel had come full cycle. The Personal Social Services Council (PSSC) in its *Report 1976* drew attention to the importance of an overview of the inter-related care systems provided by local authorities, voluntary organisations, and private bodies, taking account of the shifting emphasis on residential, day and community care and their objectives. They might work together locally, but there were few instances of collective meetings with district or county councils for joint policy making and resource planning; and for reviewing procedures for consultation with government and between voluntary organisations themselves nationally.

The first attempt to forecast voluntary organisations' manpower demands was made on behalf of the Birch working party (1976). In 1973 there were thought to be 1,700 fieldwork staff and 20,030 in residential and day care services (including Scotland). No information was given about senior staff or those who were covered by the residential and day care figures (table 1, p. 167).

In 1975 the PSSC and the NCSS initiated the first study of voluntary social service manpower resources (PSSC, 1976*b*). Information supplied by forty-four national organisations suggested that these alone employed one-sixth as many workers as the public services. They included 3,200 to 4,200 fieldworkers, 700 to 800 day care and over 8,000 residential staff (p. 15). The proportions in different organisations who held the CQSW or a residential qualification varied from nearly 100 per cent to nil (p. 20). At least 12,000 of the total required a CQSW or CSS training (p. 15). The considerable contribution of voluntary organisations to the personal social services had never been measured and no comprehensive information was available about their contribution, capacity and trends, nor about the complex interlocking of statutory and voluntary organisations, especially when some cut across statutory boundaries.

Chapter 19

Volunteers and Volunteer Service Organisers

At first volunteers worked mainly in voluntary organisations, with the exception of the youth service, the LCC School Care system and some local authority welfare departments. Then, as more trained social workers were appointed in voluntary organisations from the late 1940s onwards, there was a long struggle to distinguish the functions of each, and finally volunteers were ousted (at least for a period) from direct work with clients. Even so, there was, of course, always an infinite variety of good neighbourliness and many ancillary services which took various forms and the use of many skills.

In the early 1950s social workers might still be dominated by, and have decisions about, their cases made by committee members at a time when they were struggling to establish their identity and develop professional skills that differentiated them from the untrained. This understandably resulted in esoteric claims and possessiveness about clients. Some resisted the use of volunteers in their work because these might be dangerous amateurs who damaged clients. Some social workers were against training volunteers because, as the later Aves Report (1969) said, both they and administrators might think that 'training would enable volunteers to take the place of social workers and to undertake skilled work without further guidance' (p. 139). These arguments were natural reactions in the battle for recognition, especially when large numbers of social workers were untrained and many volunteers might be better qualified by personality and experience. It was argued, as it had been earlier in social work, that training was unnecessary, because what mattered was the willingness to give voluntary service; training would destroy spontaneity and, anyway, the suggestion that it was necessary would be indignantly rejected by volunteers.

Volunteers were used unevenly in local authority social services in the 1950s. Probably most took part in the activities organised by voluntary associations or by local authority welfare officers, such as friendly visiting of old people, help in social centres for handicapped people, or visiting the housebound.

The mid-1960s were watershed years in social work and the social services. The spread of the volunteer movement and enthusiasm for community participation stimulated fresh thought about the nature of voluntary service, and it became clearer that the roles of social workers and volunteers were complementary not identical. Some national organisations continued to give their direct service through volunteers, notably the British Red Cross Society, the Women's Royal Voluntary Service (WRVS), the CABx, marriage guidance councils, and the Samaritans. The number of volunteers in these organisations ran into many thousands. The new phenomenon of self-help cum pressure-group organisations, volunteers on their own or their children's behalf, included the Pre-School Playgroups Association (PPA), Child Poverty Action groups, welfare rights activists, Gingerbread, and many others. The Samaritans, Alcoholics Anonymous, Gamblers Anonymous, Recidivists Anonymous, and other 'anonymous' groups discovered how volunteers, sometimes those who had been in the same boat themselves, could give personal and group support and bring about changes in desperate situations. The size of these volunteer movements was very considerable, for example in 1974 there were some 17,000 Samaritans, carefully selected, trained and supported by skilled and experienced workers, and around 156,000 new clients.

Other developments, specifically to recruit and use young volunteers, included Community Service Volunteers (CSV, founded 1962) consisting mainly of young people between 17 and 19 who worked full-time for four to twelve months in many situations of social need. Task Force (founded 1964) recruited school children and other young volunteers to help old people in London. The Young Volunteer Force Foundation (founded 1968) was established with government help. It worked in different parts of the country through salaried organisers whose function was to find out what services young people could give locally and enthuse them to do so. Volunteer service by the young changed many people's picture of volunteers from middle-aged, middle-class 'do gooders' to, as Thomas (1974) expressed it, 'long haired youngsters alternating between decorating old people's flats and trying to organise a revolution' (p. 5).

A third significant volunteer phenomenon of the 1960s was the spread of local community groups which came into existence to meet some of their own and their neighbours' needs and to press for more resources (see also volume 2, chapter 18). There were also very many volunteers in the youth service, as in work with old people.

Volunteer bureaux were started by councils of social service in the 1960s and spread steadily. They were sources of advice and information for would-be volunteers, and because a wide range of openings were referred to them, they could make useful suggestions to most inquirers. They acted as a recruitment source both for statutory and voluntary agencies and for individual requests ('retired Army Colonel keen on cricket wants someone with similar interests to go for walks and sometimes to cricket matches'). By 1975 there were nearly 140, a few run by social services departments, and many with a broadened range of activities that included training and support for volunteers (Stace, 1976).

In many situations in the 1960s, when volunteers became more acceptable, they were either not being used or were frustrated by too simple or too difficult jobs with too little support, sometimes because over-pressed social workers had no time to sort out tasks that would have relieved their own pressures and have been better done by volunteers. There was always a danger of these becoming free labour or being used to relieve staff shortages rather than to enrich services and extend their scope. When local authorities began to make more use of volunteers – and they were ambivalent about this on several counts in the 1960s – it was usually assumed that these should be recruited, trained, allocated and sometimes supported by voluntary organisations.

There was no systematic inquiry into volunteers until the Aves Committee (1966–9) was set up jointly by the NCSS and the National Institute for Social Work Training (NISWT) to investigate the role of volunteers in the social services. Its Report (1969) recommended that there should be a continuous clarification of the roles and appropriate tasks of volunteers in the social services. Full- or part-time organisers of volunteers were necessary in every service in which they were used. There should be a comprehensive network of volunteer bureaux, largely financed by local authorities. There should also be active recruitment of volunteers and appropriate selection procedures: this should be followed by preparation and training closely related to the volunteer's needs. Volunteers were least used where social work was most highly developed, but social work students should be made aware of the role of volunteers and how their work related to that of professionals. A national Volunteer Foundation should be set up to act as a focus for all aspects of volunteer work. This Report helped to resolve the struggle between old and new ideas about volunteers, by clarifying their effective use in many different situations and their need for training and support. Its recommendations greatly influenced later developments, by stimulating statutory and voluntary organisations to look at their practice in regard to the training, organisation and support of volunteers, to the increase of relevant training courses, and recognition of the need for further studies.

The whole range of volunteer activity included practical or personal service or both together. Some practical service, like preparing an adventure playground, might not include any personal contact; others, like helping with holiday parties, might be a strenuous mixture of both; whereas counselling was almost entirely personal support. The essence of voluntary service was disentangled from paid activities, even though some overlap was necessary and not to be deplored. The model volunteer was flexible, enthusiastic, reliable, had unhurried time to give, could relax, listen to long-winded stories, not try to focus on agreed goals or assess underlying problems, could let a friendship develop and invite the client home. The contact might be short term in a crisis, for instance if the mother was in hospital, or comfortable reliability might be established over a far longer period than service by professionals who came and went. This continuing interest could be important in creating a personal relationship that increased the self-confidence of multiproblem families or mitigated old or handicapped people's loneliness. Some volunteers also walked corridors of power and could use their direct experience of hardship to campaign for better services or act as advocates for individuals or for improvements in familiar routines unquestioned by the staff. This gadfly responsibility might be assumed too much by some volunteers and too little by others. Matching was part of a more selective use of volunteers and it began to be realised that although many clients preferred volunteers they ought to have a choice rather than being a captive audience or forced to vote with their feet. Most volunteers liked jobs with a clear purpose, a limited commitment and visible results. Both they and the clients benefited since at its best both saw a wider spectrum of living conditions, made new relationships, profited from giving and receiving and had their experience of other people's lives enlarged.

The typical volunteer continued to be thought of as a middle-aged, middle-class woman whose children needed her less, though the Aves Report had found that 'such people no longer constitute an overwhelming majority among the total volunteer force' (p. 33). Men also gave much unrecorded voluntary service. Spontaneous help to neighbours was taken for granted whether individually or through, for example, groups of neighbouring mothers child minding for each other. This kind of help was more natural to working-class people than organised volunteering. The neighbourhood grapevine might locate many people in specific need, but did not guarantee that adequate or long-continued help was provided. Social education classes in schools, and community service associated with them, introduced school children to people in need and the concept of volunteer help: opinions differed about the value of these activities.

Personal service had intensified by the 1970s to a degree unthinkable in the 1950s, though accepted in unsophisticated forms in the 1930s and earlier. More volunteer service organisers were appointed (see below), and much more effort was invested in discovering how to use volunteers effectively. Government policy was consistently benign towards both voluntary organisations and volunteers, so that often considerable grants were given to voluntary organisations which enabled them to support the recruitment, training and use of volunteers and made possible the appointment of full-time area officers, for example by the Pre-School Playgroups Association and others.

The independent Volunteer Foundation recommended in the Aves Report finally came into being in 1973 as the Volunteer Centre, financed, like most other independent activities of the period, by trusts and public funds. Its purposes were to promote volunteering, increase its range, and act as a focal point. Its activities included the collection and dissemination of information, training, advice, technical help, and consultation about specific local developments.

The first systematic attempt to assess the effectiveness of voluntary help instead of taking this for granted was made by Hadley *et al.* (1975). This study of young Task Force volunteers who visited lonely old people showed that undirected effort without proper selection, orientation, matching and subsequent support produced a high failure rate demoralising to both sides. But it also showed that well-motivated volunteers and old people could between them overcome the worst lack of significant relationships with others which was probably the key factor in many old people's grim loneliness. In successful situations the volunteer had become a valued part of the old person's social contacts. The successful volunteers visited more frequently than others, stayed longer, gave practical help, found the relationship satisfying and were interested in and concerned about the old person. The old person must also want the volunteer and respond so that a rewarding relationship was created for both. These findings are very similar to consumers' reactions to casework (see volume 2, chapter 9). They were highly significant in showing that well-selected and supported volunteers could provide the combined affective and practical support which was a central not peripheral need for many people.

Definitions of volunteers were usually confined to those giving some direct service and thus did not necessarily include the thousands of committee members and lay magistrates, even though many had direct and responsible contacts with people in difficulty and their families, especially in juvenile and matrimonial court cases. Members of the Scottish children's hearings panels had a particularly strong claim to be included. The national and publicly financed plan for their recruitment, selection, training and subsequent support made use of and added to the best available knowledge at each stage of the process. Mapstone (1972) and annual reports on *Social Work in Scotland* (Scottish Education Department) gave useful information about the programme. Indeed, by the mid-1970s this was the best and most consistently evaluated example of the large-scale preparation and use of volunteers. Marriage guidance counsellors were a different example on a smaller scale (see volume 2, chapter 21).

In 1973 BASW raised funds for a three-year research project to examine the relations between social workers and volunteers; this action illustrated the changed attitudes by social workers towards volunteers which largely resulted from the impetus of the Aves Report. The project continued in 1975.

In the 1970s experiments in the use of ancillaries and volunteers as part of treatment grew bolder and more varied. In some circumstances volunteers from the same background as the client proved to be more not less effective than social workers. Crucial elements were initial and ongoing professional assessment of the client in his situation, careful selection and training of volunteers, and continuing support and discussion with them in relation to each client. People who had been or were having the same experience as those needing help were recruited and used for direct relations, backed up by regular, small group meetings with experienced social workers. At these sessions the 'indigenous' workers learnt more about the reasons for people's behaviour in the situation, blew off anger, frustration or confusion, clarified small immediate goals and what was happening in the situation and were supported to continue.

An imaginative form of voluntary activity was the new careers scheme pioneered by NACRO under which selected ex-offenders worked with current offenders and others, in partnership with social workers. The assumption, as with Alcoholics Anonymous and other new innovations, was that those who had been through the same experience could demonstrate that they knew it from inside. Barnardo's and Channel, a volunteer organisation in Liverpool, jointly ran a voluntary family counselling project. Volunteers were selected for qualities of warmth, realism and flexibility, trained for six weeks and supported by professional social workers in their work as counsellors to families or individuals. These were people likely to respond to close contact, but not needing long-term support or skilled casework. The volunteers took over the main responsibility for the clients, supported by individual supervision and monthly group meetings. There were also other experiments in volunteers helping newly bereaved people, with close support from experienced social workers. In-service trained workers and volunteers were also used in residential and day care centres where steady support by professional social workers and an understanding of clients' behaviour could produce positive results. Often the residents themselves were involved on an equal footing with volunteers and staff.

It had become clear that the same principles applied as in other social work situations in regard to selection, information giving, training, initial careful matching of volunteer and client or task, allocation, and continued training and support on the job.

At the time of the Aves Report only a few voluntary organisations provided training for volunteers. It was also obvious that they needed continuing support but this was seldom available. At the next stage there was an increasing number of general introductory courses for volunteers organised by university extramural departments, colleges of further education and councils of social service. Training was largely focused on specifics: what it was necessary to know about the particular organisation, about the people it served and how volunteers could help them. This included dealing with volunteers' tendencies to over identify, impose solutions and moral judgements, create dependency, expect quick results or lose heart. Professional social workers and others had also to discover both what and how to teach. Later, more use was made of audio-visual aids, role play and discussion groups to help volunteers experience what it felt like to be an old or handicapped person or someone at odds with society.

By the mid-1970s very large numbers of volunteers were active in the public as well as the voluntary social services, and mobilisation of voluntary effort in many forms and by individuals and groups had become part of the endeavour to strengthen community cohesion. There was still far to go but some essentials had been learnt and were being applied. The essence lay 'in the attitudes of society itself, and in the degree of personal responsibility which each citizen accepts for the welfare of others' (Hobman, 1969, p. 9).

VOLUNTEER SERVICE ORGANISERS

Organisers of voluntary service were first appointed by two hospitals in 1963; thereafter hospital appointments spread rapidly until by 1974 there were around 300. Organisers undertook the functions discussed below and also acted as a liaison and interpreter between volunteers, the hospital staff and patients (Finzi *et al.*, 1971).

In many voluntary agencies and local authorities, volunteers were a part-time responsibility of a staff member. A few local authorities appointed volunteer organisers from the mid-1960s, but they only began to spread after Seebohm and Scottish reorganisations and as part of the drive towards an effective community support system. The number of these appointments increased in the early 1970s, many in area teams, in attempts at closer contact with local communities. Volunteers were officially accepted in the probation service from 1966 (see chapter 7, section on 'Volunteers in the Probation and After-Care Service'). Increasingly, probation officers were expected to use volunteers and designated senior or assistant chief probation officers gave part of their time to volunteers (with ancillary help in large cities). The long-established and carefully selected voluntary prison visitors were to some extent the responsibility of senior prison welfare officers.

The Volunteer Centre, in a consultative document on *Training for Voluntary Service Co-ordinators in the Health and Social Services* (1975), defined the function as: 'Recruitment and selection of volunteers, their induction and orientation; arranging suitable placements and replacements; ensuring that all volunteers are sufficiently supported; arranging meetings, talks, social events and any further training as appropriate; in extreme situations discontinuing a service or dismissing a volunteer' (p. 11). It accepted the unlovely title of voluntary service co-ordinator.

Some organisers were primarily a link between the department and voluntary organisations, some recruited and placed volunteers and others became neighbourhood workers responsible for the identification of community resources and stimulation of self-help groups. The majority of organisers were in new posts in which they had to pioneer the service and develop its support and administrative structure. Sometimes they had a difficult, undervalued, ill-defined and isolated role, trying to keep in balance different needs and expectations and resolving tensions between the staff, the clients and the volunteers. 'Typically he is given a less than adequate and sometimes totally unrealistic job description, e.g. an appointment to serve ten hospitals covering an entire county on a part time basis or to cover, unaided, several Social Service Area Teams' (ibid., p. 13). They were struggling to clarify their own roles without supervision or guidance in situations where their employing authority often had no realistic or well-defined expectations for them – and where, moreover, they worked in isolation and under considerable pressure to try to support volunteers and discover how they could be used effectively. This delicate task had to be pioneered in situations where professionals did not necessarily welcome volunteers, a bureaucratic structure did not know what to make of them, and the volunteers themselves had to be made to feel wanted and useful to clients.

These diffuse functions had elements of organisation and management, social work and community development, and thus much in common with training officers, home-help organisers and community workers. Their ranks included social workers, teachers, nurses, personnel managers or people seeking a second career and wanting some useful experience before they took a professional training. There was a high staff turnover, said to be partly due to inadequate support, isolation, and the diffuse nature of the job.

Although the number of whole- or part-time organisers had grown rapidly from the mid-1960s, no planned training existed for them a decade later. Their varied backgrounds coupled with an ill-defined task made this difficult. The Volunteer Centre report concluded that training should be geared to organisers moving on to a career in the mainstream of social or health service administration. It proposed in-service training based on one-week full-time four to six months after appointment and another after fifteen to eighteen months. This would concentrate on the core of the task and might be supplemented by local courses. In the long term, the CCETSW certificate in social service might be appropriate, with some common elements and a special option for volunteer organisers.

The King's Fund and the NISW ran a joint short course training project from 1974–5 (King's Fund, n.d.) for organisers in hospitals and social services departments. These well-planned and evaluated five-day residential courses were thought to have been successful in conveying information about the essential nature of the job, modifying attitudes and increasing a group identification.

A working party on the National Association of Voluntary Help Organisers set up in 1975 (*Pivot*, 1976) surveyed developments and increasing diversity in the functions of volunteer service organisers. It thought 'some form of training' was essential, including induction courses, in-service training at regular intervals and longer training lasting up to two years on a modular system.

It was too early in the mid-1970s to see clearly in what ways these new appointments might develop and be related to or diverge from the mainstream of social work.

PART TWO   DEVELOPMENTS IN SOCIAL WORK STRUCTURE

Chapter 20

Supply and Demand in Social Work

THE 1950S

Failure To Take Action
In looking at the lamentable supply and demand situation in the 1950s Rodgers and Dixon commented trenchantly in their *Portrait of Social Work* (1960):

'In her 1951 report Miss Younghusband called for "an authoritative Committee to review the situation as a whole". For many years the Joint University Council for Public and Social Administration has been pressing the Government to set up an interdepartmental committee to do the same thing. It has consistently refused this approach, preferring to set up a succession of departmental committees whose recommendations regarding the recruitment, training and employment of particular kinds of social workers it has as consistently failed to implement; either because it maintained that the recommendations of one committee could not be acted upon until the next committee reported, or because the increase in the numbers of professionally qualified workers recommended for a particular field of social service were so obviously unrealistic when related to the known shortages in other fields. Much valuable time has been wasted and practically nothing achieved.' (p. 9)

This was indeed true: segments of the total field in which social workers were employed were surveyed in the 1950s by the Mackintosh Committee (1951), the Cope Committees (1951), the Underwood Committee (1955), the Younghusband Working Party (1959), the Ingleby Committee (1960), the Albermarle Committee (1960), and the Morison Committee (1962). This added up to a formidable exercise in not treading on Tom Tiddler's ground. A number of witnesses to the Younghusband working party stressed that 'a comprehensive review of the training and employment of social workers in the whole field of the social services was required in the light of experience gained since 1948' (para. 12).

Over fifteen years later the Birch Report (1976) undertook the task and tried to estimate how lost time could be made up.

In the early 1950s many local authorities looked with uncertain favour on qualified social workers compared with candidates who had gained honours in something called the university of life, a university held to be at constant and praiseworthy odds with academic institutions. Selection committees thus drew upon a comparatively limitless and unidentified supply to meet a small demand, in contrast to the known and limited supply of trained social workers and the expanding demand of later decades.

Almoners

The Cope Committees (1951) took the 1949 figures of 921 working almoners, of whom 795 were in hospitals and rehabilitation units, 57 in local authority health departments and the rest elsewhere. They said:

'We have not been able to find statistical information of a kind which would enable us to make an accurate estimate of the number of almoners needed in the National Health Service. The Institute of Almoners made available to us such information as was in its possession, but these estimates are based upon opinion and not the result of a detailed inquiry into matters of fact. It is, however, the best information available, and we would place considerable reliance upon it.' (para. 116)

They concluded that on the basis of these figures 2,500 to 3,000 almoners were needed in England and Wales and about 500 in Scotland. Lack of information made any estimate for local health authorities impossible. Demand over the coming five years would probably be limited by financial constriction. But to replace normal wastage (about 10 per cent per annum) and only to open new departments where the need was most pressing, at least an additional 150 almoners should qualify each year. This was for hospitals only. The actual output in 1951 was 106.

By 1956, of a total of 1,165 working almoners, 1,039 were employed in hospitals, 56 in local authorities, and 14 jointly between local authorities and hospitals. The Younghusband Report commented that

'The uneven geographical distribution of almoners employed by local authorities is a serious matter. In London and South-East England 44 qualified almoners, including those shared with hospitals, (more than 60 per cent of the total) are employed to serve a population of 13½ million. A similar population in Northern England is served by seven almoners only, there are two in Scotland for a population of 4.9 million, and one in Wales for a population of 2.5 million.' (para. 808)

It estimated (1959) a need for 300 almoners in these local authority services (including 30 for Scotland). This was in addition to the earlier estimate for hospitals.

Child Care

In 1952 the then head of the Home Office Children's Department in evidence to the House of Commons Select Committee on Estimates predicted that 'in the nature of things the initial demand for trained people will diminish in the course of time and the training need will be to replace wastage' (para. 793). This forecast was more wide of the mark than most.

In 1956 there were 1,037 child care officers (England, Wales and Scotland) of whom 263 were professionally qualified, 428 had a social science qualification, and 346 were unqualified. ACO returns in that year showed that counties had twice as many trained child care officers as county boroughs. The majority of trained houseparents were concentrated on southern counties. In 1958–9 13 per cent of child care officers in counties resigned, against 22 per cent in county boroughs. The geographical distribution of trained child care officers in the same year ranged from 5 per cent in county boroughs in the north-east to 45 per cent in counties in the south-east. In 1959, 167 child care officers were employed by voluntary organisations in England and Wales. In 1958 and 1959 the ACO submitted two strongly worded memoranda to the CTC drawing attention to the yawning gap between supply and demand. Figures collected by the ACO showed that in the years 1954–6 an average of 180 posts a year were filled from outside the child care service and less than 30 per cent by qualified child care officers against 50 per cent with a social science qualification only. Few men were trained, though most of the work could be performed equally well by either sex and indeed many untrained men were employed.

The average annual increase during the decade of eighty-five new child care officer posts was equal to rather over half an appointment for each local authority in England and Wales. This was insufficient to keep up with the increase in the population at risk (which included the post-war bulge in the birth rate), far less to expand the service effectively over the country as a whole. ACO calculated a need for an annual output of 190 additional, trained child care officers to allow for expansion and wastage, against an actual output of 50 to 60 a year. These figures brought out the high wastage rate in a mainly women's service and the large number of students with social science qualifications going direct into children's departments. This was inevitable without salary differentials or a promotion bar and when appointing authorities were often faced with Hobson's choice.

By 1959, 650 child care officers had been trained but of these only 357 were employed in the service. The output of training was, therefore, signally failing to meet expansion. This was all the more serious when more children's departments now accepted the need for higher standards of casework, for more time and skill to be devoted to meeting the needs of individual children, for more work with the family, and for more foster homes. Yet all these advances were delayed for lack of qualified staff.

There were no official estimates during this period of the number of houseparents needed. The Underwood Committee (1955) estimated that about 400 'house-staff' would be required over the coming decade in hostels and special schools for maladjusted children. In 1954 about 250 such staff were employed, of whom 9 held the CTC certificate in residential care.

The Mental Health and Child Guidance Services
In 1950 there were 239 PSWs in mental and general hospitals and the child guidance service; of these 8 were in the local authority mental health services and 84 in other work, notably child care. There were only 2 PSWs

practising in Wales against an estimated demand for 136 (Macintosh Report, 1951). By 1957 there were 366 PSWs in the hospital and child guidance services, 32 in local authority health departments and 90 in other work.

The Mackintosh Report estimated the demand for PSWs for all services at 1,500, including 200 for the after-care service of local authorities. In 1959 the Younghusband working party arbitrarily increased the latter figure to 300. In 1955 the Underwood Committee estimated that 420 PSWs were needed for child guidance clinics alone, on a ratio of 3 PSWs and 1 psychiatrist to every 45,000 school children (against 169 PSWs in this service in 1954 and 176 in whole-time equivalents in 1966 (Seebohm Report). These estimates must be set against an average output of 50 PSWs a year over the decade 1946 to 1956.

The Mackintosh Report estimated a need for 2 mental welfare workers per 100,000 of the population. This added up to 2,000 mental welfare workers for local authority community care as then envisaged, together with 200 PSWs. The Younghusband Report rather weakly accepted these figures (with a further 20 for Scotland). In 1956 there were 1,100 mental welfare officers (whole-time equivalents).

Other Social Workers in the Local Authority Health and Welfare Services
In 1957 there were 1,619 welfare officers (of whom 16 per cent were women) and over half had combined welfare and mental welfare duties. There were 117 chief and 69 deputy-chief welfare officers, of whom 6 were women. Sixty per cent of welfare officers, 53 per cent of mental welfare officers and 70 per cent of those with combined duties had no qualifications other than experience. Eight per cent of welfare officers and 14 per cent of mental welfare officers held a social science qualification (mainly by part-time study). Of the chief and deputy-chief welfare officers, 33 per cent held the poor law relieving officer's certificate, 9 per cent a diploma in public administration, and 5 per cent a social science qualification (usually by part-time study).

There were 601 home teachers of the blind, of whom only 35 held senior posts. Three had taken a full-time university social science course. There were about 150 deaf missioners and 6 officers employed by local authorities for work with the deaf. For work with the general classes of the handicapped there were 87 home visitors (other than welfare officers). Of these 34 were men. Two were qualified almoners, 31 per cent had a social science qualification and 53 per cent were untrained. Only 15 social workers were specifically engaged in work with families (including unmarried mothers). All these figures are taken from the Younghusband Report.

Estimated Future Need in the Local Authority Health and Welfare Services
The 1959 working party estimates were largely guesswork in the absence of any reliable information about the total number of people in any given category who needed or were likely to use the service if it were more extensively provided and known to exist. The estimates, based on a ten-year development of the services, were for 5,550–5,700 social workers, the figures included wastage, expansion, and reduction of excessive caseloads. This required an output from training rising to 500–515 annually. The actual

output in 1971 was 479. As soon as in-service training for welfare assistants was available, the Committee thought at least 200 should be recruited annually for five years. Further estimates should then be possible in the light of experience.

In addition, there was an estimated need for 300 PSWs and the same number of almoners in these services. Family caseworkers should be increasingly recruited to deal with family problems, and future requirements were estimated at 200 (including 20 for Scotland), which might be an 'unduly conservative' estimate. This total of 800 required an annual recruitment of 105 almoners, PSWs and family caseworkers over the succeeding ten-year period for the local authority services. The total output of MSWs in 1969 was 85 and of PSWs 129, though most of these went into hospital or clinical services. (Figures are from the Younghusband Report, table 44, p. 353 and *Setting the Course for Social Work Education*, CCETSW, 1973c, p. 26.)

The Probation Service

In England and Wales the probation service increased by 74 per cent between 1950 and 1961 and by 148 per cent in Scotland (Morison Report, 1962, p. 101). There was a decrease in the number of part-time officers from 136 in 1950 to 80 in 1960. Most of these either worked in thinly populated areas of Wales or Scotland or were married women with training and experience. It was official policy to make full use of all available trained caseworkers even in part-time appointments.

Direct entry continued and in 1961 just over 30 per cent of probation officers were untrained. The Morison Committee (1962) assumed that direct entry should be ended as soon as possible. It made the following estimates of future demand:

(a) to reduce caseloads an additional 206;
(b) through an increased volume of work, e.g. more court inquiries and more matrimonial work as well as compulsory after-care, an additional 150 officers;
(c) increase in the crime rate and increase of the population;
(d) more supervisory posts.

No estimates were made for the last two. A total of rather more than 2,000 officers would be needed in England and Wales 'in the near future' and a further increase of 2,750 in the next few years (para. 282). The Scottish service might well expand to a total strength of some 220 whole-time officers within the next few years (para. 283).

Wastage Rates

The Institute of Almoners recorded a resignation rate of about 10 per cent in 1956–8. The annual resignation rate of child care officers was 12·9 per cent in the three years 1954–6. In the probation service the annual average rate over the five-year period 1954–8 was 3·9 per cent. The resignation rate in the health and welfare services over a five-year period was calculated in 1957 to be about 6 to 7 per cent. It was not known what proportion left for other social work jobs, i.e. were not wastage from social work.

Table 9   The situation in the 1950s (based on the foregoing estimates)

	Approximate strength of the service	Estimated total staffs needed	Estimated annual increased output needed from training	Actual output
Almoners	1,165 (1956)	2,500–3,000 (Cope Committees estimate for hospitals, 1951) 300 (Younghusband working party estimate for local authority service, 1959)	180 (for hospital service only)	88 qualified in 1956 and 89 in 1959
Child care	1,037 (1959) (fieldstaff only)	No estimate	190 (1958 estimate)	50–60 qualified annually
Health and welfare services	3,155 (1956)	5,550–5,700 (This figure does not include an estimated need for 800 almoners, PSWs, and family caseworkers)	500–515	(No training available in the 1950s)
Probation	1,656 (1959) (excluding 80 part-time officers)	2,200–2,970		116 (in training, 1959)
Psychiatric social workers	505	2,020 including 420 in child guidance clinics and 300 in local authority health and welfare departments (Mackintosh, Underwood and Younghusband Committees'	No comprehensive estimate	(average annual output 50)

THE SITUATION IN THE 1960s AND EARLY 1970s

Problems of Manpower Forecasting

Manpower forecasting became rather more sophisticated in the 1960s with the slow acceptance of the need for trained social workers, although forecasts continued to be underestimates. And the 1950s record of gross shortages persisted. In the child care service the goal that all child care officers should be qualified was accepted by degrees. Here and in the local authority health and welfare services there was more systematic effort to estimate employers' demands and to relate expanded training to these. In probation the unachieved aim for many years had been that all probation officers should be trained before appointment. Neither the Ministry of Health nor the IMSW and APSW attempted to forecast supply and demand. To estimate demand by voluntary organisations would have been a daunting task.

The problem of output was slightly eased when students from the new two-year courses began to flow into the child care and health and welfare services. The number of trained social workers was also increased during this decade by more generous policies of secondment for training on salary of unqualified serving officers, though this did not affect total numbers. About 75 per cent of CSW students were seconded, but most child care and all probation students were new recruits.

The data on which forecasts were made were unreliable because:

(a) Little information existed about the true incidence of any given need. This varied in different parts of the country, and total incidence alone would not show the most effective form and range of services, nor the extent of the need for social work intervention, whether short-term, intermittent or long-term.

(b) If total populations 'at risk' were identified this would uncover many more potential clients. Unmet need was so great that any increase in services or better deployment of social workers increased demand, but expansion of services was limited by lack of resources.

(c) There were no criteria for good standards of service, nor what this meant in terms of skill, workloads, related services and time.

(d) Local authority forecasts were often based on what they individually thought they might be able to afford rather than on common criteria.

(e) Demographic changes were notoriously difficult to forecast, while population mobility, economic changes and changes in social habits all affected the incidence of social need, sometimes in unforeseen ways.

(f) New legislation might suddenly require additional manpower or upset the balance between services.

(g) The more efficient deployment and use of professional social work staff, for example by employment of welfare assistants or better clerical and transport facilities could, in effect, increase numbers.

(h) Changes in professional practice, for example community work, family therapy or crisis intervention could have significant consequences.

(i) Objectives were unclear and the effective use of different ways of achieving them was not assessed.

Difficulties included double counting, for example of blind people who were also old. A change in one service could also affect demand for another, for example more home helps might lessen the number of children in temporary care but conversely this might be increased by a new maternity hospital. Better housing, higher social security benefits, more day care centres, home helps, meals on wheels, and aids to daily living could lessen the need of various groups for residential care. There was much leeway to make up in meeting known needs, though this would certainly lead to increased demand and more differentiated provision. It was known that many handicapped people were ignorant of local authority services and the registration of the general classes of the handicapped was grossly inadequate. Estimates of the number of multiproblem families varied, and none of the definitions used were sufficiently precise and objective for different observers to apply them consistently. It was not known what proportion of all old people were in need of 'care and attention'. The swing over from hospital to community care for mentally disordered or handicapped people called for a large increase in social work services. The national percentage of children in care remained fairly constant but new responsibilities created demands for adequate means to meet them. Probation forecasting faced imponderables like crime rates, the sentencing policy of the courts, and extended responsibilities in the 1960s.

Official manpower forecasting – and thus output targets – for the probation and health and welfare services were based on estimates of the desirable total number of social workers in the service by a given date. In the child care service the Home Office formulated five-year plans based on the maximum feasible expansion of training.

Wastage rates were an important element in supply and demand, but still little was known about the proportion who left social work or merely transferred to another job or returned later in life. There was a high percentage of men in the probation and health and welfare services, but women heavily predominated in child care and medical and psychiatric social work. The changing sex ratio in the population as a whole meant that the reliable spinsters of the past, who remained in their posts year after year giving service to clients and not seeking advancement, were being succeeded by others who within a short period of qualification melted away into matrimony and motherhood.

Child Care – England and Wales
Returns by local authorities to the Home Office in 1964 estimated a total establishment of 3,050 child care officers by 1969. This figure, which resulted from extended duties under the Children and Young Persons Act, 1963, was almost double previous estimates, though it fell below the Home Office research unit figure of 3,175 child care officers actually needed on the basis of its 1966 workload study (Grey, 1969).

The 1966 CTC target annual output figure of 250 to 350 trained child care officers a year was subsequently raised to 675 for 1970–1 and the actual output in 1970 was 643 (including 68 in Scotland) and 805 in 1971 (including 90 in Scotland). By the time the CTC was merged in the CCETSW in 1971 and child care courses as such ended, 4,608 students had been trained (including 303 in Scotland) (CCETSW, 1973a, p. 26).

Residential Care
The Williams Report (1967) discussed the many imponderables in estimating future needs for residential care. It limited itself to a ten-year forecast of staff needs for children's and old people's homes. It was difficult to estimate future needs for children in residential care, partly owing to variations in the birth rate. If this remained roughly the same, there would be a total of about 17,500,000 children under 18 by the mid-1970s compared with 15,200,000 in 1965. If the same proportion were in residential care, this would necessitate 5,000 new places and if staff ratios in children's homes remained the same, 1,300 extra staff would be needed. There were differing views as to whether it might be possible to increase the number of children in foster homes; whether more families could be held together; or conversely, whether more children would need residential care on account of emotional disturbance. By the mid-1960s nearly all women married and most married young – and two-thirds of staff employed in all the residential homes surveyed by the Williams Committee were single women. It expected 'a dramatic increase' in the number of staff needed in hostels for mentally ill or handicapped people. It calculated that a total of 26,000 to 38,000 staff of old people's homes (depending on the staff/resident ratio) would be required by 1975. In 1974 there were in English local authority homes for the elderly 5,473 (whole-time equivalents) wardens, matrons and deputies and 30,192 (whole-time equivalents) care assistants (DHSS, 1975e).

The output of trained residential child care staff rose from 208 in 1960 to 352 (including the senior certificate) in 1970, plus 50 in Scotland. In 1970 local authority returns showed that there were 5,615 posts in all types of children's homes: 545 staff held the certificate or senior certificate in residential child care and a total of 1,853 some relevant qualification. By 1973 the total figure was 11,596 of whom 1,400 were qualified (Birch Report, table 3). When the CTC was merged in the CCETSW in 1971 there were 5,914 holders of the certificate in residential child care (including 543 for Scotland). A further 250 held the senior certificate (including 17 for Scotland) (CCETSW, 1973c, p. 29).

The CCETSW working party discussion document on training for residential work (1973d) concluded that there were about 395,000 people in residential centres of all kinds, cared for by about 65,000 staff, of whom under 4 per cent were qualified in residential work. It calculated a need for at least 11,000 more qualified residential social workers to provide one CQSW holder in every residential centre, though it was desirable that about one-third of total staff – 21,600 people – should hold the CQSW. The original DHSS ten-year plan (subsequently scaled down) would have resulted by 1983 in over 96,000 staff in extended residential provision. Other aspects of the manpower crisis in residential care are discussed in the relevant chapters.

Local Authority Health and Welfare Services – England and Wales
Returns by local authorities to the Ministry of Health estimating their need for trained social work staff for 1962–72 (Ministry of Health, 1963)

forecast a total demand for new staff of 2,362 qualified social workers by 1972 and for 2,517 'others' (para. 155). It was calculated that from 1972 this annual demand would decline from 140 to an average of 48. Revised estimates in 1966 (Ministry of Health, 1966, Cmnd 3022) were for 3,363 qualified social workers and 3,040 'others' by 1975 (table V, p. 414). The Ministry of Health laid down few guidelines for these estimates which were thus not based upon common criteria. In 1965 about 16 per cent of social workers in these services were qualified, and local authorities hoped to increase this to 52 per cent by 1975.

In 1976 the Birch Report assumed this same 50 per cent target for the mid-1980s (para. 106).

On the basis of the 1966 local authority forecast, the CTSW calculated that by the end of the decade it would require an annual intake of 650 students (allowing for wastage). This estimate was subsequently raised to 730–800. The actual output in 1970 was 456 and in 1971, 479. By the time the CTSW was merged in the CCETSW there were 2,495 holders of the certificate in social work (UK) (CCETSW, 1973c, p. 26).

The Seebohm Committee took an astringent view of the situation, which it described as 'a crisis of manpower in the personal social services'. It calculated that

'On a very conservative estimate, a population of 100,000 will on average contain 1,500 people with severe mental disorder, chiefly psychosis or subnormality, who should be offered social help of various kinds: many want and need it sorely. The entire social work staff now available to many local authorities could be usefully occupied solely in trying to support patients; helping them, their families and local communities to readjust. Whatever redeployment there may be among local authority staff, many 'area units' covering populations of 50,000 to 100,000 . . . will not inherit even one social worker trained and experienced in psychiatric problems, able to deal with crises, to supervise the untrained and inexperienced and guide the voluntary workers. Moreover, much of the time of the mental welfare staff is at present often taken up in the process of admitting and re-admitting patients to hospital. Only by breaking down the barriers between hospital and local authority, and mobilising all the trained social workers in a single service will there be a chance of deploying them where they are most needed. Widespread duplication of effort and lack of team-work among the many agencies which are involved in helping the mentally disordered are among the obstacles that must be overcome.' (para. 346)

Probation and After-Care – England and Wales
In 1964 the Conference of Principal Probation Officers estimated that the strength of the service should be 3,474 by 1969 (against the Morison Committee's figure of 2,750 'in the next few years'). The following year the Advisory Council on Probation and After-Care estimated that the total number should be 3,500 by 1970, in view of extended responsibilities for prison welfare, after-care and parole supervision. The actual number was 3,590 by December 1971 and 4,543 by 1974. The annual output target figures were raised to 550 for 1970–1. The actual output from training in 1971

was 341. By 1972 the number of Home Office sponsored places on qualifying courses recognised by the CCETSW was 630, increased to 732 in 1973, but the output was 427 in 1972 and 489 in 1973. In 1971 some officers had caseloads of 80 or more against the Home Office target of 50 for men and 40 for women. The service was 7 per cent below establishment in that year.

The Butterworth Inquiry (1972) thought Home Office calculations about future staffing underestimated the growing complexity of new tasks like parole and after-care. The Home Office estimate at that time for 1975 was 4,400 probation officers, plus an additional 400 for new duties under the 1972 Criminal Justice Act. The Butterworth Inquiry calculated that the total figure should be 5,000, i.e. a growth rate of 7·8 per cent a year compared with an actual increase of 5·4 per cent in 1971 (para. 166). The number of ancillary workers rose from 91 in 1971 to 373 in 1974.

Medical and Psychiatric Social Workers
Medical and psychiatric social workers were sometimes accused of more complacency than sense of urgency about shortages and the number of posts that could not be filled. The Ministry of Health must take much of the blame for this situation. Indeed the expansion of training, which resulted from determined efforts in the 1960s to provide a new level of service, only resulted from pressure by the professional associations and others on the policy makers and government departments. None the less it must be remembered that the probation and child care services were mandatory, whereas there was no compulsion to provide medical and psychiatric social work services universally. Neither professional association made demand forecasts. Other estimates for MSWs and PSWs in particular services are given at various points in this study. In 1969 there were 361 PSWs working in child guidance clinics and 131 vacancies (CGSIG/BASW, 1975). There was no objective measurement of workloads and staffing levels were determined on an *ad hoc* basis. When BASW and the CCETSW came into existence and specialised professional qualifications were no longer awarded, 3,615 students had qualified as MSWs and 1,773 as PSWs (CCETSW, 1973*c*, p. 26).

Estimates of Social Workers to Population Ratios
The Seebohm Report calculated a necessary ratio of at least ten to twelve social workers in social services department area teams for populations of 50,000–100,000. This would have resulted in a minimum of 4,850 and a maximum of 11,640 social workers in area teams, excluding headquarters staffs. The Report said that 'the figures are based on the *present situation* and are not optima' (italics in original) (para. 593). This range of difference was necessary to take account of different population structures, location (e.g. decaying inner city or prosperous suburban areas) and indices of social need.

Replies to the Brown and Gloyne survey (1966) gave fourteen qualified social workers in the local authorities in Scotland in 1962, of whom twelve were in children's departments (p. 47). *Social Work in Scotland* (Edinburgh University Department of Social Administration, 1969) suggested field units of 10 to 12 social workers for a population of about 50,000, taking into account necessary wastage during absence for sickness, in-service training, holidays and standby duty, together with provision for supervision and for student training. This would require 1,500 total staff (including headquarters staff) by 1974. In 1970 the actual figure was 1,365 and it had risen to 2,110 by 1973 (SWSG, 1974, p. 47).

The 1972 DHSS Circular 35/72 (1972a) requested local authorities in England and Wales to draw up ten-year development plans for their social services to 1983. A growth rate of 10 per cent per annum at constant prices was predicted. The actual returns were based on a 6½ per cent rate. Later the DHSS scaled this down to 4·6 per cent and it was succeeded by nil growth and limitations on local authority staff numbers. In 1972 local authorities had not become responsible for social work in hospitals. The Circular said that local authority experience showed that area teams should cover a much smaller population than that suggested in the Seebohm Report. In 1968 the available social work manpower represented about 15 social workers per 100,000 of the population. By 1971 this had risen to an average of 25 social workers, trainees and assistants per 100,000 population. This average masked wide differences in staff ratios, proportion of trained staff, social work assistants, the structure of the department and staff accommodation, all of which influenced the effectiveness of the service. A number of local authorities had found that they needed staffing ratios varying between 21 to 33 social work staff (including trainees and assistants) per 100,000 population – the ratios were still higher for some inner London boroughs. The ten year plan ratio was 50 to 60 per 100,000 population by 1983.

Table 10   *Estimates of social worker to population ratios in social services/social work area teams*

England and Wales		
Seebohm Report (1968)	10–12	social workers for populations of 50,000–100,000
Actual average figures (with wide variations in ratios)		
1968	15	social workers per 100,000 population
Ditto 1971	25	social workers per 100,000 population
Local authority estimated need Circular 35/72	21–33	social workers per 100,000 population
Ten Year Plan figure by 1983	50–60	social workers per 100,000 population
Scotland		
Social Work in Scotland (1969)	10–12	social workers for populations of about 50,000
Target for 1974	15	social workers for populations of about 50,000
Advisory Council on Social Work (Scotland) 1974 target for 1978	20–25	social workers for populations of about 50,000

Sources: Seebohm Report (1968), *Report of the Committee on Local Authority and Allied Personal Social Services* (HMSO) Cmnd. 3703; DHSS Circular 35/72; *Social Work in Scotland* (1969) (Department of Social Administration, University of Edinburgh).

This ten year plan was hurriedly compiled in different economic circumstances from those two years later. But for the first time local authorities had been asked to make development forecasts on common assumptions, and the government intended this exercise in long-term planning to be repeated regularly. There was some local authority indignation at being given centrally determined guidelines rather than being asked to state their general policies and social objectives or vary their ratios to meet local needs; though the then Minister of Health and Social Security said the Government 'regarded the process as a form of dialogue with the field services through which it can better inform itself of needs, priorities . . . and modify its own thinking on policy' (Joseph, 1972, p. 73).

The Butterworth Inquiry (1972) found 7·5 per cent of vacancies against establishment in the probation service; 11·8 per cent in local authorities in England and Wales, 16·9 per cent in Scotland, and 25 per cent in the hospital service. Both the probation and hospital services lost staff to the local authorities in 1971 and the probation service also suffered from recruitment difficulties. In 1971 local authority social work staffs were growing at 9 per cent per annum, probation at 5·4 per cent and the hospital service actually declining. Seniors in the probation service spent 20 per cent of their time on supervisory and administrative duties, but in local authorities the proportion was 80 per cent.

Figures for Different Periods

Tables 11–14 show the total number of social workers employed in England and Wales and in Scotland in the mid-1960s, immediately after local authority social services reorganisation in 1971 and in 1973 (English social services departments only).

The Birch Report

There was no comprehensive assessment of manpower needs until in 1974 the DHSS set up a Working Party on Manpower and Training for the Social Services (Birch Report, 1976) to estimate the trained manpower needed. It was representative of employers, professional associations, educational institutions and government departments. It concluded that a 'substantial and continuing programme of development in training should be a major national priority' (p. 3), especially in view of the low proportion of trained staff in the services. The Report did not make forecasts of demand as such. But it thought all designated social work posts should be held in time by CQSW holders; and the long-term aim should be that all staff should receive appropriate training for their role.

Training was vulnerable in a time of severe economic restraint, but this was dangerous in the long term and there should be a guarantee of protection and support for the development of training. It assumed the targets shown in table 15 by the mid- to late 1980s.

Table 11   *Trained social workers: supply and demand, 1960 and 1969–70 (England and Wales)*

	Actual output 1960	Actual output 1970	Estimated annual output needed 1960	Estimated annual output needed 1970	Actual total nos 1960	Percentage trained	Estimated total strength of service needed 1960	Estimated total strength of service needed 1969	Actual total nos 1970	Percentage trained
MSWs	98	63	No forecast since 1951			100%*	No estimate since 1951		2,273***	100%*
PSWs	57	129 (1969)	ditto			100%**	ditto			100%**
CCOs	50	575	230	675	1,100**	26%***	No estimate until 1964 1,077 (England only)	3,800 (1966 estimate)	4,014**	47% (60% of senior staff)
CSW	Nil	456	No estimate	730–800		5% (estimate)				27%
POs	91	298	ditto	650	1,633	65%		3,500	3,352	74% Scotland 48%

*   refers to those qualified to hold the title;
**   fieldstaff only;
*** total number of social workers in the NHS. Of these 72% main grade and 97% above were professionally qualified (including holders of the CSW) and the 300 PSWs in other child guidance clinics; but no information was available about other qualifications or the numbers of PSWs and MSWs in other services.

Table 12 *Numbers of social workers with the main qualifications in post, 1967 (England and Wales)*

Service	Description of worker	Total number	Number professionally qualified	Number with social science degrees, certificates, or diplomas only	Number with declaration of recognition of experience	Number of others
Children	Field officers full-time*	2,693	861	562	196	1,074†
Mental health, local authority	Senior officers whole-time	423	135	36	143	109
	Other mental health social workers, whole-time	1,202	227	104	126	745
Welfare services	Senior officers, whole-time	667	114**	73	183	237
	Other social workers, whole-time	2,004	205‡	165	169	839
Probation	Probation officers	2,479	1,706	—	—	773
Hospital services	Social workers and assistants	1,684	1,040	163***	—	481

* Field officers were those engaged primarily on work with individual children and their families, i.e. this table excludes over 700 senior staff.

† 215 of these held the Central Training Council certificate in the residential care of children or a qualification for teaching, nursing, or a profession ancillary to medicine. 119 had degrees in a subject other than social science.

** Plus 50 with the Home Teachers Certificate of the College of Teachers of the Blind and 10 with the Certificate or Diploma of the Deaf Welfare Examination Board.

‡ Plus 614 with the Home Teachers Certificate of the College of Teachers of the Blind and 12 with the Certificate or Diploma of the Deaf Welfare Examination Board.

*** Includes a few with certificate of the Council for Training in Social Work.

Source: Seebohm Report (1968), appendix M.

Table 13   *Number of staff establishments 1971*

Probation		Local authorities (England and Wales)		National Health Service	
		Directors	174		
		Deputy directors	89		
Principal POs	68	Assistant directors	229	Principal II	89
Deputy PPOs	8	Principal and senior social workers	1,115	Principal I	254
Assistant PPOs	62			Senior social workers	797
Senior POs	603	Social workers graded A.P.5	1,246		
				Social workers (a)	972
Probation officers	3,279	Main grade and A.P.4 social workers	6,951	Social workers (b)	439
Totals:	4,020		9,804		2,551

Source: Butterworth Inquiry (1972) *Report of the Butterworth Inquiry into the Work and Pay of Probation Officers and Social Workers,* table 2 (HMSO) Cmnd 5076.

Table 14   *Staffing of the statutory agencies from the years 1971–74*

Category of staff	Area covered	1971	1972	1973	1974
Probation officers	England and Wales	3,608	3,939	4,327	4,543
Ancillaries	England and Wales	91	166	—	373
Education welfare officers (LEA)	England and Wales	2,200	2,310	2,400	2,400
Local authority senior social services staff*	UK	not applic- able	3,723	4,043	5,334
Local authority social workers (including trainees and wel- fare assistants)*	UK	13,390	14,633	16,701	20,499
Home help organisers and assistant organisers	GB	1,181	1,367	1,585	1,834
Day service staff working with young children	GB	not applic- able	10,906	6,761	7,120
Other day centre staff	GB			4,541	4,944
Child care staff of community homes for children and young persons in care	UK	(GB) 12,036	12,264	12,670	14,148
Other residential care staff	GB	n/a	28,681	32,712	35,812

*The figures for 1974 (except for Scotland) include former hospital staff transferred to social services departments.

Source: Birch Report (1976) *Working Party on Manpower and Training for the Social Services* (HMSO) p. 154.

Table 15   *Training targets for the mid-1980s*

| Staff group | Provisional assumptions for CQSW: proportions of total staff in each group | | | Numbers of CQSW/CSS holders | | |
	CQSW	CSS	CQSW/CSS	In post September, 1973	Implied target for 1985 with 2% growth rate	Additional numbers required
Local authority services						
1 Senior management	70%	15%	85%	2,466	5,280	2,814
2 Field social work and social service staff*	50%	33%	83%	7,092	22,530	15,438
3 Domiciliary care organisers	25%	40%	65%	—	1,830	1,830
4 Day service staff working with young children	10%	30%	40%	—	4,350	4,350
5 Day centre staff	10%	40%	50%	1,000	5,650	4,650
6 Residential child care staff	20%	15%	35%	1,430	6,130	4,700
7 Other residential care staff	20%	15%	35%	270	13,470	13,200
8 Special schools	20%	15%	35%	200	1,745	1,545
9 Probation service (England and Wales)						
9A Probation officers (all grades)	90%	—	90%	3,185	4,815	1,630
9B Ancillaries	—	25%	25%			

* Assumes that 50% of education welfare officers will hold the CQSW by the mid-1980s. Includes child guidance social workers and assumes that 100% will hold the CQSW by the mid-1980s.
Source: Birch Report (1976), table 1, p. 106.

The Birch Report (p. 167) made the first attempt at a rough estimate of clients and social workers in voluntary organisations compared with local authorities (Table 16).

Table 16   *Voluntary social services: estimate of current staffing (based on 1973 staff and client statistics)*

	Category	No. of LA clients	No. of vol. and private clients	No. of LA 'care' staff	Estimate of no. of vol. and private staff
England and Wales	Child care	31,071	8,322	11,726	3,140
	Other residential care	111,965	53,079	30,048	14,220
	Day nursery		7% of LA	3,676	260
	Day centre		5% clients	4,455	220
	Fieldwork				1,500*
Scotland	Child care	2,850	3,806	1,100	1,470
	Other residential care	8,979	6,586	2,226	1,630
	Day nursery	3,157	798	386	100
	Day centre	3,623	883	420	100
	Fieldwork				200**

* estimate by DHSS confirmed by NCSS.
**estimate by SWSG.
Source: Birch Report (1976).

Chapter 21

Other Developments in Structure and Practice

SOCIAL WORK SALARIES, 1950–1975

Low salaries in the 1950s
Recruits to social work were deterred by the poor salary and promotion prospects which were a legacy from the origins of social work as a middle-class, female occupation in voluntary organisations. Rates in the public services began to increase in line with general salary rises and in order to attract and retain staff, especially to increase the number of men in social work.

Local Authority Salaries
Most local authorities appointed social workers on the administrative, professional and technical (APT) scales, which were flexible because of their long ranges, though this led to competition for scarce, trained staff in which better-off authorities outbid poorer ones (see table 17 for these scales at different dates).

There were some strange anomalies in the NHS scales for almoners and PSWs, whose starting salaries in 1950 were as much as £70 below the lowest APT scale. Thus a mental welfare officer with no qualifications could be graded APT II but be paid very much less if professionally qualified. This advertisement (1950) showed the absurd situation:

'Appointment of three Female Mental Health Workers . . . Preference will be given to duly qualified Psychiatric Social Workers or candidates with a Diploma or Certificate in Social Science and if so qualified the salary will be £370 – £20 p.a. – £530 p.a., commencing according to experience. For unqualified persons the salary would be £480 – £15 p.a. – £525 p.a.' (Mackintosh Report, 1951, para. 37)

An unqualified local authority officer on APT I might also be paid more than a young, trained probation officer.

Some of the worst of these anomalies were resolved by the late 1950s, though MSWs and PSWs could still earn more by leaving the hospital service. Most child care officers were appointed on APT I scales. The CTC certificate had been recognised for promotion up to the maximum of the scale, thus giving some incentive to train. In other local authority services there was no such incentive. Duly authorised officers were on the APT II scale but social welfare officers on APT I.

Probation Salaries

Salaries remained static between 1946 and 1951 in spite of many protests. In 1950 a Joint Negotiating Committee (JNC) was set up which resulted in a uniform salary scale for the first time, but equal pay for men and women was only introduced at the end of the 1950s. Salaries were finally agreed at the absolute discretion of the Home Secretary and the Secretary of State for Scotland. Twice in the late 1950s the Home Secretary whittled down JNC recommendations for reasons of government incomes policy. To probation officers this showed lack of concern for the service and for recruitment, and it gravely affected morale. In 1962 a police constable of 28 was earning nearly £100 a year more, plus substantial emoluments, than a probation officer of the same age. But from 1963 onwards the maximum for main grade probation officers was higher than for child care officers. Salary scales in Scotland were lower than in England and Wales.

All the key organisations giving evidence to the Morison Committee (1962) condemned ministerial prescription of salaries, and its Report recommended that salary scales should be freely negotiated. Rather surprisingly, the Committee was required to make detailed recommendations about actual salaries, possibly on account of the low morale in the probation service. It looked at the salaries of other social workers, but decided they were no real guide to salaries in the probation service, thus perpetuating a situation which caused much trouble later. It proposed that, as an incentive to train, direct entrants should be paid a lower salary than trained entrants for the first two years. It also proposed that regular tutor officers should be appointed in the senior probation officer grade. It recommended swingeing salary increases ranging from 20 per cent to 40 per cent. The matter went to the JNC which proposed a general interim increase of 10 per cent in the then wage freeze. But the Home Secretary used his prescriptive powers to limit the increase to the 'guiding light' of $2\frac{1}{2}$ per cent. This aroused more bitter feelings in the service and strong support for probation officers in Parliament and elsewhere. Thereafter, salaries reached Morison levels progressively by 1964. There were to be biennial reviews and a new joint negotiating committee for the probation service, exclusive of Scotland, was set up in 1966. In this same year the complicated wage-for-age system was abolished and the point of entry to the scale was determined, as for other branches of social work, by education, training and experience. Subsequently salaries rose by about $3\frac{1}{2}$ per cent a year. But after the Seebohm reorganisation probation officers felt they had suffered detrimentally in pay and prospects.

Almoners and PSWs

Almoners' and PSWs' salaries in the NHS were fixed by a Whitley Council which strictly controlled starting salaries, grading and working conditions. These scales were lower than local authority scales. In 1962 the staff side went to arbitration and the Industrial Court linked the salaries of hospital and local authority social workers.

Some Improvements in the 1960s

Though still low, salaries improved during the 1960s. Although anomalies persisted, main grade social workers in child care, mental health and welfare were on the same APT scales from 1960. Salary scales became longer and promotion prospects increased.

The 1970s

The Butterworth Inquiry (1972) was set up to review the work and salaries of probation officers and other social workers, and to make recommendations about the appropriate salary relationships between them. It found that in the probation service 80 per cent of probation officers were in the main grade, with a main grade to senior ratio of 4·1:1, thus there were restricted steps in a grade and limited promotion prospects. In the hospital service there were only three grades: main, senior and principal with a promotion ratio of 4·3:1. The Report recommended that probation and hospital social work salaries should be related to local authority scales. In the new social services departments the ratios of main grade to senior staff over the country as a whole was 2·6:1.

By the mid-1970s practically all social workers in the public services in England and Wales, except probation officers, were in social services departments, and probation was included in Scotland. Fairly large numbers were employed by voluntary organisations. From 1973 parity was achieved for all qualified social workers wherever employed, though for a long time many voluntary organisations had followed national scales. Table 17 of salary changes between 1950 and 1975 shows that some salaries had increased tenfold. These changes institutionalised social work and made it a possible professional career for men with families. Indeed, the promotion prospects in the 1970s led to jibes about more chiefs than Indians.

WORKLOAD STUDIES

Problems of Workload Assessment

Caseload or workload studies were undertaken spasmodically in different services at different times to show how social workers actually spent their time, and to clarify criteria for staffing and for use of ancillary workers. The results were of limited value and often not comparable, for example some caseloads contained dormant cases and no means were devised to measure the average amount of time·taken on a given type of case. All the following and other studies showed wasteful use of trained social workers' time.

Child Care

A study was undertaken in Scotland in 1960 to clarify demands on child care staff (Burns and Sinclair, 1963). Seven children's officers and ten CCOs kept records for four weeks. They were also asked to estimate how they thought they spent their time, and all underestimated the amount actually spent on office work and grossly overestimated that devoted to preventive work and to direct concern with the progress and well-being of children in care. In other words, they thought most of their time was spent on their proper professional function, whereas only 48 per cent of it was

Table 17   *Salary Scales, 1950–75 (England and Wales)*

	1950	mid-1960s	1971	1975
Hospital social workers				
Main grade	£330–£700	£820–£1,300	£1,290–£1,758	
Almoners—medical social workers	(under revision)	(social science qualification only)	(unqualified)	National health social workers
		£900–£1,340 (qualified)	£1,545–£1,932 (qualified)	
		£1,200–£1,545		
Senior			£1,812–£2,199	
Principal I			£2,127–£2,562	
Principal II			£2,283–£2,868	
Psychiatric social workers	£370–£550 (plus £75 for posts of special responsibility)	as above	as above	
				From 1973 all qualified social workers received the same salary irrespective of their employment. See local authority grades below:
Probation officers (Figures do not include London weighting)				
Main grade	£305–£570 (men) £290–£460 (women)	£820–£1,510	£1,395–£2,150	
Senior	£355–£620 (men) £340–£500 (women)	£1,625–£1,850	£2,298–£2,618	

Role					
Principal probation officer	£650-£1,100	Assistant principal £1,955-£2,990	Principal P.O. — Normally 75% of the principal probation officer's salary £2,823-£5,450 *according to population*	Assistant chief *according to population* £5,250-£5,721; Deputy chief £6,111-£7,695; Chief £5,250-£10,020	
Local authority social workers					
Main grade	(mental welfare) £390-£465 (boarding-out officers) £375-£525	£820-£1,200 (unqualified) £1,060-£1,435 (qualified)	£1,395-£2,457	£2,529-£3,474 (bar at £3,009 for unqualified social workers)	plus an addition for stand-by duty
Senior	£450-£710	£1,435-£2,000	£2,967-£3,075	£4,239-£5,103 Grades 1 and 2	
Principal			£2,766-£4,641	£4,689-£7,407 Range 1 and 2	
Assistant children's officers, children's officers and chief welfare officers	£390-£2,000	£2,105-£3,615			
Social services departments					
Assistant directors			£2,562-£4,641 plus	£5,613 to £13,728 according to area	
Deputy directors			£3,000-£6,000 plus		
Directors of social services depts			£3,000-£10,000 plus		

devoted to supervision, etc. of children in care and 10 per cent to preventive work.

In 1966 a similar but larger study was undertaken in England and Wales by the Home Office Research Unit (Grey, 1969) to try to formulate objective criteria for determining how many CCOs were needed for a given amount of work, and thus provide a more reliable yardstick than local struggles between conflicting claims for scarce resources in determining the number of CCOs needed to carry caseloads of given size and composition. The method used was a straightforward time study in nine different children's departments. No attempt was made (as in Scotland) to assess the quality of the work, thus it showed current practice but begged the complex question of effectiveness. The average time spent on 'work on cases' was 50 per cent (the total working time spent in actual contact with children was 16 per cent). From these findings a formula was worked out (covering all grades of non-residential child care staff) based on the caseload and time spent on it in a thirty-eight-hour working week. On this formula the total staff for England and Wales would have been 3,305 CCOs. No precise information was available about the actual numbers in post, but the formula was likely to predict a national staffing level markedly higher than the number of officers in post, yet 'it should be regarded as providing an absolute minimum criterion of staffing provision' (p. 43).

The Health and Welfare Services
In 1956 a number of fieldworkers in the health and welfare services in different types of area kept log books over two weeks for the Younghusband working party (1959). These showed that welfare officers spent on average 20 per cent of their working day on travel, 43 per cent on letter writing, record keeping, etc., 24 per cent in contact with clients and 13 per cent in discussions with colleagues. District welfare officers in one mainly rural county had average caseloads of 150, excluding old people, the removal and after-care of the mentally ill, and local home help inquiries. Caseloads of a group of home teachers of the blind ranged from 96 to 256, as against 80 to 100 recommended in 1951 by the Advisory Council for the Welfare of Handicapped Persons. A fieldworker with the deaf, who spent half his time travelling on public transport, had a caseload of 130 deaf people and 95 hard of hearing, plus 3 social clubs a week. In a rural county in 1957 an almoner had a caseload of 364, a worker for the physically handicapped 360, and the mental welfare and welfare officers had caseloads of between 159 and 608. In another county, home visitors for the handicapped had caseloads of about 200 and visited individuals on average about every fifteen weeks. They travelled by public transport. In another area where visitors had cars their caseloads were 272, 287 and 360: on average 49 per cent of their time was spent in travel, letter writing, record keeping and general administration. The four almoners in this area who kept log books spent on average 29 per cent of their time in travel, 22 per cent in contact with clients, 15 per cent in discussion with colleagues, and 34 per cent in letter and record writing and administration. Many officers had caseloads which made it impossible for them to carry out their recognised work satisfactorily, and did not allow time for more intensive work with those

who needed it or for preventive work. This, the Report said, could result in superficial assessment, wrong decisions and practically no constructive work, together with great strain on more skilled and conscientious workers. Sometimes only the most urgent cases could be selected for visiting: many clients were only seen for ten to fifteen minutes at three- to six-monthly intervals – and some were visited who did not really need it. There was no systematic investigation of the number of dormant cases in these workloads, as distinct from those which were or should have been active, nor the amount of service they needed or received.

Returns to a questionnaire sent to all health and welfare authorities by the working party showed that regular clerical help was available to fieldworkers in county boroughs, but that the majority of county councils did not provide this. A 'pool' car or an allowance for running the worker's own car was usual. Seventy-five per cent of authorities provided private rooms for interviewing, but in some situations interviews had to be held in rooms shared with other people.

In 1969 the National Institute for Social Work Training undertook a study (Carver and Edwards, 1972), financed by the DHSS, of a 10 per cent random sample of all social workers employed in health and welfare departments and voluntary organisations giving an agency service, including chief and principal officers as well as fieldworkers. The aim was to produce an accurate account of the pattern of work of these social workers, who dealt with eleven different categories of client in these services. This study over a two-week period used the diary method and was designed on much the same lines as the Home Office 1966 study of workloads in children's departments (Grey, 1969).

Unlike the earlier period in the health and welfare services, one officer in three was under 30 and only one in five was 50 or over. Fifty-eight per cent were women and 42 per cent men. Forty-five per cent of the total had less than five years' experience. Twenty-five per cent held a professional social work qualification, a further 25 per cent had a social science or a home teacher of the blind or a deaf welfare qualification. The better-educated and trained officers were in the younger age group. The remaining 50 per cent had no relevant qualifications. Only one in seven of all officers had had some substantial in-service training in the preceding two years. The majority of social workers in the health department were mental welfare officers.

Working conditions had improved, for example practically all officers used a car on the job. Nevertheless 30 per cent felt that they worked under severe time pressure with the result that they could not do the job as they thought it should be done. Nearly four out of five thought more workers were needed in their departments. A considerable proportion of time was spent on routine desk jobs, including writing and typing.

Health department fieldworkers recorded a mean number of 27·8 case contacts in the two-week period and estimated caseloads of 64·7. For welfare departments the parallel figures were 36·5 case contacts and estimated caseloads of 160·1. Less than one in five cases were mentally ill people, but they needed a substantially larger number of contacts than any other category.

Case contact time showed a high degree of stability across a wide range of variables. This worked out at a mean figure of twenty-three minutes per contact and for all the main referral categories the mean was within two minutes of the overall figure, with only small variations between different grades, qualified or unqualified officers, trainees or welfare assistants. There were also only minor differences between different local authorities. Time spent in actual contact with clients was, of course, the core of the workload, with other activities related to it. These results showed average actual, not ideal, practice over a randomly selected number of departments. The method also did not show the number of contacts per case nor attempt to determine the number required.

The results were surprisingly similar for health and welfare and children's departments, as table 13 of the National Institute's workload study showed (Carver and Edwards, 1972, p. 24, reproduced below).

Table 18 *Time spent on various activities as a percentage of total time worked in health and welfare compared with children's departments*

Department	Discussion with clients	Case-contact time Discussion with others concerned	Telephone interviews	Travel with clients	All case contact time	Other travel, etc.	All other activities
Health, Welfare and Combined whole-time equivalents =529·3	19 (health 15% welfare 22%)	6	4	2	31	16	53
Children's N=190	20	5	*	3	28	17	55

The figures used for children's departments were abstracted from Grey, *Workloads in Children's Departments* (1969), pp. 15 and 25.

* Telephone interviews were not separately reported for children's departments. They are included in the two columns headed 'discussion'.

Probation
Average caseloads in the probation service in the 1950s are shown in Table 19.

Table 19 *Average caseloads in the probation service in the 1950s*

	Men England and Wales	Scotland	Women England and Wales	Scotland
1952	61·7	59·4	42·6	43·5
1955	55·9	54·1	38·1	39·5
1959	64·9	52·1	39·9	41·4

Source: Morison Report (1962), paras 267 and 271.

Women probation officers' caseloads were fairly stable between 42·6 and 38·1 between 1952 and 1959. Men's caseloads increased steadily from 54·9 in 1954 to 64·9 in 1959. 500 men officers had caseloads of between 60 and 80. The accepted standard caseload was 50 to 60 for a man and 35 to 45 for a woman. The Morison Committee thought that workload rather than the caseload should be the standard assessment, i.e. all the probation officer's duties (para. 280). A Home Office Research Unit study of probation workloads (unpublished) had shown that it was sounder to apply workload criteria to groups of about five officers rather than to individuals, since, in a group, variations in the capacity, working methods and rates of work of individuals cancelled each other out.

PSWs' Caseloads

A sample survey of a small group of PSWs in mental hospitals and child guidance clinics undertaken for the Mackintosh Committee (1951) gave the following results:

(a) *Child guidance*

The total number of cases dealt with during a year varied between 120 and 220, in the latter there was a high proportion of cases referred for diagnosis only. In those with the lower caseload between 120 and 150 new cases a year, many were seen regularly for months.

(b) *Mental hospitals*

PSWs were trying to deal in some way or another with whatever cases were referred to them no matter how many. The number of cases on which some kind of work had been done during the year ranged from 100 to 450, this excluded the two or more out-patient clinics a week.

The Report said:

'There are grounds for believing that some psychiatric social workers in mental hospitals and child guidance centres are used for routine history taking, more than for social work, and for clerical and organising duties which persons with secretarial training could perform. We suggested in our interim report that the clerical and office routine work now performed by psychiatric social workers should in future be undertaken by clerical assistants and that employing authorities should ensure that these fully qualified workers devote the fullest measure of their time and skill to the social work for which they have been trained. We suggested too that they should be provided with telephones, suitable office accommodation in a convenient position for their work and, in addition in country districts, with home telephones and cars.' (p. 49)

A 1969 survey of child guidance clinics (CGSIG/BASW, 1975) showed caseloads ranging from under 20 to 250 (two examples). In sixty-one out of ninety-five clinics PSWs had caseloads between 20 and 60.

The Butterworth Inquiry Report, 1972
This Report concluded in 1972 that

'The demand for social workers has grown substantially in recent years and the shortage of training places as well as the need to ensure effectiveness and efficiency in the use of existing manpower makes it essential to develop more objective methods of workload measurement. This will not be a simple exercise but we are convinced that it must be tackled. The Home Office has used a form of work measurement in the probation service for some years, which now needs modification and refinement. There is no such agreed standard in the other services. Indeed, our case studies showed that few social service departments had attempted to determine the acceptable size of the individual's workload as a basis for calculating establishments. The three services need to develop some common assumptions and criteria for different types of case so that concepts of 'caseload' and 'workload' have a real and commonly understood meaning. We recommend that representatives of the three services, the Training Council and the government departments concerned should work together to this end. Until this is done there can be no valid assessment of present or future manpower needs, nor can action properly be planned to meet anticipated shortfalls of staff against establishment'. (para. 265)

Target Caseloads in the 1970s
The Scottish Advisory Council on Social Work in its study of fieldwork staffing (1974) found that directors of social work would like to reduce caseloads to about 50 (with much smaller numbers for senior social workers). The Committee itself favoured a figure of between 30 and 40. Some social services departments were reviewing caseloads to determine criteria for accepting cases and for case closure. There had been no comprehensive research on workloads since Seebohm reorganisation. Thus by 1975 there were no agreed criteria for assessing optimum workloads nor for deciding what type of case should (and should not) be allocated to qualified social workers.

PROBLEMS OF ADVANCED SOCIAL WORK PRACTICE IN ADMINISTRATIVE HIERARCHIES. A CAREER GRADE AND THE PLACE OF PROFESSIONAL SOCIAL WORKERS IN SENIOR MANAGEMENT

For years there had been a nagging unease because promotion of exceptionally good practitioners was only possible up administrative, supervision or teaching ladders, i.e. the reward of good practice was to forsake it or to stay on and earn less. None the less in the 1950s there were also complaints that social workers refused to apply for administrative jobs because they disliked administration. This was attributed partly to the concentration on casework in their training and partly to the then high proportion of less ambitious women in social work.

All social workers in the health service and most probation officers continued to practise after promotion – but they could not be promoted far.

This raised problems, discussed over the years, of how to reward two groups which were not necessarily synonymous, the excellent practitioner and the long-serving officer at the top of his salary scale.

The Seebohm Report (1968) envisaged that basic grade social workers would be promoted as seniors on merit. They would then be responsible for supervision, undertaking a few difficult cases and possibly specialising. 'The career structure of the social service department should allow a proportion of posts for highly skilled practitioners to advance in salary and status, without necessarily assuming substantial administrative responsibilities, though they would of course be expected to undertake some supervision and consultancy work' (para. 163).

At the time of the Scottish and Seebohm reorganisations, social workers and their supporters argued that senior managerial posts should be held by professionals. Indeed, power and enhanced professional status seemed to result from the capture of senior management posts. The successful social worker thus became an administrator of social services rather than an outstanding practitioner. But there were not enough to go round in both roles, the salaries were far higher in managerial posts, and alarm grew as the top-heavy structure became more obvious. A few local authorities instituted a career grade with some promotion prospects for selected practitioners, but the results were disappointing.

The Butterworth Inquiry (1972) found the probation service much concerned about the lack of more highly graded posts in casework and that probation officers had to forsake casework for career advancement. The service would like a dual hierarchy permitting promotion to both management and casework posts. Local authority social workers also thought it important that there should be more highly graded casework appointments. The Butterworth Report recommended that in the probation service there should be a new section in the main grade, open on merit to all probation officers after three years' experience. This 'B' grade would create improved salary increments for 'competent and dedicated' main-grade probation officers (the Report did not face the problem that competent is not necessarily synonymous with 'dedicated'). It grasped the nettle of selection in a way likely to cause heartburns by proposing that panels of local probation committees should take account of professional experience, performance and potential, and decide annually who should be selected for the probation officer 'B' grade.

In 1974 a BASW career grade working party was set up to look into the question of a career structure to enable fieldworkers to remain in practice yet enhance their income and status. It explored the question from the point of view of improving social work practice and clarifying the various functions which social workers should appropriately undertake, bearing in mind that complex social problems required highly sophisticated knowledge and skill. It found that social work assistants spent more time with clients than social workers, and there was naught for anyone's comfort in the strange situation 'which ensures that as a social worker gains experience and improves in competence his opportunities to practise diminish'. This was coupled with the negative incentive to remain in work with the same clients, which caused 'considerable frustration and disillusionment to social workers strongly motivated to practise social work when they found work with clients devalued' (*Social Work Today/BASW News*, 1975a, p. 283). Moreover, it honestly agreed that

'The accusation that social workers are mainly young and inexperienced is palpably true. The quality of service to clients invariably suffers, as does public confidence in social work and morale within the profession. An intolerable load is placed on the shoulders of newly qualified staff who frequently find themselves carrying a high proportion of very difficult and demanding cases, especially cases where some qualification is usually required, e.g. mental health emergencies, guardian ad litem duties, and cases of children at risk of non accidental injury. Long term clients (e.g. children in care) face repeated changes of social worker. For a profession which works primarily through relationships and which requires such a high level of maturity and continuity for its successful practice there appears to have been an abandonment of basic principles.' (p. 283)

This situation had arisen partly because social workers were used indiscriminately and neither tasks nor appropriate matching qualifications had been clearly defined. Large numbers employed as social workers were either unqualified or inexperienced and needed more supervision than experienced professionals. Senior social workers thus had to assume much responsibility for standards of practice and the practitioner only had limited accountability, which ran directly counter to professional assumptions. In such circumstances it was not clear whether practitioners were primarily social workers or local government officers. In any event, the local government hierarchical structures, with attention mainly focused on management and control of resources, was not conducive to enhancement of professional skill and responsibility by practitioners. Thus 'the administration which is theoretically designed to service the carrying out of practice has become the master and controller of practice' (p. 284). By and large, the working party said, the only settings left for good practice were the probation and aftercare service, the child guidance service and a few voluntary organisations.

This hard-hitting report went on to point out that all other professions distinguished between professional and administrative practice and valued their distinguished practitioners. This applied no less to architects' and engineers' departments in local government than to the NHS, while teachers had also achieved a clear distinction between practice and local government administration. Taking everything into account, the working party then went on to propose a 'radical restructuring of social services departments with a clear distinction made between professional practice and administration' (p. 284).

The working party recognised that this restructuring could only be done in stages, beginning with a clear division between social work and social services. The hospital hierarchies of consultants and hospital administrators provided an analogy which proved that a hierarchical structure could be used to enhance professional development. Senior social workers, who should have had at least two years of post-qualification and closely supervised experience with a particular group of clients, should be assisted by junior or trainee or assistant social workers and co-operate with residential social workers, home help organisers and others. Local government officers should be responsible for administration. The working party thought it unlikely that there would still be a 'dire shortage of social workers in the field' or of consultants if social service administration were taken over by administrators. A situation had to be created as quickly as possible in which 'it became the norm to remain in practice and the exception to go into administration' (p. 284).

Career-grade posts were an encouraging development which permitted the growth of specialisation and, if related to advanced training, could help to improve the quality of social work service. But the working party feared that 'a career grade – as an alternative to the mainstream management structure for a few social workers – will never achieve a fundamental improvement in the quality and continuity of social work services" (p. 284). These posts could be a dead end and a more desirable alternative would be to extend the social work salary scale far beyond the existing maximum. Qualified social workers could then advance up the scale, with very experienced and exceptional social workers reaching the principal officer range. Entry to this grade should depend upon a test of competence, additional to initial training and length of service. The crunch came with the nature of this test or accreditation, as had been clear with the Butterworth probation officer 'B' promotion scheme. Social work management grades would have to co-exist with the extended practitioner scale, under which some practitioners would be earning more than area officers, though responsible for their own work. No attempt was made to cost these proposals but they were a radical attempt to give status to social work practice within large departments.

Unlike the BASW working party, the Birch Report on *Manpower and Training for the Social Services* (1976) thought that a large proportion of management staff at all levels should have professional social work qualifications and management training because the quality of service by field staff depended largely on the quality of direction, supervision and guidance they received. People in these senior management posts should also ensure a high quality of professional thinking about agency policies and the special needs of particular clients. Senior management staff were also needed with qualifications in research, psychology, finance and management. The Birch Report also thought that a career grade was essential to produce senior and experienced practitioners because real skill, expertise, and special knowledge about particular clients and problems only resulted from years of practice. Without such practitioners there was little chance that standards of practice, alternative methods of, service and knowledge itself would advance.

If by the 1970s qualified social workers could expect a career in social work with promotion prospects very different from the 1950s, this had yet led to a situation in which failure to provide incentives to remain in practice was having more serious professional consequences than in the 1950s when little promotion existed and social workers were accused of shunning administration. For many years there had been concern about failure to recognise good practice. This was faced at last when the consequences of social services reorganisation were clearly having disastrous effects, but by 1975 action did not match alarm.

THE SUPPLEMENTARY BENEFITS COMMISSION

The Supplementary Benefits Commission (SBC) replaced the National Assistance Board (NAB) in 1966. For some time individual social work teachers were members of the Commission and one became vice-chairman in 1975. Stevenson (1973) analysed the functions and dilemmas of the SBC, some of the people it served, staff attitudes and training, and its relations with social workers. A post of social work adviser was created within the DHSS Social Work Service, with primary responsibility for stimulating a social work element in the SBC regional offices (the successor of the general welfare function of the NAB); liaison with social services; concern with especially difficult cases; and contributing to training. Social work service officers were also appointed to SBC regional offices.

From 1961 a category of special welfare officers (SWOs) had been created to be concerned especially with family and personal neglect, newly widowed or deserted women or others in critical circumstances, arrangements for the care of sick or disabled people, and employment or occupation for the handicapped. Many in these groups suffered from mental disorder. There were forty-seven SWOs in 1972 with caseloads of between twenty and forty. Their function clearly required social work skills, but there were unsolved dilemmas of professional specialisation with its barriers to promotion within a civil service department. 'Many of the difficulties inherent in the SWO scheme . . . arise from the attempt to graft a professional activity onto a bureaucratic structure without the benefit of the skills, experience and training which such activity would merit. SWOs handle cases which . . . are amongst the most difficult in social work' (Stevenson, 1973, p. 170). Many of these were or should also be in local authority or probation caseloads and there were unsolved tensions in spite of efforts at improved co-operation.

These comments on social work in the SBC do not deal with the much wider subject of constant conflicts between social workers and local SBC offices about the basis on which grants (especially discretionary allowances) were given or withheld. The advocacy function, increasingly accepted as part of social work, sharpened these differences and made it more important for social workers to be accurately informed about SBC regulations and for these to be administered with efficiency, understanding and courtesy. There were many intractable problems of material giving (or not giving), whether by the SBC, social services and social work departments, or voluntary organisations.

Chapter 22

Supporting Services

SOCIAL WORK ASSISTANTS

This hardy perennial experienced several changes of name on its way to recognition and had undoubtedly long existed unnamed. Social workers carrying full responsibility for a caseload could, if they were lucky, assign various tasks to intelligent secretaries or voluntary workers. The mixed feelings of social workers about disentangling this function and pressing for a recognised grade of worker sprang partly from fear that if the untrained could do much the same job, social workers' superior abilities would not be recognised, especially in the days when there was sometimes little skill component in their training. Later, the emphasis on the importance of the relationship in casework led many to think that the crucial element was not the nature of the task but the continuing relationship. This view was reinforced when small, practical services were accepted as an important means of demonstrating the caseworker's genuine concern. There was at the same time tacit acceptance, though no consistent exploration, of the possibility that many clients' identification was with a place, a small group of people and perhaps one central person. This concept, more often discussed in residential child care, helped to sooth uneasy feelings about the effects of rapid staff turnover on those clients who needed a stable, continuing relationship.

Welfare assistants (called by whatever name) might be young and fleeting, or local married women, or older people who stayed and became well known. If the personality as well as the skill of the worker can heal, it was obvious that some of the untrained rated high on personality. Some services, notably probation and child care, contended for a long time that every case was so difficult that there was no room for ancillary workers (see also chapters 2, 3, 4 and 5 on child care and chapters 6, 7 and 8 on probation and after-care).

To turn now to the emergence of the function. The first clearly differentiated group were welfare clerks in almoners' departments, referred to in chapter 9 on medical social work. Many tasks were being 'dumped' on almoners' departments which were a waste of their skill when they were in very short supply. The Institute of Almoners 1949 working party report (mimeographed) had referred to 'the careful selection of clerical staff and proper distribution of duties'. The Cope Committees (1951) endorsed this, but at no time was there analysis and experimentation to discover what was 'proper', i.e. what was consistent with the function of a hospital social service department though not a task for professional social workers. The same report recommended that the Ministry of Health or regional hospital boards should organise in-service training for welfare clerks. Nothing happened until Manchester Regional Hospital Board, in co-operation with the University extramural department and with the blessing of the Institute of Almoners, started in 1956 a one-year training course for hospital welfare workers recruited from outside (Gray, no date of publication). It was thought that welfare workers could meet patients' straightforward needs and be capable of independent action. The training consisted of two separate, two-week, residential periods and eleven months' supervised practice in almoners' departments, together with individual tutorials and small group discussions. The course included knowledge of the social services, an understanding of people's emotions and practical needs, capacity to plan with patients and to understand the limits of the job. There were several hundred applicants each year, but only about eight could be accepted. The strength of this course probably lay in tutorial support and the interest of the hospitals concerned. It did not spread, but it was a forerunner of the much later CCETSW certificate in social service.

The first clear identification of the function resulted from discussions in the Younghusband Report (1959) about services which dealt with many different needs from the most complex to practical help. It was obviously unrealistic not to look at the total range of activities revealed by the surveys undertaken for the working party and in evidence to it. This showed that there was a place for welfare assistants because, as in other services, many people primarily wanted accurate information and advice, much of it probably of a kind later identified as welfare rights entitlement, or support after initial skilled assessment. For instance,

' . . . the welfare assistant can help with practical problems such as sorting out difficulties in connection with pensions or allowances or registration for housing. He can make arrangements for holidays or a meals service, encourage attendance at club or other social activities, refer to the appropriate service for training, employment or other need and keep in touch with those awaiting admission to residential care . . . undertake follow-up visits and carry out straightforward work for the trained social worker in charge of a case.' (paras 569 and 729)

Welfare assistants should not make initial or other visits to assess need, but be attached to and only work under the supervision of trained social workers. Some might be older people or local married women working part-time, and others might be gaining useful experience before they were accepted and seconded for social work training. The working party thought that about 200 should be recruited annually for the succeeding five years: beyond that it was impossible to see how their use might develop. The Report was emphatic that they should be carefully selected, recruited in groups, and given a systematic in-service training course of related teaching and practice on the services and the human characteristics of their users.

Supervision and fuller in-service training should follow later. These were dangerous proposals for services where almost everyone was untrained, practically no in-service training existed, and welfare assistants could easily be used inappropriately and as cheap labour.

Obviously this actually happened later in some situations where welfare assistants were given demanding caseloads without supervision. But the category was widely accepted in these services, with much effort to provide in-service training, though in the days before training officers and when no one had much experience the syllabuses often resembled a two-year social science course crammed into two weeks, with the addition of talks about every department in the local authority. There were also difficulties when colleges were expected to accept seconded welfare assistants automatically for the two-year courses, until the principle was established, not without dust and heat, that the educational institution had the final say in selection. When more social work tutors were appointed these difficulties were sometimes eased by the tutor taking part in the initial appointment of welfare assistants and helping with in-service training. Later, a distinction was made between welfare assistants and welfare trainees.

The Seebohm Committee (1968) found that in 1967 there were 544 welfare assistants and 160 trainees (whole-time equivalents) employed in welfare departments (appendix F, para. 199). Figures were not given for the child care and probation services, but a trainee grade had been introduced in the child care service and the Home Office had initiated pioneer projects for the employment of ancillary staff in both the children's and probation services. These demonstrated that professional staff could be relieved of many different duties, and by degrees ancillary workers became an accepted part of each service.

The Plowden Report (1967) concluded that education welfare officers should become trained social workers. This entailed disentangling a variety of administrative tasks to be given to welfare assistants. This is an example of an occupation which began as a field administrative function then slowly emerged as social work; whereas elsewhere recognised social workers needed to shed responsibilities irrelevant to their function or else capable of being undertaken by others with less training, on the principle that the task should be related to the level of skill required. In effect, having to undertake routine tasks decreased the number of social workers, while to shift tasks elsewhere had the opposite effect. Butrym (1968) and Goldberg *et al.* (1970) in unrelated studies of different client groups each calculated that one-third of their total sample could have been effectively helped by welfare assistants.

The use of assistants varied considerably between different services, although there was a universal shortage of professional social workers. By 1971 most hospital social services departments employed more than one assistant to every four social workers, sometimes supervised by a senior medical social worker and expected to train after about a year, sometimes working on their own, sometimes limited to routine duties. In the new social services departments there was one social welfare assistant to about every thirteen professional social workers. The probation service had only just started to use ancillary workers. By 1973 there were 1,698 social work assistants and 1,492 social work trainees in social services departments in England.

In the Scottish social work departments in 1971 there were 135 social work assistants and 278 trainees to 610 field social workers. The report by the Scottish Advisory Council on Social Work on *Field Work Staffing (Scotland)* (1974) recorded 'a good deal of uncertainty about the use of social work assistants largely because . . . with the high proportion of unqualified staff they were sometimes used inappropriately. However some authorities were using them in a fairly sophisticated fashion having agreed their introduction with the staff and given them a clearly defined workload, induction training and supervision' (p. 9). It recommended a ratio of social work assistants to social workers of 1:5, with proper preparation, job allocation and supervision. It thought that trainees should be supernumeries with good in-service training and later should be seconded for training.

A 1972 CCETSW survey of trainees (Hayward, 1974) showed that 962 people were seconded for training that year, of whom over one-fifth had not been recruited as trainees. They had usually had one to three years' employment in social work and 36 per cent were graduates. Three hundred and sixty trainees failed to get places on courses. Some social services departments found difficulty in recruiting trainees, whereas others were inundated with applications. Sometimes inexperienced trainees were carrying a full workload and few authorities were able to provide good supervision and reduced caseloads.

The social work assistant category thus came into existence piecemeal as functions were slowly clarified in different services, pressure to make economical use of professional service increased, and anxieties were reduced. It is surprising that at no time was any comprehensive study made of the common range of functions in different services, who was performing these, with what effectiveness, what training and supervision they received, what job satisfaction they experienced, whether the range of functions needed redefinition, and what contribution they made to effective services to the consumer and smooth management of the services.

The question of whether there should be a separate career grade for social work assistants had been raised (Cypher, 1974) and would become more urgent when the CCETSW certificate in social service advanced beyond its first pioneer stage in 1975.

DAY CARE

Throughout the period to 1975 day care or training was started for many heterogeneous groups of people in unrelated services, provided by government departments, local authorities and voluntary organisations. They included day nurseries, old people's clubs, sheltered workshops, day training centres for the mentally handicapped, day hospitals, day training centres for offenders, and various other types. The purposes were to prevent the dependent from being left unprotected; to take a burden off the family; to give some kind of nurture, stimulus, a 'good experience', training, employment or occupation; to improve social functioning; and to keep people out of residential institutions, whether children's homes, prison, old people's homes or hospital. There were also thought to be many people who could be discharged from institutions if adequate day services were available. For an astonishingly long time the common aims with these different groups were ignored; and that the staff were not mainly caretakers with a sprinkling of occupational therapists, nurses, recreation organisers or craft instructors.

The neglect of the years could not be overtaken in a day and the CCETSW working party on day services (1975*a*) pointed out the serious humanitarian and financial effects of this neglect. Yet day services could help people to 'develop and maintain the maximum degree of independence and freedom for as long as possible' (p. 10). This could include individual development and social adaptation, with a chance to experience being both helper and helped. Little was known about the previous work experience or qualifications of day centre staffs, their problems on the job or the effect of their lack of skill. They were employed in different career structures with different opportunities, even when they worked with similar clients. In 1974 there were about 36,718 children and 64,154 adults in various forms of day services in the United Kingdom, but these figures were incomplete. The working party thought the term 'day care' too passive, paternalistic and overprotective, too much related to physical facilities and with too little concern for the stimulating, educational and rehabilitative elements in planning for individual people.

Employers had not recognised the importance of employing social workers in day services, with a few experimental exceptions like day training centres for offenders or Barnardo's and the NSPCC day centres for children in deprived neighbourhoods (Bywaters, 1972 and 1975). Some of these were started at the request of parents themselves as part of community projects. Barnardo's thought it essential that social workers should be closely connected with day care centres to help and support the families. By 1975 it had twenty-two centres covering some 600 children and others were planned. For lack of experience, most social workers had not acquired the skills peculiar to this service, though these were adaptations of professional social work competence.

Training for Day Services
It took a long time before residential social work was recognised, and even longer before the essence of day services of different kinds under different auspices for different people became so recognised. There were, indeed, large numbers of staff for whom no training existed when the CCETSW was given this responsibility. Its working party on day services report (1975*a*) concluded that all staff members needed a constellation of basic and special skills, together with consultative support from various professionals, and opportunities for further training. This training should be distinctive but within the framework of the certificate in social service. Roughly 1,800 staff would be needed within ten years to meet demand, with 40 per cent being CSS holders, 10 per cent with the CQSW (with an option in particular kinds of client and relevant day services), and the rest comprised of other professionals, for example teachers, psychologists and occupational therapists. The working party thought that day service staff primarily

needed 'the skill and ability to provide support to clients through inter-personal relationships' (p. 17). This included the ability to observe and record behaviour, to plan behavioural objectives, analyse a task, use rein-forcement techniques and plan the use of time, space and material equip-ment. All staff members needed knowledge of human development, the interaction between people and their environment, the processes of helping, and how day services fitted into community resources. Specific skills included instruction, physical care, assessment and group activities. The working party concluded that the existing diploma course for teachers of adult mentally handicapped people (about thirty-six weeks full-time) was too short even for its specific training task. Some domiciliary workers might need the same skills as day service staffs.

The proposed CSS training modules should include full-time, sandwich and day-release courses for these workers. CQSW special studies in day services should cover the impact of the setting on clients and staff, small group theory and its application, major handicapping conditions, the use of learning theory, and application of social work in day services.

By 1975 the CCETSW was discussing with several CQSW courses the inclusion of options for day services, while the seven pilot courses for the CSS were considering day service staff needs.

THE HOME HELP SERVICE

This service was originally started in 1918 for lying-in women. Organisers began to be appointed from the mid-1940s and from 1948 the service was extended by permissive powers within the NHS.

Returns in 1956 to the Younghusband working party (1959) showed that of 184 home help organisers (incomplete figures), 8 per cent had a qualifi-cation in social science, 8 per cent in nursing, and 2 per cent in domestic science. Some witnesses suggested that knowledge of social work and training in personnel management were desirable. There were divided views as to whether the service should undertake social work with clients, though all agreed that organisers should spend time discussing their cases with home helps. The working party concluded that home help organisers should be equipped to use knowledge of human relations in their own work and to co-operate with social workers. Its recommendation that caseworkers and home helps should work together, for instance in cases of potential family breakdown, was rarely acted upon.

By the 1960s the home help service clearly had a foot in both the health and social camps. The Seebohm Report (1968) recommended that it should be transferred from the health to the social services departments because it was 'both a preventive service and potentially a remedy for difficult social as well as medical situations' (para. 377).

The service only became mandatory in 1971 under the Health Services and Public Health Act, 1968 which required local authorities to provide an 'adequate' home help service. The following account is largely based on a DHSS review of the home help service (1973c) and a joint CCETSW/LGTB working party report on training (1974). At the time of the 1971 reorganisation there were 1,000 organising staff and about 70,000 home helps, mostly part-time. The service was a separate, usually low status and unevenly developed section in health departments with nursing staff closely involved in it. Social services departments had reviewed the service's objectives, internal organisation, operational problems and integration within the department. By 1973 the salaries and grading of organisers and the working conditions of home helps had been improved and more staff appointed. Some social services departments had integrated a range of home services under domiciliary service officers.

By 1974 there were in England and Wales 1,570 home help organisers and 41,500 home helps (whole-time equivalents). There were 38 organisers in Scotland in 1969 and 104 by 1974. The service was mainly provided for the elderly (80 per cent were over 65) and the acute and chronic sick. There was a marked decline in maternity work; but more help for handicapped people so that by 1974 38,700 of these received the service. Several authorities helped one-parent families (especially fathers); and one did so in emergencies like death, desertion, neglect or imprisonment. Many authorities planned to widen the service by working with families at risk to prevent children having to be received into care. This was an extension of the family aides, long since pioneered by some children's and health departments. Expansion might also include an evening, night sitter, weekend and seven-day-a-week service. In general, there had been fresh thinking about the aims of the service since reorganisation. For example, Coventry doubled the home help service in one area as an experiment to discover whether this could prevent admission to residential care, sufficiently relieve family pressure and prevent some family breakup.

The most usual organisational patterns were: (a) a central organiser who received and allocated referrals and acted as adviser; (b) a service more or less integrated with the area teams; (c) home help organisers might be in a centrally based team, advising about or responsible for domiciliary services. One authority had a home care section which included home helps, meals, day care, a neighbourly service, night sitters and short-term family care.

Home help organisers were overloaded, with large numbers of home helps to deploy and supervise and anything from 300 to 1,000 clients whose needs had to be assessed and reassessed. Their function was primarily managerial, but carried out in relation with home helps and clients and through contributing to the service's development as part of social services departments. Organisers had too much administrative and financial work which could be done elsewhere. They needed support to get more resources, to discuss difficult decisions and to let off steam.

Many organisers were also responsible for planning, staffing, forecasting, monitoring and co-ordinating the home help service. But since they worked under constant day-to-day pressure they had little time to forecast demand and plan or evaluate service effectiveness. They had always thought it crucial to see the home helps regularly, to support them and hold discussion groups. Everywhere they had too little time for periodic reassessment of clients' needs. Records were scanty, although organisers and home helps had vast knowledge of clients and their families which was not being used because few departments had devised ways of pooling information with social workers, and home help organisers complained that they were seldom consulted. Closer working relations were necessary between the home help organisers and social workers, and agreement about responsibility for assessment and review.

Organisers and assistants had a variety of backgrounds: clerical, organising, personnel management, housekeeping, nursing or other. Their prospects had much improved since reorganisation but salaries varied widely.

Home Helps

In the early 1970s there were shortages of home helps in some industrial or residential areas but waiting lists in others. Home helps themselves were the best source of recruitment. Some services had senior home helps as advisers to others, and also family aides who were more highly paid. Training schemes encouraged recruitment because they raised the standard of the service. Far back in 1918 the Local Government Board had advised that home helps should have one to three months' training (circular, 9 August 1918, para. 28). This standard was never reached, though from the 1950s organisers arranged short training courses and held regular group meetings. By 1971 some authorities had well-equipped training centres, while only thirty provided no training for either home helps or organisers. Home helps came from many different backgrounds. They often had much understanding of the personal nature of their service and of difficult and tragic situations. Some recognised the importance of being a good listener, concerned with the client's comfort and able to give companionship in crises. Some were willing to take on complex work and were equipped by former experience to do so. There were good neighbour schemes in some rural areas under which someone living close by might go in several times a day.

The Future

There were signs that a far more comprehensive service of care in the home might develop in the future to prevent social or family breakdown or to give support in crises. This would be a hybrid which comprised practical, supportive, preventive, teaching and social work skills in combination with day care facilities, volunteer help and other resources. It would affect the status of both home help organisers (probably with a changed title) and home helps (home makers or family aides?). This would also ease their incorporation in the mainstream of social services departments. It may be that this cluster of inter-related functions was going through the same stages of differentiation, as in those forms of residential care which started with the emphasis on domestic skills.

Training for Home Help Organisers

In the 1950s there was no training for home help organisers in spite of pressure by the Institute of Home Help Organisers. The Younghusband working party was clear about the importance of a function which contained 'three distinct elements: planning and organizing the service, social work and liaison with other services' (para. 482). The service itself was in an experimental stage and the working party found it difficult to recommend appropriate training for a hybrid breed who must yet not remain isolated from the main stream. It finally decided, perhaps rather lamely, that 'officers with a general training in social work and with administrative ability and experience in personnel management should be eligible for appointment as home help organisers' (para. 717). The Seebohm Report steered clear of the problem (para. 482).

The CCETSW/LGTB joint working party (1974c) found a variety of short courses differently organised and with different objectives. The Institute of Home Help Organisers certificate (revised in 1966) was usually taken as a two-year correspondence course, or in one year at a college of further education. Many organisers had taken this course, paying the fees themselves, though they were critical of its content, particularly the limited teaching about staff management. Some colleges had also started their own part-time courses in close consultation with social services departments. The working party proposed a common training for all organisers of domiciliary support services (including voluntary services). This training should include management skills, an understanding of human behaviour and needs, sociological and psychological influences on human growth and behaviour in relation to clients, the worker, superiors and subordinates; prediction of common human needs and their assessment and how to meet them; problems of specific groups such as the elderly and the mentally ill; principles and practice of interviewing; simple health knowledge and simple home management. The course should be based on block or day release, with some study modules primarily related to management, others to social work. A certificate in management flexibly organised in modules should be provided at a lower level than the existing diploma in management studies. The training should be formally assessed and lead to a nationally recognised award, giving holders a status 'comparable to that of other professions and qualifications in local government'. It was difficult to see how this could be achieved by an untried part-time course of unspecified duration. The working party said cautiously 'It may be appropriate in the longer term *to consider the development of full-time pre-employment courses for organisers*' (italics in original) (p. 49). The validating machinery should be acceptable in both social work and management fields. The working party thought that no one existing body would be appropriate, but subsequently the DHSS ruled that this responsibility belonged to the CCETSW.

In 1975 the Council suggested that its proposed new certificate in social service would be appropriate for organisers of domiciliary services because they came within 'the broad category of staff . . . who require some of the knowledge and skill . . . developed within the social work profession, combined with other substantial knowledge and skills . . . for example, management skills' (CCETSW, 1975c, p. 6). Students should be given time for study (a pious hope of all part-time courses) and have substantial and supervised practical training.

Training for home help organisers thus over the years followed a familiar pattern of: initially no training; then efforts by voluntary organisations or professional associations to provide some kind of part-time or correspondence course; followed by educational institutions coming into the picture; then government or other committees of inquiry analysed the situation and made recommendations about training, which might or might not be implemented; and finally came proposals that a national training body should sponsor qualifying courses on an agreed syllabus leading to a recognised award. Home help organisers seemed to have reached the penultimate stage by the mid-1970s.

Bibliography

Place of publication is London unless otherwise stated

ABERDEEN UNIVERSITY (1971–2), Prospectus of the Aberdeen University Two-Year Certificate in Applied Social Studies Course.

ADAMSON, GILVRAY (1973), *The Care-Takers* (Bristol, Bookstall Publications).

ADVISORY COUNCIL ON CHILD CARE (1968), *A Research and Development Strategy* (HMSO).

(1970*a*), *Care and Treatment in a Planned Environment* (HMSO).

(1970*b*), *A Guide to Adoption Practice* (HMSO).

ADVISORY COUNCIL ON SOCIAL WORK (1974), *Field Work Staffing (Scotland)* (Edinburgh, Social Work Services Group).

ADVISORY COUNCIL ON THE TREATMENT OF OFFENDERS (1963), *The Organisation of After-Care* (HMSO).

(1965), *The Adult Offender* (HMSO).

(1970), *Non-Custodial and Semi-Custodial Penalties* (HMSO).

AGE CONCERN (1974), *The Attitudes of the Retired and Elderly* (Mitcham, Age Concern).

(1975), *Manifesto* (Mitcham, Age Concern).

(n.d.), Report on *Training for Wardens of Group Housing Schemes* (Mitcham, Age Concern).

AKURST, C. R. (1973), review of *Task-Centered Casework* in *Social Work Today*, vol. 4, no. 2, p. 59.

ALBERMARLE REPORT (1960), *The Youth Service in England and Wales*, Cmnd 929 (HMSO).

APLIN, GEOFFREY and BAMBER, RALPH (1973), 'Groupwork Counselling', *Social Work Today*, vol. 3, no. 22, pp. 5–9.

APPLEYARD, GEOFFREY (1971), 'Prison Welfare?', *Howard Journal of Penology*, vol. 13, no. 2, pp. 106–13.

APTE, ROBERT Z. (1970), *Half-way Houses* (Bell).

ASHDOWN, MARGARET and BROWN, SIBYL CLEMENT (1953), *Social Service and Mental Health* (Routledge & Kegan Paul).

ASSOCIATION OF CHILD CARE OFFICERS (1969*a*), *Adoption – the Way Ahead* (ACCO).

(1969*b*), *Report of the Working Party on Professional Integrity in the Child Care Service* (ACCO).

ASSOCIATION OF CHILDREN'S OFFICERS (1953), *Cruelty to Children* (ACO).

ASSOCIATION OF COMMUNITY WORKERS (1975), *Knowledge and Skills for Community Work* (ACW).

ASSOCIATION OF DIRECTORS OF SOCIAL SERVICES (1974), 'Discussion paper', mimeographed (Association of Directors of Social Services).

ASSOCIATION OF PSYCHIATRIC SOCIAL WORKERS (1956*a*), *The Boundaries of Casework* (APSW).

(1956*b*), *The Essentials of Social Casework* (APSW).

(1958), *Working Party on the Function of PSWs in the Adult Field* (APSW).

(1960), *Ventures in Professional Co-operation* (APSW).

Annual Report 1968 (APSW).

(1969), *New Developments in Psychiatry and the Implications for the Social Worker* (APSW).

ASSOCIATION OF SOCIAL WORKERS (1953), *Notes on the Ethics of Social Work* (ASW).

(1956), *Recent Developments in Casework* (ASW).

(1960), *Morals and the Social Worker* (ASW).

AVES REPORT (1969), *The Voluntary Worker in the Social Services* (Allen & Unwin).

BALDOCK, PETER (1974), 'Community Work Experience in Social Work Training' in Jones, David and Mayo, Marjorie (eds), *Community Work – One* (Routledge & Kegan Paul).

BALLANCE, GILLIAN (1975), 'Fostering' in Stroud, John (ed.), *Services for Children and Their Families* (Pergamon Press), pp. 76–96.

BARACLOUGH, J. (1974a), 'Confidentiality', *Social Work Today/BASW News*, vol. 5, no. 4, p. 116.

(1974b), 'Confidentiality', *Social Work Today/BASW News*, vol. 5, no. 5, p. 148.

(1975), 'Code of Ethics for Social Work', *Social Work Today/BASW News*, vol. 6, no. 12, pp. 379–81.

BARNARDO'S (1969), *A Plan for the Reorganisation of the Child Care Department*, working party report (Barkingside, Barnardo's).

BARNES, L. and TAJFEL, I. (1958), 'The Teaching of Psychology in Social Science Courses', mimeographed (Joint University Council for Social and Public Administration).

BARR, HUGH (1966), *A Survey of Group Work in the Probation Service*, Home Office research studies (HMSO).

(1971), *Volunteers in Prison After-Care* (Allen & Unwin).

BARTLETT, HARRIETT (1970), *The Common Base of Social Work Practice* (New York, National Association of Social Workers).

BATTEN, T. R. (1957), *Communities and Their Development* (Oxford University Press).

BAYLEY, MICHAEL (1973), 'The Mentally Handicapped and Their Helpers', *British Journal of Social Work*, vol. 3, no. 3, pp. 319–63.

BEARD, RUTH (1970), *Teaching and Learning in Higher Education* (Harmondsworth, Penguin).

BENNINGTON, J. (1974), 'Strategies for Change at the Local Level: Some Reflections' in Jones, David and Mayo, Marjorie (eds), *Community Work – One* (Routledge & Kegan Paul), pp. 260–77.

BERRY, JULIET (1975), *Daily Experience in Residential Life* (Routledge & Kegan Paul).

BESSEY REPORT (1962), *The Training of Part-Time Youth Leaders and Assistants* (HMSO).

BIESTEK, FATHER (1961 and 1973, British ed.), *The Casework Relationship* (Allen & Unwin).

BILLIS, D. (1973), 'Entry into Residential Care', *British Journal of Social Work*, vol. 3, no. 4, pp. 447–71.

BINGHAM, J. (1961), *Do Cows Have Neuroses?* (National Association for Mental Health).

BION, W. (1961), *Experiences in Groups* (Tavistock Publications).

BIRCH REPORT (1976), *Working Party on Manpower and Training for the Social Services* (HMSO).

BOARD FOR SOCIAL RESPONSIBILITY OF THE NATIONAL ASSEMBLY OF THE CHURCH OF ENGLAND (1969), *The Church and the Social Services* (Church Information Office).

BONE, MARGARET (1972), *The Youth Service and Similar Provision for Young People* (HMSO).

BOWERS, SWITHUN (1949), 'The Nature and Definition of Social Casework', *Journal of Social Casework* (New York), vol. 30, no. 10, pp. 412–17.

BOWLBY, JOHN (1951), *Maternal Care and Mental Health* (Geneva, World Health Organisation).

(1969), *Attachment* (Hogarth Press).

(1973), *Separation, Anxiety and Anger* (Hogarth Press).

BRAITHWAITE, ROSE MARY (1959), 'The Probation Officer, His Training and Skill', *Probation*, vol. 9, no. 3, pp. 30–2.

BRANDON, DAVID (n.d.), *Women without Homes* (Christian Action).

BREE, M. H. (1970), 'Staying the Course', *British Journal of Psychiatric Social Work*, vol. 10, no. 4, pp. 170–7.

BRESLIN, ALICE and STURTON, SHEILA (1974), 'Groupwork in a Hostel for the Mentally Handicapped', *Social Work Today*, vol. 4, no. 23, pp. 722–6.

BRITISH ASSOCIATION OF RESIDENTIAL SETTLEMENTS (1951), *A Survey of Settlements, 1950* (BARS).

BRITISH ASSOCIATION OF SETTLEMENTS AND SOCIAL ACTION CENTRES (1973), 'Basic Statement of Common Purpose', mimeographed (BAS).

BRITISH ASSOCIATION OF SOCIAL WORKERS (1971), *Discussion Paper No. 1. Confidentiality in Social Work* (BASW).

(1972), *Discussion Paper No. 2. A Code of Ethics for Social Work* (Birmingham, BASW).

(1974), 'Better Services for the Mentally Handicapped: BASW Policy', *Social Work Today/BASW News*, vol. 5, no. 6, p. 173.

(1975*a*), 'Career Grade Working Party Report', *Social Work Today/BASW News*, vol. 6, no. 9, pp. 285–6.

(1975*b*), 'Confidence – in Principle and Practice', *Social Work Today/BASW News*, vol. 6, no. 8, pp. 253–4.

(1975*c*), 'The Future of Probation Officers in Borstals and Prisons', *Social Work Today/ BASW News*, vol. 6, no. 10, pp. 317–19.

(1975*d*), 'Children at Risk – BASW's Code of Practice', *Social Work Today/ BASW News*, vol. 6, no. 11, pp. 345–9.

(1977), *The Social Work Task* (BASW).

(n.d. [1974]), *Social Action and Social Work: Report of the Working Party* (Birmingham, BASW).

(n.d., adopted 1975), *A Code of Ethics for Social Workers* (Birmingham, BASW).

BRITISH MEDICAL ASSOCIATION AND THE MAGISTRATES' ASSOCIATION (1956), *Cruelty to and Neglect of Children* (BMA).

BRITISH PAEDIATRIC ASSOCIATION (1966), *British Medical Journal*, vol. 1, 'The Battered Baby Syndrome', pp. 601–3.

BROWN, G. W., BONE, MARGARET, DALISON, BRIDGET and WING, J. K. (1966), *Schizophrenia and Social Care*, Maudsley Monograph No. 17 (Oxford University Press).

BROWN, M. (1964), 'A Review of Casework Methods', reproduced in Younghusband, E. (ed.), *New Developments in Casework* (1966), (Allen & Unwin), pp. 11–37.

BROWN, S. CLEMENT (1955), 'A Study of a Sample of Trained Houseparents', unpublished (Nuffield College, Oxford).

BROWN, S. CLEMENT and GLOYNE, ELIZABETH (1966), *The Field Training of Social Workers* (Allen & Unwin).

BROWNING, JEAN and HOPE-MURRAY, E. L. (1974), 'Notes on Developing Local

Authority Social Services in England under the Chronically Sick and Disabled Persons Act, 1970', *Social Work Service*, no. 6, pp. 6–10.

BRYANT, RICHARD (1974), 'Field Work Training in Community Work', *Community Development Journal*, vol. 9, no. 3, pp. 212–16.

BULL, GRACE and BAILEY, JONATHON (1971), 'A Group for Experienced Foster Parents' in Tod, Robert (ed.), *Social Work in Foster Care* (Longman), pp. 131–7.

BURBERY, M., BALINT, E. and YAPP, B. (1945), *An Introduction to Child Guidance* (Macmillan).

BURNS, T. and SINCLAIR, S. (1963), *The Child Care Service at Work* (Edinburgh, HMSO).

BUTLER, BARBARA (1976), foreword to *Marital and Family Therapy* (Family Welfare Association), pp. 2–3.

BUTRYM, ZOFIA (1968), *Medical Social Work in Action* (Bell).

(1976), *The Nature of Social Work* (The Macmillan Press).

BUTTERWORTH INQUIRY (1972), *Report of the Butterworth Inquiry into the Work and Pay of Probation Officers and Social Workers*, Cmnd 5076 (HMSO).

BYWATERS, NANCY (1972 and 1975), 'A Survey of Day Care in Dr. Barnardo's' and 'A Second Survey of Barnardo Day Care', mimeographed (Barkingside, Barnardo's).

(1973), 'Day Care in a Large Voluntary Child Care Society', *Social Work Service*, no. 3, pp. 11 and 12.

CABINET OFFICE (1973), *Government Research and Development* (HMSO).

CADE, E. (1975), 'Therapy with Low Socio-Economic Families', *Social Work Today*, vol. 6, no. 5, pp. 142–5.

CAMERON, J. M. (1966), 'The Battered Child Syndrome', *Medical Science and the Law*, vol. 6, no. 1, pp. 2–21.

The Canford Families: A Study in Social Casework and Social Group Work (1962), Sociological Review No. 6 (University of Keele).

CAPLAN, G. (1961), *A Community Approach to Mental Health* (Tavistock Publications).

(1962), *Prevention of Mental Disorders in Children* (Tavistock Publications).

CARTER, DEREK T. (1971a), 'Attitudes of Medical Social Workers Towards Reorganisation', *British Journal of Social Work*, vol. 1, no. 3, pp. 255–75.

(1971b), 'The Deployment of Medical Social Workers', *Social Work Today*, vol. 2, no. 11, pp. 3–7.

(1976), 'The Social Needs of the Physically Sick and the Role of the Medical Social Worker' (unpublished doctoral thesis, York University).

CARVER, V. and EDWARDS, J. L. (1972), *Social Workers and Their Workloads* (National Institute for Social Work Training).

CASEMENT, P. (1973), 'The Supervisory Viewpoint' in Finn, W. H. (ed.), *Family Therapy in Social Work* (Family Welfare Association) pp. 32–6.

CENTRAL COUNCIL FOR EDUCATION AND TRAINING IN SOCIAL WORK (1973a), *Bulletin No. 1* (CCETSW).

(1973b), *Residential Work Is Part of Social Work*, report of a working party (CCETSW).

(1973c), *Setting the Course for Social Work Education 1971–73* (CCETSW).

(1973d), *Training for Residential Work*, discussion document (CCETSW).

(1973–4), *Social Work Education*, Report 2 (CCETSW).

(1974a), *Legal Studies in Social Work Education*, report of a working party (CCETSW).

(1974b), *People with Handicaps Need Better Trained Social Workers*, report of a working party (CCETSW).

/Local Government Training Board (1974c), *Training for Organisers of Home Help and Other Supportive Domiciliary Services*, report of a joint working party (CCETSW).

CENTRAL COUNCIL FOR EDUCATION AND TRAINING IN SOCIAL WORK (1975a), *Day Services: An Action Plan for Training*, report of a working party (CCETSW).

(1975b), *Education and Training for Social Work* (CCETSW).

(1975c), *A New Form of Training: the Certificate in Social Service* (CCETSW).

(1975d), *The Teaching of Community Work*, report of a working party (CCETSW).

(1975e), 'Guidelines for Post-Qualifying Studies', mimeographed (CCETSW).

(1975f), 'Principles, Procedures and Criteria for Approval of Post-Qualifying Studies', mimeographed (CCETSW).

(1976a), *Bulletin 4, Social Work Education News and Views* (CCETSW).

(1976b), *Values in Social Work*, report of a working party (CCETSW).

CENTRAL HOUSING ADVISORY COMMITTEE (1967), *The Needs of New Communities* (HMSO).

CENTRAL TRAINING COUNCIL IN CHILD CARE (1947), *Memorandum on the Training of House Parents* (Home Office Children's Department).

(1953), *Notes on the Training of House-Parents of Children's Homes* (Home Office Children's Department).

(1956), *Training in Child Care, Memorandum of Guidance by the Home Office* (Home Office Children's Department).

(1963), *Memorandum of Guidance on Practical Training for Child Care Students* (Home Office Children's Department).

(1967), *In-service Study Course for Residential Child Care Staff: Approved Guide Syllabus* (Home Office).

CENTRAL TRAINING COUNCIL IN CHILD CARE/CENTRAL COUNCIL FOR EDUCATION AND TRAINING IN SOCIAL WORK (1970), *New Perspectives in Social Work*, report of a working party (CCETSW).

CHEETHAM, JULIET (1972), *Social Work with Immigrants* (Routledge & Kegan Paul).

CHEETHAM, J. and HILL, M. (1973), 'Community Work: Social Realities and Ethical Dilemmas', *British Journal of Social Work*, vol. 3, no. 3, pp. 331–48.

CHILD GUIDANCE SPECIAL INTEREST GROUP/BRITISH ASSOCIATION OF SOCIAL WORKERS (1975), *The Child Guidance Service: Report of the 1969 Survey undertaken by Psychiatric Social Workers* (Child Guidance Special Interest Group).

CLARKE, MICHAEL (1976), 'First Year Sociology Courses: A Report of a Survey', *Sociology*, vol. 10, no. 1, pp. 83–99.

COLLINS, J. (1965), *Social Casework in General Medical Practice* (Pitman).

COLLIS, ARTHUR (1961), 'Social Work – a Current Assessment of Training and Related Topics', *Social Work*, vol. 18, no. 3, pp. 5–9.

COMMUNITY RELATIONS COMMISSION (1974), *Response to the Select Committee on Race Relations and Immigration* (CRC).

(1975), *Who Minds?* (CRC).

(1976a), *Some of My Best Friends . . .* (CRC).

(1976b), *Working in Multi-Racial Areas: A Training Handbook for Social Services Departments* (CRC).

CONFERENCE OF PRINCIPAL PROBATION OFFICERS (1968), *The Place of the Probation and After-Care Service in Judicial Administration* (CPPO).

COOPER, CHRISTINE (1975), 'The Doctor's Dilemma: A Paediatrician's View' in Franklin, A. White (ed.), *Concerning Child Abuse* (Churchill Livingstone), pp. 21–30.

COOPER, JOAN (1967), 'Residential Work with Children' (Paper read at the Conference of the Association of Hospital and Welfare Administrators, Hastings, 1967).

COPE REPORT (1951), *Report of the Committees on Medical Auxiliaries*, Cmnd 8188 (HMSO).

COUNCIL FOR CHILDREN'S WELFARE (1965), *A Family Service and a Family Court* (CCW).

(1975), *No Childhood* (CCW).

COUNCIL FOR TRAINING IN SOCIAL WORK, *Annual Report 1965* (CTSW).

(1967*a*), *Human Growth and Development as a Subject of Study for Social Workers*, working party report (CTSW).

(1967*b*), *Staff Development in Social Work* (CTSW).

Annual Report 1967 (CTSW).

(1969), 'Teaching about Utilization of Research in Social Work Courses', unpublished (CTSW).

(1971), *The Teaching of Fieldwork*, CTSW Discussion Paper No. 4 (CTSW).

(1972), *The Teaching of Sociology in Social Work Courses*, working party report (CTSW).

COURT, JOAN (1974), 'Characteristics of Parents and Children' in Carter, Jan (ed.), *The Maltreated Child* (Priory Press).

COVENTRY SOCIAL SERVICES DEPARTMENT (n.d.), *Looking for Trouble*, survey 1971–72 (Coventry, Social Services Department).

COX, D. T. and DERRICOURT, N. J. (1975), 'The De-professionalisation of Community Work' in Jones, David and Mayo, Marjorie (eds), *Community Work – Two* (Routledge & Kegan Paul), pp. 75–87.

CRELLIN, E., KELLMER PRINGLE, M. and WEDGE, P. (1971), *Born Illegitimate* (Slough, National Foundation for Educational Research).

CURNOCK, KATHLEEN (1975), *Student Units in Social Work Education* (CCETSW).

CURTIS REPORT (1946), *Report of the Care of Children Committee*, Cmnd 6922 (HMSO).

CYPHER, JOHN (1974), 'Differential Use of Manpower', *Social Work Today*, vol. 5, no. 15, pp. 452–6.

DANBURY, HAZEL (1976), 'Mental Health Compulsory Admissions', *Social Work Today*, vol. 7, no. 6, pp. 172–4.

DAVIES, BERNARD (1975), *The Use of Groups in Social Work Practice* (Routledge & Kegan Paul).

DAVIES, MARTIN (1969), *Probationers in Their Social Environment*, Home Office research studies (HMSO).

(1972), 'The Objectives of the Probation Service', *British Journal of Social Work*, vol. 2, no. 3, pp. 315–22.

(1973), 'The Criminal Justice Act, 1972 as an Expression of Social Policy', *Social Work Today*, vol. 4, no. 7, pp. 195–201.

(1974), *Prisoners of Society* (Routledge & Kegan Paul).

(1975), *Social Work in the Environment*, Home Office research studies (HMSO).

DAY, B. (1965), 'Supportive Casework in an Authority Setting', *Case Conference*, vol. 11, no. 9, pp. 389–93.

DEANE, R. (1966), 'Some Non-interpretive Casework in Families affected by Mental Illness', *Case Conference*, vol. 12, no. 8, pp. 277–81.

DEPARTMENT OF EDUCATION AND SCIENCE (1969), *Youth and Community Work in the 70s*, Report of the Youth Service Development Council (HMSO).

(1972), *Educational Priority*, *Report of a Research Project* (HMSO).

DEPARTMENT OF EDUCATION AND SCIENCE, DEPARTMENT OF HEALTH AND SOCIAL SECURITY, WELSH OFFICE (1974), *Child Guidance*, Circular 3/74 DES, HSC (15)9 DHSS, WHSC (15)5 Welsh Office.

DEPARTMENT OF HEALTH AND SOCIAL SECURITY, CHIEF MEDICAL OFFICER OF HEALTH

AND CHIEF INSPECTOR HOME OFFICE CHILDREN'S DEPARTMENT (1970*a*), Circular CMO 2/70 and LHAL 24/70.

DEPARTMENT OF HEALTH AND SOCIAL SECURITY (1970*b*), *National Health Service, The Future Structure of the National Health Service*, second Green Paper on the NHS (HMSO).

(1971*a*), *Better Services for the Mentally Handicapped* (HMSO).

(1971*b*), *Children Act 1948, Summary of Returns of Child Care Staff* (DHSS).

(1971*c*), *Fieldwork Training for Social Work* (HMSO).

(1971*d*), *Youth Treatment Centres* (HMSO).

(1972*a*), Circular 35/72 (DHSS).

(1972*b*), *Intermediate Treatment* (HMSO).

/HOME OFFICE (1972*c*), Joint Circular LASS 26/72, including a booklet on 'The Battered Baby' prepared by the Department of Health and Social Security Standing Medical Advisory Committee.

DEPARTMENT OF HEALTH AND SOCIAL SECURITY (1973*a*), *Development of Services for the Elderly*, Social Work Service Survey (HMSO).

(1973*b*), *Intermediate Treatment Project*, Development Group Report (HMSO).

(1973*c*), *Review of the Home Help Service in England* (DHSS).

/WELSH OFFICE (1974*a*), Circular LASS 13/74.

/DEPARTMENT OF THE ENVIRONMENT (1974*b*), *Homelessness*, Circular DHSS 4/74 and DoE 18/74 (HMSO).

DEPARTMENT OF HEALTH AND SOCIAL SECURITY (1974*c*), *Non-Accidental Injury to Children* (LASSL 9 (74) 13).

(1974*d*), *Report of the Committee of Inquiry into the Care and Supervision Provided in relation to Maria Colwell* (HMSO).

(1974*e*), 'The Service Delivery Study', a Social Work Service Study, *Social Work Service*, June 1975, pp. 11–14.

/WELSH OFFICE (1974*f*), *Social Work Support for the Health Service* (HMSO).

DEPARTMENT OF HEALTH AND SOCIAL SECURITY (1975*a*), *Annual Report 1974* (HMSO).

(1975*b*), *Better Services for the Mentally Ill* (HMSO).

(1975*c*), 'The Day Care of Young Children', *Social Work Service*, no. 6, pp. 14–17.

(1975*d*), *Hostels for Young People*, Social Work Service Development Group (HMSO).

DEPARTMENT OF HEALTH AND SOCIAL SECURITY STATISTICS AND RESEARCH DIVISION (1975*e*), *Local Authority Social Services Departments. Staff of Homes for the Elderly etc.* (DHSS S/F 75/6).

(1976*a*), *Consultative Document on Priorities for Health and Personal Social Services in England* (HMSO).

(1976*b*), *Guide to Fostering Practice* (HMSO).

(1976*c*), *Non-Accidental Injury to Children: Area Review Committees* (DHSS, LASSL (76) 2, CMO (76) 2, CNO (76) 3).

DINNAGE, ROSEMARY and KELLMER PRINGLE, M. L. (1967), *Foster Home Care: Facts and Fallacies* (Longman).

DONGRAY, M. (1958), 'Social Work in General Practice', *British Medical Journal*, vol. 2, pp. 1,220–3.

DONNISON, D. (1965), *Social Policy and Administration* (Allen & Unwin).

DOWLING, E. (1975), 'The Family Therapy Approach to Adolescent Disturbance' in Fiddis, B. D. (ed.), *Proceedings of the Association for the Psychiatric Study of Adolescents: Tenth Annual Conference* (APSA), pp. 39–43.

DRAKE, FRANCES (1975), 'The Position of the Local Authority' in Franklin, A. White (ed.), *Concerning Child Abuse* (Churchill Livingstone), pp. 85–94.

EDWARDS, S. R. (1976), *Treatment in Security* (Institute for the Study and Treatment of Delinquency).

ELLES, G. W. (1961), 'Collateral Treatment in a Family by Psycho-Analytic Techniques', *British Journal of Psychiatric Social Work*, vol. 6, no. 1, pp. 3–12.

(1962), 'A Family Problem and Psychopathic Illness', *Case Conference*, vol. 9, no. 4, pp. 91–5; no. 5, pp. 135–9; no. 6, pp. 153–7.

EMMET, DOROTHY, 'Ethics and the Social Worker' (1967), reproduced in Younghusband, E. (ed.), *Social Work and Social Values* (Allen & Unwin).

EVENS, P. (ed.) (1974), *Community Work Theory and Practice* (Oxford, Alastair Shornach).

FAMILY DISCUSSION BUREAU (1955), *Social Casework in Marital Problems* (Institute of Marital Studies).

(1960), *Marriage: Studies in Emotional Conflict and Growth* (Institute of Marital Studies).

FAMILY SERVICE UNITS (1976), 'Drop in Centres', *FSU Quarterly*, no. 10, pp. 27–49 (FSU).

FERARD, M. and HUNNYBUN, N. (1962), *The Caseworker's Use of Relationship* (Tavistock Publications).

FINER REPORT (1974), *Report of the Committee on One-Parent Families*, Cmnd 5629 (HMSO).

FINZI, JEAN, KING, CHRYSTAL and BOOVER, DAVID (eds) (1971), *Volunteers in Hospital* (King Edward's Hospital Fund for London).

FITZHERBERT, KATRIN (1967), *West Indian Children in London* (Bell).

FOLKARD, M. S., FOWLES, A. J., MCWILLIAMS, B. C., MCWILLIAMS, W., SMITH, D. D., SMITH, D. E. and WALMSLEY, G. R. (1974), *IMPACT, Intensive Matched Probation and After-Care Treatment*, Home Office research studies, vol. 1 (HMSO).

FOLKARD, M. S., SMITH, D. E. and SMITH, D. D. (1976), *IMPACT*, Home Office research studies, vol. 2 (HMSO).

FOLKARD, S., LYON, K., CARVER, M. M. and O'LEARY, F. (1966), *Probation Research: A Preliminary Report* (HMSO).

FORD, J. (1966), 'What Is Happening in Child Guidance?', *British Journal of Psychiatric Social Work*, vol. 8, no. 4, pp. 47–9.

FORMAN, J. A. S. and FAIRBAIRN, E. M. (1968), *Social Casework in General Practice* (Oxford University Press).

FOULKES, S. H. and ANTHONY, E. J. (1957), *Group Psychotherapy* (Harmondsworth, Penguin).

FRANKLIN, ALFRED WHITE (1974), 'The Tunbridge Wells Study Group on Non-Accidental Injury to Children', *Social Work Service*, no. 4, pp. 28–39.

FRY, MARGERY (1966), *Old Age Looks at Itself* (reprinted by the National Old People's Welfare Council).

GARRETT, ANNETTE (1942), *Interviewing: Its Principles and Methods* (New York, Family Service Association of America).

GEORGE, V. (1970), *Foster Care: Theory and Practice* (Routledge & Kegan Paul).

GIBBENS, T. C. N. (1972), 'Violence to Children', *Howard Journal of Penology*, vol. 13, no. 3, pp. 212–20.

GIBBENS, T. C. N. and WALKER, A. (1956), *Cruel Parents* (Institute for the Study and Treatment of Delinquency).

GLASTONBURY, B. (1971), *Homeless, Near a Thousand Homes* (Allen & Unwin).

GLOVER, ELIZABETH (1949), *Probation and Re-Education* (Routledge & Kegan Paul).

GOETSCHIUS, G. (1969), *Working with Community Groups* (Routledge & Kegan Paul).

GOETSCHIUS, GEORGE and TASH, JOAN (1967), *Working with Unattached Youth* (Routledge & Kegan Paul).

GOLDBERG, E. M. (1957), 'The Psychiatric Social Worker in the Community', *British Journal of Psychiatric Social Work*, vol. 5, no. 2, pp. 4–15.

(1958), *Family Influences and Psychosomatic Illness* (Tavistock Publications).

(1960), 'Parents and Psychotic Sons', *British Journal of Psychiatric Social Work*, vol. 5, no. 4, pp. 184–94.

(1961), 'The Social Worker in the Sixties', *The Almoner*, vol. 14, no. 3, pp. 96–113.

(1966a), 'Hospital, Work and Family: A Four Year Study of Young Mental Hospital Patients', *British Journal of Psychiatry*, vol. 112, no. 483, pp. 177–96.

(1966b), *Welfare in the Community* (National Institute for Social Work).

(1967), *The Families of Schizophrenic Patients* (National Institute for Social Work).

(1973), 'Services for the Family' in Wing, J. K. and Hefner, H. W. (eds), *The Roots of Evaluation: The Epidemiological Basis for Planning Psychiatric Services* (Oxford University Press).

GOLDBERG, E. M. and FRUIN, D. J. (1976), 'Towards Accountability in Social Work', *British Journal of Social Work*, vol. 6, no. 1, pp. 3–19.

GOLDBERG, E. M., with MORTIMER, A. and WILLIAMS, B. T. (1970), *Helping the Aged* (Allen & Unwin).

GOLDBERG, E. M. and NEILL, JUNE (1972), *Social Work and General Practice* (Allen & Unwin).

GOLDBERG, [E.] M., WALKER, D. and ROBINSON, J. (1977), 'Exploring Task-centered Casework Method', *Social Work Today*, vol. 9, no. 2, pp. 9–14.

GOODACRE, IRIS (1966), *Adoption Policy and Practice* (Allen & Unwin).

GOVERNMENT SOCIAL SURVEY (1964), *Staffing of Local Authority Residential Homes for Children* (HMSO).

GRAHAM, P. J. (1971), 'Some Aspects of the Relationship of Social Work to Behaviour Therapy', *British Journal of Psychiatric Social Work*, vol. 1, no. 2, pp. 197–208.

GRAY, P. G. and PARR, ELIZABETH (1957), *Children in Care and the Recruitment of Foster Parents*, Social Survey (HMSO).

GRAY, ROSEMARY (n.d.), *Training Scheme for Hospital Welfare Workers* (Manchester, Manchester Regional Hospital Board).

GRAYFORD, J. J. (1975), 'Wife Battering: A Preliminary Survey of 100 Cases', *British Medical Journal*, no. 5,951, pp. 194–7.

GREVE, JOHN (1964), *London's Homeless* (Welwyn, Codicote Press).

GREY, ELEANOR (1969), *Workloads in Children's Departments* (HMSO).

GRIFFITHS, D. L. and MOYNIHAN, F. J. (1963), 'Multiple Epiphysical Injuries in Babies', *British Medical Journal*, vol. 537, pp. 1,558–61.

GRUNHUT, M. (1954), *Practical Results and Financial Aspects of Adult Probation in Selected Countries* (Geneva, United Nations).

GUIVER, PAMELA (1973), *The Trouble Sharers* (National Marriage Council).

GULBENKIAN FOUNDATION (1968), *Community Work and Social Change* (Longman).

(1973), *Current Issues in Community Work* (Routledge & Kegan Paul).

HADLEY, ROGER, WEBB, ADRIAN and FARRELL, CHRISTINE (1975), *Across the Generations* (Allen & Unwin).

HALL, ANTHONY S. (1974), *The Point of Entry* (Allen & Unwin).

HALL, M. PENELOPE and HOWES, ISMENE V. (1965), *The Church in Social Work* (Routledge & Kegan Paul).

HALL, PHOEBE (1976), *Reforming the Welfare* (Heinemann).

HALLBURTON, P. M. and WRIGHT, W. B. (1974), 'Towards Better Geriatric Care', *Social Work Today*, vol. 5, no. 4, pp. 107–8.

HALLIWELL, R. (1969), 'Time-limited Work with a Family at Point of Being Prosecuted for Child Neglect', *Case Conference*, vol. 15, no. 9, pp. 343–8.

HALMOS, PAUL (1965), *The Faith of the Counsellors* (Constable).

HAMILTON, GORDON (1951), *Social Casework: Theory and Practice* (New York, Columbia University Press).

HAMMOND, P. (1964), 'Changing Practice in Mental Hospital Social Work', *British Journal of Psychiatric Social Work*, vol. 7, no. 3, pp. 128–35.

HARRIS, AMELIA (1968), *Social Welfare for the Elderly*, Government Social Survey (HMSO).

(1971), *Handicapped and Impaired in Great Britain, Part I*, Office of Population Censuses and Surveys (HMSO).

HAYWARD, CHRISTINE (1974), 'Survey of Trainees', *Social Work Today*, vol. 5, no. 4, pp. 117–19.

HAZEL, N. and COX, R. (1976), 'The Special Family Placement Project', mimeographed (Maidstone, Kent County Council, Social Services Department).

HEIMLER, EUGENE (1958), 'New Roads in Psychiatric Community Care', *The Medical Officer*, no. 100, pp. 295–6.

(1962), *A Link in the Chain* (The Bodley Head).

(1975), *Survival in Society* (Weidenfeld & Nicolson).

HERAUD, BRIAN (1970), *Sociology and Social Work* (Pergamon Press).

HERNE, R. (1975), 'L. A. Community Workers . . . Writers or Fighters?', *Case Con*, no. 20, pp. 20–2.

HERTFORDSHIRE CHILDREN'S DEPARTMENT (1966), *Annual Report 1965–66* (Hertfordshire County Council).

HERTOGHE, A. M. and MCLAINE, G. (1973), 'Family Therapy within a Casework Agency' in Finn, W. H. (ed.), *Family Therapy in Social Work* (Family Welfare Association), pp. 41–8.

HEWITT, SHEILA (1970), *The Family and the Handicapped Child* (Allen & Unwin).

HOBMAN, DAVID (1969), *A Guide to Voluntary Service* (HMSO).

HOLDEN, C. (1969), 'Temper Tantrum Extinction: A Limited Attempt at Behaviour Modification', *Social Work*, vol. 26, no. 4, pp. 8–11.

HOLDEN, H. M. (1964), 'The Voluntary Associate Scheme', *British Journal of Criminology*, vol. 4, no. 4, pp. 341–8.

HOLLIS, FLORENCE (1964 and 1972), *Casework: A Psychosocial Therapy* (New York, Random House).

HOLMAN, R. (1973), *Trading in Children* (Routledge & Kegan Paul).

(1975), 'The Place of Fostering in Social Work', *British Journal of Social Work*, vol. 5, no. 1, pp. 3–29.

HOME OFFICE (1948a), Circular 160.

(1948b), *Memorandum on the Principles and Practice in the Work of Matrimonial Conciliation in Magistrates Courts* (HMSO).

HOME OFFICE/MINISTRIES OF EDUCATION AND HEALTH AND SCOTTISH HOME DEPARTMENT, Joint Circular (1950), Home Office Circular 157/50 (HMSO).

HOME OFFICE (1965), *The Child, the Family and the Young Offender* (HMSO).

(1966a), *Report on Dorset County Council Child Care Service* (HMSO).

(1966b), *Residential Provision for Homeless Discharged Offenders* (HMSO).

(1968a), *Children in Trouble* (HMSO).

(1968b), *Training of After-Care Hostel Staff*, Memorandum for the Advisory Council for Probation and After-Care.

(1970), *Community Homes Project Report* (HMSO).

(1971a), *Habitual Drunken Offenders: Report of the Working Party* (HMSO).

(1971b), *Youth Treatment Centres* (HMSO).

(1972), *The Criminal Justice Act 1972, A Guide for the Courts* (HMSO).

(1975a), *Racial Discrimination*, Cmnd 6234 (HMSO).

(1975*b*), *Social Work in the Custodial Part of the Prison System* (HMSO).

Reports on the Work of the Children's Department, Sixth (1951), Seventh (1955), Eighth (1961) and 1961–3, 1964–6, 1967–9 (HMSO).

Reports on the Work of the Probation and After-Care Department, 1962–5, 1966–8 and 1969–71 (HMSO).

HOUGHTON STOCKDALE REPORT (1972), *Departmental Committee on the Adoption of Children* (HMSO).

HOUSE OF COMMONS (1952), *6th Report of the Select Committee on Estimates* House of Commons paper 235 (HMSO).

HOUSE OF COMMONS EXPENDITURE COMMITTEE (1975), *Eleventh Report from the Expenditure Committee, The Children and Young Persons Act, 1969, Vol. 1*, Cmnd 6494 (HMSO).

HOUSE OF COMMONS SELECT COMMITTEE on *Race Relations and Immigration (Session 1974–1975), Evidence* (HMSO).

HOUSE OF COMMONS SELECT COMMITTEE on *Violence in Marriage* (1975), House of Commons paper 553 (HMSO).

HOWELL, D. and PARSLOE, P. (1966), 'Working with a Family in a Child Guidance Setting', *British Journal of Psychiatric Social Work*, vol. 8, no. 4, pp. 10–20.

HUDSON, B. (1975), 'An Inadequate Personality: A Case Study with a Dynamic Beginning and a Behavioural Ending', *Social Work Today*, vol. 6, no. 16, pp. 505–8.

HUNEEUS, M. E. (1962), 'Problems related to Marital Interaction in Community Care' in *The Marital Relationship as a Focus for Casework*, Family Discussion Bureau (Welwyn, Codicote Press), pp. 33–40.

HUNT, ARTHUR (1974), 'Delinquency and the Social Services Departments' in Brown, Malcolm (ed.), *Social Issues and the Social Services* (Knight), pp. 107–21.

HUNTER, P. (1964), 'Psychiatric Social Work with Disturbed Patients in the Community', *British Journal of Psychiatric Social Work*, vol. 7, no. 4, pp. 183–90.

(1969), 'A Survey of Psychiatric Social Workers working in Mental Hospitals', *British Journal of Psychiatric Social Work*, vol. 10, no. 1, pp. 22–6.

HURST REPORT (1954), *Report of the Departmental Committee on the Adoption of Children* (HMSO).

HUTTEN, J. (1974), 'Short term Contracts', *Social Work Today*, vol. 4, no. 22, pp. 709–11.

(1975), 'Short term Contracts III', *Social Work Today*, vol. 6, no. 17, pp. 538–41.

HUXLEY, ALDOUS (1954), *The Doors of Perception* (Chatto & Windus).

INGLEBY REPORT (1960), *Report of the Committee on Children and Young Persons*, Cmnd 1191 (HMSO).

INGRAM, MICHAEL (1975), 'A Casework Study of a Disturbed Child and His Family', *Time to Consider*, Papers from a Family Service Unit (Bedford Square Press and FSU), pp. 39–51.

INNER LONDON PROBATION AND AFTER-CARE SERVICE (1975), 'Day Training Centres, First Report' and 'Is there an Alternative?', Information Bulletin No. 26, mimeographed (Inner London Probation and After-Care Service).

INSTITUTE OF ALMONERS (1949), 'Working Party on the Recruitment and Training of Almoners', mimeographed (Institute of Almoners).

Annual Report 1952–53 (Institute of Almoners).

(1953), 'Report of the Survey Committee', *The Almoner*, vol. 6, no. 2, pp. 61–9.

Annual Report 1954–55 (Institute of Almoners).

Annual Report 1956–57 (Institute of Almoners).

Annual Report 1962–63 (Institute of Almoners).

INSTITUTE OF MEDICAL SOCIAL WORKERS (1965), *Annual Report 1963–64* (Institute of Medical Social Workers).

(1969), *Annual Report 1968–69* (Institute of Medical Social Workers).

IRVINE, E. E. (1954), 'Research into Problem Families', *British Journal of Psychiatric Social Work*, vol. not stated, no. 1, pp. 24–33.

(1956), 'Renaissance in British Casework', *Social Work*, vol. 13, no. 3, pp. 187–94.

(1961), 'Psychosis in Parents: Mental Illness as a Problem for the Family', *British Journal of Psychiatric Social Work*, vol. 6, no. 1, pp. 21–6.

(1964), 'Children at Risk', *Case Conference*, vol. 10, no. 10, pp. 293–6.

(1966), 'A New Look at Casework', reproduced in Younghusband, E. (ed.), *New Developments in Casework* (Allen & Unwin).

(1967), 'The Hard to Like Family', *Case Conference*, vol. 14, no. 3, pp. 103–9.

(1969), 'Education for Social Work: Science or Humanity?', *Social Work*, vol. 26, no. 4, pp. 3–6.

'Community Care' (unpublished paper).

JACKA, ALAN (n.d.), *The ACCO Story* (Society for the Promotion of Education and Research in Social Work).

JANSEN, ELLY (1973), 'The Hostel as a Therapeutic Community and Its Implications for Training', *Residential Care* (Residential Care Association), pp. 89–97.

JEFFREYS, MARGOT (1965), *An Anatomy of Social Welfare Services* (Michael Joseph).

JEHU, D. (1967), *Learning Theory and Social Work* (Routledge & Kegan Paul).

JOBLING, MEGAN (1976), *The Abused Child* (National Children's Bureau).

JOINT UNIVERSITY COUNCIL FOR SOCIAL AND PUBLIC ADMINISTRATION (1951), 'Draft Outline for a One-Year Post-Certificate Course in Social Casework, prepared by a Sub-Committee of the Training Committee of the JUC', mimeographed (JUC).

(1952), *University Courses in Social Study* (JUC).

(1955), *University Courses in Social Administration* (JUC).

(1966), *Field Work in Social Administration Courses* (National Institute for Social Work Training).

JONES, DAVID and MAYO, MARJORIE (eds) (1974), *Community Work – One* (Routledge & Kegan Paul).

JONES, K. and HAMMOND, P. (1960), 'The Boundaries of Training', *British Journal of Psychiatric Social Work*, vol. 5, no. 4, pp. 172–7.

JONES, KATHLEEN (1964), *The Teaching of Social Studies in British Universities*, Occasional Papers on Social Administration No. 12 (Welwyn, Codicote Press).

(1967), 'Psychiatric Social Work Comes of Age', *British Journal of Psychiatric Social Work*, vol. 9, no. 2, pp. 60–5.

(1970), *The Development of Social Administration: Report of Conference on Social Administration* (Joint University Council for Social and Public Administration).

(ed.) (1972), *A History of the Mental Health Services* (Routledge & Kegan Paul).

(1975), *Opening the Door* (Routledge & Kegan Paul).

JONES, MAXWELL (1952), *Social Psychiatry: A Study of Therapeutic Communities* (Tavistock Publications).

JORDAN, W. (1970), *Client-Worker Transactions* (Routledge & Kegan Paul).

JOSEPH, SIR KEITH (1972), Address in *Report of the First National Conference of the Association of Directors of Social Services* (Association of Directors of Social Services), pp. 67–74.

JULIA, ANGELA (1967), 'Hostels for the Mentally Ill as a Stepping Stone in the Community' in *New Thinking about Institutional Care* (Association of Social Workers), pp. 68–75.

KAHN, JACK and NURSTEN, JEAN (1968), *Unwillingly to School* (Pergamon Press).

KELLMER PRINGLE, M. L. (1967), *Adoption: Facts and Fallacies* (Longman).

KELLY, A. D. (1961), 'Random Thoughts', *The Almoner*, vol. 14, no. 8, pp. 349–56.

KENSINGTON AND CHELSEA SOCIAL SERVICES DEPARTMENT (1974), *Handicap Survey Project Report* (Kensington and Chelsea Social Services Department).

KENT, B. (1974), 'The Totally Integrated Syllabus: An Experiment in Social Work Education', *International Social Work*, vol. XVII, no. 4, pp. 11–22.

KILBRANDON REPORT (1964), *Report of the Committee on Children and Young Persons (Scotland)*, Cmnd 2306 (Edinburgh, HMSO).

KING, JOAN F. S. (ed.) (1958, revised 1976), *The Probation Service* (Butterworth).

KING, ROY D., RAYNES, NORMA V. and TIZARD, JACK (1971), *Patterns of Residential Care* (Routledge & Kegan Paul).

KING'S FUND HOSPITAL CENTRE (1970), *Improving Care for the Elderly* (King's Fund Hospital Centre).

KING'S FUND HOSPITAL CENTRE and NATIONAL INSTITUTE FOR SOCIAL WORK (n.d.), 'Training for Volunteer Organizers, Report of a Joint Training Project 1974–75', mimeographed (King's Fund Hospital Centre).

KUENSTLER, PETER (ed.) (1954), *Social Group Work in Great Britain* (Faber & Faber).

LAMING, H. (1974), 'Residential Care' in *Self-Help, Participation and the Elderly*, Conference Proceedings (Southampton University).

LANSLEY, J. (1976), *Voluntary Organisations Facing Change* (Gulbenkian Foundation in association with the Joseph Rowntree Memorial Trust).

LAPPING, ANNE (1970), *Community Action*, Fabian Tract 400 (Fabian Society).

LEISSNER, A., ANGELA, K., HERDMAN, K. and DAVIES, E. V. (1971), *Advice, Guidance and Assistance* (Longman).

LEISSNER, A. and JOSLIN, J. (1974), 'Area Team Community Work: Achievement and Crisis' in Jones, D. and Mayo, M. (eds), *Community Work – One* (Routledge & Kegan Paul), pp. 118–47.

LEONARD, PETER (1966), *Sociology in Social Work* (Routledge & Kegan Paul).

LEWIS, HILDA (1954), *Deprived Children* (Oxford University Press). Local Government Board (1918), Circular 9 August 1918.

LOEWENSTEIN, C. (1974), 'An Intake Team in Action in a Social Services Department', *British Journal of Social Work*, vol. 4, no. 2, pp. 115–41.

LONDON BOROUGHS TRAINING COMMITTEE (Social Services) (1966), 'Statement of Principles for Training in the Health, Welfare and Children's Services', mimeographed (LBTC).

LONDON COUNCIL OF SOCIAL SERVICE (1974), *Community Workers and Their Employing Agencies in Greater London* (LCSS).

LONGFORD, LORD (chairman) (1964), *Crime: A Challenge to Us All*, Report of the Labour Party's Study Group (Transport House).

LYNCH, MARGARET A. (1975), 'Ill-health and Child Abuse', *The Lancet*, no. 7929, pp. 317–19.

MACKINTOSH REPORT (1951), *Report of the Committee on Social Workers in the Mental Health Services*, Cmnd 8260 (HMSO).

MALAN, D. (1963), *Brief Psychotherapy*, Mind and Medicine Monographs (Tavistock Publications).

MAPSTONE, ELIZABETH (1971), 'Social Work with the Parents of Children in Foster Care' in Tod, Robert (ed.), *Social Work in Foster Care* (Longman), pp. 98–104.

(1972), 'The Selection of the Children's Panel for the County of Fife: A Case Study', *British Journal of Social Work*, vol. 2, no. 4, pp. 445–69.

MARSHALL, TONY and ROSE, GORDON (1975), 'An Experimental Evaluation of School Social Work', *British Journal of Guidance and Counselling*, vol. 3, no. 1, pp. 2–14.

MARTIN REPORT (n.d. on Report, but actually published 1974), *Final Report of the Committee on Social Work Statistics*, Scottish Advisory Council on Social Work (Edinburgh, Social Work Service Group).

MATTHEWS, JOAN E. (1966), *Working with Youth Groups* (University of London Press).

MAUD REPORT (1967), *Report of the Committee on the Management of Local Government* (HMSO).

MAXWELL REPORT (1953), *Report of the Committee on Discharged Prisoners' Aid Societies* (HMSO).

MAYER, J. E. and TIMMS, N. (1970), *The Client Speaks* (Routledge & Kegan Paul).

MAYS, JOHN (1954), *Growing Up in the City* (Liverpool, University of Liverpool Press).

(1956), 'Social Research and Social Casework' in Association of Psychiatric Social Workers, *The Boundaries of Casework* (APSW).

MCBOYLE REPORT (1963), *Report of the Committee on the Prevention of Neglect of Children* (Edinburgh, HMSO).

MCDOUGALL, KAY (1970), 'The Advanced Course', *Case Conference*, vol. 16, no. 11, pp. 458–63.

(1972), 'BASW: The British Association of Social Workers' in Jones, Kathleen (ed.), *The Year Book of Social Policy in Britain, 1971* (Routledge & Kegan Paul), pp. 98–111.

MCKAY, ANN, GOLDBERG, E. M. and FRUIN, DAVID J. (1973), 'Consumers and a Social Services Department', *Social Work Today*, vol. 4, no. 16, pp. 486–91.

MCWHINNIE, A. (1967), *Adopted Children – How They Grow Up* (Routledge & Kegan Paul).

(1968), 'Group Counselling with 78 Adoptive Families', *Case Conference*, vol. 14, nos. 11 and 12, pp. 407–12 and 456–64.

MCWILLIAMS, WILLIAM (1975), 'Sentencing and Recidivism', *British Journal of Social Work*, vol. 5, no. 3, pp. 321–2.

MERCER, M. and ROBERTS, S. (1975), 'The Integration of Family Therapy into Social Work Practice' in Finn, W. H. (ed.), *Marital and Family Therapy* (Family Welfare Association), pp. 6–17.

MILLER, DEREK (1964), *Growth to Freedom* (Tavistock Publications).

MILLER, E. J. and GWYNNE, G. V. (1972), *A Life Apart* (Tavistock Publications).

MILLER, J. S. (1969), 'Social Work and Therapies of Control', *British Journal of Psychiatric Social Work*, vol. 10, no. 2, pp. 74–9.

MILNER HOLLAND REPORT (1965), *Report of the Committee on Housing in Greater London*, Cmnd 2605 (HMSO).

MINISTRY OF HEALTH (1963), *Health and Welfare: The Development of Community Care*, Cmnd 1973 (HMSO).

(1966), *Health and Welfare: The Development of Community Care*, Cmnd 3022 (HMSO).

(1970), Chief Medical Officer of Health and Chief Inspector, Home Office Children's Department, Circular CMO 2/70.

MINISTRY OF HOUSING AND LOCAL GOVERNMENT (1967), Report of the Central Housing Advisory Committee, *The Needs of New Communities* (HMSO).

MOON, E. M. (1958), 'The Use of Supervision in Providing a Casework Service to the Patient', *The Almoner*, vol. 11, no. 4, pp. 124–36.

(1965), *The First Two Years* (Institute of Medical Social Workers).

MORISON REPORT (1962), *Report of the Departmental Committee on the Probation Service*, Cmnd 1650 (HMSO).

MORRIS, PAULINE (1969), *Put Away* (Routledge & Kegan Paul).

MORRISON, R. L. (1967), 'The Idea of Therapeutic Communities' in *New Thinking about Institutional Care* (Association of Social Workers).

MORSE, MARY (1965), *The Unattached* (Harmondsworth, Pelican).

MOSCROP, MARTHA (1967), *In-service Training and Staff Development* (National Institute for Social Work Training).

NAPIER, HARRY (1972), 'Success and Failure in Foster Care', *British Journal of Social Work*, vol. 2, no. 2, pp. 187–204.

NATIONAL ASSISTANCE BOARD (1966), *Homeless Single Persons* (HMSO).

NATIONAL ASSOCIATION FOR THE CARE AND RESETTLEMENT OF OFFENDERS (1968), *The Training of After-Care Hostel Staffs* (NACRO).

(1976), *Training Programme and Hostel Services: 1975–1976* (NACRO).

NATIONAL ASSOCIATION FOR MENTAL HEALTH (1965), *Child Guidance and Child Psychiatry as an Integral Part of Community Services* (NAMH).

NATIONAL ASSOCIATION OF PROBATION OFFICERS (1956), 'Statement Adopted at NAPO Annual Conference, 1956', *Probation*, vol. 8, no. 10, pp. 141–5.

(December 1956), 'Generic Training for Social Work' (Notes written by an officer who had recently completed the Generic Training Course but who preferred to remain anonymous), *Probation*, vol. 8, no. 4, pp. 49–51.

(September 1957), 'Supervision in the Probation Service', *Probation*, vol. 8, no. 7, pp. 97–100.

Annual Report for 1958 (NAPO).

(June 1958), 'The Training of Probation Officers', *Probation*, vol. 8, no. 10, pp. 141–5.

(November 1966), editorial: 'Local Authority and Allied Social Services', *Probation*, vol. 12, no. 3, pp. 109–10.

(1968*a*), *Social Work in Prison*, report of a working party on prison welfare (NAPO).

(1968*b*), *Statement on Training* (NAPO).

NATIONAL CHILDREN'S BUREAU (1975), 'Children in Violent Families', mimeographed (NCB).

NATIONAL COMMUNITY DEVELOPMENT PROJECT (1974), *Inter-Project Report, 1973* (CDP Information and Intelligence Unit).

(1975), *Forward Plan 1975–76* (CDP Information and Intelligence Unit).

NATIONAL CORPORATION FOR THE CARE OF OLD PEOPLE, *Annual Report 1973* (NCCOP).

Annual Report 1974 (NCCOP).

NATIONAL COUNCIL FOR THE UNMARRIED MOTHER AND HER CHILD (1972), *Annual Report 1971–72* (NCUMC).

NATIONAL COUNCIL OF SOCIAL SERVICE (1969), *Supervision of Community Work Students* (NCSS).

(1970), *Fieldwork Supervision for Community Work Students* (NCSS).

56th Annual Report 1974–75 (NCSS).

NATIONAL INSTITUTE FOR SOCIAL WORK (1974), *An Introductory Account, 1961–1974* (NISW).

NATIONAL INSTITUTE FOR SOCIAL WORK TRAINING (1964), *Introduction to the Social Worker* (Allen & Unwin).

NATIONAL SOCIETY FOR THE PREVENTION OF CRUELTY TO CHILDREN (1974), *Yo Yo Children* (NSPCC).

(1976*a*), *At Risk*, Battered Child Research Team (Routledge & Kegan Paul).

(1976*b*), *Registers of Suspected Non-Accidental Injury*, Casework and Development Department (NSPCC).

NEILL, JUNE (1976), 'Study of Referrals', mimeographed report (Available from National Institute for Social Work research unit).

NEILL, JUNE, FRUIN, DAVID, GOLDBERG, E. MATILDA and WARBURTON, R. WILLIAMS (1973), 'Reactions to Integration', *Social Work Today*, vol. 4, no. 15, pp. 458–65.

NEILL, J., WARBURTON, R. W. and MCGUINESS, B. (1976), Social Worker's Viewpoint', *Social Work Today*, vol. 8, no. 5, pp. 9–14.

New Society (1975), Editorial, 'CDPs Writ Larger', vol. 33, no. 667, p. 122.

NEWSOME, A., THORNE, B. and WYLD, K. (1973), *Student Counselling in Practice* (University of London Press).

NEWTON, GEORGE (1966), 'The Impact of the First Two Years', *Medical Social Work*, vol. 19, no. 3, pp. 9–15.

NICHOLSON, JILL (1968), *Mother and Baby Homes* (Allen & Unwin).

NURSE, J. (1973), 'The Client, the Caseworker and the Absent Third Person', *British Journal of Social Work*, vol. 3, no. 1, pp. 39–53.

ORTHEN, MICHAEL (1975), 'Probation Welfare – Time to Think Again?', *Probation Journal*, vol. 22, no. 4, pp. 98–103.

OUNSTED, C., OPPENHEIMER, R. and LINDSEY, J. (1975), 'The Psychopathology and Psychotherapy of the Families: Aspects of Bonding Failure' in Franklin, A. White (ed.), *Concerning Child Abuse* (Churchill Livingstone), pp. 30–40.

OWTRAM, P. J. (1975), 'NSPCC Special Units', *Social Work Service*, no. 8, pp. 8–11.

PACKMAN, JEAN (1968), *Child Care: Needs and Numbers* (Allen & Unwin).

(1975), *The Child's Generation* (Oxford, Basil Blackwell).

PAGE, P. (1964), 'Mentally Ill and Homeless', a report on social work with homeless and destitute men in a reception centre, January to December 1964 (unpublished).

PARAD, HOWARD J. (1963), *Ego Oriented Casework* (New York, Family Service Association of America).

PARKER, R. H. (1966), *Decision in Child Care* (Allen & Unwin).

PAROLE BOARD, *Report of the Parole Board for 1971* (HMSO).

PARSLOE, P. (1967), 'Meeting the Needs of the Disturbed Child', *British Journal of Psychiatric Social Work*, vol. 9, no. 2, pp. 90–6.

PATERSON, J. (1949), 'The Work of an Almoner in General Practice', *The Almoner*, vol. 1, no. 11, pp. 230–3.

PEASE, K. (1975), *Community Care Orders*, Home Office research studies (HMSO).

PERLMAN, HELEN (1957), *Social Casework: A Problem Solving Process* (Chicago, University of Chicago Press).

PERSONAL SOCIAL SERVICES COUNCIL (1975), Smith, Jef, *Living and Working in Residential Homes* (PSSC).

Report 1975 (PSSC).

Report 1976 (PSSC).

Personal Social Services: Basic Information (1976a) (PSSC).

(1976b), *Social Service Manpower Resources* (PSSC).

PHILLIP, ALISTAIR E., MCCULLOCH, WALLACE J. and SMITH, NORMAN J. (1975), *Research and the Analysis of Social Data* (Pergamon Press).

PHILP, A. F. (1961), 'Character Disorders in the Socially Sick' in *Mental Health and Social Work: A Symposium: The Association of Social Workers (Gt. Britain) and the International Federation of Social Workers* (Association of Social Workers).

(1963), *Family Failure* (Faber & Faber).

PHILP, A. F. and TIMMS, N. (1957), *The Problem of the Problem Family* (FSU).

PICARDIE, M. (1967), 'Learning Theory and Casework', *Social Work*, vol. 24, no. 1, pp. 3–6.

PIERCY REPORT (1956), *Report of the Committee on the Rehabilitation, Training and Resettlement of Disabled Persons*, Cmnd 9883 (HMSO).

Pivot (1976), *Report of a Working Party on the National Association of Voluntary Help Organisers* (Berkhamsted, The Volunteer Centre).

PIZZEY, E. (1974), *Scream Quietly or the Neighbours will Hear* (Harmondsworth, Penguin).

PLOWDEN REPORT (1967), *Children and Their Primary Schools*, Report of the Central Advisory Council for Education (England) (HMSO).

POWER, MICHAEL (1962), 'Varieties of Casework', *Social Work*, vol. 19, no. 4, pp. 18–20.

PRATT, MARK (1975), 'Stress and Opportunity in the Role of the Prison Welfare Officer', *British Journal of Social Work*, vol. 5, no. 4, pp. 379–96.

PRE-SCHOOL PLAYGROUPS ASSOCIATION (1975), *Facts and Figures* (PPA).

PRICHARD, COLIN (1974), 'The EWO, Truancy and School Phobia', *Social Work Today*, vol. 5, no. 5, pp. 130–4.

PRINCIPAL PROBATION OFFICERS CONFERENCE (1968), *The Place of the Probation and After-Care Service in Judicial Administration* (CPPO).

PUGH, ELIZABETH (1968), *Social Work in Child Care* (Routledge & Kegan Paul).

RALPHS REPORT (1975), *Report of the Working Party on The Role and Training of Education Welfare Officers* (Local Government Training Board).

RATCLIFFE, T. A. and JONES, E. V. (1956), 'Intensive Casework in a Community Setting', *Case Conference*, vol. 2, no. 10, pp. 17–21.

RATOFF, LEN, ROSE, ANN and SMITH, CAROLE (1974), 'Social Workers and GPs', *Social Work Today*, vol. 5, no. 11, pp. 497–500.

RAYNOR, LOIS (1970), *Adoption of Non-White Children* (Allen & Unwin).

READING REPORT (1963), *The Place of Voluntary Service in After-Care* (HMSO). (1967), *The Place of Voluntary Service in After-Care* (HMSO).

REDCLIFFE-MAUD REPORT (1969), *Report of the Royal Commission on Local Government* (HMSO).

REHIN, G. F. (1969), 'The Practice of Psychiatric Social Work and the Future of Child Guidance Clinics', *Case Conference*, vol. 16, no. 2, pp. 42–8. (1972), 'Child Guidance at the Crossroads', *Social Work Today*, vol. 2, no. 24, pp. 21–4.

REID, W. J. and EPSTEIN, L. (1972), *Task-Centered Casework* (New York, Columbia University Press).

REID, W. J. and SHYNE, A. W. (1969), *Brief and Extended Casework* (New York, Columbia University Press).

RESIDENTIAL CHILD CARE ASSOCIATION (1969), *Residential Task in Child Care*, report of a study group sponsored by RCCA, ACCO and ACO (Banstead, Surrey, Residential Child Care Association).

RICHARDS, MARTIN (1975), 'Non-accidental Injury to Children in an Ecological Perspective' in Department of Health and Social Security, *Non-Accidental Injury to Children* (HMSO), pp. 5–12.

ROBERTS, W. L. (1968), 'Working with the Family Group in a Child Guidance Clinic', *British Journal of Psychiatric Social Work*, vol. 9, no. 4, pp. 175–9.

ROBINSON, JAMES (1971), 'Experimental Research in Social Casework', *British Journal of Social Work*, vol. 1, no. 4, pp. 463–79.

RODGERS, BARBARA (1964), *The Careers of Social Studies Students* (Welwyn, Codicote Press).

RODGERS, BARBARA and DIXON, JULIA (1960), *Portrait of Social Work* (Oxford University Press).

RODGERS, BARBARA N. and STEVENSON, JUNE (1973), *New Portrait of Social Work* (Heinemann).

ROLPH, C. H. (1970), *Homeless from Prison* (privately printed).

ROOFF, MADELINE (1972), *A Hundred Years of Family Welfare* (Michael Joseph).

ROSE, GORDON and MARSHALL, TONY F. (1974), *Counselling and School Social Work* (Chichester, Wiley & Sons).

ROSE, JUNE (1970), *Changing Focus: The Development of Blind Welfare in Britain* (Hutchinson).

ROSEMAN, R. and COOKE, J. (1964), 'Social Groupwork with Children in a Family Casework Agency', *Social Work*, vol. 21, no. 4, pp. 16–20.

ROSS, MURRAY (1955), *Community Organisation* (New York, Harper Brothers).

ROWBOTTOM, RALPH, HEY, ANTHEA and BILLIS, DAVID (1974), *Social Services Departments: Developing Patterns of Work and Organisation* (Heinemann).

ROWE, JANE and LAMBERT, LYDIA (1973), *Children Who Wait* (Association of British Adoption Agencies).

ROYAL COMMISSION ON THE LAW RELATING TO MENTAL ILLNESS AND MENTAL DEFICIENCY REPORT (1957), Cmnd 169 (HMSO).

RYAN, T. M. (1967), 'The Administrative Structure of the Child Guidance Service', *Social Work*, vol. 24, no. 3, pp. 23–7.

SAINSBURY, E. (1970), *Social Diagnosis in Casework* (Routledge & Kegan Paul).
　(1975a), 'A National Profile of FSU Families', *FSU Quarterly*, no. 8, pp. 20–30.
　(1975b), *Social Work with Families* (Routledge & Kegan Paul).

SAINSBURY, P. (1964), 'Some Aspects of Evaluating Community Care', *British Journal of Psychiatric Social Work*, vol. 7, no. 3, pp. 142–6.

SAINSBURY, SALLY (1970), *Registered as Disabled* (Bell).

SANDERS, HUGH (1963), 'Widening Horizons', *Probation*, vol. 10, no. 3, pp. 84–6.

SATIR, V. (1964), *Conjoint Family Therapy* (Palo Alto, Science and Behavior Books).

SCHOOLS COUNCIL (1967), *Counselling in Schools* (HMSO).

SCOTT, P. D. (1973), 'Fatal Battered Baby Cases', *Medicine, Science and the Law*, vol. 13, no. 3. Reprinted in *Social Work Service*, no. 4, 1974, pp. 12–21.

SCOTTISH ADVISORY COUNCIL ON SOCIAL WORK (1974), *Field Work Staffing (Scotland)* (Edinburgh, Social Work Services Group).

SCOTTISH EDUCATION DEPARTMENT (1970), *Social Work in Scotland in 1969*, Cmnd 4475 (Edinburgh, HMSO).

SCOTTISH EDUCATION AND SCOTTISH HOME AND HEALTH DEPARTMENTS (1966), *Social Work and the Community*, Cmnd 3065 (Edinburgh, HMSO).

SEEBOHM REPORT (1968), *Report of the Committee on Local Authority and Allied Personal Social Services,* Cmnd 3703 (HMSO).

SEGLOW, J., PRINGLE, M. and WEDGE, P. (1972), *Growing Up Adopted* (Slough, National Foundation for Educational Research).

SHAPIRO, PAULINE (1965), 'Children's Play as a Concern of Family Caseworkers' in Younghusband, E. (ed.), *Social Work with Families* (Allen & Unwin), pp. 71–9.

SHAW, MARGARET (1974), *Social Work in Prison*, Home Office research studies (HMSO).

SILBERMAN, M., CHAPMAN, B., SINCLAIR, I., SNOW, D. and LEISSNER, A. (1971), *Explorations in After-Care*, Home Office research studies (HMSO).

SIMON, BRIAN (1967), *The Nature and Objectives of Professional Education* (Association of Social Work Teachers).

SINCLAIR, I. (1971), *Probation Hostels for Boys*, Home Office research studies (HMSO).

SINCLAIR, I., SHAW, M. J. and TROUP, J. (1974), 'The Relationship between Introversion and Response to Casework in a Prison Setting', *British Journal of Social and Clinical Psychology*, vol. 13, no. 1, pp. 51–60.

SINFIELD, A. (1961), *Which Way for Social Work?*, Fabian Tract No. 893 (Fabian Society).

SKEFFINGTON REPORT (1969), *People and Planning* (HMSO).

SKINNER, A. E. and CASTLE, R. L. (1969), *78 Battered Children* (NSPCC).

SKYNNER, A. C. R. (1967), 'Diagnosis, Consultation and Co-ordination of Treatment' in *Report of the National Association for Mental Health Inter-clinic Conference* (NAMH).
　(1971a), 'A Group-Analytic Approach to Conjoint Family Therapy', *Social Work Today*, vol. 2, no. 8, pp. 3–11.

(1971*b*), 'Indications for and against Conjoint Family Therapy', *Social Work Today*, vol. 2, no. 7, pp. 3–5.

(1971*c*), 'The Minimum Sufficient Network', *Social Work Today*, vol. 2, no. 9, pp. 3–7.

SLUCKIN, A. and JEHU, D. (1969), 'A Behavioural Approach in the Treatment of Elective Mutism', *British Journal of Psychiatric Social Work*, vol. 10, no. 2, pp. 70–3.

SMITH, CYRIL S., FARRANT, M. R. and MARCHANT, H. J. (1972), *The Wincroft Youth Project* (Tavistock Publications).

SMITH, DAVID J. (1976), *The Facts of Racial Disadvantage: A National Survey* (Political and Economic Planning).

SMITH, D. M. (ed.) (1974), *Families and Groups: A Unit at Work* (Family Service Units).

SMITH, GERTRUDE (1975), 'Institutional Dependence in Reverse', *Social Work Today*, vol. 6, no. 14, pp. 426–8.

SMITH, JEF (1972), 'Top Jobs in the Social Services' in Jones, Kathleen (ed.), *The Year Book of Social Policy in Britain, 1971* (Routledge & Kegan Paul), pp. 16–27.

SMITH, S., HANSON, R. and NOBEL, S. (1975), 'Parents of Battered Children: A Controlled Study' in Franklin, A. White (ed.), *Concerning Child Abuse* (Churchill Livingstone), pp. 41–8.

SMITH, WINIFRED and BATE, HELEN (1953), *Family Casework and the Country Dweller* (Family Welfare Association).

SNELLING, JEAN (1970), *The Contribution of the Institute of Medical Social Workers to Education for Social Work* (Association of Social Work Teachers).

SOCIAL SCIENCE RESEARCH COUNCIL and DHSS (1974), *Transmitted Deprivation*, First report of the Joint Working Party (SSRC).

(1975), *Transmitted Deprivation*, Second report of the Joint Working Party (SSRC).

Social Work in Scotland (1969), Report by a Working Party on the Social Work (Scotland) Act 1968 (Department of Social Administration, University of Edinburgh).

SOCIAL WORK SERVICES GROUP (1971), Circular No. SW75/1971.

(1972), *Proposals for Development of Social Work Services* (Edinburgh, SWSG).

(1974), *Scottish Social Work Statistics* (Edinburgh, HMSO).

/SCOTTISH HOME AND HEALTH DEPARTMENT (1975), *Non-Accidental Injury to Children*, NHS Circular No. 1975 (Gen. 23).

SPECHT, HARRY (1975), 'The Dilemma of Community Work in the United Kingdom: A Comment', *Policy and Politics*, vol. 4, no. 1, pp. 59–71.

SPEED, MAURICE (1974), 'The Aged and the Social Services Department' in Brown, Malcolm J. (ed.), *Social Issues and the Social Services* (Knight), pp. 123–44.

SPENCER, J. (1964), *Stress and Release in an Urban Estate* (Tavistock Publications).

STACE, SHEILA (1976), *Encouraging Volunteer Bureaux* (National Council of Social Service).

STANDING CONFERENCE OF ORGANISATIONS OF SOCIAL WORKERS (n.d.), *Discussion Paper No. 1*.

STAPLETON, PAT (1976), 'Culture Clashes and the Child Minder', *Social Work Today*, vol. 7, no. 9, pp. 271–2.

STEVENSON, OLIVE (1973), *Claimant or Client?* (Allen & Unwin).

STREATFEILD REPORT (1961), *Report of the Interdepartmental Committee on the Business of the Criminal Courts* (HMSO).

STURGESS, JANET and HEAL, KEVIN (1976), 'Non-Accidental Injury to Children under the Age of 17', *Social Work Service*, no. 9, pp. 39–45.

STURTON, SHEILA (1972), 'Developing Group Work in a Casework Agency', *British Journal of Social Work*, vol. 2, no. 2, pp. 143–58.

The Teaching of Sociology to Students of Education and of Social Work (1961), Sociological Review Monograph No. 4 (Keele University).

THOMAS, DAVID N. (1976), *Organizing for Social Change* (Allen & Unwin).

THOMAS, E. I. (1969), 'Contributions of the Socio-Behavioural Approach to Inter-personal Helping in Social Work', *British Journal of Psychiatric Social Work*, vol. 10, no. 2, pp. 61–9.

THOMAS, J. E. (1965), 'Aftercare and the Prison Officer', *Prison Service Journal*, vol. 4, no. 16, pp. 18–21.

(1972), *The English Prison Officer since 1850* (Routledge & Kegan Paul).

THOMAS, MIKE (1974), *The Volunteer, Community and Society* (Berkhamsted, The Volunteer Centre).

THOMAS, N. A. (1973), 'The Seebohm Committee' in Chapman, Richard A. (ed.), *The Role of Commissions in Policy Making* (Allen & Unwin), pp. 143–73.

THOMPSON, S. (1966), 'Working with Families in a Community Service', *British Journal of Psychiatric Social Work*, vol. 8, no. 4, pp. 21–7.

THOMPSON, SHEILA and KAHN, H. H. (1970), *The Group Process as a Helping Technique* (Pergamon Press).

THORNBOROUGH, PEGGY (1974), 'Differential Treatment for Offenders on Probation', *International Social Work*, vol. 17, no. 4, pp. 36–43.

THORPE, DAVID and HORN, DAVID (1973), 'The Shape of Intermediate Treatment', *Social Work Today*, vol. 3, no. 25, pp. 8–11.

THORPE, ROSALIND (1974), 'Mum and Mrs. So and So', *Social Work Today*, vol. 4, no. 22, pp. 691–5.

THWAITES, JEAN (1950), 'Draft for a Code for Social Workers', *The Almoner*, vol. 3, no. 6, pp. 237–42.

TIMMS, NOEL (1964), *Psychiatric Social Work in Great Britain, 1939–1962* (Routledge & Kegan Paul).

(1969), *Social Casework* (Routledge & Kegan Paul).

TITMUSS, R. M. (1958), *Essays on the Welfare State* (Allen & Unwin).

(1970a), foreword to Apte, Robert Z., *Half-Way Houses* (Bell).

(1970b), preface to Goldber, E. M., *Helping the Aged* (Allen & Unwin).

TIZARD, J. (1964), *Community Services for the Mentally Handicapped* (Oxford University Press).

TIZARD, J. and GRAD, J. (1961), *The Mentally Handicapped and Their Families* (Oxford University Press).

TODD, JOAN (1967), *Social Work with the Mentally Subnormal* (Routledge & Kegan Paul).

TONGE, W. L., JONES, D. S. and HILLAM, SUSAN (1975), *Families without Hope* (Royal College of Psychiatrists).

TOWLE, CHARLOTTE (1945 and 1965), *Common Human Needs* (New York, Association of Social Workers); rev. ed. 1973, (Allen & Unwin).

(1954), *The Learner in Education for the Professions* (Chicago, University of Chicago Press).

TOWNSEND, PETER (1957), *The Family Life of Old People* (Routledge & Kegan Paul).

(1965), *The Last Refuge* (Routledge & Kegan Paul).

TOWNSEND, PETER and WEDDERBURN, DOROTHY (1965), *The Aged in the Welfare State* (Bell).

TRASLER, GORDON (1959), 'Planning a Psychology Course for Social Science Students', mimeographed (Joint University Council for Social and Public Administration).

(1960), *In Place of Parents* (Routledge & Kegan Paul).

TRISELIOTIS, JOHN (1970), *In Search of Origins, Experiences of Adopted People* (Routledge & Kegan Paul).

TUCKEY, LINDA, PARFITT, JESSIE and TUCKEY, JACK (1973), *Handicapped School Leavers* (Windsor, National Foundation for Educational Research).

TURNER, MERFYN (1961), *Norman House, the First Five Years* (privately published).

TUTERS, E. (1974), 'Short-term Contracts: Visha', *Social Work Today*, vol. 5, no. 8, pp. 226–31.

TYLER, RALPH (1950), *Basic Principles of Curriculum and Instruction* (Chicago, University of Chicago Press).

UNDERWOOD REPORT (1955), *Report of the Committee on Maladjusted Children* (HMSO).

VENABLES, ETHEL (1971), *Counselling* (Rugby, National Marriage Guidance Council).

VERCOE, K. (n.d.), *Helping Prisoners' Families* (National Association for the Care and Resettlement of Offenders).

VOLUNTEER CENTRE (1975), *Training for Voluntary Service Co-ordinators in the Health and Social Services* (Berkhamsted, The Volunteer Centre).

WALKER, A. (1970), 'Child Guidance at the Crossroads', *British Journal of Psychiatric Social Work*, vol. 10, no. 3, pp. 11–15.

WALLIS, J. H. and BOOKER, H. S. (1958), *Marriage Counselling* (Routledge & Kegan Paul.

WALROND-SKINNER, S. (1974), 'Training for Family Therapy', *Social Work Today*, vol. 5, no. 5, pp. 149–54.

(1975), 'Family Therapy: The Theoretical Background' in Fiddis, O. (ed.), *Proceedings of the Association for the Psychiatric Study of Adolescents*, Tenth Annual Conference (APSA), pp. 34–8.

WATKINS, OWEN (1971), *Professional Training for Youth Work* (Leicester, Youth Service Information Centre).

WELSH OFFICE (1974), Circular 123/74.

WILLIAMS REPORT (1967), *Caring for People* (Allen & Unwin).

WILLS, W. DAVID (1970), *A Place Like Home* (Allen & Unwin).

WILSON, HARRIET C. (1959), 'Problem Families and the Concept of Immaturity' *Case Conference*, vol. 6, no. 5, pp. 115–18.

WINNICOTT, CLARE (1955), 'Casework Techniques in the Child Care Service', reproduced in Younghusband, E. (ed.) (1966), *New Developments in Casework* (Allen & Unwin), pp. 135–54.

(1964), *Child Care and Social Work* (Welwyn, Codicote Press).

(1968), *Residential Staff in Child Care* (Residential Child Care Association).

WOOLFE, R. (1970), 'The Supply and Demand of Face to Face Youth and Community Workers in England and Wales', mimeographed (Leicester, Youth Service Association).

WOOTTON, BARBARA (1959), *Social Science and Social Pathology* (Allen & Unwin).

WRIGHT, M. (1974), 'Probation with Teeth?', *Probation Journal*, vol. 21, no. 4, pp. 103–5.

YOUNG, M. and WILLMOTT, P. (1959), *Family and Kinship in East London* (Routledge & Kegan Paul).

YOUNGER REPORT (1974), *Young Adult Offenders*, Report of the Advisory Council on the Penal System (HMSO).

YOUNGHUSBAND, EILEEN L. (1947), *The Employment and Training of Social Workers* (Dunfermline, Carnegie United Kingdom Trust).

(1951), *Social Work in Britain* (Dunfermline, Carnegie United Kingdom Trust).

(1956), 'Trends in Social Work Education', *Social Work*, vol. 13, no. 4, pp. 241–56.

YOUNGHUSBAND, E., BIRCHALL, D., DAVIE, R. and KELLMER PRINGLE, M. L. (eds), (1970), *Living with Handicap* (National Bureau for Co-operation in Child Care).

YOUNGHUSBAND REPORT (1959), *Report of the Working Party on Social Workers in the Local Authority Health and Welfare Services* (HMSO).

Index

Aberdeen University 87
adoption 73–9; illegitimate children 77; non-white children 76
Adoption Act, 1958 73
Adoption Resource Exchange 76
Advisory Council on Child Care for England and Wales 78
Advisory Council on Probation and After-Care 138, 139, 142, 292
Advisory Council on the Treatment of Offenders 98, 111
after-care 110–14; mental health 165–6, 168–70; voluntary 110–11; volunteers in 113–14
Age Concern 198, 200, 201, 256, 261
Albermarle Committee 283
Alcoholics Anonymous 170, 273
almoners 145–8, 284; see also medical social workers
approved schools 48, 58, 91; see also community homes
area health authorities 158, 160, 248
area teams 245
assessment 24, 32, 46, 211
assessment centres 58; see also community homes
Association for Group Psychotherapy 193
Association of British Adoption and Fostering Agencies 73
Association of Child Care Officers 53, 55, 75, 76, 81, 85, 239
Association of Child Psychotherapists 184
Association of Children's Officers 53, 55, 80, 81, 91, 92, 232, 285
Association of Psychiatric Social Workers 23, 162, 178, 179, 180, 181, 185, 188, 190, 191, 192, 222; Standing Advisory Committee on Training 190, 191
Association of Social Workers 30
Association of Workers with Maladjusted Children 53
Aves Report 272, 274, 275, 276

Barnardo's 37, 88, 257–8, 276, 319
Bevan, A. 249
Birch Report 34, 271, 283, 292, 295–300, 313
Birmingham Polytechnic 142
Birmingham University 133, 161
Blackfriars Settlement 83, 265
blind people 206, 214, 226, 261–2

boarding out officers 42, 80, 86; see also child care officers
Boarding Out Regulations 66
Bristol University 92, 138
British Association of Residential Settlements 265; see also British Association of Settlements and Social Action Centres
British Association of Settlements and Social Action Centres 265
British Association of Social Workers 26, 27–8, 31, 95, 118, 122, 156, 158, 159, 175, 184, 276; career grade working party 311–13; see also Child Guidance Special Interest Group
British Broadcasting Corporation 94
British Council of Churches 266
British Medical Association 184
British Psychological Society 184
British Red Cross Society 197, 273
Brown, Sibyl Clement 53
Butterworth Report 140, 293, 295, 303, 310, 311

Caldecott Community 89
Cambridge House 265
Cambridge University, Institute of Criminology 139, 143
Canford Families Study 228–9
Caplan, G. 187
care orders 48
career grades 310–13
Carlton Approved School 91
Carnegie Reports 34
Carnegie United Kingdom Trust 227
caseloads 242, 303, 306–10
case recording 23–4, 46
casework 26; in probation 101, 102–3
Caversham Project 157–8
Central After-Care Association 111
Central Council for the Disabled 261
Central Council for Education and Training in Social Work 140, 141, 174, 226, 238; courses 85–6, 96, 143, 198; working parties 33, 142, 319
Central Training Council in Child Care 53, 81–3, 85–97
Certificate in Social Service 209, 279, 318, 319–20, 323
Certificate in Social Work 292
Certificate of Qualification in Social Work 141, 142, 209, 214

SOCIAL WORK IN BRITAIN: 1950–1975

To K. E. of H. and S. K.
with gratitude

The author and publishers wish to thank the Trustees of the Carnegie United Kingdom Trust for a generous contribution to the publication costs of this volume.

Social Work in Britain: 1950-1975

A Follow-up Study

VOLUME 2

EILEEN YOUNGHUSBAND

London
GEORGE ALLEN & UNWIN
Boston   Sydney

First published in 1978

British Library Cataloguing in Publication Data

Younghusband, Dame Eileen Louise
Social Work in Britain: 1950–1975.
Vol. 2
1. Social service – Great Britain – History –
20th century
I. Title
361'.941   HV245   77–30738

ISBN 0–04–360044–1   *Hardback*

Printed in Great Britain
in 10 on 11 point Times
by Unwin Brothers Limited
The Gresham Press, Old Woking, Surrey

Acknowledgements

The Carnegie United Kingdom Trust sponsored and published my two post-war inquiries: *The Education and Training of Social Workers* (1947) and *Social Work in Britain* (1951). The Trust's generous sponsorship has also made possible this present study of some developments between 1950 and 1975. Thanks are also due to the Gulbenkian Foundation for kindly administering the grant.

I am indebted to Elizabeth Irvine for a substantial contribution and to Sylvia Watson and Fred Jarvis for sections on professional associations. Many organisations and individuals have generously contributed information, read draft chapters and given advice or permission to quote. They include Age Concern, the Association of British Adoption and Fostering Agencies, the Association of Directors of Social Services, the Association of Teachers in Social Work Education, Geraldine Aves, Mary Barker, Barnardo's, Rose Mary Braithwaite, the British Association of Settlements, the British Association of Social Workers, Sibyl Clement Brown, Megan Browne, Zofia Butrym, the Carnegie United Kingdom Trust, Derek Carter, the Central Council for Education and Training in Social Work, Olive Chandler, the Church Army, the Church of England Board for Social Responsibility, the Community Development Project Information and Intelligence Unit, the Community Relations Commission, Joan Cooper, Joan Court, Anne Cronin, the Department of Health and Social Security (Social Work Service), the Family Service Units, the Family Welfare Association, the Group for the Advancement of Psychotherapy in Social Work, Phoebe Hall, Florence Hollis, Robert Holman, the Home Office, Dorothy Howell-Thomas, Elisabeth Hunter, the Inner London Probation and After-Care Service, the Institute of Marital Studies, the Institute of Social Welfare, David Jones, Robin Huws Jones, the Joint University Council for Social and Public Administration, Ann Kelly, Bessie Kent, Margaret Lester, Katharine Lloyd, the Local Government Training Board, P. J. MacRae, Joan Matthews, Eric Miller, Richard Mills, the National Association for the Care and Resettlement of Offenders, the National Association of Probation Officers, the National Council of Social Service, the National Marriage Guidance Council, the National Institute for Social Work (including the librarians), the National Society for Mentally Handicapped Children, the National Society for the Prevention of Cruelty to Children, the National Youth Bureau, George Newton, Priscilla Norman, Jean Nursten, Pamela Page, the Personal Social Services Council, Dorothy Pettes, the Polytechnic of North London, the Pre-School Playgroups Association, Colin Prichard, the Prison Service Staff College, Hilda Rawlings, Helen Rees, Gordon Rose, Margaret Roxburgh, Eric Sainsbury, the Salvation Army, the Scottish Office (Social Work Services Group), Ian Sinclair, Adrian Sinfield, Muriel Smith, Jean Snelling, the Social Science Research Council, the Social Work

Advisory Service, the Southern and Western Regional Association for the Blind, Harry Specht, Marjorie Steel, Sara Stevens, Janie Thomas, T. Treunheuz, the Welsh Office, Reg Wright. I am also grateful to the many who helped, knowingly or unknowingly, by discussions about the past, present and future of social work and by keeping me well briefed on some activities without any specific request: they include the National Children's Bureau, the Tavistock Institute of Human Relations and the Calouste Gulbenkian Foundation. I am also indebted to the Home Office and to the Controller of Her Majesty's Stationery Office for permission to use Home Office material and to quote from Stationery Office publications, especially the Seebohm and Younghusband Reports.

Eileen Younghusband
November, 1976

Contents

Therapeutic Communities
People in Long-Stay Institutions
Caseworkers and Residential Settings
Residential Care Staff
Alternative Organisational Patterns for Residential Institutions in
Social Services Departments
Guidelines for the Future
  Training for Residential Care
Problems and Blind Spots in the 1950s
The Breakthrough of the William's Report
The Council for Training in Social Work and Courses in Residential
Social Work
The CCETSW and Training for Residential Social Work
Developments in Training within the Penal System
  Staffs of Hostels for Offenders
  Assistant Borstal and Prison Governors

Introduction and Some Conclusions
Hostels for Young People in Care
Hostels for Psychiatric Patients
Hostels for Those before the Courts
  Hostels Run by Voluntary Organisations
  Probation Homes and Hostels

PART THREE: PEOPLE WITH SPECIAL PROBLEMS

Introduction
Ethnic Minority Groups
The Homeless
Multiproblem Families
  Some Research on Multiproblem Families

Battered Children
  The Beginnings of Action
  Research Findings
  NSPCC Initiative
  Government Action in England, Scotland and Wales
  Some Pointers
Battered Wives

Focus on Unmarried Mothers
Mother and Baby Homes: A Study in the Mid-1960s
Changing Services for Unmarried Mothers in the Late 1960s
Training for Moral Welfare
One-Parent Families and the Finer Report

PART FOUR: BEYOND THE BOUNDS OF SOCIAL WORK?

List of Tables

PART ONE   EDUCATION FOR SOCIAL WORK

Chapter 1

Developments in Education for Social Work

INTRODUCTION: CHANGES BETWEEN 1950 AND 1975

By 1950 modern social work education (i.e. the application of theory in practice, learning how to make knowledge operational) had barely started, except in the mental health courses, and later only spread slowly. In the social work field as a whole in the 1950s, few people had any training, largely because no opportunities then existed apart from the small intake on social science university courses, the mental health, medical social work, child care, probation, and moral welfare trainings and various *ad hoc* specialised short courses, for instance for NSPCC inspectors or home teachers of the blind. The foundations of social work education had to be laid against many odds, and social work teachers faced conflicts in both the universities and the fieldwork agencies at a time when they themselves were struggling to discover a new identity.

The first stage was the long struggle to clarify the aims of the social science courses, i.e. whether they offered a good grounding in the social sciences, a pre-professional course, or the first stage of actual social work training. Fortunately the professionals lost the battle to make them more vocational. It was also fortunate that old university rigidities about vocational training changed, so that this began to be built on a foundation of social science, pre-professional courses.

In this second stage from about 1950, pressure was mounting for generic casework courses in the universities. This resulted in 'the Carnegie experiment' described in more detail below.

The third stage began in 1961 with two-year, integrated – i.e. social studies and professional – courses in college of further education and university extramural departments. In time in employment these students achieved equal status with university students. As a result, the essential lesson began to be learnt that any professional course must aim at competence in practice, that knowledge must be both relevant and applied. At each stage, practice and teaching related to it were forced to go ahead of verified knowledge.

Three publicly financed training councils, the Probation Advisory and Training Board (PATB) (1936), the Central Training Council in Child Care (CTC) (1947), and the Council for Training in Social Work (CTSW) (1962) stimulated, guided and to some extent financed training in their respective fields by methods discussed below in chapter 7 and elsewhere.

Throughout the period, the battles for quantity and quality had both to be fought at the same time. The alternative, in fact adopted by the Association of Psychiatric Social Workers (APSW) and to some extent by the Institute of Almoners, would have been careful, limited advance where conditions were propitious, rather than starting fresh courses with additional resources and then improving their standards by degrees. This approach placed great burdens on social work teachers, supervisors, and indeed students. But struggles to raise the level of training resulted in more people becoming clear about aims, while in some progressive services a combination of trained staff and good agency practice raised standards, so in a sense quantity was an essential foundation for quality.

The first stage began with separate, unrelated services and *ad hoc* specialised training. By the fourth stage in the early 1970s the services, training councils, and professional associations had been homogenised into personal social services (in Scotland social work) departments; the Central Council for Education and Training in Social Work (CCETSW) which had lengthened professional courses to two years and unified them on broadly comparable generic syllabuses; and the British Association of Social Workers (BASW). In this new era the problems were different but as great as they had ever been and the outcome uncertain.

PRESSURE FOR UNIVERSITY 'GENERIC' SOCIAL WORK COURSES: THE BACKGROUND OF THE CARNEGIE EXPERIMENT

The first Carnegie report on *The Employment and Training of Social Workers* (Younghusband, 1947) recommended the setting up of an independent, but university-affiliated, school of social work: the title was changed to 'institute of applied social studies' in the second report, *Social Work in Britain* (Younghusband, 1951). Its dual purpose would have been research and the training of post-graduate students on fifteen-month generic courses. The syllabus would have included social science subjects, casework and group work, and options according to students' particular interests. Theory and practice would have been closely related by caseworkers and group-work staff and by full-time supervisors. Part-time advanced courses for practising social workers and others would have been equally important. The other parallel purpose would have been social work research and examples of necessary action research were given.

In 1947 the proposal to set up such a post-graduate school of social work looked revolutionary and very costly. The Carnegie Trust convened a small joint committee of Trustees, academics and social workers to consider the proposal. This never generated any momentum: the independent members were too unclear to produce a viable blue print and the Trustees decided that financial considerations alone were sufficient to prevent them from going any further with the proposal, though they remained interested in doing what they could to improve training and encourage research. The deadlock persisted because although the professional associations and the universities both wanted to move away from wasteful, narrowly specialised and sometimes educationally unsound trainings, this was impossible for any one training organisation and the universities lacked financial resources to break fresh ground.

The Joint University Council for Social and Public Administration (JUC) held a meeting in 1949 to discuss the first report and subsequently the honorary secretary wrote to the Secretary of the Carnegie Trust to say:

'With the sections of the Report which analysed and assessed the present courses of training, there was general agreement . . . There is, again, complete unanimity in the opinion that post-credential courses of training are absolutely essential and that there is a great lack of qualified social workers who are capable of filling the higher posts or of acting as expert consultants when new projects are under discussion . . . the main discussion centred round Miss Younghusband's recommendation that a School of Social Work should be established with the dual function of training post-graduate students and carrying out research which might help us to answer some of the problems that are bothering us . . . there was a strong balance of opinion in favour of such a development though . . . there was not complete agreement with regard to the constitution and functions of such a School.' (Unpublished correspondence)

Next year the JUC set up a sub-committee of its training committee to produce a syllabus for a one-year, post-certificate course in social casework. Its report affirmed the pressure for university courses in casework which would supersede the professional courses outside the university, and emphasised the perplexities within the universities about the right way to improve the quality of what they offered. It saw skilled supervision of practical work as a key issue, and thought that the proposed course would in time produce trained social workers whose own experience of supervision would substantially help university departments and might make it possible to abandon other professional courses. The proposed course would lessen 'the threat of over-specialisation in social work', though it would be essential for professional associations and employing bodies to agree that those who completed the course would be as acceptable as others who had taken specialist courses.

The proposed 'generic' course was 'based on the assumption that the basic skill of the social worker is the same in all situations though it has of course to be adapted to the setting in which it is exercised. The social worker has in fact to be trained first and foremost to understand human beings who are the same people wherever they are' (JUC, 1951, mimeographed report).

The report suggested that as an experiment not more than two universites might run a course for fifteen to twenty students. 'There should be a full-time tutor (with adequate clerical help available) and enough good caseworkers in the district to provide opportunity for *supervised* practical work' (italics in original). It made the far-sighted proposal that agencies should appoint 'suitable persons' and that the university should pay for part of their time or (preferably) that the university should appoint three or four well-selected supervisors and 'lend them as honorary staff members' to appropriate agencies. The closest co-operation between them and the tutor would be essential and they should do some teaching on the course. They would be working members of the agency's staff and carry a caseload as well as supervising students, who would have two substantial, practical-work placements. 'The core of the syllabus would be the theory and practice of social casework in different settings.' This lecture course would run throughout the year. There would also be a course taught by a psychiatrist on psychiatric information for social workers (with a similar content to courses later entitled 'human growth and development'). There should also be a course on administration of social agencies (based on the students' practical experience); an odd, hotchpotch course on medical information for social workers; and optional courses on methods of social research, sociology, and social philosophy. There should not be an examination, but the university should award a certificate on the basis of the students' written work (including a 'reasoned report of about 5,000 words on some part of the practical work'), supervisors' reports and a viva.

The scheme would cost 'a good deal of money' (about £2,500 rising to £4,250 a year). Possible sources of grant aid were the University Grants Committee or 'some outside body such as the Carnegie Trustees'. This report is significant for its emphasis on substantial and well-supervised field-work to relate theory and practice and on the importance of properly qualified supervisors on the university staff; for what it left out as well as what it included in the syllabus; for the reliance on what was later known as continuous assessment; for its optimism about the load which one tutor could carry; and for its frank acceptance of vocational training for social work in the university. The report was unanimously accepted in principle by the JUC and the honorary secretary wrote to the Carnegie Trust to say so.

In the summer of 1950 while the supplementary Carnegie report, *Social Work in Britain* (Younghusband, 1951) was in typescript, Richard Titmuss, newly appointed to the chair in social administration at LSE, came to see the author and borrowed the draft. Subsequently he said: 'I think this is something we ought to do at LSE.' A working group was set up in the social science department and in 1951 a memorandum was sent to the Carnegie Trust on the lines of the proposal in the report, and applying for a grant of £75,000 over ten years to set up an Institute of Applied Social Studies, which might be under the wing of LSE until it had grown to independence. The Trustees unanimously turned down such a costly project, perhaps not realising its potentialities.

Of course it was easier by 1975 than in 1951 to see the difference that might have been made by an institute of this calibre which would have produced more and better qualified social workers in time for the training explosions of the 1960s; which would have developed group work as well as casework; and in which the sadly lacking research would have been as important as training. It could, indeed, have made a crucial contribution to professional and advanced training, to research, consultation, interdisciplinary seminars and at other key points. It could have provided that 'centre of excellence' so greatly needed to redress the balance when all later efforts were concentrated on basic cources – a balance which it was more difficult to redress by the 1960s and 1970s. When the National Institute for

Social Work began to fill this vacuum from 1961, ten crucial years had been lost. Undoubtedly the project would have been far more costly than the Carnegie reports and the LSE application envisaged – but not to embark on it proved more costly still in the long run.

The first breakthrough in social work education came in 1951, when the Tavistock Clinic decided to divert its resources for social work training from mental health students to a full-time, one-year advanced course for a small group of outstanding senior workers from any branch of casework. The Field Foundation (USA) gave maintenance grants and in time the Home Office (Probation) or employing authorities gave leave of absence on salary. This enabled four to six highly selected social workers each year to increase their knowledge and skill in a psychiatric setting that combined clinical practice, research and teaching. Three of these later supervised and taught on the Carnegie course. In its changing form over the years it unaccountably remained for nearly two decades the only advanced course in casework in this country (see also chapter 3, section on 'Post-Qualifying Courses').

By 1952 an *ad hoc* group, set up by the Association of Social Workers (ASW) and known as the Younghusband Discussion Group, was actively at work. It included observers from government departments as well as members from social work organisations, and its report (which it sent to the Carnegie Trust) endorsed the need for 'a general training in social work'. Later it called a meeting of professional associations to discuss its proposals, and as a result sent a letter to the Carnegie Trust signed by six of these (the Institute of Almoners wrote independently on the same lines for the second time) urging the Trust to support the proposals. The Carnegie Trustees agreed to explore the matter further.

In the same year, Professor Titmuss and the present writer went to meet several Carnegie Trustees in Edinburgh to discuss a proposal for a one-year applied social studies course at LSE. The Trustees doubted whether a generic casework course would be accepted by the main interests concerned, but later the Trust agreed to make a grant of £20,000 if LSE were willing to run such a course experimentally for four years, to contribute part of the overhead costs, and to continue it if it proved successful. This grant also depended on the bodies directly concerned being willing to grant aid students, to contribute fieldwork facilities, and to recognise the course as qualifying those who successfully completed it as caseworkers equipped to transfer from one branch of social work to another with no more than a minimum period of orientation. LSE welcomed the idea of a post-graduate, non-specialist course with teaching of an acceptable academic standard. It was also necessary to have the agreement of the Home Office (child care and probation), the Ministry of Health, the Institute of Almoners and the Family Welfare Association (FWA) (the mental health course was not included). In separate, individual discussion these all agreed to participate in an experiment to 'lower the barriers of specialisation', though the Home Office reaffirmed satisfaction with the separate courses it sponsored.

In July 1953 a joint meeting was held at LSE between representatives of the Carnegie United Kingdom Trust, the School and the foregoing bodies. They all spoke in support of the 'Carnegie experiment' and agreed to sign a 'memorandum of support'. As a result the Trustees confirmed the grant. Thus the way was clear for the next stage of appointing staff, planning the curriculum, negotiations for fieldwork supervisors and for student units, and recruiting students for the first applied social studies course, which started at LSE in October 1954.

The course itself was designed on the lines proposed in the 1947 and 1951 Carnegie reports, in that all lectures and seminars were planned by the full- and part-time lecturers in relation to each other and to the fieldwork. The Ministry of Health agreed to the appointment of additional almoners at two London teaching hospitals with substantial time for student supervision. Other supervisors were made available by the Home Office or paid for from the Carnegie grant, for example in the FWA. The chosen supervisors had themselves been supervised in training. They had reduced caseloads and were responsible for one to four students each, with teaching by both individual and group discussion. They met weekly as a group with the casework lecturer and were encouraged to attend any lectures in the course. The two full-time lecturers in charge of the course both went to the USA in 1953 to study social work education there and later Professor Charlotte Towle of the University of Chicago School of Social Service Administration came to LSE for a year as consultant to the course. The main subjects were human growth and development, social influences on behaviour, social administration, and principles and practice of casework. There were also 'settings' courses in child care, medical social work, and probation. There was concurrent fieldwork on three days a week in term time and full-time for part of the vacations and in the summer.

The actual Carnegie experiment differed from the original proposal in that it was not in an independent, university-affiliated institution; it lasted for ten months, not fifteen; it did not include group work; the staff could not undertake the amount of extramural activity envisaged in the original proposal; and it was not staffed to undertake research. These weaknesses later became apparent in the general structure of social work education as it evolved in the ensuing twenty years. What constituted the 'breakthrough' was that a financial grant made it possible to mount a generic university course based upon a social science qualification at a standard which many people had for long advocated. By 1953, it was also possible to recruit social work teachers and supervisors who could apply concepts from psychology and sociology to social work practice, and use case material to illustrate this practice.

Obviously not everyone supported what was then called 'the generic principle'. Many thought their particular clients, whether children, the ill or the delinquent, and the setting of each service too different for the essence not to be lost in a common training. This fear was revived after the 1968 and 1971 social services reorganisations, though by then it was clear that basic, generic training should be followed by opportunities to specialise. For others there were gains from the experiment because it broke down the walls of separation, so that a qualified social worker in one branch was not required to retrain to become qualified in another and it demonstrated that the common ground of casework was more fundamental than the differences; it gave other social work students the same standard of professional education as the mental health courses; and it was based upon a close partnership between the university and fieldwork agencies.

In view of later complaints about narrow, casework-oriented courses, the following extract from an article by an anonymous ex-student is illuminating: ,

'Lest it should be thought that we were solely concerned with casework, which is after all only one of a number of social work skills, we were encouraged to turn our attention to wider spheres. We were introduced to the theory of group work; we considered the role of the social worker in the community and, in particular, the place and function of the caseworker in the social services; we learned something of how social reform comes about, how casework can contribute to good administration, and, in very practical ways, of our responsibility for social policy.' (NAPO, *Probation,* December 1956, p. 51)

OTHER UNIVERSITY PROFESSIONAL SOCIAL WORK COURSES IN THE 1950s

The Institute of Almoners, in pursuit of its policy of moving training for medical social work into the universities, supported the 'Carnegie experiment' and also negotiated with Edinburgh University for a course in medical social work, which started in 1954 parallel with the established mental health course there. By 1959 professional social work courses had started in six out of the twenty-four social science departments. As in 1950, there were 3 mental health courses (LSE, Manchester and Edinburgh). There was also a PSW stream in the Liverpool course for the diploma in social administration. There were 2 child care courses (Birmingham and Liverpool) against 4 (LSE, Birmingham, Liverpool and Nottingham) in 1950; there was 1 university course in medical social work (Edinburgh) against none in 1950; and there were 3 applied social studies courses (LSE, Birmingham and Southampton) against none in 1950. Thus probation and almoner students were training in the universities for the first time and several child care courses had 'gone generic'.

There were suggestions in this period that the one-year almoner and mental health courses were too short and too hospital- and clinic-oriented when it was also urgent to train social workers with knowledge of local authority services. Debated ways of doing this were to give more relevant teaching of some subjects in the social studies and professional courses and to press for good supervision in the relevant local authority services. Action was only taken about a decade later.

By the late 1950s there was a generic trend in most professional courses as the common basis of social work became clearer, and 'generic' was no longer equated with 'elementary' and 'specialised' with 'advanced'. These courses were run in co-operation with hospitals, child guidance clinics, children's departments, probation services, family casework and other voluntary and statutory social agencies. The content was confined to casework and there was almost no provision for professional training in group work or community work.

All professional courses included study of human growth and development and individual deviance. The aim was to increase the students' understanding of the dynamics of family life, of human motivation, of normal and deviant behaviour (particularly under stress), and the ability to recognise signs of mental disorder. Some courses emphasised the needs of deprived children, others the effect of physical or mental illness, or of delinquent behaviour, according to the students' particular bent. In the generic courses there were 'settings' seminars, but only limited comparative studies. Some also included study of social influences on behaviour. A good deal was taught about the structure of particular social services and legislation, though less about administration. The study of the principles and practice of casework was important in all the courses, with analysis of detailed case records as well as general teaching. The trend was towards concurrent teaching of theory and practice, with fieldwork under supervision on two to three days each week in addition to the time spent on theoretical studies. By the mid-1950s it had become clearer that

'To run a series of separate trainings is to deny students the enrichment which comes from association with each other, to make wasteful use of scarce teaching resources, and to perpetuate a situation in which the emphasis is on administrative structure and differences rather than on similarities and educational content. Indeed, even in giving generic casework teaching, we may soon be accused of specialising, for there is already a trend towards teaching basic concepts in social work – casework, group work and community organisation – as three aspects of the necessary skill of the social worker, who will always, in fact, be concerned not only with the individual client but also with group relationships and community processes.' (Younghusband, 1956, pp. 252–3)

By this time it was usually accepted in university circles that professional courses, which were generally in sociology or social administration departments, were at least as academically respectable as some other professional courses in the universities. The universities also recognised their obligation to contribute to training for the public social services. The new, though not wholly accepted, assumption was that the universities should help to transform vocational courses from technical know-how to professional education, with a good grounding in the social sciences and the application of concepts and principles in practice. More research in the field also brought some academics into closer contact with social problems.

UNIVERSITY SOCIAL STUDY COURSES IN THE 1950s

At this point it is necessary to digress to courses in social science (sometimes called social studies), which continued to be accepted as a preparation for social work down to the early 1960s, and then return to other developments in professional courses.

The confusion of the 1940s about what should be taught in these courses slowly cleared, though each university department was a law unto itself. Economics lost its pre-eminence, sometimes subjects like physiology were dropped altogether, and by degrees social administration (including social history), psychology, and sociology became the central subjects, with social work sometimes added.

A JUC pamphlet on *University Courses in Social Study* (1952) said: 'Nearly all students choose and are selected for these courses because they wish ultimately to take up some kind of social work. Thus the courses . . . [have] a vocational bias, though they are not professional in the sense of giving a specific qualification for any particular job' (p. 3). This definition of 'professional' would probably have been accepted at the time. In that year the JUC set up a practical training committee. In 1955 the Council changed its title to the Joint University Council for Social and Public Administration. In a revised pamphlet entitled *University Courses in Social Administration* (1955) it said: 'Most of them are designed to be a preparation for professional training in one of the branches of the profession of social administration or social work and require to be completed by more specialised training and by practical experience under supervision' (pp. 3–4).

This was a· further step towards clarifying ambiguities. It was part of the continuing conflict as to whether or not social study courses should have a direct relation to social work, or whether they were also beginning to prepare students for a distinct career in social administration. Some sociologists saw no valid place for social work courses in the universities.

In evidence (1957) to the Younghusband working party the JUC made it clear that these various courses were 'academically complete', though

' . . . they do not adequately equip the student to take a responsible social work post. We now generally regard them from the vocational point of view, as a preparation for the professional training which should follow. To be recognised as fully trained, the present day social worker should both have successfully completed a general course in social studies and also have taken a social work training, usually lasting approximately a year, leading to a professional qualification.' (Younghusband Report, 1959, para. 816)

The confusion of the 1940s about the purpose of social science courses was thus resolved to the satisfaction of the universities and the professional associations. But the confusion was all the greater for employing bodies who for years had been urged to recruit 'trained' social workers, i.e. those with a social science qualification, and were now advertising for this or a certificate in child care or mental health as though they were interchangeable.

Moreover, many people with only a social science qualification were going straight into practice. Often they did not return for a professional training because there was no financial incentive to do so, and there were many more candidates than places on courses. There was much discussion about how to close 'the escape route'. The later development of three- or four-year integrated degree courses of social science and professional studies was not at that time 'consistent with university policy'.

Jones's inquiry (1964) into the university teaching of social studies in the twenty-five departments then affiliated to the JUC showed that social administration had begun to emerge as an integrative discipline which 'involved four processes: the understanding of the social situation; the recognition and formulation of social needs; the consideration of the means by which those needs might be or were being met; and the assessment of the results of social action' (p. 21).

Honours degrees in sociology, social administration, or social studies were beginning to take the place of non-graduate diploma or certificate courses. Some of the latter were still being run for older candidates and they all included some teaching on the theory and practice of social work. The number of post-graduate one- or two-year courses was increasing: these sometimes included research method and a dissertation, and all were becoming less vocational and more academic. Comparative figures for students on different social studies courses in 1950, 1955, 1960 and 1962 show the changing pattern (see table 1).

Table 1   *Students entering social studies departments in 1950, 1955, 1960 and 1962*

	Degree	Non-graduate certificate and diploma	Postgraduate diploma	Professional courses	Total
1950–1	146	387	185	98	816
1955–6	216	306	111	147	780
1960–1	322	255	192	233	1,002
1962–3	453	223	207	302	1,185
% increase/ decrease 1950–62	+210·3	− 42·4	+ 11·9	+208·2	+ 47·9

Source: Kathleen Jones (1964), *The Teaching of Social Studies in British Universities* (Welwyn, Codicote Press), p. 35.

The teaching usually included economics, philosophy, politics, psychology and history, together with either sociology or social administration. In those days the latter might cover teaching about demography and comparative culture patterns. In some universities most subjects were compulsory, in others there was a choice of optional subjects, for instance criminology, law, psychiatry, the child and the family, social aspects of health and disease, or social research method, according to what the particular university could offer. The range and depth of subjects varied considerably, therefore no general assumption was possible about the ground covered.

The inquiry showed that the amount of practical work varied from six weeks to six months, though in some degree courses there was none. This practical work was in local authority services, hospitals, probation, family casework agencies, settlements and other voluntary organisations, approved schools, borstals, children's homes, and so forth. The study identified different opinions about the purpose of this experience, which might be regarded as:

'(i)   A training in social work practice.

(ii)   An experience in the settings of social work which helps the student to decide which type of specialised training to take after graduation.

(iii)   Experience in how the less fortunate sections of the community live.

   (iv)   A maturing experience for the student.
   (v)   A way of supplementing written texts in a rapidly developing field where many of the books are out of date.
   (vi)   A valid teaching method of permanent value analogous to fieldwork in Geography or Architecture.
   (vii)   A preliminary training in research method.
  (viii)   A training in administrative method.
   (ix)   A somewhat meaningless procedure made necessary by the professional courses' preference for students with the 'Social Science Qualification'.

These views might be held in varying combinations, and with varying degrees of emphasis, and there are sometimes differences of view between members of staff in the same department.' (p. 26)

The nature and purpose of fieldwork in these courses was clarified by the JUC handbook *Field Work in Social Administration Courses* (1966) which argued that it was a necessary part of social administration teaching. But continuing confusion and lack of staff resources resulted in the unsatisfactory situation revealed by the Brown and Gloyne study of fieldwork (1966) discussed in chapter 4, section on 'The 1960s'.

Jones's study also showed that most social studies staff were in the lecturer grade irrespective of age. The ratio of professors, readers and senior lecturers was lower than for any other group in the university. Thus teachers of social studies tended to be 'older and less well-paid than other university teachers' (p. 47) and because there were few senior appointments to 'carry less weight in discussion of university policy than might be expected' (p. 47). The social work teachers were mainly women over 40 and the sociology teachers mainly men under 40. Contrary to general assumptions, nearly half the social work teachers had some research in progress at the time the survey was undertaken. Sixty of the total of 196 who answered the study questionnaire had a primary interest in social work teaching, and 20 staff members were practical-work tutor's.

Some of the tensions of this period are inherent in these figures. A new breed of young academics was coming into these departments anxious to advance in their careers by research and publication, sometimes frustrated by the lack of research opportunities and the demand that they should teach a lowly breed of student not working for a degree or specialising in any social science. Those responsible for the social studies certificate or diploma courses were still being pressed from outside to include more 'vocational' subjects or to give more 'relevant' teaching at a time when, in any event, their academic respectability was being questioned as more degrees in sociology and social administration came into existence. Perhaps it is not surprising in the circumstances that pressure by the professional associations and their supporters for teaching, of psychology in particular, more related to human behaviour in the ordinary world seemed like a demand to lower academic standards. This was all the more so when the pressure came from people who were not specialists in the subject. Possibly some of the American Fulbright fellows attached to certain universities helped to clarify confused thinking.

Unfortunately the CTC and the Probation Advisory and Training Board (PATB) never combined with the JUC to bring together social studies and social work teachers to thresh out each side's expectations and to arrive at some understanding. Only the JUC attempted this from time to time in one-day meetings and the Keele Conferences did so in more substantial residential events. The Institute of Almoners, and to a lesser extent APSW, were consequently forced into a situation where they might be making ill-judged demands. The climate changed by slow degrees throughout the 1950s and 1960s as more professional courses came into existence, thus taking some pressure off the non-graduate social studies courses, and as these themselves began to fade out.

PROFESSIONAL COURSES IN THE 1960s

By the early 1960s the ground had been cleared for the later training explosion, including two-year courses in colleges of further education. But clarification in the 1950s of the roles of social studies and social work courses did not mean the end of tensions. On the professional courses there was a constant demand by the universities for more time for academic study, and less for fieldwork or for courses on the principles and practice of social work, which might be impatiently regarded as a recapitulation of unproven assumptions, a hotchpotch of superficial study and practitioners' folklore which social workers thought constituted professional education.

There were also constant tensions as to who should have the last say about the content and balance of professional courses, the qualifications of lecturers and how to prevent recognition of courses from sliding into external control, or advice into dictation. The universities naturally claimed that they were the final judge in all educational matters, the professional associations made the same claim in relation to the standard of training, including fieldwork, while the Home Office was a rather coy piper trying to call a tune that would please everyone. The training councils (see especially chapter 7 below and elsewhere) and the JUC undoubtedly played an important part in creating situations where tensions could sometimes be profitable and almost always be contained or else resolved by discussion. Important contributory factors were that the chairmen of two (and finally all three) training councils were Vice-Chancellors; that several heads of departments and other academic staff were members of the councils and of sub-committees dealing in detail with the recognition of courses; and that the director of child care studies, the principal probation training inspector and the chief professional adviser to the CTSW had all previously been both university teachers and PSWs. This sometimes stormy partnership was built up slowly in the 1950s (primarily in relation to child care courses) until by the 1960s there was a national consultancy, negotiating and in-service training structure for the child care and probation service – and later for health and welfare – which could stimulate, support and carry forward an increase in numbers that was entirely new in social work education. There were sometimes situations in which a committee responsible for advising on acceptance of a proposed course might ask for higher standards in some directions than those suggested by a university with little relevant experience. Willingness to discuss, take advice and accept modifications sometimes triumphed over retreats into university autonomy or professional rigidity. It was equally necessary for the old hands to beware of stereotypes and unimaginative rigidities which would have prevented valuable innovations. There were at all times tensions between the not necessarily synonymous objectives of education for a profession and trained manpower for a service.

Further one-year applied social studies courses based on social studies qualifications were started during the early 1960s at Newcastle, Leicester, Bristol, Glasgow and Edinburgh Universities and at Cardiff and Swansea University Colleges. There was constant discussion about graduates in non-social studies subjects (referred to as 'non-relevant' degrees) who still had to take two separate one-year courses. It was thought that many good graduates were lost for this reason and combined social science and professional social work seventeen- to eighteen-month courses designed for them were started during the 1960s at Oxford, Liverpool, Manchester, Nottingham and Exeter Universities. In 1965 the pros and cons were discussed at a joint meeting between the Home Office and the universities concerned. The advantages were that recruitment was good and students qualified in four instead of six terms at a time when there was an urgent need for more staff and more incentives to recruitment. But some regarded this as a surrender to expediency; it caused heavy pressure on both staff and students, especially in the overlapping autumn term and resulted in insufficient time for fieldwork and essential reading on courses which ought to be of post-graduate standard. Finally each university lengthened its course to two years; and recruitment did not suffer. The pattern returned later with fifteen- to eighteen-month post-graduate courses at Bedford and Goldsmith's Colleges (London University), Brunel and Manchester Universities and Middlesex Polytechnic.

The first two-year master's degree course in social work was started at York University in 1966 through the initiative of the then Vice-Chancellor, and the first reader in social work in this country was appointed to help plan the course. The fourteen-month post-graduate course at Sussex University was later lengthened to two years and also led to a master's degree, and others came into existence at Exeter and Nottingham Universities. A new pattern of four-year, integrated social studies and social work undergraduate courses was pioneered by Bradford, Bath and Keele Universities (the latter in a slightly different form), and by three polytechnics for Council for National Academic Awards (CNAA) degrees. Students concentrated on social studies subjects for the first two years and then opted (by selection) for one of several alternatives, including social work, in the last two years. These and the two-year child care and CSW courses (not in university internal departments) were able to plan the total curriculum so that foundation and professional studies fitted together.

One of the many consequences of the training explosion of the late 1960s was a shortage of social work teachers, made all the greater by the new, better career prospects and salaries in the local authorities. This reinforced the familiar lack of time for continuing social work practice, research and contact with field teaching. There was not enough opportunity to learn how to teach, and inadequate administrative help. The JUC agreed that the Home Office staff student ratio of 1:10 for grant purposes was unsatisfactory, especially in view of the urgent need for more social work research, closer contact with practice and the opportunities for specialisation in depth by staff of large courses. The analogy of doctors responsible for training students in clinical practice was used in arguing the case.

Another difficulty was that the universities favoured generic courses, but grant aid for salaries of university tutors and other expenses was only available for child care and probation students. An unwelcome specialisation was thus forced upon the universities and they had to finance provision for other students through the quinquennial competition for University Grants Committee (UGC) allocations. As a consequence far too few graduate social workers went into the health and welfare services. If Home Office grant aid had not been available it is unlikely that pressure from local authorities and professional associations would have stimulated the great expansion in social work education in the 1960s. One result of this, however, was that the shortage of medical and psychiatric social workers grew all the greater. Pressure was brought to bear on the Ministry of Health to give grants to the universities to increase the number of places for these students. In 1968 it finally agreed to do this via the UGC, with the result that the universities provided over 100 additional places. This semed to the JUC a most undesirable endorsement of specialisation rather than generic social work education. Moreover, it helped to perpetuate a situation in which candidates had to decide on a particular field of social work before they started to train.

The rapid expansion of professional courses was a reason why the JUC Practical Training Committee was succeeded in 1966 by the Standing Sub-Committee on Social Work Education. This provided a meeting place for university teachers to discuss all aspects of professional training.

THE 1970s

In 1971 the JUC opened its membership to polytechnics offering CNAA degrees and co-opted members included the Local Government Training Board (LGTB), the CCETSW and the National Institute for Social Work. More polytechnics (in Scotland central institutions) were admitted later. By 1975 JUC membership included 56 universities (2 in Dublin) and 18 polytechnics. The Social Administration Committee had 63 members and the Sub-Committee on Social Work Education with 50 members was accorded full committee status. These committees, and indeed the JUC as such, had begun by the mid-1970s to clarify the universities' responsi-bility for standards of professional education, largely stimulated by CCETSW activities.

By the early 1970s virtually all education for social work was generic (except one course in psychiatric work and one in probation) and had begun to include social work with individuals, groups and committees.

In 1975 there were thirty-three university departments of social adminis-tration and social work. Twelve professors in these departments had profes-sional social work qualifications and a number held chairs of social work or social administration and social work. This had come with a rush when even in the early 1960s a professor of social work would have been unthinkable.

By 1975 the following courses led to the CCETSW Certificate of Qualification in Social Work (CQSW) and no distinction was made between university and other recognised courses:

(a) 35 university and polytechnic one- to two-year courses for students with relevant degrees (plus 2 in Northern Ireland and 1 in Dublin);
(b) 20 two-year university and polytechnic courses for graduates with other degrees (plus 1 in Northern Ireland);
(c) 15 four-year university and polytechnic integrated degree courses (plus 1 in Northern Ireland and 1 in Dublin);
(d) 3 courses for students with non-graduate social studies qualifications;
(e) 40 two-year courses for non-graduates (plus 2 in Northern Ireland) – six of the courses were for students of 30 plus, and
(f) 3 three-year courses for those women with family ties (non-graduates);
(g) 2 three-year courses for non-graduates of 19 plus.

Five of the foregoing courses were in Scottish universities and six in colleges of education or technology.

Some courses had emphases or options in residential social work, mental health, probation or community work. Most candidates were required to have had about a year's experience in the social services before they trained. The necessary educational qualifications ranged from a degree to five O levels, or for candidates over 25, evidence of ability to take an academic course.

In 1975 3,123 students qualified for the CQSW. This was a far cry from the 300 (93 almoners, 46 PSWs, 77 child care and 84 probation) students who qualified in 1950. But even so, only a handful completed the few post-qualification courses which existed by 1975.

TRAINING GRANTS

In the 1950s more grants for training began to be available but many anomalies still existed. Until the mid-1950s probation students trained on salary and had their fees paid (without a means test) both for social science and subsequent professional courses. Child care students received a grant and fees (on a means test) for child care courses, but not (with rare exceptions) for social science courses. They, like almoner and PSW students, were dependent upon uncertain LEA grants to take these courses. Candidates for almoner or mental health courses had first to apply for an LEA grant and only if this was refused (often late in the summer) were they awarded a means-tested Ministry of Health grant, provided they undertook to work in the NHS. Student grants were often grossly inadequate for older candidates with commitments. Thus they had to give up another job and use savings in order to train for a career in which salaries and promotion prospects were both poor. Every relevant committee of inquiry during this decade stressed that national provision of assured grants was essential both as an act of simple justice to candidates and in the self-interest of employing authorities at a time when far greater output from training was essential but many candidates could not face the lack or inadequacy of grants.

It was ironic that child care and probation which had the best salaries and career prospects also automatically provided maintenance grants and fees. For years the JUC urged the case for Ministry of Education grants for both the social science and professional courses without a condition that students should commit themselves beforehand to a particular service.

Students taking applied social studies courses were forced by grant conditions to decide their future career before they embarked on the course (unless they had an LEA grant): they might be refused a place because a section was full while a less able student might be accepted for another section; they could not be advised to or themselves decide to transfer midstream unless reciprocal arrangements existed between government departments; and they could not take employment in another service. These conditions also applied to students taking mental health or medical social work courses. It was accepted, though lamented, that the tendency of people with a social science or other qualification to take social work jobs without training was related to low maintenance grants and low status.

Untrained social workers in employment might be seconded on full or part salary by employing authorities in some services. The Home Office paid full salary and tuition fees for serving child care officers, including those employed by voluntary organisations, to train. To some extent this brought back untrained entrants after a spell in employment. There was a high proportion of seconded students on CSW courses.

Earmarked grants for students and courses finally came to an end in 1973 when responsibility was transferred from the Home Office and the DHSS to the UGC (probation and seconded students continued to train on salary). Special additional funds were allocated to the UGC until the new 1976–81 quinquennium to provide the number and type of social work courses needed. This caused a good deal of alarm and fears about the future funding of social work education in the general university competition for UGC allocations. Local education authorities became responsible for the cost of courses in colleges, and grants to students on non-graduate courses (not mandatory) while the DHSS, the Welsh Office and the Scottish Education Department were responsible for grants for students on post-graduate courses.

So came to an end the period of direct grants from central government – primarily the Home Office – for both courses and student grants. This had brought uniformity and stability into social work education for some services and speeded up expansion. Clearly it was logical in the long run to bring the financing of social work training into line with the total structure of university and college grants. But there were divided opinions as to whether that time had yet come in view of the tremendous training backlog and the competition for funds.

Chapter 2

The Changing Content
of Teaching

DEVELOPMENTS IN THE TEACHING OF PSYCHOLOGY

In the 1950s there continued to be conflicting views about the teaching of psychology in social studies courses to future social work students who were restive about academic psychology, sometimes narrowly focused on perception, intelligence, motivation, memory, habit, and so forth in isolation from developmental and social contexts. It was agreed that students needed a good grounding in general psychology before they went on to professional courses, but different universities did not give a common basis of knowledge. This increased the split between the academics and the professionals. The JUC held meetings on the subject which debated the problem of how to teach psychology to non-specialists while maintaining scientific integrity by teaching what was known, how knowledge had been obtained, and the little that was known. It was suggested that the framework should include cognitive and developmental processes and the individual in relation to his society. It should aim to demonstrate to students that the systematic study of human behaviour by scientific methods was possible, and to induce a disciplined and broadminded intellectual and emotional attitude towards human behaviour (Barnes and Tajfel, 1958; Trasler, 1959).

At least part of the controversy in the 1950s, and later, sprang from the assumption that psychology teaching in social studies courses – and indeed other teaching – should educate students to think carefully, critically and to be sceptical about evidence, but no more. Much of the content of this teaching was valid, but the process of first dissecting the corpse and then putting it together again into a full-blooded active human being created problems of learning later in the professional courses. At that stage students had to respond with their hearts as well as their heads in situations of turmoil and conflict where action was urgent but knowledge scant.

In the early 1950s psychoanalytically oriented psychiatrists were actually working with the same people as social workers and applying knowledge which seemed to 'work' in social work practice. In addition to the mental health courses, some began to teach on other professional courses as these were expanded and improved. Their clinical illustrations and dynamic teaching threw students in at the emotional deep end where, so some critics alleged, they lost their heads and their critical faculties. Individual psychiatrists taught with the emphasis on mental illness, or criminal behaviour, or child psychiatry and family disturbances. These latter probably did most to lay the foundations of the subject for social work students. They had to discover what was different in social work and help the students to find a professional identity that was not a pale shadow of psychiatry, nor primarily concerned with the past and the unconscious. In addition to difficulties about tough, intellectual learning, there were tensions when the fascination of pathology obscured interest in ordinary everyday functioning. Some social work teachers and psychiatrists were able to keep a double focus on the crucial consequences of early childhood experiences and unconscious motivation, yet relate these to clients' current reality. This teaching was based on psychoanalytic theory, though critics pointed to its many unproven assumptions. In some courses students were introduced to other schools of thought, as well as to the significance of memory, perception, habit and intelligence as essential parts of human functioning.

By the 1960s it became less academically disreputable to apply knowledge, to combine intellectual learning with imaginative consideration, and to let both play upon the human situation in the struggle to understand in order to help; a struggle, moreover, in which skill, tolerance and acceptance had to be anchored to knowledge. This was the problem of uniting scientific knowledge with a professional response to people in trouble.

It had always been assumed on the mental health courses that students must be helped to develop awareness of self and others. This was accepted on other professional courses when teaching about human growth and behaviour, and the principles and practice of social work spread and when supervision became a teaching process in which clients held up a series of mirrors to the student. This was often a painful, even if enriching, experience. 'To see ourselves as others see us is a most salutory gift. Hardly less important is the capacity to see others as they see themselves' (Huxley, 1954, p. 8). Later, another demand was added when by degrees students began to think along the two dimensions of psychodynamics and cultural values. This showed that what would be aberrant behaviour in one group was normal in another and that students, and many social workers, had to learn that their own standards of desirable behaviour might be simply an expression of their cultural values. Students therefore had to become aware not only of the effect of their own personality on others and their prejudices about or identification with particular people, but also about their culturally determined attitudes and blinkers.

From the mid-1950s it was agreed in professional and some social studies courses that human development should be taught from conception (including genetic factors) through infancy, early childhood, the school years into adolescence and adulthood, with deviations from the normal made understandable within the setting of the developmental process. In this teaching on a professional course the child had parents, school friends and teachers, but there were many complaints that he never grew up, except in the syllabus, because lecturers and students were too much engrossed for the short academic year in Freud, Jung, Piaget, Bowlby, Winnicott, Anna Freud, Melanie Klein, Erik Erikson, Fromm, Watson and others to enable the adolescent to become an adult, go to work, marry, bring up a family, become middle-aged and face old age and death. Teaching about the whole life-cycle became more possible later on in the two-year courses and when many more studies became available of adults in general and under specific conditions of handicap, bereavement, population shifts, single parenthood, or old age. Even so, a CCETSW working party report on handicap (1974*b*) found that most CQSW courses responding to their inquiry 'in their teaching about developmental processes concentrated on teaching about child development and family dynamics with a tendency to overlook even critical phases or aspects of adult life' (p. 11).

At first, much teaching about adult behaviour and family relationships was given in courses on the principles and practice of social work and the 'settings' courses on casework in child care or probation, or medical or psychiatric social work. This teaching was related to the concept of stress and the way different people coped with stress according to their personality and circumstances, their sense of identity, their degree of maturity and their defences. This became a key concept in social work, related to attempts to understand and reinforce strengths in the person and his family and social environment. Later, the many different forms of separation, loss, bereavement and discontinuities in life experiences became other key concepts. Communication also began to be studied more thoroughly as part of the casework relationship, especially in teaching about communication with children. Careful observation of behaviour and of non-verbal communication was later extended by more precise studies of 'accurate empathy' on the one hand, and of cultural elements in communication on the other, including extended and restricted language codes.

This was one of the bridges that began to be built between developmental psychology, social psychology and sociology. If it was important to understand how the individual was functioning in his current family and social situation, then it was essential to have the necessary tools of analysis. The family emerged from its sometimes exclusively Freudian framework, as understanding of its patterns of behaviour, sex roles, child-rearing practice, parental relationships and values were also clarified in sociological terms. On some courses down to the late 1960s psychoanalytic theory was taught as proven, parallel with sociology courses but neither was related to the other. In the mid-1960s the National Institute for Social Work Training ran small invitation conferences on the teaching of human growth and behaviour and of social policy, in which specialists and social work teachers debated what should be taught, for what purpose and by whom. These conferences were followed by two CTSW working party reports on the teaching of human growth and development (1967*a*) and of sociology (1972). In the 1970s the CCETSW established a tradition of setting up working parties on different subjects and published the results for further discussion and incorporation in courses recognised by the Council. The result was that in general terms priorities were clarified, though the range was greatly extended and the level at which any given subject should be taught was controversial.

Opposed interpretations of human functioning were inherent in the three major conceptual systems of psychology: the psychoanalytic, including the neo-Freudians with their greater emphasis on the ego; behaviourism and learning theory which concentrated on observable behaviour, stimulus, response and the conditioned reflex and rejected all subjective experience or motivation; and existentialism, phenomenology, gestalt psychology and other theories which stressed creativity, responsibility and self-realisation. Obviously these theories made very different assumptions about man, either swayed by largely unconscious internal drives or conditioned by external circumstances, or with limited or considerable freedom to weigh and choose alternatives. Much social work theory and practice derived implicitly or explicitly from one or other of these theories. It was not always recognised how much 'that aspect of man which is chosen for study influences the total perception of man, how readily the total possible picture is submerged in areas of special interest – or theories which seem particularly appealing' (CCETSW, 1976*b*, p. 60; see also pp. 57–62). Group dynamics and group and intergroup relations were also accepted as essential elements in social work in the late 1960s. And by the early 1970s ethology had added yet another dimension. But there was comparative neglect of the genetic basis and physical components of personality. The importance of the work situation was also neglected; as the CCETSW working party on social work with handicapped people (1974*b*) said, 'little if any attention appears to be given to the meaning of work roles and employment of the able-bodied, let alone of those with handicaps' (p. 11). And although social work had become more conscious of fathers and husbands, these were still pale shadows compared with mothers and children.

A series of action research projects in the 1950s and 1960s showed the pervasive effects of negative social situations which twisted behaviour into hostile aggression, fear and lack of confidence. This affected teaching about deviance and social pathology. It had been commonly assumed that such behaviour could be understood on the 'medical model' as a manifestation of personality disorder which could be cured or contained by individual treatment. But local studies by teams of psychiatrists, sociologists and social workers showed that 'deviant' behaviour might be a natural reponse to pathological conditions destructive of the normal development of people's drives and potentialities. 'Deviance' became more intractable when the individual no longer accepted socially ascribed norms of behaviour.

This revulsion from a clinical orientation raised fundamental questions about the very concept and causation of deviance, an important subject of teaching on social work courses. Was delinquency or even some mental illness explicable in terms of personality disorder, or were they due to bad social conditions? And was it society which forced the individual into non-conforming behaviour by scapegoating, labelling, ostracism, exclusion, the creation of institutional neurosis, giving a dog a bad name and treating him accordingly? By the 1970s for some students 'the system' had become the scapegoat, with all the pleasurable sensations of witch-hunting.

SOME CONSEQUENCES FOR SOCIAL WORK TEACHING

It is impossible to weigh up what social work students in the 1970s had gained compared with their pioneer forebears of the 1950s. Far richer and more relevant knowledge was available and to some extent there was more agreement about the content of teaching. In the first period students could reasonably absorb the required knowledge and insight, but in the 1970s for other than the most able students this became doubtful within the time limits and with the educational resources available. Trying to devise courses that were not superficial, bitty or overloaded was indeed a daunting task. On the other hand, students were more sophisticated and more know-ledgeable about common human needs. These might still be love, achievement, recognition, a sense of identity and belonging, but the subtleties and the disagreements were far greater. Capacity to cope successfully with fear, anxiety, guilt, separation and hostility, to use aggression and conflict con-structively was manifested by many people in many circumstances but not notably by the clients of social workers. There was better understanding of the strength of family bonds, in whatever strands of love, guilt and hostility they might be woven. Unconscious motivation was widely accepted; so was the concept of needs characteristic of each stage of the life-cycle, of cultural values and habits and the effect of social circumstances on individual functioning. And these had added new dimensions to social work theory and practice. The importance of relationships had been reinforced, by many different studies, including those of client reactions to casework help. These had also shown that the social work task is not necessarily or only direct work with clients, but also attempts to create stronger social networks, more group interaction and group support, and varied inter-vention to help clients to be more independent, exercise choice and control circumstances.

New developments in practice thus showed that casework was not enough, even though knowledge derived from it could be applied more widely. Group psychotherapy had burst its bonds and given the impetus to discus-sion and activity groups for many different people and purposes. Community work arrived with a rush in the late 1960s, much of it actually group work, but including community surveys, community action groups and the mobilisation of external resources, whether for specific groups of people or general neighbourhood improvement. Residential social work only began to be identified as such in the mid-1960s. To some it seemed obvious that these social work methods were not separate forms of practice but a continuum and that they should all be used in any given situation for assess-ment and action. The teaching of the different methods only began in the 1960s, with group work lagging behind, good practice in residential social work poorly explored, and community work a mixture of description and aspiration. Teaching of 'integrated social work methods' started later still, and by the mid-1970s few courses gave such teaching and it was not clear to what extent it could produce students competent to begin to use integrated methods, given the length of training and lack of such methods in field practice. Some antagonistic attitudes in community work towards casework made this more problematic. In any event, counselling, psychotherapy, group work and community work were not peculiar to social work, although other professions practised these skills in ways relevant to themselves.

In the mid-1970s social work teaching was thus at an awkward stage of development, when much more was known about casework theory and practice than about group, or community, or residential social work. Yet casework knowledge about the application of theory to practice lacked the necessary content for group and community work, though their practitioners had barely started to relate theory and practice.

Teaching of systems theory was beginning to provide another conceptual link between all four aspects of practice. The study of people's behavioural changes in total or open institutions, staff-resident relationships, and means to avoid institutional neurosis and help people to remain more alive in institutions became possible as both psychological and sociological knowledge developed and found its way into social work teaching and practice.

Naturally, the knowledge explosion, and the knowledge overlap in all the helping professions, made interdisciplinary understanding and co-operation essential. This was much discussed and sometimes practised in specific situations. But, although the desirability of interdisciplinary study of common subjects was raised sporadically throughout the period, there was no substantial common teaching of the human sciences to social work, teaching, medical and nursing students.

CHANGES IN THE CONTRIBUTION OF SOCIOLOGY TO SOCIAL WORK EDUCATION

Some of the foregoing knowledge belonged to sociology rather than to psychology. Sociology as such was not commonly included in social science or social studies courses in the 1940s and early 1950s, though some material which would now be regarded as sociological appeared in courses on social administration and social psychology. The first applied social studies course included lectures on 'social influences on behaviour' (a title devised by Richard Titmuss, who objected to 'social determinants of behaviour'). Sociology as such, i.e. the study of social interaction and social institutions, began to be an important subject in degree and diploma 'pre-professional' courses.

Social workers, perhaps dazzled by dynamic psychology, found it more difficult to use sociological concepts, and indeed students were not helped to do so. The present writer remembers substantial lectures on role theory in the mid-1940s which were not applied and seemed to the students to be of purely academic interest. It must also be remembered that until the late 1950s there were few sociological studies in this country of local cultures, social class, social interaction in given neighbourhood groups, or of social deviance or specific social institutions. In addition, although some sociologists thought it impossible to separate sociology teaching from moral philosophy or the nature of a just society, others were committed to a value-free science, i.e. what is, not what might be or ought to be. But social workers as practitioners were concerned about social change 'for the better', which led them to ask 'so what?' about sociological survey findings or theoretical systems. One result was that they and psychiatrists could communicate with each other because both were practitioners who often had to take action ahead of knowledge and were committed to enhancing mental health (whatever that might be), whereas sociology was primarily an academic discipline interested in analysis rather than action. This contrasted with a period in the early twentieth century when there were close relations between liberal, social reformist sociologists and the beginnings of education for social work: 'In both Britain and America the relationship between Sociology and Social Work has fluctuated, at one time and another, between assumed synonymity and spirited disassociation [*sic*]' (CTSW, 1972, p. 7).

Several factors no doubt contributed to the return to sociology from the late 1950s. For example, the number of sociologists and sociology degrees in the universities increased. Even so, sociology was not included in all professional courses and there were considerable variations in the amount and relevance of material even when it was taught. For example, there was more sociological knowledge in criminology than elsewhere. Moreover, students' examination scripts did not usually show an ability to apply sociological concepts in contrast to the fluency with which psychoanalytic theory tripped relevantly or irrelevantly off their pens. The concept of culture was fairly generally taught, and students read studies like Mays's *Growing Up in the City* (1954) and Young and Willmott's *Family and Kinship in East London* (1959). American field studies in criminology and urban disorganisations were also widely read, as indeed were Margaret Mead's and other anthropological studies of more simple cultures. The missing link was help to assess these findings critically in actual social situations. Thus students' case analyses were too often based upon the psychodynamics of family life, plus unexamined assumptions about 'normal' behaviour, without any recognition of different cultural values. This was partly a consequence of supervision and teaching by social workers trained in an earlier period. None the less more social work teachers were showing an interest in sociology and a few undertook substantial study and some multidisciplinary research.

Looking back at the 1950s and early 1960s, it is impossible to believe that experienced social workers can have been blind to the influence of class or family patterns, of culturally determined values, of social networks, role relationships, the effect of social circumstances on behaviour, and of other sociological concepts which later became essential elements in social work education. But the knowledge was related to specific neighbourhoods and unformulated. Role theory, which was compatible with ego psychology, was one of the first sociological concepts to be applied in practice, with ability to perform in family and social roles as a test of personal and social functioning, and the removal of impediments as a social work aim.

Sociological theories about the nature of society had much influenced social science students – from, for example, Hobhouse, Karl Mannheim and McIver earlier, to Parsons, Merton, Durkheim, Marx and Weber (rediscovered) and others at a later period. Many of these later students went on to professional courses, some convinced that sociological explanations coupled with a Marxist philosophy sufficiently explained all social problems. Non-sociology students might be equally convinced by psychoanalytic explanations of human behaviour. Each suffered from the pitfalls of either/or choices and global explanations.

Action research projects which showed the effect of social circumstances on individual behaviour and family functioning, together with developments in sociology itself, resulted in pressure to incorporate more sociological knowledge in the theory and practice of social work. A difficulty in social work education was that graduate students might come with considerable theoretical knowledge, but students taking two-year courses outside the university might have neither specific knowledge nor a scientific approach. When sociology was taught at all on such courses it tended to be a 'background' course in the first year, inadequately related to the 'foreground' of social work theory and practice. But some sociologists who taught social work students were becoming interested in their needs. For example, in the mid-1960s the curriculum for the CSW two-year course at the then North Western Polytechnic, London, had fifty sessions on sociology. In the early days of the courses in colleges of further education or university extramural departments there was a shortage of sociologists with experience of teaching professional course students who needed something different from an elementary first-year course. There was discussion and experimentation to discover whether on professional courses sociology was most effectively related to the teaching on human growth and development or to social administration, social policy and the social services.

In the enormous mass of sociological literature and conflicting views, the problem, as in psychology teaching, was how to maintain for students the integrity of the subject while selecting and applying those aspects that threw most light on practice. There was also the dilemma of how to relate the sociological, psychological and other frames of reference to each other without a deceptive reductionism, and to apply a common focus to social work theory and practice. This was agreed to entail far more interdisciplinary discussion and understanding of how students learn than had so far been undertaken. Four studies in the 1960s explored this further. These were: *The Teaching of Sociology to Students of Education and of Social Work* (Sociological Review Monograph No. 4, 1961); *Sociology in Social Work* (Leonard, 1966); *Sociology and Social Work* (Heraud, 1970) and *The Teaching of Sociology in Social Work Courses* (CTSW, 1972).

From these and other discussions, the following amongst other themes emerged: the concern of sociology with social interaction and the structure and functioning of society and of social institutions, for example the family, the church, or education within it; methods of socialisation into the culture; social values and beliefs; variations in family patterns and norms; social controls designed to maintain or restore social equilibrium, and various theories of social deviance; social relationships and connections between different social networks; the power structure; theories of role set and role relationships, including family and professional roles; exchange theory; analysis of social change; social stratification; pressure groups; and consensus and conflict theories of society. Organisation theory and the sociology of institutions also contributed to the study of the nature and function of administrative systems, the decision-making process, organisations and the bureaucratic structures in which most social work students were subsequently employed. Naturally, all these aspects had their own internal consistency as well as with each other and in their relation to psychology, philosophy, political theory and social administration. Many sociologists were beginning to accept that sociology could not be value free, though value assumptions should be clearly and objectively stated. By 1975 Clarke (1976) found from a questionnaire on the teaching of first-year sociology to a range of students that 'structural functionalism and Marxism . . . appeared in more or less well defined forms in a large number of courses' (p. 92).

The discussions in the 1960s were attempts to see the relevance of sociology in casework practice. The growth of community work began to give a different slant to the teaching of sociology, with less emphasis on the family and deviance and more on community interaction and on conflict resulting from diversity of interests and unequal distribution of power. To community workers sociology seemed far more relevant than psychology. Moreover, sociology could be given a Marxist slant which reinforced the case for structural change and 'conflict strategies'. Indeed, for many students and practitioners sociology was becoming in the early 1970s what dynamic psychology had been in the 1950s, with the result that in a swaying battle for the soul of social work Marx was in the ascendent over Freud.

PHYSICAL HEALTH, DISEASE AND HANDICAP

What and how to teach this vast subject was an unsolved problem, whether child health on the child care courses or disease processes and disability for medical social workers or handicapping conditions for CSW students. Deciding what students needed to know depended on what they were meant to do with the knowledge, and they were obviously not intended to be ersatz doctors or nurses. What could go wrong developmentally was one approach, another was congenital and acquired handicaps, a third was systems of the body and common disease processes that affected them. This might include some knowledge of the effects of certain medical, surgical and drug treatments. Social workers' use of the knowledge included knowing enough to get someone to the doctor; co-operating intelligently with doctors in hospitals, clinics and general practice; and knowing enough about the character of a particular disability to be aware of the likely effect on the individual and the family and their way of life. This included knowledge about particular handicaps and disease processes, whether they were remediable or progressive and their natural history and fluctuations, in order to know where, how and when social work help could be given. Yet problems of selection, of too little or too much, of difficulties caused by students' ignorance of physiology and anatomy, all remained.

These courses were taught either by a series of specialists or a GP trying to grasp how social workers differed from nurses, though sometimes a medical social worker was present to make the social work connections. A guideline was the distinction between intrinsic or primary physical impairment and secondary handicapping conditions which could arise from personal and family reactions and from the social situation, for example institutionalisation and undue dependence.

For several years the CTSW had a sub-committee on groups with special needs which struggled to identify the nature of social work teaching about handicapping conditions. The blind and the deaf seemed the only groups for whom specific as distinct from further knowledge was essential. The CCETSW working party on training for social work with handicapped people (1974*b*) (including the mentally impaired) explored in useful detail current deficiencies and future aims. Replies from about one in six of CQSW courses showed that all gave some teaching about mental disorder, and most about physical disease, but teaching about physical handicap and mental retardation was infrequent or minimal and there was none about deafness or blindness. Moreover, in fieldwork few students had contact with handicapped people. The working party thought it essential that all CQSW students should have improved teaching on work with them and their families and experience of working with at least one handicapped person. Professor J. E. Wing prepared as an appendix to the report an admirable outline of the desirable content of teaching, drawing on medical, psychiatric and sociological material.

ECONOMICS

From being a principal subject in earlier social science courses, economics suffered a decline in which it might not be taught at all in some degree or professional courses. Teaching of social administration should clearly take account of income maintenance, the economics of social policy and the provision and financing of public services as an element in distribution of the national income. It did so with varying degrees of adequacy. The 'rediscovery of poverty' resulted once again in more attention to the nature and causes of poverty, criteria for measurement and the groups most affected.

SOCIAL ADMINISTRATION

Well into the 1950s this subject (taught under various titles) might consist largely of descriptive accounts of health, housing, education, social security, employment and other services, sometimes buttressed by courses in social history, social philosophy, and social economics. From 1951 when Richard Titmuss was appointed to the new chair in social administration at LSE it started to take on the new dimensions suggested in his inaugural lecture: 'We are interested in the machinery of administration, which organises and dispenses various forms of social assistance . . . [and] in the lives, the needs, and the material relations of those members of the community for whom the services are provided' (Titmuss, 1958, pp. 13–14). A further dimension was added when it became obvious that larger services needed administrative competence not necessarily picked up on the job. There were criticisms that social workers were poorly grounded in administration; but there was an increasing number of degree courses in this subject from which many students went into administrative posts in central and local government.

A study of *Social Policy and Administration* (Donnison, 1965) consisted largely of the first published case studies illustrating the actual processes of administration, which he defined as 'the development of collective action for the advancement of social welfare' (p. 26). Teaching of the subject drew upon various disciplines such as sociology, social economics, political theory, social history, and legal studies, rather than being an academic subject as such. In this it did not differ from other professional studies.

By 1960 there were six chairs in social administration and twenty by 1970 (Jones, 1970). The number increased in the early 1970s with the creation of new chairs in social administration and social work, while social administration was taught in almost every British university and in many polytechnics and colleges of further education. It took on a further dimension when social services reorganisation made the need for management studies more obvious. Much additional material was added and operational research undertaken, for example by the Institute of Local Government Studies at Birmingham University, and Brunel and Essex Universities. Advanced courses (short and sandwich) and seminars were provided for senior administrators. The provision of adequate field experience was a constant preoccupation.

The content of teaching was varied and lacking in boundaries. Sometimes it included the history of the social services and changes in attitudes, as well as present-day services, whether public or voluntary and their legislative framework; identification of social needs; key social problems; allocation of resources and ranking of priorities; modes of provision; administrative structures and processes; forecasting demographic and other trends and the desirable directions of change; and value judgements in social provision. The limelight from the 1960s on poverty in the welfare state resulted in more teaching on various aspects in sociology and social administration courses.

The teaching of social administration became increasingly concerned with general social policy issues. There was also a significant increase in the teaching of administration on professional social work courses compared with the earlier period.

SOCIAL PHILOSOPHY

This had been a basic subject in the old social science courses and it continued to be so in some 'relevant' degree courses. But pressure of time eliminated it from most professional courses except 'on demand' from students or when it was brought in as social work values, or the ethics of punishment in criminology courses, or conflicts of rights and duties in various contexts. This teaching was usually given by non-specialists, and students were not engaged in rigorous logical thought. They did not receive systematic teaching about different political theories, whether democratic, capitalist, socialist or communist; or the essentials of moral judgement and 'ought' obligations; or human rights; or problems of the balance of rights and responsibilities between one person and another and the individual and society; or liberty and equality; or the nature of distributive justice. All these value assumptions arose implicitly in one form or another in all the theoretical teaching and in practice. For instance, self-determination, the value and worth of the individual, and the rights of parents and their children were social work values, but these issues were only rarely examined systematically and debated in the mainstream of the course. The CCETSW multidisciplinary working party discussion paper on *Values in Social Work* (1976*b*) examined the conflicts and complexities, but argued forcefully for an explicit examination of all hidden value assumptions.

LEGAL STUDIES

The teaching of law had always been peculiarly difficult. Students needed to know about the place of law in society, the courts and the legal system, the differences between the criminal and civil law, how legislation was passed and enforced and the legal framework of some social work practice. But they were often bemused by law lectures on the niceties of case law or the intricacies of specific legislation. It also became clear that some knowledge, for example child care legislation, was better remembered if it was reinforced by field teaching, though this needed systematic planning and might be confined to probation placements.

Legal studies were often related to courses on social history and social administration which set them within the broader context of changing social attitudes. Theories of punishment might be taught in a criminology or social philosophy course, together with the place of law in society as part of social control, the protection of the individual, the resolution of conflict, and changing social attitudes towards offenders.

New emphasis on advocacy and welfare rights created fresh problems. The teaching of law had tried to escape from factual details, which took far too much time, were learnt up for examinations and then forgotten. But here was a new demand for ability to give accurate information to clients about entitlement to a complexity of statutory benefits, the law of landlord and tenant, and family law. Some contended that social work students should acquire a detailed and extensive knowledge of relevant law: others thought this unrealistic and dangerous when what social workers really needed was enough general grasp of the law within their field to know how to get detailed and up-to-date information, and when they ought to consult welfare rights lawyers or a specialist within the department.

The CCETSW study group report on *Legal Studies in Social Work Education* (1974a) distinguished between the law social workers ought to know when they qualified and a year later. It listed fifty-four acts and regulations (England and Wales) related to the responsibilities entrusted to social workers, i.e. professional law. It was, said the study group, essential for every qualified social worker 'to have an adequate grasp of those parts of the law from which he derives authority, which set the boundaries of his statutory responsibility and which establish the administrative framework within which he must do his job' (p. 17). Social work students also needed knowledge of general law, for example family law or race relations legislation; legal aid and advice entitlement; courts and tribunals; methods of law enforcement; and the administration of justice. Information sent to the study group by 92 professional courses showed that all but 2 taught some law, 56 as a separate subject and with from 2 to 100 hours allocated to it. Thirty-seven courses did not assess students' knowledge of the law. A number made references to the law in every part of the course in its relations to human behaviour, sociology, social administration and social work. General law and administration was usually taught by an academic lawyer, 'professional' law by social work teachers, and law in society by sociologists and others. It was very difficult to find the right lecturers for courses outside the university, and most respondents were dissatisfied with the teaching of law by lecturers who were not able to relate the subject to the world of social work.

SOCIAL RESEARCH

This was an awkward subject, apt to be untaught or overtaught. It provoked terror in students unfamiliar with statistical method, and a project, long essay or dissertation often took up a disproportionate amount of time and energy. On the other hand, students learnt to gather their own information, to experience the difficulties and rewards of doing so and to realise the importance of accurate data collection for social work practice. The CTSW, in particular, gave much thought to the whole subject in relation to the two-year CSW students, and concerned itself less with 'projects' than with problems of how to help students to make better use of relevant research. Traditional university teaching aimed to prepare students to undertake research as well as to understand and assess research findings. This was appropriate when master's degrees in social work began in the late 1960s with a dissertation as an essential part of the course. But for many other students an ability to grasp and use relevant research seemed a minimum but realistic requirement. 'One of the aims of any good social work course is not only to stir the imagination of its students but also to encourage their curiosity and develop their capacity to . . . assess what they observe and what they do' (CTSW, 1969, 'Teaching about Utilization of Research in Social Work Courses'). This suggested the use at various points in social work courses of statistical information about the social services, together with research studies of particular needs and of social work effectiveness. The two-year courses faced the problem that there was no tradition of research in colleges of further education, but in the universities, too, the extent to which students knew about or took part in ongoing research varied considerably. There was constant debate as to whether all students should take a specific course on research method as distinct from efforts to incorporate research findings into all the teaching.

SUMMARY

The foregoing is a bird's eye view of some developments in the content of education for professional social work. It seemed obvious that within a common framework individual courses should decide what they could offer most effectively; that beyond certain required subjects, students should be able to choose options; and that there should be ample opportunity for subsequent in-service training and further study.

Students had to absorb, not merely learn up, a considerable body of sometimes conflicting knowledge, apply disciplined judgement to it and learn to use it differentially in social work understanding and practice. As the range of practice widened, and thus fresh knowledge had to be called upon, it was clear that this could not all be demanded for every student going into practice, which ranged from community work to psychotherapeutic relations with individuals and groups. The CCETSW working party reports on different subjects showed that some courses did not teach elements thought to be essential, because teaching resources were lacking, or some subjects were taught in greater depth at the expense of others. There were no follow-up studies to show whether students' subsequent practice suffered permanently from the omission of 'essentials' or whether these were compensated in agency supervision and subsequent study and in-service training. In any event, the greater or less teaching of given subjects differed from the whole ethos of a course. In the 1950s and early 1960s there was, so some said, too much stress on psychodynamics. By the 1970s this had shifted to sociological, political and general psychology issues, with the result, so others said, that students afterwards failed to recognise pathology when they saw it, far less were they able to intervene usefully. This sometimes had disastrous consequences. Some courses put emphasis on given aspects of social work within the framework of a generic training. It was not clear by 1975 to what extent students could be well prepared in two years for all forms of practice without specialisation or superficiality.

The CCETSW working group on *Education and Training for Social Work* (1975*b*) concluded that 'sociology, developmental social and general psychology, philosophy, political science, law, social anthropology . . . made vital contributions to the education of students for social work practice together with concepts from medicine, psychiatry and education' (p. 25). By no means all courses incorporated the 'vital contributions', bearing in mind that social administration and social work were also vital and time too limited.

Chapter 3

Curriculum Planning and Educational Method: Post-Qualifying Courses

STEPS TOWARDS CURRICULUM PLANNING

There was practically no discussion in the 1950s and early 1960s about how students learn, in addition to what they should be taught. A few courses held a post-mortem at the end when students were asked their views about the course. There was also discussion at examiners' meetings about pass or fail standards, related to implicit or explicit judgements about what students should know and be able to do at the end of the course. Some change resulted from the professional as distinct from social studies courses because tutors had to think about the content of teaching in relation to its application in practice. Supervisors also had to be helped to learn how to teach. But it was not usual to start with objectives in planning the curriculum of a new course and then translate these into the theoretical and fieldwork content of the course, and test out the most effective learning experiences and educational methods to achieve the hoped-for results. By slow degrees and largely from empirical experience, elements of the psychology of learning, culled largely from gestalt psychology and stimulus response theories, began to be applied.

University students were assumed to know how to learn, otherwise they should not be in the university. But the new two-year courses in colleges of further education were intended for students who might be older, have a more limited educational background and be unused to thinking in analytical and conceptual terms. Here, then, was another challenge to think about educational method, about objectives and how to relate these to students' ways of learning. In 1962 the National Institute for Social Work Training (NISWT) started what later became the course in educational studies to equip experienced social workers to transfer to social work teaching (see also below, chapter 6, section on 'The National Institute for Social Work Training'). This course put the emphasis on curriculum planning by objectives and the hard task of thinking out not only what, but also why and how. This entailed planning the structure and inter-related parts of the curriculum, what students were meant to do with every element in it, what were the significant connecting threads, whether there were sufficient and appropriate learning experiences to achieve each objective, and how teaching and learning were woven together. A realistic look was then taken at whether the objectives of social work education, the knowledge, skill and attitudes, could be adequately achieved by the methods to be employed within the constraints of the time available and the students' level of education and experience. Obviously there were other constraints when, even if well-qualified lecturers were available to plan special teaching (which often they were not), and, even if there were enough competent supervisors (which there were not), it usually took two or three years and much come-back from the students to discover what and how to teach.

In their anxiety to include essential knowledge, some courses became overloaded, with consequent student anxiety and failure to assimilate what they were taught. They often had too little time for reading or to learn from each other through free-floating discussion, to assimilate and think creatively, or indeed for a life of their own, when in any event courses which stretched students emotionally as well as intellectually made heavy demands upon them. This raised the whole untested question of whether in the long run it was more productive to include a wide range or to cut out some 'essentials' but cover others in depth, in the expectation that these would become part of the students' thought and a springboard for future learning. In any event, if students had to be prepared to meet change and uncertainty they must grasp and be able to apply principles and concepts. Simon (1967) concluded in an address to the Association of Social Work Teachers that 'We must aim to educate people able to bring to bear in their chosen field knowledge which they understand as relevant (though they know it is incomplete and must be added to) and skills which they may have to use or adapt in circumstances we do not know' (p. 8).

On university courses, whether pre-professional or professional, it was usual to teach from the general to the particular. But on other courses where students were used to thinking in specific rather than general terms, it was often more effective to start from where they were and work outwards. Experience of students on these courses showed that even difficult subjects could be assimilated if they were well taught. This strengthened interest in both what the teacher teaches and what the learner learns, what is heard as well as what is said. There also began to be more interest in the extent to which a well-planned curriculum could speed up learning.

A. N. Whitehead's dictum that inert knowledge was dead knowledge, and knowledge not quickly put to use was forgotten obviously applied in professional education. Few challenged the value of lectures as such, but gradually they were reinforced by discussion between lecturers and students and seminars in which students took responsibility for specific contributions, for individual and group projects, and for various observation exercises. Teachers were thus in closer touch with students' learning and attitudes. By the 1970s the distinction between learners and teachers had become blurred with the healthier assumption that everyone was at different points in the struggle to learn. Far more responsibility was placed on students to contribute by searching out material; by planned observation, for instance of small children; by direct experience; by becoming conscious of the processes of their own learning so that they might learn how to learn and contribute to curriculum revision. There was a series of intermediate goals within general objectives which reinforced learning by study, thinking, observing, seeing, hearing, discussing and doing. Students also learnt to ask significant questions, let imaginative consideration play upon these, think independently and form their own judgements. Student participation was taken for granted, but with conflicting views as to whether they as the consumers should have the ultimate say in the curriculum or whether this would be an abrogation of the staff's educational responsibility.

Social work teachers relied heavily upon case records in the 1950s and early 1960s, but students began to protest about teaching from 'dead' records and by degrees these were largely superseded by students' current cases and tape-recorded interviews. The latter were more accurate and recorded silences and inflexions of voices, though not non-verbal communication.

In time social work teachers themselves began to teach in the human growth and development courses. Some felt that the usual content did not sufficiently stretch students' imagination about how different people live, experience, grow and change, and they therefore began to use creative literature, novels, drama and poetry to reinforce learning about research findings and theories of human behaviour.

The CCETSW working group on *Education and Training for Social Work* (1975*b*) thought that 'the acquisition of skills had not been as highly valued in social work education as the acquisition of knowledge' (p. 21), and thus fieldwork was expected to carry the burden of application, whereas the educational institution ought to contribute to this. The extent to which it did so depended in part on whether or not social work teachers were also experienced practitioners. The quality of fieldwork teaching was also affected by supervisors having too little time and too little teaching experience. By the 1970s the gap between theory and practice was sometimes narrowed from the fieldwork end by the appointment of full-time supervisors with broader teaching responsibilities (see chapter 4). From the classroom end the gap was lessened by tutors who kept in touch with practice and by developments in the use of audio-visual aids discussed below. An unexplored task was to identify essentials of skill learning, break these down into their components, help students to perceive the skill to be learnt, and to master it through sufficient and appropriate opportunities for practice. Quick feedback was essential to reinforce good and extinguish bad practice. For this it was necessary to analyse social work practice, to discover how much of what elements in it, how frequently repeated in what circumstances, were necessary to develop appropriate skill. These skills were on very different levels, making different demands on the student, from administrative procedures to the ability to assess a situation systematically, to perceive distressed clients' real feelings, to communicate with them and take action that demonstrated effective concern.

These aims were far from being achieved, so the nagging question remained as to how to make better provision in fieldwork for the development of skill. Apart from the inevitable plateaux in learning, some of the despondency which students experienced at their perceived inadequacies and their failure to help might well be lessened if there were more systematised knowledge about skill learning – both for students and staff. If seconded students on courses had already experienced this systematic skill learning they would start professional training at a more advanced level, more aware of themselves, with less to unlearn, and therefore able to achieve more.

Skill learning was extremely complex in fieldwork where events were less under control and clients' behaviour urgently real. But from the late 1960s audio-visual aids began to make possible 'the thing in the middle' between the orderly second hand of the educational institution and the uncontrollable first hand of clients' needs. There follows a brief account of how these aids began to be used in conjunction with each other, with systematic teaching, and with fieldwork.

AUDIO-VISUAL AND OTHER AIDS IN SOCIAL WORK EDUCATION

Role play started in the 1950s to help students or members of refresher courses to experience different roles. These might be different kinds of interview, or a mock court, or a group, or a decision-making committee or indeed any suitable situations. There was discussion afterwards about how each participant and the audience had felt and what was learnt from the exercise. The importance of de-briefing those who had played emotionally charged roles was only realised later. Role play was based on verbal communication. Sculpting was introduced later, based on non-verbal communication through proximity, touch, posture, gestures, and facial expressions, offering another means of understanding attitudes and feelings. Sensitivity training (or T groups) on the lines pioneered in this country by the Tavistock Institute was used increasingly from the late 1950s.

Simulation exercises and games based upon one or several simple or complicated issues were added later, especially when management courses for senior officers began to be demanded from the late 1960s. The games were useful in clarifying the many different political strands, the cross-currents, the power struggles, the pressure groups, the limited range of choice, and many other constraints in determining priorities, the allocation of scarce resources and other management problems.

Films followed by discussion had been used for some time, and some, for example the Robertsons' film 'A Two-Year-Old Goes to Hospital', and their series on residential homes and foster care also had a considerable influence on practice. Tape-recorded interviews with clients began to be used spasmodically in the 1950s. But use of video-taped, live sessions with a group of students only started much later when educational institutions began to acquire expensive audio-visual equipment. Some social work teachers experimented regularly with this, but the value of these devices to speed up learning and develop communication skills had only been explored to a limited extent in social work education by the mid-1970s.

These and other aids made possible experiential learning which had a more vivid impact than discussion alone, but was easier to control than the clamorous reality of fieldwork or actual administrative responsibilities. They could be used to help students to judge their own progress and to increase empathy, the capacity to enter into, to understand and respond appropriately to other people's feelings, especially through video-taped role play; to become more self-aware and to 'see ourselves as others see us'. The study of group dynamics and interaction could also be reinforced by this live experiential learning.

By the mid-1970s a few courses were using sensitivity groups, role play, simulation exercises and practice with audio-visual aids as ice breakers with new groups of students and throughout the course to speed up cognitive learning and increased sensitivity to self and others.

Inevitably there was a risk that they might be used as gimmicks in facile exercises that ignored the complexities of real life, the depth of actual feelings and the discipline of systematic learning. But in the hands of good teachers who knew how to use them, they could be powerful ways of reinforcing knowledge, for instance about a particular social service or problem, or to change attitudes, stretch the imagination and channel emotions.

MODULES OR THEMES

Modular learning became fairly general from the early 1970s. It was based on the assumption that learning was more effective if, instead of a series of subjects being strung out over a period of time, these were concentrated in modules in which a given theme, say family therapy or priority planning in the social services, was explored in its many ramifications with a range of knowledge and learning devices concentrated upon it. It was also thought that several modules built up into larger wholes. This kind of integrated teaching made heavy demands on teachers of both theory and practice. Some CCETSW plans for further training and for the certificate in social service (CSS) were built upon this system.

PRESSURE IN THE 1970S FOR ANALYSIS OF CURRICULUM CONTENT AND EDUCATIONAL METHOD

Students who were well educated for professional practice had developed a responsible professional self capable of new ways of thinking, feeling and acting. In essence all the foregoing efforts at curriculum planning and the use of educational methodology were efforts to speed up and deepen this learning process. Assessment by both staff and students at given points in students' subsequent careers was much discussed, though some old practices persisted. For a long time it had been accepted that a period of planned orientation and consolidation in the first job was essential and this existed to some extent by the 1970s, though in too many situations newly qualifield social workers, like other field staff, were deluged with crisis work or requests for services.

It is surprising that when increasingly large funds were spent on social work education, and when every possible pattern of non-graduate, graduate and post-graduate qualifying courses existed in this country in the 1960s, none of the three training councils nor the JUC set on foot a comparative study of these different course structures, their content, and the students they recruited and trained, judged against the yardsticks of educational attainment and subsequent performance in the field. In the absence of such periodic assessments, there were entrenched beliefs and accepted practices but no means of knowing whether, for example, first laying an academic foundation in social science subjects and then adding professional education produced as good or better or worse results than 'integrated' courses; or to what extent courses outside the university with their different student body produced comparable results.

Interest in curriculum planning and teaching methods spread in British universities in the 1960s. The UGC Education Development Committee provided services, the Committee of Vice-Chancellors set up a group to promote the training of university tutors, and London University had a University Teaching Methods Unit. Its director produced a comprehensive guide (Beard, 1970) to good educational method and current knowledge about how adults learn.

It is not possible to judge the impact of these developments on social work education. The CCETSW working parties on new types of course and on the teaching of specific subjects gave admirable reasons why additional material should be added to overcrowded courses. But they did not stop there. The working party on residential social work (1973b) thought that 'all new tutors should be required to undertake extensive training in social work curriculum planning and in teaching methods' (p. 29). It estimated that at least 700 tutors would be needed in future. The working party on day services (1975a) said it was urgent for the CCETSW to develop an organised plan to train the trainers, whether teachers on CQSW or CSS courses or field supervisors. It also thought that comparative studies of the different types of training were essential to test their effectiveness. This should include monitoring the levels of skill achieved by similar students taking courses on various educational patterns.

The Council intended to sponsor preparation for teaching in short course programmes and also as part of post-qualifying studies. It produced the discussion document on *Education and Training for Social Work* (1975b) because its experience of reviewing courses made it 'aware of the need for and difficulty of achieving clarity about the objectives of social work education' (p. 5). The working group explored the nature and values of social work, and of social work education, including the importance of clarity about the aims, objectives and methods of any given course. It also discussed the common elements of social work practice that all students must acquire at an acceptable level. Its views about curriculum planning, like much in this chapter, were implicitly based on Tyler (1950) and Towle (1954).

The Ralphs Report (1975) included a valuable exercise in analysing social work tasks and translating these into knowledge, skill and attitudes, though not the learning experiences necessary to attain the objectives (pp. 57–62).

The Birch Report (1976) said: 'The preparation of teachers for social work education is an area of crucial importance where opportunity needs to be provided to acquire skills in teaching methods, as well as to conceptualise practice' (para. 7.23). Their training should be financed from the central fund which the working party proposed.

Knowledge of course planning and educational method was as important in in-service training. In the 1950s this was not recognised or discussed, but by 1975 it was taken for granted if not always applied in all types of course.

POST-QUALIFYING COURSES (ADVANCED AND FURTHER STUDIES)

There was sporadic talk about advanced training in the late 1940s and early 1950s, but the term seems to have meant a higher level of initial professional training for graduates. For a time an advanced course was run by the London University Institute of Education to fit people with relevant qualifications and experience for senior posts in residential child care. But it never became part of the CTC pattern. Advanced courses intended for experienced workers with the residential certificate in child care were started at Bristol University (1960), at Newcastle University (1963), and later at Glasgow University. From 1972 the Glasgow generic course was enlarged to include people holding senior posts in the social work services including residential care. Students' theses produced interesting material about residential child care and it is remarkable that (apart from the Tavistock Institute) the only post-qualifying courses were in the comparatively neglected field of residential care.

Throughout the 1950s and 1960s energies were concentrated on training more and more social workers on basic professional courses; some of these were much improved compared with their predecessors but they were often too short and with overcrowded or too narrow curricula. Social work practice, research and education all suffered from this concentration on basic training, and staff who lacked time for research and practice. Each year a few qualified social workers took a psychiatric social work course in order to use an increased knowledge of psychodynamics in their own field. But in this period there was little demand for advanced studies.

The improvements in social work education in the 1950s and 1960s, together with growth in the size and range of services, the need for more teaching, supervision, advanced practice, management studies, social planning and research, coupled with the growth of sociological and psychological knowledge, made it more obvious that the level and length of basic professional training must be steadily raised, social workers be given more systematic opportunity for continued learning, and advanced training be provided. No doubt continued learning resulted from in-service short courses, good practice, staff meetings, case conferences, and psychiatric and other consultation in the most progressive agencies, as well as from membership of professional associations, other activities and individual study, but this was not enough.

From the early 1950s the Tavistock Clinic one-year advanced course in casework gave a few selected caseworkers substantial interdisciplinary clinical experience, observation of normal babies in their families, and supervision and psychoanalytic teaching about child development and family life. Group dynamics teaching was added later and students were sometimes supervised on work undertaken in their own agencies. Since experienced social workers of exceptional quality were selected to take the course they were often quickly promoted to administrative posts with no opportunity for casework. This was inevitable when promotion was not geared to advanced practice. The Tavistock Clinic discussed from time to time whether the content of the only advanced course in the country was relevant to new career opportunities for social workers. Some argued that a deeper understanding of human motivation, development, and family and group relationships was essential in social work teaching and administration. Others thought the course was too heavily weighted on pathology at the expense of sociology and the structure and dynamics of institutions.

The implications of generic (applied social studies) courses precipitated discussion in the Association of Psychiatric Social Workers about advanced training. In 1956 it discussed 'an advanced university course for experienced caseworkers from all settings to give special qualifications to teachers, supervisors, administrative and research workers and other leaders in the field of social work' (Timms, 1964, p. 214). There were unsuccessful efforts to turn the LSE mental health course into an advanced course. Later a pilot advanced course for experienced social workers from various settings was run at the LSE from 1962 to 1965 (McDougall, 1970). It consisted of an academic year with optional fieldwork, attendance at seminars on methods of social work education and of social work help, research in social work and welfare, social administration, a T group, and a programme of individually planned lecture courses.

Nursten, speaking at the 1965 Child Guidance Inter Clinic Conference, argued the case for a master's degree for senior social workers in any field. Two years later she was able to pioneer such a post-qualifying course at Bradford University for social workers with at least two (later three) years' experience. This degree could be taken either by full- or part-time study and was a valuable means of raising the level of practice, supervision and teaching in the area. The syllabus included advanced casework, psychosocial development in health and disease, social policy and administration, research method, optional courses on teaching, supervision and management, and tutorials to relate theory to practice. Most past students went into social work education.

By the mid-1960s the JUC was discussing the need for a 'genuinely advanced' course in the universities for qualified social workers with substantial experience. Some members thought students who had trained in colleges of further education should be eligible on merit. There was much discussion about the importance of advanced training to make new knowledge transmissible in practice and to equip trained social workers for new tasks, especially in supervision, teaching and management. Progress was hamstrung because too few people were equipped to teach or to supervise at an advanced level, and because social workers in administrative positions could seldom be spared or paid their comparatively high salaries as seconded students. In its early years the Tavistock Clinic course was able to·give adequate senior grants from its Field Foundation (USA) Fund. Without such a grant it was only possible to select candidates from those whose employers would second them. The first attempt to run a one-year further training course at the NISWT in the mid-1960s faced the same impasse. Local authorities were seconding large numbers for basic training through pooled funds, but were understandably less willing to do this for senior staff who were on higher salaries, or even to release them without salary and run the risk that they might not return.

The CTC and the Advisory Council on Probation and After-Care (ACPAC) each gave grants for about six students a year to take further or advanced training, but these were not senior awards and there was little or no competition for them. Social Science Research Council (SSRC) post-graduate awards were only available for research and very few social workers studied for an individual PhD. By the late 1960s the CTC, which clearly recognised the importance of advanced training, was beginning to discuss senior awards, while the CTSW successfully convinced the Gulbenkian Foundation of the need for a fund from which such awards could be made. This was taken over by the CCETSW as the Fellowship Scheme for Advanced Studies. Sponsored by the Gulbenkian Foundation, the LGTB, the DHSS, and with a contribution from the Social Work Services Group (SWSG) (Scotland) it was intended for people able to make a contribution to social work or social welfare, but whose work made it unlikely that they could receive financial support from conventional educational funding. Maximum grants were normally for twelve months, but a number were for much shorter periods. In addition the DHSS made about twelve senior awards a year for recognised advanced courses.

Any course beyond basic training might label itself 'advanced', but by the 1970s a distinction began to be drawn between further training to extend knowledge and skill in some new aspects of social work practice, for example use of research findings or social work teaching or work with small groups; and study well in advance of basic training and familiar experience. A few more social workers undertook research leading to an individual PhD, while each year a few students on basic post-graduate courses for a master's degree reached an advanced level in examinations, the dissertation and fieldwork.

There were several advanced courses at the Tavistock Clinic by 1975:

(a) An interdisciplinary four-year, full-time programme of training in adult psychotherapy with seminars on theories of human growth and behaviour, the psychodynamics of family and group interaction and of various forms of therapy, together with clinical practice with individuals, marriage partners and small groups, and opportunities to practise as therapists, teachers and consultants in various agencies. About four senior social workers took the course at any one time.

(b) The one-year advanced programme for social workers included psycho-dynamic practice with adolescents, families and marital interaction, as well as seminars and opportunities to undertake teaching and consultation in other agencies. About seven students took the course each year.

(c) Part-time courses consisting of fifteen to sixty weekly sessions included needs and relationships in child care institutions, casework and social work, family therapy, marital interaction, staff supervision, techniques of crisis intervention, working with multiproblem families, short-term intervention, social work in general practice.

(d) A two-year course on one evening a week on psychotherapy for social workers. One hundred and fifty places were available on these courses and they were taken by about 100 social workers each year, though in 1975 five part-time courses had to be cancelled for lack of applicants.

The three-month, six-month and one-year, full-time courses at the NISW were a mixture of further and advanced studies and practice. They included options in management, advanced practice, community work, residential social work, social research and a six-month course in educational studies for practising or intending social work teachers (see also chapter 6, section on 'The National Institute for Social Work Training).

The one-year MA in social service planning at Essex University started in 1971. It aimed to introduce experienced students to theories and methods of social problem solving and administration including organisational theory, innovation in social service, and community power and decision making, with particular emphasis on the comparative analysis and measurement of needs. Forty students had taken the course by 1975, of whom a number were in social services departments, research or teaching.

In 1971 Brunel University started a two-year MA course in public and social administration. It consisted of four groups of subjects: theories and methods (including social research); social policy and administration; a special subject; and a dissertation which included fieldwork. The course was intended for students active in the particular service they studied. There was also an MSc course at University College, Cardiff.

The case for advanced and further training at last came into the limelight when Seebohm reorganisation was thought to have lowered the standard of services, particularly for children and mentally disordered people; when other clients like the handicapped or adolescents needed specialist knowledge and skill; when community work, residential social work and new social work skills were developing; when management, supervision, consultancy and teaching skills were obviously needed; and when the increasingly 'generalist' content of basic courses made opportunities for further study in particular fields essential.

One of the last acts of the CTSW was to explore further training on a modular system, perhaps planned over a period of years, and full-time advanced courses for much smaller numbers.

Within the first three years' term of office the CCETSW set up a group of council members to explore the objectives, pattern, organisation and siting of advanced courses in view of their importance. There was much general discussion at this time amongst those engaged in social work education about possible alternatives. These discussions reaffirmed the importance of advanced courses to improve the quality of practice and explore new knowledge. The distinction between basic, further and advanced training (though with overlapping boundaries) was usually reaffirmed, as was the feeling that all three should be provided in educational institutions able to offer research and practice experience of a high standard. Linked patterns of modular or unit opportunities for study had gained much, though not universal, acceptance. This would enable more than one educational institution (usually a university) to use other advanced teaching possibilities. On this pattern the total course might consist of several three-month, whole- or part-time modules. The relative merits of this modular system versus one-year, full-time courses required further exploration in relation to educational advantages and employers' willingness to second either for a series of shorter periods or for a year. Some thought a series of modules could hardly reach an advanced standard compared with a one-year, full-time course, and that employers found it less difficult to second for a year. It should also be possible to work out individual programmes of study and practice for people who wanted to develop some type of work for which no planned provision existed.

There were differing views as to whether social work knowledge already existed that could be taught at an advanced level. Part of the courses should be heavily practice-oriented and aim to extend the boundaries of knowledge and explore policy planning and management skills at an advanced level, without sacrificing academic excellence and with the necessary emphasis on carrying out and interpreting research. It would be necessary to compensate for inadequacies in some basic training, including too little knowledge of relevant social sciences, narrow concepts of social work and insufficient grounding in the use of research findings, i.e. knowledge that was too general and too elementary. Some social work teachers themselves might have to undertake advanced study before they could teach at that level. In short, the familiar tensions between the demands of practice, research and the quality of social work teaching *vis à vis* academic disciplines were inherent in these discussions, no doubt with potentially creative results, given common understanding and a reasonable balance of power. Discussions also emphasised the necessity of social work research founded in practice. This was essential for knowledge adequate for advanced study and should be largely undertaken by past or present practitioners. Much more extensive opportunities were needed for the study and development of skills through many different forms of continued learning, and a rapid expansion of further and advanced courses was vital for the development of social work.

There was a good deal of university heart-searching as to whether it was appropriate for the CCETSW to recognise advanced courses. Some argued that in view of limited resources it should recognise a few centres for advanced study because in any event it was responsible for setting up and maintaining standards of education, training and competence. Others thought the CCETSW would be exercising an excessive and resented power if it attempted to decide which academic institutions should initiate advanced studies when others might think they had something useful to contribute, so there should be flexible advance on a broad front. It became clear in subsequent discussions that employers would only be likely to second students to advanced courses which met CCETSW requirements, and that adequate grants would be essential for senior social workers taking such courses. In any event it would only be possible to provide post-qualifying courses for a small percentage of social workers: figures of about 150–200 a year were mentioned.

The distinction between further and advanced studies merged in a continuum of post-qualifying courses when the CCETSW sent out two documents in mid-1975 on 'Principles, Procedures and Criteria for Approval of Post-Qualifying Studies' and 'Guidelines for Post-Qualifying Studies'

(CCETSW, 1975*e* and 1975*f*). These invited proposals for such courses lasting at least three months full-time or the equivalent part-time. Proposals might be made by educational institutions and voluntary and statutory agencies independently of or in collaboration with such institutions. This was a new development. The curriculum was to include the close application of theory to practice, unless in a particular instance this was unnecessary. The level of knowledge and practice skill to be achieved was to be specified and related to defined objectives, and the staff were to be adequate in numbers and expertise. It was hoped that courses would be planned in close consultation with employing organisations and social workers. Although courses were to be for a minimum of three months, the CCETSW envisaged that some might last for up to two years. The decision to recognise a variety of courses rather than to concentrate on a few 'centres of excellence' was deplored by some, but possibly it was the only way to stimulate a variety of post-qualifying courses yet maintain standards. In any event the same procedures for recognition applied to all such courses.

The importance of training the trainers came into the limelight yet again. It was hoped that some proposals would be for educational studies in social work so that the National Institute six-month course would not remain an isolated example. The Group for the Advancement of Psychotherapy in Social Work made out a strong case for a psychotherapeutic specialisation with advanced training in social work with individuals and groups. The first post-qualifying course to be recognised by the CCETSW was in fact an MSc in mental health social work in the psychiatry department at Leeds University in 1975. This one-year course concentrated on advanced case-work, mental health, theories of human personality and behaviour and research methods. A number of other post-qualifying courses of various lengths in various subjects at various institutions were under consideration at the end of 1975. Most were for small intakes of about twelve students.

The Birch Report (1976) adopted a CCETSW proposal that all CSS and CQSW holders should have the equivalent of three months' post-qualifying training every five years and 10 per cent of CQSW holders should have a substantial period of post-qualifying training, at least to the equivalent of twelve months, at some point in their career (para. 9.55).

At least the situation was clearer by 1975 than in 1950 but there was a severe backlog in provision. It was also not certain that employers would second more social workers to take post-qualifying courses as these became available, or indeed that universities, in particular, would provide the necessary extra staff without special funds.

Chapter 4

Fieldwork and Field Teaching

THE 1950s

The Spread of Field Teaching
It was logical that if a methodology of casework was beginning to emerge in the late 1940s and early 1950s, social work teachers and practitioners should try to discover how to help students to apply this theory in practice. This meant a sea change from learning how to function in the agency, picking up as much as possible about clients from the experience of individual staff members, and learning to fulfil administrative requirements. The new demand was that the student should both learn about the agency and also apply certain concepts about human behaviour in working with individual clients. On the basis of a systematic assessment, tested in the light of subsequent response, clients should be helped to meet or come to terms with their problems and make more effective use of available social resources. This skill in personal relations obviously demanded of students an insight into their own attitudes, moral values and cultural assumptions, feelings about particular kinds of people, and ability to accept expressions of hostility, dependence, grief and pain without denying their reality. It was believed that this training resulted in general and transferable skill and attitudes as well as the knowledge of a specific service. It obviously demanded supervisors who had absorbed and were practising the 'new' casework, had more to teach than their own individual experience, and were familiar enough with the content of the course teaching to help the students to see its application in living situations.

The first move in the late 1940s consisted of summer schools and seminars for supervisors, mainly run by the Institute of Almoners and the APSW. These and the active part played by the Home Office Probation Division and the stimulus of American social work teachers are described in other chapters (see especially chapters 5 and 6). These early seminars were mainly based on casework practice because this foundation had to be laid before supervision could be realistically discussed. Sometimes this gave social workers with outmoded training enough to develop their own casework and their ability to teach, sometimes they themselves dropped out. These seminars had a tremendous impact in bringing theory and practice together and were absorbed with an enthusiasm which it is hard now to recapture.

The struggle between old and new ways caused much discussion and controversy in almoner and probation circles. Those who espoused new approaches were accused of talking unintelligible jargon and of having developed X-ray eyes. They were demanding time for uninterrupted sessions with students and there was much curiosity about the esoteric content of these sessions. This was all part of the struggle to develop a common professional language of communication and principles of practice which were neither primarily administrative nor ancillary to medicine.

Supervision in this sense faced great difficulties in the local authority services. Short periods of observation or 'accompanied visiting' were acceptable. But it was an uphill task for tutors to the first child care courses to negotiate longer placements, sanction for students to take responsibility for cases, and choice of specific supervisors. From the mid-1950s the tougher demands of the 'generic' courses helped, since the first student units were made possible by extra financing, and general attitudes changed when the service began to demand child care officers with more skills than the untrained. In contrast to child care, local authority health and welfare services remained almost wholly outside social work education until the 1960s.

The earlier practice had been to send students to the head of the service or department who then arranged for them to spend brief periods with different people to 'see all sides of the work'. When there was nothing else for them to do, they might also spend an inordinate amount of time doing chores, 'observing', or reading case records for no clear purpose. It took much tact to get this system changed to one in which a particular, selected staff member would be responsible in a teaching role for the student. Heads of agencies often found it impossible to make this kind of invidious selection if staff enjoyed having students, and 'it was only fair to let everyone have a go'. Moreover, the most senior staff members should obviously be offered the task – although they might have little systematised knowledge to teach. There were also ambivalent attitudes about students who were time-consuming, although their enthusiasm and questions were stimulating and later it became a prestige symbol to have them. It was thus no mean task to get it accepted that supervisors should be designated and that the agency and the training course should decide in consultation who was competent to supervise. Sometimes young, fairly newly qualified social workers might be preferred to their seniors who might have years of experience but nothing beyond this to teach and no knowledge of the new professional courses. This naturally caused hurt feelings, anxieties, jealousies and tensions in the agency. These practices continued for years in many residential placements.

It was also a revolutionary idea that students should be responsible for their own cases under supervision rather than go on 'accompanied' visiting or carry out too small – or sometimes too big – tasks on their own; that they should process record their interviews; take responsibility for contacts with other agencies; and have regular and substantial tutorial sessions with their supervisor. There was naturally much anxiety that clients might suffer, hence maintenance of good service to clients became an essential responsibility of supervisors. There were also problems about student accommodation, or even anywhere for them to sit, necessary clerical help and supervisors' regular participation in supervisors' meetings at the university. Social work education owes a great debt to those early tutors and supervisors who took on extra burdens, with or without the support of their colleagues, and usually without their own caseload being reduced.

Social agencies were also being asked to make the time of some of their best caseworkers available and provide accommodation when there was heavy pressure on both, and initially without any extra payment. It was also not easy to accept the careful selection of cases for students (instead of giving them a bit of everything), and gradually to build up these from two or three to no more than ten or twelve so that they might have time for reflection, detailed recording, reading and discussion. This was called learning by slow motion or learning in depth, in the belief that students would develop powers of observation, analysis, understanding of behaviour and capacity for communication which would be sufficiently ingrained to become part of their subsequent practice. Some employing agencies thought that students so trained could not cope with ordinary caseload pressures; that they were good at social diagnosis but vague about treatment; that they knew too little about administration, the decision-making process and the procedures of different agencies; and that they had too little discussion with agency administrators in their fieldwork, indeed that the difficult balance was not achieved between the development of casework skill and a grasp of administrative processes. This is significant in the light of later studies, for example of medical social work, discussed especially in volume 1, chapter 9. It led to attempts to clarify what was appropriate to training or to planned further learning in the first job. There were laments that this new kind of training had made students regrettably dependent, unable to make up their minds and take action, precious, too theoretical, too much concerned with 'deep casework', or even straying into psychotherapy. But those who experienced the value of supervision during training clamoured for it in their first jobs, even sometimes to the point of organising it by correspondence.

After a time it began to be accepted that students did not come 'fully qualified' off the assembly line, and that workloads should be built up by degrees and with regular supervision if integration of knowledge and skill was to be consolidated by experience. The probation service was the first to see the importance of supervision for serving officers, but it took some time before other social workers realised that the trained and experienced were not 'fully competent', indeed that no one is ever 'fully qualified' and that continued learning of various kinds is needed throughout a professional career.

It also took some time to realise that the new professional courses really meant it when they said that practice was as important as theory and that students must pass in both. Much time and effort were devoted at supervisors' meetings and elsewhere to working out what this entailed, how reports could be made more objective, how they could be graded and evaluated, and how to weigh them in the total assessment. Supervisors were pressed to discuss students' progress with them, to send midway reports, to discuss final reports in draft with them, and to modify these in the light of their comments or embody disagreement in the report. There was also much discussion about educational aims and expected standards of practice at the end of each placement and on what criteria students should be referred or failed. It was a hard struggle to achieve supervisors' reports which gave actual evidence of performance in support of statements. This slowly improved in courses where external examiners read supervisors' reports and could require additional evidence or ask to read case records.

The Cope Committees (1951) found no official recognition of or provision for supervision in almoners' departments. Students also had too little opportunity to become familiar with local authority social services. It recommended that 'In each hospital region, an adequate number of almoners' departments suitable for the purpose be made available for the practical training of students. Almoners giving tutorial instruction in these departments should be allowed sufficient time to do so' (para. 154).

By 1959 the Younghusband working party went further when its Report (1959) said:

'We cannot emphasise too strongly that we regard field teaching, based upon actual responsibility for a small case load, as of equal importance with theoretical study in all forms of training for social work . . . Local authorities have a vital contribution to make; indeed the training for social workers which we recommend cannot come into existence nor develop fruitfully without the active co-operation of these authorities.' (para. 884)

It also regretted that almoners and PSWs were almost entirely trained in hospitals and clinics when they should also be given supervised practice in local authority health and welfare departments.

It was a struggle at this time to convince some local councillors that training was necessary at all and that money should be spent on student training which would not necessarily benefit the particular authority. In the mid-1950s the present writer asked the chairman of the health committee of a big city what provision was made for in-service training and was told with asperity that they only employed 'fully qualified' staff and did not expect to have to spend any more on them.

Regular supervisors' meetings with course tutors were one of the most effective means of improving social work education. These only existed in a few places in the 1950s but spread rapidly in the 1960s. They enabled supervisors to know what students were being taught on the course and their own part in relating this to practice or filling in gaps, to discuss the content of supervision as an educational process, to develop norms of student performance at different stages, and to clarify standards for reports. Above all, these supervisors' meetings became strongly cohesive groups, in a valued partnership with the educational institution that sometimes led to accusations of divided loyalties and too much time spent away from the agency. A number of tutors also ran seminars for social workers who might later become supervisors. Owing to shortages, some unqualified people were used if they were good, intuitive social workers with teaching gifts, able to communicate and to know why they were doing what they were doing.

THE 1960s

By the 1960s supervision had mastered the struggles of the 1950s and was now everywhere demanded. This was a new threat to its quality, yet in spite of all the hazards genuine progress followed from the gains of the 1950s.

The starting of new university and other courses in 'desert' areas meant that social work teachers had to provide in-service training in social work for supervisors. Sometimes special supervisors had to be appointed to get courses started in such areas. This explosion in training resulted in much local confusion and competitiveness, and varying degrees of competence. The turmoil was greater in the field than on the academic side where the curriculum could be discussed in comparative tranquillity. By degrees the work of tutors and the recruitment of more qualified staff (sometimes past students) raised local standards and enabled courses to expand. As the attitudes of local authorities to employing trained social workers also changed they began to realise that to provide student fieldwork attracted trained staff.

This was reinforced, for example, by a CTC memorandum of guidance on practical training for child care students (1963). This detailed the demands of student fieldwork in the light of current good standards: it was said to have been used by children's officers to show that requests for additional resources were not a symptom of individual empire building. Pressure for and help towards better field teaching also came from the Home Office and the CTSW. In addition to supervisors' meetings at course centres there were many more refresher courses sponsored by the training councils, the professional associations and the newly formed Association of Social Work Teachers.

The best source of information about actual practice in the early 1960s was the national survey by Brown and Gloyne (1966) carried out in 1962–3. This showed that there was agreement between tutors and field staff about the aims of professional courses but much confusion about social studies students. In discussing how to relate theory to practice the authors commented pungently that

'The usual words "theory" and "practice" suggest an unreal distinction in the process of learning, as though something were picked up in one place and put down in another. The important difference lies between a live situation in which the student is in action and one in which his pursuit of knowledge and experiments in ideas are for the time being protected from immediate demands and consequences.' (p. 17)

A large majority of the supervisors interviewed thought concurrent fieldwork was a more satisfactory method of teaching and learning than block placements, in which there was too little contact between tutors and supervisors especially in distant placements. In concurrent fieldwork a much closer relationship with the course was possible and thus between theory and practice, and the students were in the agency for longer. Some favoured block placements because students were available 'for all the vicissitudes of their clients' and became more closely identified with the service, its procedures, legal sanctions and their interpretation. Block placements were having to be combined with concurrent placements on some courses because they could not expand if they relied entirely on local agencies. Later, some courses began to experiment by keeping one term wholly free for academic study and another for full-time fieldwork in the locality.

Student units had always existed in the mental health courses and were part of the Carnegie course. Otherwise, when single students were attached to different supervisors they sometimes came together regularly for group discussions. Students usually preferred group placements because there was reinforcement of learning, discussions were more stimulating, they felt more free to debate and disagree, and less afraid to put a foot wrong for fear of getting a poor report. Supervisors tended to be better qualified, they more rapidly developed norms of student performance and improved their teaching skills. On the other hand, special accommodation had to be provided and there was a risk that the student unit might become a rather precious artificial little group isolated from the pressures and general work of the department. Sometimes a member of the academic staff was seconded part-time to supervise a group of students, or a special appointment might be made to the agency, or a member of staff be released to supervise about four students and carry a reduced caseload. Such supervisors might also have some responsibility for students supervised by other caseworkers. These appointments were usually financed by trusts, by central government or by voluntary funds. At the time of the Brown and Gloyne 1962–3 study it was not possible to discover how many student units existed because their number was rapidly increasing. The study recommended the setting up of an experimental field study centre in which students placed in a variety of settings might come together for teaching. Large areas of the country were not used for students' fieldwork, for instance thirteen English counties and thirty-two county boroughs had had 0–10 students from any course in the preceding twelve months. The position was far worse in Scotland and Wales.

SOCIAL STUDIES STUDENTS

Social studies courses presented a confused picture. 'The broader social education and the understanding of social welfare policies and practices which is now more clearly seen as the focus of the social science course' (Rodgers, 1964, p. 12) had not penetrated to the practical work. There was almost no personal contact with tutors, little explanation of what kind of experience the students were expected to be given, and most agencies knew little about the content of courses. Sufficient information might not be sent beforehand, and reports on students might not be asked for or acknow-ledged. Students themselves could become bored and frustrated through having too little or too much responsibility. Many agencies were taking students from both social studies and professional courses. This added to their confusion about objectives and resulted in some feeling overwhelmed and overpressed, with supervisors 'squeezed and exhausted'. The aims seem to have ranged from general oversight of a social service to experience of agency administration, of people in different living conditions and of human relations, to some early involvement in casework practice. This last was thought at the time to be undesirable but necessary because after qualifying many social studies students were going direct into social work jobs without professional training. Rodgers found in her study of the careers of social studies students (1964) that in 1950 and 1955 over a third of all the sample went on immediately to full-time training for social work, and by 1961 over half of the rest had taken some form of training. In 1960 less than a third went on immediately to further training. Thus there was an increase in the employment of people with only a social studies qualification. So far as preferences for professional training were concerned, almoning led throughout by a comfortable margin with probation second. This indicated a recruitment incentive to social agencies to take social studies students for practical work. Many more placements of a wider range could undoubtedly have been found if tutors responsible for social studies practical work had had time to go out and look for them.

A JUC study group produced a manual on *Field Work in Social Administration Courses* (1966) which set out with admirable clarity the purposes of fieldwork in the teaching of social administration. It recognised that 'those who have tried to teach social administration to students who have had no opportunity of participating in the social services or of observing their work are well aware of gaps in comprehension and a certain lack of zest which applies to all but the best' (p. 5). The manual suggested an initial stage of participant observation which might be undertaken by students in close relation to the teaching of social administration, followed by experience with responsibility. The parallel Brown and Gloyne study had shown the unfortunate gap between the desirable and the actual situation.

THE 1970s

The 1970s started with some heavy blows to the increase of good field practice for students. There was the disruption of Seebohm reorganisation, even though despite the supervisors' preoccupation with reorganisation and their uncertainties about their own roles and future, many continued to give time and attention to students so that they were able to go on learning throughout the upheavals of 1971. Then came the aftermath with a continuous staff turnover in which almost all the best supervisors were promoted and lost to supervision; this also strained the cohesion of supervisors' groups. Newly appointed training officers were learning the job and often lessened the intimate contacts between tutors and supervisors. This was understandable, if unfortunate, when they had to juggle the demands of many courses against the needs of hard-pressed staff. By the mid-1970s these problems grew less as staff began to learn to work within large bureaucratic systems and many tutors and training officers met regularly to thresh out criteria for field placements and smoother co-operation. Even so, the poor quality of some student supervision remained a constant problem.

In 1970 the CTSW, the CTC and the LGTB jointly negotiated for the establishment of large, experimental student units in local authorities and voluntary organisations, for example a settlement, family service units and councils of social service. The NSPCC started student units in 1971 and by 1975 there were twelve of these, financed by DHSS grants. The units were part of the Society's school of social work with supervisors having a threefold responsibility to their local senior, to the school, and to the course whose students they supervised. They had monthly group supervision sessions at the NSPCC headquarters and were regularly visited by the management tutor. This kind of national cohesion had strengths when students were being given responsibility for high-risk cases and not all professional courses gave adequate support to field teachers.

Examples of the best experiments in field teaching, expanded practice and the questions being discussed were brought together in a series of CTC studies (DHSS, 1971c), a CTSW working party report (1971) and a CCETSW study (Curnock, 1975).

These were useful for the light they threw on what was actually happening in some situations, though others remained unexplored, and thus they illustrated trends rather than analysing the general situation. These surveys all showed that accepted good practice and close relations between supervisors and tutors were far from universal, indeed there was a depressing failure of communication and poor planning not necessarily caused by shortages. There was also little material available about practice in residential, community, group work or day care situations, although the CTC study covered fieldwork placements in community work, group work and children's homes as well as casework. These had developed much more slowly than casework. The courses were not sufficiently staffed to allow tutors to keep close contact with the field, to support fieldwork placements, and to achieve a good level of supervision. There was much confusion in the agencies because tutors failed to clarify expectations for fieldwork practice, especially when these aims could be met by a variety of means besides carrying a caseload. In the shortage of placements a constant search was essential for alternative means of reaching the same ends.

Students spent from 108 to 183 days in fieldwork on two-year child care courses. About 70 per cent of courses were using a block placement at some point, for example following a concurrent placement. These imposed a heavier teaching responsibility on supervisors, but students were normally recalled to the university for general and small group discussions. It was agreed that such placements should be an integral part of the course rather than being stuck on at the end. By the late 1960s group supervision was beginning to be used as a dynamic group learning process in which students brought their cases for discussion, and learning took place through group interaction which began to show the value of learning about attitudes, feelings and behaviour in a group. New students came with a more sophisticated understanding about individual behaviour and how social influences affected it than those in the past.

Almost the only information about group-work placements in the period came from returns from 50 social work (i.e. casework) courses to this CTC study group. These showed that 46 were giving some teaching on group dynamics and 38 on group-work method. On 39 courses there were opportunities for some students to work with groups in their fieldwork placements, though only 6 courses had a group-work field placement for all students. Group dynamics and group relations teaching was commonly found to be meaningless without actual group experiences. T groups, in which students freely expressed their feelings in a current student group in order to experience the dynamics of group interaction and to become more self-aware, were used in a number of courses under skilled leadership. They were controversial because the experience was thought to be damaging to some students, though many who took part in them, however painfully, reported subsequently a much greater awareness of what was going on in other group situations, a greater sensitivity to others' feelings and more awareness of themselves and their effect on other people.

Students in predominantly casework placements might be participant observers, with the social worker leading the group, or one or more students might be responsible for a group. There were real difficulties in providing supervision. Casework supervisors themselves had little theoretical understanding of group processes on which to supervise students and they sometimes found students threatening, especially if they were participant observers. As a result, a few tutors to courses undertook student supervision in group work. As in casework fifteen or twenty years earlier, it was clear that social workers using group work needed training that would give them theoretical underpinning and supervision on their work with groups, both for its own sake and as a basis for student supervision. The course in Bristol University extramural department had used group-work placements since 1967 for all students. It assumed that an understanding of group behaviour was an essential element in social work education which drew on and added to knowledge in all the other subjects. Thus students must gain knowledge, experience and skill, and a deeper understanding of group interaction through working in various groups.

The CTSW working party on field teaching was set up to clarify theory and method. It found a lack of systematic studies of fieldwork and therefore no real evidence about the optimum returns from different lengths and types of placement, or the skills, working methods and competence to be expected of students. It was extremely important to develop group and community work placements and to identify common elements in social work method. Group supervision was valuable because it created a peer-group situation, students learnt from each other and were more free to disagree with the fieldwork teacher and resolve conflicts. It would be desirable for some students to have long placements in the new social services departments and also, besides direct field and residential service to clients, to study some aspects of the department or a given group of people in difficulty. The extent to which students took part in preparing reports about themselves varied considerably, though sometimes they wrote a section on what they had learnt from the placement. The students consulted by the working party thought the fieldwork teaching was too uneven and assessment too subjective. Social workers were prejudiced against student units and there had been no study of student learning in them as against individual placements. A few large units were planned, taking ten to twenty students. It would be desirable to appoint senior fieldwork teachers for a wider teaching and co-ordination role, and to find and develop new types of placement. Fieldwork teachers were asking for help to teach more effectively, they especially needed opportunities to study concepts in social work from the social sciences and educational method. Joint planning committees between local courses were also necessary to reduce rivalries, one-upmanship and cut-throat competition for placements. These were specific suggestions for improvement rather than a pattern based on identified purposes of fieldwork.

Two seminar reports by the National Council of Social Service (NCSS, 1969 and 1970) explored the supervision of community work students, the context of the placement and the importance of training field teachers. The Gulbenkian study group's reports, *Community Work and Social Change* (1968) and *Current Issues in Community Work* (1973) both identified essential elements in community work field placements and their differences from other social work placements. These and the CCETSW (1975*d*) and Association of Community Workers (1975) reports on community work teaching are discussed in chapter 19.

Good field teaching was far from universal by the mid-1970s. Students complained of poor supervision and some placements were indeed more akin to participant observation than guided and responsible practice to turn disciplined ideas and feelings into action. Those supervisors whose own standards of practice were low were less concerned with this than whether students had fitted into the department, a situation reminiscent of the early 1950s. In addition too little effort and time had been given to relate classroom teaching about systems theory, integrated methods, and so forth to field teaching. Conversely, supervisors often complained that tutors were out of touch with what was happening in the field. The CCETSW 1973 survey of student units (Curnock, 1975) gave a more hopeful picture of the situation when special appointments were made. One hundred and ninety student units were identified and 165 supervisors answered the questionnaire, of whom 145 were responsible for groups of 3 or more students on professional courses. Another questionnaire was completed by students in 28 units. There were few units in the northern home counties and East Anglia, but a preponderance in London and Scotland. This was a remarkable contrast with the position in Scotland at the time of the Brown and Gloyne study (1966). There were more units in hospitals (54) and local authorities (46) than in voluntary organisations (21) and probation (24). In 1972–3 the units took 1,435 professional course students. Most had 6 to 15 students and the rest anything from 16 to 111. Most students liked small groups in which they could get to know each other and have seminar discussions and individual supervision. Most units took students from several courses, which must have made it difficult to relate specific theoretical teaching to practice.

Professional support for supervisors came from colleagues and tutors. Supervisors in some parts of the country had started their own organisation for support in the isolation and difficulties of the job. Some units also had advisory groups which met regularly to discuss policy, the nature of the agency's work, and the relations between ethics and field teaching. The main topics covered in supervision included the local social situation and community resources, the application of social work theory, administrative structure and procedures, and the legal framework. Unit supervisors were usually full-time but carried a small caseload, and they all had administrative responsibilities for the unit, organised the students' work experience, taught and supervised or co-ordinated other staff members to do so, and might take part in staff development. They were usually involved in management and policy decisions in the agency, which kept the unit part of the mainstream of its activities. Most were senior social workers appointed on the APT IV/V salary scales or the equivalent. Practically all had had five or more years' experience in social work before they became unit supervisors.

Students had group-work experience in 66 per cent of the voluntary organisations, 54 per cent of local authorities and about 45 per cent in hospitals and probation. Community work varied from 66 per cent in voluntary organisations to 29 per cent in probation, with casework in all of them. Groups included play therapy, discussion groups in prison, groups in day hospitals, foster-parent groups, family-therapy groups, tenants' associations, unsupported mothers' groups, therapy groups for the mentally ill, and many other groups. Community work included neighbourhood groups, detached youth work, community surveys, and some other experience not strictly community work. In some units students also worked in another agency. Students preferred working with a variety of clients and using various methods. Surprisingly, a quarter of the units relied upon individual supervision only: slightly over half had regular group supervision meetings for information giving, group discussion of cases, or for experience of group dynamics. These sessions strengthened peer-group support through students sharing knowledge and becoming more aware of themselves and others. Individual supervision was also essential.

A minority of tutors and students preferred concurrent placements. But most thought that theory and practice were more realistically related during block placements when units had an essentially educational function and could therefore overcome some of the disadvantages of such placements.

Most tutors visited units while the students were there, but some did not visit at all. Most supervisors visited the university or college, 112 did so for supervisors' meetings but 13 had no contact with at least one course. Supervisors thought that they had no influence on the content of about half the courses: but fourteen courses had joint committees on course planning and some supervisors gave priority to courses with close contact between tutors, supervisors and students. Some tutors did not discuss fieldwork objectives with supervisors, seek adequate information about the agency, or treat supervisors as equal partners. This resulted in different and unexamined expectations about theoretical teaching, students' state of knowledge, and the extent of theoretical teaching to be given by supervisors. A few supervisors taught on courses. About forty had excellent or improving relationships with courses but some others were very critical. Theoretically student units and courses were closely linked with regular contact and cross-fertilisation between them but this study showed that practice might be far different.

In most units students took part in assessment discussions. They themselves thought that supervisors overestimated the extent of this, though self-assessment with the supervisor was a realistic and effective way of judging work and progress. There were wide variations in the factors supervisors used in assessment criteria, though some ability to make, sustain and use relationships, for example, were mentioned frequently. Assessment was largely based on a student's growth and progress. Some students thought that lack of knowledge and accepted criteria for fieldwork assessment resulted in unreliable and inconsistent reports.

Information was obtained from 10 student units in residential institutions with around 160 student placements. The experience included assessment, short-term, long-term and intensive care, group sessions and group counselling, and the planned treatment of children with particular problems. Usually one staff member undertook regular student supervision and planned their work with other staff members. Some respondents thought these placements were not taken seriously by course tutors who did not always send information about the course or the students, clarify the placement aims, or visit while students were there. (One hundred and five of the 158 placements were made available by Barnardo's and the Richmond Fellowship.) Reports on students were carefully prepared by the staff, but sometimes not commented upon or even acknowledged. Better use could be made of residential experience, for example by students in a social services department spending a planned and assessed period in a residential institution. The unit teacher should be responsible for developing residential staff supervision skills.

Views about concurrent or block placements seemed to depend on fashion or personal opinion since there had never been any systematic assessment of the outcome of each. Concurrent placements were said to make a partnership between tutors and supervisors easier, to help students to relate theory and practice, and to discuss live experiences in course seminars. Block placements were thought to be less strain on students, and enabled them to see more of the agency's work and to be more available to clients.

There were different views about the best forms of field teaching, but agreement that students must develop sufficient mastery of a range of related skills and be able to use these to diagnose and take appropriate action in work with individuals, families, small groups and local community groups. Some students preferred to work primarily with individuals, families or small groups, others with community and pressure groups. Sensitivity both to social situations and individual needs was essential for all social workers.

A wider range of practice could be taught in student units than individual placements. Some students found this confusing and learnt better from concentrated practice, but students generally appreciated the range of problems and methods available in a unit. If students could give effective help to clients through short-term and contract-based work this could relieve pressure on the staff and add to the agency's service.

DEVELOPMENTS IN SCOTLAND IN THE 1970s

A Committee on Field Work Teaching, representative of all the interests concerned, was set up in Scotland in 1970 to promote urgently needed expansion. It considered all fieldwork teaching plans, pooled expenditure from the local authority rate support grant, and promoted the setting up of student units with full-time fieldwork teachers. Hospitals and voluntary organisations were making a major contribution to fieldwork and only one-third of placements were in local authorities. The Committee asked the latter to submit plans for units to be staffed by qualified fieldwork teachers and financed from pooled expenditure. Social work teachers helped local authority staffs to develop skills in field teaching, and short courses were run by the SWSG to improve practice in departments as a whole. By 1974 42 fieldwork teacher appointments had been made in local authorities (against 8 in 1970), and 8 in voluntary organisations, and more were pending. This was the chief means by which professional social work training was dramatically increased in Scotland from an output of 120 in 1970 to 298 in 1974, though there were great difficulties in recruiting sufficient, well-qualified fieldwork teachers to staff the units. The Committee made the enlightened assumption that about 20 per cent of fieldwork teachers' time should be spent in developing their own professional skills as social workers and social work teachers, in order constantly to incorporate new skills and new knowledge into their teaching.

POINTERS TO THE FUTURE

The CCETSW survey of units taking nearly 1,500 students a year was a far cry from the two student units for the LSE mental health course in 1950. There was no comparable information about the constantly changing number of individual fieldwork placements, the experience of these supervisors, what and how they taught, whether they had close contact with courses, what were the merits and demerits of individual and student unit placements, whether the apparent swing in favour of block placements was significant in individual supervision or resulted from more field teaching in student units. The CCETSW discussion document *Education and Training for Social Work* (1975*b*) deplored the tendency to separate theory and practice. The academic institution had become the primary learning base, rather than there being a shared responsibility for creating learning experiences in which practice teachers were fully involved and explicit about their objectives and methods. Much effort was needed on all sides to close the gap between theory and practice.

The chief change between 1950 and 1975 was that by slow degrees field teaching became accepted as an essential part of social work education. Only the Tavistock Institute combined teaching, supervision, practice and research, and thus solved problems of theory and practice failing to keep in step with each other because they were pursued in different institutions primarily dedicated to teaching or practice and often in little contact with each other. But students needed the cut and thrust of diverse points of view in an educational institution, as well as closely knit theory and practice.

Proposals had been made, but not implemented, for 'centres of excellence', well staffed to give student teaching at a high standard of related theory and practice and at levels appropriate to both basic and advanced training. In the meantime, the best of what was known in the early 1950s was still often not applied by 1975. Difficulties in providing a coherent experience for students, coupled with constant pressure of other work, made achievement sometimes disappointing. Perhaps the next step would be for individual social services departments, probation and after-care services, and voluntary organisations to set about substantial educational experiments in partnership with specific universities or colleges, somewhat on the lines of teaching hospitals. If theoretical teaching played a bigger part in fieldwork there would be less split in course objectives, research studies might be better used, and there would be closer understanding between educational institutions and service agencies.

The objectives of knowledge, skill, attitudes and values for field placements and how to realise them were too often vague: thus criteria for student assessment in these different aspects still lacked precision. But the focus of supervisors' reports had shifted from the students' personality to actual performance backed by evidence.

Field teaching was still a chief educational problem facing social work training by 1975. Clearly much was being achieved by courses which had regular, close contacts between tutors, supervisors and students. Other steps towards closing the gap were, on the one hand, more field teaching which used the application of theoretical concepts in practice and study of the local social situation; and, on the other, in the classroom use of role play, audio-visual aids, sensitivity groups, and other methods contributing to skill learning and the awareness of self and others.

Chapter 5

In-Service Training and Staff Development

THE 1950s

There were many efforts from the early 1950s to provide refresher courses, seminars and conferences to introduce social workers, whether trained and experienced or unqualified, to new knowledge and new methods. They aimed to increase knowledge, to loosen rigidities and broaden horizons, to shake self-satisfaction, excite curiosity, and contribute to common standards of practice. There was limited understanding about how people learn, but the considerable investment in these courses – which were provided for hundreds every year in the child care and probation services (see volume 1, chapter 8) and for substantial handfuls elsewhere – was an essential complement to professional training. In-service training and later staff development covered residential as well as other staff.

From its first days the CTC accepted a need to encourage continued learning by child care staff, whether trained or untrained. The Home Office Memorandum of Guidance on Training in Child Care (CTC, 1956) pointed out that newly qualified staff members should work for a time under guidance in order to consolidate and continue learning. Untrained staff had more extensive needs. One or two large authorities had appointed a senior child care officer to plan orientation sessions. In the 1960s the Universities of London and Manchester extramural departments ran one-year, day release courses for child care staff and other such courses were regularly run for residential staff. Every year the CTC made available a national programme of refresher courses with places for several hundred child care officers and residential staff. These courses consisted of a limited number of formal lectures but much discussion of actual problems being dealt with by the participants. They aimed to help older, experienced workers to combine intuitive wisdom and skill with systematic learning.

It was both a strength and weakness of in-service training courses that they were run outside the actual work situation, though by degrees they were recognised as complementary to, though not a substitute for, supervision, and it became possible in some situations to provide both. Information is not available about the proportion of social workers in any given service who were able to take these courses, nor at what intervals in their careers.

Often they arrived on residential courses too weary to respond for the first day or two, while on day release courses they were usually carrying their normal caseload or feeling guilty about the extra burden on colleagues. One tutor of the 1950s said in a personal communication: 'I remember how exhausted they were on arrival, and teaching elementary casework theory wasn't easy because the current British approach then was anecdotal and their own cases might be written up in a couple of paragraphs.'

Throughout the 1950s professional associations, notably the Institute of Almoners, the Association of Psychiatric Social Workers (APSW), and the Association of Social Workers (ASW), ran two- or three-day seminars and conferences on supervision, casework, group work and professional ethics. This new spirit had begun amongst almoners in the late 1940s when a succession of visiting Australian medical social workers and some pioneer almoners demonstrated a blend between American casework principles with British traditions of attention to practical needs and social action. The Institute of Almoners and the FWA jointly raised funds to bring over an American casework consultant in 1954. The Institute's annual report for that year said about the visit: 'There is no doubt that it will have provided valuable information for further thought on the possibilities of applying this method which American social workers call "supervision" in the practice of casework in the U.K.' (p. 6).

Some experienced almoners had been trying for a long time to improve the level of casework practice in their own departments through systematic supervision (Moon, 1958). Later ASW financed a consultant from Canada to conduct a series of seminars in different parts of the country for social workers in any service. In this period there was a hunger amongst social workers in every setting for seminars on casework, for discussion of members' own cases, for chances to learn more, to gain more knowledge and skill, more understanding in order to be more helpful.

In 1951 the Mackintosh Committee recommended a system of in-service training for local authority mental welfare officers (MWOs) under the supervision of experienced psychiatric social workers (PSWs) or MWOs. Newly appointed MWOs should have a preliminary period of training under an experienced worker to give them a general background and to test their suitability for the work. This should be followed by in-service training. This recommendation resulted in little action for a decade or more. But APSW sponsored a scheme under which trainees were appointed for not more than two years to approved posts in mental hospitals and local health authorities, where they worked under the supervision and guidance of trained PSWs. Suitable trainees were then accepted for one of the university mental health courses.

Refresher and other courses for workers in the health and welfare services were provided by the Institute of Almoners, APSW, ASW and the Institute of Social Welfare. Valiant attempts to fill the gaps in training for residential staffs were made by the National Association for Mental Health (NAMH) which ran a variety of courses for residential staffs of hostels and homes for mentally ill or handicapped people. The National Old People's Welfare Committee did their best to introduce some kind of training by running three-week, residential refresher courses for heads of old people's homes. In the late 1960s the National Association for the Care and Resettlement of Offenders (NACRO) started to run courses for wardens of after-care hostels (see chapter 13). All these courses provided by voluntary effort could only cater for small numbers compared with the number and variety of refresher courses for the child care and probation services.

Apart from these refresher courses, in-service training in local health and welfare authorities mainly consisted of individual training 'on the job' under the guidance of a more experienced worker. Some local authorities arranged for MWOs to be regularly present at mental hospital ward rounds and clinics and to take some lectures given to hospital staff. In others, a newly recruited worker would visit for about a couple of days with an experienced worker and then be left to get on with it. An MWO described his experience in the mid-1950s as follows:

'There appear to be no arrangements for in-service training and most of the workers rely on their own intuition and experience in dealing with people rather than on any systematic learning since they entered the service. I am appalled at the total absence of any system of training or selection in the appointment of duly authorised officers. I have experienced and observed new appointments to this important post recruited from general clerical grades having no previous experience of any type of social work. Some of those appointed were immature and quite incapable of appreciating the impact of mental illness on an individual, his family or the community around him. Their only training was to receive incoming telephone calls from doctors, hospitals, etc referring cases to be dealt with under the Lunacy Acts. After one or two weeks of this duty they were allotted to an observation ward. Some time later these officers will be expected to go into the field and to resolve serious mental illness problems objectively to the advantage of the patient, his family and the community.' (Younghusband Report, 1959, para. 854)

The Younghusband working party was emphatic that far more systematic in-service training was needed in the health and welfare services. This should include planning by senior staff of various kinds of in-service training, whether run by the authority or available elsewhere. In addition to the usual forms, it should include well-planned staff meetings, field manuals, bulletins and a staff library. All newly appointed staff should have systematic orientation and work for a time under supervision. Welfare assistants should take planned in-service training courses on appointment. To turn the desirable into the possible took a long time.

If the purpose of in-service training was to enable workers to give a better service and to get more personal satisfaction, then formal courses were not the whole answer. Much learning resulted from small group discussions, whether amongst colleagues or elsewhere, from consultation with a more experienced worker or a psychiatrist about an individual case, from case conferences, from groups set up to gather information about some specific need, and from personal observation, reading and 'imaginative consideration'.

THE 1960s

In-service training was naturally an important part of the whole upsurge of training in the 1950s and 1960s. The task was immense, considering that the majority of social workers and residential care staff were unqualified, that new recruits were constantly added, that in-service training should not be a once-for-all exercise, and that qualified social workers also needed such opportunities regularly in their careers. Yet staffs were usually overworked, social work tutors were in short supply, and resources for in-service training had to be balanced against the needs of qualifying courses. There was still no information about the numbers in each service taking in-service training courses at different points in their careers, what effect these had on their practice, and whether the learning got fed back to their colleagues. The amount and range of in-service training in the child care and probation services were both increased, which obviously meant much pressure to add to teaching resources. When more local authorities appointed their own training officers (with up to two-thirds of their salaries paid by the LGTB) the national CTC programme changed from general provision for all staff to specific subjects for senior staff. From 1966 the programme concentrated on a main theme each year, for example supervision, organisation and administration, the effects of new legislation, or the use of new methods like group work or family therapy. Increasingly the short courses were planned jointly for field and residential child care staff (see also volume 1, chapter 5). These courses were a substantial reinforcement to full-time training and by the late 1960s were taken by over 800 participants annually. A 1948 Home Office Circular (1948a) said that it was intended from time to time to plan residential conferences for children's officers to discuss matters of common interest. The first such conference was a seminar at Oxford in 1964, perhaps stimulated by the National Institute for Social Work Training's consultations all over the country for chief welfare officers. Not surprisingly it was a great success and soon repeated.

From 1962 the new Council for Training in Social Work actively promoted in-service training, though its policy was not to run courses itself. For example, it sponsored short courses for senior staff with training responsibilities, for older field workers, for potential short course tutors, unqualified social workers, and welfare assistants and trainees.

The NISWT ran multidisciplinary and other courses lasting for a day to three weeks in all parts of the country. These included short courses and consultations to improve communication and discussion across departmental, organisational and professional boundaries; courses for specific groups like chief welfare officers, residential staff, senior administrators, elected members of local authorities, or training officers; interdisciplinary courses, for example for doctors and social workers, research workers and social workers; and courses on specific subjects, for example prediction in social work, evaluating the effectiveness of a social service, or the place of research knowledge in social work education.

Training officers began to be appointed from the late 1950s and by 1967 nearly sixty children's departments had one or more. The CTSW discussion paper on *Staff Development in Social Work* (1967*b*) affirmed local authorities' recognition that staff selection and training would become an increasingly important part of their contribution to a better social work service. It found that 'in some of the larger authorities this work has proved sufficiently extensive to justify a whole time appointment' (p. 3). Training officers would need organising and training abilities as well as their professional social work experience. Sometimes they were called staff supervisors or tutors, often they only gave part of their time to training and usually they had to discover for themselves what the job entailed, what to teach, how to teach, sell in-service training to their colleagues, and co-operate with senior staff in discovering how to use it to improve the administrative and service performance of staff. A few big local authorities had staff training centres where orientation and other courses were run. Far the most substantial of these was the London Boroughs Training Committee, set up in 1965 to provide a service for the twenty-eight London boroughs when the LCC ceased to exist. It sponsored interdisciplinary in-service training courses, which included residential staff. It ran many forms of in-service training from day conferences to day release courses lasting for a year on many different aspects of social service provision and for chief officers and councillors, training officers and senior and field staff. Its staff was widely consulted and worked closely with the universities and other educational institutions in London about new professional courses and the extension of all forms of in-service training. In the 1960s the courses it provided or sponsored were taken by about 2,000 participants a year (London Boroughs Training Committee, 1966). In six months in 1975–6 it ran over eighty short courses and study days.

When the NISWT first assessed gaps in training in the early 1960s there was clearly a need to help local authorities to learn what was meant by staff development, an almost unknown North American concept, and how to provide it.

'The term in-service training had been familiar here for some years but it tended to mean either going away for refresher courses or else spending a few days on a new job going round the department and doing a little accompanied visiting before being turned loose. The idea that social agencies should themselves take responsibility for the planned orientation of their staff, whether trained or untrained, and that staff development is a continuing process was not generally recognised.' (Moscrop, 1967, p. 5)

As part of the effort to systematise staff development, a Canadian consultant came to the NISWT in 1964 for eighteen months on a Ford Foundation grant. She had a British counterpart worker on the CTSW staff and a CTC training inspector was attached to the project. Teaching materials were produced, a national seminar was run for experienced social work teachers, and other courses both nationally and locally for training officers. There were also two in-service training demonstration projects in a big city and a rural county, in which an essential condition was attendance by social workers from every department. An innovation in the consultant's approach was the emphasis on educational method in planning the content of a course, in teaching and in evaluating the outcome. The focus was first on the needs of those for whom the service existed, its structure and the task of untrained or inexperienced social workers in it, attention then shifted to the trainee's current level of knowledge and understanding and what he needed to become more competent. This was very different from a series of talks on different social services, or other staff development activities planned with little reference to objectives or educational method.

The project understandably stimulated the acceptance of staff development. The CTSW in its second annual report (1965) said:

'The term "staff development" may be unfamiliar. It implies an overall plan for continued opportunities for staff to learn, whatever their stage of experience. The responsibility for such plans lies with local authorities who are in the best position to assess the needs of their individual members of staff and to organise a staff development programme.' (p. 3)

The project also reinforced the case for appointing training officers at a senior level and thus with more status.

By the end of the decade extensive in-service resources existed to train welfare assistants and trainees (or others with the same function), for newly appointed social workers, and for experienced social workers and administrators wanting to study a specific topic. It had also begun in community work where practitioners came from a variety of different backgrounds and were learning from their own and their colleagues' experience. The Gulbenkian study group (1968) thought that in-service training was a high priority and, in the dearth of qualified community workers, the most realistic way of improving performance, adding to knowledge and laying the groundwork for professional training.

In general there were varied patterns of in-service training, including two- or three-day or up to five- or ten-day, full-time courses, day or half-day release courses over a period, and sandwich courses. These consisted of a short, full-time period followed by a return to work, usually with a project to complete for discussion in the further full-time period. Coming together again after an intervening period seemed to reinforce learning; group interaction was also potent on day release courses if participants were not overtired and preoccupied.

There was almost no study of the effectiveness of these various patterns and time intervals nor the effect of group dynamics on learning. In 1966, the NISWT set up an interdisciplinary working party to study the content and methods of short courses under one month for social workers. Its interim report (unpublished) discussed teaching methods and patterns of courses in relation to aims, the characteristics of members and their motivation for learning, the significance of age, the importance of language and of hetero/homogeneity in relation to learning. Teaching methods – including lectures, group discussions, reporting back, group projects, role playing and the use of audio-visual aids, tutorials, reading and written work – and various patterns and lengths of courses and evaluation were also considered. The whole subject proved more unexplored and complex than had been foreseen owing to the lack of 'hard' knowledge, for example about the most effective length of short courses, how to plan courses in relation to what could be achieved with a particular group using given educational methods, and objective criteria for follow up and evaluation.

THE 1970s

By the 1970s more was known about the use of group dynamics in in-service training, timing, and the choice of course content to stimulate learning, broaden perspectives and bring about attitude shifts and more self-awareness. Discussion groups with a knowledgeable leader and experiences in small discussion sessions were found to be more effective in strengthening common feeling and improved communication, especially if combined with simulation exercises and audio-visual aids, than lectures to the whole group by an outside speaker followed by discussion.

Before and immediately after the social services departments came into operation the DHSS initiated and the LGTB sponsored a series of study conferences for the new directors, for example at LSE, the Institute of Local Government Studies and the NISW. In these courses new directors, with the aid of leading national experts, worked in plenary sessions and small groups on some of the problems and priorities of reorganisation. Later, short courses for directors and deputy directors, for example on social planning, became a regular part of the CCETSW's central programme of short courses.

From the start, the CCETSW accepted in-service training as an important part of its functions and sponsored an annual programme of short courses for specific participants, notably for mixed groups of social workers; for tutors and lecturers; for people engaged in staff development and student supervision; for directors and assistant and area directors; and for research staff. The courses included priorities in the social services, work with groups, intermediate treatment, community work, family therapy, integrated social work methods, curriculum planning, and teaching methods. They were either run by the Council's staff or by educational bodies on its behalf.

Before 1968 in-service training courses in Scotland were mainly provided in co-operation with the Scottish central departments by the training councils and the NISWT. After 1968 the SWSG became responsible for a much enlarged, short course programme. When the CCETSW opened an office in Edinburgh in 1974, it took over this responsibility with the intention of identifying general needs and those peculiar to Scotland.

CONCLUSION

This was the pattern of in-service training as it emerged from 'refresher' courses in the 1950s sponsored by voluntary organisations, professional associations and the Home Office. By the 1970s there was a national frame-work with a far more extensive range of courses of varied lengths on specific topics for particular groups (which might be multidisciplinary), run under various auspices and largely sponsored and financed by the LGTB or the CCETSW. In the 1950s local authorities had no thought of making them-selves responsible for staff development, but in 1971 the new social services departments made training units part of their structure to assess all training needs and see that they were met. Provision varied; for example in one London borough in 1974 a staff member combined training with other responsibilities, but another borough had thirteen training officers. All training officers required skill in negotiating with other senior staff about in-service training, secondment, and indeed about manpower policies, in planning courses (especially induction courses), and in working with those who taught in them. Some training officers might have no teaching responsibilities themselves. They had a difficult assignment in a complex administrative hierarchy when they often had insufficient status and initially little experience of teaching, assessing training needs and structuring training programmes. Training Officers were appointed in large numbers after the 1971 reorganisation. This led to much discussion about their tasks and needs, and in 1975 the National Association of Training Officers in the Personal Social Services came into existence with much support from related organisations. By 1975 the principle of continuing education at every level in administrative hierarchies was taken for granted, even though plans were curtailed by economic recession. There can be no doubt of the enormous contribution made by in-service training in those twenty-five years to raising the level of practice, reinforcing professional education, and bringing together social workers and others for mutual learning, enrichment and exploration of current issues.

Chapter 6

Contributions to Social Work Education

THE AMERICAN AND OTHER INTERNATIONAL IMPACT UPON SOCIAL
WORK EDUCATION AND PRACTICE IN BRITAIN

In the 1940s some leading social workers, drawing on their reading, continuing contacts and pre-war experience, thought that a good deal could be
learnt from the more systematic development of social work practice and
education in the USA. By the early 1950s regular exchanges began. These
were made possible by American generosity that enabled British social
workers and students to go to the United States for observation and study
under the Fulbright and Smith-Mundt Programs and through the activities
of the British Committee for the Interchange of Social Workers and
Administrators (which covered other countries as well). American social
work educators also came here under the Fulbright Program and other
auspices. They usually had university or other attachments for a year: during
that time they helped to plan new applied social studies courses, or, more
frequently, ran seminars for practising social workers. These discussion
seminars in different parts of the country to which members brought their
own 'live' case material helped to create a climate in which it was easier
to admit how much there was to learn. They led to an orderly working
method in which some social workers became more adept at assessing a
situation, learning to pose relevant questions in their work, to observe
significant interactions, to become more aware of their own attitudes and
to evolve some criteria by which to assess progress or the lack of it. Social
workers from different settings discovered, sometimes to their astonishment,
that they shared common assumptions about the range of human behaviour
and reactions to stress and the use of a professional relationship to help
people to cope better; and that the clients of one agency were no different
or more complex than those of another.

In spite of what was said later, the earthy common sense of the American
social workers anchored psychoanalytic theory to the current reality. The
principle of self-determination also helped to erode current paternalism.
Enormous and undifferentiated earlier claims grew more modest so that
social workers became less prone to 'casework' someone who really needed
a home help or to expect to bring about sea changes in the personalities of
grossly disturbed or deprived people. In brief, 'These contacts were of very

great value, both on account of the professional teaching accomplished, and in helping to create a climate of feeling in which it became easier to admit how much there was to learn, and to accept the idea of in-service supervision as well as of more intensive student-supervision' (Irvine, 1956, p. 191).

At first there was a good deal of resistance to 'American casework' because 'American clients were quite different' from British people who were not accustomed to expressing their feelings. British caseworkers claimed to be quite as good as the Americans but 'they had time to talk about it while we were busy doing it'. One real difference was that the Americans, with perhaps more inquiring minds, had, unlike the British, worked hard to apply relevant findings from the behavioural sciences to practice, and to distil theory from recorded experience, even with all the weaknesses that were later so eagerly revealed. Not everyone agreed that consultation and supervision were needed or that the new knowledge (primarily based upon psychoanalytic theory) was either relevant or desirable, when the primary task as it seemed to many was to give practical help with sympathy and understanding.

The other decisive overseas contribution was made by the UN European seminars on casework, largely taught by leading American social work educators such as Gordon Hamilton and Florence Hollis. The first was held in Vienna in 1950. Thereafter they took place annually, always with a number of participants from Britain. At the 1954 seminar in Leicester half the group leaders were American and half British (the latter all psychiatric social workers by training). The UN European Regional Office also collected case records and distributed these as well as reprints of articles in professional journals, thus making good teaching material available for full-time and in-service training courses. In the succeeding years British social workers regularly contributed to and benefited from the annual programme of UN seminars on a wide variety of social issues, as well as from congresses and seminars run by the International Association of Schools of Social Work of which the JUC was a member.

This North American contribution, including British social workers who went to American and Canadian schools of social work, helped not only to change views about practice, and to bring members of different professional associations closer together, but also to prepare groups of social workers to supervise students and colleagues, to act as consultants and social work educators, and to write.

Unfortunately these gains and the foundations laid for further advance were confined to casework. The two leading American group-work teachers who came here for a year in the 1950s were not able to make much impact and though seminars given by Grace Coyle on a short visit were enthusiastically attended they had no continuing result. This may have been partly because the only attempts by social workers to use groups in conjunction with casework were primarily therapeutic groups in psychiatric treatment settings. The youth service was almost wholly in the education field, and only the YWCA through its American contacts was beginning to use social group-work methods.

In course of time an increasing number of British social work practitioners and teachers built up continuing contacts with the USA and Canada by study or work there, while leading Americans regularly came to this country. As British social work incorporated what proved to be relevant aspects of American research and professional experience and as social workers added to this from their own experience, earlier rejection or overidentification died down. Moreover, the exchange steadily spread far beyond the bounds of casework and included social research as well as practice. This was helped by the Americans' recognition that they might sometimes have something to learn from us, as well as by the generosity of their response which created in time a basis of greater equality. The gain was not all one way, many Americans welcomed the chance to test out theories in another country which spoke roughly the same language but had a different culture. This was illustrated by American emphasis in the mid-1950s on 'putting the social back into social work' and the discovery that the British, in spite of a heady flirtation with the transference, had never taken it out.

In this country, as elsewhere, many American books and journals were found of great value and widely used: notably standard textbooks like Gordon Hamilton's *Social Casework: Theory and Practice* (1951), Helen Perlman's *Social Casework: A·Problem Solving Process* (1957), Charlotte Towle's *Common Human Needs* (1945, 1965 and 1973), and *The Learner in Education for the Professions* (1954), Florence Hollis's *Casework: A Psychosocial Therapy* (1964 and 1972), Annette Garrett's *Interviewing: Its Principles and Methods* (1942), Howard J. Parad's *Ego Oriented Casework* (1963), Father Biestek's *The Casework Relationship* (1961 and 1973), Harriett Bartlett's *The Common Base of Social Work Practice* (1970), W. J. Reid and A. W. Shyne's *Brief and Extended Casework* (1969) and many others. These are only the most familiar of many others regularly read and used in Britain. The writings of American sociologists and psychiatrists, like Robert Merton, Talcott Parsons, Erich Fromm, Erik Erikson, Gerald Caplan and Franz Alexander, also got into the bloodstream of British social work.

Most of the new innovations in social work method came from the United States. These included generic casework as distinct from a series of specialisations, 'aggressive casework' with 'hard-to-reach clients', casework in authoritarian settings with acting-out delinquents, crisis intervention, family therapy and brief task-centred casework. Because group work had been little explored compared with casework, while community work was new, American material was read and used though not applied to the same extent. American explorations in integrated methods courses were only slowly explored in Britain because there was comparatively little use of integrated work with individuals, groups and communities in practice, because social work teachers had too little experience and because most of our social work courses were too short for effective teaching over a wider range of practice.

American social work methodology and social research were obviously developed within the American culture. It was therefore essential to discover in applying it here what was relevant for British social workers, whether universals of human experience or common to both cultures. Unfortunately because of the limited research and systematically recorded practice in Britain, much was either applied piecemeal or not applied, or taken on trust. A number of American research findings, for instance on aspects of adoption or delinquency or the behaviour of disturbed children, became familiar in relevant circles and were sometimes used in common with British studies as a basis for experimentation or further research.

It is sometimes said that the Americans rediscovered poverty before the British did. The anti-poverty program and radical writings, highlighting the outrage of poverty with its destruction of human dignity, certainly influenced radical social workers in Britain. But the identification of many social and community workers from the late 1960s with the deprived and the powerless, their anger at social injustice, had its own indigenous roots.

American publications, American practice and American research are not specifically referred to at other points in this study but their very considerable influence must be taken for granted throughout the whole period.

The Australian influence mainly consisted of exchanges of MSWs between the two countries though other Australian social workers also settled here and contributed to practice. Various fellowship schemes also made it possible for British social workers to have periods of observation of particular social service in other European countries, while large numbers of social workers from other continents came to this country under UN, British Council or other auspices and contributed to a fruitful international exchange of views and experience.

THE NATIONAL INSTITUTE FOR SOCIAL WORK TRAINING: (FROM 1973 THE NATIONAL INSTITUTE FOR SOCIAL WORK)

The Younghusband working party's recommendation (1959, paras 949–55) for a 'staff college' financed by a national trust originated at a drafting weekend in a chance remark by a member in the lunchbreak. Immediately the Report appeared the proposal was taken up by the Nuffield Foundation and the Joseph Rowntree Memorial Trust. They initiated discussions with interested people, including various members of the working party, to explore the most effective contributions a staff college could make, particularly in the neglected health and welfare field, where action was needed on a broader front than basic training alone.

There were practical questions of location, finance and staffing to settle before the experiment could be launched. This meant clarifying its immediate purposes and its probable long-term development within the entire field of the statutory and voluntary personal social services. The dilemma of location was solved when someone closely connected with the project proposed the Mary Ward Settlement building in Tavistock Place. The Settlement, which was short of funds, agreed to sell Mary Ward House to the Nuffield Foundation, provided it could remain in the large building next door (formerly a school for physically handicapped children).

The project was welcomed by government departments, local authorities, professional associations, voluntary organisations and others because it would provide a national centre and focus for social work, a power house, a meeting ground and, to vary the metaphor, the spring board which social work had always lacked.

The National Institute for Social Work Training (NISWT) came into existence in 1961 with an annual grant of £35,000 for ten years (of which £6,000 was paid back in rent). This was reasonable for those days, as the Carnegie Trust grant of £20,000 to LSE for four years to start the first applied social studies course had been in 1953. By 1975 the annual budget of the National Institute was around £250,000 a year from various governmental, trust and other sources, including fees.

Its first aim was sometimes expressed succinctly as 'helping everyone to jump on the same bandwagon'. Translated into sober operational terms this was to include:

(a) pioneering one of the new courses in social work;
(b) providing short refresher courses for senior staff;
(c) pioneering a course in social work education to prepare professional social workers as tutors in charge of the new two-year courses;
(d) preparing and making available teaching materials, especially case records and reprints of useful articles, and taking the initiative in stimulating research and publications in social work;
(e) providing a specialised library in social work and closely related subjects;
(f) progressively becoming a centre of information, for research, and for meetings, discussions and conferences between senior administrators, social workers, academics and members of other professions.

Initially one of its tasks was to answer coherently the question 'What is social work?', to demonstrate its relevance to the health and welfare services, to state convincingly why social workers needed training and what local authorities must contribute to it.

Within a total strategy, when change from the old to the new had to be accelerated and made coherent by various means, one of the NISWT's most fruitful early activities was the three- or four-day residential consultations held all over the country for senior administrators in the health and welfare services and social workers. These consisted of exchange of information, coupled with consultation between those running services for clients with particular disabilities, and social workers able to be clear about their own practice. Membership of a consultation was by invitation so that key people in each locality took part, the discussions resulted in a less oversimplified perception of needs which slowly resulted in better services. Later, joint meetings were organised to promote interprofessional understanding, for example between doctors and social workers.

Parallel with these consultations the NISWT gave much help in setting up the initial two-year courses in colleges of further education, and itself pioneered the first one-year course for experienced but untrained social workers in the health and welfare services – and also child care – to complement at middle-management level what was being done by the consultations and other means for top management. The aim was to select people with sufficient intelligence and desire to learn who had not become rigid in a bureaucratic structure. There was no shortage of applicants nor unwillingness to second them. In the early 1960s there were still middle-aged men and women of good native intelligence who had won grammar school scholarships in the pre-war depression years but had been forced to forego them. They seized upon, as one said, 'the second chance I never thought life would give me'. The course was a demanding combination of theory and practice (with one fieldwork placement focused on administration and the other on casework). The lecturers realised the personal and intellectual upheavals faced by these mature students as they became more aware of themselves, of the dynamics of human relations, and of the, stresses and deprivations they met in their work. It was soon 'realised that whenever an individual or a small group of people is given some extra training and thus set apart from a larger group, tensions are engendered which make it difficult for the two groups to re-integrate, or even to communicate freely' (Irvine, 1956, p. 189). This led to consultation with chief welfare officers and medical officers of health on how to receive back and provide the right setting and support for seconded staff members in order to consolidate rather than waste their new skill and knowledge. This pioneer course ran for the planned five years, though others on similar lines were started later in different parts of the country.

As another aspect of the whole expansion of training courses, it was obviously necessary to 'train the trainers' more adequately than was possible in short seminars. In its earliest days the National Institute started a six-month course in social work education to help professional social workers make the considerable shifts in their own attitudes, in roles and in knowledge necessary to change from being social work practitioners with clients to become social work teachers in an essentially educational relationship to students. The course included teaching practice as well as seminars on the nature of social work, other related subjects, curriculum planning, and work with supervisors. The change of focus from individual clients to the nature and purpose of social work, coupled with hard thinking about the contribution of the social sciences, was not easy. In the first few years when two-year, general social work courses and similar child care courses were being started, it was often made a condition of appointment that the tutor should be chosen well in advance and be able to take the NISWT course ahead of the planning for a new two-year course in a particular college. The course was also taken by social workers hoping for a teaching appointment, and, as time went on, by experienced tutors given leave of absence to take it, as well as by some teachers of other subjects in social work courses, by those specialising in residential care or as training officers. Surprisingly, though numbers increased over the years and the curriculum was enriched, by 1975 similar courses had not been started elsewhere in spite of the obvious need pointed out in the Seebohm Report (1968, para. 573) and by other reports in the early 1970s. This was part of a strange assumption that an education qualification is needed to teach children but not adults.

At a time when the teaching of human growth and behaviour, sociology, social administration and indeed social work itself were all at a fluid stage, the NISWT's conferences on these subjects brought lecturers within or outside the universities together for joint discussion.

It is an interesting sidelight on the lack of social work publications even in the early 1960s that no book existed which explained social work in clear, comprehensible terms as practised in the British scene. The NISWT tried to fill the gap with *Introduction to the Social Worker* (1964) and *Welfare in the Community* (Goldberg, 1966*b*) as part of its whole endeavour to spread social work understanding and practice in the social services. Its series of publications later included research studies in social administration, adoption, fostering, maladjusted adolescents in a residential situation, the homeless and the rootless, and policy problems in supplementary benefits administration.

Its first research project was a national inquiry into the field teaching of social work students (summarised in chapter 4). Subsequently the research unit undertook several substantial action research projects (summarised in relevant chapters) on social work in general practice, workloads in the local authority health and welfare services, community work, the effectiveness of social work, and chronic schizophrenic patients and their families; while a series of interrelated action studies in two social services departments and studies of task-centred casework and day care centres were in progress in 1975. The research unit staff also took an active part in consultancy and advisory work and in teaching on the post-graduate professional courses and various of the short courses. There was much emphasis on the use and testing of research findings in social work practice.

One of the NISWT's earliest American consultants was a leading professor of group work, but like others, the Institute only began to contribute effectively to social group work training and practice in the 1970s. In the late 1960s when teaching in community work theory and practice was becoming popular, the National Institute decided that rather than try to adapt American material to the British scene, it would run its own five-year project in Southwark. The project's purposes were to stimulate active and self-supporting community groups, and services better geared to local people's needs, as well as to record and evaluate these processes and provide field placements for Institute students. This was an isolated example of an educational institution setting up a project with the twin purpose of providing a service to local people, and fieldwork placements and teaching material for its students. In practice the project concentrated on its community work function (D. Thomas, 1976).

The NISWT rapidly became a common meeting ground for consultations and the exchange of views, for information seeking and for the planning of new projects. An enormous contribution was made by a series of Fulbright Fellows and other leading Americans who spent up to a year at the NISWT, contributed to teaching and research at the Institute and elsewhere and sometimes came back for more. There was also a regular series of visitors from Europe and Asia. In time, leading members of all three political parties and senior administrators came for discussions and to ask the Institute's help on various aspects of the social services. These informal dining-club discussions and other activities aired new ideas and contributed to action. The Aves and Williams Committees (see later chapters) and subsequent developments in training for senior residential care staff and for organisers of volunteers were examples of successful initiative. This initiative also led to the setting up of the Social Work Advisory Service (SWAS).

By the early 1970s when the size and complexity of the social services and the range of knowledge and research needed were all greatly increased, the content of the National Institute's work expanded to include developments in residential care, day care, management, community work, task-centred casework, integrated social work methods and social planning; indeed the NISW was one of the pioneers in the study and promotion of management in the social services. Its short course programme, planned in co-operation with the CCETSW was much extended, particularly to meet the needs of senior- and middle-management training officers, social work teachers, homes advisers, senior residential staff and research officers. Subjects included organisational structure, priorities in the social services, objectives and values, in-service training programmes, and research in the social services. Its interdisciplinary, interorganisational and interservice contributions grew in the 1970s and it developed more direct consultancy services. In 1973 it dropped 'Training' from its title.

The original course in social work education (renamed educational studies) continued and two others were added – a one-year course in further social work studies with options in community work, management or in-service training and supervision for experienced social workers; and a twelve-week sandwich course with an agency-based study in the intervening period, intended for senior social workers responsible for community work, management, in-service training, supervision or residential care services. For some time these three courses were taught separately and students suffered from a lack of teaching contact with each other, particularly since the courses were meant for social workers who would be influential in deciding the quantity and quality of social welfare provision. In 1971 it was decided to bring together students on all three courses for certain parts of the teaching. The main themes were: social policy and social planning, social work intervention, management and organisation, philosophy and the social sciences, and special study and practice in a specific field.

Between 1961 and 1975 the NISWT pioneered, or contributed with others, and in its totality became an essential part of the social work scene at a time of great expansion when what it offered was crucial to a total strategy. This was largely because it provided a neutral meeting ground where many different interests could come together, agree or disagree but meet in an institution which had broad interests but no party-line axe to grind. Its aim was to be sensitive and responsive to the needs of the social services at any given time (NISW, 1974).

THE LOCAL GOVERNMENT TRAINING BOARD

The LGTB was set up in 1967 on the initiative of local authority associations in consultation with the main trade unions representing local government employees. It was a national body responsible for developing training for all types of staff employed by local authorities. It operated in England and Wales, not Scotland, and was financed by a voluntary levy on local authorities until 1975 when the Board's finances came from a deduction from the needs element of the rate support grant. The LGTB's responsibilities ranged far more widely than the training of social workers, yet by the mid-1970s it was grant aiding many more students for social work training than for any other qualification. In this field it financed some training officer appointments and student unit supervisors, spread in-service training and grant-aided local authority staff to take these courses. It played an important part in the development of local authority training policy and was instrumental in increasing management training for senior administrators in the social services departments.

THE SOCIAL WORK ADVISORY SERVICE

The case for a unified advisory service, which had been argued from the 1940s, naturally grew stronger as social work expanded. In its absence people sought information and advice from university appointments officers or individual staff members, professional associations, the training councils, the National and other Councils of Social Service, local probation services, children's departments, CABx, social workers and anyone else who seemed able to give it. Sometimes the information was up to date, accurate and comprehensive, sometimes not, while the advice usually applied to a particular service when would-be candidates ought to have been encouraged to consider the whole range of possibilities. This process was both time-consuming and inefficient.

Finally in 1963 when the social work explosion had begun and recruitment was vital, a joint working party of the Standing Conference of Organisations of Social Workers and the NISWT brought together the main statutory and voluntary organisations to discuss what ought to be done about the wasteful confusion of the current situation. The Calouste Gulbenkian Foundation gave a three-year grant to make the project possible, every major statutory and voluntary interest was represented on its Council of Management; and in 1967, four years after the initial discussions, SWAS was set up with an office in London. Its aim as a national clearing house for advice and information was to answer inquirers, whether school leavers or older people, about training and career prospects, and to supply information to careers teachers, university appointments board officers and others who gave vocational advice and guidance. It regularly gathered, stored and collated information about every aspect of social work and training, while its careers leaflets and other publications were always produced in consultation with the relevant training body and professional association. Most inquiries were dealt with in this way. In course of time there were regional offices, together with part-time consultants, all over the country so that individual counselling interviews became possible and close links were made with local statutory and voluntary social services.

The service had become well established and publicly financed by 1970. Its work increased greatly after the reorganisation of the social services, and by 1970 the London office alone was dealing with over 2,000 inquiries a month. It was an essential national source of referral for advice and information at a time when many more people were becoming interested in social work as a career.

The greater number of candidates for training and of training courses meant that many of the former were taking long and expensive journeys for interviews, sometimes for several interviews, and might be turned down for a course when there were vacancies elsewhere. Much staff time was taken up by processing applications, while referees might be asked for several references in different forms for the same candidate. The CTC had started to run its own clearing house for the two-year child care courses, which provided the first unduplicated count of applicants. Later, after discussion about the design of a common application form and letter to referees and how to avoid limiting candidates' freedom of choice, SWAS began in 1970 to operate a clearing house for the child care, non-graduate courses and dealt with 8,000 inquiries in the first year.

Discussion in the JUC at this time showed that English universities had seven to twelve times and Scottish universities five to six times as many applications as there were places. Most agreed to join in a clearing-house scheme, and (with some compromises) an application form, the wording of a request for an essay or personal statement and the form of the letter to referees were agreed. This scheme was also operated by the SWAS clearing house from 1971. All applications were submitted to the candidate's first-choice course and only if this failed to his second choice, and so on.

In 1974 SWAS as such was taken over by the CCETSW as a semi-independent activity and in 1975 integrated as part of the Council's information and advice service for individual inquirers and careers advisers. The post-graduate clearing house continued but became a CCETSW responsibility as part of a wider clearing house for both post-graduate and non-graduate courses.

Chapter 7

Characteristics of the Training Councils in the 1960s: the Seebohm Report's Recommendations on Training; and the Early Days of the Central Council for Education and Training in Social Work

DIFFERING PRACTICES OF THE TRAINING COUNCILS IN THE 1960s

The pressure for expanded training in the 1960s would have faced overwhelming obstacles from piecemeal and slow development and more uneven standards if it had not been for the initiative, standard setting and support services of the training councils – the CTC, the CTSW and the Training Committee of ACPAC. The Institute of Medical Social Workers (IMSW) and the Association of Psychiatric Social Workers (APSW) also played important parts in training. None the less there were obvious disadvantages in all these separate activities.

In the 1960s there were only two meetings between the JUC and representatives of the three councils, each for *ad hoc* discussion; and for a number of years only one person served on all four bodies. The result was that members of each were ignorant of the activities, aims and point of view of the rest; strong loyalties and competitiveness developed amongst them and a natural desire to advance the training interests of a particular service without taking account of the others. Moreover, those who worked in each service had a long history of close identification with it. By contrast there was consultation between the staffs of the three councils about proposals to start new courses, though there was no over-riding responsibility to assess the total demand for social workers and plan training resources accordingly.

It was part of CTC later strategy to spread courses all over the country, particularly the north-east and Wales. To pioneer in desert areas required not only an external stimulus and tactful negotiation with a university or college and discovering whether appropriate teaching was or could become available, but also an investment in in-service training and special supervisor appointments. After the first increase in the number of courses the CTSW decided to expand existing courses. This made it possible to appoint two or three (later more) tutors to each course and to evolve a closer partnership with local social agencies. Those responsible locally for existing courses might not be consulted or informed when any given new course was proposed although competition for field placements was acute. Sometimes a joint committee was set up locally to improve provision and allocate resources (in one area this was nicknamed the cut-throat committee). There was also competition from the social studies courses which included practical work – and the CTC was actively trying to increase the intake to these courses to improve recruitment for the child care courses.

Pooling of local authority expenses for fieldwork was an important incentive to expansion in their services. CTC and CTSW training policies included new recruitment and making inroads in the large numbers of untrained staff. Secondment reached considerable proportions, especially in the health and welfare services, and, coupled with in-service training, helped to introduce common principles of practice.

By the end of the decade there might well be CTC, CTSW and probation courses in a university, an extramural department and a college of further education in the same city, indeed sometimes two small separate courses each with tutors in charge in the same educational institution. This was wasteful of valuable teaching resources and could lead to friction, especially where the sources and level of grant aid, fees paid to lecturers in the same subject and tutor/student ratios were different, and a greater or lesser amount of clerical help, accommodation and library facilities were provided. Gradually, more shared teaching was introduced in parallel two-year courses. This naturally led students to demand that they should receive both the CTC letter of recognition (the child care certificate was discontinued in 1960) and the certificate in social work.

The move towards closer relations dated from 1965. In that year the newly formed Association of Social Work Teachers brought together tutors from all types of full-time courses. In the same year the chairmen of the three councils met the then Lord Privy Seal to discuss common policies, and some form of amalgamation began to be in the air. Training councils' staffs consulted regularly and in 1966 a working party was set up to explore similarities and differences in policies and the possibility of joint discussions with educational institutions about the recognition of post-graduate or Council for National Academic Awards (CNAA) degrees which led to two or more social work qualifications. As things were, those initiating a new course might have to negotiate for recognition with five separate bodies, the CTC, the CTSW, ACPAC, IMSW and APSW. This resulted in much duplication of work, waste of time and sometimes conflicting curriculum revision demands. Finally in 1966 the CTSW and the two professional associations set up a joint committee to examine proposed new university or CNAA courses and to make recommendations to its members about recognition. The JUC nominated two observers but the other two councils remained aloof from this attempt to introduce a joint committee for initial negotiations and standard setting. There were fears in university circles that it was an attempt to impose tighter controls and increase specialisation rather than to lessen duplication and conflicting demands.

Each of the three councils had different admission requirements for students (the universities – other than extramural departments – had their own admission standards and assessment procedures). The procedure for recognising new courses also differed. The training committee of ACPAC exercised little detailed control over courses but the CTC and the CTSW both had committees with university and social work members which received and commented upon the draft syllabus for any proposed new course and made recommendations to their respective councils, to the accompaniment of a loud or muted background chorus on academic freedom. As a result of these discussions, proposed curricula were often improved after an exchange of views between the experienced and the newcomers. The risk of strait jackets and stifled initiative was rightly raised but usually avoided: its alternative appellation was common national standards. There was a constant struggle to achieve balance and inter-relation between the main subjects and theory and practice, to prevent the curriculum from being heavily overloaded, to weigh up whether particular groups of students could realistically absorb all that was expected of them in the available time, to encourage well-thought-out innovations, and to try to achieve some minimum standard in fieldwork placements.

The CTC and the training inspectors were too overburdened in the 1960s to review existing courses. But the CTSW recognised any course for a three- or five-year period and then reviewed it in considerable detail. It also appointed assessors to each course as a chief means of creating and monitoring comparable national standards. The CTSW was never involved in university courses, but in the pioneer situation in colleges of further education this tight control was probably necessary, indeed a support to the staffs of the courses, until standards had been tested and accepted, when the controls began to be relaxed.

CTC working parties produced several papers on fieldwork (discussed in detail in chapter 4). And the CTSW set up working parties to produce reports on the teaching of human growth and behaviour, sociology, and fieldwork: while its curriculum development group reviewed existing curricula in the light of new knowledge, changing demands and increased teaching experience. Published information about CTC and ACPAC training activities consisted of a few brief paragraphs in Home Office Children's or Probation and After-Care Department reports but the CTSW published its own reports which reviewed specific topics in detail. The Advisory Council on Child Care had a research and development committee which both initiated and co-ordinated research and the CTSW also had a research committee which was active in promoting research utilisation. Like the CTC at an earlier period, it found itself hamstrung in forecasting by a lamentable lack of up-to-date information about the number of social workers in the health and welfare services, retirement rates and numbers needed in relation to future demands for the services.

THE SEEBOHM REPORT AND TRAINING FOR SOCIAL WORK

It is worth summarising the Seebohm Committee's (1968) views on training because these embodied much current thought by social workers, educators, administrators and interested observers in the mid-1960s. The Committee envisaged an initial basic generic training which, after experience, would give the social worker competence to cope with a wide range of social need, provided he had the support of adequate consultation and other resources. This should be followed by the opportunity to develop further skill in the light of new knowledge and changed circumstances. The increasing importance of teamwork pointed to the need for a good deal of interdisciplinary training and the ability to develop new ways of meeting individual, family and community needs within a comprehensive social service department. Professional social workers should constantly draw upon the results of relevant work in the behavioural sciences and be trained to assess the effectiveness of different ways of meeting need. The then situation of separate recruitment, finance and specialised practice were all impediments to a unified training in principles and skills common to all forms of social work with individuals and families.

Nearly all the evidence to the Seebohm Committee supported integration of training, including the probation and after-care service: this was agreed by the National Association of Probation Officers (NAPO). A common basic training in university and other courses was essential rather than the existing separate trainings. The hard and fast division between two kinds of higher education created a gap, said the Report, which 'although comprehensible is nevertheless deplorable' (para. 540).

Well-qualified social workers trained outside the university should be admitted to university courses in social work beyond the basic level. Universities should continue to provide basic professional training and also accept the major responsibility for experiment and developments in new forms of training. The Committee felt strongly that social work teaching was bound to suffer unless those who taught continued to practise as social workers, even though a combination of teaching and practice would entail an increase in the staff/student ratio. Fieldwork teachers also needed training in educational planning and methods, in new areas of knowledge and practice, and the application of research findings. By the mid-1970s expansion of demand in relation to supply had made these desirable aims as remote as ever. The Report thought that expansion in training was impossible without substantial additional funds both from local authorities and the University Grants Committee (UGC). The latter should make special earmarked funds available both for basic training and for professional postgraduate training, research and experiment.

The content of professional training for social work should lay more stress on work with groups and communities and also on social planning and the administrative structure of the organisations in which social work services were provided. Experiment was needed with a wider concept of generic training to equip students to work as appropriate with individuals, groups and communities.

'The justification of this approach is the belief that the divisions between different methods of social work are as artificial as the difference between various forms of casework and that in his daily work the social worker needs all these methods to enable him to respond appropriately to social problems which involve individual, family, group and community aspects. This newer concept of generic training has obvious attractions as a preparation for work in the social service departments.' (para. 558)

The Report recognised that owing to the shortness of training, students might only acquire a superficial acquaintance with a range of methods and not develop a soundly based professional skill in any one of them. No experience existed to show whether it was possible for students on basic courses to reach real, initial competence in all three methods or only one, together with sufficient knowledge of others to enable them to do their own job properly. The alternative would be optional courses at greater depth in basic training, with the opportunity to develop skill to a higher level in subsequent training. This should include advanced studies in particular areas of knowledge and practice, for example delinquency or mental health, group and community work and residential social work, as well as in research methods and the application of research in social work. This was necessary for a greater understanding of scientific method, a more critical approach, and more commitment to the importance of extending more systematic, empirical knowledge than existed at the basic training level.

'We were concerned to find that staff who teach social work in university departments and in colleges of further education today, seldom carry the research responsibilities expected in other departments. It was urged on us in evidence that this was due to the teaching load and administrative commitments of social work teachers and to the voluntary work in the social services which they undertake outside their departments. Extending the boundaries of knowledge is no less important for the development of social work than for other professions which claim to be based on scientific knowledge. Concentration of interest and resources on training to the neglect of research is bound to be counter productive. Without the stimulus and the underpinning of research, training itself will not be able to meet the challenge presented by new problems and new ideas.' (para. 562)

The Committee was also concerned with the training of residential staff, home help organisers, volunteers and social work aides as well as the importance of in-service training, staff development and 'training the trainers'. It was also very well aware of the need for

'. . . a constant dialogue between those in the social services and those responsible for training, so that the trainers are continuously examining how relevant is the training they provide to the needs of the community. The more resources that are put into social services, including training, the more important it is that the community should have evidence of what this investment achieves. There is in every profession a danger of fossilisation around ideas and practice which become sacrosanct and thus impervious to empirical challenge. The wish of many social work teachers to continue to practise as well as teach should, if it can be realised, help to reduce the danger of separating training from the needs of the field. In short, there should be an on-going review of training in relation to needs, and evaluation should be built into training developments in order to determine the effectiveness of different methods and degrees of training.' (para. 580)

So far as the central organisation of training was concerned, the Committee said trenchantly that

'. . . the existence of three separately administered training councils for social work, each advertising for students, each directly or indirectly competing for teaching staff and field placements, each setting up or promoting separate courses, sometimes in the same building, adjacent but not integrated, is educationally and professionally unsound; we believe it involves an indefensible waste of scarce resources which should not be continued.' (para. 533)

The Committee proposed that a new advisory council for the personal social services should take on these responsibilities through a training committee. This met with almost universal dissent in view of the size of the task, which included training responsibilities beyond the boundaries of the local authority personal social services (para. 533).

THE CENTRAL COUNCIL FOR EDUCATION AND TRAINING IN SOCIAL WORK

In the event, powers which already existed under the Health Visiting and Social Work (Training) Act, 1962 were used to bring together the CTC, the CTSW and the Training Committee of ACPAC to form the Central Council for Education and Training in Social Work (CCETSW). This Council, which came into existence in 1971, covered the United Kingdom. It was independent of a government department though financed by the DHSS (probation students continued to be financed by the Home Office). Its functions were to promote education and training in all fields of social work to recognise training courses and to award qualifications, to recruit students and to undertake research in social work education. Like the CTC and the CTSW, it was also responsible for training social workers for voluntary agencies. Before its official starting date it met informally to look at the different practices and responsibilities of the three councils and of APSW and IMSW to determine the most urgent priorities, notably about recognition of existing courses and the qualification to be awarded to students.

When the CCETSW came into formal existence it quickly announced that it would award a certificate of qualification in social work (CQSW) to all students successfully completing recognised courses, and also continue to award in its own name the previous CTC and CTSW qualifications in residential care. It took over staffs of the three councils but some of these were civil servants who only remained for a limited period. It had to fuse different procedures and evolve new ones, particularly in relation to residential social work, community work and social work with handicapped people. It thus had to tidy up, keep the best of what already existed, strengthen the foundations, create channels of communication, and expand to meet the new needs of social services departments. It decided that the 150 qualifying courses for which it became responsible should be two years in length, other than those for residential social work or based upon a social studies qualification. As a result some existing courses added a further year or merged with another two-year course; others became phase III courses (described below). The probation one-year courses were lengthened for an interim period by supervision and planned study in the first year of service before the qualification was awarded. The Home Office recognised the CQSW as the qualifying award for the probation service, as it had from the start recognised an applied social studies qualification. Specialised child care, CSW, mental health and medical social work courses ceased to exist and were 'reconstructed to provide a basic qualification for professional social work with less emphasis on a particular setting' (CCETSW, 1973*c*, p. 3). A common core of knowledge and skill could be combined with a variety of expertise through options, for instance in work with children, or old people, or delinquents, or the mentally ill, or physically handicapped, or in method of social work with individuals, families, groups or communities, or in residential settings. It was planned that a proportion of social work staff in residential and day services should hold the CQSW. It was hoped to expand the number of available places by 60 per cent by 1976 and to keep an even balance between graduate and non-graduate students. By mid-1975 it looked as though these plans might be affected by cutbacks in secondment and LEA student grants. The Council also took responsibility for recognition and review. It required detailed information within a standardised form – earlier a bone of violent contention between the CTC and the universities – and visits by a panel of assessors.

The CCETSW took over the child care emergency courses (now generic) and continued them into the mid-1970s. Largely because of their close-knit staff teams, these courses achieved a high standard of teaching and at least one (at Leeds Polytechnic) pioneered a new experiment with a 'totally integrated' syllabus of which 'the core . . . lies in the idea that all teaching should seek to further the students' understanding of the human being in interaction with his environment, the needs he brings to his social interactions, the provisions made by others to meet these needs, problematic areas of need-meeting, and the place of social work in the problem solving' (Kent, 1974, pp. 1–2).

There were many regrets when these courses were discontinued and their teams disbanded. 'Emergency' courses as such must always end but if financial difficulties can be overcome it is desirable to keep staffs with strong group feeling together and use their expertise in more permanent patterns of training. This was done to a limited extent in two-year courses for mature students.

The three-phase plan (to include Scotland) had been worked out jointly by the CTC and the CTSW for experienced but unqualified officers over 35 with five or more years' experience at 31 March, 1972. It was implemented by the CCETSW in 1971. Phase I consisted of twenty-four study days in six months at an educational institution under the direction of a study supervisor who would help to relate theory to practice. Phase II comprised thirty-six study days in twelve months and related the earlier studies to social work. There was no selection or assessment. Those who completed the two phases were eligible to be selected for a one-year, full-time qualifying course in certain universities and polytechnics. The quality of the teaching and the supervision given by study supervisors in the first two phases varied from routine to very good but it improved with experience and, contrary to expectations, a very high proportion of eligible students completed phases I and II and applied to take the full-time qualifying course. Some had already taken the Josephine Butler or NSPCC courses, a substantial minority held senior social work posts and some 'had been the backbone of the service over many years' (CTC/CTSW, 1970). There was a strong demand for these courses to continue beyond 1975 and the CCETSW announced that spring that they would 'cease when eligible students have been catered for'.

The CCETSW set up two series of working parties to undertake social work curriculum studies, and to produce discussion papers (followed by policy statements) on specific forms of training, for example for residential social work. Its plans for residential and day services training and for education welfare are described in chapters 13 and 21.

The Council's most controversial proposal was for a certificate in social service (CSS) (CCETSW, 1975c) to be started experimentally in 1975. Students had to be at least 18 and employed in a public, voluntary or private social service. The course was based on release to take three units, each comprising 240 or 320 hours of formal study (plus reading and project work), the total to be completed in not less than two or more than five years. The teaching was to be linked with learning on the job by study supervisors provided by employers and given time for regular contracts with students and tutors. To avoid supervision being an additional burden for hard-pressed staff some part-time appointments might be made. But in the current shortage of supervisors for qualifying courses it was hard to see who would be available. There were also to be liaison officers between the employing agencies and the colleges. All students were to take a common unit on the development of individuals in families and the community, human needs and the extent to which they were met, national and local social policy formulation, and social service provision. Students were to contribute their own experience. The standard options were focused on life stages – i.e. children and adolescents, adults, the elderly – or the community. The special options were to prepare students for a defined range of tasks related to their own work. Each student was to choose one standard and one special option. The units were to be taught in colleges (except the specialist option) either by day release study (with a minimum of ten days in residence) or block periods, and students' workloads were to be reduced. A college statement was to be issued to each student satisfactorily completing a unit. Students whose college and work assessments for three units were satisfactory would receive the CCETSW certificate in social service. Schemes would only be approved by the Council if satisfactory provision could be made by employing agencies and colleges. It was thought that the

CSS would be appropriate for those who needed management training and technical skills in addition to some social work knowledge and skill: examples were organisers of domiciliary services, day services staff, mobility officers for the blind, or advisers on welfare rights. A second category included assistant residential or day service staff with substantial but not general responsibility for clients. It was thought that there would continue to be many assistant and support staff for whom these courses would not be feasible but who needed in-service training. Pilot schemes had started at five colleges by October 1975.

In an altered form, these were the three grades previously identified by the Younghusband working party (1959) as inherent in the realities of the work situation. The CSS proposal was controversial because it raised the question of the CCETSW's boundaries, because many appointing committees might not distinguish between the CQSW and the CSS, because scarce resources might be diverted from professional training, and because in a period of recession local authorities might release staff to take units at the local college rather than seconding them for full-time CQSW courses.

The CCETSW came into existence at a time when enormous and quick expansion in social work education was demanded, whether for field or residential workers, of qualifying and post-qualifying courses and of in-service training. This was made necessary by the high proportion of untrained social workers, coupled with the overwhelming demands on the reorganised personal social services, and the new duties and expectations that faced probation officers. This social work explosion took place at the same time that the reorganisations of 1971 and 1974 created upheavals in local authority services and resulted in large numbers of experienced social workers being promoted to administrative posts and lost to practice and student supervision. Moreover, from 1974 the DHSS ceased to be responsible for grant aiding either courses or non-graduate students, which created fresh uncertainties about what might happen to university courses when earmarked grants ceased at the end of the quinquennium and how staff/ student ratios in polytechnics and other colleges might be affected (see also chapter 1). On top of all this, the economic blizzard descended in 1974–5 leading to sharp cuts in public spending and many 'frozen' posts. It is remarkable in these circumstances that the government announced an increase in the CCETSW grant from about £600,000 in 1975 to over £1,000,000 by 1976. As a result five regional offices were opened and the professional staff increased to over fifty.

The CTC, the Training Committee of ACPAC and, in other ways, the CTSW had faced many of the criticisms about interference and the arbitrary use of power later levied against the CCETSW. This may be an occupational hazard, and there were strong arguments for separating training from a government department, but it had the disadvantage of loss of continuous contact with what was happening in the field.

The first tensions between the JUC and the CCETSW began when the CCETSW introduced plans to expand training in certain universities and polytechnics, with resultant anxieties about the basis of selection and the effect of expansion on academic standards. Subsequently additional tensions were created by the detailed material and the visits required for recognition and review of all courses (including those in universities), though conversely some took these procedures for granted and found them helpful. Perhaps no one foresaw when the CCETSW was set up that the linkage between its recognition of courses and salary scales would give it a stranglehold, since no course it did not recognise could give an award that conferred the accepted qualification. There was no appeal from its decisions but the Council itself was composed of representatives of all the interests concerned. In addition, a range of people beyond actual council members was involved in its work through membership of review panels and co-option to committees.

The problem of how to reconcile the Council's power with university freedom and the needs of the field was far from being resolved by 1975, but tensions sometimes resulted in improvements if they did not lead to entrenched attitudes and if decisions were almost always jointly made. These were the turbulent circumstances in which the CCETSW had to decide upon and implement policies after much consultation, conflicting views and criticism, initially to bring separate courses into line with each other and then continuously to expand training. These policies were designed to create a coherent pattern from what already existed and to chart a new course for social work education.

After temporary upheavals of recognition and continuing problems of expansion the next conflict came when the Council began to engage in a necessary if controversial mopping-up operation. This was essential in order to bring within a coherent pattern small specialised courses on the margins of social work outside the scope of the previous councils and to initiate training where none had existed before. In 1974 the DHSS made the Council responsible for day care training, including teachers for the mentally handicapped, who could not logically be separated from residential care staff. From the outset it had been responsible for training for social work in the education service (see chapter 21, section on 'Social Work and Education Welfare'). There were discussions as to whether it should become responsible for training home help organisers (see volume 1, chapter 22, section on 'The Home Help Service'). More controversial still, it decided to promote the CSS described above. This represented expansion beyond recognised social work (with the exception of education welfare) and raised the problem of whether its function was solely the education of social workers or included the training of staff at various levels for the personal social services. The latter task might confuse the issues and dissipate the Council's resources. But as more and more functions in the social services seemed to require a measure of skill for which no training existed it was argued that the CCETSW should pioneer this. The Council itself discussed the problem of boundaries in its 1973–4 report (pp. 36–7). It drew a distinction 'between professional social work and other forms of social service closely allied with social work'. It thought it was essential to make this distinction crystal clear in order to relate the Council's activities to the reality of the work situation and to uphold high standards in professional education for social work. This would force it, in co-operation with other bodies, to be more explicit in defining what it meant by social work and education for it, and to clarify training responsibilities for other groups.

The Social Work Education Committee of the JUC, the Association of Teachers in Social Work Education, BASW, NAPO, the Association of Directors of Social Services, the Directors of Social Work (Scotland), the Conference of Chief Probation Officers and the Residential Care Association all had a stake in this debate as interested parties and whether as gadflies, dissidents, stimulators, contributors or clarifiers.

PART TWO DEVELOPMENTS IN SOCIAL WORK THEORY AND PRACTICE

Chapter 8

Changes in Casework Theory and Practice: Social Work with Groups

CHANGES IN CASEWORK THEORY AND PRACTICE

New Dimensions in the 1950s

Until the 1950s there were hardly any studies of actual practice by British social workers. Accounts ranged from wide philosophical aims to why the office walls should be painted primrose. A standard book on probation (Glover, 1949) spoke of fifteen-minute interviews as 'probably sufficient for regular contact' (p. 275). The 'new' casework superseded stereotyped assumptions about people's behaviour in which social workers took their personal reactions at face value. In the 1950s they began to try to understand the reasons behind behaviour and to assess the situation in an orderly way before deciding how to use the relationship to help the client with his difficulties. At first American case records were used in seminars for practising social workers, but in time more British records were produced and, perhaps naturally, these were usually success stories, showing the effectiveness of the 'new casework' so that the need seemed to be for social workers to learn more of the same. The new knowledge from dynamic psychology was heady wine because it seemed to show the goal-directed nature of apparently irrational behaviour, even though some goals were self-defeating. Process recording of interaction with the client illuminated the processes of change over a period and the effect of accepting and respecting people rather than telling them what they ought to do or rebuking them for their behaviour.

For the first time the client's expression of hostility was recognised as positive rather than a failure to be avoided, because social workers aimed to be friendly people who 'brought out the best in others'. But hostility was there in any event and if the client displaced it onto the worker and was helped to express it this might drain off tension, stress and antagonism in other relationships and make it more possible for the client to face current reality. He was helped to feel that the negative and destructive parts of his personality were accepted and that the worker remained friendly and concerned, so that ambivalent feelings were less likely to be denied or frustration to be built up. 'Enabling people to express their hidden anxieties and despair can bring considerable relief. Instead of investing so much energy in hiding problems from the outside world and letting them fester inside . . . the very fact that they are discussed makes them seem more manageable' (Goldberg, 1966*b*, p. 34). In the new climate, social workers who had previously relied largely on their own experience learnt to reflect upon the significance of what was happening in the interaction between themselves and the client, to listen and to sense the meaning of what was said or not said and the strength – or absence – of feeling behind it, and also to be aware of non-verbal communication. They saw the importance of understanding mixed motives, their own as well as the client's, recognising defence mechanisms, and clarifying the essential nature of the problem as it affected the client, rather than concentrating on presenting symptoms: 'We need to get the client's overwhelming, sprawling, difficulty into a manageable size . . . to shrink it' (ASW, 1956, p. 8).

This approach had strengths and weaknesses. In some local authority service there was at that time too much tendency for untrained workers to focus on symptoms rather than people and to rely on pep talks. Conversely, trained social workers were accused of prying into people's intimate affairs as a condition of giving them some simple service which they needed. There was indeed a tendency to denigrate practical services and to regard 'material needs' as distracting attention from the 'real problem'. A dichotomy also grew up amongst professional social workers between the advocates of practical services and material giving and those who put the emphasis on making a relationship in which the client experienced and expressed ambivalent feelings, anxieties, fears and hostility. Practical services, so some held, undermined independence, created a dependency situation, and material giving was a form of bribery. This decreased interest in the current social situation, resulted in some people being considered unsuitable for casework because they were not motivated to co-operate, or were too aggressive or immature, or had too little capacity for insight. In other words, the person was unsuitable for treatment, not the treatment for the person.

Throughout this earlier period some caseworkers were struggling to discover whether psychiatric social work in particular was a kind of second-best form of psychotherapy or an entity in its own right with its own independent professional competence – and if so, what this was. There was emphasis on early, unconscious experience, the client's inner world, with comparatively little interest in the current social environment, though there was still much to be learnt about the interlocking of personality, family relationships, behaviour and social circumstances. Home visits were similarly frowned upon by a few authors. They argued that if the client really wanted help he would come to the office where uninterrupted interviews based upon verbal communication could take place free from distraction on calm neutral ground. In any event, it was more important to explore what the client thought about home circumstances than what these were really like, even though the caseworker remained ignorant of clients' social circumstances. Such methods were not appropriate for unwilling clients who did not keep appointments, or for those who found difficulty in communication or shunned formal interviews. Heimler (1958) describing a practice ahead of its time said 'Many . . . patients could only be induced to accept help provided this was offered in an informal and in a quasi-social manner . . . social work must still be based on psychoanalytical theories and principles, but the technique must be radically adapted to meet the needs of the patient . . . We are part of the community, a new brand of specialist' (p. 296).

For many caseworkers who could not avoid dealing with current external circumstances, their problem was how to apply psychodynamic concepts to the handling of these current situations and environmental problems. They sometimes had to work with clients for whom office interviews based upon verbal communication were meaningless. And they had to try to help people for whom psychiatric treatment had little to offer: acting-out clients, psychopaths, immature or mentally dull people, and indeed normal people in stressful situations. Many caseworkers also had to undertake complex tasks with little opportunity for professional learning or stimulus, unlike those in psychiatric settings where there was psychiatric leadership and constant stimulus and opportunity for professional learning.

Already in the early 1950s some caseworkers in their practice and teaching emphasised discovery of and support for strengths rather than delving into pathology, supporting the ego by evoking the client's co-operation and evaluating his behaviour in the 'here and now'. The caseworker's spontaneous concern, 'feeling response', and desire to help were agreed to be of over-riding importance.

Various seminars and working parties resulted in three widely read and quoted pamphlets of the time: *Recent Developments in Casework* (ASW, 1956), *The Essentials of Social Casework* (APSW, 1956*b*) and *The Boundaries of Casework* (APSW, 1956*a*). These analysed the nature of casework, the situations where it was appropriate, and those in which it was not needed because help could be given by untrained workers with opportunities for supervision and consultation by caseworkers. The 'one to one relationship' was assumed, but 'the caseworker must be able to take into consideration the needs of all the individuals concerned in a situation, and the setting in which they live' (APSW, 1956*b*, p. 2). The following deductions were drawn from so doing: 'The severity of a problem, however, is not necessarily determined by a particular group of symptoms or social ills. It is dependent, rather, upon the extent to which personal difficulties or inadequacies interfere with the client's ability to solve his difficulties unaided' (ibid., p. 1).

In *The Essentials of Social Casework* it seemed to be assumed that the social services were adequate if only the client was able to use them and little attention was paid to bad housing, poverty, life at the margin, or a destructive social environment. In the casework writing of the time it was not contested that housing and other environmental factors were important but they were held to be secondary, i.e. that the client would be able to surmount them but for his inner conflicts. Unemployment might be due to frustration or an inability to accept authority, and there were striking examples of people being helped back into employment through casework (Heimler, 1962). Family relationships were studied, largely through matrimonial and child guidance work. There was stress on, indeed a zest for, more knowledge and improved skill but little reference to the need for research in social work, to a wider range of casework practice, to social work with groups and communities, or as Mays put it at the 1956 APSW symposium, to 'an unravelling of the complex threads of the ways in which the individual relates to his social environment rather than an examination of the possibly pathological psychology of the individual' (Mays, 1956, p. 70).

These were obvious shortcomings but understandable at the time when mixed groups of social workers had only recently started to reflect systematically upon the nature of their practice and were still deeply immersed in trying to understand people who for one reason or another (and granted the diagnosis of reasons was sometimes too limited or inappropriate) were not able to cope with their personal and social difficulties. Most professional social workers of the 1950s believed in their ability to help people, believed in what they were doing, and in the effectiveness of the new methods they were beginning to learn. Their inherent desire to help people was reinforced by a deeper understanding, particularly of irrational behaviour, and a methodology that seemed to make help more possible, and at last they had a common language for communication. They were struggling hard to discover what was unique to casework as distinct from either psychotherapy or 'welfare' and it is not surprising if at that time the boundaries of casework were narrowly drawn. As was pointed out by Brown (1964): '. . . much of the casework literature published in this country during the 1950–60 decade focuses on the interpretive type of work appropriate for relatively mature and well integrated individuals, and students and others seemed to be gaining the impression that this was the method *par excellence* to use with all clients' (p. 36).

The growing use of psychoanalytic theory in casework led in some quarters to an emphasis on the transference, which was always present in the casework relationship, whether recognised or not, and a source of unconscious fantasy interfering with perception of current reality. Some caseworkers used their understanding as a guide to their own response to behaviour. Others stressed the insight-giving process, the intensification and use of a relationship in which transference phenomena were interpreted. *The Caseworker's Use of Relationship* (Ferard and Hunnybun, 1962) was a clear and well-argued analysis of casework which relied heavily on the use of the transference relationship, on interpretation, on client self-determination, and an understanding of the unconscious effect of early experience on current behaviour. In some circumstances with some clients this was an appropriate and helpful method. But with many others it was more important to support the ego than to bring unconscious fantasies to the surface. This might be achieved by a therapeutic use of the relationship to provide experiences the client had lacked and which were necessary for maturation. Later this technique was also used in various therapeutic groups. As Power (1962) said in a review article, the method 'described in this book may be best used to help people whose ego is reasonably well developed and who have a fairly clear sense of identity, but who are beset with problems, the solution of which seems elusively beyond their grasp and who need additional insight before they are able to attain sufficient control over their own feelings and their environment' (p. 20).

Casework as a means of communicating with children also came into the limelight as the child care service grew. This meant being able to give them information, to talk with them, to listen, to help them to express their feelings about leaving home and their fears about the future, and to be a reliable figure in their lives. Child care workers had a particularly difficult task in casework with parents (who often felt intensely guilty at their parental failures), with actually or potentially damaged children, and in a partnership role with foster parents. Yet

'The child's primary need is not for a casework relationship but for an environment which can provide for him and within which he can be cared for successfully. The main therapeutic experience for the child will not be in the relationship with the caseworker but in his relationships with his foster parents. Of course, the caseworker will be needed to help the child to deal with his feelings about his own parents and to adjust to and make use of his foster home; as well as to select and support the foster parents.' (Winnicott, 1955, p. 138)

New consciousness of the effect of culture and of physical circumstances on behaviour partly resulted from such studies as *Growing Up in the City* (Mays, 1954) and *Family and Kinship in East London* (Young and Willmott, 1959), which suggested that norms of behaviour varied according to culture or subculture, so that social workers must be careful not to use their own cultural assumptions and moral codes as yardsticks of normality or psychopathology.

Goldberg (1961) summed up the scene at the end of the 1950s thus:

'Having by now securely incorporated into the theory and practice of social casework the basic tenets of dynamic psychology, we might usefully rediscover the social environment in which our clients move, not as a static framework but as a dynamic process continually interacting with inner personal forces. This may well become our main practical and theoretical task in the coming years.' (pp. 104–5)

Expansion in Casework Theory in the 1960s
By degrees it began to be realised that while psychoanalytic theory illuminated the behaviour of a wide range of people, including normal people under stress, it must be used as a basis for a more comprehensive range of techniques than those of the analyst. Several articles at the time, notably 'A Review of Casework Methods' (Brown, 1964) and 'A New Look at Casework' (Irvine, republished 1966) united divergent concepts and practices and were widely used because they each emphasised that 'skill in casework lies in the understanding of the different needs of different people in various social circumstances and in the provision of different appropriate kinds of help' (Brown, 1964, p. 3).

This bypassed a number of more or less fruitless arguments by concentrating on what the client needed rather than

'. . . the use of a small range of techniques directed towards the development of self-knowledge, although this does demand skill of a kind, but in the careful assessment of the social situation, personality structure, stage of development and source of anxiety of each individual, and then in the sensitive, flexible, discriminating use of appropriate methods of help. Depending on the changing needs of the client at any particular time, we may be warm or detached, active or passive, directive or permissive, verbal or silent, moralistic or non-judgmental in our approach.' (Brown, 1964, p. 34)

This was in line with the early use of role theory in casework and new developments in ego psychology which stressed the client's current life situation and the possibility of growth and change through interaction between him and his environment. 'Real' casework was no longer identified with a method akin to psychotherapy; it now began to be seen as a wide repertoire of verbal and non-verbal communications and methods of work based upon a sensitive and changing assessment of the client's needs in his family and social context. This made it easier to think of practical services, non-verbal communication, and indeed the use of authority, as elements in a casework process, particularly with immature people, and of 'reaching out' to those who would never of their own volition go near a social work agency. It also resulted in a new perception of casework as encouraging a maturation process through a stable relationship in which the caseworker showed himself concerned, well-disposed and understanding, while able to resist the client's efforts at manipulation. The essential point was a repertoire of communication methods which made possible the differential use of relationship. As Irvine pointed out in 'A New Look at Casework', 'stable parents provide a model which is more useful in many casework situations than that provided by psychoanalysis' (republished 1966, p. 41).

This was part of a slow move away from the medical model of specific treatment and cure which had been understandably adopted by medical and psychiatric social workers through their identification with the medical profession. The emphasis on the importance of interviewing skill, on assessment and on appropriate treatment goals continued.

Recognition of the influence of the current social environment, of the whole family as a unit and the interaction within it, led to an emphasis on modifying attitudes within a social context as well as improving social circumstances. Thus the home visit became recognised as a more effective means of understanding and influencing the client's interaction in his family and the reciprocal relations between him and his environment. It was often possible to communicate more easily in the home than in a hospital, office or clinic setting, to see the family functioning as a group, the dynamics of family interaction, roles in family life, the modes of family communication and their social conditions.

In line with these developments, practical services and material giving began to be integrated into the casework process, providing they were used with a full understanding of their purpose, as means of meeting psychological need because for many clients deeds spoke louder than words, especially when they urgently needed practical help or material necessities. But if these were a valid part of casework, was their provision also sometimes simply a welfare function? And on what criteria should the judgement be made? Could it only be determined by skilled intake interviews? If not, who should make the initial decision and on what criteria? Were all practical needs the tip of a psychosocial iceberg that should be explored? This debate about the relations between social work and the giving of financial and material help swung back and forth over the years with little clarity, because there was scant systematic analysis and few facts by which to determine when such decisions by the in-service trained were plain common sense or when undetected social casualties were being swept under the carpet.

Long-term casework was still in the 1960s regarded as the desirable norm, intended to bring about a major change in the client and his way of life. Short-term contact and limited goals were still often thought not to be 'real' casework.

Caseworkers were clarifying their relations to administration. They began to ask about the extent to which the administrative structure and policies facilitated or hindered casework relationships with clients; whether the ways in which the agency, as such, operated demonstrated good human relations; and the contribution which caseworkers could make to general policy through their first-hand experience of the effect on people of the implementation of social services. Conversely, various studies referred to in other chapters showed the limitations that resulted from newly qualified caseworkers' ignorance of administration and the functions of related professions.

Developments in Casework Method in the Early 1970s
(by Elizabeth Irvine, AAPSW, formerly Reader in Social Work, York University)

The pursuit of this subject has emphasised the selective and partial nature of published work as evidence of trends and processes in the profession. As pointed out by Bree (1970), the journals at any one period are liable to over-represent some interests and under-represent others. Social work journals from 1970 to 1975 were naturally preoccupied with problems of organisations in the new social services departments, and reflected a gradual struggle to distinguish the proper functions of professional social workers from those services which could be performed by aides or voluntary workers. There was also an interest in new types of service, such as intermediate treatment, and in the study of particular client groups, such as violent parents or drug abusers, and research studies on aspects of social work or relevant subjects. There was also evidence of a considerable ferment at the theoretical level, particularly in the use of general systems theory to construct a unified framework for the three traditional methods of social work and for any new ones which might develop.

The general trend reflected in these journals is undoubtedly away from the close study of the individual and personal service to him towards a preoccupation with the provision of large-scale material services and the problems of ways and means. The counter-current is not so well reflected and there is little sign, for instance, of the existence of the flourishing Group for the Advancement of Psychotherapy in Social Work (GAPS) largely concerned with the clarification of the concept of psychotherapy and the integration of new developments into this concept (see chapter 12). GAPS was also concerned with promoting the conditions in which psychotherapeutic casework could be practised in social agencies, particularly in the revival of specialisation and the creation of posts for senior practitioners to enable the therapeutic worker to continue to practise this skill without financial sacrifice.

Little space was devoted in the journals to questions of casework method, but the few articles published reflect a considerable creative ferment. The search for greater economy and effectiveness was represented by the similar methods known as short-term contracts and task-centred casework, and some attention was also paid to aspects of family therapy.

Crisis Intervention. These methods emphasised the importance of crisis intervention, derived mainly from the work of Gerald Caplan (1961, 1962), who maintains that the vulnerability of the individual during the crisis produced by changes in life situations involves not only the risk of impaired future functioning but also the possibility of long-term improvement. Individuals differ in their vulnerability and capacity to mobilise their latent potential, on the basis of previous experience, but Caplan maintained that the quality of social support can considerably influence the outcome. Friends and relations may be able to give all the social support required to ensure a favourable outcome, but if these are lacking, or encourage rigid, brittle and maladaptive defences, it is important that professional helpers, such as social workers, should be ready and able to intervene in favour of solutions which will increase the individual's (or the family's) self-confidence, maturity and ability to cope with stress.

Caplan conducted a number of annual seminars in London for members of the helping professions, and his influence was widely disseminated. Crisis theory was applied sporadically by the establishment of special crisis services for the bereaved and of walk-in services for adolescents, and in the efforts of some child guidance clinics to eliminate the waiting list. It also constitutes an important element in family therapy and short-term casework. It was clearly of capital importance to social services departments contending with an acute shortage of trained social workers and an apparently unlimited demand. Hope of further economies arose from the findings of Reid and Shyne (1969) that within an experimental population of families with problems in relationships those receiving short-term help (eight interviews, the number specified beforehand) made more progress than others assigned to long-term, open-ended help.

Task-Centred Casework. This of course raised urgent questions as to why less should be more effective than more. Building on this preliminary study, Reid and Epstein (1972) formulated and tested a model of 'task centred casework'. In an able review of their book, Akhurst (1973) said:

'The basic elements of their scheme are the identification of specific problems, the selection of related tasks and the development of helping techniques. The contact with the client begins the exploration of the problem which the client is prepared to work on. The agreement of the client is essential to the process, and it entails singling out a target problem the resolution of which will be the main focus of help. The process then moves on to the selection of tasks which are appropriate to the resolution of the problem. These are tasks for both the client and the worker. Once again, the involvement of the client is crucial.' (p. 59)

Compared with traditional casework, the emphasis was on cognitive rather than emotional modification as a basis for behavioural change. The client was helped to achieve a better understanding of the unsatisfactory current situation of which he complained; an understanding both of other participants in it and of the nature and dynamics of his own behaviour and interaction with them. Deeper awareness was only sought in case of blockage, when it became necessary to explore the nature and origin of obstacles to task performance, including, if necessary, some relevant early history.

Where clients presented multiple problems, the target problem was selected in accordance with the clients' priorities if he was able to formulate or select them, otherwise according to the degree of affect with which he spoke of them. Once problem, goal and task were formulated, the worker took responsibility for holding the client to the task, even if the latter found he would prefer to work on one of his other problems, and even if this appeared to be a more fundamental one.

A number of action projects were carried out to test the value of this method in various settings and with various types of problem. Among these was a study by Goldberg, Walker and Robinson (1977) on the use of this method in a social services department area office. As the authors point out, the method is clearly inappropriate for many of the cases referred to these departments, such as multiproblem families whose parents learn, if at all, very slowly and in the context of a strongly nurturing relationship; or the many cases demanding open-ended surveillance of young delinquents, children at risk, the mentally ill or handicapped and the disabled. It required a certain degree of ego strength in the client – i.e. the ability to learn fairly rapidly and to carry out agreed tasks – and seemed to be most successful in relatively simple situations where clients are motivated for change, rather than with those bombarded by many vicissitudes. In many cases the need was not for casework but for information or advice to enable the client to solve his own problem, or for an assessment of the eligibility of applicants for various domiciliary services, or for residential or day care, and the mobilisation of the services required.

Of the sixty-eight cases referred to the workers in the project during the course of one year, only twenty-two were considered to be suitable for task-centred casework; the others fell into the various categories mentioned above, with a few who were unable to select one of their numerous problems to work on, or who refused to consider any help but immediate financial aid to stave off a crisis. In this small experimental sample, problems of inadequate resources proved most amenable to task-centred casework. Underlying problems such as marital difficulties or physical or mental disability were often left untouched as being less important or too chronic and unalterable, but the client was usually better able to manage them when the financial problem was solved.

Dissatisfaction in social relationships also appeared to be a promising field: loneliness and isolation in the elderly, and relationships impoverished owing to physical or mental handicaps (such as agoraphobia). Some cases where serious and chronic problems were untouched demonstrated the feasibility and advantages of aiming at limited and attainable objectives whilst not ignoring intractable difficulties.

This aspect of the method had in fact been taught in the USA for many years under the title of 'partialising the problems' but had more or less dropped out of use by the 1960s, and so had to be born anew. There are also striking parallels between the task-centred method and the 'functional' (Rankian) style of casework which flourished in some centres in the USA and was for a time strongly opposed by the orthodox Freudian, or 'diagnostic', school of thought. Both approaches emphasised the value of a brief, planned period of service or co-operation, as tending to mobilise greater effort in the client. Emphasising the importance of the present, neither particularly encouraged the search for early experiences to illuminate present attitudes and behaviour, though such memories were accepted and used if they appeared unbidden. However, task-centred casework was considerably more directive, in view of the finding that many clients preferred active and goal-directed help to passive, exploratory techniques.

This element recurred in family therapy, where Skynner (1971*a, b, c*) noted that family therapists found it necessary to adopt a more active, controlling role in spite of the bias towards therapeutic passivity in their previous psychotherapeutic training: 'Active, challenging, stimulating interventions are . . . striking in the protocols of most workers in this field' (Skynner, 1971*b*, p. 5). Skynner also advocated brief interventions of from one to ten sessions as being often able to produce 'striking and satisfactory change within a few sessions' (Skynner, 1971*a*, p. 4), and specifically included among suitable clients 'the more inadequate types of families, often referred to child guidance clinics' (Skynner, 1971*b*, p. 5). We shall return to this method later.

Brief Focal Intervention. One feature of this model, fairly widely adopted here, was the formulation and negotiation of specific limited aims with the client, commonly seen in terms of establishing a contract. It appeared that this should include, for maximum effectiveness, the stipulation of a limited period for co-operative work on the problems, and towards the goals agreed. This approach had considerable appeal for workers in social services departments, but in practice goals and frequency of visits were specified more often than time limits. The Tavistock Clinic set up a Brief Focal Intervention Programme, which provided advanced training for qualified and experienced social workers. Members of this unit contributed most of the scanty British literature on this subject. Hutten (1974) established the rationals for such work with reference to prevention theory, crisis theory and the work of Reid and Shyne described above, linking these also to Malan's research (1963) on brief psychotherapy. Tuters (1974) described a three-month, time-limited piece of focused work with a mother and her latency-age daughter following the sudden death of the father, to enable them to get in touch with their bereaved feelings of loss, anger, despair and disbelief, and 'to rebuild a relationship of trust and respect together' (p. 226).

A third paper, again by Hutten (1975), illustrated with a number of short case studies the indications and opportunities for brief focal intervention, including situations of sudden loss by death or separation, and of breakdown in intrafamilial communication. The method was also recommended for reluctant clients who wanted help only on their own impossible terms. 'Here the focal task is to explore what, if any, contract can be made' (p. 538). A number of clients, who were unprepared at first to share responsibility for the outcome of the contract, were enabled by this method to make a responsible commitment to work on their difficulties over time, and to discover that a limited contract was possible and worth while. Conversely, the method was also recommended for clients 'whose chronicity is as much determined by the professionals' behaviour as by the defects of the client' (p. 540). Thus families beset by an incurable handicap in one of their members can be helped in a limited time to share and accept their grief about the handicap and to mobilise their strength to adapt more creatively and independently to the situation.

This method was clearly related to task-centred casework, differing mainly in a greater emphasis on the ventilation of feeling than on behaviour and in a less directive stance for the caseworker. Probably for this reason it was found to be effective in cases of bereavement or sudden loss, which proved relatively unresponsive to task-centred casework in the study by Goldberg, Walker and Robinson (1977). Here they were classified among 'problems of social transition', a sociological category which perhaps directed attention away from the psychological problem involved.

These short-term models naturally appealed to intake teams in social services departments, which usually took responsibility for short-term casework as well as assessment and referral (according to the few published accounts of their work). Loewenstein (1974) described the work of such a team in terms of crisis intervention. She was concerned that such work might prove uncongenial to some social workers, and suggested that many might wish to do it for limited periods only. She also found that fieldwork training often failed to develop in students the requisite skills of rapid assessment and of working under stress in crisis situations, despite the manifold opportunities for such training. She thought it might be necessary for social workers to acquire expertise in this field by in-service training in crisis work with families, including conjoint family therapy.

Family Therapy. Family therapy was first conceptualised and formalised in child guidance clinics. Social workers had, of course, often been confronted with several family members on home visits, but had often tried to isolate their particular 'client' from children, relatives and neighbours, even from the spouse. When interviews intended to be private had to be conducted in public the interruptions and distractions were regarded as a regrettable hazard of the home visit. Some caseworkers were able to accept the situation and turn it to account. Day (1965) and Deane (1966) described such work, one with a very demoralised family visited on behalf of the NSPCC, the other as a probation officer whose client's mother had recently returned from a mental hospital, while other children were gradually returning from care. The Family Service Unit (FSU) habitually dealt with whole families, as described by Halliwell (1969). Goldberg (1960) also described some dynamic family interviews carried out as part of a research project.

Casework with families shaded into family therapy, but by 1970 the latter term was generally used to refer to a process based on a theory of family interaction and on an explicit contract that the whole nuclear family (at least) would meet regularly with the therapist. The first British account of such work in a social agency appeared in *The Canford Families* (1962), an account of an action research project staffed mainly by PSWs, and based on an *ad hoc* social agency for early intervention with families whose children appeared to be at risk of delinquency or of mental ill-health. All the families chose to be visited at home, and the regular weekly visits were timed to include or exclude the children, as seemed most appropriate (see volume 1, chapter 15). Regular one-hour visits 'framed' the work and distinguished it clearly from simple social interaction; it was found that the parents themselves excluded relatives and neighbours. Keen attention was paid to non-verbal communication, which was also used by the workers as appropriate, and to the frequent use of the children by the parents as channels of communication. Home visits necessarily constituted 'life space interviews', and the worker sometimes arrived in the middle of a family crisis. Despite its relevance for social workers, *The Canford Families* fell on stony ground, and the later development of family therapy was mainly office-based with clinical models.

The sudden explosion of interest in family therapy as a tool for social workers in the 1970s seems to have been sparked off by Skynner (1971*a, b, c*). These articles by a psychiatrist with a background in child guidance and analytical group therapy, stimulated some members of the Family Welfare Association (FWA) to experiment with family therapy. Later publications rarely refer to literature published before 1970.

At an FWA conference on family therapy in 1973, 140 people attended out of 1,000 who had inquired. The papers showed the influence of the Institute of Marital Studies which had familiarised social workers with the concepts of projective identification (the attribution to others of lost or repudiated aspects of the self) and of counter transference, both as a source of information about the clients and as a temptation to collude with one or other client. Some family therapists considered that the use of this method minimised transference to the therapist because so much was transferred between family members, but the FWA speakers commonly found themselves to be the object of transference, and considered it appropriate to accept this and use it by interpretation or in other ways. At the first FWA conference Casement (1973) made a useful distinction between 'the counter transference response', which was personal to the worker, and must be carefully monitored and if possible dispelled, and the 'diagnostic response', the feelings aroused in him by the client's behaviour towards him, which was an indication of the client's state of mind and the nature of his transference. He also advocated 'the supervisory viewpoint', i.e. awareness and study of the way the problems of a family often reproduce themselves in the relationship of the co-therapists, another phenomenon of great diagnostic value. Other concepts of particular value to social workers in agencies with scarce resources of time, were those of 'the bearable movement target' and 'the minimum sufficient move' (Hertoghe and McLaine, 1973) which related the aims of intervention both to the fragility of the clients and the limited time available.

In 1971 a Family Institute was established by Barnardo's in Cardiff to experiment with the differential use of family group therapy, based on systems theory and small group dynamics. Walrond-Skinner (1974) described the main aspects of the work at the Institute as 'orientation to the family group, an emphasis on shared responsibility for problem-solving, the culture of openness, the inter-disciplinary staff, the use of co-therapy and the concentration on brief intervention' (p. 150). Skynner's influence was acknowledged, particularly in the context of correctly identifying the boundary of the family system to be treated. General systems theory also contributed the concepts of homeostasis and circular casuality (a major contrast with the medical model). Family therapy based on this body of theory was described elsewhere by Walrond-Skinner (1975) as having three stages: 'The challenge of the dysfunctional sub-system boundaries and the experimentation with new healthier alliances within the system . . . a restructure of more functional sub-systems . . . and individuation of family members . . . which involves the growth of individual members towards becoming separate within their family system' (p. 42). See also Dowling (1975).

Another member of the Institute, Cade (1975) reported that a planned series of six to ten sessions, at intervals of three weeks, could bring about significant improvement in the relationships and functioning of a number of poor and disorganised families (see also Roberts, 1968). Cade also described various 'action techniques' such as sculpting and role playing, 'an experiential way of working with a family's relationship difficulties' in which the therapist played a more active and directive role than was usual in casework.

The East London FSU described its work with families in a useful monograph (Smith, 1974) using models for insight-oriented and communications-oriented family therapy derived from Satir (1964) and Skynner. Such techniques were not considered appropriate for all the Unit's clients, and the case illustration shows the worker varying her role and technique according to her perception of the client's changing needs. Speakers at the second FWA conference on marital and family therapy (1975) also emphasised the need to translate 'into terms appropriate to a social work setting the model of family therapy which has been developed in a clinical one' (Mercer and Roberts, 1975, p. 6). They found that few clients of FWA were willing to engage in 'family therapy strictly defined' by participating in 'a conscious decision by both worker and family to work together on the family interaction, using the here and now of their experience in a regular and time-limited session' (ibid., 1975, p. 6). However, they found that 'more important . . . than the family's explicit agreement is the social worker's perspective on the family and its problems', and the fact that 'the whole family is seen as the client and continually related to as an entity' (ibid., p. 7). The mere offer of family therapy 'makes a statement to the family itself about who is being focused on, which will have treatment implications' (ibid., p. 9). In a fascinating case illustration, considerable improvement was brought about in what had seemed a desperate situation simply by encouraging the school counsellor (the only contact with the family) not to be manipulated into panic action, and by offering two whole family interviews, neither of which was accepted. Pressure was taken off the scape-goated school child and the general level of anxiety in the family seemed to have dropped.

Virtually nothing was written about the practice of family therapy in social services departments, although it was known that some of these were encouraging the use of this method, often with the help of the Family Institute and the Family Therapy Project of the Tavistock Clinic in conducting study days or short courses for their staff. As an economical method, effective with some at least of the disorganised families which proved least responsive to traditional methods and most prone to chronicity, family therapy had much to offer these departments.

Counter Transference and the Diagnostic Response. We have seen how the counter transference and diagnostic responses were distinguished by Casement (1973) in the context of family therapy, together with 'the supervisory viewpoint'. Although these responses had not yet been distinguished and labelled, the diagnostic value of the social worker's emotional response to the client had been mentioned by Huneeus (1962), Timms (1964) and E. Sainsbury (1970). Jordan (1970) particularly studied the collusion which often results from uncritical acting out of the social worker's personal counter transference, and the value of developing Casement's 'diagnostic response' by recognising at least part of the worker's feeling as representing the role which the client, consciously or unconsciously, projects or displaces onto him, and tries to induce him to play.

Nurse suggested that the failures of communication, the apparently unbridgeable cognitive gap between some clients and their workers reported by Mayer and Timms (1970) could not be adequately explained simply in terms of incompatible conscious assumptions and expectations (see also chapter 9). 'It is unbridgeable for reasons outside, and controlling, the actual meeting of the people concerned' (Nurse, 1973, p. 40). He described a type of client who complains bitterly about some near relative, demanding that the worker take urgent action to control or separate him, without actually meeting him, and often withdraws at any attempt to induce him to explore his own contribution to the situation, or even at further questions about the absent villain. Nurse found that if the worker abandons his attempt at rational evaluation and exposes himself to the full impact of the client's communication, he himself becomes acutely anxious lest refusal to comply with the client's demands should result in total breakdown or violent crime on the part of the client and/or his absent partner. He has allowed the client to succeed in inducing in the worker a replica of his own terror, and is tempted to avoid the threatened disaster by accepting responsibility for the partner. The temptation must be avoided, but the relationship is one into which 'both worker and client must become locked' if progress is to be made; the worker has to enter the client's nightmare before he can lead him out of it. The worker's only hope of helping is to get behind the presenting problem by speaking appropriately and directly to the client about his own needs and distress, thus enabling him to tell the worker of events or periods in his own life that were his own 'shorthand' for long

standing difficulties that were compounding the present problematic situation
. . . The central point is . . . that the social worker is enabling the client
to express needs of his own in a way which does not include them in the
relationship that is . . . going wrong (p. 51). Following this, it was sometimes found possible to obtain permission to see the third party, but
sometimes this proved unnecessary.

Behaviour Modification. Jehu (1967), the earliest exponent of behaviour
modification as a method of social work, described the theory and its
teaching application in *Learning Theory and Social Work* and included them
in the social work curriculum of the Leicester University School of Social
Work alongside those of traditional casework. The topic was further
expounded by Picardie (1967) and E. I. Thomas (1969), while critical articles
were published by Irvine (1969) and J. S. Miller (1969). Holden (1969)
illustrated the technique by a case study in which parents were enabled,
by a combination of advice and operant conditioning, to extinguish the
bed-time tantrums of their 3-year-old daughter by ignoring her screams.
The author suggested that many more children than at present could be
helped by teaching parents to understand and use behavioural techniques,
but many social workers felt misgivings lest parents be given such tools of
increased control without adequate exploration of the dynamic situation in
the family, of which the child's symptoms might be a danger signal.

Further articles advocating behavioural methods were reassuring in that
they clearly demonstrated the authors' sensitivity to emotional factors.
Sluckin and Jehu (1969) reported the treatment of elective mutism in a
child of 4, precipitated by illness in both mother and child. At the onset
of treatment, the child would only speak to her own family. The behavioural
techniques employed included the withdrawal of positive reinforcement for
inappropriate behaviour (the mother stopped responding to the child's
non-verbal communication); *in vivo* desensitisation to the presence of a
stranger (the social worker); positive reinforcement (sweets and approval)
for appropriate modes of behaviour (reading aloud and speaking in the
social worker's presence). Eventually having started school, the child was
induced to read to her headmistress in her mother's presence, and eventually
she suddenly began to speak spontaneously to most people. This behavioural
treatment followed some casework with the mother, who recalled traumatic
episodes in her own childhood which had led her to warn her children too
strongly of the danger of speaking to strangers.

Only occasional articles on this subject were published subsequently.
Graham (1971) described her role as PSW in a behaviour therapy team:
she stressed that learning theorists had recently come to see that the
generalisation to the real-life situation of attitudes and behaviour towards
which treatment is directed depends very largely on whether the spouse or
other close relative reinforces or discourages it. Thus the traditional
approach of treating the patient under laboratory conditions, and leaving
social events to take care of themselves was giving way to the strategy of
training relatives to discourage or ignore maladaptive behaviour and to
encourage adaptive behaviour, as carried out by Holden. Graham summed
up the tasks of the social worker in the behavioural team:

'She may assess the patient–relative interaction and identify those who are important sources of social reinforcement. She must attempt to predict their response to any possible change in the patient's behaviour as a result of treatment. She may train relatives in behavioural modification techniques and monitor any alterations in relatives' behaviour in response to a change in the patient's behaviour.' (p. 206)

Her importance in identifying the patterns of social reinforcement in patient–relative interaction is particularly emphasised.

Finally, Hudson (1975) presented a case study with a dynamic beginning and a behavioural ending. The client, a woman with an 'inadequate personality', enjoyed her relationship with the caseworker, recounted relevant material about her early experience, and developed a considerable understanding of her self-defeating behaviour, but she became very dependent and her problematic behaviour did not diminish. 'All we seemed to have achieved was an excellent relationship!' (p. 507). The worker now decided to use this relationship as a basis for intervention or behaviour treatment by behavioural techniques. She reformulated her task in terms of teaching her client 'a number of new behaviours', both practical and interpersonal, 'hoping that her feelings of failure, despair and friendlessness' would 'change as a result of outer changes' (p. 507). Having explained her change of approach to her client, she initiated a programme of conditioning with social reinforcement. Success was rewarded by expressions of pleasure, while failure elicited disappointment and a briefer visit. Eventually visits became conditional on task performance, as reported by telephone.

The close resemblance of this method to task-centred casework showed the extent to which learning and behavioural theory were becoming integrated into casework practice. Moreover, behavioural therapy was beginning to involve families along with individuals, and thus apparently approaching family therapy. However, a vital difference was that in the behavioural model, therapy was focused on an identified patient and parents, siblings or spouses were included on the footing of co-therapists, which must itself have questionable implications for the distribution of control in the family; whereas family therapists refused to accept an identified patient and insisted that they were only concerned with the problems of the family as a whole.

A further type of brief social work intervention involving the use of the Heimler scale of social functioning, originally designed to measure movement in clients, was gradually refined and developed as a sensitive diagnostic tool. Based on the empirical finding that success in social functioning is closely related to satisfaction in life, the scale consists of a questionnaire concerning the subject's level of satisfaction in the five areas of work, finance, friendship, primary and secondary family relationships, and sexual and other intimate relationships. The level of frustration is also elicited and scored, together with 'escape routes' (ineffectual attempts at relief) and the degree of rigidity or uncertainty in the subject's account of his state of mind.

A therapeutic use of the scale was then developed (Heimler, 1975). While administering the questionnaire, the social worker pauses at intervals to delineate the general pattern of the responses, thus sharpening the subject's awareness of himself and his predicament, and eventually encouraging him to do this for himself. Significant shifts in perception occur in the course of this process, and the client becomes strongly motivated to take some action to improve his situation and discusses with the social worker the possibilities which occur to him. The method is described as being highly economical of time, with the advantage of avoiding a dependent relationship with the worker. It is said to be effective with the majority of social work clients, while those for whom it is not indicated can be detected during a careful preliminary interview and other methods prescribed. Short courses in the diagnostic use of the scale were provided by the Institute of Social Functioning at Great Missenden, Buckinghamshire, leading to an international qualification which confers the right to use the scale, while a further course confers the right to use it therapeutically. These uses of the scale spread gradually in Britain during the 1970s, especially in the probation service.

SOCIAL WORK WITH GROUPS

Group Work in the 1950s

As in the 1940s, there was much work in the 1950s with recreational groups, and elsewhere some developments in group therapy under psychiatric guidance, but little practice or understanding of social group work as a social work method. Maxwell Jones (1952) *Social Psychiatry: A Study of Therapeutic Communities*, Foulkes and Anthony (1957) *Group Psychotherapy*, and Bion (1961) *Experiences in Groups* were widely read. *Social Group Work in Great Britain* (edited by Kuenstler) appeared in 1954. He himself regarded social group work and community organisation as two forms of social work characterised by

'(i) a common agreement as to the conscious use of a process of relationships; (ii) the use of activities as a method of relationship; (iii) an interest in understanding more about the behaviour of individuals; (iv) the acceptance of the role of a leader as a person consciously establishing a relationship with individuals through the activities in which they participate; (v) the utilisation of these skills for the improvement of the community.' (p. 17)

But succeeding chapters were almost wholly descriptive.

The Canford Families (1962) included therapeutic social group work sessions for some of the children,.though not for adults. It was assumed that disturbed family relationships had deprived the children of certain developmental experiences which could be supplemented in a therapeutic group that would also modify behaviour which brought the child into conflict with his environment. These activity groups used play as the child's natural and satisfying means of communication which made interaction possible and led to a 'mothering' relationship with the group worker. It defined therapeutic group work as 'a method which uses the potential of group dynamics to help individuals to solve personal problems' (p. 120). These dynamics could also be destructive, which made it essential for the group worker to understand the process.

This and the Bristol Social Project (1953–8) were pioneer studies, valuable for the detailed records of changing individual and group behaviour over a period of time and within a theoretical framework. The Bristol Project was largely based on local groups, whether of 'ordinary residents'˙ or 'initiated for the specific purpose of helping the members to improve their social relationships' (Spencer, 1964, p. 12).

Work with groups of many different kinds expanded during this period but without the conscious use of group dynamics and interaction. The Younghusband Report (1959) suggested that its proposed national staff college should pioneer training in group work and community organisation. It said:

'At present, there are no facilities for such training in this country, except to a limited extent for youth work. We regard this training as highly desirable for workers with the handicapped, for home help organisers, for some staff of residential institutions, and for more senior officers, who must learn how to mobilise community resources on behalf of mentally ill and mentally or physically handicapped people and to keep them, as well as old and difficult people part of the community. Much work with the handi-capped, whether at handicraft centres or in clubs, necessitates a knowledge of group relationships and of how to help individuals to get the greatest possible satisfaction from their membership of the group. In the long run, when experience has been gained and teachers become available, we would hope that all those taking the two year course would have some training in the use of these other social work methods.' (para. 950)

But in the 1950s these were alien ideas far removed from practice.

Group Work in the 1960s and Early 1970s
By degrees the concept of the therapeutic community (Maxwell Jones, 1952) gave an impetus to the use of group processes rather than or in addition to individual therapy, as a means of giving residents more say in the daily régime, and breaking down staff authoritarian attitudes. But these ideas spread slowly. Group psychotherapy reinforced the development of group counselling and group discussion, while role theory clarified leadership roles and ascribed or assumed roles in a group, for example scapegoating.

Work with small groups developed, though in a piecemeal fashion, as it became more obvious that the individual is constantly interacting with others in group situations and that group dynamics could have a powerful effect on attitudes and relationships and thus be an effective medium for decision making and change. Roseman and Cooke (1964) described a three-year project in the East London FSU where social group work with children was used to supplement the Unit's basic service – family casework. This article well illustrated current attitudes about group work as supple-mentary to the main one-to-one relationship. By the end of the 1960s group discussions and group activities were spreading, either in planned or spon-taneous settings, for therapeutic, information giving, planning, decision-making, or 'experiential' purposes. For instance, groups might be run for adopters or would-be adopters, for foster parents, hospital patients facing the next stage, for multiproblem family children and parents, for ex-psychiatric patients, for maladjusted or withdrawn or delinquent children and adolescents, for prisoners' wives; or in various residential situations, including prisons; or by self-help groups like Alcoholics Anonymous; as well as for 'normal' people in a variety of stress situations or wanting to change or else prevent change in their environment. Groups might be carefully selected, or composed of anyone who turned up, for instance in an old people's home. They might have an activity from the beginning like a play group, or flounder until they discovered their own objectives, like some neighbourhood groups. They might be time limited from the beginning or continue indefinitely with a changing membership. These groups were run by settlements, community centres, youth clubs, the FSU, psychiatric hospitals and many other residential institutions, and by psychiatrists, psychologists, probation, child care and mental welfare officers, medical and psychiatric social workers and family caseworkers, and by many community groups.

Sturton, an American-trained group worker, discussed (1972) the processes of gaining acceptance for group work in a local authority area team of caseworkers, the false starts and the final successful establishment of various client groups. Laming (1974) described how the same group-work adviser was able to start groups in old people's homes and other residential institutions. These were planned joint discussions for residents and staff which opened up communication between them, and made it possible for residents to have more say in practical arrangements and also to express feelings about loneliness, illness and death. A result was a closer understanding between staff and residents, and more resident participation and influence in the running of the home. Breslin and Sturton (1974) described the effective development of a staff and residents group in a hostel for mentally handicapped women.

The main purposes of groups were as an aid to diagnosis, to give some 'good' experiences to deprived people, to facilitate sharing and the ability to take action by a group with similar experiences, to generate capacity to carry through the processes of decision making, to enable group members to try new roles, to support each other in stress situations, to lessen anxiety and increase self-confidence, to facilitate personal growth, and to act as a supportive service in many different situations.

In the late 1960s a further impetus came from community development activities, the strong emphasis on participation by consumers – whether in neighbourhood groups or receivers of a service – and the discovery that group-motivated activity was an important democratic process that could counter inertia, overcome communication barriers, apathy and dependence and gave people a sense of achievement. Groups with their network of relationships could also play a crucial part in helping to counter isolation and alienation, heighten awareness of self and others, and sometimes change destructive attitudes. In some circumstances it was easier for people to play out roles and to express their feelings of anxiety, anger, frustration, hostility, or mourning at separation with the protection of a group. Naturally there were characteristic processes in the life history of a group, and the understanding and use of these was an important element in group work skill. A number of social workers began to have experience of group dynamics, interaction and communication in therapeutic communities of various kinds; for example Grendon Prison was specially designed for offenders with psychiatric problems: the emphasis was on group therapy and in 1975 the staff consisted of seven psychiatrists, and an equal number of psychologists, together with prison welfare and prison officers. This was a new experience for many caseworkers trained to assess how past experiences were affecting the individual's behaviour rather than to be alive to and able to listen to the subtle cross-currents, the various levels of current group interaction in intergroup relations, and to relate to the group rather than individuals. In addition to the carefully planned small group meeting on the worker's own ground there were more daring experiments in going out to meet existing groups on their own ground, sometimes with the use of indigenous workers or 'linkers' as in NACRO new careers or Family Planning Association (FPA) grapevine experiments referred to in other chapters. Imaginative forms of intermediate treatment and more varied activities with offenders in the community in day training centres or through community service orders were other examples at this end of the spectrum. At the other end were the changes in the whole focus in residential and day care and clubs, discussed in other chapters.

The majority of those who experimented with groups had to learn from their own experience, reinforced by reading available material on group dynamics and group work.

There was much discussion amongst practising social workers and in training courses as to whether group work was becoming an essential part of social work education, or an optional extra, or a separate stream in its own right. It was obvious that, as in community work, very substantial opportunities for in-service training were essential if group work was to become an accepted part of social work education and practice. Bernard Davies (1975) in a comprehensive study, based on the assumption that group work should be in the main stream of social work practice, summed up the situation in the mid-1970s thus:

'Lip service has been paid for years to the value of group work and the need for social workers to see it as an additional medium of work . . . Overwhelmingly, however, despite the changes which have taken place in the last decade, social work in Britain still means casework.' (p. 13)

He continued:

'At the outset, this may well mean that social work in Britain has to pull itself up by its bootstraps . .. Yet, if social workers do not actually begin to practise more often and in a more deliberate fashion in group situations, if they do not include pre-service students in them, and act themselves, or force senior staff to act, as teachers of such students – if, that is, they do not proceed *as if* the resources already existed – then those resources will in fact never be created.' (pp. 140–1)

Group work was included in an increasing number of CQSW courses but there was an extreme shortage of competent supervisors. Social workers were being enabled to take various part-time courses run by the Tavistock

Institute, the Grubb Institute of Behavioural Studies and the Institute of Group Analysis. Over the years some social workers also participated in the 'Leicester Conferences' in group relations part-sponsored by the Tavistock Institute.

An Illustration: Group Work in the Probation and After-Care Service in the 1960s

The probation service was a good example of sensitive experiments in group work. In the 1960s more probation officers began to practise group work on the assumption that for some probationers this was an important reinforcement to a one-to-one relationship; and that, as Alcoholics Anonymous was demonstrating, group members who know each other's problems from the inside and who formed a reference group, could sometimes help the individual more effectively than the social worker alone. A group work seminar was held in 1962 at Leicester University, others followed and by 1966 nearly fifty probation officers had been at one of these seminars and had had experience in running groups of their own and their colleagues' probationers. In 1963 the Tavistock Institute provided the chairmanship for a working party of probation officers to examine the place of group work in the probation service, the form it should take, and what training was needed for it. This was followed by a Home Office sponsored conference to discuss what had been learnt about the scope for group work amongst probationers and what the training needs were for probation officers.

By then about 5 per cent of probation officers had used group methods at some time. Individual probation officers were experimenting with group sessions with probationers and finding that group membership gave support, with greater freedom to express negative feeling and to relate to fellow members rather than simply to an authority figure. A number of useful descriptions of individual experiments with groups appeared in the NAPO journal *Probation* during this period. These articles, together with the Home Office Research Unit *Survey of Group Work in the Probation Service* (Barr, 1966), showed significant results in the use of groups. For some years probation officers had run probationers' camps as part of their treatment. A few had seen group psychotherapy in practice at the Henderson Hospital and the Tavistock Clinic and group-counselling programmes in certain prisons and borstals. The double stream of psychoanalytic and sociological theory was resulting in a greater understanding of behaviour in small groups and the effect of the group on the individual. Some probation officers, frustrated by the little that they could accomplish with boys individually away from their own setting, were experimenting with group discussions or activities with an entire delinquent gang or a mixed group. Boys were more willing to talk and to air grievances in the group than individually, which lessened guilt and anxiety and helped them to express bottled-up feelings. This also gave an opportunity to observe interpersonal relationships. The probation officer was put in a less dominant role and some negative aspects of authority were eased. Group work was especially useful for people with problems about authority, communication and relationships. Group relationships also helped to carry individual boys over the break up of school friendships and the formation of work friendships. Some groups mainly used verbal communication and others activities, though some made fruitful attempts to combine both. It was probably easier to cope with aggression in discussion groups when members were seated than in activity groups when there was more opportunity for physical conflict between members. On the other hand, there was value in the constructive expression of physical aggression. There was no evidence that the dangers of contamination or of the group becoming too difficult for the probation officer to handle were real, while, conversely, individual members often got help from the group. Most probation officers leading groups thought of themselves primarily as therapists rather than teachers, i.e. giving clarification, insight, interpreting the group's behaviour. The groups themselves tended to exercise support and control, though there was sometimes a conflict between the non-directive, permissive attitude of probation officers in groups and their use of authority with individuals. From the probation officer's point of view the group showed up problems of relationships and communication and revealed the real person and the feel of the local teenage situation more quickly, especially as adolescents were seen in a setting nearer to everyday life than in one-to-one interviews. Group work proved a valuable additional activity for assessment, an adjunct to diagnostic interviews but not a substitute for them. Tension in the group tended to be focused on problems common to most of the members and individual personal needs might be neglected. Group work was largely a means of dealing with problems of communication, particularly with the young, inarticulate and inhibited. It might be more relevant to the needs of psychologically normal offenders whose problems sprang from stresses in the environment. The influence of the group could be harmful as well as beneficial, for example through scapegoating or ganging up.

The Home Office study concluded that group work with parents was also desirable. Here, too, for some time there had been isolated experiments by individual probation officers. If group work was to be used on a larger scale it was also important to be able to evaluate the results. This would entail classifying offenders, knowing that some types might benefit from a particular treatment and others be unaffected, and yet others probably detrimentally affected. Probation officers using group work needed training for it and also to be able to recognise more clearly what they were trying to do, to define the aims and methods for each new group in relation to the assessed treatment needs of the selected members. More systematically recorded accounts of group discussions, either transcripts or tape recordings, were also needed to test theories about the way in which groups develop and the mechanisms at work, and also to develop counselling skills and techniques (see also volume 1, chapters 6 and 7).

Chapter 9

Consumer Reactions to Casework

INTRODUCTION

INTRODUCTION

For a long time it was assumed in social work, as in other helping professions, that the professional judged the quality and relevance of the given service on the basis of professional knowledge not available to the client. Caseworkers commonly assessed 'movement in the case' by changes in the client's behaviour, but failure might be ascribed to resistance or lack of motivation to benefit from casework help. The distinction between the underlying and the presenting problem was valid when people did not recognise the source of their trouble or lacked the courage to talk about it or could not find words to express it. But it reinforced the assumption that professional caseworkers knew best what people really needed, whereas in practice much casework was short-term, related to specific situations in which the client's own view of whether he could cope better as a result of help was highly relevant. What the client wanted and whether he thought he would get it, was also one of several ways that might have been used to test the effectiveness of a service.

Change began in the late 1950s when the Younghusband working party (1959) was strongly criticised for not undertaking consumer research and felt called upon to be apologetic about this on grounds of lack of time. But, as a leading social work educator said at the time, 'It was all a matter of expectations: if they did not know what to expect they had no standard by which to gauge their satisfaction. This applies particularly to casework help.' The present writer feared that to test consumer reactions by research in poorly developed social work in the health and welfare services would reveal low levels of expectation that would damage the case for improved services. Moreover, it would not have been easy to undertake research in these services when anyone who visited the home was assumed to be 'from the welfare', and clients did not know what kind of help could be expected. Later the Seebohm Committee (1968) faced the same criticism and gave the same explanation.

SOME STUDIES OF SPECIFIC CLIENT REACTIONS TO CASEWORK

Attempts to discover client reactions began from the mid-1960s, perhaps as part of wider moves towards participation. Butrym in her study of medical social work in a large hospital (1968) asked a small number of patients their views about the medical social work service they had received. The responses were overwhelmingly positive, indeed, as in some other studies, more patients than social workers rated a service successful. Medical social workers were regarded as people 'who have an interest in patients and do all they can for you', who are helpful 'at a time when one is desperate with worry'. Their most desirable attributes were: kindness, sympathy, desire to help, tact, ability to listen, warmth and a capacity to understand.

Hewitt (1970) in a study of the families of 180 spastic children in the Midlands found that mothers wanted practical advice about management (particularly as the child grew older and heavier to carry), equipment, gadgets and facilities for short-term care. They also appreciated someone who was interested in them and their children, an understanding person to talk to, especially in the first shock of realisation that the baby was handicapped, and for detailed information about the condition and how to meet the consequent difficulties. But the social worker must have practical experience of looking after handicapped children. Hewitt commented:

'In this situation of scarce and inadequate provision, which applies particularly to the mentally handicapped who also have physical handicaps, the case worker is in a very difficult position. Faced with a family who are suffering strain because the community services are inadequate to meet their practical needs, how can he or she approach them?' (p. 169)

Of the total sample, 18 per cent thought social work visits made no difference, 52 per cent welcomed social workers without reservation, while 23 per cent gave them a qualified welcome, i.e. liked their visits but felt these had no useful result.

Goldberg *et al.* (1970) found in an action research study of casework with frail old people that of the special group, who had more visits and by the same professional social workers, 77 per cent found the visiting helpful, compared with 48 per cent of the comparison group. Seven per cent in the special group and 15 per cent in the comparison group thought the visits were no help, while 16 per cent in the special and 35 per cent in the comparison group were non-committal. 'What permeated these positive comments above all is the pleasure about the needs being met, both material and psychological, the feeling of being cared for, and the sense of security arising from knowledge of where to turn in time of need' (p. 178).

An exploratory study of working-class people's impressions of casework, *The Client Speaks* (Mayer and Timms, 1970) was based on the views of clients who had recently completed treatment with the London FWA either for personal problems, primarily matrimonial, or economic difficulties. The aim was to discover whether and why they were satisfied or dissatisfied with the service. The study was valuable for the clients' comments which probably revealed common attitudes and sometimes confusions based on unexplored or inappropriate assumptions. Even in this family casework agency over two-thirds of the study group clients had had six interviews or less.

It was clear that clients did not go to social work agencies unless they were in much distress, indeed at their wits' end. But people did not necessarily, as was supposed, go first to relations or friends, they often feared lack of sympathy, revealing failure and losing face, overburdening other people, lack of confidentiality, and going against values of self-reliance and independence. Those who told their worries had been given conflicting or inadequate advice.

The FWA's dissatisfied clients who had interpersonal problems expected that after one or two sessions the social worker would reach a conclusion about the rights and wrongs of the situation, make a moral judgement and take steps to change the offender's – i.e. the other person's – behaviour. He should come to decisions, give advice about what to do and take sides. Clients expected this, but attempts to clarify causes and delve into the past were puzzling and irrelevant. The social workers, on the other hand, were trying to give these clients a better insight into their problems and increased self-awareness. Both the client and the social worker wanted the other party to the difficulty to take part in treatment but for different reasons. Some thought the social worker was not interested in them, did not trust them, lacked authority, or did not understand them because he had not had similar experiences. Thus clients and social workers operated in ignorance of the other's view about problem solving. The social workers thought that discontinued treatment was due to the anxieties it aroused rather than to different cultural assumptions. 'Each of the parties assumed that the other shared certain of his underlying conceptions about behaviour and the ways in which it might be altered' (p. 77).

The satisfied clients in this group had experienced relief through talking freely, 'getting it off one's chest'. They saw situations more clearly as a result of airing problems and received emotional support, enlightenment and guidance. It appeared that clients could only feel emotional support if the social worker was manifestly interested in them, was concerned, really seemed to care what happened. Practical action, not just listening, demonstrated this concern, 'We'll solve the problem or sort something out'. Suggestions, advice, information and guidance were welcomed, coupled with reflective insight which led to better understanding of the situation. Some differences between the two groups seemed to be that the satisfied clients received more support and guidance and the social worker was active on their behalf, whereas the unsatisfied clients felt that their social workers had given them little support and guidance, not taken action, but had tried to get the client to see her own contribution to the problem. It is not clear whether other factors, for example different personality types, were also relevant.

The clients who asked for help with material problems had struggled for some time before they forced themselves to face the disgraceful admission that they could not fend for themselves and might be seen as paupers or cadgers. They expected a moralistic, punitive reaction from social workers, who would be strict, stern and abrupt, give them a good telling off, investigate their past life and inspect the home. The satisfied clients got the material help they needed. They were surprised that social workers were people to whom they could talk, who were interested in them and lessened their shame. They also experienced the relief of talking, of emotional support, guidance and enlightenment. Activity by the social worker was the main indication of interest and concern. The grant also showed the social worker's belief that they were telling the truth and were not cadgers. Nearly all the dissatisfied clients had not received material help, in their recollection the social worker started with an insight-oriented approach, with irrelevant discussion of the marriage, etc., and was not interested in the financial problem. They repeatedly went over the same ground in a series of interviews when the financial need was urgent. If a grant was given this was appreciated but the casework process was much resented.

Mayer and Timms concluded that to offer psychological help to such clients without meeting their material needs failed to come to grips with their problems. These clients

'. . . were consumed with worry over debts, the possibility of an eviction, the cutting-off of their electricity, and it is absurd to expect that the urgency of their needs could be met by a non-material approach, whether this be a matter of offering insight, providing friendship, or the opportunity to unburden themselves to a sympathetic listener.' (p. 140)

There were psychological factors of greater or lesser degree in a need for money but the authors concluded that 'In their preoccupation with psychological matters, social workers have tended to develop an occupational blindness to economic realities' (p. 141).

Social workers' adherence to the general professional assumption of the right to explore intimate aspects of clients' lives in strict confidence in order to give effective help was alien from client assumptions no matter what took them to the agency. Thus they were often resentful and offended ('She'd no right to ask such questions'). They did not distinguish between a professional relationship and the reciprocal relation of friendship: indeed the problem of where to draw this boundary for different people of different degrees of sophistication at different times in different circumstances constantly preoccupied social workers and led to conflicts about treating clients as equals versus a professional relationship. Not surprisingly, the authors saw no easy way to bridge the chasm between clients' moralistic, judgmental 'find the offender and deter him' attitudes and insight-oriented casework, which were simply not on the same wavelength. The study did, however, demonstrate that some casework is effective in the eyes of some clients, and thus the importance of a wider range of social work techniques and more study of clients' views.

Holman (1973) in a survey of 100 private and 100 local authority foster mothers found that one-third of the former and 73 per cent of the latter had positive views about CCOs. Over half of the first and 25 per cent of the second had mixed views, while eight and one foster mothers in each group were negative. As in other studies, a high proportion found social workers genuinely concerned, friendly people, but distinguished between this and being able to help. About two-thirds of the local authority foster mothers found the CCOs' visits helpful, whereas the same proportion of private foster mothers did not. Foster mothers who received practical help or who had known the CCO for a long time were the most likely to think she was helpful.

Social Work in Prison (Shaw, 1974) included material on the attitudes to welfare of men in two prisons. Prison Welfare Officers (PWOs) did not have substantial daily contact with inmates, yet the welfare officer was mentioned as the person with whom they would discuss personal affairs, largely because he was not part of the prison system, information would be confidential and he treated the man as a normal person not as a prisoner. Nearly two-thirds thought that other people had a poor opinion of 'the welfare' though the personal views of over a quarter were favourable. It is common to find in studies of institutions that perceptions of other people's views contrast with private opinions, so that opposition to the staff is over-estimated. 'The basis of the criticisms was whether or not they felt the officer had "solved" their problems on demand' (p. 53). The time sense of an overworked PWO obviously differed from that of a prisoner anxious for action which would demonstrate that he had some minimum control over events. Other factors such as the frequency and nature of the contact, previous experience of probation officers or of other social workers influenced attitudes; while 'working class expectations that social work should consist of direct practical action may be carried over to the welfare officer' (p. 55). At one prison where the welfare officer was in the prison wing and the men had frequent contacts, 50 per cent had gone to the PWO with personal problems but only 10 per cent at the prison where the officer was in the administrative block.

Over half the men who had long and systematic casework interviews showed favourable attitudes, compared with 28 per cent of the controls, and half expressed considerable satisfaction at being able to 'get down to the problem and thrash it out'. Three-quarters felt that they had been helped in some way and only 13 per cent that it had been a waste of time, as against one-third of the control group.

The views of a group of men probationers given 'intensive' casework treatment by a special unit in the London service were summarised in IMPACT (Folkard *et al.*, 1974). Of the forty who had confidential interviews with a member of the Research Unit almost three-quarters thought their probation officer was most like a teacher or welfare officer and least like a policeman; in regard to relationship roles, more than half thought him to be most like a friend and least like a busybody. Almost all probationers liked their probation officers, were treated fairly by him and believed he wanted to help them. Overall attitude scores showed that the vast majority had a very favourable attitude. The probation officers were less prone to believe that clients thought well of them, thought they would be seen as busybodies more often than they were, and sometimes predicted incorrectly that clients would think they were not understood. There was an indication that the greater the number of previous convictions and the higher the risk of reconviction the more favourably was the probation relationship seen by the probationer under intensive supervision. This might be related to the three-quarters who thought that probation would help them to keep out of further trouble. Over two-thirds of the probationers said that they confided in their probation officers, the large majority that they were given support, encouragement and practical help, and that they were helped to understand themselves and their behaviour. Less than a third thought that their probation officers were strict but a quarter thought they ought to exercise more control. More than half were satisfied with the amount of contact with the probation officer but a third would prefer less.

The most effective meeting of clients' emotional and material needs and accuracy in judging their attitudes towards the worker was manifested in E. Sainsbury's (1975*a*) study of twenty-seven FSU multiproblem families. The purpose was to discover what clients thought was good practice and the right personal qualities for social workers. It was difficult to distinguish the families' regard for the moral and ethical aspects of helping from their views about emotional and material help. Material and other forms of help were sometimes linked emotionally, especially in crises when one might symbolise the other. The clients' memories were often more detailed and accurate than those of the social workers (as checked against each other and case records). In their contacts with other social services they thought that 24 had been helpful and 10 unhelpful (10 Supplementary Benefits Commission contacts were rated helpful and 13 unhelpful).

The attitude of the intake worker and the speed and scope of his response to expressed need coloured all subsequent impressions. 'Little is known about the effects upon those needing help of inconsistency and contradiction in the attitudes of those whose job it is to make help available. Assuming that more harm is achieved than good, the evidence provided by these families draws attention to an important but neglected aspect of social work practice' (p. 24).

Immediate material needs, including debts, were the primary problem in 23 cases and the wife's severe depression in 4. In 25 cases the family was completely satisfied with the help received, and partially satisfied in 2. No family thought that there was a big difference between the help asked for and received. It was the practice of the Unit to meet clients' stated needs immediately if possible, regardless of other help offered later.

Every family except one received material help, usually clothing or furniture. Eighteen families went to the unit play groups, teenage groups and mothers' groups. Several thought that the mothers' groups were vitally important chances to share problems and learn from others. Practically all the families were visited weekly. The most important subjects of discussion were money matters, the health and feelings of the wife and care of the children. Health was a significant problem and although material needs were regularly discussed because they were the most frequent referral problems, the families mentioned the well-being of the wife, emotional support and reliable friendship more often than these referral problems. The clients remembered that the most 'helpful help' had been material aid and budgeting, emotional support and reliability in crises, negotiating with other agencies and regularly collecting the family's debts.

Support through directive help fitted in with the families' views about their needs and sometimes made possible professionally sophisticated help with feelings, attitudes and response. This help was not necessarily incompatible with friendship which included clients' knowledge about the workers' personal lives. This quality of friendship made acceptable both firmness and the exercise of authority and power, direct advice, and moral or emotional pressure, for example to carry out a particular task or meet certain social obligations. 'The capacity of the social workers to take control (of people as well as of events), to be firm and to limit personal destructiveness, was widely referred to as a valuable attribute' (p. 25). There was an interdependence between acceptable firmness and accurate empathy. Thus the feeling of being really understood made it possible to blend permissiveness with authority: the families did not expect total 'permissiveness from the worker and thought that clients had obligations. 'The way in which these other qualities are blended . . . will depend on the social worker's accuracy in perception, his emotional integrity and self-discipline, and his views of his own obligation and purpose' (p. 85). Practically every family expressed confidence in and goodwill towards their social worker.

The most important quality in a social worker was his 'concern and activity, his trust, his ability to lessen feelings of shame in seeking help, and material aid' (p. 70) and his 'homeliness': 'They never let you feel as if you are poor . . . you feel as if you are just talking to a neighbour or a friend'; 'She helps you to talk and listens to what you have to say'; 'He's interested in us as people, as a family'; 'They say what they think you ought to do, but they don't say you've got to do it.' This was manifested in spontaneously wanting to help, equality in the relationship, and friendliness, understanding, listening, reliable emotional support and availability in crises, the ability to take hold when one is at one's wit's end, moral goodness, keeping confidences and being completely trustworthy. There was close agreement between the responses of the families and the social workers' views about what these would be.

The social workers were asked to assess change as measured against initial assessment in several aspects of family functioning: financial, marital, parent/child, relationships, employment, and ability to cope. Fourteen families showed some satisfactory movement but six had increased difficulties in financial or employment matters. There was little change in the remaining seven. The commonest improvement was in the ability to cope with internal distress and the least was in employment,

'A high level of congruence was discovered between the problems presented and the help offered . . . the Unit's clients need particular help in their interfamilial role-performances, and in respect of their personal feelings of distress; and . . . the Unit's greatest success lies in the help provided in those areas . . . it seems likely that the greatest single impact upon the clients' perceptions of the services received was made by the quality of relationships formed with the social workers and that functional changes were most apparent in the area of personal and family feelings.' (p. 98)

There was no association between these feelings and achievements in social functioning.

The social workers thought that good casework, which safeguarded the feelings, needs and rights of clients, was the basis of achievement but not in itself identified with it. 'Successful social work consists of the achievement of both long-term and short-term goals and the awareness of their causal and experiential connectedness; the achievement and the awareness being present in the minds of both worker and client' (p. 122). But ' "success" was regarded with suspicion by workers, who were especially alive to the possibilities of manipulating behaviour unscrupulously and without the consent and comprehension of the client' (p. 117). 'There is a positive relationship between the extent of the client's identification with the values and objectives of the worker and the extent of changes in his social functioning' (p. 120).

All the foregoing studies were based on small samples of particular groups of clients, though the common factors that emerged were significant for practice and for planning of services. The first attempt to get the views of a random sample of clients (McKay *et al.*, 1973) covered 305 people in Southampton social services department. Compared with the total Southampton population, proportionately more 'consumers' were separated, widowed or divorced women or elderly people, or large families; and more were living in overcrowded conditions or were unskilled and semi-skilled workers. Half were elderly or disabled, two-fifths had child care or family relationship problems, but less than 10 per cent were suffering from mental disorder. The distribution in relation to the general population indicated that the department was reaching those most in need.

Rather less than one-third of the clients did not know what to expect or did not think they would be helped. They usually expected, and received, such practical help as services, bedding, or aids to daily living. Over one-third said that they felt less anxious and depressed, more confident and stable, as a result of help. Clients expected social workers to act as advocates for them about housing and other difficulties. Ninety per cent said they had received some kind of help. Those under 60 mainly mentioned advice, information and casework help (it seemed possible that the emotional and social needs of older people were being ignored). Two-thirds of the total were satisfied and less than one-fifth dissatisfied. Nearly all thought that the social workers were good listeners and made appreciative comments about their personalities and the help received. Those who saw the social worker most frequently were the most satisfied. Nearly all appreciated being visited. Of the fifty-four dissatisfied clients, one-third had children in care and wanted them back, and twelve elderly or physically handicapped people wanted to be visited more often. The qualities that clients most valued in social workers were understanding, sympathy, a pleasing personality and social skills.

The majority of social workers thought that clients expected to discuss personal problems and receive advice, sympathy and information, but in fact less than 10 per cent of clients expected this. There was no discussion of attitudes amongst those who had or had not received this kind of casework help but staff shortages probably made it rare, even though it was what social workers felt that they ought to be giving. The clients were far less negative about the services than social workers thought they would be.

CONCLUSIONS

These studies were conducted at different times with small groups of different types of client with or without control groups and not within a common frame of reference, yet they produced the markedly similar results brought together in table 2.

Table 2   *Attitudes to Casework*

		Helpful	Doubtful	Not helpful
Hospital patients (Butrym, 1968) who MSWs thought needed professional social work help	N=32	27	4	1
Mothers of cerebral palsied children (Hewitt, 1970)	N=180	52%	23%	18%
Prisoners (Shaw, 1974)				
intensive contact	N=75	75%		13%
ordinary contact	N=75	28%		25%
Probationers (Folkard *et al.*, IM-PACT, 1974)				
intensive treatment	N=40	the 'vast majority'		
FWA clients (Mayer and Timms, 1970)	N=61	15 clients interviewed whose cases were closed by consent		46 clients interviewed who had failed to continue
Old people (Goldberg *et al.*, 1970)				
special group	N=150	77%	16%	7%
contrast group	N=150	48%	35%	15%
Social services department (McKay *et al.*, 1973)	N=305	90% 'some help' 67% satisfied		20% dissatisfied
Foster mothers (Holman, 1973)				
local authority	N=100	73%	25%	1%
private	N=100	33%	over 50%	8%
FSU multi-problem families (E. Sainsbury, 1975a)	N=27	25 families 'completely satisfied'	2 families 'partially satisfied'	

Not all inquiries distinguished between attitudes to social workers and whether or not their help was effective. Far more clients than the social workers expected found them 'nice kind people who would help you if they could', though often they could not. This seemed to show that a good relationship was only helpful to the client if some need as they perceived it was met. Sub-cultural or individual differences in perception could create barriers to which social workers were sometimes insensitive. The outstanding fact was that the more frequent the contact the more helpful the social worker was thought to be. The Hawthorne effect must be given its due weight – but not more – where there were experimental and control groups. Frequency of contact built up a relationship in which the client began to trust the worker; trust came from manifest concern, accurate empathy, interest and a desire to help. This was not primarily manifested by attempts to discuss personal problems but by providing the practical help and services that the client needed – being efficient, active, an advocate, able to give information. This was what demonstrated the social worker's care and concern, it was indeed in itself psychological help and often resulted in the client being able to let off steam, discuss personal problems and receive emotional support. The social workers' attitudes and quick material giving allayed the intense shame felt at asking for help, because it met poverty and powerlessness with equality and friendship. These studies were a view through the other end of the telescope of essential conditions for an effective professional service.

Chapter 10

Had Social Work Become a Profession? Values and a Code of Practice

STEPS TOWARDS A PROFESSION

In the 1950s social workers primarily thought of themselves as almoners or probation or child care officers or PSWs, or whatever it might be, rather than as social workers. By the late 1960s this had changed but social work was still largely equated with casework; group work was its handmaiden, or else allied to education; while many vocal community workers were anxious to get both social work and professionalism out of their hair. The drives to achieve a unified profession culminated in the British Association of Social Workers (BASW), and professional status become synonymous with a recognised training.

The hallmarks of a profession were generally taken to be: recognition by society and a test which conferred the right to practise; a coherent body of knowledge; tested and transmissible skill characteristic of the particular professional practice; professional integrity coupled with a commitment to give an impartial service; and a code of ethics or professional conduct. On these criteria social work had travelled hopefully in the twenty-five years since 1950, but views differed as to whether it had begun to arrive as a profession. Its boundaries continued to be fluid, but that was true of other professions; and it had frequently tried to clarify a central purpose unique to itself. Unlike medicine, the law and some other professions, it did not give an independent, fee-paying service (in this country at least) to private individuals, so were its functions and boundaries determined professionally or by employment and administrative decisions?

Basic knowledge from psychology and sociology had increased in range and relevance. But problems of selecting and of bringing different disciplines within a common frame of reference remained. It was hard to encompass this varied and still patchy knowledge and, even if much of it seemed to 'work', to discover how to translate it into peculiarly social work knowledge and practice, 'what' worked best, with 'whom', 'how', and even 'why'. Far more tested knowledge and skill became essential when, in addition to the increasing demands of modern direct practice, social workers took on far more extensive administrative, managerial, planning and policy-making responsibilities. Moreover, practice itself had broadened from the 'one-to-one relationship' to include the family as a group, the social and physical environment, various groups within a neighbourhood and residential situations.

Social workers were commonly described as agents of social change, ideally of change for the better. They were responsible for acting as regulators between change and stability to help to cushion the strains on family life caused by too great discontinuities in life-styles in a more affluent, mobile and permissive society – a society whose own values were full of dissent, fluid and uncertain, and which generated acute problems of isolation, conflicting values and sometimes insoluble dilemmas of choice. In practice social work only made a piecemeal contribution on this wide stage, though in the 1970s the newly formed BASW became active about urgent social and political issues.

It was also increasingly obvious that a varied range of resources was needed for the effective practice of social work because

'. . . "effectiveness" heavily depends not only on the general infrastructure of social service institutions but on their variety, distribution, accessibility and range of specialised functions; from particularly experienced home helps for motherless families to half-way homes for young male schizophrenics discharged from mental hospitals. If these are absent, inaccessible or grossly inadequate the social worker is as much handicapped as the doctor is today in most parts of Africa.' (Titmuss, 1970*b*, p. 14)

Interdisciplinary and interservices co-operation was equally essential in fulfilling a social and personal caring function. These advances in knowledge, organisation, problem identification and interdisciplinary relatedness had forced social workers to evolve the wider range of practice skills referred to in other chapters.

By the 1970s the social work function was accepted by society. Although the majority of workers did not hold the CQSW, the universally recognised professional qualification, some tested and transmissible skill existed even if not sufficiently tested or transmitted. There was concern to safeguard professional integrity, and social workers were becoming exercised about some of the complications of a code of ethics discussed below.

VALUES IN SOCIAL WORK

The other element in a profession – attitudes, values, a code of ethics – has not been mentioned elsewhere in this study. It proved more elusive, more difficult to pin down without false claims, than even knowledge or skill, not least because views differed about the functions of social workers. But better techniques seemed to imply a moral responsibility to be critical of the purposes for which they were used. Moreover, professional practice from within ever larger administrative structures conferred power, which made its responsible, differentiated use imperative. To legitimise professional practice conferred the right to do things, to ask questions about intimate affairs, which would otherwise be a gross intrusion. Social workers, whether trained or not, had been given such rights within the social services, though not by all their clients (Mayer and Timms, 1970), and in the absence of a code of practice there were between 1950 and 1975 very different attitudes amongst different social workers, whether trained or untrained, in the last resort because value systems reflect different views about human nature. These attitudes raised problems about confidentiality, the allocation of resources, responsibility and the right to intervene, which no longer seemed so simple as when it was assumed that the worker's good intentions and people's obvious need conferred the right. This was the 'daddy knows best' view that the client 'doesn't know what he wants and won't be happy till he gets it', in contrast to the Benthamite view that each man is the best judge of his own self-interest, which became fashionable later.

So-called permissive casework faced the charge that it used knowledge about the client's unconscious, irrational motivation to bring about behaviour consistent with the caseworker's values. Its practitioners contended that this was a necessary stage in helping the client towards a better sense of reality, to improved capacity to perceive and respond appropriately to people in the current reality situation. It was essential for the social worker to recognise irrational motivation and prejudices, his own as well as other people's, and that he himself was 'the product of a particular sub-culture which may have a value system at variance with that of the community in which he is doing his professional work . . . All social workers should be expected to be critical of their own irrationality' (Gulbenkian Foundation, 1968, p. 84).

Values, other than cultural or individual preferences or prejudices, essentially expressed what people thought they ought to do. Yet the concept of 'ought' varied over time and in different social groups. Thus the concept of values might refer to conflicts between the cultural values of the client and the worker and the dilemmas of misunderstanding or confusion this could create. For instance, a local community group might gang up against rather than accept immigrants or rowdy adolescents; or individual clients might lay the blame on others and expect moral judgements to be meted out to them. In such a non-meeting of value assumptions what was the role of the social worker? Were social work values in some sense 'better' than some clients' values? Indeed 'can one really believe that all people's ideas about ways of life are equally good, including those that involve neglecting children and not paying the rent?' (Emmet, 1967, p. 17).

Some held that social workers should not make their own values known to clients, others that the client would sense them anyway and it was more honest to have them out in the open where they could be discussed. 'The client does not want to be eternally hitting a blancmange, he wants to get some affirmative reactions from the worker and to know the worker's values, even if he rejects them' (ASW, 1960, p. 26).

The growth of professional responsibility rested on assumptions about good practice and social workers' increasing claim to make decisions on the basis of their own professional judgement rather than carrying out those made by the medical profession, magistrates, administrators or a committee. This was a claim to be able in some circumstances to assess a given situation in the light of general knowledge about human behaviour with sufficient accuracy to predict the probable future outcome, given certain courses of action. It included accountability for the results of the decision. The greater the accuracy of prediction the less did decisions between alternatives enter in. Yet many decisions were a choice of evils in tangled, broken or non-existent relationships, or rigid constraints of circumstances, or in clashes of interest, for instance between a severely handicapped child and the family as a whole, or between the generations. These clashes became more acute as the focus shifted from the isolated individual to family interaction, especially in situations where the point of effective intervention might long since be past. These were often value choices about the lesser of two evils and workers might have to act on the basis of incomplete knowledge and scanty resources. This reinforced the case for a code of practice that would clarify elements in these choices, as well as a commitment to research, to good agency procedures, to clarity about aims, and to social reform.

In many situations social workers were caught in conflicts about balancing their responsibilities to the client, their employer and their professional integrity. Several dramatic conflicts in the 1960s between social workers and their employers raised the issue of whether they should make public a particular dispute, strike, take it to arbitration, resign, or stay on in the hope of bringing about improvement. It was also not obvious what support they should receive from their professional association, for example to 'black' an employing authority or to strike might result in a deteriorating service to clients but seem the only remaining sanction against bad practices.

Social workers gave an uncomplicated allegiance to the principle of self-determination in the period when they were struggling to discover why people acted as they did and to help them to make their own choices rather than to force moralistic solutions upon them. The principle became less clear-cut when attention shifted to the family, the group and the local community. Self-determination began to seem part of an individualist philosophy, and anyway who or what was the 'self' that determined? Culturally imposed values, together with the irrational elements in human behaviour and the constraints of poverty or ill-health, further narrowed freedom of choice or self-directed action and reinforced a deterministic philosophy in which self-determination was an illusion. Most social workers were little troubled by philosophical arguments about determinism and negative or positive freedom – freedom from and freedom to. Indeed, the day-to-day significance of the principle· might be an attitude of respect for people's ability to reach decisions, their right to have a say in those that affected them, a belief in the value of diversity in society, and thus a safe-guard against manipulating people to conform. The concept of participation, which came into the limelight in the 1960s, was an aspect of self-determination under a more fashionable name. For some social workers this included the acceptance of each person as uniquely himself and of his right to be different but not to behave in ways which injured others. Naturally this principle was riddled with question marks. Did the right to be different include a self-destructive way of life? If behaviour is an aspect of personality, could they be separated and was it possible to control one without the other, or did the concept of 'acceptance' mean an attitude of active good will towards a person in spite of his behaviour? This concept was part of the effort to understand people and treat them as individuals, to place them in relevant rather than irrelevant categories, and to recognise that there was in most people a central organising principle, a self related to other people and the outside world which it was a major aim of social work to protect against internal assaults and from damage to its integrity from other people and circumstances. Closely related to this was the perennial problem of a balance between rights and responsibilities, especially in family relationships where one member's right to self-determination might conflict with others' rights.

Clearly none of these values was unique to social work, indeed some could only be practised if they were widely accepted. Their essence was 'an effort to relate factors making for change in society to the inherent general needs of persons including their need for stable and congenial relationships with other persons' (Gulbenkian Foundation, 1968, p. 80). But social workers were at the storm centre of clashes between deviants and society, at the place where the frail, the powerless and the overwrought called for compassion, protection and independence. Thus social workers were caught up in value conflicts and decisions which were essentially value choices and where, moreover, because one value pressed too far violated others, it was essential to keep relative values in balance. They were also engaged in a constant struggle for administrative procedures that enhanced the well-being of people, especially the powerless. Indeed there were acute dissensions within social work itself, and it was practised in the midst of unresolved administrative, moral and social conflicts, even though the reality of conflict was a dynamic condition that could lead to better practices. Under the reorganised social services of the 1970s professional social workers were employed in still more senior positions and in increasingly large administrative services, though unfortunately to a decreasing extent in direct practice. This increase in bureaucratic power and more monolithic control over resources made it crucial for social work to advance as an independent profession and to clarify a generally accepted code of professional practice (with disciplinary implications), rather than relying on individual decision or else simply acting as servants of the social services. Moreover, it was obvious that the social services themselves, including the penal system, operated on avowed, or unexamined, or conflicting values.

Dilemmas about the use of social workers as agents of social control became obvious to professional social workers in the 1950s

'. . . particularly in those cases where help is not sought and its need not recognised by the client . . . In many situations the social worker is acting as the agent of authority, and the "help" expected of him by authority is sometimes interference to produce conformity. He may in fact be expected to reform the client.' (ASW, *Morals and the Social Worker*, 1960, p. 9).

This conflict spread as some social workers came to the conclusion that they were being used to manipulate powerless clients into conformity to 'establishment' values by making this a condition of essential material help. Did social workers give some people a bad name and then casework them into inferiority rather than self-confidence? Some later results of treating deprived people as colleagues rather than clients seemed to demonstrate significant responses to differences in ascribed roles.

On some sociological views, deviance or mental disorder was largely due to labelling and scapegoating rather than to psychiatric, physical or genetic factors. Thus, it was said, social workers were being used to reinforce the labelling process rather than to help change the social attitudes responsible for it. In contrast, a demand also grew in the early 1970s for more direct intervention, especially in families where children were ill-treated or neglected, or to ensure that some babies who would otherwise be bandied about from pillar to post should be 'freed' for adoption.

Were these views polar opposites or attempts at more accurate identification of an inevitable care and control continuum in social work practice? Were they a slippery slope or a great divide? Was care itself control by the powerful over the powerless or were there situations in which care could only be given within control, even though there should never be control without care for the individual? To some, controls were a denial of respect for the clients' freedom of choice, to others the dilemma was unreal because attitude change was only motivated through relationship and thus control as such was not only unethical but ineffective – it failed to pass the pragmatic test. But what about changes that could be induced by behavioural modification techniques? Here once again was the issue of power and on some value assumptions the responsibility to use positive and negative reinforcement within the constraint of respect for the individual, and aimed to make him more independent. On more extreme behaviourist assumptions these constraints were irrelevant. Was the community worker who incited local groups to political action fundamentally different from the caseworker attempting to clarify the 'real problem'? Did daddy go on knowing best? Or were each from within a different ethos striving to enlarge the client's freedom of choice – if such a thing existed?

Obviously, what to some was the use of controls to manipulate clients into conformity in a basically unjust, class-ridden system, was to others a necessary use of controls in some circumstances for the protection of other people and indeed the individual himself. This might be constructive with people who were at a given time not capable of sufficient self-direction, provided it was used as part of a process in which some of the hurly-burly was lessened, life simplified – or enriched – as a means of enlarging their freedom of choice, ability to live independently, and meet their social responsibilities. This included helping the client to achieve more hope and self-confidence, more accurate insight into himself, his relationships and his circumstances, coupled with all-round efforts to improve these. On this view, process and change rather than a static state were inherent in the concept of control. The aim was control as a stepping stone to independence rather than punitive control over the scapegoats of society. Thus in the perpetual dilemma of balancing the interests of the individual and society, means had to be found both to change social circumstances and to combine control with care for destructive and damaged people.

This illustrates growing conflict about means, since the problem was to discover the means to achieve desired ends such as greater freedom of choice. It was accepted by many social workers that these ends were part of a constellation centred on respect for the integrity and inherent dignity of the unique individual, a moral obligation to enhance his humanity and to do nothing to detract from it, to treat him thus because he was a human being and as though his behaviour or his physical or mental condition merited such treatment. Some social workers contended that this was a liberal, individualistic ethic, whereas they subscribed to a collectivist philosophy which laid emphasis on society rather than the individual. To many young social workers of the 1970s a code of practice embodied bourgeois values of an élitist profession when the real challenge was to identify with the poor and the powerless in order to bring about structural social change. Indeed the gap widened between those who saw the answer primarily in terms of the class struggle, and those who, while emphasising the ill-effects of social conditions, were yet conscious that personal problems of living cut across class boundaries and that social classes I and II enjoyed no immunity from tangled human relationships or separation, ill-health, loneliness and death. The increased political involvement of social work could be interpreted either as its professional adolescence or recognition that a profession embedded in social problems was inherently political.

A fair amount of social philosophy had been taught in the old social studies courses and sometimes related to the social sciences, although it was not often applied or immediately relevant, but there was greater diversity from the mid-1950s in the new degree courses. The professional, one-year courses were increasingly overloaded so that students concentrated on social work method to the exclusion of a rigorous examination of social work aims and values.

A CCETSW interdisciplinary working party produced a discussion document on *Values in Social Work* (1976b) which examined conflicting views and drew attention to the unsatisfactory situation in which much teaching of psychology, sociology, social administration and social work was riddled with unexamined value assumptions. In the range from existentialism to behaviourism, maximum freedom of choice or none might be assumed. For a penetrating discussion of the place of values in social work see Butrym (1976).

PROFESSIONAL ASSOCIATION STUDY GROUPS ON SOCIAL WORK VALUES AND PROFESSIONAL ETHICS, 1950–1975

In 1950 a study group set up by the British Federation of Social Workers produced a draft code for social work. The Federation thought that to adopt such a code would 'greatly facilitate co-operation . . . by recognising certain moral obligations to the client, the profession and the community' (Thwaites, 1950, *The Almoner*, pp. 237–42). (There was no mention of employing agencies.) The obligations to the client were to observe strict confidence, to take all relevant information into consideration and to act on accurate knowledge; to balance this with responsibility to the community and to keep 'the public' informed about social needs. The duty to the profession was to help fellow social workers within the constraints of confidentiality; to teach and advise; and to contribute from experience to 'form a corpus of knowledge and skill'.

Two years later the Association of Social Workers (ASW) held a study conference on the ethics of social work, prepared for by ten local study groups. The outcome showed a striking difference from the earlier document, particularly in its emphasis on the client's rights and enhancing his ability to reach his own decisions. There was general agreement that the rights of the client included respect for his right to order his life and reach his own decisions within the limits of the law; the right to courtesy and consideration; and the right to protection from unnecessary or irrelevant probing into other aspects of his personal concerns. The social worker should 'stick to the practical aspects of the situation stated by the "client" ' though showing 'interest, sympathy, encouragement, patience and understanding' (ASW, 1953, p. 8). Clients must be encouraged to understand their responsibilities and fulfil their duties. Social workers must have enough faith in themselves and others to accept failure from time to time. Their professional obligation must over-ride their personal emotions or their own convenience. They must collectively press for better training and working conditions and salaries that made it possible to fulfil their function. Social workers had a duty to respect man's dignity and to recognise that reverence for life is essential in social work. From this stemmed the duty to arouse the social conscience, to keep the community aware of social needs, and to play an active part in social reform.

The need for research was fully recognised by this 1953 conference, but it was 'an expert's job' and few field workers had time to undertake it. Social workers had a duty to get a professional training 'now usually accepted to be a university certificate or degree in social studies which includes practical work or a degree in other subjects plus a year's experience with a professional agency' (p. 17). There was conflict about the desirability of drafting a professional code. It would help to protect individual social workers against administrative pressures and clarify the minds of its own members, but since there was no single, recognised basic qualification which distinguished social workers and the profession was not a coherent whole it would not be strong enough to take disciplinary action against those who violated the code.

In 1959 ASW held a further conference on morals and the social worker which discussed the ethical warrant for social work, explored moral problems in social work, and the personal and professional attitudes and conduct of the social worker. The main issues debated were the right to intervene and the danger of social workers being used as agents of conformity, contrasted with their attempt to make 'the second class citizens, the deviants and the misfits, feel that they belong, that society cares about them' (Association of Social Workers, 1960, p. 2). The conference also discussed confidentiality, permissive techniques and problems of value conflict, the relation between social work values and social and agency pressures, and conflicts in social work obligations to society, a particular institution and the individual.

These study groups and conferences during the 1950s were obviously discussing pressing daily problems. They concentrated on morals or ethics rather than a code of practice. There seems to have been much implicit if little explicit acceptance of the latter amongst professional social workers in circumstances where low salaries, poor promotion prospects, and status and constant overwork demanded considerable motivation. In recorded discussions social workers seem to have recognised that they were driven by a mixture of compassion, guilt, caring, personal satisfaction, rescue motives and identification with the underdog. They needed a degree of tolerance, dogged patience, warmth and single-mindedness in dealings with clients beyond ordinary human expectations in private life.

By the late 1960s principles and practice were better defined in relation to each other. The processes of judgement and decision making and the respective roles of professional staff and committee members were more realistically analysed than in earlier discussions. The Association of Child Care Officers (ACCO) set up a working party in 1969 'to examine the conflict of loyalties imposed on child care staff when they are compelled by their employing authority to act in complete contravention of their professional principles' (ACCO, 1969*b*, p. 2). The report concluded that although 'all social workers who are professionally qualified, experienced and supported by supervision should be held to be competent to make professional judgments' (p. 2) yet some decision making, for example assumption of parental rights over a child, should be a local authority committee responsibility.

The principle of confidentiality was obviously violated when case records began to include more than purely factual information, but might be left lying about in an office, or personal information that included clients' names might be sent to committee members or passed on to another service without the client's knowledge or consent, or be used at case conferences where professionals might have different views about confidentiality from other members. The British Association of Social Workers' (BASW) first exploratory discussion paper, *Discussion Paper No. 1. Confidentiality in Social Work* (1971) spoke of the 'multiplicity of problems concerning confidentiality experienced by social workers from different settings, working for different agencies with different traditions, and with employing bodies in some instances having little understanding of the necessity, in this context, for establishing trust and maintaining secrecy' (p. 4). The social worker accepted intimate and confidential information on behalf of the agency, which had a duty to safeguard records and only to pass on information with the client's knowledge (with a few exceptions). This exploratory discussion paper was confined to casework. It did not explore the nature of confidentiality in group work or community work. The Seebohm Committee (1968) thought that professional views about confidentiality as between individuals and clients, or patients, were 'anachronistic' in the situation of large organisations and teams treating individuals over long periods. A new code of practice to meet the changed situation should be worked out between the professions concerned (para. 662). The Scottish Committee on Social Work Statistics (the Martin Report, n.d., but actually published in 1974) concluded that 'conceptually what has taken place is a translation from the notion of the authorized individual to that of the authorized group' (p. 19). The BASW discussion paper on confidentiality in social work (1971) and the questions formulated by the working party on confidentiality (Baraclough, 1974*a* and 1974*b*) did not explore this aspect.

In 1971 BASW set up a working party to advise the Association on a code of ethics in the belief that 'a unified organisation of social workers ought . . . to adopt an ethical code which could be a unifying statement of the basic values of social work' (BASW, 1972, p. 1). The working party issued a discussion document and remained in being to amend it in the light of members' comments. A further draft 'Code of Ethics for Social Work' was produced in 1975 (Baraclough, 1975) and after further discussion and amendment it was adopted by BASW in 1975 as an initial statement to be tried out in practice (BASW, *A Code of Ethics for Social Work*). It assumed that professional practice included 'obligations beyond those of the ordinary citizen', and that 'members of a profession have obligations to their clients, to their employers, to each other, to colleagues in other disciplines and to society'. The code and principles of practice were more precise than earlier discussions in that they differentiated between professional ethics in general, ethical principles especially relevant to social work, and rules of conduct for the application of these in practice. The primary purpose of the code was to make explicit those ethical principles implicit in practice which prescribed professional responsibilities for the protection of clients. The basic social work principle was 'recognition of the value and dignity of every individual human being, irrespective of origin, status, sex, sexual orientation, age, belief or contribution to society [and] . . . a responsibility to encourage and facilitate the self realisation of the individual person with due regard for the interests of others' (p. 379). The social worker, being concerned with the enhancement of human well-being, had a commitment to serve these purposes with integrity and skill. This entailed complementary rights, including the exercise of professional discretion, to carry out the obligations. There were responsibilities to meet needs, to contribute to social planning and social action and to co-operate with other professions, within the context of economic resources. There was also an obligation to contribute to the increase of professional knowledge, as well as personal knowledge and skill. Social workers were accountable to those under whose authority they worked and responsible for the efficient performance of their professional task and their management of the organisation's resources. This included upholding the clients' rights and making public those circumstances which created or contributed to hardship and suffering.

This statement of general principles was translated into principles of practice which made it incumbent upon each BASW member to the best of his ability to:

(a) contribute to policies for human welfare and not permit his knowledge, skills or experience to be used to further inhuman policies;
(b) respect clients as individuals;
(c) not act out of prejudice or selectively towards clients;
(d) help to increase clients' range of choice and power to make decisions;
(e) not reject a client, even if obliged to protect others against him or acknowledge inability to help him;
(f) put his professional responsibility before his personal interests;
(g) take responsibility for his standard of service and recognise that continued professional education was essential;
(h) collaborate with others in the client's interest;

(i) make it clear when he was speaking or acting publicly in a personal or official capacity;
(j) be responsible for helping clients to obtain all the services and rights to which they were entitled;
(k) respect confidential information;
(l) work for conditions in employing agencies which enabled social workers to accept the obligations of the code.

The comments on the principles of practice (abridged) clarified their meaning and application, the implication that employers should recognise the code and the obligation on BASW members to uphold it.

The code was intended to be tested in practice and periodically amended in the light of this. It was challenged by a minority of BASW members as a disciplinary, conservative, élitist professional document, but accepted by the majority as a step towards better possibilities for good practice. Obviously it also referred by implication to bad practice, and sanctions and expulsion. These were related to BASW's continuing work on disciplinary procedures. These attempts to clarify aims were an example of the view that 'Professional associations give quite concrete and explicit expression to the otherwise rather abstract idea of a profession as a shared system of ideals, methods and knowledge' (Rowbottom *et al.*, 1974, p. 23). Many of these principles were ideals only capable of partial fulfilment so it remained to test out their power in the day to day practice of social workers.

Chapter 11

Social Work and Social Research

SOME DEVELOPMENTS IN SOCIAL RESEARCH IN THE 1950S AND 1960S

Various studies in psychology, sociology and criminology in these decades added greater precision either to knowledge or ignorance about personal and social functioning, although these studies were at different levels of abstraction or based upon different theoretical concepts and thus difficult to co-ordinate in specific social work practice. There was often failure to take the crucial next step of testing and incorporating relevant findings and concepts in social work or social agency practice, and so enlarging the boundaries of practice by more flexible, imaginative, objective and evaluated use of knowledge or hypotheses. Unfortunately, there was no planned endeavour by selected social agencies to test findings systematically and make the results generally available.

A number of research studies were analysed by Barbara Wootton in *Social Science and Social Pathology* (1959) in an attempt to sift 'hard' and 'soft' knowledge. Her criticisms of social work were in turn both criticised and quoted but they were useful in forcing social workers to face the gap between aspiration and achievement, as well as too exclusive concentration on the individual's emotional problems compared with the social stresses and deprivations which encompassed him.

From the 1950s the Institute of Community Studies publications helped to bring into social work more awareness of the effect of culture, including the social worker's own cultural assumptions, on behaviour and values. The National Children's Bureau from its foundation in 1963 added greatly to knowledge about child nurture, in particular through the National Child Development Study which followed the growth through the years of children born in one week in 1958, and in greater depth what happened to those who were illegitimate, adopted, members of one-parent families, handicapped or exceptionally gifted. Various studies by the Cambridge Institute of Criminology, by the Social Medicine Research Unit of the Medical Research Council and by the Home Office Research Unit (referred to in more detail elsewhere) cast light on various aspects of individual, family and social malfunctioning.

A number of universities and other institutions, notably the Tavistock Institute of Human Relations and the National Institute for Social Work (NISW), undertook studies financed by the Home Office, the DHSS, the

Social Science Research Council (SSRC), various foundations or from other sources. Some were fact-finding surveys, others action research projects.

The Family Discussion Bureau, renamed the Institute of Marital Studies (IMS) in 1968, was the only substantial example of a service based upon systematically recorded and evaluated casework. It published *Social Casework in Marital Problems* (1955), *Marriage: Studies in Emotional Conflict and Growth* (1960), and later other studies of casework and marital problems. It worked upon psychoanalytic assumptions about conflicts which each partner unconsciously expressed through the other. The IMS focused increasingly on marriage as a potential container for the conflict that is inseparable from emotional growth, and on the interaction between the couple, though the concept of interaction and the use of the term did not figure in its literature until the mid-1960s.

Isolated action research was undertaken by the FWA and Family Service Units and elsewhere in the 1950s and 1960s. There was also more attempt by individual social workers to learn more about people with particular personalities and their families for instance (Goldberg, 1958 and 1967). Individual researchers also undertook fact-finding studies, notably in the child care service, but the samples were inevitably small and they tended not to be replicated elsewhere. None the less, as interdisciplinary research in family life and the social field increased, more social workers had opportunities to become familiar with social research methodology.

ATTITUDES OF SOCIAL WORKERS TOWARDS RESEARCH

Social workers were criticised for not assessing the effectiveness of their actual performance more systematically than by individual and subjective records of 'successful' or 'unsuccessful' cases, or by articles in professional journals reporting studies with small and ill-selected samples. None the less: 'Of very great importance are the "success stories". Clients responding against the trend should be studied to see if the crucial features can be identified and used to help other clients' (Robinson, 1971, p. 479).

Inadequate recording systems, which often did not provide even basic data and were not standardised, were partly due to employing agencies' lack of interest in evaluating the effectiveness of a social work service, to inadequate secretarial help for overpressed social workers, as well as to individual social workers, the profession as a whole and social work training, which all showed a strange indifference to research and evaluation.

The difficulty of assessing social work effectiveness included the severe methodological problems of determining what constituted 'success' or 'failure' and how to measure the effects of intervening variables or spontaneous remission. By the late 1960s social work objectives became modest compared with the Aladdin's lamp claims of earlier enthusiasts. More attention was given to specific favourable changes which might be achieved within a defined time span, what variables were significantly related to outcome, and what kind of social work, or other help might be most effective. It was more usually recognised that in a research project everyone in the experimental and control groups must suffer from the same problem, as identified by clients as well as researchers; that the given treatment tested must be relevant to all members of the sample; that the size of the sample affected the significance level, i.e. the smaller the sample the greater the likelihood of failure to identify positive findings. Also that it might sometimes be better to have a large treatment sample and compare various sub-groups rather than a small treatment sample and a control group.

If social work could be effective, neutral or actually harmful in its impact upon different kinds of people in particular circumstances, then it was crucial to have more standardised, verified, transmissible and cumulative knowledge to make differential assessment and treatment possible. This pointed to observation and assessment procedures which sifted out relevant from irrelevant information as a basis for deciding on the most effective social work intervention, and other services, to use, based upon agreement with the client or clients about aims. It was also essential that social workers should systematically record and check their practice by regular evaluation in the light of change. Social work still had far to go in acquiring and constantly adding to a relevant body of knowledge and proven methods of practice. Studies of various client groups suggested that, like clients of other professions, many were untreatable in the sense that major change could not be expected, though evidence suggested that increased ability to cope with problems, if not the ability to solve them, could result from social work help. But effective action might only have been possible at some earlier critical point in such life histories.

There was much concern from about the mid-1960s about research consumption, since social workers tended to accept unproven theories, to affirm the uniqueness of each individual as a reason for not analysing similarities, to treat statistics with frightened aversion and not to use available research findings. This sprang partly from a failure to recognise that 'the requisites of "production" are not identical to those of "consumption". The producer must have required numerous skills in order to carry out research . . . The consumer of research need not possess these particular skills, but he must understand selected basic principles and be able properly to appraise the results of studies' (Phillip *et al.*, 1975, p. 12).

The need for quantitative assessment was inherent in research assumptions, since power in prediction was the desired outcome. But even though 'success' and 'failure' might be measurable against limited and specific objectives, they also involved value judgements of 'better' or 'worse' and difficulties of relating objective evidence of changed behaviour to clients' subjective feelings of improvement or decline: moreover, behaviour might change at the expense of emotional adjustment or without attitudes being affected.

It was extremely difficult to interpret apparent improvement when 'intervention may merely cause the underlying pathology of behavioural disorder to choose a different path'. Or 'improvement may set up a chain reaction, which will throw out of balance a long-established social equilibrium' (Goldberg, 1973, p. 283).

The reluctance of social workers to think in statistical terms sprang partly from realising that since much of social work was based upon relationships, there was also the elusive effect of different personalities upon each other to be taken into account. Moreover, the full-blooded richness of human life, its tragedies, its loves and its dreams could only be captured in one-dimensional form by research. The creative imagination of artists and poets was, some said, an equally valid form of knowledge in the practice of human relationships. But both dimensions began to seem essential to effective practice.

TWO ACTION RESEARCH STUDIES OF SOCIAL WORK EFFECTIVENESS

In order to eliminate the possibility that different outcomes were due to initial differences in risk rather than treatment, it was necessary to conduct controlled experiments with random allocation to experimental or control groups, to compare like with like and to ensure that factors other than treatment were evenly distributed. A few research projects of this type are summarised in other chapters.

Helping the Aged

The most substantial study in this country to test the relative effectiveness of social work, *Helping the Aged* (Goldberg *et al.*, 1970) was conducted under the auspices of the National Institute for Social Work with 300 elderly clients who had applied for help to a welfare department. These were randomly allocated to two professional social workers in an experimental group and to untrained but experienced welfare department staff in a control group, after each old person had been assessed by a doctor also qualified in psychological medicine and by a social worker. Unlike previous studies, the criteria of success were specified and measured before as well as after treatment. Social work was interpreted to 'include concern with the external social situation, with the acceptable delivery of appropriate services, with the enrichment of social relationships in the community as well as with the therapeutic impact of the casework relationship on feelings of depression, frustration and loneliness' (p. 34). Hypotheses about possible changes resulting from social work concerned environmental change and social contacts, changes in personal interests and activities, attitudes to their situation, a decrease in social needs, and improvements in severe emotional disturbance. Nearly half the clients were over 80, two-thirds lived alone, a quarter suffered from a serious disease, and almost half were in poor housing. They had frequent contacts with other people, very few were isolated and only about 5 per cent seemed to be in need of residential care.

Morale turned out to be a crucial factor in outcome and a sensitive indicator of change. By the end of ten and a half months of the experiment the old people in the special group had received twice as much help as those in the comparison group (the welfare department's untrained social workers carried about 120 cases against a maximum of 75 each for the professionals). The trained social workers saw more problems and laid more emphasis on casework and contacts with relatives and medical and voluntary agencies. They made greater efforts to enrich the old people's lives by introducing them to clubs and volunteers and encouraging holidays and outings, and they worked more selectively according to individual people's needs. The social and medical assessors, reassessing on the same criteria as the initial assessment, did not have access to their original assessments nor know who was in the special or the control group. At the end of the project both groups had significantly fewer practical needs. The special group's morale had improved significantly, more were going to clubs, had had a holiday, felt satisfied with life, had a positive attitude, had fewer worries and personal problems or practical needs, were significantly more active and less depressed than clients in the control group. These differences in social functioning and practical needs were statistically significant and five of the seven hypotheses were upheld. Also a significantly higher proportion of clients themselves in the special group thought that the social worker's visits and practical services had been helpful. As in other studies, it appeared that intensive focused effort in the first months was more effective than long-drawn-out, open-ended casework. Size of caseload affected the results, for instance the input of the project caseworkers was twice that of the social workers in the welfare department. There were other factors besides size of caseload which stemmed from the professional social workers' perceptions and techniques, and their fuller diagnoses, especially of more subtle difficulties in social and emotional functioning. Thus they encouraged more discussion of feelings and of interpersonal relationships and combined this more often with practical services. They also worked more selectively in more sensitive relation to clients' needs than the local authority social workers. The outcome may also have been affected by the motivation of the project social workers to achieve results within the ten months' time limit of the project and by regular team discussions which kept goals firmly in view. Thus there was evidence that motivation, skill and a goal-directed approach significantly affected outcome. It also appeared that the project social workers' training contributed substantially to their ability to make a comprehensive assessment of their clients' social situation and to work differentially in relation to needs. The old people's comments showed that they rejected an impersonal, service-oriented approach or a personal one which ignored their practical needs.

In the judgement of the research team, about one-third of the sample only needed occasional review visits by a welfare assistant working under the supervision of a trained social worker, and provided there had been a competent initial assessment, which could be made by a qualified social worker in about one interview. The authors ended by affirming their belief that

'. . . if social workers were prepared to define their middle-range goals in more precise operational terms, to describe and where appropriate to categorize and measure their social work activities, to tolerate independent assessments and to heed their clients' evaluations, then we could take a great leap ahead in any sphere of social work we cared to study. We could gradually get closer to determining the relative effectiveness of different types of intervention in different situations. Training and deployment of limited resources could then be based, at least partially, on tested evidence rather than on commitment to certain methods of social work.' (pp. 200–1)

Goldberg herself (1973) questioned whether the more favourable results in the experimental group were 'due to differences in social work skills brought about by training, or are personality, natural gifts, enhanced motivation, more intensive attention, lower caseloads, and more opportunities for regular team discussion the crucial ingredients responsible for a more favourable outcome in the special group' (p. 294).

Social Work in Schools
Rose and Marshall (1974) described a five-year project to discover to what extent school social work could be effective in reducing delinquency or maladjustment. They regarded a social worker as 'anyone whose main function is attempting to help children and their families to solve, or to adjust to, personal and/or social rather than educational or vocation problems' (p. 13). Five social workers, variously trained, were appointed to five mixed schools, while two control schools without social workers were used for some comparisons.

In all, 557 children in the experimental group were helped, some very briefly, though many cases were spread over a period of time, with periods of inaction or crises. The controls were the untreated children, plus children from the control schools.

Questionnaires answered by the children themselves were administered to each of three successive year cohorts. These covered aspects of the child's behaviour, environment, personality and attitudes, and related to home, school, peer group and the self and were completed in their second and fourth years at school. These tests yielded fifty-four variables, which were subjected to factor analysis and showed two basically different types of adjustment (a) the child's social adjustment to other people and society in general, and (b) to himself, for example anxiety or self-esteem. Behaviour reports were also obtained from parents, teachers and police records. It was found that the children varied widely in the degree to which they manifested their problems in their behaviour, that is how well they could cope with their difficulties.

Analysis of the adjustment and behaviour scores showed that in the untreated children an improvement in social adjustment (conformity) was accompanied by lower personal adjustment (anxiety) and vice versa, 'The children treated by the school social worker did not however manifest this association . . . it appeared that social casework or counselling could effect improvement in one dimension without adversely affecting the other' (p. 6). Social adjustment was largely affected by difficult family relationships and poor attainment at school, the more the social workers did and 'the more the work was aimed at the child's environment rather than at the child himself, the more successful they were' (p. 160) in ameliorating environmental problems.

Treated and untreated children from both groups of schools were matched on predicted outcomes, using a range of information over a period of time, so that differences in outcome could be ascribed to treatment differences. 'The results of the work of the school social workers were shown to be clearly positive: both behaviour and social adjustment scores improved by comparison with untreated controls' (percentages not given) (p. 8). Children dealt with by police juvenile liaison schemes, a court appearance or probation showed that social adjustment scores deteriorated with more controlling treatment, while the more supportive the treatment the more social adjustment scores improved. Police records showed that after boys from the experimental schools had left for two years or more their delinquency rate was two-thirds that for the controls.

The authors pointed out the importance of a statistical design for research to evaluate behavioural change which takes into account the interaction of test scores, behaviour and treatment as ongoing processes, rather than relying on a rigid 'before and after' framework.

THE HOME OFFICE RESEARCH UNIT'S PROBATION STUDIES

The Home Office Research Unit (founded in 1958) started in 1962 a large-scale and continuing study of probation. The aim was to clarify differences in outcome for different types of offender who had been dealt with in different ways on probation, in order to facilitate the matching of treatment to offender, since a probationer's record was not a sufficient criterion of the success of the method. It was also necessary to know whether and how far probation had altered his conduct and how far the outcome would have been different if the court had selected some other method at its disposal, for example whether probation achieved better results than a fine or absolute or conditional discharge, and whether it was less successful with particular types of offender than other methods. Several studies showed success rates of about 70 per cent but this was the classic success rate claimed for almost any form of penal and correctional treatment (Grünhut, 1954).

The wider range of treatment for offenders started in the 1960s and 1970s, extended the responsibilities of the probation and after-care service and led to a series of Research Unit studies discussed, for example, in volume 1, chapter 7.

SOME DEVELOPMENTS IN THE LATE 1960S AND EARLY 1970S

By the 1970s more knowledge was available about developmental psychology, reactions to loss, separation, crises and continued stress and the nature and extent of various social problems, though limited – and very costly – operational research usually demonstrated many ramifications in any given problem. Moreover, ideological views differed sharply about the concepts of social pathology and deviance, and the extent to which the sickness lay in the individual or society.

The Advisory Council on Child Care in an effort to stimulate and co-ordinate relevant research produced a research and development strategy (1968) which set out current Home Office supported research and possible future research, with the hope that there might be consultation about priorities and co-ordination of projects. The purpose was to throw light on real and urgent problems, while other research was designed to add to fundamental psychosocial knowledge. It gave priority to comprehensive studies of residential child care and foster-home placement. These remained in limbo until several years later.

The Social Science Research Council (SSRC) was set up in 1965 to support, encourage and carry out research in the social sciences, to provide advice and to disseminate knowledge concerning the social sciences and also to grant aid post-graduate students. It financed several projects which added to knowledge about particular social work client groups. The most important of these for social work orginated in 1972 when in a speech the then Secretary of State for Social Services, Sir Keith Joseph, used, but did not coin, the phrase 'the cycle of deprivation'. A campaign ensued to focus attention on this, particularly in families where it recurred in successive generations, and to undertake research in a complex and controversial subject. A joint DHSS and SSRC working party was set up: it decided that the cycle of transmitted deprivation was researchable, commissioned a review of the literature and examined some of the complexities (First report on *Transmitted Deprivation*, SSRC, 1974). Deprivation included being delinquent, in poverty, chronically dependent on social services, unemployed, ill-housed or emotionally disturbed. It might or might not persist. People with multiple difficulties were likely to find it more difficult to escape from one generation to another. Intergenerational transmission might result from environmental rather than family factors. Yet there was evidence of intergenerational continuity, even though the causal mechanisms were little understood. The distinguishing personal or environmental characteristics of those who broke out of the cycle, compared with those who did not, could be highly significant. Intensive study of deprived families in their social milieux could also yield useful hypotheses, as well as more knowledge about continuity of problems throughout the individual's life. The many studies of social and individual deprivation tended to concentrate on a given point in time, whereas it was obviously necessary to have information about intergenerational continuities over long periods of time, such as the National Child Development Survey, or studies in small local areas. In all such research, genetic factors should be taken into account as far as possible. Theories of social stratification required systematic testing, as well as follow up of deprived people from various social classes.

In 1973 the DHSS agreed to finance and the SSRC to administer a seven-year programme of research into the cycle of deprivation, especially continuities and the processes and mechanisms which sustain or inhibit these continuities. Two years later a number of proposals had been considered and eleven accepted, with a strong emphasis on psychology and psychiatry, whereas the aim was to support varied research to try

'. . . to establish the extent to which the deprived groups of today are the descendants of the deprived groups of the past and that can suggest some causal explanations for the continuities and discontinuities . . . The mechanisms in question could, of course, operate within the family, the local community or institutions of the wider society' (Second report on *Transmitted Deprivation*, SSRC, 1975, pp. 2 and 5).

RESEARCH AND THE PERSONAL SOCIAL SERVICES

The Seebohm Report (1968) summed up the situation as follows:

'The personal social services are large-scale experiments in ways of helping those in need. It is both wasteful and irresponsible to set experiments in motion and omit to record and analyse what happens.' (para. 455)

And:

'Research is necessary in order to identify and measure the problems with which the personal social services should be grappling, and to assess the methods of dealing with them. Most research will therefore be concerned with two broad tasks. First, the collection and analysis of basic data and, second, the clarification, evaluation and costing of the main options available in tackling the problems.' (para. 459)

In the personal social services throughout most of the 1960s there was only limited and uneven collection and sharing of basic data; very little analysis of comprehensive information about the services, local conditions and the extent and nature of different needs in different parts of the country; and thus little clarity about the aims of the services and priorities, indeed only one children's department had a research unit. But the 1968 and 1971 reorganisations made it crucial to estimate the inter-related present and future social needs of an area in the light of census data about demographic and other change; to decide on plans to meet them, co-ordinated with other services; and continuously to evaluate all types of provision and treatment in order to make the most effective use of resources in the light of changing or newly identified need. This pointed to a joint responsibility by central and local government, the universities, voluntary organisations and the professions. After the social work and social services departments came into being most set up research and intelligence units. At first these were largely concerned with data collection and area surveys for more effective deployment of staff. Later they began to undertake inquiries or research related to particular client groups, sometimes in co-operation with university or other research teams.

Edinburgh and Glasgow Universities set up a joint university social work research unit in 1972, financed by the Social Work Services Group (SWSG). It estimated the 'hidden' demand for social work services in different areas and conducted workload studies. Brunel University had a social services organisation research unit from 1971 which undertook action research in social services departments and Bradford University set up a social work research unit. The Birmingham University Institute of Local Government Studies (INLOGOV) also undertook research, ran seminars and provided the Clearing House for Local Authority Social Services Research, which was a means of making individual authorities' research and inquiry results known. Manpower organisation and planning (MOP) at the NISW studied human behaviour in organisations, personnel and caseload management, and research consumption and evaluation. The NISW research unit created instruments for continuous review and monitoring of social work and social services provision.

All of these and other research activities were concerned with helping social services departments to define objectives, whether for the whole department or individual workers' decision making, intake systems, methods of defining and assessing need, the use of social indicators, the deployment of resources, and problems of balancing priorities. To a considerable extent this type of research was a post-Seebohm phenomenon in the personal social services. By the mid-1970s such studies were adding essential new knowledge about effective provision of services and new dimensions to social work.

A government White Paper, *Government Research and Development* (Cabinet Office, 1973), laid down general principles to regulate the relations between research councils and government research. It said: 'Ministers must ensure that departmental objectives are properly backed by applied research and development programmes directly related to these objectives.'

The DHSS undertook research and development in the personal social services, commissioned 'extramural' research, and gave research grants. In 1974 it set up research liaison groups to promote research, development, assessment, and assimilation of the results. There were groups on social handicap, children, old people, mental health and handicap, and the local authority personal social services.

A memorandum (mimeographed, 1974) to the research committee of the Association of Directors of Social Services proposed classifying research according to the main groups of uses of the services and the principal services available to meet needs.

The Personal Social Services Council concluded in its first annual report (*Report, 1975*) that 'a considerable body of important research in the personal social services is currently being undertaken in central government, local authorities, voluntary organisations and in the academic world' (p. 11). Its own research and intelligence committee intended to concentrate upon short-term, small-scale projects.

The various categories of relevant research which had been clarified by the mid-1970s were thus:

(a) basic research in the behavioural and social sciences, which contributed to better services;
(b) social work research to add to knowledge and improve practice;
(c) research in the social services to identify present and future needs, to evaluate means of meeting need and whether alternative means would do so at less cost; to assess management and service utilisation effectiveness, priorities in the deployment of manpower and other resources, and response to social trends.

Much of this was essentially interdisciplinary. It was doubtful whether the volume of available research findings was yet being effectively incorporated in overpressed social services departments' policies, organisation and practice. Or, indeed, whether accepted good practice was being tested, added to and generally applied. Moreover, many pointers which came to light in unconnected action research studies were seldom seized upon and pursued further. Thus this chapter records a number of isolated studies not evaluated within an agreed framework. Albeit there were great improvements in measuring devices, social work research design, identification of fallacies, and more realistic hypotheses.

Chapter 12

Some Professional Associations in Social Work

INTRODUCTION

In the early 1950s the most influential professional associations were the long-established Institute of Almoners (later the Institute of Medical Social Workers (IMSW), the Association of Psychiatric Social Workers (APSW) and the National Association of Probation Officers (NAPO). They continued to struggle for recognition of their distinct professional expertise and raise standards of practice, within the health service where the primary function was medical or the penal system where it and social work were sometimes at odds. By the early 1950s three child care associations, the Association of Children's Officers (ACO), the Association of Child Care Officers (ACCO) and the Residential Child Care Association (RCCA), had come on the scene with the birth of the child care service. They all grew rapidly in membership and effectiveness, with influential annual conferences, fact-finding studies and close relations with the Home Office and local authority associations. Indeed, the quality of the new child care service – professionally, administratively and in the collection of evidence on which new legislation was based – owed a great deal to them: as did developments in the probation service to NAPO and the Conference of Principal Probation Officers.

Different specialised social workers came together in university, Association of Social Workers (ASW), or other seminars and, sometimes to their surprise, discovered that they 'spoke the same language'. The impact of these joint seminars, often led by visiting American social work educators, is frequently referred to in periodicals and reports of the period and was part of a steady move towards the exploration of common ground. Small groups of local social workers often met in each other's homes for mutual consultation based on case discussions.

The membership of the three child care associations and the Institute of Social Welfare, like that of NAPO, was based on employment in the particular service rather than professional qualifications, though from 1964 ACCO confined its membership to qualified child care officers.

IMSW and APSW only admitted to membership holders of their specialist qualifications irrespective of employment. But ASW affiliated social workers irrespective of qualification or employment. APSW and the IMSW never doubted that membership should be confined to the qualifications they recognised nor NAPO that it should be based on employment, but later the British Association of Social Workers (BASW) was rent by this problem when large numbers of untrained people were carrying the burden and heat of the day. There were also several other smaller but sometimes effectively vocal professional bodies, like the Association of General and Family Caseworkers (AGFCW) and the Association of Moral Welfare Workers. These were primarily composed of caseworkers. The National Association of Youth Service Officers, based on employment by local education authorities, and the Community and Youth Service Association, with a training condition for membership and its journal *Rapport* remained separate from the social work scene.

Each professional association developed its own strong individuality and ethos, and although their activities were similar their 'personalities' were highly characteristic of their particular membership's attitudes.

APSW and the Institute of Almoners were as much concerned with standards of training as with improvement of professional practice and recognition of their function by employers and the medical profession. They both underwent struggles to find their identity as social workers rather than being adjuncts to the medical profession. After some years of drawing nearer together they agreed in 1961 upon a close working relationship to make the best use of resources and increase professional solidarity. To a considerable extent their similar interests in the health field covered the same ground in negotiations with other bodies and thus duplicated expenses.

PROFESSIONAL JOURNALS

There were many separate professional or closely related journals in the 1950s and 1960s, *The Almoner, ACCORD, Child Care News, The Child in Care, The British Journal of Psychiatric Social Work, Probation* (later the *Probation Journal*), *Social Work, Case Conference, Social Service, Crucible, Social Welfare* and others, as well as substantial reports of annual conferences. *Case Conference*, started in 1954, was widely read in Britain and overseas and had more influence than the others as a general forum for social work. When BASW came into existence in 1970 most of these were merged in new periodicals (see below).

In the 1970s two new social work periodicals appeared, *The Social Worker* and *Community Care*. *Case Con* was started in 1970 and described itself as 'a revolutionary comic for social workers'.

THE NATIONAL ASSOCIATION OF PROBATION OFFICERS
(incorporating notes by Fred Jarvis, OBE, Chief Probation Officer, Leicestershire Probation and After-Care Service)

In 1950 NAPO had rather less than 900 members and an annual income of about £2,000. By 1975 the membership was over 2,700 and the income more than £60,000 a year. Probation officers regarded themselves as 'servants of the court' until their functions were greatly extended in the 1960s. Some were more conscious of their place in the judicial system than with other social workers, though to others social work was their primary professional identity. Probation officers themselves constituted the service, and one in which – like child care – universal coverage was essential. Thus NAPO struggled throughout the period for an end to direct entry, reduced case-loads, more recruitment, increased in-service training and improved salaries, and recognition of the professional status of probation officers.

In the 1950s probation officers were preponderantly middle-aged or elderly. The religious influence was still considerable and most officers would have admitted to a strong sense of vocation. They tended not to criticise society, accepting it as it was and trying to improve the situation of the individual client within the existing structure. By 1975 the typical probation officer had taken a generic CQSW course, questioned society's structure, was impatient of authority and tended to locate the blame for crime in society rather than the individual. NAPO had thus become very different from twenty-five years earlier. Members had moved towards the concept of a main grade officers' organisation because many identified the upper grades with 'management' and there was much support for registration as a trade union and negotiations for a closed shop.

Relationships between the Home Office and NAPO improved over the years. During the 1950s NAPO was trying to raise the status of probation officers. Their small salary increases had kept pace to some extent with the rising cost of living, but the Association was unable to achieve any sub-stantial improvement which would mark probation officers' growing pro-fessional outlook. In 1956 it pointed out to the Joint Negotiating Committee (JNC) the changed character and increased duties of the service, the wider responsibilities of probation officers, their long hours of work, and the growing knowledge which they had to master. These salary negotiations resulted in distrust of the Home Office, which had done much to develop the service (see volume 1, chapters 6 and 7). The situation improved from the mid-1960s and increasingly the Home Office, NAPO and the Conference of Principal (later Chief) Probation Officers worked together.

NAPO's part in the Standing Conference of Organisations of Social Workers is described later. The argument raged throughout 1968 and at the 1969 annual conference a resolution was passed affirming that it was not possible to protect the interests of NAPO members or their clients within a unified association of social workers. Next year in a referendum of members a substantial majority supported an independent organisation.

NAPO had a good deal of support in Parliament at crisis points. Its annual conferences were a meeting point for its own members and other colleagues at which major current issues were debated. Its journal *Probation* (later the *Probation Journal*) contained commendably diverse views about new developments in the field of delinquency. Its handbook, *The Probation Service* (King, 1958, revised 1976) was a major and much-used publication of a type not produced by any other professional association.

THE INSTITUTE OF ALMONERS – LATER THE INSTITUTE OF MEDICAL SOCIAL WORKERS

The story of the Institute is largely told in volume 1, chapter 9 on medical social work and the training of medical social workers. Its members, almost wholly women, kept steadily in view their function as an independent profession rather than medical auxiliaries. The history of the Institute from its beginnings in 1905 was the story of a long struggle with very limited resources in what was often an uncomprehending setting, without the support that NAPO and the child care associations received from the strong Home Office probation and child care councils. The Institute thus also had to face university ambivalence at what sometimes seemed invasions of university freedom. None the less almoning was for years the favourite career in social work and before it came to an end the Institute had done much to clarify the social work function and raise standards of practice.

THE ASSOCIATION OF PSYCHIATRIC SOCIAL WORKERS
(by Elizabeth Irvine, AAPSW, formerly Reader in Social Work, York University)

When APSW celebrated its silver jubilee in 1954 it had grown in numbers and influence and there were nine local branches, many of whose members were never able to attend the general meetings in London. The demand of the branches for more influence in the counsels of the Association became insistent, and two spare-time liaison officers were appointed to improve communication and help the centre to be more responsive to the views of the provinces, and eventually a revised constitution provided for branch representation. The branches were particularly active in the recruitment drive undertaken in 1958 in a frantic effort to expand training in view of the latest increase in demand for PSWs.

APSW, like the then Institute of Almoners, restricted its membership to practitioners whose qualifications it recognised. Although not a training body it exercised considerable control over training, particularly over the quality of fieldwork placements. In 1961 it established a register of qualified PSWs whose members were entitled to the protected appellation of Associate of APSW. Until 1956 APSW performed the trade union function of negotiating with the Whitley Council but in that year it decided to negotiate in future through NALGO, which had more forceful and experienced negotiators. The situation improved considerably after this, though it never became wholly satisfactory (see also volume 1, chapter 21, section on 'Social Work Salaries, 1950–75').

The 1958 annual report noted that preparation of evidence for government committees and working parties had become a major part of the Association's activities. This proved to be a continuing trend. The Association was consulted by the Ministry of Education about the implementation of the Underwood Report on maladjusted children (1955), and sent memoranda on various subjects to the Ministries of Health, Education, and Labour. Evidence was also given to various Scottish Committees.

Occasionally evidence was given jointly with the National Association for Mental Health (NAMH) or through co-operation with ASW. Active co-operation with other professional bodies was a constant subject in the annual reports. Standing joint committees were set up with the Royal Medico-Psychological Association, the Society of Mental Welfare Officers, and the Society of Chief Administrative Medical Officers of Health, the latter mainly concerned with plans for the training of MWOs. In 1961 APSW joined the Federation of Associations of Mental Health Workers.

In 1954 APSW started negotiations with comparable associations overseas for reciprocal recognition of professional qualifications. These negotiations were lengthy and difficult because the American and Canadian master's degree, with which parity was claimed by APSW, were two-year courses, compared with the one-year PSW training. An agreement was reached after some years with the Canadian Association, but agreement was not finally reached with the American National Association of Social Workers (NASW) until 1967 through the Standing Conference of Organisations of Social Workers.

APSW also developed an important function in providing such further training for its members as was possible on a shoestring. In 1956 a number of short weekend courses were organised on supervision and consultation. A series of annual discussions for tutors and supervisors involved in the training of PSWs was inaugurated in 1963, and the following year a course in group work was launched with the help of the Association for Group Psychotherapy (AGP). This became an annual event, but was eventually taken over entirely by AGP and run on interdisciplinary lines. Refresher courses and study weekends were also organised with increasing frequency as time went on, a number of the former providing the material for such publications as *The Boundaries of Casework* (1956a), *Ventures in Professional Co-operation* (1960) and *New Developments in Psychiatry and the Implications for the Social Worker* (1969).

APSW constituted a small professional élite of well-qualified social workers who were deeply and proudly committed to the maintenance of high professional standards. It was thus able to sustain a degree of solidarity and personal comradeship among its members, many of whom keenly felt the loss of this when APSW finally merged its identity in the larger and more powerful BASW.

THE ASSOCIATION OF CHILD CARE OFFICERS

ACCO originated in 1948 when a student on one of the first child care courses wrote to the rest suggesting that they should get together and form an association. This they did the following year with an initial income of £1.50p. Active individuals soon started lively regional groups which sent ideas to the Executive and were asked for their advice and opinions. In time there were local discussion groups, a number of joint activities with ACO and RCCA and two periodicals, *ACCORD* and *Child Care News*. The annual conference became in its way as important an event in the child care world as the ACO conference. This association learnt how to use the mass media effectively on a number of issues, prepared evidence for various committees of inquiry and published a series of monographs, for example *Adoption – the Way Ahead* (1969a). Together with ACO and RCCA it sponsored the Castle Priory study group which resulted in the much-used report *Residential Task in Child Care* (RCCA, 1969) (see also volume 1, chapter 3, section on 'Residential Child Care in the 1960s'). It used political influence effectively through well-informed public relations and by recruiting

MPs of all parties who agreed to present its point of view. It was also acceptable to the Home Office and local authorities because of its sound views about the development of the statutory and voluntary child care service. What it accomplished in its twenty-one years of zestful life certainly repudiates the accusation that social workers are indifferent to social action and social reform. It was indeed 'politically the most effective and mature of the social work organisations' (Jacka, n.d., p. 67). Its key role in the Seebohm Implementation Action Group is referred to in volume 1, chapter 16. When it merged in BASW in 1970 its membership had grown from 35 in 1949 to nearly 3,000 by 1969 and its annual income from £1.50p to nearly £10,000.

THE ASSOCIATION OF CHILDREN'S OFFICERS
(by Sylvia Watson, OBE, Children's Officer, Hertfordshire County Council 1948–70)

ACO was founded in 1949, primarily because children's officers needed the support of colleagues in carrying out their uncharted, difficult and often lonely job. Many of them were new to local government and knew nothing of its rules and protocol: in some councils, fellow chief officers, particularly those who had lost part of their empires to children's departments, treated children's officers with suspicion verging on hostility. Children's committees and assistant staff turned to their children's officer for guidance, but these had few guidelines and little to help them apart from their own determination and optimism.

The Association obviously met the need because almost every children's officer in England and Wales soon joined it. Scotland established its own Association; discussions took place over the years about merging the two but this never happened and contact was maintained largely by representative attendance at each other's conferences.

ACO was work-oriented and its stated aim was 'to further the welfare of children deprived of a normal home life': 'to encourage and assist in the preservation of the family' was added in 1952. Children's officers learnt from each other by discussion, exchange of views and dissemination of information. Regional branches were established from the start and well supported, particularly in more scattered areas where children's officers travelled long distances to attend meetings.

The *ACO Bulletin* was important because it spread news throughout the country, stimulated thought and gave guidance to children's officers on many difficult problems. The annual national conferences in different parts of the country were lively events attended by most children's officers, by councillors, by representatives of government departments, kindred associations, distinguished guests and eminent speakers who used the conferences as occasions to make important speeches on a wide range of topics concerning the welfare of children. Children's officers were accompanied by councillors, many of whom returned home with new ideas and strengthened in their determination to fight in their councils for the interests of children.

ACO was initially established to help children's officers in their work through discussions and the straightforward giving and exchange of information. As the scope of the work of children's departments widened ACO activities expanded. It became increasingly concerned with the promotion of good professional standards, the stimulation of thought on a wide range of social problems concerning children and families, and influencing public opinion to achieve its ends. Initially it concentrated on the welfare of individual deprived children but soon found that these could generally be best helped by support given to the family, which involved environmental changes and the improvement of social and economic conditions. It came to see that there was a close link between deprivation and delinquency and that to tackle both it was necessary to work on a broad front.

This wider scope made ACO more outward looking, which involved working with other associations, national bodies and the Home Office. It led to setting up working parties and sub-committees on special subjects and the adoption of a positive role. ACO became an increasingly effective pressure group which fought for more training and better conditions for staff, provided evidence for national committees and government departments and influenced legislation and public thought. This had a snowball effect when its work won public recognition and its views were increasingly sought by national bodies and government departments.

ACO was an effective professional body in its internal and external relationships. It was important to children's officers because it helped them to improve the quality of their work, gave them professional companionship and support, and was a channel through which they could express their views. Members served on the County Councils Association and the Association of Municipal Corporations and contributed significantly to the views put forward by these two important local authority Associations on adoption, child protection, juvenile delinquency, staff training, and on draft government circulars and child care legislation. It made a forceful contribution through its membership of the Central Training Council in Child Care and the Advisory Council on Child Care, and through the pressure it exerted, particularly for increased provision of training. It initiated and encouraged co-operation with other social work associations and finally worked for its own demise through its support for implementation of the Seebohm Report (1968).

THE ASSOCIATION OF SOCIAL WORKERS

ASW, which grew out of the British Federation of Social Workers, was born in 1949, nearly died for lack of funds and members two years later, but was reborn and ran a school for supervisors. During the 1950s and 1960s it ran a series of discussion groups, followed by national seminars on the ethics of social work, group work, supervision and administration. These resulted in a series of widely used pamphlets. It had an influence beyond its size because it could bring specialist social workers together and its Uncle Tom Cobley and All membership included university social work teachers and some leading social work practitioners who deplored the separations in social work and, like many members of the specialist bodies, wanted to see a unified professional association. From the early 1960s holders of the certificate in social work discovered that it was the only professional association they were eligible to join. Many 'generically' trained social workers also became members.

THE INSTITUTE OF SOCIAL WELFARE

The Institute of Social Welfare was founded in 1953, largely for workers in the local authority welfare services, and pressed for training and better conditions in those services. By 1975 membership was open to those working in the statutory or voluntary social services, and affiliate membership to anyone in sympathy with its objective of improving the social services. It published a monthly journal, *Welfare*, and had about 1,500 members in 1975.

THE ASSOCIATION OF SOCIAL WORK TEACHERS – LATER THE ASSOCIATION OF TEACHERS IN SOCIAL WORK EDUCATION

The original Association was started in 1965 on the initiative of a few people and 130 social work teachers were invited to the inaugural meeting. Many more social work courses were being started and there was an obvious need for tutors to form a group, as the constitution said, 'to promote study and provide a means of common action amongst members on matters affecting training for social work'. Full membership was confined to those who taught social work method on professional or other organised courses. Supervisors were only admitted to associate membership. A representative of the Standing Conference of Tutors to Residential Child Care Courses was welcomed at the first annual meeting, i.e. at a time when moves had begun to include residential care in social work. The Association had an active nucleus of members and ran several successful conferences during its life-time.

When the specialised courses ceased and the whole concept of social work was changing, it became essential to set up a more comprehensive association. In 1971 the Association of Social Work Teachers, the Association of Tutors to the Certificate in Social Work and Residential Social Work, the Standing Conference of Tutors to Residential Child Care Courses, the Mature Entrance Tutors Group and the Tutors' Group of Probation Officers Training Courses all came together to discuss what should be done. The last four were tutors to specialised courses whose meetings had been financed from public funds. Tutors in university courses also held regular regional meetings under JUC auspices. The working party recommended that all these different groups should unite in a new Association of Teachers in Social Work Education. The first meeting was held in 1972 and a constitution adopted. Full membership was extended to all teachers on social work courses leading to the CQSW, even though they themselves were not professional social workers. The following year the constitution was amended to include 'practice teachers of social work' employed in designated posts, primarily to supervise students. In 1975 full membership was broadened still further.

The Association worked through local branches, published an informative newsletter, and ran well-attended day and residential conferences on such subjects as methods and objectives in social work teaching, research in social work, training for residential social work, and the management of expansion in social work education. It also held discussion meetings on advanced and further training and the relation of community work training to social work. It met regularly with related organisations. It was allocated three seats on the CCETSW and met periodically with the staff. The Association's purposes included the relation of social work practice and training, identification of the professional core of social work, promotion of research studies and research into social work education, curriculum planning, teaching methods and conditions of training. Obviously there was a need for such an association in the total pattern of responsibility for social work education but it faced the same difficulties as other professional organisations in securing enough support from hard-pressed people.

THE GROUP FOR THE ADVANCEMENT OF PSYCHOTHERAPY IN SOCIAL WORK

GAPS was initiated in 1971 and spread rapidly. By 1972 its membership was over 400. It brought together. social workers and residential workers who wished to advance the use of the psychodynamics of relationship, both conscious and unconscious, in social work practice with individuals and groups.

The aims were to establish psychotherapy as an appropriate social work specialisation, to encourage training in psychotherapeutic skills and opportunities for their practice, to provide a support group to social workers interested in psychotherapy, and a means of communication between them and those in other professions with similar interests. The Group's discussion papers pointed out that the range of social services should include social work which made use of psychotherapeutic skills, since there were many clients of both statutory and voluntary agencies who suffered from personality and relationship problems for which they needed an effective service. The relationship between the client and worker was central to work which aimed to bring about psychological change, and which entailed working with the client's external relationships and his own inner experiences. In determining the appropriate use of psychotherapeutic work in any one instance the factors involved were the social worker's competence and skill in various methods, the nature of the client's personality and needs, and the agency's function.

The worker's competence depended on his personality, level of self-awareness, the amount and depth of his theoretical and practical training, the quality of supervision and the availability of continuing support. Owing to the shortage of training facilities, many workers had had to develop their skills as best they might, and the Group was anxious for an increase of courses in psychotherapeutic work at advanced levels as well as for the teaching of a psychodynamic approach in all generic courses.

MOVES TOWARDS A UNIFIED PROFESSIONAL ASSOCIATION

The Joint Standing Committee of AGFCW, APSW and the Institute of Almoners was part of the move towards greater unity, and from 1959 it was actively engaged in discussion of common standards. In the same year ASW initiated the Joint Training Council for Social Work composed of representatives of nine different organisations. In 1961 this Council and the Joint Standing Committee set up a working party composed of representatives of the Institute of Almoners, APSW, AGFCW, and ASW to explore the possibility of a national federation of social workers. It reported in 1962 and after discussion with all the constituent bodies it was decided to set up a Standing Conference of Organisations of Social Workers (SCOSW). This was a key point in the move away from specialisation and isolation towards identification of social work as a whole. The Institute of Almoners *Annual Report 1962–63* commented that

'The officers and chairman were chosen by general consent on the grounds of the obvious qualifications of each for his or her particular job, and the keenness and enthusiasm with which this new federation of organisations has settled down to its work augurs well for the attainment of its primary aim of establishing a unified national association of trained social workers.' (p. 7)

It was composed of ACCO, AGFCW, the Association of Moral Welfare Workers, APSW, ASW, IMSW, NAPO and the Society of Mental Welfare Officers.

SCOSW soon gathered sufficient momentum to initiate several standing committees and to hold many discussions. In 1965 it set up a working party to make recommendations on the future organisation of social workers. The subsequent discussion paper (*Discussion Paper No. 1,* n.d.) outlined as alternatives either a federation which would take over some common interests of its constituents but otherwise leave them to carry on with their specialist functions; or else a national association in which all the existing organisations would be merged. The second proposal would mean loss of identity for professional associations which had their strong individuality and had struggled to raise standards of practice and training in particular services. This decision was particularly hard for one of the leaders in the move for unity, IMSW, which had been in existence in one form or another for over sixty years and had more direct responsibility for training than any of the other associations. Yet the ground swell towards greater unification in services, in training and in social work practice, the growing sense of a common profession of social work, was so strong that the discussion paper brought most of the organisations concerned into common accord. The effect on NAPO was the reverse. It had been a partner in the first negotiations but it began to take fright when the Scottish White Paper, *Social Work and the Community* (Scottish Education and Scottish Home and Health Departments, 1966), suggested that the probation service in Scotland should be merged in general social work departments. Many probation officers felt strongly that they were different from other ·social workers because of their ties with the courts and the correctional system, the element of legal compulsion in their work and their knowledge of criminal, anti-social behaviour. NAPO was also split on the question of whether probation and after-care would be most effective inside or outside comprehensive local authority personal social services. A majority of NAPO was only prepared to consider a federated structure for the proposed BASW rather than unification, with individual membership based upon recognised qualifications, and specialist sub-sections, which the other associations favoured. These alternatives were further discussed up and down the country by members of all the constituents of SCOSW. Finally, with nostalgia for the past but solid hope for the future, the working party was asked by a majority to prepare a draft constitution for a unified association. This was agreed by all the members of SCOSW except NAPO. Complicated negotiations followed to reconcile the different practices of the eight constituent organisations, decide the future of journals, conditions of membership, and so on (McDougall, 1972).

THE BRITISH ASSOCIATION OF SOCIAL WORKERS

Finally BASW came into existence in 1970. It obviously had to find a new and different identity from that of its predecessors. This was not easy in a far bigger group with more diffuse interests. Fortunately enthusiasm for 'Seebohm' and the first stages of implementation gave it an initial rallying cry and by degrees a new generation of social workers became active on its committees and working groups. Its fortnightly publication *Social Work Today* covered more ground and sometimes at a better standard than earlier small journals and incorporated *BASW News*. The *British Journal of Social Work* took over and maintained the high standard of the *British Journal of Psychiatric Social Work* but with a wider range of interests, while *Parliament and Social Work* was published during parliamentary sessions.

BASW soon showed a desire to use political influence and intervene in public affairs characteristic of the new era in which it was born. It set out to affect decision making in Parliament and local government besides making known its views about the needs of social services consumers, to speak in the name of social work on relevant current issues and improve public understanding of social work, in the press, broadcasting and television, at a time in the 1970s when social work faced mounting criticism.

BASW's code of practice is discussed in chapter 10: it produced a variety of discussion papers and explored the pros and cons of registration and accreditation. In 1974 it set up a working party to identify the social work task, the functions of trained and untrained staff and the development of specialisations. This it did in some detail in an important report published in 1977. Membership was extended in 1973 to qualified residential social workers; associate membership, based on employment, was opened to community workers, prison governors, housing welfare officers and a few others. A number of probation officers joined as full members.

In 1975 it decided, after heated debate and strong feelings, not to admit unqualified social workers to membership, though they were in a majority in the social services departments. Some radical social workers regarded BASW as an élitist, professional closed-shop organisation, but others saw professional solidarity and standard setting as essential means of improving practice and giving social workers an independent professional voice. A procedure for the accreditation of qualified social workers with defined experience began to be discussed at this time.

The structure consisted of sixty-eight branches (some more lively than others) and six (later eight) standing commit'ees on membership, salaries and service conditions, public relations and social policy, education and training, publications, and international relations. By 1975 the previous four sections had become national committees on general health, mental health, child and family care, and the treatment of offenders. These ran national conferences in their particular field and produced reports on specific subjects. Any group of members could apply to be registered as a special interest group and report annually to the Council. By 1975 there were seven such groups; they were a flexible means of focusing members' interests and BASW encouraged their expansion. Both they and the small meetings in the big annual conference were means of bringing members together about their special concerns and making it possible for them to get to know each other. Inevitably it was more difficult to feel identified with a professional association far larger and wider ranging than the small groupings of the past. BASW was indeed part of the institutionalisation of social work and in its first five years it began to find its feet and to develop a new collective 'personality'. Its total membership was 8,539 in 1970 and 9,993 by 1975.

THE ASSOCIATION OF COMMUNITY WORKERS (NOT A PROFESSIONAL ASSOCIATION)

ACW began in 1968 with training requirements for full membership. This posed difficulties because some of the best community workers were untrained, others had different qualifications, for example in planning or adult education, while community workers did not want to be confined within any one profession or to paid work which may be indistinguishable from what others do unpaid (Cox and Derricourt, 1975, p. 83). These training requirements were dropped in 1973 and an occupational criterion substituted. Its aim was to become an 'ideological pace-setter for "client-centred" community work' (p. 87) and the principal centre for debate on the whole subject. It regarded itself as a national forum rather than a professional association.

THE RESIDENTIAL CARE ASSOCIATION

RCA grew out of the active Residential Child Care Association which campaigned vocally and effectively from the 1950s for better residential standards and more knowledge. The Association included workers in residential and day-care settings for children, the handicapped and old people, and continued to have an influential voice. It published a periodical, *Residential Care* (later *Residential Social Work*) and annual reviews of specific aspects of residential care. It supported good standards of training and practice but thought that membership should be open to all staff irrespective of qualifications.

THE ASSOCIATION OF DIRECTORS OF SOCIAL SERVICES

ACO was absorbed in the new Association of Directors of Social Services (with its Scottish counterpart) in 1971 as a result of Seebohm reorganisation.

It had a membership of close on 120 directors and worked through an Executive Committee, standing committees on training and research and various *ad hoc* special interest groups. Its aim – which illustrates new concepts in the social services – was 'to promote a comprehensive social service for individuals, families and communities'. In operational terms this aim obviously meant influencing the formation of national policy by making the Association's views known to government departments and by submitting evidence to committees of inquiry. The Association worked closely with professional associations like BASW, with the CCETSW, the Personal Social Services Council (PSSC), and others, and with national voluntary organisations. It had an influential voice not only in these ways but also through its biennial conferences, the first on 'The Process of Planning and the Settlement of Priorities' (1972) and the second on 'The Expectations of the Social Services' (1974).

The Training Committee was primarily concerned with necessary expansion of training to meet increasing and changing demands and problems related to training. It worked in close liaison with the CCETSW and other national training bodies like the JUC and the Local Government Training Board (LGTB). The research committee's aim was to identify research activity particularly significant to directors of social services, to promote such research and the implementation of necessary findings both at policy and practice levels.

The Association came into existence in the full flood of reorganisation when unfamiliar services had to be welded together and common policies evolved. In its first years the social services expanded rapidly but then it had to face the effects of the second reorganisation on its own structure and to try to keep many difficult balances in the next period of severe retrenchment.

There was a separate Association of Scottish Directors of Social Work.

Chapter 13

Functions and Staff in Residential Care: Training for Residential Care

FUNCTIONS AND STAFF IN RESIDENTIAL CARE

BEGINNINGS OF THE 'CARE' FUNCTION

At the beginning of the 1950s some voluntary organisations and a few new children's departments probably achieved the best, all-round standards of personal care in institutions. It was assumed that the purpose of other residential institutions was either custodial, or moral reform, or to provide physical care or treatment, a 'good upbringing' or rehabilitation. During the next twenty-five years static complacency was punctured by the manifest failures of some institutions, by staffing difficulties, and by a few pioneers who began to look at what happened to the residents as people, to ask whether many need be there at all, and whether institutions were only a refuge from life or could be used to enable people to find themselves and live more fully.

At first the only positive analogies ready to hand were the family or the public school: hence the emphasis on family group homes for children, or creating a homelike atmosphere in hostels for offenders or ex-psychiatric patients whose inability to tolerate family life was often a main symptom of their difficulties; or approved schools or borstals modelled on public schools. Rehabilitation when applied to some people in some types of institution was another early recognition of the 'total person' or care function, though not of its complexities or the changes it demanded in institutional régimes and staff attitudes. Yet these beginnings gave a new direction to residential care. The revolutionary concept of the therapeutic community only came later and spread unevenly to different institutions.

Children's homes (discussed in volume 1, chapters 2 and 3) and mother and baby homes were the only residential situations in which a specific nurturing or growth function began to be accepted before 1948, notably in the staff training schemes of the National Children's Home, Dr Barnardo's and Josephine Butler Memorial College. Elsewhere it was thought that the 'right personality' or else another training, primarily for teaching or nursing, or experience in the armed services was sufficient. To a large extent the function was tacked onto these professions in such titles as housemaster or matron. Unfortunately there is no word in English to describe the creation of a milieu in which people can grow as people and be enabled to succeed in some particular life task that faces them. For convenience the term 'the care function' will be used here though it is inadequate and has been recently shot at for being paternalistic.

Naturally it first became clear in relation to children who needed nurture away from their own homes and to whom damage might already have been done in the family, the outside world, or in negative institutions. By degrees experiments in reversing emotional deprivation were pioneered in various residential settings for disturbed children and adolescents or young delinquents. There were few experiments for the long-term physically handicapped or for old people.

The shift partly resulted from the concept of institutional neurosis and concern about delinquents who 'came out worse than they went in', mentally disordered or handicapped people whose spirits died, or long-stay children many of whom became institutionalised. The common missing factor seemed to be the stimulus to sometimes painful individual development, sufficient independence and freedom of choice, contact with the ordinary world and a climate in which bonds of affection – relationships – could grow between people and reinforce their sense of personal worth and identity. This had been regarded in many institutions as a byproduct or something not to be expected, particularly for prisoners, vagrants, or homeless people, or those needing considerable physical care. The change in thought and practice which began in relation to differently labelled categories of people in these decades was a progression from deterrence through mainly custodial or good physical care to conscious efforts to make residential situations more alive and stimulating, more effective than an impoverished outside environment.

The situation seemed comparatively simple when effort was concentrated on some aspect of the total human being: treatment for an illness, physical care for a handicapping condition, vocational rehabilitation and industrial training, or deterrence for offenders. But it is always total people with their own individualities, a past, present and future, as well as ailments, lacks, failures and potentialities who go into institutions and the revolutionary change during the period was the realisation that because they atrophy or grow as people through their experiences in an all-encompassing milieu, this itself should make the well-being of persons a central aim in its particular treatment or custodial functions. This was essentially a dynamic rather than a static concept; it meant discovering how to give appropriate shelter and support to different people where they could be ill, dependent, protected, controlled, comforted, challenged, have anxiety heightened, encouraged to regress as the first stage in growth to independence, recovery, self-development and a better sense of reality.

There were several strands in these developments: first, perception of the function and recognition that unless people grew in any 'total institution' they became withdrawn or anti-social. Secondly, until the 1970s there was a failure to perceive this common factor in unrelated forms of residential living such as prisons or old people's homes. Thirdly, difficulties of staff recruitment delayed the start and spread of training, the systemisation of experience and knowledge, the growth of action research and the fruitful application of research findings. Problems of recruitment also delayed the recognition of this function as essentially residential social work with standards of professional practice, knowledge, training and recognised status. Fourthly, discoveries about the effects on people of institutionalisation and of separating children, in particular, from their families resulted from the late 1950s in emphasis on community care, with long-term effects on the type of residents in institutions.

Other discoveries also had to be made about the design and location of buildings because of the effect these had in promoting or frustrating group and intergroup relations between the staff, residents and the community. Long-stay hospitals and prisons in particular were 'trapped in history' through the social attitudes expressed by the building. Purpose-built institutions only became possible from about the mid-1950s when much was learnt and mistakes made about translating objectives into bricks and mortar. Management skills also had to be developed for régimes that embodied new concepts. The selection, care and after-care of residents posed very different problems if the selection and planning of treatment groups were possible, than if all comers had to be accepted. Views about the régime also shifted from paternalistic 'doing things for' to democratic 'doing things with' assumptions.

The seminal discoveries were made not by social workers but by pioneer educationalists, primarily in schools for maladjusted children, and by psychiatrists. Naturally, too, the care function was fulfilled to a marked degree by many individual teachers in boarding schools, nurses in homes for old or handicapped people and other individual staff members, whether trained or untrained, sometimes in spite of difficulties in combining this with their primary role.

Some of the unsolved problems of identifying and providing appropriate therapeutic treatment in hostels are discussed in chapter 14. These illustrate the inherent problems of all institutions intended for personal growth and the prevention of social handicap, even though many differences existed, on the one hand between institutions designed for short-term or intermittent care in a crisis or as part of a continuing treatment plan; and on the other 'total' institutions with their self-enclosed life, including those where residents remained for storage rather than treatment because no alternative existed, and some of which were end-of-the-road institutions.

All institutions were prone to suffer from isolation for geographical and other reasons and to become inward-looking. This created tensions for the staff as well as the residents, even though visiting committees and others often made valiant efforts to relate the institution to the local community, to encourage visitors to come in, and residents and staff to go out.

THERAPEUTIC COMMUNITIES

The concept of the therapeutic community, pioneered at Belmont Hospital, by the 1960s began to seem a better answer than either family or public school assumptions. Attempts to create such communities, usually under psychiatric guidance, began in a handful of children's homes, approved schools, schools for maladjusted children, psychiatric hostels and Grendon Psychiatric Prison, and were later extended. The Williams Report (1967) described the therapeutic community as:

'. . . one in which deliberate effort is made to use to the fullest possible extent, in a comprehensive treatment plan, the contribution of all the staff and of all the patients . . . Staff and staff, staff and residents, residents and residents, are the communication links in mutual exchanges of ideas and attitudes which become part of the living community and change its nature. When communications are opened up like this there is much less likelihood of the residents feeling pushed around by "them", and they are more likely to appreciate staff problems and be more co-operative and make fewer unreasonable demands.' (pp. 136–7)

The idea of the therapeutic community contributed much to an understanding of the residential situation as capable of being positive and creative in itself rather than simply to provide custodial care, or education, or physical treatment, or comfortable physical living conditions. Morrison (1967) analysed essential criteria as agreement by staff and residents about the therapeutic aims of the institution and how to achieve them and a genuine effort to make full use of residents' capacities to contribute to the task 'a recognition that self-regulation . . . is preferable to passive adjustment; [and] . . . a concept of community life as a "safety zone" for practice with interpersonal relationships where new forms of behaviour can be "tentatively tried out for size", and new skills, ideas and values tested out' (p. 44). Residents' participation with the staff in choices and decisions about running the institution generally began to be considered desirable by the 1970s as a means of diluting staff power, 'them and us' relationships, the tendency of residential institutions to be run for their own benefit, and of residents to be deprived of choice and decision making. Parallel with an emphasis on institutions with highly skilled staff and a carefully planned régime, there were hopeful new experiments for the early 1960s to help groups of inadequate, or deviant, or mentally disturbed people to run their own living arrangements, given the physical setting and skilled outside psychiatric or social work support, sometimes through weekly therapeutic group sessions.

PEOPLE IN LONG-STAY INSTITUTIONS

The first analysis in depth of the nature of the task in total institutions was made in Miller and Gwynne's study (1972) of twenty-two voluntary and local authority homes, and of wards in long-stay hospitals for severely physically disabled people. Significantly, the project resulted from the initiative of residents at Le Court Cheshire Home for severely physically handicapped people. Its aim was to clarify what residential care involved for incurable people and what improvements were possible, on the assumption that in addition to physical care it was essential to cope with psychological and social factors, because 'If emotional and psychological needs are denied or discounted, the most expert and devoted care of the body can destroy the person' (p. 88).

For most people the entry into such institutions was the point of no return, with the prospect of increasing dependence, disability and finally death after years of such living. The hospital chronic sick wards tended to be almost wholly concerned with medical and nursing care, with 'helpless bodies to be processed', thus they were characterised by depersonalisation and apathy for the patients and none of the usual medical satisfactions for the staff. The local authority and voluntary homes varied in the extent to which they recognised that people with crippled bodies had unsatisfied drives and capacities and that the function of the staff was not to treat incurable disabilities but, in addition to good physical care, to provide opportunities for individual development, self-expression and means of exercising independence. This included the chance to make relationships that were emotionally satisfying, to marry, to share in the management of the home and policy decision making, to run a variety of activities and organise work.

There was inevitably considerable physical and often financial and emotional dependence. Thus the dependence/independence balance was more difficult than in ordinary life because 'dependence which was complete and inevitable in some aspects of life spilled over into others where it was not' (p. 19).

In order to build a culture and structure appropriate to the task, it was essential neither to accept nor deny but rather to examine the differences between being able-bodied or physically handicapped, recognising that each institution is a social system created by residents and staff who function in a given environment. The problem was that the residents could not belong to a variety of social systems, as in the outside world; while the myth of the happy home denied the reality of deterioration and death and led to feelings of impotence and failure, instead of an acceptance of the reality but action about the difficulties.

Because of their physical and economic dependence, residents were apt to see themselves as being at the mercy of the management and staff, since they were permanent and the staff comparatively transient. This created constant apprehension about the sensitivity and skill with which their physical needs would be met and their personality respected. It was important to counteract these feelings by a substantial share in management. The staff worked under considerable stress owing to the powerful emotional effect of close contact with highly disabled people and 'impartiality' could lead to stereotyping, for example scapegoating or canonisation, and relating to the label not the person. The staff needed their defences, but opportunities for regular discussion and counselling by a psychotherapist or social worker were important for both residents and staff.

The authors concluded that 'It is possible both to arrive at more effective concepts of residential care and to recruit staff and train them to operate more successfully' (p. 15). This study was an influential contribution to understanding what needed to be done, how and by whom in many residential situations.

CASEWORKERS AND RESIDENTIAL SETTINGS

In the late 1940s and early 1950s there were attempts to employ caseworkers on the staffs of approved schools, schools for maladjusted children, or in borstals to help individuals in various specialised institutions. Some health or welfare departments used social workers to visit residents in institutions and to provide the rudiments of a casework service. A few borstal assistant governors were seconded to take mental health or applied social studies courses, though these were not the right answer when a main concern was with group interaction. Some probation officers worked in approved hostels. This was part of the struggle, particularly in the delinquency services, to find some appropriate professional skill and teaching for residential work. Caseworkers might understand the pain of separation, the effects on family relationships, the shallow emotions, the depersonalisation, the institutionalisation and the difficulties of a satisfactory adjustment to ordinary life suffered by people in institutions. But casework as such lacked the necessary skills in group relations, the dynamics of group living and management techniques, while the emphasis was on individuals rather than the group situation. The pattern that emerged by degrees made caseworkers responsible for particular residents and their families – often before admission – in co-operation with the resident staff, as well as for after-care.

Later on, experienced social workers began to be appointed as consultants to staffs of some residential institutions. Roles, functions and expertise became rather clearer as a result of therapeutic responsibilities, the professionalisation of residential social work, and the emergence of leading experts in this field. This gave more – though not enough – status to residential staff. The change from authoritarian régimes added enormously to staff stresses and made it crucial to support them by consultation, in-service training and involvement in the mainstream of the agency's work. Assessment before admission, preparation for admission, specific objectives for improvement in residents' social functioning, work with the family, and periodic reviews began to be practised and certainly received lip service. But there was continuing confusion about the respective roles and responsibilities of field and residential workers for residents and their families.

RESIDENTIAL CARE STAFF

Obviously to fulfil new and extremely demanding aims for residential care required changes in policy, higher staff ratios, and better trained staff with the desired attitudes, skill and considerable work satisfaction. This heightened problems of recruitment and incentives. Almost nothing was known about the numbers and staffing of different types of home until on the initiative of a few individuals the National Council of Social Service and the National Institute for Social Work Training (NISWT) raised funds to set up an unofficial committee, the Williams Committee, in 1962 to inquire into the recruitment, retention, training and field of work of staffs of residential accommodation. The Committee decided to limit its inquiry (published in 1967) to 'those institutions whose principal purpose is the provision of a home or social education for the many different groups in the community for whom this is required'. Unfortunately this ruled out three institutions – long-stay hospitals, prisons and common lodging houses – where the care function was most neglected. But the Committee, like most others, was limited by the practicable rather than the logical. Clearly, however, many of its findings applied generally. It set on foot the first comprehensive survey ever undertaken into the organisation and staffing of homes for old, or mentally or physically handicapped people, children and adolescents (including delinquents), and unmarried mothers and young children in need of accommodation. Information was gathered through this survey about more than 7,000 homes caring for over 250,000 people.

About half of all homes for old people were run by local authorities and catered for two-thirds of old people in residential care. The typical home had between 16 and 56 residents though some had over 250. Half the residents were 80 or over and women outnumbered men by 3:2. The ratio of full-time care staff to residents was 1:6, of whom 82 per cent were full-time and 65 per cent non-resident. A substantial majority of heads of voluntary homes were completely satisfied with the staff accommodation, but the majority was much smaller in local authority homes. There was a 25 per cent annual staff turnover. Over 80 per cent of the full-time care staff had no qualification other than experience. This was much higher in local authority than in voluntary homes. Most of the small percentage of trained staff were state registered nurses; only 2 per cent of all full-time staff had taken the fourteen-week course run by the National Old People's Welfare Council.

The survey showed a ratio of full-time care staff to residents of 1:4·1 in mother and baby homes, 1:4·3 in homes for physically handicapped people, and 1:6·3 in homes for the mentally handicapped. Over four-fifths of all staff were full-time, and between one-fifth and a quarter were non-resident (62 per cent in homes for physically handicapped adults). Ninety-seven per cent of the staff of mother and baby homes were single women, whereas over two-thirds of the staff of homes for mentally handicapped people were married. Over two-thirds of all full-time staff had no other qualification but experience. In mother and baby homes one-third of the staff were unqualified, of the remaining two-thirds 29 per cent had nursery nursing or residential child care qualifications and 65 per cent nursing qualifications. The average number of residents in mother and baby homes was 13. In homes for the mentally ill or retarded the average number was 19, and 40 in homes for physically handicapped adults. The figures for children's homes are summarised in volume 1, chapter 3, section on 'Residential Child Care in the 1960s'.

The Committee recognised that the work required much knowledge and skill, though they were criticised later for not analysing what was actually done by the staff and thus clarifying functions. They thought that the predilections of people for work with children, or old or physically handicapped people, or others might change in time so that residential care became one profession. This and subsequent developments are discussed below. Part of the staff discontent and frustration arose from a general failure to recognise the responsibilities of the work, while lack of recognised credentials lowered its status. The Committee members were

'. . . constantly struck by the amount of sheer goodness we have encountered – by the sympathy and humanity shown by so many in the approach to their jobs, despite difficult conditions, and by readiness to sacrifice their own leisure and interests. Naturally enough, there have been times when we have not fully endorsed the methods employed . . . but . . . we all became convinced . . . that the large majority give themselves to their work not only with devotion, but with respect for their fellow human beings who need their help; and . . . that the happiness and satisfaction they experience in their work, despite its restrictions and frustrations, stem from their belief that they are doing a job that is so obviously worth while.' (p. 17)

This impression of many residential staff (including nurses) was repeated in other field studies at various times.

In many homes poor accommodation and long working hours restricted the freedom and independence of the staff. Yet it was possible for a much higher proportion to be non-resident, and residence ought to become a matter of choice.

The Committee recommended that there should be frequent meetings of staffs of residential institutions within an area to discuss their common problems and work in general. Homes advisers should be appointed to act in an advisory and supportive capacity, to promote the interchange of ideas and experience, to provide an outlet for the feelings of junior and senior staff, and also to begin to build up an articulate body of knowledge and experience. These appointments became general within the framework of the reorganised social services after 1971. But there were complaints that the double role of adviser and service manager was ill-defined.

Jef Smith found in a survey for the Personal Social Services Council (PSSC, 1975) that poor accommodation still affected recruitment and not enough use was made of non-resident staff. It was thought that poor pay and unsocial hours discouraged recruitment, while staff turnover was related to the nature of the work, lack of support and a poor career structure. It was not clear whether support was best provided by 'professional care officers' able to discuss human and social problems, or by administrators expert in physical management. Both were needed but seldom available. Most support was aimed at heads and senior staff, with little in-service training for junior staff. The inadequate quality of the staff employed dominated all other problems, but all respondents to the survey were convinced that it was possible and urgent to alter the situation. A number of inquiries showed great satisfaction or much dissatisfaction in the work, but little attempt to discover what kind of people were at the two extremes or whether and why the transient dissatisfied sometimes became the settled satisfied.

Sometimes new homes could not open or numbers in others had to be reduced because of staff shortages. This was the reality against which the Birch Report (1976) concluded that to meet the daily living, social and therapeutic needs of residents, staff/resident ratios must be improved. This was essential because of

'. . . the need for staff meetings and other forms of consultation and training both in and outside the establishment; involvement of residential staff in work with the families of residents and in relationships with the community, the development of or participation in a range of activities to enrich the lives of residents or to promote their social and intellectual growth.' (6.12)

ALTERNATIVE ORGANISATIONAL PATTERNS FOR RESIDENTIAL INSTITUTIONS IN SOCIAL SERVICES DEPARTMENTS

In the social services departments responsible for an increasing range of residential institutions, there was usually an assistant director of residential care (sometimes including day care). Decisions about admission to residential care naturally became more complex than in small specialised departments where it was easier to achieve common standards by direct discussion. Billis (1973) described an action research model developed by the Social Services Organisation Research Unit of the Institute of Organisation and Social Studies at Brunel University. This was designed to ensure equal assessment standards between areas and the best use of resources. The project identified several decisions essential to a satisfactory residential placement:

(a) whether residential care was needed;
(b) whether the application was an emergency or there was time for better choice and adjustment;
(c) the most suitable residential milieu for the particular client.

Various patterns had evolved between the two extremes of area teams having full control of residential facilities in their areas through a homes liaison officer (a decentralised geographical pattern), or control resting with the headquarters assistant director of residential care (a functional pattern). There were inadequate contacts between field workers and homes on account of staff shortages, resistance amongst senior residential staff, and lack of understanding of some residents' need for social work, as well as of the importance of residential staffs becoming part of area teams.

GUIDELINES FOR THE FUTURE

A PSSC working party, set up to produce guidelines on principles and practices in residential homes for adults reported in 1975. In *Living and Working in Residential Homes* it defined residential care as 'the produce of two different responses to social problems; the creation of group-living to meet people's needs for suitable accommodation and possibly their social and emotional needs; and the provision of care' (p. 2). The aims should be therapeutic or nurturing the resident's ability to cope with the demands of daily living. The principles, based upon an agreed philosophy about the purposes of residential care, were that physical care is not enough, personal identity and independence must be actively maintained through a choice of alternatives, made possible by comprehensive and co-ordinated services; active resident participation; an environment that is better than the resident's previous situation; a regular, six-monthly review of progress;

a support system for residents and staff, including in-service training, discussion and consultation for the staff; and close relationships with the local community. These principles summarised enlightened views about residential care in the mid-1970s. They had become clear, slowly and in piecemeal fashion, throughout the preceding twenty-five years. Their translation into practice depended upon a better calibre of well-equipped and sufficient staff, support and management, action research and experimentation, and more resident and local community involvement. This also depended upon close co-ordination between residential and community services, upon adequate support services to keep people in the community as long as possible, sometimes with intermittent use of residential care, and wherever possible to return them to ordinary living as quickly as possible with adequate after-care. An inevitable consequence of keeping people out of residential care was that these institutions were being asked to provide constructive services for more and more difficult, damaged, frail, or handicapped people.

TRAINING FOR RESIDENTIAL CARE

PROBLEMS AND BLIND SPOTS IN THE 1950s

There was little interest in the residential task in the care or control of adults during the 1950s and 1960s compared with residential child care. Efforts were made by the Prison Commission to discover and provide the appropriate training for assistant prison governors (discussed below): and there were spasmodic efforts to persuade probation officers to become wardens of approved hostels at some point in their careers. This was an early – and abortive – attempt to recognise residential work as social work. For many years Josephine Butler Memorial College in Liverpool provided a training for the staff of mother and baby homes (see chapter 17) which was the same length as residential child care courses but – like them – attracted too few recruits. The National Old People's Welfare Council and the National Association for Mental Health made valiant attempts to provide in-service training courses, in management and personal care respectively, for matrons of old people's homes and staff of homes and hostels for mentally disordered people. There was no non-nursing training for the residential care of physically handicapped adults. The assumption was that senior staff of residential establishments for old, or handicapped, or disordered people should be nurses and the rest only needed to be kindly and competent people. The shortage of residential staff was bemoaned but the task itself was largely conceived as one of running an establishment that provided good physical care.

It was typical of prevailing attitudes that the Younghusband Report (1959), whose proposals revolutionised the training of field staff, was blind to the training needs of residential staffs and made no attempt to suggest suitable publicly sponsored training courses for them.

THE BREAKTHROUGH OF THE WILLIAMS REPORT

The move that finally brought training for this work within the mainstream of social work began in 1962 when the Williams Committee started work. Its main concern was training and its report was published in 1967 – over twenty years after the Curtis Committee (1946) had thought training for residential child care so urgent that it issued an interim report.

The Williams Committee concluded that residential care had distinctive characteristics which could make it a professional career in its own right. It recommended that comprehensive two-year courses should be accepted as the normal preparation for residential work. In the existing situation one-year courses should be run for work with the elderly and the physically and socially handicapped. Nurses wishing to undertake residential care should be expected to train for it. In-service training and staff development programmes should be stepped up and co-ordinated, including short courses for those undertaking wider or special responsibilities for particular aspects or new developments. There was also a need for a variety of advanced courses for all types of residential work, some at post-graduate or post-certificate level; courses for qualified and experienced staff should be provided by universities.

Two-year courses were desirable because they would give opportunity for the development of group methods in the residential setting at a higher level than was possible in one-year courses. They should have a common basis, with options in work with children and young people, the elderly, the physically handicapped of all ages, and the socially handicapped with special reference to mental disorder and social maladjustment.

The Report provoked much discussion. There was general agreement that training was both necessary and feasible for what was clearly a distinctive professional task, though it would not be possible to attract recruits of the necessary calibre unless their status, salaries, training and working conditions were substantially improved. In the meantime it was difficult to see how to alter the imbalance between supply and demand. There was fairly general agreement that the Committee had been unrealistic in thinking that all forms of residential care would become one profession providing a life-long career. An alternative was to provide courses in residential work and also to recognise the function as residential social work with emphasis on the dynamics of group living, and to start residential options in applied social studies courses to qualify students as both field and residential social workers. They could then work in either situation during their professional life. It was optimistically hoped that this would reverse the one-way movement from residential care to fieldwork.

THE COUNCIL FOR TRAINING IN SOCIAL WORK AND COURSES IN RESIDENTIAL SOCIAL WORK

Fortunately the CTSW had the structure, the staff and the necessary contacts, and in 1968 the Ministry of Health empowered it to promote and approve training courses for staff of residential homes in the health and welfare field. It was thought wisest to start with existing senior staff of old people's homes and hostels for adult mentally disordered people. Other experienced candidates were also eligible. Five one-year qualifying courses were started in colleges of further education which already had CSW courses and in 1970 twenty-two students qualified. After some discussion the plunge was taken to adopt the title 'residential social work' in the belief that residential work would not, as the Williams Report thought, develop as a separate profession. The next plunge came in 1969 when the first 'Williams' two-year course 'across the boundaries of age and handicap' was started at Enfield College of Technology (later the Middlesex Polytechnic). It was jointly recognised by the Central Training Council in Child Care (CTC) (with a child care option) and the CTSW. The syllabus had similarities with a social work course: it included group dynamics and group practice, and also courses on health and household management and an early attempt to formulate the principles and practice of residential social work. The separate national qualifications (CTC and CTSW) were the same as those for the one-year courses and recruitment was poor, nine students for the first course, six for the second, and no intake for the third, with the result that the course was discontinued. This may have been inevitable when it was competing with one-year courses. But some people thought that a two-year training was educationally far sounder and that for various reasons a generic course of this type never had a fair chance to develop, even alongside courses with options in fieldwork or residential work.

The one-year courses spread slowly on account of problems of recruitment and because there was hardly anyone competent to teach or to supervise students – the same problem that faced those trying to promote training for staffs of hostels for offenders. The necessary knowledge and skill had the two elements of relationships with residents, the community, staff and colleagues in the social services; and management, catering and physical care. On the first one-year courses there was also the question of specialised or generic training. By 1971 there were eight full-time qualifying courses only open to existing senior staff. Most of those who took them were from old people's homes.

In 1969 the CTSW also started to work out an in-service training scheme for residential staff, substantially on the same lines as the CTC scheme. 'Notes of Guidance' were prepared, related to the main objectives of the courses, designed to encourage students to think afresh about the essential purpose of residential care and to increase their understanding of the residents. By 1971 there were fifty-two such courses.

THE CCETSW AND TRAINING FOR RESIDENTIAL SOCIAL WORK

By the time the CCETSW came into existence there was thus a pattern of training for health and welfare as well as child care residential staff. There was also discussion, but almost no action for lack of candidates, about training of staffs of hostels for delinquents, deviants or homeless people.

The CCETSW soon amalgamated the child care and health and welfare groups in the preliminary and in-service study schemes. One of its first acts was also to set up a working party on training for residential work. This discussion document (1973*d*) recommended a single pattern of training for residential and field staff but made the controversial proposal of different qualifications for social work and welfare work. The term 'welfare' was still too much of a hot potato, but later the certificate in social service (CSS) was accepted as a qualification for many residential and other staff. The discussion document defined residential social work as 'a method of social work in which a team of workers operates together with a group of residents to create a living environment designed to enhance the functioning of individual residents in the context of their total environment' (p. 15). Its suggested training objectives were that all staff with a social work function should hold the CQSW in a ratio of one to every two other staff. On the basis of existing staffing this added up to about 21,600 CQSW holders – 3,200 a year over a ten-year period, about the same as the number of field workers. This was a formidable task indeed when in addition to children, old people and the handicapped, residential institutions included prisons and borstals, probation and after-care hostels, other hostels of various kinds, family rehabilitation units, temporary accommodation and other residential situations. Some people still thought that residential care was different from social work with its own distinctive body of knowledge and skills.

The discussion document sparked off considerable response before the working party issued its final report. The CCETSW accepted its recommendation that training for residential work should be of the same length and standard as fieldwork within a single pattern of training, leading to a common qualification; and that there should be more than one type of qualification for both field and residential work (1973*b*, p. 9). There should be some teaching about residential social work in all courses and the possibility of a residential option in some.

This bold pattern of training for residential social work (and for another level which later became the CSS) was accepted. Following the Council's decision, integrated field and residential courses were promoted; this necessitated a thorough reappraisal of training for social work in order to clarify common elements in different settings. Nagging fears about poor recruitment persisted and the risk that combined courses would lead to an even greater fall in numbers of residential workers. Table 3 shows the few recruits to residential social work who qualified in 1975.

Table 3   *Students completing various courses in 1975*

Certificate of qualification in social work	3,123
Certificate in residential social work	104
Senior certificate in residential care of children and young people	34
Certificate in the residential care of children and young people	518
Preliminary certificate in residential care	797

Source: CCETSW (1976a), *Bulletin 4, Social Work Education News and Views* (CCETSW), pp. 18–19.

DEVELOPMENTS IN TRAINING WITHIN THE PENAL SYSTEM

Staffs of Hostels for Offenders

The training of wardens and assistant wardens for hostels for offenders was an almost insoluble problem. The service was small, the hostels scattered and the prospect of advancement non-existent; yet the job itself was immensely difficult and demanding, with little support. The Home Office was conscious of the need for training but in the circumstances pre-service training would have been unrealistic and, so far as training of existing staff was concerned, the problem was how to bring enough people together in any one place at any one time for a long-enough period or at regular-enough intervals to enable any worthwhile training to be given. Some of the problems were much the same as those for staffs of psychiatric after-care hostels from the early 1960s. But these were under different statutory or voluntary auspices, the responsibility of a different government department, and although their clientele had similarities the twain did not meet.

Even by the late 1960s there were few professional social workers or social work educators well informed about the realities of hostel life with offenders or the inadequacies and urgencies of the existing situation. A report by the National Association for the Care and Resettlement of Offenders (NACRO) working party on training and after-care of hostel staffs (1968) 'shared the professional assumptions and attitudes of the Williams report' and was reluctant to think in terms of stopgap emergency courses which might prevent more fundamental solutions. The members saw little value in short introductory courses which allowed insufficient time for first-hand experience or the development of appropriate attitudes, insight and self-awareness. They argued that sustained in-service training should be given to the best existing field staff in order to create a nucleus of people able to conduct in-service training on part-time courses. Courses should be experimental and evaluated so as to provide more effective training in future. The most practicable possibility was day release courses (a day a week for a year) for several types of residential workers with a good balance of theory and practice based on lectures and discussions followed by small group sessions on practical problems. They should concentrate on the common features of a wide range of hostel situations. In view of current ignorance about the specialised facilities needed for specific types of people it was premature to consider sophisticated training.

It was essential to look at training in relation to recruitment, working conditions, salary structure and career prospects. It was undesirable and impracticable to train people solely for hostel work. Movement should be facilitated between various forms of residential care and probation. The development of a comprehensive system of training must be a combined exercise and buttressed by continuous support and consultation for hostel staffs. The latter would probably do more than anything else to raise standards, lessen stress on staff and improve the staffing situation. It was an essential reinforcement to training.

A Home Office paper for the Advisory Council for Probation and After-Care (ACPAC) (1968b) suggested that introductory courses should include: the practicalities of housekeeping; normal human growth and development;

the personalities and behaviour of offenders generally; special problem cases; the penal system, the effects of penal institutions on offenders; the dynamics of group living; social aspects of hostels as small transitional communities; the community and the social services, how these can be used in the resettlement of offenders.

By 1975 the training programme organised by NACRO and financed by the Home Office covered staff working in after-care hostels, probation homes and hostels, projects for alcoholics and drug dependents, and other residential facilities for homeless people. The programme included local seminar groups, a variety of residential project courses, a sandwich course in counselling; and an introductory training course for new entrants consisting of three months, full-time, followed by short residential courses during the next nine months. Staff were also encouraged by NACRO to take the CCETSW in-service study courses and the new CSS.

Assistant Borstal and Prison Governors
From 1954 it was possible to enter the assistant governor grade either by promotion within the service or direct from outside. Promoted prison officers had a six-month training. In 1957 it was decided that all new recruits, who included graduates and others with university or professional backgrounds, should be trained. Initially this was a six-month residential course at the Prison Service Staff College, with a syllabus that included short courses on psychology, sociology and criminology, as well as training in the technical and practical skills necessary to the work, and attachments to penal institutions.

From time to time a few assistant governors were seconded to take a psychiatric social work course and in 1957 two took the LSE applied social studies course, and one the Tavistock Institute advanced course in casework. Apparently the Prison Commission (as it was then) decided that casework was a suitable training for assistant governors and the seconded staff were intended on their return to train others. In the event, this plan was not developed as originally intended and was superseded. There were about 100 assistant governors at that time, most of whom were in borstals.

By degrees there was greater emphasis on a 'social casework orientation' in the Staff College course, and related theoretical subjects such as human growth and development were included in the syllabus. The ACTO report on *The Organisation of After-Care* (1963) recommended that assistant governors should have a

'. . . longer grounding in casework methods (including group work), taught by experienced social workers; a widened practical knowledge of social and behavioural problems affecting young delinquents and of the relevant social services in the community; and spells of practical experience not only in penal institutions but in probation and other community agencies.' (para. 94)

This supported the trend towards a social casework basis for training.

In 1963 a senior lecturer was seconded from Leeds University to the Staff College as adviser on studies to the college principal; and the college structure was altered to make possible a concentration on social studies, particularly in the training of assistant governors. The residential course was extended to eight months in 1965 and some casework practice was undertaken in nearby penal establishments and probation offices. During this developmental period the possibility of seconding all entrants with the necessary qualifications to take university casework courses was considered. But the main training continued to be undertaken by the Staff College.

In 1966 escapes from a maximum security prison led to the Mountbatten Inquiry which increased emphasis on security. The programme for assistant governor training was not curtailed or immediately altered in content, but there was more concentration on the training needs of prison rather than borstal assistant governors. Until 1971 these changes were made within the eight-month residential training pattern but by then it seemed necessary to review the whole situation. This resulted in a job-related training for all assistant governors, based on job analyses and using a modular pattern of sandwich training over two years.

From 1971 the two-year course began with a three-month introductory programme, which differed for promoted prison officers and direct entrants. For the latter it consisted of a two-week prison officer training course and a period of supervised practice as a uniformed officer in a local prison. The remaining nine months of the first year included ten-week courses at the College followed by seven months' supervised practice in the field. The College programme comprised seven modules lasting from three days to two weeks. Each module was a cluster of assistant-governor tasks (for example, maintenance of good order; resettlement and parole); with theoretical teaching provided by Leeds University and Manchester Business School and technical training by the College tutors. Each module began in the College and continued through supervised practice in the field in order to emphasise the relevance of theory to practice. During the two years, students were also attached to their local probation and after-care service for thirty-six working days under the supervision of individual probation officers. They also spent ten days in a psychiatric hospital under the supervision of a senior nursing officer to study the organisation of treatment in an institution and the community.

If the objection is made that a separate Prison Staff College was an anachronism, cut off from the main stream of social work or other experiments in field teaching and theoretical studies, it must yet be accepted that prisons themselves were still isolated. Much thought had gone into restructuring this training over the years and valiant efforts were made to use professional training in casework, though this would have been only partially relevant for assistant governors, who needed more comparative study of 'total' and other custodial or treatment institutions; group dynamics; staff/inmate relationships; objectives and problems of achieving these factors in success or failure; relations with the outside world, including the family and the social milieu; alternatives to custody; and the institution in relation to prevention, diagnosis, rehabilitation and after-care. This is not to deny the importance of understanding individuals, the ability to gain their confidence and to play an appropriate role with other staff in bringing about attitude changes, whether amongst staff or inmates. Ultimately perhaps the need may be met within the framework of CCETSW professional qualifications in residential social work.

Chapter 14

Social Work and Hostels for Special Groups

INTRODUCTION AND SOME CONCLUSIONS

Hostels for people able to work but needing special help for a period in order to live independently developed slowly during the period and with a number of false starts. They catered for some extremely damaged, aggressive or withdrawn, dependent, hostile and disturbed or delinquent people, and although their potentialities as a sheltered entry to ordinary life were recognised, these potentialities were only realised in individual instances. More was written about hostels for offenders than those for young people in care or for ex-psychiatric patients; while unfortunately these accounts were full of gaps and usually not comparable. None the less a common pattern ran through them, a pattern of régimes that were sometimes too restricting or too unstructured, with ill-defined aims, unsuitable premises and overwhelming demands on the staff. Staffing was naturally the key issue. Everything depended upon the warden, but often the staff/resident ratio was insufficient, there was a heavy staff turnover, assistant staff were young, inexperienced and untrained, staff accommodation was poor and added to stress, while in most instances there was too little support for the staff from the service concerned. In any event, many residents were far too disturbed to be effectively helped with the resources available. What was clearly indicated – though not undertaken – was a major research-orientated inquiry into the separate and unrelated provision of an essentially similar service, in order to identify its strengths, how these could be reinforced, and the weaknesses eliminated or reduced.

HOSTELS FOR YOUNG PEOPLE IN CARE

The 1948 Children Act empowered children's departments to provide hostels for young people in care, and a number did so. There was no comprehensive survey of these hostels, until the DHSS social work service undertook one in 1971 (*Hostels for Young People*, 1975d). At that time there were 200 hostels in England and Wales. They catered for young people experiencing pressing adolescent problems owing to personal and family stresses, especially those from unsatisfactory homes or who would not fit into lodgings; and for disturbed young people who might otherwise be in community homes with education on the premises (the successor euphemism for 'approved' schools).

The study showed that a number of local authorities had no hostels, and voluntary organisations had been responsible for a large proportion of the total. There had been very few local objections to hostels being started, and more than half had good relations with their neighbours.

Most of the residents were under 18 and had come from foster homes or community homes. They stayed for a year or two at most, though usually for a shorter time. They had little real choice of whether or not they went to a hostel because there was often no alternative. The hostels catered for boys and girls in employment, though some were in full-time education. They generally accepted and tried to help young people with considerable behaviour problems, some with a family history of mental illness, and many with destructive and aggressive behaviour. Hostels seldom asked for anyone to be removed, yet 'the problems they presented were so serious as to question whether their needs had ever been adequately assessed or realistic consideration given to the resources necessary to provide for their needs in the hostels' (p. 14). Most residents when they left went home, into lodgings or a flat, to relatives or friends, to residential employment or the services, or via the courts to what was referred to as 'a more structured environment'.

A number of hostels had married couples in charge as warden and matron, though seven of the girls' hostels were wholly staffed by single women. There were too few staff posts for work with difficult adolescents and many posts were vacant. There was also a high staff turnover, many assistants were inexperienced and untrained and could not be left in charge if the warden and his wife went out. The staff saw their task as helping residents to develop and lead a normal life in the community and to understand themselves and their backgrounds better. This included 'providing a substitute home, [a] secure environment and supportive or caring atmosphere, and thereby trying to encourage personal development, maturation, stability, self control, confidence, standards and a sense of values' (p. 21). More than half the staff expressed job satisfaction but there was also considerable uncertainty and frustration. They obviously needed the support, reassurance and help which many received from their headquarters. Closely linked with these difficulties were inadequacies in staff accommodation. Many were satisfied with their accommodation, but there were complaints of lack of privacy, noise, and the need for self-contained separate accommodation. More staff than formerly were taking in-service training courses.

Hostel régimes varied from flexible and informal to paternalistic and authoritarian. Only a minority of hostels involved residents in day-to-day decision making and some residents were very resentful of the failure to consult them about matters of daily living. Rules might be unknown to the residents and apparently arbitrary. Only four out of the fifty-four hostels studied had some form of group work. Residents were interviewed at a number of hostels. They were very dissatisfied in a small minority of hostels where there was no resident participation or consultation. Many thought there was too little privacy or opportunity to talk with friends and visitors.

Hostels were part of complex services and could not perform their task in isolation from a professional and administrative network, including the field staff responsible for individual boys and girls and contacts with their families. Decisions and treatment plans were usually made jointly between the field and residential staffs. There were often considerable efforts to maintain and strengthen family contacts. Unfortunately, there was little continuity of relationship owing to frequent changes of field and hostel staffs. The hostel domestic staff was much more stable but the survey did not explore the importance of this for the residents.

In 1964 a Home Office Children's Department internal working party had recommended that pre-release hostels should be established experimentally at a few approved schools. By 1971 there were twenty-five for girls and nine for boys linked to the renamed community home with education on the premises. Staff were shared to some extent and boys and girls knew them and the hostel well before they went there. These staffs were 'genuinely enthusiastic' about their work: there were always professional colleagues nearby for consultation and support, medical and psychiatric services were shared, the staffing situation was relatively stable, and a higher proportion were qualified than in other hostels.

On the whole, staff had a clear motivation for their work and, in spite of the difficulties, experienced considerable satisfaction and sense of achievement. They recognised that these disturbed and damaged young people were at a particularly vulnerable period in their lives and needed help to become self-supporting and establish responsible relationships, particularly with the opposite sex, and to learn to adjust to the community at large. 'But . . . in most cases the task was greater, particularly in terms of staff and buildings, than the resources provided to meet it' (p. 60). There were far too few staff posts, many staff were working very long hours, there was a need both to recruit and to retain many more trained staff. In many hostels staff 'suffered living conditions likely to tax their equanimity and lead to unnecessary tension and friction' (p. 60). For the residents too 'in many cases the buildings presented severe constraints to the achievement of their maturation, independence and socialization which were the objectives of the hostels' (pp. 60–1). This included 'the need to have a place to be alone, even to learn to be able to be alone' (p. 61), an essential experience for 'a group of human beings who by definition find personal relations difficult' (p. 61), and a means whereby much explosive behaviour might be avoided. To have to share living arrangements day and night stretched self-control to breaking point, whereas 'single bed sitting rooms could make a major contribution to the development of work in hostels' (p. 61).

This study cast some light on hostels as they had probably been for some time. Unfortunately, there was no detailed study of residents and their views or any follow up of their subsequent life histories. The impression was that the hostels were making good and necessary provision for many young people, though there was no actual evidence of this, nor of the proportion of fairly ordinary to very difficult young people. Nor was there evidence of continuous and comprehensive professional assessment and treatment, especially for the most difficult young people who needed much closer and more skilled help than overburdened, untrained staff could give them.

HOSTELS FOR PSYCHIATRIC PATIENTS

The 1959 Mental Health Act faced local health authorities with the problem of having to start residential provision from scratch in a largely unexplored field and with a good deal of local resistance. There were fears that the hostels might simply become chronic wards in the community, and, as can happen with a new service, some of the first hostels had difficulty in filling their beds (Apte, 1970).

The ratio of staff to residents in hostels for mentally disordered people slowly improved and more hostels were started by local authorities, mental hospitals and voluntary organisations. But the aim of a short stay and quick discharge was not being realised. They were designed 'to provide an ex-hospital patient with a sheltered setting that will both enlarge his opportunity for remaining out of hospital through a graduated encounter with the community and increase his capacity for more self-sufficient and independent living' (Apte, p. 9). It clearly required considerable skill to provide a widely graduated experience for a group of recovering ex-psychiatric patients. The Royal Commission on the Law relating to Mental Illness and Mental Deficiency (1957) thought someone trained in mental nursing would be 'the ideal person to take charge of such a home'. Indeed there was no other relevant qualification at that time.

In 1963 Apte, an American PSW, studied a number of psychiatric hostels. He traced 43 in England and Wales, 26 operated by local authorities, 11 by voluntary organisations, and 6 by hospitals. Two-thirds of the residents were admitted from mental hospitals, the rest had been living alone, with relations or friends, or elsewhere. Some hostels were intended to give long-term care to rootless people or those whose parents had grown old or died. Others were finding that a time-limited service was often unrealistic since there were large numbers of unattached people in the hostels who needed long-term support. They had an average of eighteen residents and three staff. Chief mental welfare officers were responsible for the supervision of most local authority hostels and wardens, and patients were usually referred for admission through mental welfare officers. Ten out of twenty-five wardens were mental nurses, but eleven had no relevant training. Eighty per cent had had many years experience in hospitals and tended to reproduce an institutional régime. Many had stereotyped and institutional attitudes towards the residents. They thought that the hostel was intended to provide a normal home environment and would not tolerate 'sick behaviour'. Recruitment was a considerable problem and there was a high staff turnover. Salaries were low, hours long, and there was a lack of privacy. The ratio of staff to residents varied from 1 : 4 to 1 : 33.

Many institutionalised and apathetic residents needed to be actively revitalised and given fresh motivation, but few wardens were aware of their own potential influence in this. In two voluntary hostels, wardens with relevant experience were giving individual psychotherapy. In four other hostels the wardens were willing to discuss emotional and social problems with residents. Only four hostels fostered resident participation or self-government and only two regularly ran therapeutic groups: these were led by psychotherapists who encouraged patients to express their feelings and discuss the running of the hostel. Few hostels had any recreational activities but a few residents from some hostels went to social therapeutic clubs.

Because skilled social work help was not available to see residents over a stressful period of moving out on their own, the hostels were forced to keep on many who were able to leave. The resident's clinical contribution was the key variable in his return to health or his continued dependency, but administrative practices and the reciprocal relationship between the resident and social environmental factors tipped the scales for many. Custodial and authoritarian régimes kept residents dependent and did little to change their badly damaged self-image, whereas permissive régimes induced beneficial psychological change and were significantly more successful in returning people to the community. There was some degree of psychiatric and social work support for the wardens in about half the hostels (only eight hostels had PSW help) and there was a significant relationship between this and the number of residents returned to the community.

The effectiveness of the hostels was limited by a failure to recognise the amount of planning and professional resources they needed, when the task demanded sophisticated understanding of individual and group dynamics as well as technical skills. But there was no suitable training. Wardens had inordinate demands made upon them and had not been equipped to accomplish rehabilitative tasks with residents who were often suffering from long-standing emotional difficulties and acute anxieties. Much more knowledge was needed (including comparative studies) about the right kind of transitional environment for different people. The low bed occupancy in many hostels was partly due to a failure to plan in co-operation with local mental hospitals, which led to tensions on both sides.

As in other studies of the period, residents' views were not sought. But staff weaknesses, dissatisfaction and lack of professional support were common in studies of residential care. There was the same aim of creating 'a homelike atmosphere' as in hostels for ex-offenders, but a failure to analyse or provide for the complexities of the rehabilitation and resettlement task, including the sudden or graduated transition from institutional to hostel conditions. In contrast with the rapid turnover of residents in hostels for offenders, ex-psychiatric patients tended to remain dependent and stay too long.

Julia (1967) described a hostel with regular group meetings between staff, residents and a social worker. Many residents moved out into local lodgings but continued to receive hostel and casework support. She concluded that the régime of such hostels should provide 'conditions in which the patient can "test out", in an atmosphere of acceptance and understanding, his difficulties in relating to others, learning new and more constructive ways of relating, learning to cope with demands of reality and . . . building up his confidence and sense of independence' (p. 68). Richmond Fellowship hostels were started in 1959 through one person's initiative and by 1974 there were twenty-four hostels for people suffering from emotional and social breakdown. Jansen (1973) found from experience that the staff needed training, which included knowledge of developmental and social psychology, psychiatry, discussion of their own casework and group work problems, experience in and understanding of group dynamics and practical aspects of the work.

The local authority ten year plan (Ministry of Health, 1963) envisaged 16,000 places in hostels, i.e. 0·3 of the population, by 1972 against 0·323 in 1962. In the second plan (1966) 42 per cent of local authorities actually cut down on their projected places. This was partly because hospitals had not used the hostels as much as had been expected. Far more than the then existing provision was also needed for the severely subnormal.

HOSTELS FOR THOSE BEFORE THE COURTS

Hostels Run by Voluntary Organisations

Approved hostels for boys and girls, run by voluntary organisations with Home Office grants, had a long and partially successful history when the right warden could be found.

The first Norman House was opened in 1954 to provide a home for homeless adult recidivists. It was based on the assumption that 'going straight' only had meaning as a consequence of attachment to people. 'The . . . social isolation that characterises homeless recidivists makes nonsense of acceptable living because there is none to support and approve of it' (Turner, 1961, p. 7). Norman House was most successful with inadequate men who had experienced a succession of social failures but could respond in sympathetic, highly supportive living conditions.

In the Norman House type of hostel the staff lived entirely with the residents in a close family group with the aim of unfreezing isolated people. Only exceptional married couples could stand the strain of this way of life. Northways for ex-borstal boys described by Derek Miller (1964) was the outstanding example of a hostel with considerable psychiatric support for both residents and staff, designed to develop insight.

When responsibility for prison after-care was transferred from discharged prisoners' aid societies to the probation service a number of these societies and others turned their attention to the provision of hostel or other residential accommodation, for example the Margery Fry Foundation, the St Leonards Housing Association and the Simon Community. The Reading Committee in two Reports (1963 and 1967) which gave a fresh direction to thought and action urged that a range of hostels should be provided for homeless offenders both for after-care and as a possible alternative to prison. These should include multi-purpose hostels at the disposal of local probation and after-care services; 'bed-sitter' type hostels; specialised hostels for alcoholics, for the work shy and for elderly institutionalised offenders. The Carnegie Trust immediately advanced funds for voluntary organisations to set up five such experimental hostels and a Trust was created for the purpose. The bed-sitter, multi-purpose and aged-offender hostels all gained useful experience. The hostel for the work shy never got started after months of delay owing to the strength of local opposition – as contrasted with the multi-purpose hostel which was accepted elsewhere by local residents in a comfortable middle-class area. An experienced investigator (Rolph, 1970) thought they were

'. . . examples of what can be done to make a hostel comfortable, welcoming, socially demanding, and (within obvious limits) homelike. They happen to have found suitable premises, which is important: but they have also found suitable wardens and staff, which is absolutely vital. And there is not the smallest doubt that in these hostels, as indeed in most hostels, there are men who would otherwise be in prison.' (p. 32)

Rathcoole House for alcoholic men was interesting because of its wider implications. It had a slow start, because it aimed to foster self-help largely by means of a weekly group meeting with a visiting psychiatrist and the warden. Later an Alcoholics Anonymous group was formed and in time residents decided that there should be no fixed length of stay but anyone who drank at all should be asked to leave. A second house was opened in 1967 and then a third. By degrees all decisions were made at the weekly house meeting and Rathcoole House was run by a non-residential social worker (Home Office, 1971*a*).

Homeless women were not studied separately until a small group in the 1960s, mainly of alcoholics who went the rounds of prison, common lodging houses or sleeping rough. They were in poor physical and psychiatric health, with erratic employment and few stable relationships. In a residential project for them started by Christian Action in the late 1960s (Brandon, n.d.), it was found that they suffered from severe sleeping difficulties, depression, general tenseness and various physical problems which required both medical and social work help. They all came from large families and had suffered from failing health, loss of children, imprisonment. In this project the trend was away from short-term stay to better social diagnosis and individual treatment. There were no age limits and the residents could stay for indefinite periods. Attendance at the house meetings was compulsory since each resident was encouraged to speak her mind about her personal problems and house difficulties, as well as making the community rules. Illicit drugs and alcohol were prohibited. Some women had violent and self-destructive tendencies which could only be contained by some outlet for their anger and hate.

By 1966 the Home Office was giving grants to many voluntary after-care hostels and the following year a rapid survey of twenty-four of these was undertaken by the Research Unit (Silberman *et al.*, 1971). Its purpose was to clarify what the hostels were trying to do, how they were doing it, what were the roles of those who controlled them, what were their tasks and what problems they faced. Most wardens aimed to give residents 'a firm sense of belonging', a breathing space, and possibly a long-term stay in the difficult period after release from prison.

The hostels' standard of physical comfort varied from reasonable to good. Seventy-five per cent of the residents left within three months, but the proportion who stayed for more than six months varied from 6 per cent to 28 per cent in different hostels. Thus for the vast majority of residents the hostels were half-way houses, but little was known about the accommodation to which they went, what happened to them, or their way of life. Young homeless offenders were far more likely to be reconvicted than older ones. There was a high chance of reconviction in the first three months after release.

There were some doubts about the value of these small hostels run on a family model for a varied range of offenders. 'No one can fully understand the emotions which the quasi-family situation of a hostel may arouse in a disturbed person, nor what feelings of guilt or regret he is likely to have when he leaves it' (ibid., p. 78). The hostels did not succeed in providing a satisfactory substitute for home or in meeting whatever were the causes of homelessness. If wardens could not cope with the problems of running hostels they either became too authoritarian or permissive, in what were usually emotionally exhausting situations. 'To a large extent the problem may be not that of getting wardens with better personalities but of enabling wardens to make better use of their personalities' (p. 88). The hostel residents and staff each appeared to lead isolated lives and there was almost none of the support from committee members and close integration with the local community envisaged in the Reading Report.

Salaries were low, hours were long and sometimes wardens without a responsible deputy could not take all their annual leave. Only five out of twenty-four hostels had a pension scheme. Wardens had almost no opportunities for training or even for discussions with other hostel wardens. Eighty-two per cent of the wardens had no training of any kind and their previous experience varied enormously. They were all having to undertake an extremely difficult and demanding job almost without support, which, as the Williams Report (1967) commented, was fair neither to them nor the residents. There was a very high staff turnover because most people could not stand the strain for long.

The weaknesses of this situation were not compensated for by the strengths because the hostels were too scattered to make an adequate consultation and support system possible; wardens had little relief; and on account of the difficulty of finding a temporary replacement, it was almost impossible to second someone to take the CTC one-year residential child care course on work with difficult adolescents. Training was thus limited to short two-week courses or *ad hoc* local provision. Even to combine this with the training of probation and after-care hostel staffs would have made little difference in what was essentially a scattered cottage industry. Yet – as in other residential work – provision of outside support for hostel staff was 'absolutely essential'. This included the management committee, the local community and outside specialists and professionals, for example consultation from social workers and psychiatrists.

In 1967 the Home Office set up eight regional consultative committees to advise the voluntary movement about the provision of additional after-care hostels. It also started the Bridgehead Housing Association to acquire suitable houses for hostels and turn them over to voluntary organisations to administer, but there was no systematic body of knowledge and experience about running such hostels. One of the regional committees commented that it 'could see no real progress being made . . . until proper training and prospects of a career are made available to hostel staffs'. Thus it echoed what had been fruitlessly said in various circumstances over a number of years.

The NACRO report (1968) on the training of after-care hostel staffs found the existing situation 'almost completely unsatisfactory'. Many of those responsible for hostels were not at all convinced of the need to train hostel staff, whether any training was necessary, and if so, how much, what kind and what content. There were different views about the value of knowledge and skill versus character and personality, coupled with a lack of clarity about the objectives and régime for different types of hostel. The result was that different objectives were being pursued in the same situation, with attempts to cater for the needs of a mixed clientele at different levels and in different ways. This had resulted in the policy of development of multi-purpose hostels as a basis for future diversification.

By the end of 1969 there were 73 hostels with accommodation for 793 residents, and by 1972 about 150 hostels with 1,500 places. These included provision for alcoholics, drug addicts, very disturbed young offenders, insti-tutionalised elderly men, and those who needed employment in a hostel with a sheltered workshop.

Probation Homes and Hostels
Sinclair's Home Office Research Unit study (1971) of boys' probation hostels carried out between 1965 and 1967 showed wide variations in absconding and further offence rates. These differences were not explained by selection, the liaison probation officer, the policy of the court, or other social factors. But they were highly correlated with the personality of the warden, which seemed to determine both the number and type of boys who failed. Under some wardens older boys were more likely to fail and under others younger boys. Some wardens took back few absconders and most failed: others took back more and succeeded. Successful régimes had a common pattern in which the discipline was strict and consistent, but the warden showed warmth and understanding of the boys' problems and was well supported by his wife. These findings seemed to show that delinquent behaviour in institutions is a product both of the institution, the residents and the kind of relation-ships created in them, and that treatment aimed at changing the individual rather than his environment is not likely to have much success. The findings also clarified the problems of very small residential institutions which depended essentially on one man, when individual wardens and particular boys may or may not get on with each other.

The Advisory Council on the Treatment of Offenders (ACTO) report on *Non-Custodial and Semi-Custodial Penalties* (1970) was clear about the need for further experiments in the use of hostels for adult offenders in addition to the recently expanded programme of hostels for adolescents – many of which would in future be provided by local authorities under the Children and Young Persons Act, 1969. Many adolescents were, in any event, quite unsuitable for hostel life, while some immature and inadequate offenders in their twenties could probably be successfully contained in hostels.

The first four probation hostels for men who would otherwise have gone to prison were opened in 1970. They demonstrated that some inadequate, immature and socially irresponsible men could be helped to adjust to living in the community in the stable, supportive environment of a hostel. The courts were willing to make probation orders with requirements of residence in hostels even for men who had a substantial number of previous convictions and had run the gamut of institutional treatment including several prison sentences. Substantial expansion of probation hostels for adults aimed to provide 110 hostels with 1,650 places. It was thought necessary to involve the probation service more closely in the new hostels. The Criminal Justice Act, 1972 enabled probation and after-care committees to set up and run such hostels; forty-seven committees were doing so by 1975 and the probation service was involved in the new hostels, which it was hoped would provide closer support. Some men who were usually given short prison sentences were so institutionalised or inadequate as to need sheltered work at least for a time, and the probation home concept, which included work training on the premises, began to be extended experimentally to adult offenders. Probation officers were beginning to spend a period as hostel wardens on senior probation officer salaries.

Martin Davies (1974) expressed a sharply contrasting view that

'Life in a sheltered hostel can . . . subject the resident to additional stresses and render him more liable to breakdown . . . because of the proximity of support/control agents, [this] suggests that . . . rationally designed systems of accommodation . . . may be less successful . . . than . . . the more normal absorption of the ex-prisoner into the society whence he came . . . Part of the answer may be far more general provision of flatlets and bed-sitters . . . "All I want is a room somewhere" may well be an appropriate comment for the ex-prisoner, with the emphasis on *all*: no social worker, no warden, no artificial family atmosphere, no rules and regulations, no therapeutic group techniques, no segregation from ordinary people, and no subjection to further institutionalisation at the very time when the ex-prisoner is expected to rediscover his independent role in society.' (p. 103)

The second Reading Report (1967) spoke of 'the pressing need for research even at the simplest descriptive levels – who can do what for whom, and what happens to the fall out and those who refuse help?' (para. 144). But there was no long-term research into the effect of different types of hostel régime for different offenders.

The Younger Report (1974) placed much faith in hostels, flatlets and lodgings as part of non-custodial control for young offenders, though it did not examine the known complexities. A selected private landladies scheme, with close social work support, began to develop and by 1972 the Home Office was grant-aiding social workers' salaries in five such schemes.

The bail hostel experiment began in London in 1971. It did not confirm the general impression that many men were being remanded in custody who could be released on bail if hostel accommodation were available, but this might have been due to restrictive criteria for admission. A limited expansion of the experiment was therefore decided upon and the courts made full use of hostels with less restrictive conditions.

PART THREE   PEOPLE WITH SPECIAL PROBLEMS

Chapter 15

Social Work and Groups with Special Problems

INTRODUCTION

Two groups of people more vulnerable than most emerged into prominence from the 1950s. They were ethnic minority groups and the homeless. This chapter also includes multiproblem families who by definition needed social work help. Drug addiction and alcoholism were also increasing problems at different points in the period.

ETHNIC MINORITY GROUPS

Immigrants of different races, religions, languages and customs from the new commonwealth only came to this country in large numbers from the 1950s. Their arrival resulted once again in the rejection of an alien body and the prejudices and problems of assimilation which accompany immigration and have to be faced on both sides. For the host country it meant accepting as equal fellow citizens people of other races, who in turn faced difficult problems of gaining acceptance, of accommodating to life in an unfamiliar culture and climate, of trying to integrate or learn to live comfortably in two cultures. There were many problems of racial prejudice and discrimination in housing, employment, schools, higher education, career opportunities, relations between the sexes and acceptance in clubs and pubs. Better relations were made difficult on both sides by barriers of language and misunderstandings caused by different cultural assumptions, especially about husband and wife obligations and child-rearing practices. Authoritarian values clashed with those of an increasingly permissive society which was unclear about its own values or sense of direction but frequently unwilling to think that other ways of living were as good as its own or to accept cultural pluralism.

A common pattern before severe restriction on immigration was for the father to come first, establish himself and save up enough to bring over his wife and children. Some of the worst problems arose when children, brought over after years of separation, might feel outsiders and not even recognise their parents, be expected to fit in easily, sometimes be rejected when they caused conflicts and jealousies in the family; and even be brought before the juvenile court if they failed to adapt. These were some of the most difficult situations that faced probation officers and others. Such young people did not belong, were not accepted anywhere, and might become rootless drifters unless family tensions could be lessened or they could be helped through adolescence into independence. It was more usual for a number of family members to arrive within a comparatively short time and go to areas of immigrant settlement where members of extended families or people from the same villages or islands were close enough to form support networks, which lessened their demands on social work help in crises. None the less many new immigrants were subject to stress and crises in which social work help with cultural understanding might be needed, though often not available. Most newcomers had shown by their initiative and effort in migration that they were competent people able to cope given initial help and a fair chance. Large numbers were unfortunately forced to congregate in inner-city areas in overcrowded conditions, often working long hours for low wages or else unemployed.

It was a social work task – not necessarily fulfilled – to become familiar with the stages of adaptation, some of the crisis points of initial strangeness and homesick reactions, the anxieties, loneliness, change in roles, disillusionment and fears of rejection, the different customs, the pressure to conform too soon, the separation from all that was familiar which immigrant families faced. These were essentially transplant reactions. But unless they were lived through and newcomers were accepted here they could degenerate into hostility and chronic difficulties on both sides.

Ideally it was part of the social work task to try to bridge these gaps: to learn how to communicate with immigrant families; to offer them warmth, kindness and understanding, and to demonstrate this by the ability to give practical help and advice; to discover how to lessen ambivalence and tensions on both sides by interpreting different cultures to each other; to create situations of give and take, for example those that brought Asian women out of their isolation; and in every social work situation with non-European clients to contribute the necessary extra dimension of knowledge and understanding about their ways of life. This included taking part in the many organised efforts at mutual understanding undertaken by community relations councils, the churches, community centres and clubs, schools, and many others. Group and community workers in particular required – though they frequently did not have – a sound understanding of the sociology of racial prejudice, acceptance that different cultural values might be as good as their own, and knowledge of how to lessen local hostility and rejection. These extra demands were particularly pressing in poor urban areas, where there might well be constant tensions between non-Europeans and local people, and where social workers, like others, were criticised either for extra efforts to help with minority groups' serious personal and emotional problems or for ignoring special needs.

Unfortunately, throughout the period there were far too few social workers from the same backgrounds or with sufficient knowledge of different cultures and languages. Thus many social workers had little information, understanding or awareness of the real situation and what action might be appropriate. Some suffered from racial prejudice or did not realise that it was essential to understand and respect other cultural values. The Community Relations Commission (CRC) issued a training handbook for social services departments (1976*b*) which argued strongly for some special training for social workers in multiracial areas, both in initial and in-service courses.

It was important to understand in what ways non-Europeans differed from local people, what were their typical ways of coping with crises, what were their values. For instance, there was the constant difficulty of assessing whether given behaviour was culturally normal, a reaction to stress or a manifestation of pathology. Cheetham (1972) in a valuable analysis of immigrant characteristics and social work said: 'For example, does extreme passivity and resignation in the face of an imminent eviction or other crisis reflect a tradition of abandonment to Fate or Divine Providence, or is it a sign of acute depression? How far is the severe treatment of children or wives customary or a sign of a serious breakdown in relationships?' (p. 195). Talking things over with children or exploring various alternatives, explorations of the past, of relationships and feelings were all alien concepts to both Asians and West Indians. Each might think of social workers as powerful people who could take some desired action, act as advocates or make authoritarian decisions: in any event there were no traditions of asking for outside help with emotional problems. Some social workers' failure to understand these different assumptions and to learn to use direction and control constructively caused much confusion and did not help the client. The West Indian's strong expression of feelings, contrasted with Asian formalised relationships, made communication with each group difficult for British social workers. There were also language difficulties with the many Asians who did not speak English. Attitudes to time and to office appointments also caused problems. These misunderstandings were acute in the 1960s though they persisted later. By 1975 about 40 per cent of these non-Europeans had been born here. They thus understood, if they did not necessarily accept, local cultural assumptions.

Muslim families had a strict code of conduct and extended family obligations. Many settled down in Britain to a conventional family life within the Islamic code or saved money to return home ultimately. Problems arose from the extremely lonely life of wives expected to remain in the home, though by degrees more husbands allowed them to join the many classes in English started for small groups of Asian women, and sometimes to go out to work. The children could be torn between a permissive régime at school and the conformity demanded at home, sometimes with severe punishment for disobedience. Social workers, and other professionals, had a delicate task to understand this extended family culture and to try to lessen its rigidities without undermining family cohesion or adding to the inevitable intergenerational conflicts. Not surprisingly, many Asians thought British society immoral and feared for their children's contamination. This, coupled with feelings of rejection and insecurity, might lead them to withdraw into their own ethnic groups. Social work values also had to be differently interpreted in Asian families where traditionally situations were discussed with and decisions made by the male head of the household, and self-determination and confidentiality were alien concepts.

In the very different West Indian family pattern it was acceptable for a woman to have children by a series of men before marriage at a later age. These children were cared for successively by their own mothers or by grandparents or aunts who usually accepted a responsibility to do so. Children were not thought to suffer from these changes or from rigid discipline. This was baffling to British social workers who accepted the stable nuclear family as the norm, were puzzled by violent expressions of feeling, and did not recognise the temporary rejection of the pregnant adolescent as a ritual bow to Queen Victoria. Special difficulties were created for the child care service when mothers who were used to having their children reared by other people saw children's community homes as a means of getting good care and education for their children. Fitzherbert (1967), from her knowledge of the West Indian family structure and her experience in a London children's department, concluded that intensive work at the point of application for care often resulted in finding relations able and willing to recognise West Indian family obligations and to look after a child at a point of crisis. She thought that CCOs were making too little effort to trace fathers and press their obligations; or to use the strengths of the extended family and mobilise other services to keep the child in his own setting. Once removed from it and received into care there might be little chance of his return. Hence there were a number of West Indian children in long-term care whose ultimate social integration might be more problematic than if they had remained in an extended family group. Thus, she argued, social workers in trying to avoid racial discrimination were failing to understand West Indian family patterns, when the extreme step of removing a child from his family was rarely justified in the long run.

There was difficulty in recruiting black foster parents and a disproportionately large number of West Indian children and children of mixed race were in children's homes. Too few residential staff came from the same ethnic groups, knew about their background and culture, or about Asian dietary prohibitions and religious observances. Children often had too few toys and stories related to their own backgrounds and too little help in sorting out their own identity.

As usual in immigrant situations, children and adolescents were at the family storm centre of conflicting standards of behaviour, trying to adapt and make friends at school or work but unsure of peer-group acceptance and sometimes creating family conflict by their demands for greater freedom. The first generation went through stresses at school with their language and learning difficulties but they and their parents could look back to the country which was home, whereas many of those born here might have little sense of identity or of belonging in Britain or elsewhere. The many facets of racial disharmony included lack of career opportunities that matched abilities; taboos on intermarriage; obvious, subtle or fancied discrimination; and constant uncertainties about local people's responses. This second generation wanted to live as equal citizens here, though 'what they suffer from is not unfamiliarity with our ways, but familiarity with the consequences of prejudice . . . which unless it is tackled successfully will lead to alienation and all that involves' (Community Relations Commission evidence to the House of Commons Select Committee on Race Relations, 1975, p. 83). These stresses, and the evils of high unemployment, particularly amongst young West Indians, were forcing them to evolve their own culture and sometimes leading to explosive situations and the alienation of the young.

These non-Europeans were unalterably denied the ability to fade into the background as previous waves of immigrants had done. By the mid-1970s Britain was a multiracial society but it was still not clear whether prejudice, discrimination and resentment were temporary or permanent, whether non-European children who grew up in a prejudiced white society would be able to think of themselves with pride as black and British. All this and much more were important elements in social work practice, especially in those deprived inner-city areas where non-Europeans might be scapegoated for behaviour common in the neighbourhood.

A national survey was carried out by Political and Economic Planning (PEP) in 1974, based on a random sample of 3,300 adult members of ethnic minorities and a matched sample of white men. Results (David Smith, 1976) showed that the minority groups were in less skilled jobs, and were less well-paid, even those with the same qualifications. They were also in poorer housing. These disadvantages did not improve over time.

A 1975 CRC survey (CRC, 1976a) of 1,000 white and 1,000 coloured people showed that young whites were markedly more tolerant than their parents, indeed the majority were liberal and optimistic. But there were realistic fears about the consequences of racial discrimination. As a Home Office White Paper on racial discrimination (Cmnd 6234, 1975a) said

'If, for example, job opportunities, education facilities, housing and environmental conditions are all poor, the next generation will grow up less well equipped to deal with the difficulties facing them. The wheel then comes full circle, as the second generation find themselves trapped in poor jobs and poor housing. If, at each stage of this process, an element of racial discrimination enters in, then an entire group of people are launched on a vicious downward spiral of deprivation.' (p. 3)

Social workers co-operated with and were employed by the CRC, local community relations councils, the many voluntary organisations with a particular interest in non-Europeans, the churches and special organisations set up to help them. In some localities probation officers, social workers in social services departments, community and youth workers, and day nursery and community homes staffs gave regular service to immigrants at different stages of their settling-in period or with later problems. A number of self-help groups were set up by members of different minorities and religions, and it was often good practice for social workers to mobilise these and the strengths of the extended family rather than trying to work only with someone in difficulty.

The CRC was set up under the 1968 Race Relations Act to encourage harmonious race relations. It concerned itself with the consequences of prejudice and discrimination and efforts to 'achieve a genuine equality of opportunity'. It also attempted to change British people's hostile attitudes. By 1975 there were eighty-five local, autonomous community relations councils, consisting of affiliated organisations and individual members, backed by the services of the CRC's regional development officers. These councils had 216 staff members by 1974 of whom a number were social workers. The councils varied considerably but all aimed at an effective local and national movement to represent the interests of ethnic minorities. Those working on their behalf stressed the cultural enrichment that had resulted from every wave of immigrants over the centuries and could do so in a multiracial society. In some areas there was discrimination in employment and other injustices leading to extreme racial tensions and sporadic out-bursts of violence by or towards West Indians or Asians. In other situations, people of different races were living and working amicably with each other, so the long-term outcome was less clear than the contributions that social workers and members of other professions could make.

THE HOMELESS

Housing problems had social consequences for very large numbers of people, whether through overcrowding, lack of repairs or essential amenities, unsuit-able housing especially for old or handicapped people, and ignorance about the laws relating to landlord and tenant. Indeed, housing was one of the biggest problems in social workers' caseloads throughout the period and the many forms of unsuitable housing severely affected family relationships, but this section is only concerned with actual homelessness.

The number of homeless families greatly increased in the post-war housing shortage and there was a squatter problem, especially where squatters took over disused Army camps. People might have had to leave furnished lodging or tied cottages, or been turned out after a quarrel, or evicted for overcrowding or rent arrears. They included deserted, unmarried or otherwise unsupported mothers and children, as well as families and single people. People in these groups were very different from each other in the severity of their problems ranging from normal families to rootless single people.

'During the first few years after 1948 many local authorities were over-whelmed by the sheer numbers for whom accommodation had to be pro-vided, the difficulty of re-establishing many of the families in the community during an acute housing shortage and the complexity of the social problems which came to light, some without precedent in the experience of local government officers.' (Younghusband Report, 1959, para. 500)

By the late 1950s their numbers were swollen again by rising rents, insecurity of tenure, and the decontrol of property to let. Homeless families either fended for themselves or went into what might be extremely un-suitable local authority temporary accommodation. Many local authorities refused to admit fathers, which naturally increased the risk of permanent family break up. This was strongly discouraged by the central departments concerned and ceased from the mid-1960s. There was sometimes co-operation and sometimes a tug of war betwen housing, welfare and children's depart-ments to prevent the children from having to be received into care. A hand-ful of authorities provided intermediate housing. Voluntary organisations did what they could, for example the Liverpool Council of Social Service operated a casework service for the rehousing and after-care of families who seemed permanently settled in temporary accommodation, and found that support was needed to enable families to come through the shock of finding themselves homeless.

There had been sporadic concern about single people, tramps, people sleeping rough and those who used National Assistance Board (NAB) reception centres or Salvation Army and other common lodging houses. But almost nothing was known about the size of the problem of homeless single people until an NAB national survey was undertaken on a night in 1965 (NAB, 1966). Nearly 30,000 were in hostels, of whom only 10 per cent said they lived that way from choice; a third had left home after their marriage had broken down, because of a dispute with or death of a relation, or because they had never had a home. About 60 per cent of the men were working, 28 per cent (60 per cent in NAB reception centres) said they were ex-prisoners. Drink, mental disorder or illness were all significant factors, so was family disintegration. Many middle-aged men had gone to pieces after the death of their mothers with whom they had lived. There were just on 2,000 men and 60 women in NAB reception centres. Nearly 1,000 people were found sleeping rough (only 45 women). Nearly half gave lack of money or accommodation as the reason. They varied from local eccentric characters who got much attention to the true wanderer. Many were in employment and many had children, but once they became unsettled it was almost impossible to grow roots again, whether they drifted from place to place or slept rough locally. Many common lodging houses and reception centres housed 100 or more unstable and rootless people under the same roof. In 1964 a professional social worker in an NAB reception centre analysed the situation thus:

'Many men, although unable to grow to independent maturity, seemed nevertheless to have reached some balance in life through relationship to another person. When this relationship was disrupted there was insufficient inner strength to fall back upon and the man . . . fled from all he knew . . . Many arrived on the rebound from divorce or separation, and although now technically "unencumbered", seemed quite unable to recover, spending year after year in depression and squalor, either wandering from place to place, or appearing nightly at the Centre . . . they are running both from their own crippling fears about themselves, and also from officialdom in any form, which they picture as condemning and hounding them – and the less competent they become in carrying their responsibilities, the more hounded they feel, and the more elusive they become . . . the Reception Centre staff is being called upon to "influence" those men whose intractable problems have led the "helping" services to turn their backs in despair. Can it really be supposed that they have the vital skills needed to give personal help to a shifting population topping 400 of jobless, penniless, unhappy misfits a night? . . . Reception Centres and large hostels are often cut off from modern psychological and social thinking and are generally ill-equipped for the burden we place on them . . . Most of these men were not well enough to fend for themselves. Placing them in large hostels only wedges them more firmly into the depersonalised way of life which accen-

tuates their disabilities . . . the effects of a long-term stay in short-term
accommodation can only be destructive. Because of the large and shifting
population, discipline is strict, and a man has little legitimate opportunity
for self-direction or responsibility; he eats, sleeps, works, goes out, comes in
as ordered, day in, day out. He has no rights, no place of his own, probably
no possessions, no money. He is a shadow with neither past nor future.
He seldom has a friend or anyone who knows him personally, and treats his
fellows with aloof suspicion, often well justified . . . present laws relating to
mental illness force an increasing number of men into helpless degradation,
dishonesty, and deterioration because the decreased use of hospital beds
has not been accompanied by an appropriate increase in community provisions.' (Page, unpublished)

In 1959 the DHSS financed research into homelessness in greater London
and in Wales and the west of England. In London Greve (1964) found that
the main causes were domestic friction aggravated by overcrowding, evictions
and a chronic housing shortage at rents that people could afford. Families
with acute housing difficulties formed a growing hard core amongst those in
temporary accommodation. Most had come from poor housing with few
amenities, high rents with little or no security of tenure, and were homeless
after eviction or moving out of furnished accommodation. Some had been
subject to terrorism. Many had tried and were still trying persistently to
find their own accommodation but could not do so at rents they could
afford and landlords were increasingly refusing to take families with young
children. To test the situation in 1962 seven family service units undertook
a systematic search for low rent housing; this covered house agents, advertisements, and shop window cards. This entire systematic effort only produced three rooms for one family. The Milner Holland Report (1965)
analysed the intractable problem of multi-occupation in greater London
and also concluded that hardship was 'heavily concentrated in privately
rented housing' (p. 90).

In Wales and the south-west Glastonbury (1971) found the housing
shortage itself far less severe. But there was a higher proportion of social
breakdown, particularly domestic friction and rent arrears, amongst homeless families. The majority were young parents with young children. There
was also a number of chronically unemployed men. Over a quarter of the
sample had no housing of their own and either shared with others, or lived
entirely in institutions or rough. The rest depended on private housing.
About 25 per cent of large families admitted to temporary accommodation
had earnings below the supplementary benefits scale.

Around two-thirds of the families in both studies going into temporary
accommodation were already in the caseloads of social work agencies,
including a considerable number of problem families. Social workers thought
that their supportive help was generally successful but there was very little
actual constructive rehabilitation because of shortage of qualified staff
and the authorities' unwillingness to allocate sufficient resources to work
which did not bring quick results. 'The distinction between "deserving" and
"non-deserving" families, based on an assessment of the families' blame-
worthiness for the loss of their previous homes, affected a majority of

housing authorities' (Glastonbury, 1971, p. 220). There were generally strict regulations and moral attitudes towards council rehousing. The ideology of the poor law and the laws of settlement still coloured the outlook of some housing and welfare department officials, but the children's departments were usually more sensitive and less judgmental in helping the homeless. Equality of provision in the social services was still a distant goal. Greve commented:

'It is tragic, but probably inevitable, that professional skills and techniques in welfare work should lag behind continual changes in the conditions which they are designed to alleviate . . . It is not that professional social workers are reluctant to develop new skills but more often that policies do not sufficiently recognise or accept the need of the untidy or ungrateful for help from trained specialists.' (1964, p. 22)

Glastonbury identified three elements in the needs of the homeless: housing, material aid and social work. The rent guarantee schemes which most local authorities operated (often in effective combination with preventive social work) helped to prevent eviction and should be extended to tenants of private landlords. Assessment of the causes showed that although much was due to housing conditions, the major reasons could most appropriately be the concern of social workers and thus the task of prevention should rest primarily on the social services departments. An early warning system was essential and, in addition to actual rehousing, a much wider use of social workers in relation to the personal and social inadequacies which often led to homelessness. No department wanted the task of rehousing the homeless because of their often intractable problems. An adequate social work after-care service was also necessary to re-establish the family and to prevent periodic homelessness from becoming part of a family's way of life. Intermediate housing schemes with after-care services, and long-term sheltered housing in the community were valuable and should be part of specialised housing provision by the social services department.

The Seebohm Committee (1968) thought that housing departments should shoulder the full range of housing responsibilities and that 'to relieve them of responsibility for dependent or unreliable tenants would discourage them from looking at the housing needs of their area as a whole and create or reinforce degrading stigmas and social distinctions' (para. 401).

'Nevertheless, the problem remains of the vulnerable families who have little hope of getting (or, in some cases, keeping) a council house for a long time. The problem is not solved by leaving certain families to fend for themselves, or shuttle between accommodation for homeless families, "half-way housing", unlicensed caravan sites, unsatisfactory lodgings and the streets.' (para. 398)

The Committee drew a distinction between accommodation for homeless families and special residential care. They said:

'By the latter we mean provision in rehabilitation or recuperative units of various kinds which take a family (including the husband where there is one) for a temporary period and provide them with accommodation, respite, support and any necessary training to give them a reasonable chance of being able to manage on their own again, if necessary with help from the personal social services. Provision such as this, even though some of the families concerned may also be homeless, should be the responsibility of the social service department.' (para. 404)

In 1965 there were about 12,500 families in local authority temporary accommodation, two-thirds of whom were evicted tenants. But by 1970 DHSS figures showed 25,274 people living in temporary accommodation and this figure rose to some 33,000 in 1973. Partly owing to different authority policies, including the exclusion of adults without dependent children from the figures and different methods of recording homelessness, the true extent was unknown. An unknown number of homeless people turned first to their relations and found somewhere to live with them, with friends, or through voluntary organisations before they approached the authorities.

The Finer Committee (1974) drew attention to the acute problems faced by lone parents in finding accommodation, their insecurity of tenure, their poor conditions and risk of becoming homeless. The Committee recommended that wider use should be made of rent guarantees under the Children and Young Persons Act, 1963.

In 1974 under a joint DoE and DHSS Circular (DHSS, 1974*b*) temporary accommodation and responsibility for rehousing the homeless were to be transferred after a transitional period to the housing department, but the social services departments would remain responsible for personal social services connected with homeless people, who indeed often had not one but many different problems. Children were not to be separated from their parents on account of homelessness, nor the father from his family.

The rate of house building fell every year from 1968 and private tenancies declined. Throughout the period housing authorities' policies about early-warning systems, eviction, and willingness to co-operate varied widely. The difficulties created by the existence of different authorities for personal social services and for housing in some areas were perpetuated in the 1974 local government reorganisation. In Scotland most housing departments had early-warning systems. 'In some authorities this resulted in few eviction orders and in one authority there were no evictions for many years' (Scottish Education Department, 1970, para. 2.3). The decrease in house building resulted in increased homelessness and longer periods in temporary accommodation – which effectively decreased the number of units available. Social services departments could do no more than relieve problems of homelessness: the only answer was more housing where it was most needed.

Voluntary organisations became increasingly active. From the late 1960s onwards Shelter campaigned on behalf of the homeless and by effective publicity made the general public aware of the human consequences of the problem and stirred local authorities to make better provision. Shelter Housing Aid Centre (SHAC), the Catholic Housing Aid Society and the Single Homeless and Rehabilitation Project (SHARP) helped many homeless people to find accommodation. A number of voluntary housing associations helped to prevent homelessness, for example St Leonards Housing Association for married ex-prisoners and their families.

Various projects were started for single homeless people. These included the Cyrenians, Centre Point (Soho) with overnight accommodation and a referral service for young drifters, the Brighton Archways Venture, the Blenheim Project, the Campaign for the Homeless and Rootless (CHAR), and an increasing number of others. Some projects were for rootless young people who had left home because of a quarrel or had been pushed out; they might be from approved schools or children's homes and have a poor education and work record but be skilful at exploiting resources; they were adolescents who needed to be rescued from travelling any further along the road to failure. Many common lodging houses (renamed hostels) closed down in the 1970s which increased the number of people sleeping rough. Many were homeless because of the housing shortage and high rents but others were rootless people suffering from alcoholism, drug addiction, personality disorder, mental illness, physical illness or disability, or were ex-prisoners.

By the 1970s the number of homeless families with children had also greatly increased, so that local authorities in some urban areas were forced to house them in bed and breakfast hotels, an expensive and highly unsatisfactory arrangement, particularly when families with small children were forced to be out all day. Squatting and squatters associations had become a common phenomenon recognised by some enlightened local authorities which made empty accommodation available to them pending its demolition.

Bad housing and actual homelessness had always been a running sore. The provision of new housing, the demolition of outworn accommodation and abatement of overcrowding all failed to keep pace with the growth of population between 1950 and 1975. The result was that homelessness reached crisis proportions in some situations; while social workers were being forced to do frustrating palliative work when the solution was more housing.

MULTIPROBLEM FAMILIES

Services for multiproblem families were associated with the family service units (FSU) which had set out in the 1940s to help multiproblem families by friendship, practical services, material help, and a unit house where people could come and there were play groups for the children. Indeed their well-recorded, intensive family casework service was the chief source of knowledge about methods that succeeded or failed in helping such families. The main emphasis in this account is therefore on their experience, though many social workers in other voluntary and public services were also trying to help multiproblem families. In 1950 there were five units, but by 1975 they had increased to twenty-three with staffs of from three or four, to ten or twelve social workers, some student units and considerable public financing. Each unit was a more or less autonomous, close-knit team, which enabled individuals to bear the disintegrating anxieties and frustrations of the work.

Social workers with multiproblem families were employed in these teams and by a few local authority health or children's departments. FSU experience demonstrated that membership of a group which functioned as a team, together with good consultation, were essential supports for individual workers. Elsewhere there were conflicting views about concentrating staff on difficult and depressing work which often showed small result because knowledge about assessment and how to bring about change was still very limited in relation to families overwhelmed by their difficulties. None the less, a number of these families, many of them large ones, were held together and supported.

In the 1950s the FSU experimented with 'aggressive' casework techniques, reaching out to the unreached, who otherwise would consistently fail to seek help. 'Aggressive' casework was being pioneered in the USA at the time and caused much interest here. It faced the charge that in trying to reach poorly functioning people at odds with themselves and society, it lured them into conformity to standards imposed upon them by skilful manipulation. On a contrary view, it strove to help them to become more competent in managing their lives, more aware of social reality, more free to make their own choices. It had become clearer that major behaviour change was unlikely in such families and many could only function better (with intermittent crises) if they were given confidence, and felt cared for by a benign parental figure over indefinite periods of time. Thus emphasis was shifting from a view of problem families as genetically 'poor stock' to a view of them as immature people with little impulse control, sometimes unable to make good personal relationships, often immobilised by anxiety and depression.

Both experience and research showed that most of these inadequate families laboured under burdens of ill-health, poverty and bad housing that would tax the most competent, and thus their very failure showed their need for positive discrimination in general social service provision. In addition, there was clearly a need for a more varied range of personal services, including practical and supportive help, with therapeutic play groups and other help for the children and adolescents. Many of these extremely deprived parents also needed opportunities for play and to feel accepted. Services thus needed to be comprehensive, co-ordinated and coherently provided by members of whatever profession could become acceptable to and learn how to help such families.

In the 1960s material help and practical service became secondary, only to be used as part of a wider casework plan for families entangled in constricted circumstances and their own weaknesses, and with the emphasis on relationships with the whole family rather than individual family members. Casework itself had to be used selectively to deal with one or more problems at a time.

Until the advent of family therapy the FSU was the only social agency which set out to work with the family as the unit, as distinct from individual members within their family context; they also undertook some group work. From about the mid-1960s social work methods were broadened to include group therapy, especially for children who had had few happy experiences, consistent relationships or boundary setting in their disorganised lives. Assessment of family dynamics and environmental stresses had become more precise, with a series of limited targets and an effective use of learning theory to achieve realistic objectives. By the 1970s some thought it a social work task not only to be constantly supportive, but also to create new situations in which clients could learn to take more responsibility for themselves. The experience of the late 1960s also showed clearly that, because the causes of difficult family situations are complex and inter-related, effective intervention required an agency able to provide varied though complementary resources and methods of work. As a result, many units moved beyond seeing group work, play schemes or community work merely as subsidiary extras to the main stream of casework. The freedom of units to try out new responses to local need resulted in considerable differences in their services. These included welfare rights, publicity, counsel-ling, advocacy, drop-in centres, a school for truants, and other projects for children with school difficulties, and play activities with children and with mothers and children together. Group work might consist of therapeutic groups for adults or children or might give compensatory experiences in both activities and relationships. There were imaginative experiments in community work in deprived neighbourhoods, with an FSU house as a base and with some early success in enabling people to develop neighbour-hood resources and relations.

The FSU had always thought it important as part of their befriending and caring activities to have a base to which families could come where there was play for the children, a bed in an emergency, and sometimes a clothing and furniture store. Later some units experimented with drop-in centres to relieve family pressures, to enable people to get to know and help each other, to relieve loneliness and to act as an escape place for people under stress (FSU, 1976, pp. 27–49).

Ingram (1975) gave a horrifying case study of the twenty social agencies involved unhelpfully, usually with delays and inefficiencies, in the treatment of one severely disturbed child. Case studies in *Time to Consider* (1975) and E. Sainsbury (1975b) reinforced earlier assessments of multiproblem families, including the need for better basic services.

Treatment techniques and evaluation had been much widened and improved with a new concern with processes at work in group and inter-group relationships. Some units were also extending their neighbourhood services in the belief that they were stigmatising multiproblem families. There was a new note of light-hearted enjoyment in some FSU accounts of community music, drama, festivals and play schemes. The aim was to enable people to have good and enjoyable human experiences as an element in the early preventive action which remained as urgent as ever, not least to prevent destructive family experiences becoming for the children the seed-bed of later social failure, as these had been for their parents before them.

Some Research on Multiproblem Families

The FSU had always regarded research as part of their total activity. From 1952 to 1958 a PSW studied some of the major factors which created diffi-culties for 129 multiproblem families receiving long-term casework (Philp, 1963). The great majority of these were in the lowest socio-economic group; one in four had cash incomes below National Assistance Board standards. About 12 per cent were on National Assistance, usually because the father suffered from a long-term disability, chronic unemployment, was serving a prison sentence, or had deserted the home. The families had an average of over five children, with a range from one to fourteen per family. One-third were living in overcrowded conditions and another third in accommodation rated poor or bad. Sixty-two per cent had had one or more moves in the last five years and in 44 per cent of the sample these moves had been associated with relationship difficulties. Ill-health was one of the most important handicaps from which the families suffered. Only a quarter of the fathers and one-third of the mothers were free from physical illness, defect or undiagnosed symptoms. One-quarter were incapacitated to a considerable extent. Most had problems of interpersonal relationships in the family or outside it. There was only one family in which neither parent had shown some symptom of physical or psychological disability in the recent past, whilst just over 10 per cent of the parents had a history of severe mental illness. Only four of the families had no problems related to the health and adjustment of the children. Seventy per cent had multiple problems related to housing, income, home care, child care, health and personal relationships. Nearly 40 per cent of the children showed signs of disturbance.

Most parents came from large families but had almost no contact with their brothers and sisters, although most were still in touch with their mothers, many of whom lived at a distance and did not play any effective part in the family. A third had links with close relatives who provided some support in crises, and friendly and helpful relationships with neighbours, but the majority had neither. Only seventeen families had no male head. Sixty-nine per cent of the men and 66 per cent of the women had suffered from broken homes or marked marital disharmony in their own childhood.

There were current problems of physical neglect of the children, cruelty, harsh treatment or other problems of parent/child relationships in 74 per cent of the families. At the time of the study over 21 per cent of the children were away from home (over 12 per cent either adopted or in care, the latter usually on account of the mother's confinement or illness). Most of the mothers and many fathers gave their babies much emotional warmth and physical contact. But they were not able to respond appropriately to the demands and needs of older children.

'The great majority of parents were handicapped by some form of personality disturbance, the general characteristics of which were impulsive behaviour, an inability to tolerate frustration and a concern with aggressive feelings. These men and women seemed to have little self confidence and self esteem. While they often seemed insensitive to the needs and feelings of others, they showed that they badly needed approval and they tended to be exceptionally apprehensive of the opinion of others.' (pp. 269–70)

Philp and Timms (1957) reviewed the available knowledge about problem families. It was thought that well-recorded casework would increase 'understanding of their overwhelming emotional needs, their serious dependency problems and their unsatisfied infantile demands' (p. 20). Such unresponsive families were a nightmare to the social services, consuming a disproportionate amount of resources in a series of crises for little more than intermittent holding operations. None the less they were very far from being a clearly definable or homogeneous group.

Irvine (1954 and 1967) attempted to isolate the type of instability characteristic of problem families. She concluded that they had little appreciation of the value of money, no sense of time and little of property, and that the whole internally consistent group of symptoms were manifestations of extreme immaturity – 'a picture of children of three or four keeping house'. From this it followed that the most effective forms of help were frequent visiting, practical help in household tasks, and spontaneous warmth on the part of the worker. Obviously differential assessment was essential to distinguish between degrees of immaturity, disorder, schizoid withdrawal, paranoid and psychopathic reactions, and those whose feelings of inferiority led them to anticipate rejection.

Wilson (1959) argued that the immaturity explanation was impressionistic rather than based upon systematic psychiatric investigation. Her own sociological study of fifty-two 'hard core' families in Cardiff showed that many were faced with excessively stressful conditions. The father was either dead, elderly, or suffering from physical or mental disability in thirty-nine of the families. Ten men in good health were in steady work, but five of the wives were in poor physical or mental health. An unstated number of families had from four to eleven children and suffered from chronic economic strain which heightened the stresses of parenthood. Thus 'a large proportion of the families had to face extreme stress situations for considerable periods, which could not entirely or even partially be explained in terms of inevitable consequences of immature personalities' (p. 116). The majority of these families had no relations to give them support, when in any event they were continuously exposed to psychological and economic strains which might well produce a regressive response. These parents might have suffered emotional starvation in childhood, and so clearly did a number of their children.

Philp (1961) commented:

'We cannot reasonably consider as "socially sick" families who are condemned by circumstances to live in conditions which . . . make such demands on people that they become depressed or which can only be weathered at the cost of chronic irritability, antisocial behaviour or illness. And the fact that some disturbed individuals will seek or create situations which confirm or maintain their illness must not blind us to the fact that very unsatisfactory social environments may still exist in our society.' (p. 51)

Tonge, Jones (both psychiatrists) and Hillam (1975) suggested a possibly important clue to understanding problem families. They studied thirty-three multiproblem families in Sheffield, against a comparison group of matched families in order to evaluate the part played by psychiatric illness and personality disorders. Clinical diagnoses showed 58 per cent of the problem families men and 55 per cent of the women to be suffering from mental illness or personality disorder. The latter predominated in the men and neurosis – possibly a reaction to their husbands – in the women. Disturbed attitudes to their own fathers were common amongst both sexes with psychiatric disorders. This suggested that fathers play a more important part than had been supposed in the genesis of problem families. Twelve per cent of the comparison group suffered from neurotic and psychosomatic disorders. There were no significant differences in physical ill-health. Many more problem than comparison families were living in squalid poverty, were in debt, unemployed, of lower intelligence, caring inadequately for the children, delinquent, subject to gross marital discord. Forty-six out of 200 problem family children were suffering from psychiatric illness (against 13 comparison children). Physical health and truancy did not differ for both sets of families.

This was a classic picture of the problem family but to the authors 'a nagging doubt remained'. They realised late in their investigation that the families' choices which were not directly controlled by economic necessity or psychiatric disturbance expressed their values and affected their social behaviour. These were summed up in failure to plan and a striking refusal to notice the discomfort in which they lived. Their characteristic choices could not be fully accounted for by mental pathology, poverty or membership of a sub-culture. But they might well be a sign of living without hope. Faced by criticism, rejection and their own self-condemnation for massive failure, the families withdrew demoralised into social isolation. Denial of squalor and social norms was symptomatic of the anxiety engendered by overwhelming stress and an inability to continue struggling with failure. This could be the basis of 'the intuitive recognition of problem families by social workers' (p. 119). This type of unstable personality might result from inconsistent affection and poor care in childhood which arrested their emotional development at the earliest stage and led in adult life to regressive responses. There might also be a constitutional factor in these vulnerable and damaged personalities. The authors concluded 'We were not dealing with different types of abnormal families but with a mosaic of social and individual pathology' (p. 115).

E. Sainsbury (1975*a*) constructed a 'national profile' of the 1,014 families in the caseloads of ninety-six caseworkers in nineteen FSUs in early November 1972. Questionnaire returns showed an average of 4·2 per cent children in each family against a national average of 2·4 per cent; 27·3 per cent were fatherless families, 5·4 per cent were in ESN schools (national average 0·7 per cent), 35·7 of fathers were at work and 36·8 per cent unemployed. There were 'serious debts' in 45·3 per cent of the families and in 19·5 per cent one or both parents had been before a criminal court or subject to a court order in the past year. The caseworkers rated the principal problem at the time of referral as financial and/or housing (30 per cent); disturbed family relationships and inadequate child care (44·2 per cent); major personality disorder or serious distress (23 per cent); and physical ill-health (2 per cent). There were considerable local variations in each category, which Sainsbury suggested might have been due more to variations in local services and policies than to family behaviour (see also chapter 9).

Chapter 16

Social Work and Violence in the Home

BATTERED CHILDREN

The Beginnings of Action

Battered children and battered wives had always existed. In the 1950s and 1960s the children slowly became more 'visible' in the public eye through the work of individual paediatricians, the NSPCC and others. Some were removed from their homes under place of safety orders and brought before the juvenile courts under the Children and Young Persons Act, 1933 as being in need of care or protection. The co-ordinating committees of the 1950s (discussed in volume 1, chapter 15, section on 'Co-ordinating Committees') were a first step towards earlier identification and co-ordinated action by different professionals and services, both statutory and voluntary. Then came the Ingleby Committee (1960), charged to suggest how to prevent 'cruelty to . . . juveniles'. Its Report led to the Children and Young Persons Act, 1963 which gave children's departments wider powers to do preventive work.

The perennial difficulty was how to discover what went on inside the home, where child battering usually took place; what precipitated child abuse; how to intervene sufficiently early; what were the personality characteristics of battering parents; whether they could respond to what kind of treatment; whether or not the family could be held together without further risk to the children; what were the limits of confidentiality; at what point the children's (later social services) departments or the NSPCC should exercise their responsibility and remove the child from his home; and, if the court made a fit person (later care) order, whether, and with what safeguards, he should be allowed to return.

In a memorandum on *Cruelty to Children* (1953) the Association of Children's Officers (ACO) said hopefully 'Physical ill-treatment is comparatively rare and the law provides adequate penalties . . . The machinery for detecting and combating physical violence appears to us to be adequate' (pp. 3 and 8). It thought the prevention of mental ill-treatment was 'a much wider problem'. A Joint Committee of the BMA and the Magistrates' Association, reporting in 1956 on *Cruelty to and Neglect of Children*, said more realistically 'There can be no doubt that a large number of cases of cruelty and neglect are never brought to notice' (p. 10) and 'in many cases children have been the subject of neglect or cruelty over a considerable period' (p. 14). The report summarised evidence from many witnesses and analysed forms of cruelty and neglect which ranged more widely than physical violence. It discussed underlying causes and their medical, legal and social aspects. It concluded that 'psychological disturbances and deviations in one or both of the parents constituted one of the commonest and most far reaching causes of cruelty and neglect. It is largely in the minds of the parents that we must seek the underlying causes of both these conditions. Relatively little is known about them and it is obvious that research is urgently required' (p. 26). It also thought that 'gross forms of physical maltreatment of children are probably rare'. There was, it said, inadequate co-ordination between the various services and much could be done to remedy this. Nearly twenty years later the Maria Colwell Inquiry (DHSS, 1974d) identified this as a key factor in failure to prevent her death.

Research Findings

The following is a summary of some research findings in Britain in the short period since the risk of non-accidental injury was first recognised. The samples were small and

'It is often difficult or impossible to draw general conclusions from these studies, as the representative status of the sample studied is unclear. Often the size and characteristics of the base population from which the sample is drawn is not known and, without such data, estimates as to "rates of incidence" and discussions of, for example, age distributions of injured children and their families are likely to be misleading. Frequently the procedures by which the sample of children came to be identified are also not stated, and the small size of the samples used makes extrapolations to the general population of dubious validity.' (NSPCC, 1976b, p. 5)

In 1953 the Prison Commission agreed, on the suggestion of that great penal reformer and friend of children, Margery Fry, to notify to a forensic psychiatrist, Dr T. C. Gibbens, particulars of men and women imprisoned during the year for violent cruelty to children. He and Walker (1956) found that 29 out of 32 men and all 7 women were either mentally abnormal or aggressive, unstable, inadequate or mentally subnormal. Three men and no women were 'normal'. They had experienced rejection, indulgence and hostility in their own childhood. This suggested that 'cruelty to children cannot be adequately dealt with by warnings and punishments, but calls for concentrated and skilled social work, directed often towards the whole family' (p. 24).

The finding which ultimately changed the picture in this country resulted from the work of Silverman, an American radiologist, who in 1952 suggested that when an X-ray showed healed fractures, non-accidental injury must always be suspected whatever explanations parents might give for falls out of a cot, downstairs, or off a scooter. In 1962 Dr Kempe of Denver coined the term 'the battered child syndrome'. Two orthopaedic surgeons (Griffiths and Moynihan, 1963) first described the condition in this country. They were followed by Cameron (1966) who concluded that 'the syndrome . . .

[was] associated with various forms of social, biological and intra-psychic stress' (pp. 2–21). A number of his findings were confirmed by subsequent research.

On the initiative of two paediatricians actively concerned about child battering (renamed non-accidental injury to children), a working group of doctors, nurses, lawyers and social workers came together to discuss how to improve the 'management of' (in social work terminology 'services to') such families and to provide a link between the medical professions, the social and health services, the legal profession and the police. The group's Tunbridge Wells Conference (1973) was a landmark, the papers were subsequently published (Franklin, 1974) and the working group remained in being.

In Scott's study (1973) of twenty-nine cases where the father had killed a child of the household under 5 years old, less than half was a biological parent. There had usually been previous injuries and there was always a precipitating stimulus from the child, e.g. crying, or refusal of food, which the fathers interpreted as wilful defiance, a battle of wills, not loving or understanding him (i.e. role reversal). Twelve fathers had also assaulted their wives and in eight cases were already being visited on account of previous child abuse. Unlike the Gibbens and Walker study, no father was diagnosed as mentally ill or subnormal; but they had very immature or aggressive personalities and nearly all showed difficulty in controlling themselves or coping with stress. Nineteen came from punitive families but ten apparently had normal homes.

Cooper (1975) studied 136 children with non-accidental injuries seen between 1965 and 1971. The death rate was 10 per cent and in 30 per cent permanent brain damage resulted. Ounsted *et al.* (1975) in their study of children and families at Park Hospital, Oxford, found one-third of the families untreatable, and thus the child's permanent placement in a stable family was essential. Some parents suffered from serious mental illness or inadequate personalities; many had themselves been violently treated and were unloved children to whom little was given but much was demanded. The mother and other brothers and sisters as well as the injured child were routinely admitted to the hospital for 'total care' and a family diagnosis in which both parents took part. Also at Park Hospital, Lynch (1975) suggested that 'episodes of ill-health in vulnerable families during pregnancy, delivery and early childhood put the parent/child bond at risk' (p. 319).

Smith *et al.* (1975) studied 134 battered children under 5 and 53 controls. Seventy-five per cent of the injured children as against 31 per cent of the controls came from social classes IV and V. Seventy-six per cent of the mothers and 64 per cent of the fathers had mild or severe personality disorders. Twenty-one per cent of the fathers had a criminal record and one-third were diagnosed as aggressive psychopaths.

In 1974 the Home Office Research Unit undertook for the Probation and After-Care Department a study of clients for whom probation officers were responsible on account of non-accidental injury to the children (Sturgess and Heal, 1976). At that time only twenty-two out of sixty-seven areas had formal area review committees and where they existed the probation service was often not represented. The inquiry identified 334 children (75 per cent under the age of 4) in 297 families. Between a quarter and a third of the children had died from injury, caused by either mothers or fathers. Forty-four per cent of the surviving children were still living at home and about the same proportion were in care. Most parents were young and most fathers were in unskilled jobs. In nearly half the families one or both parents had at least one previous criminal conviction and 43 per cent had had previous contacts with the probation service. Seventy-six per cent were in current contact with other social agencies. In 19 per cent of families the same or other children had previously been injured.

NSPCC Initiative

78 Battered Children (Skinner and Castle, 1969) was a retrospective survey of children under the age of 4 known to NSPCC inspectors. The records showed 'a reluctance by the medical profession to initiate measures to protect the child', whether suffering from bruises, fractures or burns, who was often returned home without any satisfactory provision being made to modify family stresses, and subsequently more severely injured. There were more women batterers than men. The group seemed to divide into those adults who were habitually aggressive (47 per cent) and those whose emotionally impoverished personalities could not sustain child-nurturing relationships. Some social workers showed considerable sensitivity in concentrating on the protection of the child by reducing the stresses in the total family situation and forming a helpful relationship with the parents. Others exhibited varying degrees of authoritarianism. Many social workers found it difficult to accept the reality of child battering and reacted with anxiety or withdrawal, which limited their ability to help. It was not possible to draw any conclusion that a given type of intervention increased or decreased the risk to a child, though actions which added to existing family tensions seemed to increase the risk of battering. A few cases in the non-aggressive group responded to a skilled social worker able to devote considerable time to the relationship. Multiplicity of workers and over-frequent observation of battering families could increase family stress and 'a type of supervision of a family which is limited to an anxious watchfulness without specific treatment goals isn't in the child's interest' (p. 20).

In 1970 the NSPCC Battered Child Research Department mounted a three-year social work action research project in order to learn more about the nature and treatment of the syndrome. A treatment centre was started in London to which local hospitals and other services could refer children under 4 who had received non-accidental injuries. There was a day nursery with much mothering and physical comforting, mothers' discussion groups and intensive casework with the families, including a twenty-four-hour, on-call service by a staff of five caseworkers. The project was guided by a multidisciplinary scientific Advisory Committee and had psychiatric and paediatric consultation. Unfortunately there were delays in referral, a tendency to 'go it alone', and a common failure to recognise that a multidisciplinary approach, case conferences, a co-ordinated plan, and clearly defined and observed procedures for communication and decisions about responsibility were all essential.

At Risk (NSPCC, 1976a) recorded the project and its findings in relation to the twenty-five families treated. The case records were carefully analysed (though not also by outside assessors) after eighteen to twenty-one months of intensive therapy. There was severe marital tension in eighteen cases and nine husbands were violent to their wives. None of the parents took drugs or had a history of in-patient psychiatric treatment but nine fathers had a drink problem. All but two parents had themselves suffered rejection, disruption of care during early childhood, loss of a parent figure, severe discipline and subsequent emotional starvation. They did not suffer from poverty or physical neglect. Many of the mothers had had pregnancies and heavy responsibilities in adolescence. The families were overcrowded, lonely, without relatives or friends. 'An overwhelming conglomeration of disadvantages and mischance had dogged their childhood and adolescence and still shadowed their adult lives' (p. 93), reinforced by their lack of trust and self-confidence. Money was a major problem largely owing to high rents. They moved frequently. Most of the mothers felt a 'lack of emotional support, of communication, of being cared for, understood and valued . . . trapped, . . . lonely and out of control of their lives' (p. 86). Most seemed depressed and highly defended against their feelings. They were solitary often dependent people.

The team assumed that these deprived parents had an impaired ability to care for their children and expected them to give rather than receive love and thus disappointment and finally battering would result. The team offered a therapeutic relationship aimed at fostering the parents' emotional development with the hope that they would then be more able to care for their children and decrease their unrealistic demands on them. Treatment included acceptance, reliability and help with practical problems. Most parents thought the difficulty lay in the children rather than themselves. Most fathers remained untrusting throughout the earlier period but the mothers varied from trusting to unapproachable. It was thought that in the first year the parents developed some basic trust and became more assertive and independent. But usually the worker became too much part of the family circle to be able to continue as a therapist about other problems.

After treatment terminated the fathers were more satisfied at work, the mothers were less isolated in their local community, the family was better housed and there was marked improvement in some marital relationships though ten out of twenty-five couples had separated. There was less financial disorganisation; the mothers' energy and motivation increased and they were more assertive and emotionally mature. Both they and the fathers were physically healthy. Immature and ineffectual, or rigid and highly defended fathers showed little change but some improved in psycho-physical functioning. Psychological tests showed that battering parents were consistently more reserved and detached, with poorer emotional control, more aggressive and less realistic and practical than the controls. Battering fathers were abnormally introverted. This suggested that the complexities underlying battering might include genetic traits. These findings contrasted significantly with E. Sainsbury's study (1975a) of intensive FSU casework with multiproblem families in which the commonest improvement was in interfamilial relations and the least in employment.

The crucial outcome, i.e. relations between mothers and battered children, was disappointing and there were many doubts about the effectiveness of the treatment in improving the quality of mothering or the children's relations with their mothers. 'The majority of mothers were not even fairly accepting of the battered children after twenty-one months of treatment' (p. 171). A later review showed that 'only eight out of a possible twenty-three children seemed to be making reasonably satisfactory and sustained developmental progress' (p. 174). With hindsight the team thought that they had stressed the therapeutic claims of the parents over those of the children; that those temporarily removed from home would have benefited from fostering; that the children should have had more individual therapy; that 'some situations would have been better resolved by the child's being permanently removed and offered a good alternative home' (p. 120). Seven out of thirty-two siblings were thought to have been physically injured by their parents. Some of the battered children had periods of residential care in hospital or children's homes during the project. All those who attended the project nursery improved developmentally but later they showed signs of emotional disturbance. Twenty of the children were at home at the end of the project and long-term follow up was planned for them.

In 1974 the NSPCC enlarged its Battered Child Research Department by setting up the National Advisory Centre for the Battered Child which continued to undertake research, consultation and education, coupled with a treatment service in the immediate district. It was decided (Owtram, 1975) to set up special units offering a twenty-four-hour service, each staffed by three well-qualified social workers, with paediatric/psychiatric and legal advice available and in close co-operation with the local social services and area health authorities. The units provided social work services to families where there was proven or suspected non-accidental injury to a child; consultation to promote good practice; and a register of all suspected cases in the area. The Manchester unit started in 1973 and by 1975 others had followed in Leeds, Newcastle upon Tyne, Coventry and Northampton. It proved necessary to offer help to any child under 16. The number of actual treatment cases was very small compared with those where there was consultation, registration and monitoring at three-monthly intervals. The NSPCC was planning to establish a unit in Glasgow to give service to families in co-operation with statutory social work and health authorities.

In cases treated by a unit at least half the children had to be removed from home and day care was needed for those who stayed at home. The unit staff acted as an extended family for the parents, with group meetings, individual therapy, and other means of making them feel accepted, apparently much on FSU lines. Access to the special unit registers was confined to doctors and named people in the area health authority or social services department. It was hoped by means of these registers to build up information on defined criteria from a range of medical and social agencies and thus make it possible to compare cases in particular localities with characteristics of the general population. This should 'enable detailed comparisons to be made on such factors as age distribution, family size, household composition and socio-economic status' (NSPCC, 1976*b*, p. 5) as well as more accurate estimates of the extent of non-accidental injury.

Government Action in England, Scotland and Wales

In 1970 the chief medical officer of health and the chief inspector of the Home Office Children's Department sent a joint letter to local authorities (DHSS, 1970*a*, CMO 2/70). This was followed by a further letter (DHSS, 1970*a*, LHAL 24/70) enclosing a memorandum prepared by the standing Medical Advisory Committee of the Central Health Services Council.

In 1972 the Home Office and DHSS issued a joint circular (DHSS, 1972*c*, LASS 26/72) to local authorities suggesting they should set up joint consultation groups of all the interests concerned to make arrangements which ensured that all necessary protection and help was made available to the child, others at risk in the family, and to the parents and other adults. It gave precise advice about action and co-operation between GPs, hospitals, local health authorities, the social services department and the NSPCC, and repeated some recommendations of the British Paediatric Association's 1966 memorandum on 'The Battered Baby Syndrome' (*British Medical Journal*, 1966).

Further DHSS and Welsh Office circulars (DHSS, 1974*a*, LASS 13/74; and Welsh Office, 1974, 123/74) recommended the joint establishment by local authorities and area health authorities of area review committees. A similar Scottish circular (Social Work Services Group/Scottish Home and Health Department, 1975, NHS Circular 1975 (Gen. 23)) was issued in 1975. This gave guidance on aspects of professional practice, identification of vulnerable families, action where there was actual or suspected injury and local control and review procedures.

By 1975 there were 100 joint local and area health authority area review committees, covering the whole of England and similar committees in Wales. Senior members included all relevant professions, the probation service and voluntary agencies like the NSPCC. Practically all had set up strictly confidential central registers accessible only to senior staff of named agencies. Not all provided for regular review of cases or distinguished on the register records between known injury or suspected risk. Case conferences were composed of those directly concerned in an individual case, while review committees of senior professionals monitored policy. Returns from authorities covering about 90 per cent of the child population recorded some 5,700 cases (40 fatal) of known or suspected non-accidental injury in nine months of 1974 (DHSS, 1976*c*). Identification was essential but appropriate treatment posed an even bigger problem. Some thought that too much effort had gone into detection of children at risk in comparison with other urgent and numerically larger problems but a good deal was learnt about clear lines of communication, identification, interdisciplinary co-operation, decision and action.

Some Pointers

By 1975 research studies, NSPCC special units, Home Office and DHSS pressure, local review committees, watch-dog activities by local authorities, advances in understanding the nature of the problem contrasted markedly with the static complacency of the 1950s. This resulted primarily from initiative by paediatricians and psychiatrists, followed by social workers and lawyers, and led to interdisciplinary study and government action. Much use was made of American experience and there were regular exchange visits.

Different investigators stressed the pathology of the abuser; or of family interaction; the part played by the child himself in the dynamic process; pre- or post-natal environmental experiences; constitutional or congenital factors; or socially produced stress factors such as poverty or bad housing (NSPCC, 1976*b*). The following pointers emerged from research and experience:

(a) The mortality rate from injury was 10 to 20 per cent and the risk of brain damage high.

(b) Battered children were often born to young mothers ill-prepared for motherhood who had several pregnancies in quick succession.

(c) Premature and low birth weight babies were over represented in all samples of non-accidental injury. It was not known whether this was due to the mother's perception of the baby, its possible handicap, how she looked after it, or the baby's early separation from her in an intensive care unit.

(d) A particular child in the family might be the scapegoat but injury tended to be an ongoing family problem, and the siblings might suffer considerable emotional damage.

(e) Persistent crying, with parents' loss of sleep, could lead to extreme frustration and feelings that the baby was rejecting and criticising them. 'Children, right from the moment of birth, are very different from each other and some are much easier to love than others . . . Frequent crying, piercing cries, regular waking at night, feeding problems, vomiting after feeds and non cuddliness are all often mentioned in case histories' (Richards, 1975, p. 8).

(f) Failure to thrive was a danger signal, as well as bruises, fractures or other injuries not satisfactorily explained.

(g) Unlike neglectful parents, these parents often gave their children good physical care but were lacking in ability to mother, indeed they expected the baby to meet their dependency needs and to give them love.

(h) Families were often subject to severe economic, social and personal stress. They might be isolated, in poverty, lone parents, in poor housing, fearing eviction or complaints from neighbours if the baby cried too much. Marital relationships might be unhappy with frequent tension, quarrelling and separation. They had no helpful relations or friends, they moved frequently; and the battering often happened at some point of crisis or extreme fatigue. 'The lonely, yearning sense of inferiority, lack of self esteem, tensions and suspicion, pervasive anxiety and depression, lack of empathy towards their babies, and inability to nurture are all extensively described in the literature' (Court, 1974, p. 29).

(i) Some research showed a high concentration of battering parents in social classes IV and V, others that social class was less relevant, though child abuse was unlikely to be suspected in the professional classes.

(j) It was essential to act quickly when battering was suspected and to admit the child to hospital immediately. The first slight injuries might be a parental cry for help. Some frustrated or hopeless parents desperately wanted help and might be able to admit this, given adequate social or psychiatric therapy. Far more serious injuries might otherwise result. This also pointed to the need for day nurseries, mothers' groups and other ways of diluting stress for mothers who might otherwise reach breaking point.

(k) A high proportion of identified battered children were under 2. There was some suggestion, however, that older children also suffered unsuspected non-accidental injuries to which school teachers might be helped to become alert.

(l) Parents were most open to treatment at the crisis point when the doctor diagnosed non-accidental injury. It was essential that skilled and sensitive social and psychiatric therapy should be available at this point. The aim should be to reduce the demands parents made on their child by giving them alternative sources of satisfaction. Criticism or use of authority could be positively harmful. It might be too risky to let the child go home but continuing support to the parents might prevent injury to subsequent children.

(m) Research studies differed as to the amount of mental disorder amongst such parents from nil to around 10 per cent. Immaturity and aggression were common factors. There was much evidence that the parents' own experience of rejection, cruel punishment and lack of mothering was a crucial factor. A primary aim of treatment by social workers should thus be to provide a warm, non-critical relationship in which dependency was freely accepted.

(n) Less was known about battering fathers than mothers and there had been fewer attempts at study and treatment.

Jobling (1976) in an annotated bibliography on child abuse drew attention to the lack of evidence about the long term emotional development of seriously ill-treated children. Treatment techniques to help either battering parents or the abused child were both lacking. Arrangements to identify and protect children at risk far exceeded knowledge about or provision of treatment.

Social work opinion had begun to swing from preserving the blood tie at all costs to the view of a leading paediatrician with much experience of battered children that 'The mistaken notion that separating a child from his family is always a last resort and harmful is widely believed by social workers. In fact the contrary is true. Whatever the age of the child, the removal from traumatic physical and emotional battering is always beneficial if the substitute care provides adequately for the child's needs' (Cooper, 1975, p. 27).

In 1975 BASW produced a detailed code of practice for social workers with responsibility for children at risk (BASW, 1975d). But social work knowledge had barely begun to be formulated and systematised, nor what might be the indications for temporary or permanent removal, for intensive care and mothering in day centres or the home, and how to provide 'good experiences' for the child and each parent. The NSPCC study *At Risk* (1976a) showed, as other long-term studies of intensive casework had done, that changes can be brought about in some though not all aspects of family functioning. Unfortunately least change resulted where change was most desired. This raised the question of whether other methods, including intensive group therapy, would be more successful or whether some parents were for reasons not yet clarified incapable of emotional bonds with a child. In any event, permanent removal of the child from the home might be indicated rather than continuing emotional damage while the parents were being treated. The problems of how to provide the necessary interdisciplinary skilled resources and how to protect the siblings remained. Once again it was clear, as in child care in general, that

'. . . working with parents to change their attitudes and behaviour towards the child is not enough. The children themselves need someone to help them to learn that it is possible to trust an adult and that love is not always conditional on the gratification of adult needs. They also need help in coping with the inevitable anger, hopelessness and depression which accompanies being beaten for no good reason. At the same time the stress on professional workers who undertake direct work with these children and are able to share in their pain should not be overlooked and they, in turn, need support themselves.' (National Children's Bureau, 1975, p. 4)

BATTERED WIVES

Obviously cases of violence between husbands and wives have been known to social workers for years, but identification of certain patterns and multi-disciplinary study and action only really began in the late 1960s. In 1973 the Chiswick Women's Aid Shelter for battered wives was set up by the initiative of one pioneer. It provided refuge at any hour, and was always overcrowded. Grayford (1975) in his study of 100 cases of battered wives and their children, mainly at the Centre, found that many boys showed a disturbing picture of uncontrolled violence. The girls on the other hand were passive and withdrawn (Pizzey, 1974). Other centres, flats offering temporary accommodation and women's aid groups spread rapidly all over the country, many of them members of the National Women's Aid Federation. Their experience showed that often battered wives did not leave home because there was nowhere for them and the children to go. They needed far more effective legal, financial, housing and counselling help than was available by 1975.

A report of the House of Commons Select Committee on *Violence in Marriage* (House of Commons paper 553, 1975) deplored the little information available in government departments. It recommended that twenty-four-hour family crisis centres should be 'readily and rapidly' available in very large towns, together with many more refuges for battered wives.

There was a known relationship between drunkenness and battering but hardly any research into causes or remedies, though there was 'increasing evidence from retrospective data on the backgrounds of parents who abuse their children, husbands who seriously assault their wives, and murderers that physical violence figures prominently in their childhood experiences' (NCB, 1975, p. 3). There was a complex inter-relation of social, cultural, sexual and pathological elements in many such cases. Obviously some cases of non-accidental injury to children came from such families, and many children suffered severe emotional trauma from witnessing violence between parents or from one parent to the other and sometimes trying to act as mediators.

The NSPCC pilot study in 1973 of twenty-three violent matrimonial cases showed the children's rootless lives, frequently leaving home and returning again to recurrent violence; the preoccupation of the parents with their own unmet needs, inability to discuss problems, and use of the children as pawns in the conflict. The parents mentioned sex as the most frequent cause of conflict. The study suggested that skilled use of authority and understanding care is necessary in social work with the parents and direct casework help by social workers able to communicate with children (*Yo Yo Children*, 1974). The NSPCC had plans to extend this work, recognising that long-term emotional damage might be more serious than physical injury.

Chapter 17

Social Work with Unmarried Mothers: One-Parent Families

FOCUS ON UNMARRIED MOTHERS

Until the late 1960s attention was concentrated on unmarried mothers and their children rather than widows or deserted, divorced or separated parents, perhaps because the urge for reform was uppermost. Support for unmarried mothers consisted largely of moral welfare work by the Anglican and Roman Catholic Churches and the Salvation Army, with the emphasis on personal relations, especially in marriage. Their main activities, in addition to sex education, were casework with unmarried mothers, together with mother and baby homes, 'shelters' and training homes staffed by matrons and assistants, of whom some took the Josephine Butler House 'indoor' course for residential work. A number of moral welfare associations were also registered adoption agencies; and many moral welfare workers co-operated closely with maternity MSWs.

In the 1950s there began to be more questioning of the whole concept of moral welfare confined to sex relations outside marriage, and of the disproportionate investment of the churches' resources in this work. Even though pressing problems of illegitimate pregnancy required family casework, the service was separate from the main stream of child care and family welfare, and indeed from the matrimonial work of the probation service. It was also argued that the moral welfare associations were too small and too specialised to give the essential range of services and were only able to deal with comparatively few cases in their districts. Moreover, it was hazardous to concentrate on one special form of human need, particularly one which aroused strong emotions, entwined with cultural and religious attitudes and taboos, while unmarried mothers were sometimes forced by Hobson's choice to accept help from a religious organisation with an unfortunate title. Conversely, it was contended that to help them and their children was a traditional commitment of the church; moral welfare combined social work with distinctively Christian spiritual help; and anyway statutory services relied upon the church to provide the service, often using moral welfare associations as an agency service. Some people argued that thereby local authorities purchased on the cheap a service which otherwise they would have had to provide at greater cost and more comprehensively themselves.

By 1956–7 only sixteen local authorities had appointed staff to work with unmarried mothers. These were almoners or other social workers, or health visitors. This was a decrease of 50 per cent in the number of local authority staff specifically appointed for this work since 1948. But, said the Younghusband working party (1959, para. 425) '. . . we see no advantage in isolating the care of these mothers either from similar work with unsupported mothers, or from the work of a family caseworker employed by the health department'. Lone fathers were still invisible.

There was radical rethinking in the 1960s of the moral welfare approach and indeed whether the churches should directly engage in professional social work at all. A detailed study of *The Church in Social Work* (Hall and Howes, 1965) was initiated in 1958 by the Church of England Moral Welfare Council to explore moral welfare in the context of the social services and as part of the church's pastoral ministry. The authors said, 'Nowhere in our casework investigations did we find any clear indication that, apart from its traditional identification with the unmarried mother and her child, moral welfare work could be distinguished from that undertaken by other social work agencies in either avenue of referral or type of case referred' (p. 190). Of the workers themselves they said,

'Terribly complicated situations involving illegitimate children of married people, divorcees, etc. are taken as they come . . . at its best, their attitude towards their cases combined realism with compassion and adherence to church teaching and standards with the capacity to accept patiently, tolerantly and at times with a pleasant sense of humour, the most daunting manifestations of human waywardness.' (p. 247)

The authors concluded that 'the overall long-term effect of current developments in social policy is likely to lessen both the need and the opportunity for the Church to make its own corporate contribution in this particular form of social service' (p. 262).

Great efforts were made to improve standards and employ more staff but, as with all services aiming at national coverage through small autonomous voluntary units, the standard of work by diocesan moral welfare associations (the title was now generally altered to family welfare) varied from good to poor, partly as a result of differences in grant aid, since some local authorities were quite unrealistic about the cost of the services they were securing by small grants. At its best, an association consisted of an organising secretary and several other trained social workers, well supported, with good office facilities and able to offer a professional service both to unmarried mothers and as an adoption agency. At the opposite extreme an overburdened organising secretary might be struggling on her own with little backing to undertake an extremely demanding task and to fill a number of ill-defined roles as administrator, adoption officer, caseworker and money raiser or an unqualified or partially qualified worker without supervision might offer no more than an inadequate welfare service. Clients with much need for support, information, practical help, and a chance for regular discussion with a competent caseworker might have only one or two interviews and little relief for all their anxieties, especially about whether to part with or keep the baby.

At the peak in the late 1960s there were about 350 social workers, and diocesan adoption agencies placed 2,000–2,500 children a year for adoption. There were some 170 mother and baby homes in England and Wales catering each year for over 11,000 out of around 70,000 unmarried mothers. Eighty per cent were run by religious orders, the Salvation Army, small independent associations, or local health authorities. There were several surveys of these homes in the 1950s and 1960s.

MOTHER AND BABY HOMES: A STUDY IN THE MID-1960s

In 1964 a substantial study of twenty-six mother and baby homes in the north and south of England (Nicholson, 1968) was undertaken on the initiative of the National Council for the Unmarried Mother and Her Child. Matrons and social workers were interviewed (twenty-five out of fifty-one of the latter were Church of England moral welfare workers). This survey is especially useful because 250 residents were also interviewed, whether singly or in groups. A few of the premises were modern and cheerful but on the whole they were large, draughty, old-fashioned houses, costly to heat and maintain, and with a gloomy, shabby appearance. They were often furnished with other people's discards, though it must be remembered that this was then usual in most voluntary organisation homes. Many alterations and improvements were in hand at the time of the visits and poor equipment was mainly due to the financial position of voluntary bodies.

The investigators found that the staff in the twenty-six homes, who were the single most important factor in the standard of care, were often depressed by poor material standards and inadequate equipment and accommodation. Most matrons had worked in mother and baby homes for many years. All had a heavy burden of responsibility for staff and residents, for supervising work, for administration, for maintaining harmony, for filling in gaps and frequently for being on call at night in addition to long daily hours of work. Few matrons had any training (this finding is surprising in view of the Williams Committee survey returns – see below). Some made a happy home in the most unpromising conditions and helped residents with the personal problems of illegitimacy. When they established good relations with residents this was largely due to their own personal qualities, especially if they had a genuine understanding of and liking for the residents, a sense of humour, a capacity to evoke respect and an ability to comfort those in distress. All the twenty-six homes had at least one other staff member, but the establishment was inadequate in some homes and there were acute staff shortages in many. It was difficult to find staff who were suitable for work with long hours, poor working conditions and the strain of constant contact with unhappy people, and who also fitted in well with existing staff. The result was that candidates known to be unsuitable might be appointed, or the post left unfilled. Some matrons were so overburdened with household chores and routine administration that they had no time to help residents with social and emotional difficulties. Yet this ought to be the matron's primary function while other staff were seeing to the cooking, cleaning, and other domestic and clerical work. It was essential for the staff to know the residents' world, to understand their attitudes and to lessen their feelings of social rejection, ostracism and guilt. But as in all residential homes, there was a risk of the staff losing contact with the ordinary community and changing social attitudes.

The care function was essentially the comfort and support which residents sought as an asylum and safe shelter from a hostile environment. This support they largely gave through their efforts to help each other as a group through the comfort of being together. The survey interviewers had lively group discussions on a variety of subjects which revealed strong views. There was an obvious sense of group unity and support, though the residents often felt that unmarried staff could not understand the agony of deciding the baby's future or the pain of parting with it for adoption. Well-conducted group discussions by matrons or social workers on this crucial decision, on fostering and on adoption would have greatly helped to lessen tensions and anxieties, and dispel ignorance and confusion. The most important issue of all, whether or not to keep the baby, was always on their minds and they were desperate to sort things out. Some took their troubles to the matron but often they had no one to talk to except other very worried residents. Most of the matrons would not discuss plans until the baby was two or three weeks old – and the social worker might well not be available. The investigators concluded that the residents needed someone who could help them to formulate and face up to the problem. They did not want anyone else to make the decision for them but they very much wanted help from someone who could tell them all the factors they should consider and help them face the practical and emotional consequences of their decision. Practical problems were often dealt with kindly and helpfully, but support in emotional and social difficulties was usually not available, nor in fact recognised as necessary.

Only about half the residents had seen a caseworker since they came into the home, often because moral welfare workers were satisfied with the care in the home and thought that contact was unnecessary, or the matron resented it, or long distances made continued contact too difficult (a resident might have chosen to go far away from her own neighbourhood). Most moral welfare workers interviewed knew that clients were seen too infrequently, caseloads were too heavy and there was often little chance to build up a good relationship over a series of interviews. In contrast, those residents whose caseworkers had sufficient time or were within travelling distance said how understanding they had been in giving practical help and a chance to talk things out. But most were vague about their caseworkers: they were nice, kind people who would help you if they could; they arranged admission to the home and would help with adoption, but that was it. The study concluded that the objectives of casework with unmarried mothers should be to support and help them in making plans for the baby and to help with unresolved problems of which the illegitimate pregnancy might be a symptom. If possible this would include working with the family and the baby's father.

Mother and baby homes were valuable if they provided accommodation not otherwise available for girls who wanted the comfort and companionship of being with other unmarried mothers; and if they helped them to meet the social and emotional problems of their illegitimate maternity. The rules, restrictions, invasion of privacy and erosion of responsibility were too great in most of the homes surveyed to make this possible. These findings have been summarised in detail because they also clearly illustrate some of the inherent difficulties and the lack of individual help or group discussions common in various other residential institutions.

CHANGING SERVICES FOR UNMARRIED MOTHERS IN THE LATE 1960s

The Williams Committee Report, *Caring for People* (1967) included a summary of questionnaire returns from 109 mother and baby homes. The typical home had thirteen residents of whom 73 per cent were aged 15 to 20. The ratio of full-time care staff to residents was 1:4·1. Ninety-seven per cent of the staff were single women (42 per cent aged over 50). The Report commented: 'In mother and baby Homes where the work would appear to be particularly suitable for married women, and there is some evidence that the girls prefer married matrons, it seems surprising that practically no married women are employed' (p. 84). Two-thirds of the staff had a qualification, of these 65 per cent were in nursing and 29 per cent in nursery nursing or child care. The Report failed to mention the Josephine Butler House training.

The closing of many mother and baby homes in the late 1960s was largely due to staff shortages and decreased referrals. Flatlets began to be provided for unsupported mothers where they could keep their babies and enjoy secure accommodation. The 'pill', legalised abortion and more tolerant attitudes towards unmarried mothers and their children contributed to this change. But there were fears that the wholesale closing of mother and baby homes would leave too little support for unstable and unsupported mothers adrift with their babies. In any event, many of them suffered from poverty, poor accommodation, isolation and anxiety – and thus their children suffered too. In the 1960s it became more usual also to try to see and help the putative father. Adoption agencies, in particular, began to discover that he often had strong feelings about the welfare of his child.

By the late 1960s a number of diocesan associations had changed their moral welfare title, freed themselves to broaden the scope of their work and escaped from an out-dated image. Some were transferring work to children's departments: others met with stone-walling by local authorities not keen to take on any extra commitments; and there was, as elsewhere, confusion and anxiety about possible Seebohm changes. It is probably true to say that the moral and social welfare councils welcomed the provision of a basic service for unmarried mothers by the new social services departments. Local pressure might be necessary to ensure an adequate service, and withdrawal by diocesan associations over a period in consultation with the local authority services. Some which were also societies registered for adoption planned to continue this service in co-operation with a range of other supporting services, housing associations and 'sheltered' housing projects for unsupported mothers, youth counselling services, and the like. Various aspects of this wider view of a partnership between the Anglican

Church and the public services to create a 'caring community' were explored in *The Church and the Social Services* (Board for Social Responsibility of the National Assembly of the Church of England, 1969).

Thus 'moral welfare', an integral part of social work for many years, was coming to an end as such, though in some dioceses family welfare services were still primarily for unmarried mothers (or fathers). At an earlier period it was urgently necessary to help prostitutes and to protect outcast and neglected unmarried mothers and vulnerable children, but it is questionable whether the service should have been continued in this particular form for so long without more pressure on local health authorities to exercise their responsibilities and for adequate provision within general family and child care services. There was also too little recognition of the isolation that may result from attempts by voluntary effort to provide universal coverage for narrowly defined groups, rather than to pioneer and demonstrate standards for a service which then becomes part of universal and general provision. Moral welfare associations themselves were exploited by the failures of public provision, with the result that they continued for too long and attempted too much. In the circumstances many sensible people felt impelled to devote themselves to this work, to persevere with few resources in spite of much frustration because they were faced with the urgent daily needs of defenceless and unsupported women and girls for whom no alternative care existed.

The Seebohm Committee (1968) recommended that there should be 'a clear assignment of responsibility to the social service department for ensuring adequate social care and advice for both the unmarried mother and her child' (para. 211). Although social services and social work departments assumed this responsibility, the provision of 'adequate social care' remained an aspiration, especially of decent and secure housing and financial resources.

TRAINING FOR MORAL WELFARE

The pattern of the Josephine Butler Memorial College courses for 'indoor' and 'outdoor' workers remained substantially unchanged from the pre-1950 period. A handful of students took the three-year courses which included the Liverpool University social science diploma and others took some lectures at the University. A one-year course was started in 1965. From that year the students, who now included men, took some subjects in the CSW course at the Polytechnic instead of the University. The total syllabus included theology, as well as social science and social work subjects and fieldwork. Increasingly the Josephine Butler courses began to suffer the fate of other specialised *ad hoc* courses when a coherent national pattern of training began to emerge. There were discussions with the CTSW about recognition of the casework course, and similar discussions with the CTC about the residential care course. But it was not the policy of either training council to recognise specialist courses which were not conducted in a general educational institution. Moral welfare workers who had taken these courses thus fell between two stools, and no 'conversion' courses were provided for them. Finally in 1972 the courses came to an end and the College was changed into a hall of residence, though it still provided refresher courses and seminars relating to illegitimacy and adoption.

The London course was started during the Second World War to meet an immediate need, but continued on into the 1960s as a short specialised training with two months' theoretical work and four months' practice for women over 40. It made a substantial contribution to the number of moral welfare workers.

Of 289 moral welfare workers covered by a survey in 1968 13 had taken a social science and Josephine Butler Memorial College qualification, 63 the College's two-year course and 23 the older entrants course, while 19 had professional social work qualifications. The largest single group, 77, had taken the London course. Of 74 staff of mother and baby homes, 21 'had some social work training'.

ONE-PARENT FAMILIES AND THE FINER REPORT

The common disadvantages suffered by all types of one-parent families only became 'visible' in the late 1960s, when the Finer Committee was set up to study the legal, financial and social difficulties from which divorced, separated, deserted and widowed marriage partners or unmarried mothers suffered. Its Report (1974) explored the many disabilities that could be the lot of more than a million children and their parents, yet it recognised that

'One-parent families do not share a common affliction in the sense that this might be said of all who suffer from a physical disablement of a certain kind. Many of the parents and children in such families are successful in their own relationships, form rewarding relationships with others, attain a measure of personal and social competence and success, and enjoy a level of happiness which in no way differentiates them from other families or groupings of families in the community. In all these matters they vary, like all other families, among themselves . . . For some . . . the withdrawal of a violent husband and father or a neglectful wife and mother may create better, even if still unsatisfactory, conditions in the home than existed previously. It would be untrue of 'one-parent families and do an injustice to them if an account of the disadvantages from which they suffer were to categorise them as a section of our society united in inadequacy, whether self-made or imposed.' (para. 8.3)

The 'inadequacies' changed over time from the crisis of an illegitimate pregnancy, or the death or desertion of the wife or husband with consequent feelings of grief, loss, rejection or humiliation, to the enduring strain of poverty, the necessity to cope alone without a partner, to suffer loneliness yet try to fulfil both parents' roles for the children. Many lone parents were forced, and often wished, to work, but women's wages were low and provision for the care of the children during working hours quite insufficient. Many were on supplementary benefit, others had earnings below that level. The result was that the child might

'. . . have to cope with a mother who is constantly worried with the effort of making the money go round, who has nothing to spare for extras which most other children take for granted, and who is lonely and depressed. Such a child may have to fend for himself because his parent is working, carry a share of domestic responsibilities beyond his years and capacity, and so be compelled to frequent absence from school.' (para. 8.12)

The Committee found that children in one-parent families tended to show more stress symptoms than other children. There were 13,200 places in day nurseries in 1973 but 250,000 one-parent families with children under 5. In 1970 over half the children in long-stay care were from such families. Housing was also an acute problem because of the scarcity of private accommodation to let, high rents and reluctance to take children, coupled with long waiting lists for council housing. Poverty and housing difficulties were the two biggest material disadvantages suffered by one-parent families and obviously added greatly to emotional and social stress. Less than 15 per cent of all lone parents were unmarried mothers. One in six were lone fathers, many of whom wanted to make a home for the children in a culture which assumed it was 'unmanly' for a man to give up work, care for children and do household chores. They thus received no kudos for that which was considered commendable in a woman. Sometimes their higher earnings made it easier for them to pay for help in working hours but often there was no alternative to the children being received into care. Lone fathers had begun to be identified as a group whose particular disabilities were acknowledged, and they were accepted in the self-help groups started by women single parents in different parts of the country for mutual support and pressure.

Housing projects included short-stay accommodation in converted houses, sometimes with residential supervision. Over 100 such schemes were known to the National Council for the Unmarried Mother and Her Child by 1972 (*Annual Report*, p. 21). Some mothers who could manage on their own were living in such accommodation, but there was practically nothing for mothers with multiple problems and severe emotional difficulties. Long-stay housing projects faced the dilemma of whether special provision should be made for one-parent families with mutual support, or whether this labelled and segregated them. In some areas one-parent, self-help and discussion groups were successful but in others, mothers' groups as such were more acceptable.

The Finer Committee's recommendation of a guaranteed maintenance allowance for children in one-parent families would have dealt with the worst uncertainties and deprivations of poverty, though the range of care and support services for children and parents remained gravely lacking and the housing situation worsened. The Report's proposals had not resulted in action by 1975 in spite of much pressure from the Finer Implementation Action Group and elsewhere. It was significant of a new concern that the National Council for the Unmarried Mother and Her Child, established in 1918, changed its title in 1973 to One-Parent Families and extended its responsibilities.

By 1975 it was clear that:

(a) unmarried mothers were only a small proportion of all one-parent families;

(b) such families were more 'at risk' than others, and therefore additional financial, housing and social services help was necessary to lessen stress and loneliness;

(c) concern for the children's welfare should over-ride judgements about parental adequacy or inadequacy;

(d) provision in a special one-parent category should be avoided unless it was clearly indicated.

PART FOUR   BEYOND THE BOUNDS OF SOCIAL WORK?

Chapter 18

Community Work

Community work in a conceptualised form, with training, an association of community workers and a body of literature only dated from the late 1960s. It had actually been undertaken for years by settlements, community centres, clubs and councils of social service. Many self-help groups also existed, started for their own purposes and making their own decisions. But these diverse activities did not rest upon a common body of knowledge nor were they an identifiable movement.

The need for community work was demonstrated by the social consequences of large-scale urban development, mobility in employment, the growth of new housing estates, the persistence of deprived neighbourhoods and the increasing number of immigrants. All these resulted in the severing of neighbourhood ties and of old close-knit communities. Community work as a distinctive activity thus finally emerged in response to problems of massive population change, large-scale deployment of resources remote from democratic control, industrial developments and areas of urban blight, which resulted in a need for a complex variety of other services and fresh responses to new patterns of living. This pointed to the necessity for integrated social planning in order to give proper weight to the human consequences of technological change.

The emergence of community work as a subject of special study, practice and training was also probably an aspect of lessening paternalism in the social services, a growing belief that people have a right and duty to participate, to be respected as equal citizens, to have their say in social action which affects their lives, to express their views, take part in decision-making processes, and to achieve self-chosen goals, rather than having things done for them, without their knowledge or consent. It was also a reaction against the growing size and bureaucracy of the public services and thus the inability of elected representatives to fulfil their ascribed function.

Sociologists differed about the meaning or usefulness of the concept of community, including its imprecise use with a variety of loose meanings. Cheetham and Hill (1973) in analysing these suggest 'it is important to acknowledge that areas which are changing rapidly, and these areas are often focuses of attention for community workers, are particularly likely to be socially heterogeneous' (p. 333). None the less the term was a useful shorthand to describe various group and intergroup activities of people with common interests in a locality or with a community of interests, or attempts from outside to stimulate community involvement where this was obviously lacking.

There was far from being a gradual and progressive development in community work over the whole period. The Bristol Action Research Project (Spencer, 1964) was a pioneer attempt to 'establish practical means of tackling . . . strains and stresses . . . encouraging local initiative and getting local residents to take a greater degree of responsibility for their community life' (p. 3). Such an enterprise was new in this country at the time, with no guidelines as to methods or criteria for evaluation. The Project met with much hostility and its direct achievements were limited. Nevertheless its work with local groups demonstrated the powerful effect of social pressures on individual attitudes and behaviour, and later action research studies benefited from its experience.

From the mid-1950s the London Council of Social Service, in common with other attempts elsewhere, pioneered community work with already existing tenants' associations on local authority housing estates. These groups were autonomous but needed more organisational and social skills to work for their self-chosen aims without endangering their independence. Goetschius' study of these activities (1969) was an early attempt to identify community workers' functions which he defined as providing information, acting as a go-between and giving direct help, encouragement and support. This was also the first attempt to use detailed case records to illustrate common principles in community development. It emphasised the importance of detailed record keeping and concluded that a specialised training was needed for community work which 'can be regarded either as adult education or as social work, depending on the nature of the sponsoring agency' (p. 161). It was only concerned with pre-existing groups and did not discuss the inherent conflicts and power struggles which later became a dominant theme in community work. Its title indicated uncertainty about the boundary between group and community work. It assumed that community work was a method of social work and one which had been gravely neglected in comparison with casework.

The range of community activities as they began to emerge during the 1960s included a variety of self-help groups, whether pre-school play groups, tenants' associations, squatters' associations, or others. Some of these were able to manage their affairs but others needed help to sustain interest, build up confidence, find a meeting place, learn the necessary social skills, discover particular needs in a neighbourhood, stimulate people to come together and form an active committee, run the committee and decide upon and carry through projects, fact-finding surveys, money-raising efforts, publicity campaigns, deputations to the local authority, and so on. This was largely the non-directive type of community work which began to be systematised around the mid-1960s.

There was much discussion of the need to stimulate local community care for old or handicapped people or acceptance of ex-prisoners or psychiatric patients or of social dropouts: community relations activities on behalf of coloured immigrants also became important as their numbers and the consequent tensions increased. This type of community work with predetermined goals, namely attempts to change local attitudes through outside action, was little developed in practice.

Initially community work was seen in rather one-dimensional terms of helping people to think, decide and act. This was the consensus model advocated by Batten (1957) and Ross (1955). Later American influence, stemming from juvenile delinquency and anti-poverty programs reinforced the view that much community group activity was about the redistribution of scarce resources and helping deprived people to gain more power. In the United States and later in this country this resulted in the realisation that the aims of community groups may be frustrated by powerful vested interests or entrenched attitudes and that, since conflict is sometimes inevit-able, community workers should include political and public relations skills in their practice. There was no agreement as to whether the primary aim of community work was that the people concerned should achieve results important to them, or better social relationships, or concentrate on a power struggle to induce structural change. There was also disagreement amongst community workers who either saw themselves as helping groups to achieve their own self-chosen objectives, or aimed to influence or select groups to respond to the community worker's own view of desirable objectives.

In 1966 the Gulbenkian Foundation set up a study group to analyse present and future objectives in community work and to make recommenda-tions about training. Its report (1968) played an influential part in clarifying confused thought about community work as it was then emerging, and contributed to dramatic developments in the late 1960s. It concluded that community work was

'. . . only one aspect of the far broader issue of how to meet people's needs and give them an effective say in what these are and how they want them met. It is part of a protest against apathy and complacency and against distant and anonymous authority. It is also part of the whole dilemma of how to reconcile the "revolution of human dissent" with the large-scale organisation and economic and social planning which seem to be inseparably interwoven with the parallel revolution of rising expectations. This boils down to the problem of how to give meaning to democracy.' (p. 4)

'Community work is essentially about the interrelations between people and social change, how to help people and the providers of services to bring about a more comfortable "fit" between themselves and constant change, how to survive and grow as persons in relation with others.' (p. 29)

The study group narrowed down this broad analysis in operational terms to: direct community work with local people; agency and interagency co-ordination; community planning and policy formulation (p. 35). These might be separate or interlocking functions performed by the same agency or community worker in different contexts. For some time there was marked resistance to this broad definition, since the energies of community workers were concentrated on neighbourhood community work. This began to change in the mid-1970s as neighbourhood community workers took on wider responsibilities and the limitations of neighbourhood work itself became more apparent.

At the time there was much heart-searching as to whether or not community work should become a definable separate activity, possibly full-time and with a professional training. It was cogently argued that an informed understanding of the 'community dimension' was a necessary part of the professional task of senior administrators, members of various professions, local councillors and planners, rather than something which should become an occupation in its own right. But the study group concluded that 'common experience suggests that where no category of professionally employed people is primarily committed to the exercise and development of a particular function regarded as socially desirable it is likely that it will remain subsidiary to other professional purposes' (p. 28). The views of those who thought both were necessary prevailed. Much discussion of 'the community dimension' was primarily about possible trends, hopes and aspirations, even a denial of realities. Developments in Scottish social work departments in the 1970s were first steps towards implementing the concept.

The report identified five phases in community work with their accompanying analysis and action. These phases were: exploration and study; creation of a structure and supports; formulating policy; implementing plans; and evaluation (pp. 68–9). This framework applied in many different forms of community work and at different levels, including the interactions within and between different groups, relations between officialdom and local groups, between different organisations, and in relation to struggles for resources.

The later and much enlarged Boyle Group, also sponsored by the Gulbenkian Foundation from 1970–3, concentrated on *Current Issues in Community Work* (1973). Even in this short period, the climate had changed considerably. 'Community oriented' attitudes were still far from universal, though stimulated by frustration or a more general desire for participation; community activists and pressure groups were more numerous and more community workers were employed in a variety of settings, while fundamental conflicts about the aims and methods of community work were more starkly apparent (p. 18). It was also more obvious that 'some of the more difficult assumptions about community work relate to concepts of authority, power and the distribution of resources' (p. 21).

There were fluid boundaries between group work and community work, indeed group and intergroup work was an essential element in all community work though much group work was not in any sense community work. In so-called grass-roots community work the worker needed a competent knowledge of the local authority and voluntary services; and to be able to interpret life as seen through the eyes of local people, the priorities as they saw them for lessening the pressures and constrictions from which they suffered. Much community work required for its success an ability to stretch the imagination and shake the rigidities of many of those in authority. Comprehensive social data were essential to analyse the effect on people of economic, population and other changes in order to make possible across-the-board social planning of services through interdisciplinary and interagency co-operation.

Controversy began during the 1960s as to whether it was essential for community workers to hold appointments built into the power structure in order to bring about change; or whether in such circumstances they became effectively gagged, unable to protest against the activities – or inertia – of their employers, particularly if they worked in one local authority department and caused trouble with others. It was thus essential, some said, for community workers to be outside the power structure, preferably employed by community groups, and free to help groups to clarify their dissatisfactions and take action. Community workers employed by voluntary organisations might also be able to support unpopular pressure groups unless this seriously affected the organisation's fund-raising efforts. In contradistinction, Cheetham and Hill (1973) argued that local authorities were not monolithic structures and that community workers could be effective if they presented plans and projects 'sensibly and cogently' (p. 344).

Explorations in the use of community work were beginning to be made by agencies which had hitherto put all their eggs in the casework, group-work or education baskets. Such varied studies as the Plowden Report (1967), *Probationers in their Social Environment* (Davies, 1969), *Advice, Guidance and Assistance* (Leissner *et al.*, 1971), *Stress and Release in an Urban Estate* (Spencer, 1964), the Seebohm Report (1968), *The Needs of New Communities* (Ministry of Housing and Local Government, 1967), and many others all demonstrated the ineffectiveness of trying to foster social improvement by concentrating on individuals and groups without changing the quality of the environment in which they had their roots, or were rootless. The Seebohm Report stressed

'. . . the need for the personal social services to engage in the extremely difficult and complex task of encouraging and assisting the development of community identity and mutual aid, particularly in areas characterised by rapid population turnover, high delinquency, child deprivation and mental illness rates and other indices of social pathology. Social work with individuals alone is bound to be of limited effect in an area where the community environment itself is a major impediment to healthy individual development.' (para. 477)

Some growing points in community work were manifested in tenants' associations, the beginnings of the welfare rights movement fostered by the Child Poverty Action Group and by individual supporters, squatters' associations, family advice centres run by children's departments, local activities of community relations councils, the Young Volunteer Force Foundation, and many other forms. For example, in some situations the amount of unmet need uncovered by a neighbourhood family advice centre made it obvious that preventive work must include play centres and youth clubs, information services (including housing and social security), material help and social work services. Such centres 'were community based and aimed at fostering community participation, . . . they were *not* aimed at replacing existing services, but at supplementing them, or at providing services where the relevant agencies had failed to do so' (italics in original) (Leissner *et al.*, 1971, p. 315).

These detached centres in high-need communities 'showed a marked tendency to regard the community as the basic client unit and to allocate much time and effort to community work' (Leissner and Joslin, 1974, p. 122).

From another angle, the Department of the Environment undertook from 1973 four inner area action research studies to examine the functioning and needs of each area from the point of view of the people living there, including housing, transport, environmental services and education, employment, health and social services.

As community work experience accumulated an essential element in it was clearly an ability to understand the impact on local people of their living conditions, to discover why services did not reach them effectively, and to stimulate both their's and service agencies' participation in improving the situation. The causes included local people's ignorance about existing services and how to approach them; fragmented and inaccessible services; complex and differing eligibility requirements; the negative attitudes of some services; gaps or overlapping in services; and rigid, inadequate or non-existent provision. This liaison, stimulating, interpreting role in an intricate web of public and voluntary agencies proved as complex as the abilities needed in working with neighbourhood groups, bearing in mind that these groups themselves were likely to be split by a variety of alignments and vested interests rather than presenting a united front.

David Thomas (1976) described and analysed the Southwark Community Project sponsored by the NISW which was a comparatively untried form of community interaction when it started in 1968. The aim was a dual approach through service agencies and local groups to improve 'outside' material resources of housing and employment and planning and co-ordination between services; and to stimulate local groups to influence these decision-making processes. This case history, very different from others referred to above, showed the emergence by the 1970s of the double commitment of community work, the frustrations of inability to remedy unemployment or bad housing, or to improve services, and thus the tensions for community workers trying to negotiate more external resources to help local people to improve the quality of their lives. A number of other action research projects were started in the late 1960s and early 1970s, whether under public or voluntary auspices. Some were time-limited, three- or four-year projects but many were continuing activities by local authorities, settlements, councils of voluntary service, or self-help groups.

The Seebohm Committee saw the situation through the other end of the telescope when they said

'If the services are to meet effectively the complex range of individual, family and community problems, then effort devoted to investigating the needs of an area, and to the overall planning and co-ordination of services and resources, both statutory and voluntary, is clearly of the utmost importance. The staff of the social service department will need to see themselves not as a self-contained unit but as part of a network of services within the community. Thus effective co-ordination with other services and individuals and the mobilisation of community resources, especially volunteers, to meet need are as important aspects of the administration of the social service department – and demand as much skill – as its internal management.' (para. 478)

They were certainly right in their final comment. This type of co-ordination was an example of the community focus in administration and applied to local authorities as such.

Both the Seebohm Committee and the Scottish White Paper *Social Work and the Community* (Scottish Education and Scottish Home and Health Departments, 1966) envisaged that the new unified social service or social work departments would be committed to encouraging community participation and efforts to contribute to community well-being. Senior posts in community work would be necessary to develop these aspects and to act as consultants to area teams, whose staffs should be skilled at working with and in the community. A number of such appointments were made in the early 1970s, but often to co-ordinate and support local voluntary organisations rather than to stimulate neighbourhood community action.

A leading American expert, Specht (1975), concluded from his observations that in Britain the concentration on local neighbourhood community work seriously limited its scope, functions and potential. Small local groups could only have limited capacities, resources and goals, in contrast with representative statutory and voluntary councils and planning bodies covering wide areas which could use community work to increase their understanding of and links with local communities. Overconcentration on organising the poor ignored the reality that effective support for social change must involve a broad cross-section of those in key positions, including central government financial and political support. Moreover, deprivation was not concentrated in localities, for example most children in disadvantaged areas are not deprived. He found that community workers themselves were despondent and disillusioned at not having achieved much in relation to their aspirations. This raised the question of whether community work was a social movement or a profession. Many young community workers were motivated by an ideological drive to bring about massive social change. This was based on a theory that provided a simple, straightforward explanation of a social evil along with directions for its elimination. Professionals, on the other hand, have an enduring function and must develop a broad spectrum of ideas, theories and practices to meet a variety of community problems. A social movement ideology would not give community workers the range of knowledge and skill needed for the task. In his view there was also a neglect amongst British community workers of the structural and organisational aspects of change, of communication systems, and the evaluation of results. The primary interest of community workers in group and intergroup activities, social planning and structural change raised continuing questions about the relations between community work and casework with its primary interest in individuals.

COMMUNITY DEVELOPMENT PROJECTS

The principle of selectivity expressed as positive discrimination, i.e. making more resources available where there was high social need, was implemented in the late 1960s through the urban aid programme, education priority areas (EPAs) and the Home Office-sponsored community development projects. In the urban aid programme a 75 per cent government grant was available in many areas of high social need. Under it, many imaginative projects run by local authorities or voluntary organisations were sponsored. Educational priority area projects (which stemmed from the Plowden Committee's recommendations, 1967) were based on local schools. At their most idealistic they aimed at 'a curriculum realistically related to the EPA environment and designed to equip the rising generation with the knowledge and skills to cope with, gain power over and in the end to transform the conditions of their local community' (DES, 1972, p. 12). It was recognised that EPAs were only a part of a comprehensive social movement of community development.

In 1969 the Government decided to set up four – later to be increased to twelve – community development projects (CDPs) in areas of high social need. The aim of the experiment was to discover over a five-year period more effective ways of meeting the needs of people suffering from inter-related forms of social deprivation. It was thought that they did not know the 'true nature' of their problems, or how to use the social services, partly because these latter were vertically organised, whereas many problems required horizontal, co-ordinated services. The CDPs were therefore intended to diagnose the local community's problems, discover how to help them to establish social relationships, to use the social services, and to function with less need for special support. Client participation was not written into the Home Office scheme (Lapping, 1970). It was based heavily on the American anti-poverty program experience but was to be operated through local authorities. Formulated criteria for success included increased personal care, better family functioning and child-rearing practices, and improved physical conditions in the neighbourhood. These differed substantially from some later community development criteria when conflict about the reasons for community deprivation increased.

Small areas with about 10,000–20,000 population were to be centrally chosen in co-operation with the local authorities concerned, with 75 per cent finance from the urban programme and 25 per cent from the local authority. Interservice teams consisting of two or three full-time and additional part-time members, with the participation of all the local statutory and voluntary services, were to identify needs, stimulate better co-ordination and accessibility of services, and foster community involvement, with better communication between local people and local services. There was also to be a Home Office central team, with the whole project closely related to the urban aid programme and EPA projects. Research and evaluation provided by local universities or polytechnics was to be built in from the beginning. The central team started in 1969; and a central information and intelligence unit came into existence in 1973. Two local CDPs started in 1970 and the last three of the twelve in 1972.

Originally it was assumed that the research teams would provide data, act as consultants to the action teams, and evaluate the results of their activities. This separation resulted in friction because action research could not be carried on smoothly by two separate groups. Consequently the two moved closer together; in some projects research team members were also involved in action. Differences in basic assumptions in different CDPs resulted in a critical assessment of different methods and a radical view of the whole experiment.

Several different types of area were chosen, some suffering from industrial decline, others in small areas of urban blight in the midst of regional growth. Within this diversity, most projects found 'lower than average incomes; disproportionately high rates of unemployment; high dependence on state benefits . . . and poor housing, lack of amenities, overcrowding, dilapidation or stigma (National Community Development Project, 1974, p. 8).

The initial assumptions that multiple deprivation originated in the pathology of the local people and could be overcome by improving the local services and communication links and generating self-help activities had therefore been challenged, and it began to be assumed that

'Problems of multi-deprivation have to be re-defined and re-interpreted in terms of structural constraints rather than psychological motivations, external rather than internal factors . . . the symptoms of disadvantage . . . cannot be explained adequately by any abnormal preponderance of individuals or families whose behaviour could be defined as "pathological". Even where social "malaise" is apparent it does not seem best explained principally in terms of personal deficiencies, so much as the product of external pressures in the wider environment.' (p. 8)

Unskilled and semi-skilled workers, immigrants, unsupported mothers, large families and the elderly were likely to be concentrated in areas of the worst housing with poorer public facilities and services. This reinforced the view that large-scale structural change was essential to redress the unequal distribution of goods and services, which led to the powerlessness of the poor to remedy their lot without massive external resources.

Within the general context, local teams concentrated on different forms of action based on different ideas about how to achieve change. These ideas could be grouped into the following assumptions. Firstly, concensus assumptions that social problems could be cured by better communication and co-ordination. Secondly, pluralist assumptions that social problems are largely due to failures of participation and an imbalance of interests in the political arena; change therefore results from negotiation between the policy makers and the disenfranchised. Finally, the structural conflict assumption that social problems are due to fundamental conflicts of interest between social classes, the problem is the unequal distribution of power, and change can only result from working with organised groups.

Most CDPs operated on a mixture of these assumptions and used community development, community organisation and community action methods. These included social planning aimed at changes in policy as a result of analysis of the physical, social and economic aspects of a given situation; changes in organisational practices through better management and administration, including better communication, leading to improved co-ordination and more efficient services; and community development aimed at improving the functioning of local communities, and especially the development of community relationships. Better co-ordination and communication had been to some extent achieved by the project teams, for example through community education programmes, better services for young people, support for community groups, lively information and advice centres, and welfare rights campaigns. But these methods were ineffective where major policy changes were needed, for instance in urban redevelopment schemes.

Each project selected a set of local issues for an inter-related attempt to tackle these problems through action and research in the light of an analysis of the area's problems. Interproject discussion clarified common key issues. Some of these were: unemployment (both structural and of particular groups), income and income maintenance, much unmet need, ignorance about welfare rights, and housing (especially the whole question of publicly provided housing and 'ghetto' estates). Related to these key issues were projects for the old, the young, and for better race relations. The organisational and community development activities related to these key issues were the promotion of neighbourhood action. This included making available to local community groups information, advice and technical expertise, running community newspapers and providing equipment. Some teams responded to every issue raised locally, while others decided in advance what problems to tackle. Some local authorities started multiservice centres in team areas.

These activities entailed many studies and surveys by the teams, contributions by local authorities and central government, use of other relevant knowledge and experience, discussions with local residents and consultations with a variety of agencies knowledgeable about the areas and their problems. The results were sharpened perceptions, wider social networks and better communication between many different groups and interests, including local authority departments and government local offices. Projects changed rapidly, which made it impossible to give an accurate picture of their action and ethos over a period of time.

Bennington (1974) described through a detailed case study how experience in the Coventry CDP had led to the view that 'many of the critical problems identified by the Project study area are not inherent in or specific to that neighbourhood, but are manifestations of wider processes in society . . . the wider class structure within which 'deprivation' has to be examined' (p. 275). This was reiterated in the National CDP *Forward Plan 1975–76* (1975): 'Poverty is seen to be a consequence of fundamental inequalities in our present political and economic system . . . Improved co-ordination of existing social and welfare services can at best make only a marginal impact' (p. 1). This conclusion was inevitably controversial.

'The CDPs were surely accurate in overturning the one sided belief on which they were founded: that run-down neighbourhoods were created by socially incompetent inhabitants whose ills could be righted simply by extra social service support and participation policies. It was . . . well known long before 1970 that local people could not cure the bad housing, the housing policies, the poverty and unemployment which constricted their lives and in some was accompanied by manifestations of malfunctioning.' ('CDPs Writ Larger', *New Society*, July 1975)

In 1975 the Home Office decided to launch a comprehensive community project (CCP) under the aegis of its new urban deprivation unit. This was to cover much wider geographical areas than CDPs and embrace regional economic planning boards, area health authorities and all local government departments. Pilot projects were to be started in Gateshead, Bradford, the Wirral and Wandsworth. In most debates there was an either/or assumption between self-help participation and better local authority services on the one hand, and on the other politically motivated change with a massive injection of national resources.

COMMUNITY ACTION

Spontaneous groups coming together for some kind of common action – whether to run an outing, protect their interests, protest, or get something changed – were a familiar part of social life. But in the late 1960s community action became more clearly defined as the poor and the powerless taking action on their own behalf. This sprang partly from the shortcomings and aloofness of central and local government, and the persistence of multi-deprivation in certain neighbourhoods in regard to housing, environmental conditions and poverty. It was an essential element in community action that groups, whether or not they received outside help, consisted of local people who were themselves leaders and decision makers and had discovered that by banding together as tenants against property developers, or as welfare right claimants, or as parents they could get grievances listened to and learn how some part of 'the system' could be modified. For example, the Southwark Community Project generated local community groups which stayed together and raised funds to employ community workers when the Project ended.

In the 1970s many social workers aligned themselves with community action groups and supported them with information, help in finding places to meet, resources to run the group, and the know-how to present a case to public authorities. This could help to bridge the communication gap between two groups of people whose orderly or spontaneous ways of working and different language codes often made each incomprehensible to the other, which of itself generated hostility. Social workers sometimes found themselves at odds with their employers if a group became too militant in its actions or radical in its demands.

Some community activists accepted an obligation to make poor people politically conscious about an unjust system; to others this was an element in the work but not the whole of it; yet others were not concerned about inducing change by political means. This boiled down to belief in community action as a means to secure more resources through a process that enabled people to become socially effective, or else a commitment to induce structural change as the only means of altering an essentially unjust social system. On this last view, 'Community work can be seen as a new technique to cover over the more open sores of the capitalist urban structure' (Herne, 1975, p. 20). Community action projects were more likely to employ conflict than consensus strategies.

THE EMPLOYMENT OF COMMUNITY WORKERS

The clarification of community work as a distinct method of practice with significant common elements only gathered momentum in the late 1960s. Previously those newly identified as community workers had been designated according to the post they occupied, whether as wardens of settlements, social development officers in new towns, secretaries of councils of social service, community relations officers, or others. New discoveries about the effects of the social environment cast light on the importance of the community work element in the functions of many teachers, youth leaders, caseworkers in various settings, planners, the clergy, architects, local councillors, some doctors, and administrators in many services, whether statutory or voluntary.

In 1967 the Gulbenkian Study Group tried to collect information about the qualifications and tasks of those employed in existing posts in community work, as well as about salaries and career prospects. This proved a frustrating exercise because of the rapidly changing scene, the variety of auspices, the different designations of jobs, so that some people were called community workers though their primary function was different, while others where it was indeed the primary function had a variety of different titles. From the limited data available, it seemed as though the majority of those with a clearly defined community work function were employed by voluntary organisations, though pioneer appointments were also being made by public authorities. It was obvious that often the appointing body did not know what community work was or what could be expected from it, but was hopefully appointing someone to find out and achieve the impossible.

Salaries were either on the Whitley, Burnham, APT or civil service scales and varied widely in relation to the level of responsibility. Some community workers (for example, a few secretaries of councils of social service or settlement wardens, social development officers and community relations officers) had a social science qualification or youth leadership training, but the majority had no academic or relevant qualifications and none were required for appointment. This was not surprising in a situation reminiscent of casework in the mid-1940s.

In interviews for the Gulbenkian Group with community workers they identified four main functions: fact finding, fostering local initiative by helping local groups in defining and working to achieve what they wanted, administration of the community work agency, and direct service to the community to provide a communication link between the people and organisations. These functions translated into skills included the ability to gather and analyse information quickly, to establish and maintain good relations with many different individuals, groups and organisations; and competence in administration and committee work. The essentials of community work were identified in terms of competence required in day-to-day activities with a guiding purpose, though the report itself, *Community Work and Social Change* (Gulbenkian Foundation, 1968) included a more sophisticated analysis. There were no criteria for measuring the effectiveness of specific community work projects. In interagency community work constant committee meetings, telephoning, letter writing, memoranda and discussions made it difficult to remain clear about objectives, about what was relevant or irrelevant in a hurried and overbusy life. No matter where or how it was practised, the boundaries of community work were bound to be indeterminate and the central core easier to define in theory than in day-to-day practice.

The picture, then, in the mid-1960s was of an increasing number of community work appointments by a variety of different agencies, but chaotic employment conditions, no career structure, ill-defined promotion prospects and no relevant training. The situation was, perhaps inevitably, equally chaotic from the point of view of the varied legislation under which community workers could be employed and the various local authority departments where they might be found. Probably the two most clearly defined groups were secretaries of councils of social service (of whom there were over 100 in 1967) and new towns social development officers (of whom at that time there were 17 with 34 assistants).

The Gulbenkian Foundation undertook for the Boyle Group a further survey in 1970–1 of all advertised posts in five national publications, which seemed to be primarily community work. Two hundred and thirty-three posts (by this time six out of ten were advertised by public authorities) were identified and further information was obtained about 153, of which over half were new posts. Confusion about the nature of community work continued so that over half the local education authority posts were in youth or community centre work, similarly some social services department posts were primarily casework or community care. A higher proportion of community work appointments than previously were being made by planning or housing departments, new towns corporations, or the Community Relations Commission. Voluntary bodies included councils of social service and a variety of independent local groups which had raised funds to start a community project. There were also new openings for community work teaching and research. Each local authority department decided for itself whether the salary of a community worker should be on the Burnham, JNC, Soulbury or APT scales. Appointing bodies were still both unclear and overoptimistic.

'Many employers seemed to think of the community worker as someone who, once employed and "on the ground", would automatically resolve community stress or remove specific difficulties. Community work appeared also to be understood by some employers solely as a means for the co-ordination of services in deprived areas (rather than as a means of eliciting community participation), or to be regarded as a panacea for a social malaise which had defied conventional remedies.' (Gulbenkian Foundation, 1973, p. 85)

The London Council of Social Service undertook a survey (1974) of full-time community workers employed in greater London. Details were given of the activities of roughly 250 community workers in a wide variety of statutory and voluntary agencies (sometimes several in one agency), as co-ordinators, for specific groups, to 'improve community relations' or on particular projects. Objectives were clearly specified and a number were joint activities between local authorities and voluntary organisations. This study did not cover the whole range of community work but it illustrated the growing employment of community workers and more realistic ideas about what they could do.

Fieldwork members of the Boyle Group analysed their roles and functions and agreed that

'since they are practitioners in group situations they must have a knowledge of group dynamics, what is happening in a group, the interaction of individuals and the effect of different personalities, including how to cope with natural leaders who may dominate the group. The essential skills in human relationships include how to work effectively with different groups ranging from those with practically no social skills to others with a wide span of knowledge and social competence, how to maintain interest, how to make constructive use of conflict as well as agreement, how to communicate with indigenous groups on the one hand and with senior officials and members of other professions on the other hand. This would include giving practical information, collecting data and presenting it in statistical form, using adult education methods and communication skills, as well as systematically recording what is being done in order to evaluate methods and outcome.' (Gulbenkian Foundation, 1973, p. 110)

This was a significantly more sophisticated appraisal than the previous one (Gulbenkian Foundation, 1968) and many other accounts brought out the high degree of self-awareness, the capacity for well-planned use of working time, for accurate assessment and evaluation needed to estimate the most helpful level of involvement in a particular project, when and how to intervene, support or withdraw.

Chapter 19

Training for Community Work

THE BEGINNINGS OF TRAINING FOR COMMUNITY WORK IN THE 1960s

Training for community work only began in the mid-1960s. In 1967 a questionnaire asking for information about community work teaching was sent to university social studies and adult education departments and colleges of further education with social work courses. This information was published in *Community Work and Social Change* (Gulbenkian Foundation, 1968, pp. 48–59). Many respondents did not understand the term or thought that any discussion of the community implications of the workers' professional task was community work. Theoretical teaching in social studies departments ranged from short optional courses or occasional lectures by visiting lecturers to a 220-hour course of lectures and seminars. Nine applied social studies courses had some teaching on community work. In seven departments field placements in community work were compulsory for students taking a community work option and were optional in some others. The length varied from six to eight weeks.

The University of Manchester Department of Adult Education ran a one-year diploma of advanced studies in community development. Practical work was confined to fact-finding surveys. The Adult Education Department at Edinburgh University had a similar course. University College, Swansea, ran a two-year diploma in social development and social administration with a community work option. Fieldwork occupied eighteen weeks during the two years. The London University Institute of Education had a long-established, three-month course for senior officers. All these courses, primarily designed for overseas students, were taken by an increasing number of British students intending to work in this country.

The LSE had newly started a community work option in its one-year course in social work studies. One two-year child care course had a lecture course and related fieldwork in community development. Several CSW courses included lecture courses and field placements in community work. The two courses in Scotland for the diploma in youth and community service included the principles and practice of community development and field placements in group work in the community. The Westhill College two-year course for community centre wardens included substantial periods of fieldwork. There were short lecture courses on community work, variously interpreted, in a number of other courses. It was clear, however, that training for community development overseas was the only well-established example in the late 1960s, although there was a limited study of community work in other professional courses usually as an aspect of another main function. There were substantial lecture courses on community development in thirteen degree or diploma courses.

This was inevitably a rudimentary start when the subject was a secondary one for most lecturers, when experience in this country was both limited and in the main unrecorded, and the practice of community work had not been conceptualised or related to theoretical knowledge from the social sciences. Moreover, fieldwork still lacked a framework or practitioners qualified to supervise, while some still thought community work was simply an extension of casework. But here, too, a beginning had been made in plans for field teaching units.

In this situation a good deal of the 1968 Gulbenkian Study Group report was devoted to analysing aspects of the social sciences, methods of social investigation, social administration, political theory and social philosophy relevant to training for community work. It assumed that the central issue was 'to determine the basis for selection. In community work, as in other spheres where given sciences are used to underpin practice, this necessitates clarity about the central task – what configuration of activities and purpose distinguishes any particular practice from others' (p. 102).

It stressed the relation of this knowledge to the theory and practice of community work and gave much attention to various forms of fieldwork and the training of field teachers. It suggested that community work should be an option in some applied social studies courses, and in certain circumstances for administrators or teachers, in order that students might take a broad qualification rather than a specialised training. In view of the lack of people competent to teach or supervise community work and the need to build up teaching material, a theory of practice and student units in fieldwork, it proposed that initially resources should be concentrated in two or three full-time courses, but that in-service training should be rapidly expanded.

DEVELOPMENTS IN THE EARLY 1970s

There were a number of developments between 1967 and the later Gulbenkian Foundation Boyle Group Study, *Current Issues in Community Work* (1973). The three separate social work training councils had been merged in the Central Council for Education and Training in Social Work (CCETSW), which had community work related to social work within its terms of reference. The four two-year courses which succeeded the one-year course at the National College for the Training of Youth Leaders were entitled training for youth and community work (see chapter 20, section on 'Training for the Youth Service'). A specialised course in community work had been started at York University and there were streams or options in community work in ten other courses including University College, Swansea, LSE, Birmingham Polytechnic's four-year CNAA sociology degree, and Aberdeen and Glasgow Universities, in addition to the long-established community development courses at Manchester and Edinburgh Universities.

In 1968 the JUC set up what became an active group on community work to be concerned with fieldwork assessment, the recognition of courses and their sponsorship and financing.

Some respondents to the Boyle Group inquiry thought that community work was not part of social work, others that 'the theory and practice of community work should be an integral part of social work training' (Aberdeen University Prospectus 1971–2) or conversely, that it had no teachable body of theory and practice. The following were contrasting points of view from social work courses: '. . . if the social and personal problems which face many citizens are to be dealt with in more than a largely irrelevant manner it will be necessary to extend social work practice into the area of community work' (p. 107). 'Community work does not have a direct bearing on individual cases and therefore could not be regarded as a kind of social work' (p. 160). In short, the intervening five years had clarified confusion and conflict.

The demand for community workers in the new social services or social work departments, together with broader concepts of the nature of social work and reinforced by students' demands, were resulting in more community work teaching in social work courses.

'There has been a shift from concentration on casework to a new concept of social work, based on ability to assess a social situation and intervene in whatever seems to be the most effective way, whether primarily with the individual, family, group or community or with other social systems; this has led to the conclusion that even social workers who will practise primarily as caseworkers must have some abilities in and intelligent understanding of community work.' (p. 107)

Even so, only nine out of forty-six social work courses which gave some teaching on community work had lectures and seminars lasting for two or more terms. There was no agreement about the content of this teaching and only four aspects were commonly taught: roles and techniques of the community worker (53 per cent), social change or social action (79 per cent), pressure groups and other means of intervention (82 per cent), conflict, contest and consensus (66 per cent). About one-third of the courses with this teaching did not include related fieldwork. Some fieldwork consisted of student projects which might or might not include relations with a local community. Only a minority had any substantial provision for community work placements. The picture was more hopeful in intention than practice. There were plans for future expansion of community work – and often the lack of community work teaching was due to the overloaded curricula of one- or two-year courses, to overburdened teachers with little time for study or for contact with practice and the heavy commitments entailed in creating fieldwork placements, training supervisors and facing other problems of relating theory to practice. (Evens (1974) produced a valuable pioneer collection of case studies and articles on supervising by community work teachers and practitioners and, later, *Community Work – One* (Jones and Mayo, 1974) produced on behalf of the Association of Community Workers, also included analytical descriptions of specific projects.)

The situation was compounded by the scarcity of suitable placements, the diffuse nature of much community work and consequent student frustration, the difficulty of giving students responsibility for planning and carrying through a project in the time available; uncertainty about the nature of community work and the skills students should begin to acquire; the teaching content of field supervision in relation to classroom studies; planning the students' work; and the nature of the reports to be required on and by students. This difficult exercise was further confused by a clash of views. One group thought this supervision should use the same educational method (though not with the same content) as casework supervision. For instance, Goetschius (1969) held that

'Supervision in community work is only different from supervision in casework and social group work in its frame of reference. Both supervisor and student or worker operate from their understanding of the community process and the possibilities of intervention in it. Apart from this, supervision has the same purpose of helping the worker to be more objective, to see his work in a proper context, to develop and improve skills and techniques and to come to terms with field work problems.' (p. 167)

A CTC study of *Fieldwork Training for Social Work* (DHSS, 1971c) described in detail community work placements by Liverpool, Leicester, Aberdeen and Oxford Universities. Bryant (1974), in reviewing current inadequacies in both fieldwork and theoretical studies, proposed that educational institutions and fieldwork agencies should jointly set up training projects. Baldock (1974) described supervision in a community work student unit.

Fieldwork was but one aspect of the ideological confusion about community work, and the lack of any systematic study of the processes in different types of community work and the personality, knowledge and aptitudes which these demanded. In spite of these hindrances and the failure to make more adequate provision in a few 'centres of excellence', the Boyle Group found advances in fieldwork, for instance at Glasgow University where the lecturer in community work was in the field for a day a week, the full-time student unit supervisor taught in the classroom and both held monthly meetings for thirty to fifty community workers. There were several other student units with full-time supervisors, financed by government departments or trusts. Community work teachers were finding it essential to run in-service training courses for community workers in the neighbourhood as a means to raise standards. Both sides gained from these group discussions.

In addition to expanded training within the social work orbit, some of the ten new youth and community work courses included teaching and practice in community work (see chapter 20, section on 'Training for the Youth Service). A significant new development was the two- or three-year part-time courses in community work run by extramural departments of universities and by polytechnics, leading to a certificate or diploma. These were taken by practising community workers and as 'conversion' courses by youth leaders, caseworkers and teachers.

Little information existed about the nature and range of in-service training. The NCSS had initiated interdisciplinary part-time courses at five universities. University extramural departments, polytechnics and colleges of further education were all running more part-time courses focused on community issues. The Association of Community Workers (ACW) was also energetically promoting this. Part of the value of in-service training, broadly interpreted, was the exchange of experience, different points of view and disputes about controversial issues. In its various forms it was the best means of raising the level of performance amongst the increasing number of full- or part-time community workers. This and the production and dissemination of teaching materials (including audio/visual aids) was also a means of enriching theory and practice, though much more was needed.

It was generally accepted that although work with communities was an essential part of social work, yet much community work was independent of it. The Boyle Group analysed various points of view about community work (Gulbenkian Foundation, 1973, pp. 113–15). Some saw it as a distinct professional activity related to but separate from both social work and education. To others community work was obviously a facet of adult education but unrelated to social work. Others again saw it as part of modern concepts of administration. To yet others it was essentially a political activity aimed at structural change and the redistribution of power which would inevitably cause dissension; thus community activists should be well grounded in political theory and social action techniques. Others recognised the community element in a variety of professions dealing with how people live, but thought real community work was essentially spontaneous and local. They agreed with those who argued that to train professional community workers would destroy their identification with deprived people, create yet one more self-aggrandising, élitist profession and a remote bureaucratic structure. Everyone recognised that, in any event, professionally trained community workers, in whatever camp they might be, would only be a small minority of all those doing community work. Some argued that, since the number of people employed full-time was steadily increasing, instead of limited experience they needed the support of training in a method applicable in a variety of situations, a sense of identity, responsibility embodied in a code of practice, knowledge backed up by research, and a strong association. This, moreover, would provide some protection for the public against irresponsible activities.

Following upon earlier discussions, the CCETSW was approached by both community work and social work courses for its views about community work. A CCETSW working party recommended recognition of courses with an option in or solely for community work, provided they had a broadly based core content, together with teaching and fieldwork related to the social services. In 1973 the CCETSW decided to recommend community work options in social work courses which it recognised. There were divided reactions to this, some had long been wanting recognition of such options, but to others this savoured of an attempted social work takeover in the absence of a national body concerned with community work as an independent career.

The CCETSW study group on the teaching of community work (1975*d*) accepted that there were radically different views about the existing and future relations between community work and social work, and hoped that these would be put to the test in teaching and practice. It was split on the issue of whether community work was a social work method with similar aims and objectives but with characteristic skills, many of which were shared with other social workers. Those who saw it as part of social work argued that the objectives and values of social work and community work were identical. To separate work with individuals and families from that with community groups would lead to an inadequate understanding of people's needs and the fragmentation of services. The techniques of advocacy, negotiation and group work were accepted as essential elements in social work. Social workers might be involved with many groups whether of single mothers, physically handicapped people, claimants' unions, tenants' associations, pre-school play groups, intermediate treatment projects, and so on.

The opposing side argued that many community work techniques were used by planners, adult educationalists, the clergy and others: and that community work was different from social work because it dealt with processes at work within the whole community, rather than specifically therapeutic activities. It also focused upon the allocation of resources and the development and reassertion of political consciousness in local communities. Community workers suspected social workers of assuming that

'. . . problems lie with the powerless and deprived themselves, rather than with structures and processes which have gradually eroded the democratic system. They [social workers] are still pre-occupied in therapeutic work with individuals, families and small groups and . . . far removed from the broader political perspectives and intervention at quite different levels of society.' (p. 24)

Most community workers would deeply resent any attempt to equate them with social workers because they feared that this would stifle new and more radical developments. On the other hand, both theoretical and fieldwork training for community work seemed to have close parallels with existing social work courses.

ACW also published a discussion paper on *Knowledge and Skills for Community Work* in 1975. Both documents accepted the need for substantial training for a skilled and difficult task, and were landmarks as far as thought about the content of training was concerned. The ACW paper took the range of community work jobs and analysed necessary knowledge and skills from community action to social planning. The CCETSW working group said 'community work is about policies, resources, conflicts of interest and mutual aid and also about achieving greater degrees of equality and social justice and . . . therefore it is also concerned with politics in its broadest and most important sense' (p. 11). Its involvement in the exercise, use and control of power might result in conflict, protest or co-operation. Community work also included many undramatic routine tasks aimed at improving social life in a locality.

Both documents stressed that in the course of training students must become clear about community work assumptions, their own values and motivation and how they affected others. They must learn to be involved yet detached, not subject to manipulation, able to say no, and to cope under stress and without support. This meant learning to think realistically about what community work could and should achieve and to understand the issues with which it dealt. Training must help students to assimilate a solid basis of workable theory related to practice (CCETSW), 'give students the basis on which to make judgments in relation to a range of conflicting values and interests' (ACW, 1975, p. 8). The ACW document saw objectives in down-to-earth terms: understanding people in their local environment, working with them, providing services to achieve community goals and fostering community care, self-help and integration. This required skills in working with groups, including communication, listening, liaison, mediation, public relations, ability to discuss issues honestly with local people and officials, and to increase the group's self-confidence. Individual counselling skills were also needed.

The ACW document was only concerned with the content of training not how, where or for how long. Some community workers thought educational institutions far too theoretical and that training should be based on field training centres, apprenticeship, and day release schemes. The more orthodox CCETSW discussion document's curriculum proposals were based on two-year qualifying courses. Students should be helped to view community work as part of a complex network of formal and informal processes of individual and social interaction. The central teaching themes should flow from the essential tasks and skills of community work. This would include a framework of knowledge from social administration, social anthropology, sociology, social psychology and social history; analysis of a network of social relationships and institutions of many kinds; aspects of moral philosophy and political theory; and the ethical issues implicit in all social intervention. Any course should have a sound conceptual framework with theory tested in a variety of practice situations. The ACW group thought that in order to understand people in their environment students needed 'bits out of several disciplines', especially sociology (including the sociology of organisations), psychology (including group processes), political theory and the economic system. The group was sharply divided about 'conventional psychology'. 'Some members thought it and social psychology offered little help to community workers who work with a range of "normal" individuals . . . in a variety of roles' (p. 15). Others thought 'community workers should have the best psychology can offer' (p. 15).

Otherwise both discussion documents were broadly agreed about the content of training, though the ACW group emphasised that much of the most essential knowledge did not yet exist and that much work was also needed to identify and use relevant knowledge from the social sciences.

Since community work had developed very rapidly there was little available material about its actual practice. There was also much controversy about the principles on which it rested and a dearth of transmissible teaching about key issues identified from case studies and based upon actual processes and skills. Many students who had taken community work courses felt that the teaching was excessively theoretical and did not adequately reinforce community work practice. Community work teachers should have direct experience and be able to continue to learn through practice, reading and research. Tensions were created if academic studies became a symbol of intellectual or other pressure toward objectivity and social distance, or fieldwork a symbol of anti-intellectual pressures to emotional commitment and over-identification.

Both discussion documents agreed that in fieldwork students should have well-guided opportunities for fact finding and social study, for assessment of current needs, for discussion with fieldwork teachers, fellow students and community groups, and for time to stand back and assess their work. They needed adequate opportunities for practice in communication, administration, practical tasks, recording, finance and budgeting. They should be helped to integrate their studies by relating theory to practice and the contributory disciplines to the central aims, skills and tasks of community work. Because there were many isolated first jobs in community work with very little support and with almost no chance of supervision, fieldwork should prepare students to work alone in their first appointments.

Placements should include interorganisation and social planning settings. Both concurrent and block placements could be valuable. Courses with large numbers of students required a full-time professional staff member to find and develop placements, and increasingly such appointments were being made. Supervisors on the college staff could make it possible to use settings where no field teaching would otherwise be available. Extra staffing should allow field teachers and course tutors sufficient time to formulate concepts and clarify theoretical implications in field situations. Everyone, including other lecturers and students, must take responsibility for the development of the total course. Field study centres, for example, would make it possible for students from different disciplines to share field experience. At this early stage in the development of community work a variety of placements should be used.

The evaluation of fieldwork was an essential part of the overall assessment of each student's performance. This might include material obtained by the student about local community resources, analysis of situations, preparation of memoranda and records of his own work. Each student should contribute to the evaluation of his work.

The CCETSW working group thought it desirable to concentrate on certain 'centres of learning', able to offer various types of training from short courses for local residents to advanced training and research. It was also desirable to run post-graduate and other careers' courses in the same department. Short courses and day release courses for supervisors were also 'vitally necessary', and opportunities for further study for community workers going into posts which entailed consultation, participation in multi-disciplinary teams and interagency work. It would be necessary to appoint extra staff to set up community work options or to start new community work courses.

The CCETSW group also recognised that a wide range of courses and institutions could provide teaching in community work for volunteers, 'indigenous' workers, members of other professions, experienced untrained workers; and courses in further and advanced studies. Modular, day release, and short courses would meet some of these needs. In the absolute shortage of good fieldwork placements, courses for fieldwork teachers were urgently necessary, as well as more student units.

By 1975 the CCETSW had recognised the community work option in the four-year CNAA degree course at Birmingham Polytechnic and the youth and community work course at Goldsmiths College. Other applications were pending. The long-established university courses designed for overseas students continued. There were also day release courses of various lengths. There had been no systematic evaluation of the different trainings in relation to past students' subsequent work performance.

The two Gulbenkian studies and the CCETSW and ACW discussion documents span ten years of effort to clarify community work and promote training for it. By 1975 more courses were training for community work, though training developments were modest. In contrast with earlier confusion, and in spite of conflicting purposes, there was a good deal of agreement about the skills needed in community work. Its essence was group interaction to achieve community objectives and its boundaries ranged from very practical routine tasks to social planning and political action. There was agreement that knowledge from the social sciences was essential (though psychology was controversial); that teaching should not be too theoretical; and that students must acquire appropriate values and adequate skill for practice. Sociology and social psychology were weak in their application to day-to-day practice, though it was not clear whether the knowledge itself was missing or time and competence to identify, apply and add to it. Conceptualisation in community work had begun and an active search for sources of knowledge could take it further. Some joint appointments by field agencies and educational institutions were hopeful signs. The divisions in community work and comparatively limited interest in training made the outcome more problematic. It is worth noting that casework had been in this situation in an earlier period, but had worked hard to identify and learn to apply relevant knowledge. This made it important to carry forward the highly diverse rank and file so that training for community work might find its sense of direction. Many community workers were ambivalent about training, partly because of uncertainties about their own identification, and desire to dissociate themselves from social work, and deep suspicions of professional élitism. For many different reasons community work training had been a confused mixture of resistance, desire to climb on the bandwagon, and pressure of other work. By 1975 ACW and the JUC Community Work Group were pressing for an independent training council in community work on the grounds that community work was part of various professional activities and a practice in its own right.

Chapter 20

The Youth Service: Training for the Youth Service

THE YOUTH SERVICE IN THE 1950s

The youth service was originally pioneered by national voluntary organisations and local clubs. It only came into being during the Second World War in association with the education service. After the war the youth service lost its momentum, so far as public authorities were concerned, though national voluntary organisations and local clubs continued to sustain in old and new ways 'the service of youth'. By the 1950s the voluntary clubs were still struggling to maintain existing services or to experiment with new methods and to raise a large part of their expenditure by their own efforts. Local authority youth service provision was a patchwork, sometimes with a close partnership between voluntary organisations and their own youth service officers, sometimes in active competition, sometimes the local authority had decided to go it alone or else to make no provision at a time when their hands were full with problems of finding enough school places and teachers for the increasing child population.

The Albermarle Committee was appointed in 1958 to review the contribution which the youth service could make to helping young people to play their part in the life of the community. In a hard-hitting Report (1960) it made clear the 'critical condition' of the youth service because those who worked in it felt themselves 'neglected and held in small regard, both in educational circles and by public opinion generally' (para. 2). Lack of encouragement by the Ministry of Education since the 1940s had also 'checked the momentum with which the service was launched and betrayed the high hopes of those who believed in it' (para. 36).

This was indeed one of the series of government inquiries from 1950 to 1960 which drew attention in strong terms to the failure of government departments to secure the provision of necessary manpower and other resources for particular services, although Parliament had given them adequate powers to do so. The Albermarle Report recommended that the Minister of Education should initiate a ten-year development plan with the guidance of a Youth Service Development Council. This was done.

The vast majority of youth leaders were either volunteers, or else part-time paid leaders (often teachers) of whom about 4,600 were employed by local education authorities. The Albermarle Report concluded that

'Leadership within the Youth Service has also suffered from shortage of money and lack of encouragement. Leaders feel unsupported and unappreciated: they look for some sign that their work is nationally recognised as important, but find it neither in official expressions of policy nor in the rewards of a salary scale for those who are full time which would put their work on a level with cognate professions. They seem to themselves to be in danger of becoming cut off from the march of social and educational advance. And there is a considerable volume of evidence that full time posts fail to attract good applicants.' (para. 42)

This situation could 'only be dealt with by a rapid growth in the Service, by improvement in the quality, training and conditions of service of its leaders and workers, and by new approaches towards the young' (para. 156).

The full-time service consisted of youth leaders, including wardens of large youth centres with other staff, organisers and youth service officers (predominantly development officers and consultants in later terminology), single-handed youth leaders and social group workers with unattached youth. Single-handed club leaders had to run the building, recruit and support voluntary workers and teachers, be in close touch with other services and professionals in the neighbourhood, keep the management committee happy, raise money; and above all attract club members to engage in recreational, social and educational activities and enable them so far as possible to run the club themselves. The leader was supposed to achieve a variety of aims which might or might not be realistic, though he received little training or support in clarifying means as well as ends. Indeed, he might be expected to 'spend hours of the day in cleaning his building, stoking the boiler or raising money to pay his own salary' (para. 243).

THE YOUTH SERVICE IN THE 1960S AND EARLY 1970S

By the 1960s the number of commonwealth immigrants and general geographical mobility within the country were both increasing; there were more young people adrift in the cities; educational facilities had vastly increased and a substantial number of adolescents were in full- or part-time education, though over half remained untouched by it. The average age of marriage had fallen and the age of majority had been lowered to 18. A distinct teenage culture of pop music, dress, language and hair-style had emerged which cut right across class difference. Higher earnings meant that young people could choose to spend their leisure in such settings as pubs or discotheques where they were independent, rather than in youth clubs which were often too juvenile and restrictive. Most youth work was still in clubs with traditional forms of membership and activities. These also continued to separate young people of 14 to 20 from the rest of the community instead of treating them as part of community development activities.

Between the two extremes of the traditional club or uniformed organisation (both valuable for younger members) and unattached workers, there were clubs with no membership requirements, together with encouragement and support for spontaneous friendship or interest groups which only needed a place to meet. Some youth clubs, community centres, evening institutes and colleges of further education were full of lively groups and many activities, mainly because those who ran them succeeded in creating an atmosphere in which small groups could plan, discuss, find friendship and create things together that gave them satisfaction.

In the 1940s the whole emphasis had been on a club programme full of activities and the leader was thought to be failing if the members 'just sat about doing nothing but talk – in short if an easy informal setting had been created which was a desired aim in the 1960s. Young adolescents had a good deal of physical energy to discharge but older ones wanted to relax after the day's work. By the 1960s young people were probably taking part in a wider range of activities than ever before, in sport, cycling, canoeing, the arts, climbing, swimming, trekking or travel. But they were doing these things from time to time rather than at regular club sessions, where it was now agreed there should be an informal atmosphere but no obligatory programme.

What had begun in the 1940s as the service of youth changed, then, in the 1960s to a broader concept of enabling adolescents and young adults to cope with personal problems and conflicts, to increase their confidence in themselves and their ability to create and run self-governing groups for a variety of purposes. At the other end of the scale, it was obvious that the under-fourteens needed much better provision, the result being that pre-school and other play groups spread all over the country. Joint appointments began to be made of teacher/youth leaders or tutor/youth leaders to develop youth work in schools and carry it forward for school leavers, to do similar work in colleges of further education and also lead a youth club. Of 500 such appointments by 1969 a quarter were held by qualified youth leaders. Predictably, the new term 'counselling' was beginning to be used in recognition that youth workers (who always had seen it as part of their job to listen to and help adolescents suffering from family, personal and social stress) needed some specific training and skill to make good use of this relationship. In youth work, as elsewhere, the person already known in the situation was likely to be turned to because 'most young people . . . need – and sometimes need desperately – the comfort of a good listener and the chance to sort out their ideas in the presence of an experienced and emotionally uninvolved adult' (DES, 1969, p. 92).

In 1969 a survey was undertaken for the Department of Education and Science (DES) (Bone, 1972) to assess the use made of the youth service and the extent to which it met the needs of young people. The survey revealed that 65 per cent of all young people between 14 and 20 went to clubs but 93 per cent left before they were 21. The least educationally and socially privileged were also least likely to join clubs. For most of these the problem was to increase the attractions to them of joining organised groups before they left school so that they were less prone to become unattached later. Of the unattached the survey said

'The unattached appear to lead less satisfactory lives than the attached. More of them were bored, unenthusiastic about varied experiences, preferred the company of people they knew and had little interest in anything which was going on beyond their immediate experience . . . They appeared to be more timid and more socially inept but, judging by the greater prevalence of boredom amongst them, and the smaller number who claimed to be very happy, not very satisfied with their condition.' (p. 181)

In the 1960s youth work was still an isolated career with newly qualified leaders or untrained people often having to take full responsibility for a club because there were practically no assistant appointments and too few youth service officers to give support. There were also inadequate promotion prospects. But by degrees youth service officer appointments covered the whole country. By 1970 the total number of full-time youth leaders in employment (both qualified and unqualified) was about 2,000. In 1972 the figures had risen to 2,700 with about 500 vacancies. These figures only included those employed by local education authorities or in grant-aided voluntary organisations, i.e. they did not include youth and community workers employed by social services departments or non-grant-aided voluntary agencies.

From 1961 those who had taken a recognised youth leadership course, all qualified teachers, any holder of a university degree or diploma in social science, and untrained youth leaders who had completed five years' satisfactory service by that date were regarded by the Ministry of Education as qualified youth leaders. Qualifying courses lasting from seven weeks to six months for untrained practising youth leaders and community centre wardens with less than five years experience were organised by the Ministry and voluntary youth organisations. Those who had taken a youth leadership course had to start from the beginning to qualify as teachers or social workers.

The shortcomings and tensions of being poised between the education and social services and the consequent love-hate relationship inevitably continued. Full-time workers in the youth service suffered the familiar frustrations of not knowing where they belonged and being given too little support and recognition. In the late 1960s the tensions were greatly (and to some extent creatively?) increased by the rise of community work. The Youth Service Development Council report, *Youth and Community Work in the 70s* (DES, 1969) expressed the hope that its proposals for longer training would create opportunities for advancement through teaching, further education or social work. This same hope had been expressed, though unfulfilled, since the early 1940s.

There was also the dilemma of where youth and community work belonged in the whole structure of the social services. The DES decided not to accept the report's proposal for a youth and community service and to restrict its interest to educationally based services and the related voluntary youth organisations. It is arguable that to have done otherwise would have increased overlapping at central government level. Locally a broad range of services for young people continued to develop, whether through pioneer voluntary effort or expanded services under local education authority or social services department auspices. There was obviously more overlapping and confusion about functions when intermediate treatment began and social services departments sponsored more pre-school and other play groups.

There was much discontent with the 'traditional' youth service and its failure to attract young adults, more radical youngsters and, above all, children and young people in deprived areas. In short, so it was alleged, the youth service did most for those who needed it least and was dominated by buildings instead of getting out into the community to make relations with young people on their own terms. *The Wincroft Youth Project* (Smith et al., 1972) expressed this point of view:

'The use made of professional effort in the Youth Service is determined by two central features of its organisation: its location in educational administration, both nationally and locally, which leads to its dependence upon the objectives and skills of further education, and now, increasingly, of the schools; and its reliance upon the mixed youth club as its major method. Despite the brief and sporadic flirtations of the Youth Service with work with the 'unattached' no serious efforts have been made to use the social-work method within its structures. Moreover, despite the fashionable talk of relating the work of clubs to the communities in which they are located, clubs are still very isolated from communities. The club that has a parents' association or involves many parents in its functioning is exceptional . . . and their work is shaped by the way in which young people present themselves for membership, and, usually, how long they choose to stay. Little effort is made to meet them before they join or to follow them up after they leave. It is likely that the more socially deprived youngster does not join clubs as frequently as other ordinary working-class young people, and when he does join he does not sustain his membership for as long.' (pp. 251–2)

There was abortive pressure for a comprehensive review of the needs of young people; for social care within the education system, for school leavers especially through the youth employment service; for all forms of leisure and local provision through the youth service and elsewhere for children through to young adults setting up home; for physically or mentally handicapped young people; for young delinquents, drug addicts, dropouts, drifters and young homeless people. Such a review would have been within the terms of reference of the Seebohm Committee, but because of pressure of time it contented itself with saying that such an inquiry was overdue and should be undertaken urgently. The urgency still remained seven years later.

SOME EXPERIMENTS IN UNATTACHED YOUTH WORK

Mays (1954) studied the cultural background, behaviour and social attitudes of eighty boys, well known to him, growing up in a deprived, poverty-stricken Liverpool neighbourhood. Results showed the normality of their group delinquent behaviour in their social circumstances and reinforced the case for community studies. It concluded that 'in certain urban areas with a tradition for anti-social behaviour, children tend to react to personal difficulties or to strained relationships in the home by delinquent activity' (p. 114). After some pioneer projects with 'unclubables', work with unattached youth began with several well-recorded and widely read experimental projects. Morse (1965) described the process of becoming accepted by and understanding groups of unattached young people. Goetschius and

Tash (1967) similarly recorded the processes and what was discovered from a coffee-bar project. There were other well-planned projects from which much, whether positive or negative, was learnt. Isolated individual appointments of unattached youth workers were also made with too little realisation of the amount of support, supervision and consultation needed by such workers, who were necessarily young and often vulnerable. Moreover, unattached youth work

'. . . attracts many people who share the adolescent conflict with respectable adult society or are so individualist that they find it difficult to co-operate with other workers. The workers should be secure in themselves, able to stand a high level of stress over a long period, resourceful enough to exploit situations to the advantage of their client and capable of explaining their client's needs to unsympathetic officials.' (Smith *et al.*, 1972, pp. 262–3)

These experiments were the beginning of systematic work in coffee bars, pubs, dance halls or in the streets with the increasing number of the unattached, alienated and drug addicts. Many such projects were run by local authorities and voluntary youth organisations, with a few financed from a DES experimental fund. By 1968 there were over 100 full-time detached youth workers, and by 1975 40 in London alone. This was a small proportion of the total number of workers in the youth service, particularly when these and other pioneer experiments had demonstrated some of the conditions under which it was possible to make contact and work with alienated young people. Other examples were the Soho and Blenheim Projects in London which gave jobless, homeless, rootless and addicted young people 'somewhere to be' where they were unquestioningly accepted and supported.

The most substantial action research project of the period was *The Wincroft Youth Project* (Smith *et al.*, 1972), undertaken from 1965 to 1969 in a blighted urban area similar to many others. There were 54 boys in the project and a matched control group in another area: about 600 other adolescents were also affected by the project. Boys aged 15 plus were selected because they were delinquent or else maladjusted in the sense of being unable to sustain social relationships. 'The project was concerned not merely with adjusting young people to their environment but also with helping them to change it. They were to be helped to become more conscious of the factors, both personal and social, which shaped their lives and the ways in which they could exert more control over their own destinies' (p. 6). It was also hoped to discover methods of working with difficult young people in an unstructured setting.

The method used was social group work, with casework introduced later with isolated boys or to reinforce group experience. It became a constant problem to keep the demands for casework within reasonable bounds. With very isolated young people the one-to-one relationship was like a friendship in which the individual got to the point of being able to face and share problems.

By and large the boys' parents showed little interest in them, they and their fathers kept out of each other's way and their fathers only took an interest in them when something went wrong. They were socially segregated from the responsible adult world and their adolescent friendships were tenuous or non-existent. These adolescents belonged to a loose social network centred on pubs and commercial cafés and their hostile and uncooperative attitudes to strangers were partly a result of their cultural deprivation. An aim of the project workers was to help to create more stable and satisfying groups than the informal friendship groups which constantly sprang up and collapsed. Most of the work was done in cafés, in the streets, in expeditions and in cars and minibuses. The latter turned out to be excellent settings for group work or casework in the course of a journey or a lift home. Transport made it possible to go on expeditions further afield or to visit relatives or friends in borstal or approved schools. The project used premises from time to time but these were expendable and discarded once they had served their purpose.

At the end of the evaluation period there was a statistically significant difference between the project group and the controls on certain measures of delinquency, i.e. the social work programme did prevent delinquency. But on improved adjustment with parents, leisure and peers, the project was only marginally effective.

The four professional workers functioned as a team 'whose abilities and temperaments complemented each other and resulted in mutual support'. Probably this kind of close team membership was necessary to withstand the strains of the work and to clarify by discussion what was happening in fluid, unstructured, quickly changing situations.

'Group work did, however, offer something that casework could not – the opportunity for more accurate diagnosis, as a result of workers being able to see the way that a boy reacted to his peers, and thus the possibility of his receiving support from friends who were part of his social milieu, which may well have meant more to him than the efforts of adult social workers who were not.' (pp. 250–1)

This project brought out, as did others discussed in this study, that intensive and skilled work can bring about change in some though not all aspects of behaviour; and that, with very deprived people, it may be essential to work within their own environment and try to give them richer experiences and more freedom of choice.

THE YOUTH SERVICE AND INTERMEDIATE TREATMENT

Intermediate treatment was a threat and a challenge to the youth service. Voluntary youth organisations and individual settlement had pioneered imaginative projects such as holidays on a barge, coffee bar projects and unattached youth work and holiday adventure courses. But these were isolated activities by those with imagination, whereas intermediate treatment was backed by public funds, national in scope but on everyone's doorstep. The response of the youth service was predictable if contradictory. Many said they had their hands full already and saw no reason why the ordinary good member should be short-changed for the prodigal son; others that intermediate treatment was nothing new, they had being doing it all the time and they were so successful at containing young people at risk that most members did not become delinquent. Or else, delinquents were welcomed into the club and settled down there; or it was recognised that a problem existed but those at risk were different from actual offenders who should be dealt with elsewhere and not as part of the youth service. Finally, to some in the youth service it was their responsibility to discover new forms of help for such boys and girls even if not necessarily in the traditional club framework.

In some areas there was a good deal of tension between the youth service and social services departments: resentment at not being consulted when the youth service had years of experience, or being made use of without support when a boy or girl was sent to them, or feeling rejected when no one was sent, even though the local court might be making few orders. When intermediate treatment officers started to work co-operation developed in many areas. The anxieties and sense of rejection experienced by the youth service partly sprang from thinking that it was expected to 'do' intermediate treatment rather than to be an important element in the resources available to supervisors.

None the less, intermediate treatment posed once again questions about the changing purpose of the youth service and what its priorities should be. In any event, there was potential and sometimes actual overlapping between education and social services departments in the provision of youth group activities, pre-school play groups for children of one-parent families or whose mothers were at work, or for school children after school hours and in the holidays, or for others who were delinquent or 'at risk'.

TRAINING FOR THE YOUTH SERVICE

Professional training for the youth service, and indeed the service itself, steadily sank into the doldrums in the 1950s. All but one of the university one-year youth service courses were discontinued for lack of candidates, though the Westhill College two-year course for youth leaders and community centre wardens was started in 1952. The then National Association of Mixed Clubs and Girls Clubs valiantly continued to run its eighteen-month course based on a university social science qualification, but with practically no candidates.

The earlier *ad hoc* specialised university courses had had well-planned curricula, teaching and practice, and full-time tutors who were in close contact with the students' fieldwork as well as their university studies. But the courses suffered from weaknesses common at the time. The students

'. . . learned some psychology, some social administration, perhaps some sociology, all of a fairly academic kind, and something about the structure and administration of the Youth Service. They no doubt discussed practical problems with experienced people, and spent time on practical work and acquiring activity skills, but they had no opportunity to learn a method or professional discipline, and they did not meet the term "social group work" . . . The lack of a professional method meant that the theoretical understanding they acquired could only be applied in a "hit and miss" way, and that for most of their practice they were thrown back largely on ingenuity and intuition.' (Matthews, 1966, p. 44)

If the courses had continued and been properly integrated and expanded, they could have established group work as such and brought a valuable element into the new pattern of university courses in casework. As it was, they wilted and died for lack of students. Reasons for this were the dead-end career, the 'unsocial' demands of evening and weekend work, and the isolation faced by a single-handed club leader, often torn between contrary pressures from the management committee and the club members.

The Albermarle Committee (1960) calculated that it was necessary to raise the number of full-time youth leaders (which had fallen from 828 in 1954 to 700 at that time) to 1,300 by 1966. This could only be done by emergency training. The Report recommended that a national college should be started, but did not examine the alternative case for several courses in different parts of the country where theory and practice could have been more closely related and general standards raised. None the less the extreme scarcity of qualified teaching staff would probably have made this impracticable.

The Committee thought that in the long term, apart from the proposed emergency course, professional youth leaders should be recruited from teachers, social workers and 'mature persons with a natural gift for leadership'. Teachers should be the main source of recruitment and there should be a youth leadership option in the courses at some teacher training colleges. In relation to social workers, the Report commented that certain recommendations in the Younghusband working party Report (1959) were of great importance for the youth service. It said

'. . . we are interested to see that a particular function of the College [the proposed staff college] will be to pioneer training in group work and community organisation, for which no proper facilities yet exist in this country. Pioneering in this field would in time influence the content of professional training courses in universities; and we hope that in the years ahead students interested in social group work with adolescents will be offered particular opportunities for preparing themselves for this work as a possible option in university professional courses.' (para. 251)

The Albermarle Report further suggested that mature but unqualified students should take the two-year course at Westhill College. There should be three-month transfer courses for candidates with other relevant qualifications.

The Report was silent about the content of training for social work students, but it proposed that the content in teacher training for youth leadership should include: 'Adolescent psychology, problems of personal relationships, the transition from school to work, the youth employment service, adolescent physiology, and health and sex education . . . preparation for marriage, group behaviour and the principles of group work, and personal relationships of the young worker' (para. 251).

'In his theoretical studies the student training for youth work will need to consider the history, aims and organisation of the Youth Service as a part of further education, and the techniques of club work and club administration. He will have a special interest too in the structure of industry and in apprenticeship and industrial training. His practical work will, we hope, include regular experience in local group leadership under supervision, with opportunities for real responsibility, as well as visits of observation to different kinds of youth group. Adequate club practice under guidance seems to us one of the most vital elements of his training.' (para. 260)

Matthews (1966) commented that the Report seemed to imply that training in social group work was important for professional youth workers, 'but in its section on the content of training, it makes only brief mention of the subject and does not explain what it is, or how training in it might be carried out' (p. 12).

On the day in 1960 when the Albermarle Report was published the then Minister of Education announced that he had accepted its recommendations for an emergency one-year course. Eleven months later premises had been found at Leicester, the governors, principal and staff appointed and ninety students selected for the first course at the National College for the Training of Youth Leaders, wholly financed by the Ministry of Education. This showed what could happen if some people knew what they wanted and were determined to get it. As with most other emergency courses, its life was extended, in this instance beyond the original five years. Perhaps emergency courses generate enthusiasm and are well planned because as Dr Johnson said, 'When a man knows he's to be hanged in a fortnight, it concentrates his mind wonderfully'. The College closed in 1970 after qualifying 1,099 students in nine intakes.

In its size, its large special staff and some of its curriculum construction it had much in common with the emergency child care courses, though there was no educational or other connection between them. They differed in that the National College students were resident in a single-purpose college and had to cram everything into one year, whereas the child care emergency course students were in polytechnics and had a second year of continuing contact and supervised practice before they qualified (see volume 1, chapter 5, section on 'The Training of Child Care Officers').

The main subjects in the National College course were: principles and practice of the youth service (including administration); social studies; social group work; and social psychology (including human growth and development). Social group work was regarded as 'the distinctive professional skill of the youth worker'. Watkins (1971) described it as

'. . . a method of promoting individual development through group experience. It is based on the observation that we develop as persons largely through the quality of our interaction with others. Whether this interaction helps or hinders the realization of our potential and does or does not promote social harmony is usually a matter of chance. The social group worker's task is to foster in a particular group setting the conditions that will be most helpful to those involved, thus lessening the element of chance in the situation and to help his clients to grow in the understanding of their situation and to relate to a variety of people in a variety of conditions. The worker does this by trying to understand the factors at work in group processes, such as the goals, values and expectations that people bring with them, the degrees of understanding that they display, the needs they express by their behaviour and the way they react to one another.' (p. 25)

Owing to the neglect of group work in this country there were few qualified practitioners or teachers in 1961. Fortunately, one of these later joined the staff of the course and developed social group work teaching and field practice within it.

Adequate fieldwork related to theory naturally posed great difficulties in a course of 100 or more students in a service where supervision was almost non-existent, and where, moreover, there was no grant from central government funds towards supervisors' salaries. The fieldwork consisted of an evening a week in term time, four weeks full-time near the beginning, and eight weeks near the end of the course. The students went to different parts of the country in groups, each with a tutor. Each student was under the joint supervision of a youth leader and a college tutor. In the early years the tutor had to do most of the supervision because many club leaders had no idea what field practice meant and looked on students as extra helpers. It became obvious, as in similar pioneer situations, that the tutor had to help the field supervisor to talk through and systematise his own work and to understand the purpose of training before he could begin to help students to identify the components of professional practice in their day-to-day experience. Students' process recording showed their part in interaction with the group and helped to increase self-awareness. These records were sometimes used in joint sessions between the tutor, the field supervisor and the student. In addition, they helped supervisors to relate their first-hand knowledge to the student's grasp of theory. There were also group tutorials to discuss characteristics of the local community, the youth service in relation to other services, professional ethics and principles, and to increase skill in helping individuals and groups to develop socially.

After the early stages, when more youth leaders had experience of supervision, in-service training courses were provided and past students who had themselves been supervised became available, the quality of supervision improved. None the less, although nearly all the early students had considerable youth work experience, it is unlikely that three months of supervised fieldwork was enough for someone who would take on single-handed and with little support varied responsibilities as an administrator, manager, group worker, counsellor, educator and someone competent in public relations.

The College staff consistently urged the need for supervision for youth leaders in their first post to give them support in taking the full burden of responsibility, to help them to consolidate their training and to apply their theoretical knowledge, to think and observe in a disciplined way, and to make decisions with more awareness and confidence.

The following summary of the National College course, which illustrates some of the educational processes, tasks and dilemmas inherent in professional training, draws heavily on the lively discussion by Watkins (1971).

Decisions about the qualifying award were made by periodic assessment of students' performance and discussion of this with them. The minimum standard was defined in behavioural terms. A student had to be able: (a) to make and use satisfactorily relationships with young people and adults, and to help young people to use group membership to further their own development; (b) to manage a unit of work, to cope with administrative demands and to use time efficiently; (c) to understand and be articulate about youth leadership and his own methods.

This continuous assessment sometimes caused considerable tension in a residential college where students thought they were being assessed by the staff even at meal times and in leisure activities. They did not always believe staff reassurances to the contrary. The assessment of personal qualities aroused the most anxiety because students felt that they were being judged as people. This often led them to repress hostile feelings or controversial views and they were easily discouraged from frank and free discussion if they thought this might count against them. It was also difficult for tutors to reconcile helping students to perform at their best with the demand for objective assessment. These are well-known difficulties of a continuous assessment of performance but they may have been compounded in a closed residential setting, when tutors also played a large part in the fieldwork. There are some analogies between this situation and the Rainer House one-year probation course where students faced anxieties about being selected, taught, assessed, and later inspected by the same powerful figures (see volume 1, chapter 8). A subsequent follow-up study of National College past students to assess the predictive function of assessment showed no statistically significant correlation between College gradings and subsequent career patterns.

From the first, the staff concluded that social workers had done more than anyone else to analyse the principles of professional practice in interpersonal relations. But obviously it was necessary to clarify the different situation in youth and community work where the focus was on the group rather than the individual, where people came for pleasure and peer group relations and not with a problem, compared with agencies offering a casework service to people in difficulty. Nevertheless there was thought to be a basic understanding common to all the helping professions which applied in the teaching and practice of youth work.

From 1964 onwards, when the experiment was to be continued, the College pressed for a two-year course because one year put too great a strain on both staff and students. Neither had sufficient time for reflection or more detailed study and the curriculum was packed with information which could not be assimilated. The students needed more time to discover and overcome their individual learning difficulties, to make the transition from a non-professional to a professional role, and to follow up issues arising from their fieldwork. Also, in a one-year course essential common ground had to be covered and there was no chance to specialise where additional knowledge and skill were needed, for example in unattached youth work, in counselling, in group work in schools, residential work, community centres, clubs in immigrant areas, community schools, play group leadership or adult education. The Department of Education and Science (DES) – as the Ministry of Education became in 1964 – was not willing to lengthen training to two years on grounds of expense and the effect on numbers. These were the same grounds on which the Home Office unsuccessfully resisted the universities' case for lengthening the seventeen-month, post-graduate applied social studies courses to two years for essentially the same educational reasons.

The other recognised youth leadership courses were the post-graduate Diploma in Youth Work at Manchester University; courses at University College, Swansea; the National Association of Boys' Clubs course at Liverpool; and the YMCA course in London; together with the two-year course at Westhill College. Altogether there were nearly eighty places on these courses. In Scotland there were two-year diploma courses in youth and community service at Moray House and Jordanhill Colleges of Education.

In 1960, when teacher training was lengthened to three years, a few colleges of education started a youth leadership option. By the end of the decade this was offered by thirty colleges, and by 1973 at fifty-three colleges. It was not a mainstream subject and there was confusion about the purpose and content of the fieldwork. A number of teachers who took it worked in youth clubs on one or two evenings a week.

The Bessey Report (1962) on part-time training, established the important principle that the basic content of training must be the same as for full-time courses. Since the early 1950s the National Association of Youth Clubs had run two-year, part-time courses with experienced tutors in charge. These consisted of lectures, guided reading, tutorial meetings and written work, with most of the practice being in students' own clubs. 'Bessey' part-time courses spread all over the country in the 1960s. They were run by local authorities and voluntary organisations and taken by over 5,000 students within ten years. They were not standardised and might last from six weeks to three years. The best of these part-time courses probably reached a higher standard than similar courses in social work, but they remained isolated and lessons learnt from them were not applied elsewhere. Much other in-service training was offered by local education authorities and the voluntary youth organisations. The need to 'train the trainers' was recognised and it was officially suggested that regional courses should be provided. Some regional programmes were made available under the Regional Advisory Committees for Further Education but these did not meet the general need.

In 1970, the DES plans allowed for an annual recruitment of 185 full-time students to cover existing replacements, expansion and wastage. Over the preceding ten years the minimum annual recruitment had been around 200 full-time youth leaders. There was a high annual turnover and many posts took months to fill (Woolfe, 1970).

When the National College came to an end it was succeeded by two-year courses – variously named – in youth and community work at Leicester College of Education, Manchester Polytechnic, Westhill College of Education, Goldsmiths College (University of London), University College, Swansea, the National Association of Boys' Clubs (NABC), (in co-operation with Liverpool and later Durham University) and the YMCA National College (in co-operation with the Polytechnic of North East London). Further courses were added later at Matlock College of Education, Bulmershe and Crewe Colleges of Higher Education and Sunderland Polytechnic. These courses, several of which were not new, aimed to equip students as professional workers in social education, community social work, youth work, community centres, play groups and community relations. The emphasis was thus on adolescents and young adults in neighbourhood settings, and on group work and counselling skills rather than on the youth service as such. There was a good deal more concurrent fieldwork, often alternating with block placements. The main subjects of study were psychology, sociology, social structure and the principles of youth and community work. The courses at Moray House and Jordanhill Colleges of Education continued on the same lines and others in Scotland were added later. About 10 per cent to 15 per cent of students from these two-year courses went into social services departments as community workers. They were technically unqualified if the course was not recognised by the CCETSW. It recognised the course at Goldsmiths College in 1975 and other applications were pending.

This expansion of full- and part-time training was essential, but it was all concentrated on minimum basic training and there were no national plans for more substantial or advanced training to produce the first-rate practitioners, supervisors, consultants, group work teachers and competent researchers whom the service needed to make headway in the immensely difficult tasks it was setting itself. For one reason or another it had always been in a state of emergency since its inception in 1939 and by the 1970s there was little sign of a total strategy that would give it the solid underpinning of a universal and professional service.

Chapter 21

Counselling and Education Welfare

COUNSELLING

All forms of counselling had much in common. The term came to be used either as an aspect of all the helping professions, as in Halmos (1965) *The Faith of the Counsellors*, or an element in other professional practice, for example the law, or, increasingly, as an activity in its own right. It might be either individual or group counselling. As Thompson and Kahn (1970) pointed out, it drew upon dynamic theories of group behaviour but used these in a different way and also theories of social casework, but was not a technique for use solely by social workers.

Marriage Counselling
The term first became general in marriage guidance from the foundation in 1938 of what became in 1946 the National Marriage Guidance Council. Both it and the Catholic Marriage Advisory Council relied almost wholly on trained volunteers. Counselling sessions consisted of interviews with husband or wife separately or together or group discussions. Venables (1971) stressed that

'The aim is to help the person . . . to a greater awareness of the nature of his difficulties so that he is able to find an acceptable way to resolve them . . . The method used is to offer him a relationship with a person – a counsellor – not emotionally involved in his difficulties – a relationship which is bounded by a structure which should be well-defined and understood by both parties. The quality of this relationship and its effectiveness in achieving the aim of counselling will clearly depend on the nature of the counsellor.' (p. 91)

She continued: 'Counselling is a way of dealing with emotional and relationship distress by concentrating at least as much on the person and his feelings as on his problem' (p. 137).

In the early post-war years applicants for marriage guidance had an initial interview to decide whether the problem was primarily legal, medical or religious and then were referred accordingly. As understanding of the primacy of emotional and relationship factors in marriage increased, the emphasis shifted so that marriage counsellors worked with all clients; but a panel of legal and medical consultants was available to local marriage guidance councils, and individual counsellors could consult a psychiatrist in cases of apparently severe emotional disturbance. As a matter of principle marriage counsellors did not pay home visits.

Selection and training was discussed in detail by Wallis and Booker (1958), and the position in the early 1970s by Venables (1971) and Guiver (1973). What follows is based mainly on the latter. There was a rigorous selection procedure under which applicants were initially interviewed by about three members of a local sponsoring committee. Its report and two references determined whether the candidate should go forward for selection and training by the National Marriage Guidance Council. In the 1950s, indeed down to 1967, this consisted of a two-day residential selection board, modelled on the Civil Service Selection Board procedure. Later this was reduced to a one-day, non-residential selection. Each group consisted of about eight candidates and three selectors. It started with short written tests followed by group discussions 'designed to assess individual reactions to various random statements, fictional marital problems and relationship situations in terms of prejudice, vulnerability and self awareness' (p. 133). Individual interviews with two selectors were designed to clarify personal suitability in greater depth. The selectors made the final decision on all available data. There was a shortage of counsellors but only about half the candidates passed the selection procedure. Successful candidates first undertook some set reading. They then trained for a total of forty-eight hours in groups of about twelve with two tutors, starting with role play and video-taped counselling interviews, with discussion of the group's reactions and feelings. They then practised for sixteen weeks under supervision before an introduction to group work, concentrating on learning about group interaction, education in personal relationships, and preparation for marriage. This was followed by study of aspects of human growth and behaviour. The final section consisted of further aspects of counselling and a general summing up of training. Not more than one section might be taken in a term and the total course was spread over approximately two years. Less than 10 per cent either failed to finish the course or did not reach the required standard. Each student had six tutorials a year, attended fortnightly group discussion on cases led by regional tutors and had to record every interview. Counsellors also learnt the 'techniques of group discussion' since most counsellors also worked with groups of young people or engaged couples or marriage partners.

There were in 1974 about 1,450 marriage guidance counsellors who had completed this training and were practising. This nationwide service by volunteers contrasts with the sophisticated research-based practice of the Institute of Marital Studies (IMS). In the 1960s joint activities began when members of the National Marriage Guidance Council staff took the one-year, part-time course at the IMS, which also provided consultation services and seminars.

Wallis and Booker (1958) and Venables (1971) both discussed the difficulty of testing effectiveness. This was being attempted in social work and should not be impossible in this important field. It would also be valuable to know how the performance of volunteers given this type of training compared with that of both in-service trained and professionally qualified, full-time social workers. The Aves Committee (1969) said

'We believe that increased co-operation between Marriage Guidance Councils and social workers would enable the Councils to give a better service to their clients than they do at present. We hope that there may be a move towards a greater use of social workers in this service, particularly for the selection and allocation of cases; and to provide consultation and guidance for the carefully selected, appropriately trained, and often gifted volunteers.' (p. 177)

In 1975 the Home Office set up a working party on marriage guidance to collect information about the use being made of marriage counselling, and to co-ordinate knowledge and treatment methods, training, and research.

Vocational Guidance and School Counselling

Vocational guidance and careers advice were long established, whether in schools or institutions of higher education or youth employment bureaux. The new factor was an understanding based on experience that it was as important to take account of a child or young person's emotions, irrational and non-rational attitudes, desires and unconscious or cultural assumptions as of his intelligence, school attainments and aptitudes. This was related to the emergence of school counselling which was concerned with educational, vocational and personal, family or classroom difficulties, or personality problems from aggression to withdrawal and including the many problems that children might present in school – problems that often could not or would not be dealt with in a clinic. This showed the exceptional possibilities 'of the school as a potentially therapeutic as well as an educational institution, which has the care of children over a number of years' (Schools Council, 1967, p. 60). School counselling required a wide range of competence which included close liaison with individual teachers and the school system as a whole, besides liaison with the children's (later the social services) department, the probation and after-care service and education welfare officers. The action research study *Counselling and School Social Work* (Rose and Marshall, 1974) is discussed in chapter 11.

The new teacher counsellor appointments were controversial. It was strongly contended that if school counselling were so intimately bound up with the school, then no one who was not part of the teaching profession could perform it effectively. On another view it was essentially social work, for the child's life in his family and neighbourhood was quite as, if not more, important as his school life, moreover the pre-school years and adolescence were crucial and thus the comprehensiveness and continuity of the social services department with all its resources, its knowledge of the community, and its expertise in child care and family relationships made it the appropriate service to assume this function rather than to duplicate it within the education system.

Teachers began to be seconded to take the one-year courses in counselling established during the 1960s at Manchester, Keele, Reading, Exeter and Leeds Universities or the course for consultants in higher education. Most of these courses included educational statistics, test construction and individual testing, measurement and guidance related to a pupil's ability and aptitude for the purpose of educational and vocational guidance, and to help with personal and social problems. Each year the Tavistock Institute ran a one evening a week seminar covering three terms. Students brought illustrative material from their own counselling work in schools and explored its processes and implications in the light of lecture/discussions on child development, individual and group dynamics and other psychological and sociological topics. There was a variety of other short in-service training courses.

Newsome *et al.* (1973) described, with case illustrations, the student counselling service at Keele University and its importance in helping students with many different educational, vocational and personal problems ranging from a need for straightforward information to contemplated suicide. The authors define counsellors as 'educators who aim to create through the exercise of their skills an environment in which students can face and explore their own feelings without fear, learn how to cope more effectively with decision-making and examine their values and objectives without risk of condemnation' (p. 6).

Other Developments in Counselling
Counselling as a distinct function with some training had also developed amongst the clergy, youth leaders, doctors, lawyers and some of those working with students, immigrants, the handicapped, and elsewhere. Youth counselling centres with supporting psychiatric, legal and medical services began to be pioneered for young people who wanted to talk to people who did not know them and whom they would not necessarily see again, but which offered a drop-in confidential service. There were about sixty of these by 1972.

Age Concern (Scotland) started two pilot projects in 1973 to select and train volunteer counsellors for old people and their relations, including financial, health, housing and personal matters.

Most counselling was based on Carl Roger's theory of client-centred counselling with its emphasis on the importance of the relationship with the client, exploration of feelings and interviewing skills. Caseworkers' emphasis in the 1950s on the worker/client relationship which later brought them into disrepute subsequently became acceptable as counselling, indeed its core. It drew heavily on casework literature and some descriptions by leading exponents are hard to distinguish from 'pure' casework. Obviously counselling was a more attractive term than casework; it was not associated with social breakdown, pathology or lack of material resources, and it was validly practised by people trained to do so but who primarily belonged to some other profession.

In 1971 the Standing Conference for the Advancement of Counselling was set up through NCSS initiative and by 1975 had 123 member organisations covering many professions and volunteer counsellors. It was concerned with standards, adequate opportunities for consultation and supervision, and professional and volunteer training. Counselling was clearly an addition to some professions to enable them to do their own job better or an extension of a professional role or, as in social work, an intrinsic part of the main function. But there were different views as to whether or not it was or should be emerging as a new profession in its own right.

SOCIAL WORK AND EDUCATION WELFARE

During the 1950s education welfare officers were primarily concerned with school attendance and applications for free meals, shoes and clothing. They were also responsible for enforcing regulations about the employment of children and in some areas they undertook the after-care of children from special schools. They had no powers to deal with any problems of child care not connected with school attendance. They were each responsible for the school attendance of an average of 3,000 children, with a range from 2,000 to 7,500. They might make from 150 to 350 visits each week. Most were men and a large number were in late middle-age, having been recruited from the police or the services. By the 1970s recruitment had spread to other occupations.

Some EWOs were familiar with individual family problems in their districts over a long period of time. But without a great reduction in their caseloads, opportunities for training and changes in organisation and support, they might be able to do little more than advise or admonish on questions of school attendance. As Rodgers and Dixon (1960) found in the late 1950s:

'The duties of education welfare officers vary in different authorities . . . and more or less emphasis is placed on their social work responsibilities according to the sympathies of their senior officers. Thus a very mixed body of men with no common training are performing different duties in different districts with a varying amount of supervision and few common principles to guide them. Inevitably the amount of social work they do depends on the intelligence and interest of individual men.' (p. 59)

They were primarily concerned with normal families rather than with families 'at risk', yet they were in a strong position to identify such families, since failure to attend school included school phobias and truancy, both symptoms of family disturbance. Increasingly in the 1960s, this still largely unrecognised service tried in varying degrees in different parts of the country to give help and support to families and to act as a link with other social services. Over the years it had taken on wider functions and many EWOs recognised that previous authoritarian methods were not relevant to symptoms of social and emotional stress. But they were ill-supported in spite of the service's potentialities for identifying children at risk. And many EWOs thought that school phobia was 'a name invented to prevent them from securing the attendance of some children who were "getting away" with their absence from school' (Kahn and Nursten, 1968, pp. 202–3). Prichard's survey (1974) showed that in EWOs' 'hardcore' caseloads there were many highly disturbed children who required skilled assessment.

In Glasgow, social workers, usually with a social science qualification, were responsible for education welfare as distinct from school attendance. There were sixteen with nine assistants in 1967. After the Social Work (Scotland) Act, 1968 the service was transferred to the Social Work Department. The London County Council school care system, which had existed since 1907, made volunteers responsible for a wide range of welfare and health functions, with the support of about eighty children's care organisers by the 1960s. School attendance duties remained with school inquiry officers. There were also special inquiry officers, often with much knowledge and shrewd judgement, attached to the London juvenile courts. In 1970 the Inner London Education Authority (ILEA) introduced a unified education welfare service composed of area teams of EWOs and voluntary workers to offer social work support to school children and their families. Some staff were seconded to take professional social work courses. This service thus remained separate as to both boundaries and auspices from the Inner London boroughs social services departments.

In general, salaries were low, promotion prospects limited, and there was no general training. Varying amounts of supervision were available but there were no common guiding principles. In the early 1960s the Council for Training in Social Work (CTSW) agreed to initiate opportunities for selected EWOs to take the two-year or one-year courses. Implementation was deferred in spite of pressure on the DES, first for the Plowden Report (1967), then for the Seebohm Report (1968), and then pending clarification of the role of the service in relation to the new social services departments. With some justification, EWOs felt themselves neglected, isolated and often not consulted when they had valuable knowledge. They struggled for years to achieve recognition and training but the DES showed little interest in improving either their qualifications or their status.

In 1963 the Local Government Examinations Board introduced a certificate in education welfare based upon examination results on papers on central and local government, the social services, the education welfare service, child welfare and the use of English. By 1973 ten colleges provided day release courses in these subjects for some 140 students, but large areas of the country were not covered, there were no fieldwork requirements, workloads were not reduced for study, and the certificate was awarded purely on written examination results. There was a failure rate of about 50 per cent and by 1971 only roughly 8·5 per cent of EWOs held a certificate which many felt was not relevant to their needs. It was phased out by 1974.

The National Association of Chief Education Welfare Officers calculated in its evidence to the Plowden Committee that of its 1,200 members over 300 had been studying for this certificate and that 30 had a university social science qualification (Plowden Report, para. 220). The Plowden Report, which was the first government report to pay attention to education welfare, concluded that many school attendance visits were a waste of time. It proposed that

'Welfare officers should be enabled to concentrate on the real problem cases and have time to give them the benefit of general casework. If some of the welfare officers are to carry increasing responsibilities for social work, and we think they should after training, a distinction must be made between their welfare duties and the administrative work which ought to be done by others.' (para. 228)

Education welfare officers should be free to transfer if they so wished or else to remain on the administrative side of education departments. They should be enabled to take in-service training in social work or else one of the two-year social work courses. Much routine work was purely clerical or could be done by correspondence, telephone, or by welfare assistants.

One of the most difficult decisions that faced the Seebohm Committee concerned social work in schools. It was argued that the welfare of children was an intrinsic part of the school's responsibilities and that teachers would not co-operate with an outside service, which in any event would not be effective unless it was intimately part of the school set up. But the Committee was clear that children must be thought of in their total environment which included their family and neighbourhood as well as their school, and that one department should be dealing with the whole range of the family's personal and social needs, including children under school age and school leavers. School children may be affected by economic hardship, marital disharmony, or bad parent/child relationships: the schools could often spot these danger signals, sometimes manifesting themselves in truancy, aggression or withdrawal, and enable the social service department to take prompt action. Social workers in area teams would be more effective because in their work in schools they would have behind them the resources and consultative services of the social services department, rather than working on their own in isolation, and incidentally perpetuating the system of segmented *ad hoc* social work services with limited career prospects. Social workers in the social services department should be attached either whole- or part-time to particular schools. They should be knowledgeable about the education service in order to have the confidence of school staffs. Conversely, teachers should be better equipped to understand the social factors which affect children's behaviour and more knowledgeable about the social services. Neither the Seebohm Report (1968) nor the later Ralphs Report (1975) referred to the importance of understanding the school as a social system, wherever the professional responsibility for this might be located, and its impact on teachers, pupils and parents.

The Local Authority Social Services Act, 1970 left the siting of the education welfare service to local authority discretion. A few transferred it to the social services department to be run as a secondment service like hospital social work or probation officers in prison welfare. Otherwise, area teams developed various forms of co-operation with EWOs from *ad hoc* discussions to regular meetings.

Rose and Marshall (1974) concluded, as a result of an action research project in attaching social workers to schools, that casework with individual children produced improvements in social adjustment (see also chapter 11). The effectiveness of fieldworkers depended on the setting, it was therefore important that social workers should be personally acceptable, given a clearly defined function within the school system, and accept the school norms and values. Conversely, though the relations between the social worker, the child and the family were largely confidential, teachers should be willing to accept a social worker's judgement about a child and sometimes change their own handling in consequence. Some teachers saw personal counselling as part of their function and were competitive with social workers. The authors said: 'Our conclusion is that despite the claim of the teaching profession and the views of the education departments, it does not appear to be necessary to be teacher trained to carry out those various duties described as personal guidance or social work' (pp. 185–6).

Educational counselling was not part of social work, but the relations between teachers and a new breed of EWOs trained in social work remained to be defined in the light of experience.

A working party set up by the Local Government Training Board (LGTB) investigated the functions and appropriate training of EWOs. Its report (the Ralphs Report, 1975) was the first thorough review of the subject. It found an extraordinary range, and variety of duties in this 'sadly neglected' service with no uniformity and no national guidance about the work, though 'it is clear the education welfare officer's role at present is that of a social worker within an educational setting' (p. 19). This included physically, mentally and materially handicapped children, and relations between the school, the community and the home. The education welfare service was not being given the opportunity it sought to measure up to its functions. Indeed it had 'suffered from consistent neglect'.

Some authorities were appointing various specialist staffs, whether school social workers, teacher social workers, or school counsellors, which inhibited the development of the education welfare service. Most of these experiments were designed to meet specific needs, whereas the education welfare service could be developed to promote the educational well-being of the child as a whole. Little consistent thought had been given to its development in the past and 'little recognition of its future potential in the new field of socio-educational need' (p. 43). Analysis of depth studies undertaken by the working party reaffirmed that in this 'undervalued and under-developed service' the neglected potential of education welfare could only be realised within a reconstructed service and with adequate training. In the vast majority of local education authority areas there was a ratio of one officer to 4,000 pupils or less, but a wide variation of functions throughout the country, apart from school attendance. Detailed analysis in nine areas showed not only the many clerical and administrative tasks but also that EWOs should exercise a social work role in an educational setting, yet there was a considerable amount of conflict between them and social workers. In 1972 there were 2,380 EWOs in England and Wales, of whom one-third were over 55 and only 15 per cent were women. There was little wastage, it was a service characterised by stability and maturity, but EWOs were almost wholly unqualified.

The working party thought that the future role of EWOs should include assessment of social, emotional and educational problems related to the child's ability to benefit from education; a supportive relationship with and between teachers, children and parents, including interpreting family and social situations to teachers; appropriate referrals; enforcement of legislation; and functions in relation to pre-school children. The Report did not mention the transition from school to work. The enlarged functions required social work and educational skills, but the working party was against isolated specialist courses which would petrify the service in its existing state. It came down in favour of EWOs taking the CQSW with additional courses in the theory, sociology and administration of education and the education of children with special needs. Fieldwork placements should be developed in educational settings. About 250 places would be needed annually. The Report particularly favoured the CCETSW-sponsored 'phase III' courses and in-service training for older long-serving officers who would continue to be the backbone of the service.

Training alone would be ineffectual without a national statement of policy by the DES giving official recognition and status to the education welfare service. The Department should also take responsibility for common standards of practice essential for an effective professional service.

The Report's recommendations were accepted by the LGTB and the CCETSW, which became responsible for training social workers for the education service. Discussions were started with the DES and representatives of education services, while several courses were encouraged to develop field placements and teaching to equip students for this service. By 1975 education authorities intended to second 160 to 190 existing staff and trainees each year to take the courses. Pilot courses were also started to train supervisors for fieldwork in education welfare; and the LGTB set out to plan a national programme of post-experience courses at various educational institutions.

The Birch Report (1976) based its training projections on the assumption that the education welfare service 'would move professionally into line with social workers in the local authority social services departments' (para. 9.8). At long last policy moves had begun to bring EWOs in out of the cold.

Bibliography

Place of publication is London unless otherwise stated

ABERDEEN UNIVERSITY (1971–2), Prospectus of the Aberdeen University Two-Year Certificate in Applied Social Studies Course.

ADAMSON, GILVRAY (1973), *The Care-Takers* (Bristol, Bookstall Publications).

ADVISORY COUNCIL ON CHILD CARE (1968), *A Research and Development Strategy* (HMSO).

(1970*a*), *Care and Treatment in a Planned Environment* (HMSO).

(1970*b*), *A Guide to Adoption Practice* (HMSO).

ADVISORY COUNCIL ON SOCIAL WORK (1974), *Field Work Staffing (Scotland)* (Edinburgh, Social Work Services Group).

ADVISORY COUNCIL ON THE TREATMENT OF OFFENDERS (1963), *The Organisation of After-Care* (HMSO).

(1965), *The Adult Offender* (HMSO).

(1970), *Non-Custodial and Semi-Custodial Penalties* (HMSO).

AGE CONCERN (1974), *The Attitudes of the Retired and Elderly* (Mitcham, Age Concern).

(1975), *Manifesto* (Mitcham, Age Concern).

(n.d.), Report on *Training for Wardens of Group Housing Schemes* (Mitcham, Age Concern).

AKURST, C. R. (1973), review of *Task-Centered Casework* in *Social Work Today*, vol. 4, no. 2, p. 59.

ALBERMARLE REPORT (1960), *The Youth Service in England and Wales*, Cmnd 929 (HMSO).

APLIN, GEOFFREY and BAMBER, RALPH (1973), 'Groupwork Counselling', *Social Work Today*, vol. 3, no. 22, pp. 5–9.

APPLEYARD, GEOFFREY (1971), 'Prison Welfare?', *Howard Journal of Penology*, vol. 13, no. 2, pp. 106–13.

APTE, ROBERT Z. (1970), *Half-way Houses* (Bell).

ASHDOWN, MARGARET and BROWN, SIBYL CLEMENT (1953), *Social Service and Mental Health* (Routledge & Kegan Paul).

ASSOCIATION OF CHILD CARE OFFICERS (1969*a*), *Adoption – the Way Ahead* (ACCO).

(1969*b*), *Report of the Working Party on Professional Integrity in the Child Care Service* (ACCO).

ASSOCIATION OF CHILDREN'S OFFICERS (1953), *Cruelty to Children* (ACO).

ASSOCIATION OF COMMUNITY WORKERS (1975), *Knowledge and Skills for Community Work* (ACW).

ASSOCIATION OF DIRECTORS OF SOCIAL SERVICES (1974), 'Discussion paper', mimeographed (Association of Directors of Social Services).

ASSOCIATION OF PSYCHIATRIC SOCIAL WORKERS (1956*a*), *The Boundaries of Casework* (APSW).

(1956*b*), *The Essentials of Social Casework* (APSW).

(1958), *Working Party on the Function of PSWs in the Adult Field* (APSW).

(1960), *Ventures in Professional Co-operation* (APSW).

Annual Report 1968 (APSW).

(1969), *New Developments in Psychiatry and the Implications for the Social Worker* (APSW).

ASSOCIATION OF SOCIAL WORKERS (1953), *Notes on the Ethics of Social Work* (ASW).

(1956), *Recent Developments in Casework* (ASW).

(1960), *Morals and the Social Worker* (ASW).

AVES REPORT (1969), *The Voluntary Worker in the Social Services* (Allen & Unwin).

BALDOCK, PETER (1974), 'Community Work Experience in Social Work Training' in Jones, David and Mayo, Marjorie (eds), *Community Work – One* (Routledge & Kegan Paul).

BALLANCE, GILLIAN (1975), 'Fostering' in Stroud, John (ed.), *Services for Children and Their Families* (Pergamon Press), pp. 76–96.

BARACLOUGH, J. (1974*a*), 'Confidentiality', *Social Work Today/BASW News*, vol. 5, no. 4, p. 116.

(1974*b*), 'Confidentiality', *Social Work Today/BASW News*, vol. 5, no. 5, p. 148.

(1975), 'Code of Ethics for Social Work', *Social Work Today/BASW News*, vol. 6, no. 12, pp. 379–81.

BARNARDO'S (1969), *A Plan for the Reorganisation of the Child Care Department*, working party report (Barkingside, Barnardo's).

BARNES, L. and TAJFEL, I. (1958), 'The Teaching of Psychology in Social Science Courses', mimeographed (Joint University Council for Social and Public Administration).

BARR, HUGH (1966), *A Survey of Group Work in the Probation Service*, Home Office research studies (HMSO).

(1971), *Volunteers in Prison After-Care* (Allen & Unwin).

BARTLETT, HARRIETT (1970), *The Common Base of Social Work Practice* (New York, National Association of Social Workers).

BATTEN, T. R. (1957), *Communities and Their Development* (Oxford University Press).

BAYLEY, MICHAEL (1973), 'The Mentally Handicapped and Their Helpers', *British Journal of Social Work*, vol. 3, no. 3, pp. 319–63.

BEARD, RUTH (1970), *Teaching and Learning in Higher Education* (Harmondsworth, Penguin).

BENNINGTON, J. (1974), 'Strategies for Change at the Local Level: Some Reflections' in Jones, David and Mayo, Marjorie (eds), *Community Work – One* (Routledge & Kegan Paul), pp. 260–77.

BERRY, JULIET (1975), *Daily Experience in Residential Life* (Routledge & Kegan Paul).

BESSEY REPORT (1962), *The Training of Part-Time Youth Leaders and Assistants* (HMSO).

BIESTEK, FATHER (1961 and 1973, British ed.), *The Casework Relationship* (Allen & Unwin).

BILLIS, D. (1973), 'Entry into Residential Care', *British Journal of Social Work*, vol. 3, no. 4, pp. 447–71.

BINGHAM, J. (1961), *Do Cows Have Neuroses?* (National Association for Mental Health).

BION, W. (1961), *Experiences in Groups* (Tavistock Publications).

BIRCH REPORT (1976), *Working Party on Manpower and Training for the Social Services* (HMSO).

BOARD FOR SOCIAL RESPONSIBILITY OF THE NATIONAL ASSEMBLY OF THE CHURCH OF ENGLAND (1969), *The Church and the Social Services* (Church Information Office).

BONE, MARGARET (1972), *The Youth Service and Similar Provision for Young People* (HMSO).

BOWERS, SWITHUN (1949), 'The Nature and Definition of Social Casework', *Journal of Social Casework* (New York), vol. 30, no. 10, pp. 412–17.

BOWLBY, JOHN (1951), *Maternal Care and Mental Health* (Geneva, World Health Organisation).

(1969), *Attachment* (Hogarth Press).

(1973), *Separation, Anxiety and Anger* (Hogarth Press).

BRAITHWAITE, ROSE MARY (1959), 'The Probation Officer, His Training and Skill', *Probation*, vol. 9, no. 3, pp. 30–2.

BRANDON, DAVID (n.d.), *Women without Homes* (Christian Action).

BREE, M. H. (1970), 'Staying the Course', *British Journal of Psychiatric Social Work*, vol. 10, no. 4, pp. 170–7.

BRESLIN, ALICE and STURTON, SHEILA (1974), 'Groupwork in a Hostel for the Mentally Handicapped', *Social Work Today*, vol. 4, no. 23, pp. 722–6.

BRITISH ASSOCIATION OF RESIDENTIAL SETTLEMENTS (1951), *A Survey of Settlements, 1950* (BARS).

BRITISH ASSOCIATION OF SETTLEMENTS AND SOCIAL ACTION CENTRES (1973), 'Basic Statement of Common Purpose', mimeographed (BAS).

BRITISH ASSOCIATION OF SOCIAL WORKERS (1971), *Discussion Paper No. 1. Confidentiality in Social Work* (BASW).

(1972), *Discussion Paper No. 2. A Code of Ethics for Social Work* (Birmingham, BASW).

(1974), 'Better Services for the Mentally Handicapped: BASW Policy', *Social Work Today/BASW News*, vol. 5, no. 6, p. 173.

(1975*a*), 'Career Grade Working Party Report', *Social Work Today/BASW News*, vol. 6, no. 9, pp. 285–6.

(1975*b*), 'Confidence – in Principle and Practice', *Social Work Today/BASW News*, vol. 6, no. 8, pp. 253–4.

(1975*c*), 'The Future of Probation Officers in Borstals and Prisons', *Social Work Today/ BASW News*, vol. 6, no. 10, pp. 317–19.

(1975*d*), 'Children at Risk – BASW's Code of Practice', *Social Work Today/ BASW News*, vol. 6, no. 11, pp. 345–9.

(1977), *The Social Work Task* (BASW).

(n.d. [1974]), *Social Action and Social Work: Report of the Working Party* (Birmingham, BASW).

(n.d., adopted 1975), *A Code of Ethics for Social Workers* (Birmingham, BASW).

BRITISH MEDICAL ASSOCIATION AND THE MAGISTRATES' ASSOCIATION (1956), *Cruelty to and Neglect of Children* (BMA).

BRITISH PAEDIATRIC ASSOCIATION (1966), *British Medical Journal*, vol. 1, 'The Battered Baby Syndrome', pp. 601–3.

BROWN, G. W., BONE, MARGARET, DALISON, BRIDGET and WING, J. K. (1966), *Schizophrenia and Social Care*, Maudsley Monograph No. 17 (Oxford University Press).

BROWN, M. (1964), 'A Review of Casework Methods', reproduced in Younghusband, E. (ed.), *New Developments in Casework* (1966), (Allen & Unwin), pp. 11–37.

BROWN, S. CLEMENT (1955), 'A Study of a Sample of Trained Houseparents', unpublished (Nuffield College, Oxford).

BROWN, S. CLEMENT and GLOYNE, ELIZABETH (1966), *The Field Training of Social Workers* (Allen & Unwin).

BROWNING, JEAN and HOPE-MURRAY, E. L. (1974), 'Notes on Developing Local

Authority Social Services in England under the Chronically Sick and Disabled Persons Act, 1970', *Social Work Service*, no. 6, pp. 6–10.

BRYANT, RICHARD (1974), 'Field Work Training in Community Work', *Community Development Journal*, vol. 9, no. 3, pp. 212–16.

BULL, GRACE and BAILEY, JONATHON (1971), 'A Group for Experienced Foster Parents' in Tod, Robert (ed.), *Social Work in Foster Care* (Longman), pp. 131–7.

BURBERY, M., BALINT, E. and YAPP, B. (1945), *An Introduction to Child Guidance* (Macmillan).

BURNS, T. and SINCLAIR, S. (1963), *The Child Care Service at Work* (Edinburgh, HMSO).

BUTLER, BARBARA (1976), foreword to *Marital and Family Therapy* (Family Welfare Association), pp. 2–3.

BUTRYM, ZOFIA (1968), *Medical Social Work in Action* (Bell).

(1976), *The Nature of Social Work* (The Macmillan Press).

BUTTERWORTH INQUIRY (1972), *Report of the Butterworth Inquiry into the Work and Pay of Probation Officers and Social Workers*, Cmnd 5076 (HMSO).

BYWATERS, NANCY (1972 and 1975), 'A Survey of Day Care in Dr. Barnardo's' and 'A Second Survey of Barnardo Day Care', mimeographed (Barkingside, Barnardo's).

(1973), 'Day Care in a Large Voluntary Child Care Society', *Social Work Service*, no. 3, pp. 11 and 12.

CABINET OFFICE (1973), *Government Research and Development* (HMSO).

CADE, E. (1975), 'Therapy with Low Socio-Economic Families', *Social Work Today*, vol. 6, no. 5, pp. 142–5.

CAMERON, J. M. (1966), 'The Battered Child Syndrome', *Medical Science and the Law*, vol. 6, no. 1, pp. 2–21.

The Canford Families: A Study in Social Casework and Social Group Work (1962), Sociological Review No. 6 (University of Keele).

CAPLAN, G. (1961), *A Community Approach to Mental Health* (Tavistock Publications).

(1962), *Prevention of Mental Disorders in Children* (Tavistock Publications).

CARTER, DEREK T. (1971a), 'Attitudes of Medical Social Workers Towards Reorganisation', *British Journal of Social Work*, vol. 1, no. 3, pp. 255–75.

(1971b), 'The Deployment of Medical Social Workers', *Social Work Today*, vol. 2, no. 11, pp. 3–7.

(1976), 'The Social Needs of the Physically Sick and the Role of the Medical Social Worker' (unpublished doctoral thesis, York University).

CARVER, V. and EDWARDS, J. L. (1972), *Social Workers and Their Workloads* (National Institute for Social Work Training).

CASEMENT, P. (1973), 'The Supervisory Viewpoint' in Finn, W. H. (ed.), *Family Therapy in Social Work* (Family Welfare Association) pp. 32–6.

CENTRAL COUNCIL FOR EDUCATION AND TRAINING IN SOCIAL WORK (1973a), *Bulletin No. 1* (CCETSW).

(1973b), *Residential Work Is Part of Social Work*, report of a working party (CCETSW).

(1973c), *Setting the Course for Social Work Education 1971–73* (CCETSW).

(1973d), *Training for Residential Work*, discussion document (CCETSW).

(1973–4), *Social Work Education*, Report 2 (CCETSW).

(1974a), *Legal Studies in Social Work Education*, report of a working party (CCETSW).

(1974b), *People with Handicaps Need Better Trained Social Workers*, report of a working party (CCETSW).

/Local Government Training Board (1974c), *Training for Organisers of Home Help and Other Supportive Domiciliary Services*, report of a joint working party (CCETSW).

CENTRAL COUNCIL FOR EDUCATION AND TRAINING IN SOCIAL WORK (1975a), *Day Services: An Action Plan for Training*, report of a working party (CCETSW).

(1975b), *Education and Training for Social Work* (CCETSW).

(1975c), *A New Form of Training: the Certificate in Social Service* (CCETSW).

(1975d), *The Teaching of Community Work*, report of a working party (CCETSW).

(1975e), 'Guidelines for Post-Qualifying Studies', mimeographed (CCETSW).

(1975f), 'Principles, Procedures and Criteria for Approval of Post-Qualifying Studies', mimeographed (CCETSW).

(1976a), *Bulletin 4, Social Work Education News and Views* (CCETSW).

(1976b), *Values in Social Work*, report of a working party (CCETSW).

CENTRAL HOUSING ADVISORY COMMITTEE (1967), *The Needs of New Communities* (HMSO).

CENTRAL TRAINING COUNCIL IN CHILD CARE (1947), *Memorandum on the Training of House Parents* (Home Office Children's Department).

(1953), *Notes on the Training of House-Parents of Children's Homes* (Home Office Children's Department).

(1956), *Training in Child Care, Memorandum of Guidance by the Home Office* (Home Office Children's Department).

(1963), *Memorandum of Guidance on Practical Training for Child Care Students* (Home Office Children's Department).

(1967), *In-service Study Course for Residential Child Care Staff: Approved Guide Syllabus* (Home Office).

CENTRAL TRAINING COUNCIL IN CHILD CARE/CENTRAL COUNCIL FOR EDUCATION AND TRAINING IN SOCIAL WORK (1970), *New Perspectives in Social Work*, report of a working party (CCETSW).

CHEETHAM, JULIET (1972), *Social Work with Immigrants* (Routledge & Kegan Paul).

CHEETHAM, J. and HILL, M. (1973), 'Community Work: Social Realities and Ethical Dilemmas', *British Journal of Social Work*, vol. 3, no. 3, pp. 331–48.

CHILD GUIDANCE SPECIAL INTEREST GROUP/BRITISH ASSOCIATION OF SOCIAL WORKERS (1975), *The Child Guidance Service: Report of the 1969 Survey undertaken by Psychiatric Social Workers* (Child Guidance Special Interest Group).

CLARKE, MICHAEL (1976), 'First Year Sociology Courses: A Report of a Survey', *Sociology*, vol. 10, no. 1, pp. 83–99.

COLLINS, J. (1965), *Social Casework in General Medical Practice* (Pitman).

COLLIS, ARTHUR (1961), 'Social Work – a Current Assessment of Training and Related Topics', *Social Work*, vol. 18, no. 3, pp. 5–9.

COMMUNITY RELATIONS COMMISSION (1974), *Response to the Select Committee on Race Relations and Immigration* (CRC).

(1975), *Who Minds?* (CRC).

(1976a), *Some of My Best Friends . . .* (CRC).

(1976b), *Working in Multi-Racial Areas: A Training Handbook for Social Services Departments* (CRC).

CONFERENCE OF PRINCIPAL PROBATION OFFICERS (1968), *The Place of the Probation and After-Care Service in Judicial Administration* (CPPO).

COOPER, CHRISTINE (1975), 'The Doctor's Dilemma: A Paediatrician's View' in Franklin, A. White (ed.), *Concerning Child Abuse* (Churchill Livingstone), pp. 21–30.

COOPER, JOAN (1967), 'Residential Work with Children' (Paper read at the Conference of the Association of Hospital and Welfare Administrators, Hastings, 1967).

COPE REPORT (1951), *Report of the Committees on Medical Auxiliaries*, Cmnd 8188 (HMSO).

COUNCIL FOR CHILDREN'S WELFARE (1965), *A Family Service and a Family Court* (CCW).

(1975), *No Childhood* (CCW).

COUNCIL FOR TRAINING IN SOCIAL WORK, *Annual Report 1965* (CTSW).

(1967a), *Human Growth and Development as a Subject of Study for Social Workers*, working party report (CTSW).

(1967b), *Staff Development in Social Work* (CTSW).

Annual Report 1967 (CTSW).

(1969), 'Teaching about Utilization of Research in Social Work Courses', unpublished (CTSW).

(1971), *The Teaching of Fieldwork*, CTSW Discussion Paper No. 4 (CTSW).

(1972), *The Teaching of Sociology in Social Work Courses*, working party report (CTSW).

COURT, JOAN (1974), 'Characteristics of Parents and Children' in Carter, Jan (ed.), *The Maltreated Child* (Priory Press).

COVENTRY SOCIAL SERVICES DEPARTMENT (n.d.), *Looking for Trouble*, survey 1971–72 (Coventry, Social Services Department).

COX, D. T. and DERRICOURT, N. J. (1975), 'The De-professionalisation of Community Work' in Jones, David and Mayo, Marjorie (eds), *Community Work – Two* (Routledge & Kegan Paul), pp. 75–87.

CRELLIN, E., KELLMER PRINGLE, M. and WEDGE, P. (1971), *Born Illegitimate* (Slough, National Foundation for Educational Research).

CURNOCK, KATHLEEN (1975), *Student Units in Social Work Education* (CCETSW).

CURTIS REPORT (1946), *Report of the Care of Children Committee*, Cmnd 6922 (HMSO).

CYPHER, JOHN (1974), 'Differential Use of Manpower', *Social Work Today*, vol. 5, no. 15, pp. 452–6.

DANBURY, HAZEL (1976), 'Mental Health Compulsory Admissions', *Social Work Today*, vol. 7, no. 6, pp. 172–4.

DAVIES, BERNARD (1975), *The Use of Groups in Social Work Practice* (Routledge & Kegan Paul).

DAVIES, MARTIN (1969), *Probationers in Their Social Environment*, Home Office research studies (HMSO).

(1972), 'The Objectives of the Probation Service', *British Journal of Social Work*, vol. 2, no. 3, pp. 315–22.

(1973), 'The Criminal Justice Act, 1972 as an Expression of Social Policy', *Social Work Today*, vol. 4, no. 7, pp. 195–201.

(1974), *Prisoners of Society* (Routledge & Kegan Paul).

(1975), *Social Work in the Environment*, Home Office research studies (HMSO).

DAY, B. (1965), 'Supportive Casework in an Authority Setting', *Case Conference*, vol. 11, no. 9, pp. 389–93.

DEANE, R. (1966), 'Some Non-interpretive Casework in Families affected by Mental Illness', *Case Conference*, vol. 12, no. 8, pp. 277–81.

DEPARTMENT OF EDUCATION AND SCIENCE (1969), *Youth and Community Work in the 70s*, Report of the Youth Service Development Council (HMSO).

(1972), *Educational Priority, Report of a Research Project* (HMSO).

DEPARTMENT OF EDUCATION AND SCIENCE, DEPARTMENT OF HEALTH AND SOCIAL SECURITY, WELSH OFFICE (1974), *Child Guidance*, Circular 3/74 DES, HSC (15)9 DHSS, WHSC (15)5 Welsh Office.

DEPARTMENT OF HEALTH AND SOCIAL SECURITY, CHIEF MEDICAL OFFICER OF HEALTH

AND CHIEF INSPECTOR HOME OFFICE CHILDREN'S DEPARTMENT (1970*a*), Circular CMO 2/70 and LHAL 24/70.

DEPARTMENT OF HEALTH AND SOCIAL SECURITY (1970*b*), *National Health Service, The Future Structure of the National Health Service*, second Green Paper on the NHS (HMSO).

(1971*a*), *Better Services for the Mentally Handicapped* (HMSO).

(1971*b*), *Children Act 1948, Summary of Returns of Child Care Staff* (DHSS).

(1971*c*), *Fieldwork Training for Social Work* (HMSO).

(1971*d*), *Youth Treatment Centres* (HMSO).

(1972*a*), Circular 35/72 (DHSS).

(1972*b*), *Intermediate Treatment* (HMSO).

/HOME OFFICE (1972*c*), Joint Circular LASS 26/72, including a booklet on 'The Battered Baby' prepared by the Department of Health and Social Security Standing Medical Advisory Committee.

DEPARTMENT OF HEALTH AND SOCIAL SECURITY (1973*a*), *Development of Services for the Elderly*, Social Work Service Survey (HMSO).

(1973*b*), *Intermediate Treatment Project*, Development Group Report (HMSO).

(1973*c*), *Review of the Home Help Service in England* (DHSS).

/WELSH OFFICE (1974*a*), Circular LASS 13/74.

/DEPARTMENT OF THE ENVIRONMENT (1974*b*), *Homelessness*, Circular DHSS 4/74 and DoE 18/74 (HMSO).

DEPARTMENT OF HEALTH AND SOCIAL SECURITY (1974*c*), *Non-Accidental Injury to Children* (LASSL 9 (74) 13).

(1974*d*), *Report of the Committee of Inquiry into the Care and Supervision Provided in relation to Maria Colwell* (HMSO).

(1974*e*), 'The Service Delivery Study', a Social Work Service Study, *Social Work Service*, June 1975, pp. 11–14.

/WELSH OFFICE (1974*f*), *Social Work Support for the Health Service* (HMSO).

DEPARTMENT OF HEALTH AND SOCIAL SECURITY (1975*a*), *Annual Report 1974* (HMSO).

(1975*b*), *Better Services for the Mentally Ill* (HMSO).

(1975*c*), 'The Day Care of Young Children', *Social Work Service*, no. 6, pp. 14–17.

(1975*d*), *Hostels for Young People*, Social Work Service Development Group (HMSO).

DEPARTMENT OF HEALTH AND SOCIAL SECURITY STATISTICS AND RESEARCH DIVISION (1975*e*), *Local Authority Social Services Departments. Staff of Homes for the Elderly etc.* (DHSS S/F 75/6).

(1976*a*), *Consultative Document on Priorities for Health and Personal Social Services in England* (HMSO).

(1976*b*), *Guide to Fostering Practice* (HMSO).

(1976*c*), *Non-Accidental Injury to Children: Area Review Committees* (DHSS, LASSL (76) 2, CMO (76) 2, CNO (76) 3).

DINNAGE, ROSEMARY and KELLMER PRINGLE, M. L. (1967), *Foster Home Care: Facts and Fallacies* (Longman).

DONGRAY, M. (1958), 'Social Work in General Practice', *British Medical Journal*, vol. 2, pp. 1,220–3.

DONNISON, D. (1965), *Social Policy and Administration* (Allen & Unwin).

DOWLING, E. (1975), 'The Family Therapy Approach to Adolescent Disturbance' in Fiddis, B. D. (ed.), *Proceedings of the Association for the Psychiatric Study of Adolescents: Tenth Annual Conference* (APSA), pp. 39–43.

DRAKE, FRANCES (1975), 'The Position of the Local Authority' in Franklin, A. White (ed.), *Concerning Child Abuse* (Churchill Livingstone), pp. 85–94.

EDWARDS, S. R. (1976), *Treatment in Security* (Institute for the Study and Treatment of Delinquency).

ELLES, G. W. (1961), 'Collateral Treatment in a Family by Psycho-Analytic Techniques', *British Journal of Psychiatric Social Work*, vol. 6, no. 1, pp. 3–12.

(1962), 'A Family Problem and Psychopathic Illness', *Case Conference*, vol. 9, no. 4, pp. 91–5; no. 5, pp. 135–9; no. 6, pp. 153–7.

EMMET, DOROTHY, 'Ethics and the Social Worker' (1967), reproduced in Younghusband, E. (ed.), *Social Work and Social Values* (Allen & Unwin).

EVENS, P. (ed.) (1974), *Community Work Theory and Practice* (Oxford, Alastair Shornach).

FAMILY DISCUSSION BUREAU (1955), *Social Casework in Marital Problems* (Institute of Marital Studies).

(1960), *Marriage: Studies in Emotional Conflict and Growth* (Institute of Marital Studies).

FAMILY SERVICE UNITS (1976), 'Drop in Centres', *FSU Quarterly*, no. 10, pp. 27–49 (FSU).

FERARD, M. and HUNNYBUN, N. (1962), *The Caseworker's Use of Relationship* (Tavistock Publications).

FINER REPORT (1974), *Report of the Committee on One-Parent Families*, Cmnd 5629 (HMSO).

FINZI, JEAN, KING, CHRYSTAL and BOOVER, DAVID (eds) (1971), *Volunteers in Hospital* (King Edward's Hospital Fund for London).

FITZHERBERT, KATRIN (1967), *West Indian Children in London* (Bell).

FOLKARD, M. S., FOWLES, A. J., MCWILLIAMS, B. C., MCWILLIAMS, W., SMITH, D. D., SMITH, D. E. and WALMSLEY, G. R. (1974), *IMPACT, Intensive Matched Probation and After-Care Treatment*, Home Office research studies, vol. 1 (HMSO).

FOLKARD, M. S., SMITH, D. E. and SMITH, D. D. (1976), *IMPACT*, Home Office research studies, vol. 2 (HMSO).

FOLKARD, S., LYON, K., CARVER, M. M. and O'LEARY, F. (1966), *Probation Research: A Preliminary Report* (HMSO).

FORD, J. (1966), 'What Is Happening in Child Guidance?', *British Journal of Psychiatric Social Work*, vol. 8, no. 4, pp. 47–9.

FORMAN, J. A. S. and FAIRBAIRN, E. M. (1968), *Social Casework in General Practice* (Oxford University Press).

FOULKES, S. H. and ANTHONY, E. J. (1957), *Group Psychotherapy* (Harmondsworth, Penguin).

FRANKLIN, ALFRED WHITE (1974), 'The Tunbridge Wells Study Group on Non-Accidental Injury to Children', *Social Work Service*, no. 4, pp. 28–39.

FRY, MARGERY (1966), *Old Age Looks at Itself* (reprinted by the National Old People's Welfare Council).

GARRETT, ANNETTE (1942), *Interviewing: Its Principles and Methods* (New York, Family Service Association of America).

GEORGE, V. (1970), *Foster Care: Theory and Practice* (Routledge & Kegan Paul).

GIBBENS, T. C. N. (1972), 'Violence to Children', *Howard Journal of Penology*, vol. 13, no. 3, pp. 212–20.

GIBBENS, T. C. N. and WALKER, A. (1956), *Cruel Parents* (Institute for the Study and Treatment of Delinquency).

GLASTONBURY, B. (1971), *Homeless, Near a Thousand Homes* (Allen & Unwin).

GLOVER, ELIZABETH (1949), *Probation and Re-Education* (Routledge & Kegan Paul).

GOETSCHIUS, G. (1969), *Working with Community Groups* (Routledge & Kegan Paul).

GOETSCHIUS, GEORGE and TASH, JOAN (1967), *Working with Unattached Youth* (Routledge & Kegan Paul).

GOLDBERG, E. M. (1957), 'The Psychiatric Social Worker in the Community', *British Journal of Psychiatric Social Work*, vol. 5, no. 2, pp. 4–15.

(1958), *Family Influences and Psychosomatic Illness* (Tavistock Publications).

(1960), 'Parents and Psychotic Sons', *British Journal of Psychiatric Social Work*, vol. 5, no. 4, pp. 184–94.

(1961), 'The Social Worker in the Sixties', *The Almoner*, vol. 14, no. 3, pp. 96–113.

(1966*a*), 'Hospital, Work and Family: A Four Year Study of Young Mental Hospital Patients', *British Journal of Psychiatry*, vol. 112, no. 483, pp. 177–96.

(1966*b*), *Welfare in the Community* (National Institute for Social Work).

(1967), *The Families of Schizophrenic Patients* (National Institute for Social Work).

(1973), 'Services for the Family' in Wing, J. K. and Hefner, H. W. (eds), *The Roots of Evaluation: The Epidemiological Basis for Planning Psychiatric Services* (Oxford University Press).

GOLDBERG, E. M. and FRUIN, D. J. (1976), 'Towards Accountability in Social Work', *British Journal of Social Work*, vol. 6, no. 1, pp. 3–19.

GOLDBERG, E. M., with MORTIMER, A. and WILLIAMS, B. T. (1970), *Helping the Aged* (Allen & Unwin).

GOLDBERG, E. M. and NEILL, JUNE (1972), *Social Work and General Practice* (Allen & Unwin).

GOLDBERG, [E.] M., WALKER, D. and ROBINSON, J. (1977), 'Exploring Task-centered Casework Method', *Social Work Today*, vol. 9, no. 2, pp. 9–14.

GOODACRE, IRIS (1966), *Adoption Policy and Practice* (Allen & Unwin).

GOVERNMENT SOCIAL SURVEY (1964), *Staffing of Local Authority Residential Homes for Children* (HMSO).

GRAHAM, P. J. (1971), 'Some Aspects of the Relationship of Social Work to Behaviour Therapy', *British Journal of Psychiatric Social Work*, vol. 1, no. 2, pp. 197–208.

GRAY, P. G. and PARR, ELIZABETH (1957), *Children in Care and the Recruitment of Foster Parents*, Social Survey (HMSO).

GRAY, ROSEMARY (n.d.), *Training Scheme for Hospital Welfare Workers* (Manchester, Manchester Regional Hospital Board).

GRAYFORD, J. J. (1975), 'Wife Battering: A Preliminary Survey of 100 Cases', *British Medical Journal*, no. 5,951, pp. 194–7.

GREVE, JOHN (1964), *London's Homeless* (Welwyn, Codicote Press).

GREY, ELEANOR (1969), *Workloads in Children's Departments* (HMSO).

GRIFFITHS, D. L. and MOYNIHAN, F. J. (1963), 'Multiple Epiphysical Injuries in Babies', *British Medical Journal*, vol. 537, pp. 1,558–61.

GRÜNHUT, M. (1954), *Practical Results and Financial Aspects of Adult Probation in Selected Countries* (Geneva, United Nations).

GUIVER, PAMELA (1973), *The Trouble Sharers* (National Marriage Council).

GULBENKIAN FOUNDATION (1968), *Community Work and Social Change* (Longman).

(1973), *Current Issues in Community Work* (Routledge & Kegan Paul).

HADLEY, ROGER, WEBB, ADRIAN and FARRELL, CHRISTINE (1975), *Across the Generations* (Allen & Unwin).

HALL, ANTHONY S. (1974), *The Point of Entry* (Allen & Unwin).

HALL, M. PENELOPE and HOWES, ISMENE V. (1965), *The Church in Social Work* (Routledge & Kegan Paul).

HALL, PHOEBE (1976), *Reforming the Welfare* (Heinemann).

HALLBURTON, P. M. and WRIGHT, W. B. (1974), 'Towards Better Geriatric Care', *Social Work Today*, vol. 5, no. 4, pp. 107–8.

HALLIWELL, R. (1969), 'Time-limited Work with a Family at Point of Being Prosecuted for Child Neglect', *Case Conference*, vol. 15, no. 9, pp. 343–8.

HALMOS, PAUL (1965), *The Faith of the Counsellors* (Constable).

HAMILTON, GORDON (1951), *Social Casework: Theory and Practice* (New York, Columbia University Press).

HAMMOND, P. (1964), 'Changing Practice in Mental Hospital Social Work', *British Journal of Psychiatric Social Work*, vol. 7, no. 3, pp. 128–35.

HARRIS, AMELIA (1968), *Social Welfare for the Elderly*, Government Social Survey (HMSO).

 (1971), *Handicapped and Impaired in Great Britain, Part I*, Office of Population Censuses and Surveys (HMSO).

HAYWARD, CHRISTINE (1974), 'Survey of Trainees', *Social Work Today*, vol. 5, no. 4, pp. 117–19.

HAZEL, N. and COX, R. (1976), 'The Special Family Placement Project', mimeographed (Maidstone, Kent County Council, Social Services Department).

HEIMLER, EUGENE (1958), 'New Roads in Psychiatric Community Care', *The Medical Officer*, no. 100, pp. 295–6.

 (1962), *A Link in the Chain* (The Bodley Head).

 (1975), *Survival in Society* (Weidenfeld & Nicolson).

HERAUD, BRIAN (1970), *Sociology and Social Work* (Pergamon Press).

HERNE, R. (1975), 'L. A. Community Workers . . . Writers or Fighters?', *Case Con*, no. 20, pp. 20–2.

HERTFORDSHIRE CHILDREN'S DEPARTMENT (1966), *Annual Report 1965–66* (Hertfordshire County Council).

HERTOGHE, A. M. and MCLAINE, G. (1973), 'Family Therapy within a Casework Agency' in Finn, W. H. (ed.), *Family Therapy in Social Work* (Family Welfare Association), pp. 41–8.

HEWITT, SHEILA (1970), *The Family and the Handicapped Child* (Allen & Unwin).

HOBMAN, DAVID (1969), *A Guide to Voluntary Service* (HMSO).

HOLDEN, C. (1969), 'Temper Tantrum Extinction: A Limited Attempt at Behaviour Modification', *Social Work*, vol. 26, no. 4, pp. 8–11.

HOLDEN, H. M. (1964), 'The Voluntary Associate Scheme', *British Journal of Criminology*, vol. 4, no. 4, pp. 341–8.

HOLLIS, FLORENCE (1964 and 1972), *Casework: A Psychosocial Therapy* (New York, Random House).

HOLMAN, R. (1973), *Trading in Children* (Routledge & Kegan Paul).

 (1975), 'The Place of Fostering in Social Work', *British Journal of Social Work*, vol. 5, no. 1, pp. 3–29.

HOME OFFICE (1948a), Circular 160.

 (1948b), *Memorandum on the Principles and Practice in the Work of Matrimonial Conciliation in Magistrates Courts* (HMSO).

HOME OFFICE/MINISTRIES OF EDUCATION AND HEALTH AND SCOTTISH HOME DEPARTMENT, Joint Circular (1950), Home Office Circular 157/50 (HMSO).

HOME OFFICE (1965), *The Child, the Family and the Young Offender* (HMSO).

 (1966a), *Report on Dorset County Council Child Care Service* (HMSO).

 (1966b), *Residential Provision for Homeless Discharged Offenders* (HMSO).

 (1968a), *Children in Trouble* (HMSO).

 (1968b), *Training of After-Care Hostel Staff*, Memorandum for the Advisory Council for Probation and After-Care.

 (1970), *Community Homes Project Report* (HMSO).

 (1971a), *Habitual Drunken Offenders: Report of the Working Party* (HMSO).

 (1971b), *Youth Treatment Centres* (HMSO).

 (1972), *The Criminal Justice Act 1972, A Guide for the Courts* (HMSO).

 (1975a), *Racial Discrimination*, Cmnd 6234 (HMSO).

(1975*b*), *Social Work in the Custodial Part of the Prison System* (HMSO).

Reports on the Work of the Children's Department, Sixth (1951), Seventh (1955), Eighth (1961) and 1961–3, 1964–6, 1967–9 (HMSO).

Reports on the Work of the Probation and After-Care Department, 1962–5, 1966–8 and 1969–71 (HMSO).

HOUGHTON STOCKDALE REPORT (1972), *Departmental Committee on the Adoption of Children* (HMSO).

HOUSE OF COMMONS (1952), *6th Report of the Select Committee on Estimates* House of Commons paper 235 (HMSO).

HOUSE OF COMMONS EXPENDITURE COMMITTEE (1975), *Eleventh Report from the Expenditure Committee, The Children and Young Persons Act, 1969, Vol. 1*, Cmnd 6494 (HMSO).

HOUSE OF COMMONS SELECT COMMITTEE on *Race Relations and Immigration (Session 1974–1975), Evidence* (HMSO).

HOUSE OF COMMONS SELECT COMMITTEE on *Violence in Marriage* (1975), House of Commons paper 553 (HMSO).

HOWELL, D. and PARSLOE, P. (1966), 'Working with a Family in a Child Guidance Setting', *British Journal of Psychiatric Social Work*, vol. 8, no. 4, pp. 10–20.

HUDSON, B. (1975), 'An Inadequate Personality: A Case Study with a Dynamic Beginning and a Behavioural Ending', *Social Work Today*, vol. 6, no. 16, pp. 505–8.

HUNEEUS, M. E. (1962), 'Problems related to Marital Interaction in Community Care' in *The Marital Relationship as a Focus for Casework*, Family Discussion Bureau (Welwyn, Codicote Press), pp. 33–40.

HUNT, ARTHUR (1974), 'Delinquency and the Social Services Departments' in Brown, Malcolm (ed.), *Social Issues and the Social Services* (Knight), pp. 107–21.

HUNTER, P. (1964), 'Psychiatric Social Work with Disturbed Patients in the Community', *British Journal of Psychiatric Social Work*, vol. 7, no. 4, pp. 183–90.

(1969), 'A Survey of Psychiatric Social Workers working in Mental Hospitals', *British Journal of Psychiatric Social Work*, vol. 10, no. 1, pp. 22–6.

HURST REPORT (1954), *Report of the Departmental Committee on the Adoption of Children* (HMSO).

HUTTEN, J. (1974), 'Short term Contracts', *Social Work Today*, vol. 4, no. 22, pp. 709–11.

(1975), 'Short term Contracts III', *Social Work Today*, vol. 6, no. 17, pp. 538–41.

HUXLEY, ALDOUS (1954), *The Doors of Perception* (Chatto & Windus).

INGLEBY REPORT (1960), *Report of the Committee on Children and Young Persons*, Cmnd 1191 (HMSO).

INGRAM, MICHAEL (1975), 'A Casework Study of a Disturbed Child and His Family', *Time to Consider*, Papers from a Family Service Unit (Bedford Square Press and FSU), pp. 39–51.

INNER LONDON PROBATION AND AFTER-CARE SERVICE (1975), 'Day Training Centres, First Report' and 'Is there an Alternative?', Information Bulletin No. 26, mimeographed (Inner London Probation and After-Care Service).

INSTITUTE OF ALMONERS (1949), 'Working Party on the Recruitment and Training of Almoners', mimeographed (Institute of Almoners).

Annual Report 1952–53 (Institute of Almoners).

(1953), 'Report of the Survey Committee', *The Almoner*, vol. 6, no. 2, pp. 61–9.

Annual Report 1954–55 (Institute of Almoners).

Annual Report 1956–57 (Institute of Almoners).

Annual Report 1962–63 (Institute of Almoners).

INSTITUTE OF MEDICAL SOCIAL WORKERS (1965), *Annual Report 1963–64* (Institute of Medical Social Workers).

(1969), *Annual Report 1968–69* (Institute of Medical Social Workers).

IRVINE, E. E. (1954), 'Research into Problem Families', *British Journal of Psychiatric Social Work*, vol. not stated, no. 1, pp. 24–33.

(1956), 'Renaissance in British Casework', *Social Work*, vol. 13, no. 3, pp. 187–94.

(1961), 'Psychosis in Parents: Mental Illness as a Problem for the Family', *British Journal of Psychiatric Social Work*, vol. 6, no. 1, pp. 21–6.

(1964), 'Children at Risk', *Case Conference*, vol. 10, no. 10, pp. 293–6.

(1966), 'A New Look at Casework', reproduced in Younghusband, E. (ed.), *New Developments in Casework* (Allen & Unwin).

(1967), 'The Hard to Like Family', *Case Conference*, vol. 14, no. 3, pp. 103–9.

(1969), 'Education for Social Work: Science or Humanity?', *Social Work*, vol. 26, no. 4, pp. 3–6.

'Community Care' (unpublished paper).

JACKA, ALAN (n.d.), *The ACCO Story* (Society for the Promotion of Education and Research in Social Work).

JANSEN, ELLY (1973), 'The Hostel as a Therapeutic Community and Its Implications for Training', *Residential Care* (Residential Care Association), pp. 89–97.

JEFFREYS, MARGOT (1965), *An Anatomy of Social Welfare Services* (Michael Joseph).

JEHU, D. (1967), *Learning Theory and Social Work* (Routledge & Kegan Paul).

JOBLING, MEGAN (1976), *The Abused Child* (National Children's Bureau).

JOINT UNIVERSITY COUNCIL FOR SOCIAL AND PUBLIC ADMINISTRATION (1951), 'Draft Outline for a One-Year Post-Certificate Course in Social Casework, prepared by a Sub-Committee of the Training Committee of the JUC', mimeographed (JUC).

(1952), *University Courses in Social Study* (JUC).

(1955), *University Courses in Social Administration* (JUC).

(1966), *Field Work in Social Administration Courses* (National Institute for Social Work Training).

JONES, DAVID and MAYO, MARJORIE (eds) (1974), *Community Work – One* (Routledge & Kegan Paul).

JONES, K. and HAMMOND, P. (1960), 'The Boundaries of Training', *British Journal of Psychiatric Social Work*, vol. 5, no. 4, pp. 172–7.

JONES, KATHLEEN (1964), *The Teaching of Social Studies in British Universities*, Occasional Papers on Social Administration No. 12 (Welwyn, Codicote Press).

(1967), 'Psychiatric Social Work Comes of Age', *British Journal of Psychiatric Social Work*, vol. 9, no. 2, pp. 60–5.

(1970), *The Development of Social Administration: Report of Conference on Social Administration* (Joint University Council for Social and Public Administration).

(ed.) (1972), *A History of the Mental Health Services* (Routledge & Kegan Paul).

(1975), *Opening the Door* (Routledge & Kegan Paul).

JONES, MAXWELL (1952), *Social Psychiatry: A Study of Therapeutic Communities* (Tavistock Publications).

JORDAN, W. (1970), *Client-Worker Transactions* (Routledge & Kegan Paul).

JOSEPH, SIR KEITH (1972), Address in *Report of the First National Conference of the Association of Directors of Social Services* (Association of Directors of Social Services), pp. 67–74.

JULIA, ANGELA (1967), 'Hostels for the Mentally Ill as a Stepping Stone in the Community' in *New Thinking about Institutional Care* (Association of Social Workers), pp. 68–75.

KAHN, JACK and NURSTEN, JEAN (1968), *Unwillingly to School* (Pergamon Press).

KELLMER PRINGLE, M. L. (1967), *Adoption: Facts and Fallacies* (Longman).

KELLY, A. D. (1961), 'Random Thoughts', *The Almoner*, vol. 14, no. 8, pp. 349–56.

KENSINGTON AND CHELSEA SOCIAL SERVICES DEPARTMENT (1974), *Handicap Survey Project Report* (Kensington and Chelsea Social Services Department).

KENT, B. (1974), 'The Totally Integrated Syllabus: An Experiment in Social Work Education', *International Social Work*, vol. XVII, no. 4, pp. 11–22.

KILBRANDON REPORT (1964), *Report of the Committee on Children and Young Persons (Scotland)*, Cmnd 2306 (Edinburgh, HMSO).

KING, JOAN F. S. (ed.) (1958, revised 1976), *The Probation Service* (Butterworth).

KING, ROY D., RAYNES, NORMA V. and TIZARD, JACK (1971), *Patterns of Residential Care* (Routledge & Kegan Paul).

KING'S FUND HOSPITAL CENTRE (1970), *Improving Care for the Elderly* (King's Fund Hospital Centre).

KING'S FUND HOSPITAL CENTRE and NATIONAL INSTITUTE FOR SOCIAL WORK (n.d.), 'Training for Volunteer Organizers, Report of a Joint Training Project 1974–75', mimeographed (King's Fund Hospital Centre).

KUENSTLER, PETER (ed.) (1954), *Social Group Work in Great Britain* (Faber & Faber).

LAMING, H. (1974), 'Residential Care' in *Self-Help, Participation and the Elderly*, Conference Proceedings (Southampton University).

LANSLEY, J. (1976), *Voluntary Organisations Facing Change* (Gulbenkian Foundation in association with the Joseph Rowntree Memorial Trust).

LAPPING, ANNE (1970), *Community Action*, Fabian Tract 400 (Fabian Society).

LEISSNER, A., ANGELA, K., HERDMAN, K. and DAVIES, E. V. (1971), *Advice, Guidance and Assistance* (Longman).

LEISSNER, A. and JOSLIN, J. (1974), 'Area Team Community Work: Achievement and Crisis' in Jones, D. and Mayo, M. (eds), *Community Work – One* (Routledge & Kegan Paul), pp. 118–47.

LEONARD, PETER (1966), *Sociology in Social Work* (Routledge & Kegan Paul).

LEWIS, HILDA (1954), *Deprived Children* (Oxford University Press). Local Government Board (1918), Circular 9 August 1918.

LOEWENSTEIN, C. (1974), 'An Intake Team in Action in a Social Services Department', *British Journal of Social Work*, vol. 4, no. 2, pp. 115–41.

LONDON BOROUGHS TRAINING COMMITTEE (Social Services) (1966), 'Statement of Principles for Training in the Health, Welfare and Children's Services', mimeographed (LBTC).

LONDON COUNCIL OF SOCIAL SERVICE (1974), *Community Workers and Their Employing Agencies in Greater London* (LCSS).

LONGFORD, LORD (chairman) (1964), *Crime: A Challenge to Us All*, Report of the Labour Party's Study Group (Transport House).

LYNCH, MARGARET A. (1975), 'Ill-health and Child Abuse', *The Lancet*, no. 7929, pp. 317–19.

MACKINTOSH REPORT (1951), *Report of the Committee on Social Workers in the Mental Health Services*, Cmnd 8260 (HMSO).

MALAN, D. (1963), *Brief Psychotherapy*, Mind and Medicine Monographs (Tavistock Publications).

MAPSTONE, ELIZABETH (1971), 'Social Work with the Parents of Children in Foster Care' in Tod, Robert (ed.), *Social Work in Foster Care* (Longman), pp. 98–104.

(1972), 'The Selection of the Children's Panel for the County of Fife: A Case Study', *British Journal of Social Work*, vol. 2, no. 4, pp. 445–69.

MARSHALL, TONY and ROSE, GORDON (1975), 'An Experimental Evaluation of School Social Work', *British Journal of Guidance and Counselling*, vol. 3, no. 1, pp. 2–14.

MARTIN REPORT (n.d. on Report, but actually published 1974), *Final Report of the Committee on Social Work Statistics*, Scottish Advisory Council on Social Work (Edinburgh, Social Work Service Group).

MATTHEWS, JOAN E. (1966), *Working with Youth Groups* (University of London Press).

MAUD REPORT (1967), *Report of the Committee on the Management of Local Government* (HMSO).

MAXWELL REPORT (1953), *Report of the Committee on Discharged Prisoners' Aid Societies* (HMSO).

MAYER, J. E. and TIMMS, N. (1970), *The Client Speaks* (Routledge & Kegan Paul).

MAYS, JOHN (1954), *Growing Up in the City* (Liverpool, University of Liverpool Press).

(1956), 'Social Research and Social Casework' in Association of Psychiatric Social Workers, *The Boundaries of Casework* (APSW).

MCBOYLE REPORT (1963), *Report of the Committee on the Prevention of Neglect of Children* (Edinburgh, HMSO).

MCDOUGALL, KAY (1970), 'The Advanced Course', *Case Conference*, vol. 16, no. 11, pp. 458–63.

(1972), 'BASW: The British Association of Social Workers' in Jones, Kathleen (ed.), *The Year Book of Social Policy in Britain, 1971* (Routledge & Kegan Paul), pp. 98–111.

MCKAY, ANN, GOLDBERG, E. M. and FRUIN, DAVID J. (1973), 'Consumers and a Social Services Department', *Social Work Today*, vol. 4, no. 16, pp. 486–91.

MCWHINNIE, A. (1967), *Adopted Children – How They Grow Up* (Routledge & Kegan Paul).

(1968), 'Group Counselling with 78 Adoptive Families', *Case Conference*, vol. 14, nos. 11 and 12, pp. 407–12 and 456–64.

MCWILLIAMS, WILLIAM (1975), 'Sentencing and Recidivism', *British Journal of Social Work*, vol. 5, no. 3, pp. 321–2.

MERCER, M. and ROBERTS, S. (1975), 'The Integration of Family Therapy into Social Work Practice' in Finn, W. H. (ed.), *Marital and Family Therapy* (Family Welfare Association), pp. 6–17.

MILLER, DEREK (1964), *Growth to Freedom* (Tavistock Publications).

MILLER, E. J. and GWYNNE, G. V. (1972), *A Life Apart* (Tavistock Publications).

MILLER, J. S. (1969), 'Social Work and Therapies of Control', *British Journal of Psychiatric Social Work*, vol. 10, no. 2, pp. 74–9.

MILNER HOLLAND REPORT (1965), *Report of the Committee on Housing in Greater London,* Cmnd 2605 (HMSO).

MINISTRY OF HEALTH (1963), *Health and Welfare: The Development of Community Care*, Cmnd 1973 (HMSO).

(1966), *Health and Welfare: The Development of Community Care*, Cmnd 3022 (HMSO).

(1970), Chief Medical Officer of Health and Chief Inspector, Home Office Children's Department, Circular CMO 2/70.

MINISTRY OF HOUSING AND LOCAL GOVERNMENT (1967), Report of the Central Housing Advisory Committee, *The Needs of New Communities* (HMSO).

MOON, E. M. (1958), 'The Use of Supervision in Providing a Casework Service to the Patient', *The Almoner*, vol. 11, no. 4, pp. 124–36.

(1965), *The First Two Years* (Institute of Medical Social Workers).

MORISON REPORT (1962), *Report of the Departmental Committee on the Probation Service*, Cmnd 1650 (HMSO).

MORRIS, PAULINE (1969), *Put Away* (Routledge & Kegan Paul).

MORRISON, R. L. (1967), 'The Idea of Therapeutic Communities' in *New Thinking about Institutional Care* (Association of Social Workers).

MORSE, MARY (1965), *The Unattached* (Harmondsworth, Pelican).

MOSCROP, MARTHA (1967), *In-service Training and Staff Development* (National Institute for Social Work Training).

NAPIER, HARRY (1972), 'Success and Failure in Foster Care', *British Journal of Social Work*, vol. 2, no. 2, pp. 187–204.

NATIONAL ASSISTANCE BOARD (1966), *Homeless Single Persons* (HMSO).

NATIONAL ASSOCIATION FOR THE CARE AND RESETTLEMENT OF OFFENDERS (1968), *The Training of After-Care Hostel Staffs* (NACRO).

(1976), *Training Programme and Hostel Services: 1975–1976* (NACRO).

NATIONAL ASSOCIATION FOR MENTAL HEALTH (1965), *Child Guidance and Child Psychiatry as an Integral Part of Community Services* (NAMH).

NATIONAL ASSOCIATION OF PROBATION OFFICERS (1956), 'Statement Adopted at NAPO Annual Conference, 1956', *Probation*, vol. 8, no. 10, pp. 141–5.

(December 1956), 'Generic Training for Social Work' (Notes written by an officer who had recently completed the Generic Training Course but who preferred to remain anonymous), *Probation*, vol. 8, no. 4, pp. 49–51.

(September 1957), 'Supervision in the Probation Service', *Probation*, vol. 8, no. 7, pp. 97–100.

Annual Report for 1958 (NAPO).

(June 1958), 'The Training of Probation Officers', *Probation*, vol. 8, no. 10, pp. 141–5.

(November 1966), editorial: 'Local Authority and Allied Social Services', *Probation*, vol. 12, no. 3, pp. 109–10.

(1968a), *Social Work in Prison*, report of a working party on prison welfare (NAPO).

(1968b), *Statement on Training* (NAPO).

NATIONAL CHILDREN'S BUREAU (1975), 'Children in Violent Families', mimeographed (NCB).

NATIONAL COMMUNITY DEVELOPMENT PROJECT (1974), *Inter-Project Report, 1973* (CDP Information and Intelligence Unit).

(1975), *Forward Plan 1975–76* (CDP Information and Intelligence Unit).

NATIONAL CORPORATION FOR THE CARE OF OLD PEOPLE, *Annual Report 1973* (NCCOP).

Annual Report 1974 (NCCOP).

NATIONAL COUNCIL FOR THE UNMARRIED MOTHER AND HER CHILD (1972), *Annual Report 1971–72* (NCUMC).

NATIONAL COUNCIL OF SOCIAL SERVICE (1969), *Supervision of Community Work Students* (NCSS).

(1970), *Fieldwork Supervision for Community Work Students* (NCSS).

56th Annual Report 1974–75 (NCSS).

NATIONAL INSTITUTE FOR SOCIAL WORK (1974), *An Introductory Account, 1961–1974* (NISW).

NATIONAL INSTITUTE FOR SOCIAL WORK TRAINING (1964), *Introduction to the Social Worker* (Allen & Unwin).

NATIONAL SOCIETY FOR THE PREVENTION OF CRUELTY TO CHILDREN (1974), *Yo Yo Children* (NSPCC).

(1976a), *At Risk*, Battered Child Research Team (Routledge & Kegan Paul).

(1976b), *Registers of Suspected Non-Accidental Injury*, Casework and Development Department (NSPCC).

NEILL, JUNE (1976), 'Study of Referrals', mimeographed report (Available from National Institute for Social Work research unit).

NEILL, JUNE, FRUIN, DAVID, GOLDBERG, E. MATILDA and WARBURTON, R. WILLIAMS (1973), 'Reactions to Integration', *Social Work Today*, vol. 4, no. 15, pp. 458–65.

NEILL, J., WARBURTON, R. W. and MCGUINESS, B. (1976), Social Worker's Viewpoint', *Social Work Today*, vol. 8, no. 5, pp. 9–14.

New Society (1975), Editorial, 'CDPs Writ Larger', vol. 33, no. 667, p. 122.

NEWSOME, A., THORNE, B. and WYLD, K. (1973), *Student Counselling in Practice* (University of London Press).

NEWTON, GEORGE (1966), 'The Impact of the First Two Years', *Medical Social Work*, vol. 19, no. 3, pp. 9–15.

NICHOLSON, JILL (1968), *Mother and Baby Homes* (Allen & Unwin).

NURSE, J. (1973), 'The Client, the Caseworker and the Absent Third Person', *British Journal of Social Work*, vol. 3, no. 1, pp. 39–53.

ORTHEN, MICHAEL (1975), 'Probation Welfare – Time to Think Again?', *Probation Journal*, vol. 22, no. 4, pp. 98–103.

OUNSTED, C., OPPENHEIMER, R. and LINDSEY, J. (1975), 'The Psychopathology and Psychotherapy of the Families: Aspects of Bonding Failure' in Franklin, A. White (ed.), *Concerning Child Abuse* (Churchill Livingstone), pp. 30–40.

OWTRAM, P. J. (1975), 'NSPCC Special Units', *Social Work Service*, no. 8, pp. 8–11.

PACKMAN, JEAN (1968), *Child Care: Needs and Numbers* (Allen & Unwin).

(1975), *The Child's Generation* (Oxford, Basil Blackwell).

PAGE, P. (1964), 'Mentally Ill and Homeless', a report on social work with homeless and destitute men in a reception centre, January to December 1964 (unpublished).

PARAD, HOWARD J. (1963), *Ego Oriented Casework* (New York, Family Service Association of America).

PARKER, R. H. (1966), *Decision in Child Care* (Allen & Unwin).

PAROLE BOARD, *Report of the Parole Board for 1971* (HMSO).

PARSLOE, P. (1967), 'Meeting the Needs of the Disturbed Child', *British Journal of Psychiatric Social Work*, vol. 9, no. 2, pp. 90–6.

PATERSON, J. (1949), 'The Work of an Almoner in General Practice', *The Almoner*, vol. 1, no. 11, pp. 230–3.

PEASE, K. (1975), *Community Care Orders*, Home Office research studies (HMSO).

PERLMAN, HELEN (1957), *Social Casework: A Problem Solving Process* (Chicago, University of Chicago Press).

PERSONAL SOCIAL SERVICES COUNCIL (1975), Smith, Jef, *Living and Working in Residential Homes* (PSSC).

Report 1975 (PSSC).

Report 1976 (PSSC).

Personal Social Services: Basic Information (1976a) (PSSC).

(1976b), *Social Service Manpower Resources* (PSSC).

PHILLIP, ALISTAIR E., MCCULLOCH, WALLACE J. and SMITH, NORMAN J. (1975), *Research and the Analysis of Social Data* (Pergamon Press).

PHILP, A. F. (1961), 'Character Disorders in the Socially Sick' in *Mental Health and Social Work: A Symposium: The Association of Social Workers (Gt. Britain) and the International Federation of Social Workers* (Association of Social Workers).

(1963), *Family Failure* (Faber & Faber).

PHILP, A. F. and TIMMS, N. (1957), *The Problem of the Problem Family* (FSU).

PICARDIE, M. (1967), 'Learning Theory and Casework', *Social Work*, vol. 24, no. 1, pp. 3–6.

PIERCY REPORT (1956), *Report of the Committee on the Rehabilitation, Training and Resettlement of Disabled Persons*, Cmnd 9883 (HMSO).

Pivot (1976), *Report of a Working Party on the National Association of Voluntary Help Organisers* (Berkhamsted, The Volunteer Centre).

PIZZEY, E. (1974), *Scream Quietly or the Neighbours will Hear* (Harmondsworth, Penguin).

PLOWDEN REPORT (1967), *Children and Their Primary Schools*, Report of the Central Advisory Council for Education (England) (HMSO).

POWER, MICHAEL (1962), 'Varieties of Casework', *Social Work*, vol. 19, no. 4, pp. 18–20.

PRATT, MARK (1975), 'Stress and Opportunity in the Role of the Prison Welfare Officer', *British Journal of Social Work*, vol. 5, no. 4, pp. 379–96.

PRE-SCHOOL PLAYGROUPS ASSOCIATION (1975), *Facts and Figures* (PPA).

PRICHARD, COLIN (1974), 'The EWO, Truancy and School Phobia', *Social Work Today*, vol. 5, no. 5, pp. 130–4.

PRINCIPAL PROBATION OFFICERS CONFERENCE (1968), *The Place of the Probation and After-Care Service in Judicial Administration* (CPPO).

PUGH, ELIZABETH (1968), *Social Work in Child Care* (Routledge & Kegan Paul).

RALPHS REPORT (1975), *Report of the Working Party on The Role and Training of Education Welfare Officers* (Local Government Training Board).

RATCLIFFE, T. A. and JONES, E. V. (1956), 'Intensive Casework in a Community Setting', *Case Conference*, vol. 2, no. 10, pp. 17–21.

RATOFF, LEN, ROSE, ANN and SMITH, CAROLE (1974), 'Social Workers and GPs', *Social Work Today*, vol. 5, no. 11, pp. 497–500.

RAYNOR, LOIS (1970), *Adoption of Non-White Children* (Allen & Unwin).

READING REPORT (1963), *The Place of Voluntary Service in After-Care* (HMSO). (1967), *The Place of Voluntary Service in After-Care* (HMSO).

REDCLIFFE-MAUD REPORT (1969), *Report of the Royal Commission on Local Government* (HMSO).

REHIN, G. F. (1969), 'The Practice of Psychiatric Social Work and the Future of Child Guidance Clinics', *Case Conference*, vol. 16, no. 2, pp. 42–8. (1972), 'Child Guidance at the Crossroads', *Social Work Today*, vol. 2, no. 24, pp. 21–4.

REID, W. J. and EPSTEIN, L. (1972), *Task-Centered Casework* (New York, Columbia University Press).

REID, W. J. and SHYNE, A. W. (1969), *Brief and Extended Casework* (New York, Columbia University Press).

RESIDENTIAL CHILD CARE ASSOCIATION (1969), *Residential Task in Child Care*, report of a study group sponsored by RCCA, ACCO and ACO (Banstead, Surrey, Residential Child Care Association).

RICHARDS, MARTIN (1975), 'Non-accidental Injury to Children in an Ecological Perspective' in Department of Health and Social Security, *Non-Accidental Injury to Children* (HMSO), pp. 5–12.

ROBERTS, W. L. (1968), 'Working with the Family Group in a Child Guidance Clinic', *British Journal of Psychiatric Social Work*, vol. 9, no. 4, pp. 175–9.

ROBINSON, JAMES (1971), 'Experimental Research in Social Casework', *British Journal of Social Work*, vol. 1, no. 4, pp. 463–79.

RODGERS, BARBARA (1964), *The Careers of Social Studies Students* (Welwyn, Codicote Press).

RODGERS, BARBARA and DIXON, JULIA (1960), *Portrait of Social Work* (Oxford University Press).

RODGERS, BARBARA N. and STEVENSON, JUNE (1973), *New Portrait of Social Work* (Heinemann).

ROLPH, C. H. (1970), *Homeless from Prison* (privately printed).

ROOFF, MADELINE (1972), *A Hundred Years of Family Welfare* (Michael Joseph).

ROSE, GORDON and MARSHALL, TONY F. (1974), *Counselling and School Social Work* (Chichester, Wiley & Sons).

ROSE, JUNE (1970), *Changing Focus: The Development of Blind Welfare in Britain* (Hutchinson).

ROSEMAN, R. and COOKE, J. (1964), 'Social Groupwork with Children in a Family Casework Agency', *Social Work*, vol. 21, no. 4, pp. 16–20.

ROSS, MURRAY (1955), *Community Organisation* (New York, Harper Brothers).

ROWBOTTOM, RALPH, HEY, ANTHEA and BILLIS, DAVID (1974), *Social Services Departments: Developing Patterns of Work and Organisation* (Heinemann).

ROWE, JANE and LAMBERT, LYDIA (1973), *Children Who Wait* (Association of British Adoption Agencies).

ROYAL COMMISSION ON THE LAW RELATING TO MENTAL ILLNESS AND MENTAL DEFICIENCY REPORT (1957), Cmnd 169 (HMSO).

RYAN, T. M. (1967), 'The Administrative Structure of the Child Guidance Service', *Social Work*, vol. 24, no. 3, pp. 23–7.

SAINSBURY, E. (1970), *Social Diagnosis in Casework* (Routledge & Kegan Paul).
   (1975*a*), 'A National Profile of FSU Families', *FSU Quarterly*, no. 8, pp. 20–30.
   (1975*b*), *Social Work with Families* (Routledge & Kegan Paul).

SAINSBURY, P. (1964), 'Some Aspects of Evaluating Community Care', *British Journal of Psychiatric Social Work*, vol. 7, no. 3, pp. 142–6.

SAINSBURY, SALLY (1970), *Registered as Disabled* (Bell).

SANDERS, HUGH (1963), 'Widening Horizons', *Probation*, vol. 10, no. 3, pp. 84–6.

SATIR, V. (1964), *Conjoint Family Therapy* (Palo Alto, Science and Behavior Books).

SCHOOLS COUNCIL (1967), *Counselling in Schools* (HMSO).

SCOTT, P. D. (1973), 'Fatal Battered Baby Cases', *Medicine, Science and the Law*, vol. 13, no. 3. Reprinted in *Social Work Service*, no. 4, 1974, pp. 12–21.

SCOTTISH ADVISORY COUNCIL ON SOCIAL WORK (1974), *Field Work Staffing (Scotland)* (Edinburgh, Social Work Services Group).

SCOTTISH EDUCATION DEPARTMENT (1970), *Social Work in Scotland in 1969*, Cmnd 4475 (Edinburgh, HMSO).

SCOTTISH EDUCATION AND SCOTTISH HOME AND HEALTH DEPARTMENTS (1966), *Social Work and the Community*, Cmnd 3065 (Edinburgh, HMSO).

SEEBOHM REPORT (1968), *Report of the Committee on Local Authority and Allied Personal Social Services*, Cmnd 3703 (HMSO).

SEGLOW, J., PRINGLE, M. and WEDGE, P. (1972), *Growing Up Adopted* (Slough, National Foundation for Educational Research).

SHAPIRO, PAULINE (1965), 'Children's Play as a Concern of Family Caseworkers' in Younghusband, E. (ed.), *Social Work with Families* (Allen & Unwin), pp. 71–9.

SHAW, MARGARET (1974), *Social Work in Prison*, Home Office research studies (HMSO).

SILBERMAN, M., CHAPMAN, B., SINCLAIR, I., SNOW, D. and LEISSNER, A. (1971), *Explorations in After-Care*, Home Office research studies (HMSO).

SIMON, BRIAN (1967), *The Nature and Objectives of Professional Education* (Association of Social Work Teachers).

SINCLAIR, I. (1971), *Probation Hostels for Boys*, Home Office research studies (HMSO).

SINCLAIR, I., SHAW, M. J. and TROUP, J. (1974), 'The Relationship between Introversion and Response to Casework in a Prison Setting', *British Journal of Social and Clinical Psychology*, vol. 13, no. 1, pp. 51–60.

SINFIELD, A. (1961), *Which Way for Social Work?*, Fabian Tract No. 893 (Fabian Society).

SKEFFINGTON REPORT (1969), *People and Planning* (HMSO).

SKINNER, A. E. and CASTLE, R. L. (1969), *78 Battered Children* (NSPCC).

SKYNNER, A. C. R. (1967), 'Diagnosis, Consultation and Co-ordination of Treatment' in *Report of the National Association for Mental Health Inter-clinic Conference* (NAMH).
   (1971*a*), 'A Group-Analytic Approach to Conjoint Family Therapy', *Social Work Today*, vol. 2, no. 8, pp. 3–11.

(1971*b*), 'Indications for and against Conjoint Family Therapy', *Social Work Today*, vol. 2, no. 7, pp. 3–5.

(1971*c*), 'The Minimum Sufficient Network', *Social Work Today*, vol. 2, no. 9, pp. 3–7.

SLUCKIN, A. and JEHU, D. (1969), 'A Behavioural Approach in the Treatment of Elective Mutism', *British Journal of Psychiatric Social Work*, vol. 10, no. 2, pp. 70–3.

SMITH, CYRIL S., FARRANT, M. R. and MARCHANT, H. J. (1972), *The Wincroft Youth Project* (Tavistock Publications).

SMITH, DAVID J. (1976), *The Facts of Racial Disadvantage: A National Survey* (Political and Economic Planning).

SMITH, D. M. (ed.) (1974), *Families and Groups: A Unit at Work* (Family Service Units).

SMITH, GERTRUDE (1975), 'Institutional Dependence in Reverse', *Social Work Today*, vol. 6, no. 14, pp. 426–8.

SMITH, JEF (1972), 'Top Jobs in the Social Services' in Jones, Kathleen (ed.), *The Year Book of Social Policy in Britain, 1971* (Routledge & Kegan Paul), pp. 16–27.

SMITH, S., HANSON, R. and NOBEL, S. (1975), 'Parents of Battered Children: A Controlled Study' in Franklin, A. White (ed.), *Concerning Child Abuse* (Churchill Livingstone), pp. 41–8.

SMITH, WINIFRED and BATE, HELEN (1953), *Family Casework and the Country Dweller* (Family Welfare Association).

SNELLING, JEAN (1970), *The Contribution of the Institute of Medical Social Workers to Education for Social Work* (Association of Social Work Teachers).

SOCIAL SCIENCE RESEARCH COUNCIL and DHSS (1974), *Transmitted Deprivation*, First report of the Joint Working Party (SSRC).

(1975), *Transmitted Deprivation*, Second report of the Joint Working Party (SSRC).

Social Work in Scotland (1969), Report by a Working Party on the Social Work (Scotland) Act 1968 (Department of Social Administration, University of Edinburgh).

SOCIAL WORK SERVICES GROUP (1971), Circular No. SW75/1971.

(1972), *Proposals for Development of Social Work Services* (Edinburgh, SWSG).

(1974), *Scottish Social Work Statistics* (Edinburgh, HMSO).

/SCOTTISH HOME AND HEALTH DEPARTMENT (1975), *Non-Accidental Injury to Children*, NHS Circular No. 1975 (Gen. 23).

SPECHT, HARRY (1975), 'The Dilemma of Community Work in the United Kingdom: A Comment', *Policy and Politics*, vol. 4, no. 1, pp. 59–71.

SPEED, MAURICE (1974), 'The Aged and the Social Services Department' in Brown, Malcolm J. (ed.), *Social Issues and the Social Services* (Knight), pp. 123–44.

SPENCER, J. (1964), *Stress and Release in an Urban Estate* (Tavistock Publications).

STACE, SHEILA (1976), *Encouraging Volunteer Bureaux* (National Council of Social Service).

STANDING CONFERENCE OF ORGANISATIONS OF SOCIAL WORKERS (n.d.), *Discussion Paper No. 1*.

STAPLETON, PAT (1976), 'Culture Clashes and the Child Minder', *Social Work Today*, vol. 7, no. 9, pp. 271–2.

STEVENSON, OLIVE (1973), *Claimant or Client?* (Allen & Unwin).

STREATFEILD REPORT (1961), *Report of the Interdepartmental Committee on the Business of the Criminal Courts* (HMSO).

STURGESS, JANET and HEAL, KEVIN (1976), 'Non-Accidental Injury to Children under the Age of 17', *Social Work Service*, no. 9, pp. 39–45.

STURTON, SHEILA (1972), 'Developing Group Work in a Casework Agency', *British Journal of Social Work*, vol. 2, no. 2, pp. 143–58.

The Teaching of Sociology to Students of Education and of Social Work (1961), Sociological Review Monograph No. 4 (Keele University).

THOMAS, DAVID N. (1976), *Organizing for Social Change* (Allen & Unwin).

THOMAS, E. I. (1969), 'Contributions of the Socio-Behavioural Approach to Interpersonal Helping in Social Work', *British Journal of Psychiatric Social Work*, vol. 10, no. 2, pp. 61–9.

THOMAS, J. E. (1965), 'Aftercare and the Prison Officer', *Prison Service Journal*, vol. 4, no. 16, pp. 18–21.

(1972), *The English Prison Officer since 1850* (Routledge & Kegan Paul).

THOMAS, MIKE (1974), *The Volunteer, Community and Society* (Berkhamsted, The Volunteer Centre).

THOMAS, N. A. (1973), 'The Seebohm Committee' in Chapman, Richard A. (ed.), *The Role of Commissions in Policy Making* (Allen & Unwin), pp. 143–73.

THOMPSON, S. (1966), 'Working with Families in a Community Service', *British Journal of Psychiatric Social Work*, vol. 8, no. 4, pp. 21–7.

THOMPSON, SHEILA and KAHN, H. H. (1970), *The Group Process as a Helping Technique* (Pergamon Press).

THORNBOROUGH, PEGGY (1974), 'Differential Treatment for Offenders on Probation', *International Social Work*, vol. 17, no. 4, pp. 36–43.

THORPE, DAVID and HORN, DAVID (1973), 'The Shape of Intermediate Treatment', *Social Work Today*, vol. 3, no. 25, pp. 8–11.

THORPE, ROSALIND (1974), 'Mum and Mrs. So and So', *Social Work Today*, vol. 4, no. 22, pp. 691–5.

THWAITES, JEAN (1950), 'Draft for a Code for Social Workers', *The Almoner*, vol. 3, no. 6, pp. 237–42.

TIMMS, NOEL (1964), *Psychiatric Social Work in Great Britain, 1939–1962* (Routledge & Kegan Paul).

(1969), *Social Casework* (Routledge & Kegan Paul).

TITMUSS, R. M. (1958), *Essays on the Welfare State* (Allen & Unwin).

(1970a), foreword to Apte, Robert Z., *Half-Way Houses* (Bell).

(1970b), preface to Goldber, E. M., *Helping the Aged* (Allen & Unwin).

TIZARD, J. (1964), *Community Services for the Mentally Handicapped* (Oxford University Press).

TIZARD, J. and GRAD, J. (1961), *The Mentally Handicapped and Their Families* (Oxford University Press).

TODD, JOAN (1967), *Social Work with the Mentally Subnormal* (Routledge & Kegan Paul).

TONGE, W. L., JONES, D. S. and HILLAM, SUSAN (1975), *Families without Hope* (Royal College of Psychiatrists).

TOWLE, CHARLOTTE (1945 and 1965), *Common Human Needs* (New York, Association of Social Workers); rev. ed. 1973, (Allen & Unwin).

(1954), *The Learner in Education for the Professions* (Chicago, University of Chicago Press).

TOWNSEND, PETER (1957), *The Family Life of Old People* (Routledge & Kegan Paul).

(1965), *The Last Refuge* (Routledge & Kegan Paul).

TOWNSEND, PETER and WEDDERBURN, DOROTHY (1965), *The Aged in the Welfare State* (Bell).

TRASLER, GORDON (1959), 'Planning a Psychology Course for Social Science Students', mimeographed (Joint University Council for Social and Public Administration).

(1960), *In Place of Parents* (Routledge & Kegan Paul).

TRISELIOTIS, JOHN (1970), *In Search of Origins, Experiences of Adopted People* (Routledge & Kegan Paul).

TUCKEY, LINDA, PARFITT, JESSIE and TUCKEY, JACK (1973), *Handicapped School Leavers* (Windsor, National Foundation for Educational Research).

TURNER, MERFYN (1961), *Norman House, the First Five Years* (privately published).

TUTERS, E. (1974), 'Short-term Contracts: Visha', *Social Work Today*, vol. 5, no. 8, pp. 226–31.

TYLER, RALPH (1950), *Basic Principles of Curriculum and Instruction* (Chicago, University of Chicago Press).

UNDERWOOD REPORT (1955), *Report of the Committee on Maladjusted Children* (HMSO).

VENABLES, ETHEL (1971), *Counselling* (Rugby, National Marriage Guidance Council).

VERCOE, K. (n.d.), *Helping Prisoners' Families* (National Association for the Care and Resettlement of Offenders).

VOLUNTEER CENTRE (1975), *Training for Voluntary Service Co-ordinators in the Health and Social Services* (Berkhamsted, The Volunteer Centre).

WALKER, A. (1970), 'Child Guidance at the Crossroads', *British Journal of Psychiatric Social Work*, vol. 10, no. 3, pp. 11–15.

WALLIS, J. H. and BOOKER, H. S. (1958), *Marriage Counselling* (Routledge & Kegan Paul.

WALROND-SKINNER, S. (1974), 'Training for Family Therapy', *Social Work Today*, vol. 5, no. 5, pp. 149–54.

(1975), 'Family Therapy: The Theoretical Background' in Fiddis, O. (ed.), *Proceedings of the Association for the Psychiatric Study of Adolescents*, Tenth Annual Conference (APSA), pp. 34–8.

WATKINS, OWEN (1971), *Professional Training for Youth Work* (Leicester, Youth Service Information Centre).

WELSH OFFICE (1974), Circular 123/74.

WILLIAMS REPORT (1967), *Caring for People* (Allen & Unwin).

WILLS, W. DAVID (1970), *A Place Like Home* (Allen & Unwin).

WILSON, HARRIET C. (1959), 'Problem Families and the Concept of Immaturity' *Case Conference*, vol. 6, no. 5, pp. 115–18.

WINNICOTT, CLARE (1955), 'Casework Techniques in the Child Care Service', reproduced in Younghusband, E. (ed.) (1966), *New Developments in Casework* (Allen & Unwin), pp. 135–54.

(1964), *Child Care and Social Work* (Welwyn, Codicote Press).

(1968), *Residential Staff in Child Care* (Residential Child Care Association).

WOOLFE, R. (1970), 'The Supply and Demand of Face to Face Youth and Community Workers in England and Wales', mimeographed (Leicester, Youth Service Association).

WOOTTON, BARBARA (1959), *Social Science and Social Pathology* (Allen & Unwin).

WRIGHT, M. (1974), 'Probation with Teeth?', *Probation Journal*, vol. 21, no. 4, pp. 103–5.

YOUNG, M. and WILLMOTT, P. (1959), *Family and Kinship in East London* (Routledge & Kegan Paul).

YOUNGER REPORT (1974), *Young Adult Offenders*, Report of the Advisory Council on the Penal System (HMSO).

YOUNGHUSBAND, EILEEN L. (1947), *The Employment and Training of Social Workers* (Dunfermline, Carnegie United Kingdom Trust).

(1951), *Social Work in Britain* (Dunfermline, Carnegie United Kingdom Trust).

(1956), 'Trends in Social Work Education', *Social Work*, vol. 13, no. 4, pp. 241–56.

YOUNGHUSBAND, E., BIRCHALL, D., DAVIE, R. and KELLMER PRINGLE, M. L. (eds), (1970), *Living with Handicap* (National Bureau for Co-operation in Child Care).

YOUNGHUSBAND REPORT (1959), *Report of the Working Party on Social Workers in the Local Authority Health and Welfare Services* (HMSO).

Index